QUEEN OF FRANCE

Queen of France

A BIOGRAPHY OF MARIE ANTOINETTE

BY ANDRÉ CASTELOT

TRANSLATED FROM THE FRENCH
BY DENISE FOLLIOT

HARPER & BROTHERS
NEW YORK

This book is published in England and France under the title of
MARIE ANTOINETTE

To Madame S.-R. Carré

Contents

Introduction

"Les pièces originales sont là, telles quelles, elles parlent ou elles se taisent, elles font foi. Les conditions modernes de l'Histoire sont à ce prix."

Sainte-Beuve

This book was made possible thanks to unpublished documents principally from the French National Archives and the *Haus-Hof und Staatsarchiv* of Vienna. I did not wish to encumber the pages with footnotes and the reader will find the sources used assembled and commented on at the end of the book. But I would like here to thank M. Bernard Mahieu, of the National Archives, for the valuable help he so kindly gave me during the three years in the course of which I constantly harassed him with endless questions.

Thanks to Mlle la Comtesse Coreth I was able to make use of the unpublished documents concerning Marie Antoinette's childhood and marriage which are preserved in the Vienna Archives. I should like to express my gratitude to her and to M. Nemeth, who carried out very detailed researches for me. I should also like to thank my good friend the doctor and historian Paul Ganière, whose remarkable and valuable explanations can be read; M. Ch. Mauricheau-Beaupré, Keeper of the palaces of Versailles and Trianon, who allowed me to wander through the Château; my friends Pierre Géraudel and Pierre Labracherie, of the National Archives, whose great kindness made my work easier; and finally Mme la Comtesse du Bouchage and her daughter, Mme Maurice Firino-Martell, who were good enough to let me make use of the as yet unpublished *Mémoires* of their ancestor, General Comte de Caraman.

As an unbiased attitude is of first importance I considered it indispensable to give the words of eye-witnesses as often as possible.

A.C.

QUEEN OF FRANCE

1

❀

"A Dainty Morsel"

TOWARDS THE END of the winter of 1770 the servants installed a second bed in the Empress Maria Theresa's enormous and draughty bedroom in the Hofburg at Vienna. Every evening it was occupied by a fair-haired little girl of fourteen, who had no longer been a child since Thursday, 7 February, at precisely a quarter past five in the evening—an intimate piece of information which gave the Empress "extreme pleasure" and which a messenger of the French Embassy carried at full gallop to Versailles, to Louis XV, whose pleasure, it appears, was no less keen.

The girl sharing the imperial bedroom was Maria Theresa's youngest daughter, the Archduchess Antonia—such was Marie Antoinette's name at that time—who in two months was to marry the Dauphin of France and who would one day rule with him over the finest kingdom in the world.

Antonia was to be married!

Only the summer before she had been scampering breathlessly about with her brothers and the little princesses of Hesse through the shrubberies of Schoenbrunn's Tyrolean garden. And it was not so very long since Maria Theresa, passing through the long gallery where the little Archduchess was "playing at marriage" with Mozart, had heard the young prodigy ask:

"I shall be your husband, shan't I?"

"Oh yes, no one but you!" cried Antonia earnestly and with shining eyes.

What a child she had been then!

1

With an affectionate motherly eye the Empress watched her little Archduchess fall asleep each evening, this girl who was her favourite, perhaps because Maria Theresa felt her to be unarmed against life.

The Empress had certainly settled her children very well. Apart from two daughters given to the Church—the Abbesses Marie-Anne and Marie-Elisabeth—Marie-Christine was Princess of Saxe-Teschen, Marie-Amélie was the reigning Duchess of Parma and Marie-Caroline was Queen of Naples. Of her sons the eldest, Joseph, King of the Romans, Emperor since the death of Francis I, reigned, together with Maria Theresa, under the name of Joseph II, and Leopold was Grand Duke of Tuscany. There were two more sons. It would not be difficult for Maria Theresa to find them a place, or even a throne, in her mosaic of States which was like Europe in miniature.

Within its thick walls the Hofburg was wrapped in silence. How many times during the eight weeks preceding her daughter's departure must "King Maria Theresa," as the Hungarian grandees called her, have leant over the bed of this fair-haired child to whom she had reserved the finest role.

Little Antonia was not pretty—she was something better. In spite of a high, rounded forehead, irregular teeth, a somewhat aquiline nose and a lower lip which was already full of disdain, she was adorable. Her tutor, the Abbé de Vermond, who was of a reserved nature, nevertheless said with enthusiasm:

"You might find faces which are more regularly beautiful, but I doubt if you could find one more attractive."

Another witness praised the silky texture of the girl's fair hair, went into ecstasies over "her eyes, blue but not insipid," and particularly admired her "Greek neck" and the "pure oval of her face." However, a foreigner—admittedly an Englishman—found this oval "too elongated" and thought her eyes unpleasantly "excited." But there was one point on which everyone in Vienna was in agreement—and which was soon to delight Versailles: the pearly whiteness of Madame Antonia's complexion, a "dazzling" complexion, as some said.

One of La Tour's pupils, the pastellist Ducreux, who had come to Vienna the year before to do a portrait of "Madame Antoine," had caught his young model's somewhat proud way of holding her head, "so poised that every movement was full of nobility." The picture gives a hint of that graceful bearing which would one day become Marie

Antoinette's celebrated "queenly carriage." On the occasion of a festivity at Laxenburg in the previous summer the Abbé de Vermond had also been amazed by her "noble and majestic posture," which was really surprising in a child of that age. He had described it to the Comte de Mercy-Argenteau, Austrian Ambassador to Paris, adding, "If she grows a little taller the French will need no other indications for recognizing their sovereign."

For a long time Maria Theresa mused at the bedside of the delicate child who symbolised the end of the series of wars which had for centuries set Bourbons against Hapsburgs. During her youth the Empress had seen her father, Charles VI, struggle against France; in those days they fought, for Poland, on the Rhine and in Italy. A year after her accession, in 1741, the Empress had in her turn to fight France in order to save her inheritance. She had not been able to stop Frederick II, an ally of Louis XV, from snatching Silesia from her. But Louis XV, callously abandoned by the King of Prussia, and with his Spanish and Italian cousins as his sole support, had turned towards Vienna. As a result, France and Austria, who had fought each other for so long, after the astonishing reversal of alliances of 1 May 1756 fought side by side. But on each occasion France was the loser. In seven years she had sacrificed, in helping Frederick II win Silesia from Maria Theresa, as much in men and money as she had spent over another seven years in trying, vainly, to reconquer it. Louis XV had certainly toiled for no reward in the service of the King of Prussia— that Prussia which, through the fault of France, had ominously risen from obscurity.

And, after thirty years of slaughter, all the spilt blood, all the forgotten victories, the shameful defeats and the degrading treaties led to the bed where little Antonia slept, the symbol of the alliance between France and Austria, or rather, between two peoples—Louis XV and Maria Theresa, backed by their Ministers, Choiseul and Kaunitz. All four strove to maintain the union, in spite of the violent opposition of their peoples and in spite of the French King's unfortunate daughters, who had been anti-Austrian because their father's mistress, the Pompadour, was not, and would continue to be so because the du Barry was not either.

For his part the Austrian Emperor was undoubtedly in favour of the "Alliance," but he was extremely censorious and refused to flirt with

Versailles. According to Kaunitz, Maria Theresa's son "often forgets that one must flirt with Mme la France, just because she is France." To which Choiseul, stung by having his country compared to an elderly coquette, replied, "If the Emperor is not in the mood to make advances, the King is not of the age or temperament to receive them."

But Maria Theresa had not only her son's francophobia to combat. The French diplomats, realising how much the Empress wanted to make her daughter Queen of France, tried to derive as much profit as they could from the situation. M. de Durfort, Louis XV's Ambassador, was given definite instructions: "Leave Maria Theresa in doubt without actually discouraging her."

However, the matter was well settled in Louis XV's mind. The marriage of a son of France with the "daughter of the Caesars" would prevent Austria from drawing too close to Russia and Prussia. The union would consolidate the Alliance and stabilise the balance of Europe. Prussia, Russia and England would be on one side; France, Austria, Spain and Italy on the other. In May 1766 Louis XV had received the Comte de Mercy, and after the interview the Ambassador was able to write to his sovereign, "The King spoke his mind in such a way that Your Majesty may look on the scheme as settled and certain." Louis XV, indeed, appeared pleased at the thought of the arrival at Versailles of a princess whose youth would enliven the court. He too, like Louis XIV, would have his Duchesse de Bourgogne.

Yet for three years, since the Marquis de Durfort's arrival in Vienna at the beginning of 1767, a kind of ballet could have been observed: the Empress offering her daughter and the Ambassador at once refusing and accepting her.

It was one of the Austrian Ministers, Prince Starhemberg, who fired the first shot, in April 1767, by asking Durfort "what he thought of the Archduchess Antonia."

"She is very attractive."

Pleased with this, the Prince went on, "She will be a charming wife for M. le Dauphin."

But Durfort immediately checked this enthusiasm by replying coldly and emphasising the final words, "The morsel is dainty and will be in good hands, *if that is the case.*"

Maria Theresa then decided that she herself would offer the "dainty morsel." After a grand concert given at Schoenbrunn she approached the Ambassador, who in company with the Spanish Minister, Comte de Lahoni, was watching the future Dauphine, and made an undisguised allusion to her daughter's marriage and departure for France.

"I hope she will find success there . . ."

As M. de Durfort remained unresponsive, the Empress turned laughing to Lahoni. "We two can speak more freely, for the French Ambassador has not yet said anything to me about it."

"I pretended not to hear what I could hear very well," sighed Durfort, telling Choiseul of the incident, and he added, "I thought I ought to tell you of a scene which the Empress's air and manner made a rather embarrassing one for me." Choiseul was not concerned with the embarrassment of France's representative at the Hofburg. "You were quite right to be non-committal. The King wishes you to continue to act with the same circumspection until further orders from His Majesty."

The Ambassador's "circumspection" became even more marked when a second scheme was grafted on to the first: the second marriage of Louis XV. As Maria Leczinska had died on 24 June 1767, why should not the King of France also marry a young princess? The Viennese court, which had an ample store of archduchesses, immediately offered one of its daughters, and Antonia's elder sister, Elisabeth, appeared at a masked ball in a domino adorned with *fleurs de lis.* "I fear that this was done on purpose," wrote Durfort, somewhat alarmed by Maria Theresa's eagerness to put into execution the motto of the Austrian monarchy: *Bella gerant alii; tu, felix Austria, nube.*

It was Mercy who had had the curious idea of marrying the two sisters to the grandfather and grandson. At first Louis XV had not said no, "as long as her face was such as not to displease him." But the plan came to nothing and Elisabeth was left to take the *fleurs de lis* off her domino.

Maria Theresa, who always pretended to consider the first scheme settled, busied herself actively with her daughter's education. And heaven knew she needed it! Her governess, Mme de Brandeiss, wrote all her pupil's exercises in pencil and Antonia had only to go over them in ink. The child herself admitted this to her mother. Maria Theresa then instructed the Countess of Lerchenfeld to take the Archduchess's education in hand. But the result was no more successful. Admittedly, as a pupil of Metastasio, Antonio spoke Italian fluently; admittedly she danced with grace under the instruction of the dancer Noverre from Paris; admittedly, thanks to her teacher Gluck, she played the clavichord well; but her French—a Parisian actor had given her some lessons in diction—was studded with germanisms, her German was full of grammatical errors and she wrote with appalling slowness. Through the good offices of Mercy the Empress had finally summoned a French tutor from Paris.

The choice fell on the Abbé de Vermond, "Doctor in the Sorbonne" and librarian in the college of Quatre Nations. He was a typical "blunt courtier," who considered knowledge as good as birth and "treated more highly born people as his equals, sometimes as his inferiors." It was too much for M. de Durfort! He had heard nothing about the "expedition" until the Abbé's arrival and consequently took offence. Vermond paid no attention and set to work—not without difficulty. He explained matters to Choiseul: "A little laziness and much frivolity make it very difficult for me to teach the Archduchess. She understands perfectly well when I put clear ideas before her. Her judgment is nearly always good, but I cannot get her into the way of exploring a question, although I know she is capable of it." Antonia, indeed, was full of good will; she displayed some obstinacy; her character was eager and engaging; but her mind, although intelligent, was not able to concentrate. Furthermore, her mocking nature and constant distractions "counteracted her talent for learning." She neatly evaded her tutor's reproaches and he got results only by "amusing" his pupil.

The Abbé did not succeed in amusing her with writing, and he sighed: "I must confess this is the subject in which I have made least progress." He was more fortunate with French history: "The Archduchess has in this given proof of reasoning ability and good judgement." This is not just a flattering compliment. We possess proof of it in one of Antonia's exercises, an unpublished text which has been preserved by the Vienna *Staatsarchiv* and which one cannot read today without emotion, for in it the future Queen of France judges herself. The little girl, who was then only 12 or 13 years old, draws a comparison between two princesses of the house of Savoy, both daughters of Duke Amédée, the future King of Sardinia. The elder, Marie-Adelaide, Duchesse de Bourgogne and mother of Louis XV, remained something of a Savoyarde even at Versailles, although she had become French by her marriage with Louis XIV's grandson. The younger,

Marie-Louise, Queen of Spain and wife of Philip V, had unhesitatingly adopted her husband's nationality. And Antonia writes:

"The Duchesse de Bourgogne was very scheming. She tried first of all to insinuate herself into the mind of Madame de Maintenon, with whom she tried to do all she could for her father, but not for France, by providing ill counsels and bad generals, who could not lead an army.

"As for the Queen of Spain, she behaved much better, for she interfered in nothing, although she had much to suffer from her father, who caused her much grief and wished to unthrone her, proclaiming Archduke Charles King of Spain. For myself I think that the first was very wrong, for if she wished to have an establishment she should also have been loyal to it and not betrayed the State, and for the other I think she acted well in not interfering in anything and in so loving her husband and her father.

"To continue speaking of the Queen of Spain, I must say that she was not only virtuous, but she had much resolution in affliction . . ."

And referring to various acts and answers showing the "greatness of soul" of the little fifteen-year-old Queen, Marie Antoinette concluded:

"I fear that I should not have done the same!"

She was wrong. After having acted like the Duchesse de Bourgogne, whom she judged so severely, she who would then be called the "Widow Capet" would show even more grandeur "in affliction" than that Queen of Spain, little Louison of the "fiery heart," whose contemporaries described her as "super-natural."

Antonia's reaction to the Duchesse de Bourgogne's "treachery" was the result of Maria Theresa's good advice. In thinking of her daughter's "establishment" Maria Theresa foresaw with apprehension the young Archduchess's bewilderment on encountering the corruption at Versailles after spending all her youth at a homely court—even bourgeois, if Goethe is to be believed—where talent ranked above birth, where etiquette appeared only on ceremonial days and where, in the Prater, the court carriages were passed by the first cab. Maria Theresa constantly repeated to the child: "You must not mention what is customary, nor expect it to be followed. On the contrary, you must adapt yourself entirely to what the French court is accustomed to do."

For, in conformity with her strategy, the Empress continued to act as though the marriage were official. She instructed M. de Mercy to deal with the trousseau in Paris and asked him to send the hairdresser Larseneur. Moreover, in June 1769, on the eve of the feast of St. Antony, she gave a great entertainment in her daughter's honour and placed her next to the Marquis de Durfort. So that there should be no doubt at all in the minds of the guests, the evening ended with a set piece of fireworks showing a dolphin spouting columns of flame through its nostrils.

This audacity had its reward for in the same month Maria Theresa received a letter from her "good brother and cousin Louis XV," who wrote to her without irony that he could "no longer delay" giving expression to his satisfaction at "the forthcoming marriage of his grandson to the Archduchess." And their betrothal was at last officially announced.

The diplomats of both countries were at once assailed by terrible problems. In June 1769, at the request of M. de Choiseul, the Marquis de Durfort went to see Kaunitz to ask him a number of questions about "the marriage contract, the public entry, the solemn demand, the escorting of the bride, the place and formalities for the Remise (or transfer), and the ceremonial to be observed towards the King's Ambassador Extraordinary in all the functions he would have to carry out."

"I promise to fulfil all requests as quickly as possible," Kaunitz had assured him, but six months later, in spite of dozens and dozens of trips by messengers between Vienna and Versailles, hardly any progress had been made. However, Kaunitz constantly claimed to be "making haste." He quite forgot to indulge in his peculiar habits; he no longer smeared his face with egg-yolks, nor was he to be seen cleaning his teeth after dinner with a sponge and a scraper. So that his wig might be evenly powdered he used to walk slowly between two rows of valets armed with bellows which surrounded their master with a cloud of powder. Now Kaunitz paid no attention to his hair-dressing; he had too much to do. How was he in ten months to settle the all-important questions of precedence, etiquette, protocol, ceremonial and gifts so as to avoid any incident? Kaunitz might well be "strong in body, genius and principles," but problems like these can be disconcerting. At Versailles, Choiseul, who was quite as overweening as his Austrian colleague, lost his reputedly unquenchable gaiety; this business forced him to abandon a frivolity which had become a matter of principle, and he bombarded Durfort with proposals and counter-proposals. Who would sign the contract first? The presence of Joseph II, who reigned with his mother, would be another tiresome complication. Would two copies be drawn up, one for France and the other for Austria? In what language would they be written? Louis XV hoped it would be French, "since the law and customs of France will be more exactly and clearly expressed in that language than in any other." And in what order would the Ambassadors, Ministers and commissioners sign? One must read the voluminous correspondence between the diplomats which is preserved at both the Quai d'Orsay in Paris and the Minoritenplatz in Vienna, to grasp all the problems arising out of the marriage of two children. Above all M. de Durfort was to be careful not to invite the future Dauphine to the entertainment he was to give in her honour on the occasion of the marriage by proxy. Why? Had not the Archduchess already visited the Embassy? M. de Choiseul gave him bluntly the reason for this order: "The respect that M. de Durfort, as a subject of the King, will from that moment owe the princess will no longer permit him to seek or invite this honour." "As a result of this same respect" the Ambassador should no longer take an "equal seat" when in the presence of the fiancée. What should he do if he were offered one at the Hofburg? He must manage as best he could! And without a smile Choiseul ordered him "to use all suitable tact in this matter."

These gentlemen blackened reams of paper but hardly mentioned the future married pair. We only know that at the end of February Antonia had a cold, but that blowing her nose "has not effected the slightest change in her countenance or her gaiety." The correspondence is even less expansive regarding the fiancé. Mercy had summed matters up once and for all: "Nature seems to have denied everything to M. le Dauphin" and he appeared, moreover, to possess "only a limited amount of sense." The Ambassador had not dared to put these last words in the plural. Two months before the marriage the Empress realised that her daughter had received no other picture of her fiancé than that of a brilliant, sparkling dolphin belching fire into the sky at Laxenburg. The unfortunate girl risked being somewhat disappointed on her arrival at Versailles. The Empress therefore asked Durfort if she might be sent a portrait of her future son-in-law.

Louis XV hastened to send to Vienna three engravings representing "the Dauphin ploughing." This was hardly gallant ... At the beginning of April, therefore, two portraits of Louis-Auguste in ceremonial dress were at last given to Antonia, who put them "in the room where she sits." "I cannot tell you how much satisfaction these portraits have given," wrote the Ambassador. She who in a few days would be the Dauphine of France mused for long before the image of her future husband. But Maria Theresa warned her that princesses have no right to expect love.

"Domestic happiness consists in mutual trust and kindness," she insisted. "Passionate love soon disappears!"

In the vast bedroom with its heavy white and gold sculpture the Empress continued to pour forth advice.

"Don't show curiosity; this is a point on which you give me great anxiety."

Another question worried her: place-hunters.

"You must know how to refuse ... Don't undertake any recommendations. To avoid trouble don't listen to anyone."

When she thought of her daughter's age—she was fourteen—Maria Theresa trembled. Admittedly, at that time babies who were scarcely weaned became colonels in the musketeers, but for all that the Empress was anxious.

"Don't be ashamed to ask advice from everyone and don't do anything of your own accord."

Until then the Queens of France had always tried to forget their original nationality. Maria Theresa was of another opinion and gave advice which was later to prove serious: "Remain a good German!"

Antonia's temperament gave her the most anxiety. "I realised that her character comprised much frivolity, lack of application and obstinacy in following her own will, together with adroitness in evading intended reproaches." She strove tirelessly to put some ballast into that light head and to tame the stubborn will she could already perceive behind that little round forehead.

On the morning of 15 April 1770, Easter Sunday, M. de Durfort, *Ordinary Ambassador* of His Most Christian Majesty, left Vienna—to return an hour later as *Ambassador Extraordinary,* as though he were coming from France. Little Antonia, together with her sister Maria-Christina, the future Governor of the Low Countries, watched the spectacle from Countess Trauttmansdorff's house.

And what a spectacle it was!

It cost more than 100 million francs of present-day money and M. de Durfort had received only half this from Versailles to pay for all the celebrations. The Ambassador Extraordinary might have ruined himself, but he could at least boast that he had not disappointed the Viennese, who were dazzled by the passage of 48 carriages, each drawn by six horses. Incidentally, the whole stable—including six led saddle horses—was sold the next day by M. de Durfort to help replenish his exchequer.

In fact the Ambassador had had to pay for only 46 carriages, as two travelling coaches had been presented by King Louis XV to his future granddaughter. The Archduchess gazed admiringly at the two enormous carriages with which she was to travel to Versailles, and which had cost 40 million francs of our money. They were the work of the saddler Francien, but had been designed by Choiseul himself. The first was upholstered in crimson velvet on which Trumeau had embroidered the four seasons; the second was upholstered in blue velvet and on its doors were displayed the four elements. On top were bouquets of flowers in gold of different colours and so supple that they nodded gracefully in the slightest breeze.

The two gala coaches were empty, but in the others were the officers of the Ambassador Extraordinary and round the carriages were pages, grooms and servants. In all there were 117 persons dressed in "rich stuffs" of blue, yellow and silver.

On the following day M. de Durfort, after passing through a double rank of noble German and Hungarian guards, was publicly received in audience by the Queen-Empress and the Emperor Joseph II. This was for the official proposal. The Ambassador performed three accomplished bows and made ready to begin his speech, but then—as had been carefully arranged by Choiseul—the Empress invited him to put on his hat, which gave Durfort the opportunity to give another deep bow, cover himself and—in a further improvisation provided by etiquette—immediately remove his hat once more. On ending his speech the Ambassador turned towards the door and made a sign to a rider who seemed at that moment to have arrived from France. He brought Marie Antoinette a letter from her fiancé and a portrait. This was the sixth in six weeks—they were making up for lost time! Maria Theresa summoned the Archduchess, who was waiting in an adjoining room. She came in, made her curtseys and with her mother's approval fastened the "portrait," brought by the rider, on her bosom. One must conclude that the portrait was a miniature. "All this," Durfort related, "took place amid profound salutations." We can well believe it.

On the next day—17 April—in the presence of her mother, her brother, the Marquis de Durfort and all the Ministers, Antonia performed her first political act: her renunciation of the hereditary Austrian succession. In the great hall looking on to the Burgplatz the future Queen Marie Antoinette, having first signed the act drawn up in Latin and later to be ratified by Louis XV and the Dauphin, took the oath before the Coadjutor of the Prince-Bishop of Laylach. It was, in fact, Cardinal Migazzi, Archbishop of Vienna, who should have handed the Testament to the Archduchess and asked her to swear, but the Marquis de Durfort had cried out in protest. In that case he would have had to take second place to the prince of the Church! The Ambassador had accordingly succeeded in arranging that the Cardinal should not take part in *any* ceremony. In the evening Antonia was received by her brother at a great supper in the Belvedere for 1,500 guests. The meal was followed by a ball to which there thronged 6,000 masks and white dominos. A vast ballroom, lit by 3,500 candles, was erected for the purpose, adjoining the palace. The façade, walls and balconies were covered with "appropriate" decorations: it was all torches of love, dolphins, glowing vases borne by seraphim, garlands, hearts and flowers. The Empress had thought of everything: 800 firemen with damp sponges spent the whole evening extinguishing the sparks which fell from the chandeliers. "H.I.M.'s motherly care," the official account tells us, went so far as to order dentists to stand by during the feast in case any sudden toothache required an immediate extraction.

On the evening of the next day, Wednesday, it was M. de Durfort's turn to extend princely hospitality to the Austrian court in the Liechtenstein Palace, in the suburb of Rossau, which he had hired for the occasion. All along the route three rows of illuminated pines gave a light as bright as day, and between each tree and the next was placed a dolphin carrying a lantern.

The feast was given on the eve of the nuptial ceremony, so that Marie Antoinette, not yet the Dauphine, could attend without derogation to her rank. Here, too, flaming dolphins sparkled in the night, but the Ambassador had not considered this symbol to be enough, and pictures lit by 8,000 lamps were disposed on pyramids. One saw Hymen ordering Louis-Auguste to wed the goddess of beauty, then the Danube and the Seine lovingly mingling their waters, and finally "H.R.H. the Dauphine" walking to France "on a carpet of flowers sown by Love."

The classic fireworks, accompanied by the fashionable strains of Turkish music, preceded the supper, which was served by 800 servants to 850 guests.

On Thursday, 19 April, at six o'clock in the evening, the whole court went in great pomp, and to the sound of trumpets and kettle-drums, through the gallery of the Palace to the Church of the Augustines, where the marriage by proxy was to be celebrated. Little Antonia, all smiles, advanced with her mother and brother. She looked enchanting in her dress of cloth of silver.

Archduke Ferdinand, 17 months older than the bride, took the Dauphin's place and knelt at his sister's side before the altar. The *prie-Dieu* for the "married pair" were covered in red velvet embroidered with gold. In order to please Durfort the Cardinal had been asked to stay at home and the Papal Nuncio, Mgr. Visconti, officiated, assisted by the court curé, who bore the warlike name of Briselance.

It was in the vestry of this same church, on 3 November 1755, that little Maria Antonia Josepha, born on the preceding day—all Souls' Day and the day of the Lisbon earthquake—had been baptised in the presence of the Emperor Francis.

The married pair knelt and replied *"Volo et ita promitto,"* to the question put to them by the Nuncio. The rings, one of which Marie Antoinette would give the Dauphin, were blessed and then Briselance drew up the act of celebration, Kaunitz certified it and Durfort legalised it. After the *Te Deum* a salvo was fired in the Spitalplatz and it only remained for them to go to supper—without Durfort, as the Ambassador did not want to yield precedence to Prince Albert of Saxe-Teschen, Marie Antoinette's brother-in-law. Versailles had asked the latter not "to cause any difficulty" and "to arrange matters as best he could." The Prince gave way as far as church was concerned, but being very greedy he wanted to go to the supper; so, in order to avoid dishonour, the Marquis stayed at home. The feast was no less of a success on that account, and the Comte de Saint-Julien, grand master of the imperial kitchens, worked wonders. A hundred and fifty guests were summoned, not to dinner, but to admire the nine princely guests eating off gold plate, while the artillery set off a peal at "the first draught drunk by Their Majesties."

The next day, the eve of the departure for France, was devoted to a final public repast, to leave-taking and to correspondence. Maria Theresa wrote no fewer than three letters to Louis XV, asking the King "to be indulgent towards any thoughtless act" that might be committed by "her very dear child." "I commend her to him yet once more as the tenderest pledge that exists so sincerely between our States and Houses . . ." For her part, Antoine—it was thus that she signed her letter—wrote in a very childish hand to Louis XV, begging "his indulgence" and asking him also "to obtain in advance that of the Dauphin." No document in the archives gives us any details of that last night in the Empress's bedroom, but we can imagine the tears of the little girl who doubtless knew that she would never again embrace her mother, the mother she feared yet adored, and those of the woman who not without anguish saw the departure of the child "who was her delight," but of whose frivolity and thoughtlessness she was also aware. "I am bathed in tears," she wrote the next day when the cavalcade of 366 horses had borne her child away into the distance.

She did not weep alone. The Dauphine's foster-brother wrote: "We did not return home until we had lost sight of the last courier following her, and when we did it was but to mourn among the family for a common loss . . ."

On Saturday 21 April the long procession of 57 carriages preceded by three postillions blowing their horns left the suburb of Mariahilf and passed before Schoenbrunn.

Schoenbrunn!

Never again was Marie Antoinette to see the long yellow façade with its green shutters, nor her apartments on the ground floor where, after hours of play, she and her brothers and sisters would eat pyramids of Viennese cakes dripping with whipped cream.

A few more revolutions of the wheels and the coach crowned with its bouquets of flowers passed the exact spot where, on a summer morning five years earlier, Antonia had embraced her father for the last time. The Emperor Francis, who was on his way to Innsbruck

for the celebration of the marriage between Archduke Leopold—the
future Leopold II—and the Infanta Maria Luisa, had gone to Schoenbrunn to embrace his children. But when he was a little way from the
castle, on the same road now followed by the Dauphine, he had,
perhaps, some presentiment of his coming death and stopped his
coach.

"Go back for the Archduchess Antonia; I must see her again."

He had gazed at her with indescribable tenderness, and for the rest
of her life Marie Antoinette was never to forget that look.

Did she remember too the advice the Emperor left for his children?
"Never be indifferent before what appears to you to be evil, nor
attempt to find it innocent . . . We are not put into this world merely
to amuse ourselves . . . What kind of people we should frequent is
also a delicate matter, for they may often lead us into many things
against our will . . . Friendship is one of the pleasures of life, but one
should be careful to whom one entrusts this friendship and not be too
prodigal of it . . . This is why I advise you, my dear children, never
to be in a hurry to place your friendship and trust in someone of whom
you are not quite sure."

The future friend of Mme de Polignac and Baron de Besenval was
only fourteen years old; one could not hope that she would remember
all this advice. Would she even read the recommendations her mother
had just given her, which contained a summary of their evening talks?
At fourteen one could not expect from her anything more than that
her heart should beat faster every time someone in her suite pronounced
in her hearing the magic word *Versailles*. Under the orders of Prince
Starhemberg, Commissioner Plenipotentiary "in charge of the remise,"
there were 132 persons: ladies-in-waiting, serving women, hairdressers,
secretaries, dressmakers, surgeons, pages, furriers, chaplains, apothecaries, lackeys, cooks and menservants of all kinds, not to mention
an escort of noble guards and above all a grand postmaster, the Prince
of Paar, assisted by nine masters and 25 employees. They were not too
many to watch at each stage over the 376 horses needed for the
procession. As the horses were changed at least four or five times a
day, a stable of more than 20,000 horses had had to be distributed
on the route from Vienna to Strasbourg. All along the road the bells
pealed and the artillery fired salutes.

On the first day, after eight hours' travelling, the cavalcade slept at

Mölck, where the Dauphine was welcomed by her brother, Joseph II. At the Benedictine convent, where she spent the night, the pupils performed an opera for her, the monks providing the orchestra. The performance was extremely bad—so bad that Marie Antoinette was "very bored" and became gloomy, at least if we can believe Durfort, who had accompanied the Archduchess so far. Perhaps, however, it was grief at leaving everything she loved.

The following morning she embraced her brother and, alone in her carriage with the Princess of Paar, took the road to Enns, where the Prince of Auersperg received her in his castle. On the 23rd she left the Danube valley and slept at Lambach; on the 24th, after six hours' travelling, she reached Altheim; on the 25th she crossed the Inn and spent the night at Alt-Oettingen; she spent the 26th and 27th not far from Munich at the castle of Nymphenburg, where she was greeted by Maximilian-Joseph, the Elector of Bavaria. There was no etiquette, and, as we are told, "confusion" was the rule. On the 28th she was at Augsburg, and on the 29th nine hours' journey brought the coach to Günsburg, where Marie Antoinette was to spend two days with her aunt, Princess Charlotte of Lorraine, Abbess of Remiremont. The great entertainment offered her was a distribution of food to the people and a visit to the Lorraine chapel of Königinbild, on the Burgau road. As she left twelve young girls presented the Dauphine with wild flowers simply and attractively bound with ribbon, and one of them recited a poem hoping that "the most serene couple" would live more than a hundred years. Then they sat down to table, and 132 people consumed, among other dishes, a trifle of 150 chickens, 270 lb. of beef, 220 lb. of veal, 55 lb. of bacon, 50 pigeons and 300 eggs.

On the next day, 1 May, the long procession of carriages took the road to Ulm and reached Riedlingen. On 2 May they rejoined the Danube, and on the evening of this ninth *Nacht Station* Marie Antoinette stopped at Stockach. On 3 May the suite arrived at Donau-Eschingen, and on the following day, having been nine and a half hours on the road, spent the night at Fribourg. They rested there on the 5th and on the 6th. Having crossed the Black Forest, Marie Antoinette finally arrived at the Abbey of Schüttern, the last stage before the "remise." She had hardly arrived when she received a visit from the Comte de Noailles, Ambassador Extraordinary charged by the King with her reception, who had come from Strasbourg with the Comte de Mercy. This post, which he owed to his friend Choiseul, filled Noailles with pride. He had insisted for himself on "the honours of cannon and troops," and above all on plenty of money. The Treasury being, as usual, in difficulties, the Count had been offered some flattering decorations, but he had replied arrogantly: "I already have enough!"

Choiseul therefore decided to give him a sum corresponding to a good 12 million francs of present-day money, advising him "to be satisfied" with that. The Count consoled himself by thinking that his mission took on the aspect of a family affair, since his wife and his son, the Prince de Poix, were among the imposing suite sent by the King to meet his granddaughter.

M. de Noailles did not stay long with his future sovereign; serious problems were oppressing him and he had to consult with Prince Starhemberg. Three words in the deed of remise—the *Consegna*, as it was called in Austria—stuck in his throat: "Their Imperial Majesties *having been willing* to accede to the King's wish . . ." In this way Maria Theresa and Joseph II seemed to be granting a favour to Louis XV. Could it not rather be said that in common accord Their Imperial and Royal Majesties were "agreed"? Starhemberg gave way, for he too had something to request: in accordance with Austrian etiquette he wanted a dais to be placed in the *salon de remise*. Noailles agreed, and becoming bolder suggested that Louis XV should be named first in the official document. Starhemberg nearly fainted. It was impossible! They went on arguing, night fell, and—to make an end—a compromise was reached: as in Vienna, two documents would be drawn up. In the one for France the King would have precedence, whereas in the one intended for Austria he would come after Maria Theresa and Joseph II.

Everyone then went to bed, except for the secretaries who had to work all night to change the documents. Marie Antoinette, who from now on would bear these names only, was sad. Tears flowed from her eyes and during this last night on German soil her thoughts turned towards her mother. Her ladies heard her sigh through her tears: "I shall never see her again!"

For the official remise it had first been planned to use a house situated on an island in the Rhine and belonging to a Master Gelb. However, it would have been necessary to pull down the partitions, build a reception room on to the brick façade and fill in a pond in front of the house. The scheme was abandoned, much to Master Gelb's relief, and a house was built nearby with two entrances—one French and one Austrian—two antechambers, four offices and a large hall where the ceremony would take place. The room was adorned with carpets lent by the Prince of Lorraine and tapestries borrowed from the old Cardinal de Rohan, Archbishop of Strasbourg. According to Louis XV's envoys everything was done "in order to safeguard the feelings of both courts," but for all that the tapestries caused Goethe much indignation. He was then twenty and often left the courses of the University of Law at Strasbourg in order to visit the hall and look at the tapestries, whose "choice of subjects" revolted him. "They were a copy of pictures painted by very good French masters, but these pictures represented the story of Jason and Medea. On the right of the throne could be seen the unhappy betrothed in the throes of all the anguish of a cruel death; on the left, Jason, seized with horror at the sight of his murdered children, while the Fury rose into the air in a flaming chariot. Such subjects appeared to me to be so little in harmony with the circumstances that I could not help exclaiming out loud: What! At the moment when the young princess is about to step on to the soil of her future husband's country, there is placed before her eyes a picture of the most horrible marriage that can be imagined! . . . Might one not say that the most awful spectre has been summoned to meet the most beautiful and happy betrothed?"

One can guess, in spite of young Goethe's anger, that the tapestries did not find their way back to the archbishopric.

In spite of what Mme Campan said—and after her all the other historians—the little Dauphine was not stripped naked on the Rhine island on the morning of the 7th, so that she might not retain so much as a piece of ribbon from her former homeland. That old custom had been abandoned. As the archives relate Marie Antoinette simply put on, in one of the Austrian rooms, a ceremonial dress brought from Vienna. Her grand mistress of the robes, her tiring woman and her Kammerfraülein, who accompanied her, did the same in the other room and the ladies of her suite dressed in the Gelb house. The little bride was even able to keep on her maiden jewellery: chain necklace, aigrettes, *prétension, boutons de compère, boucles de chien* and a *bec de diamants* for her hair.

Followed by her Austrian escort, the little Dauphine, giving her hand to Starhemberg, entered the *salle de remise* and stood before the large table symbolising the frontier and covered with crimson velvet. On the other side there were only three people: Noailles and his two assistants, the commissioners Bouret and Gérard. Behind her the door giving on to Germany remained open, whereas the French door was still shut. An unpublished document preserved in the National Archives actually informs us that behind the latter door the Prince of Poix and the gentleman usher were looking "through the keyhole." The scene was a short one: Marie Antoinette took her place on the dais dear to Starhemberg—the Lutheran University had had it constructed that very morning. She listened to M. de Noailles making a speech of exceptional banality and submitted to a recital of the official act by Bouret.

That was all: the Archduchess was now French. The Austrian ladies kissed her hand, the French door opened to admit the Comtesse de Noailles and the Comte de Saulx-Tavannes, gentleman-in-waiting. What trouble that entrance had given the Ambassador Extraordinary! The detailed report preserved in the Archives relates: "The Comte de Noailles having informed the usher that he wished the Comtesse de Noailles to come in side by side with the gentleman-in-waiting, who was supposed to give her his hand to enter, the usher, to please the Comte de Noailles, arranged that the second half of the door should be pushed open by the lady-in-waiting's skirts, which might have happened accidentally." The usher, doubtless preoccupied by this manoeuvre, opened the door somewhat too early and from the French antechamber "all could see the leave-taking of the Austrian ladies."

When the former suite had left the German door was closed and the young Dauphine went to meet Mme de Noailles. Surrounded as she was by strangers—only Starhemberg remained present—the poor girl must have felt at a loss, and she threw herself into the arms of her lady-in-waiting, as though for safety. But the severe Comtesse de Noailles considered that this effusion did not come within the protocol and she hastened to introduce M. de Noailles to the Dauphine, to whom he had already been presented the day before. But this time it was in his quality of grandee of Spain and, according to the custom, Marie Antoinette embraced him. Mme de Noailles, who was in her natural element with etiquette, then presented the girl's household to her. Her mistress of the robes, the Duchesse de Villars, and her other ladies of honour, the Duchesse de Picquigny, the Marquise de Duras, the Comtesses de Mailly and de Saulx-Tavannes, had formerly, together with Mme de Noailles, been in the household of Maria Leczinska. In order to avoid intrigue and rivalry, Louis XV had preferred to maintain the former household of the Queen. For years these six ladies had shared the slow-moving existence of their deserted mistress, and neither in their faces nor in their behavior was there any breath of youth or gaiety. Marie Antoinette must certainly have shuddered a little when she thought that she must henceforth spend the greater part of her time with these mature ladies.

However, she smiled politely as she walked gracefully towards the antechamber—and towards France.

The dull rumbling of a storm died away towards the Black Forest, a triple peal of artillery sounded from the ramparts, the bells rang in all the churches and the coach crowned with its bouquets of gold flowers stopped at the first houses of Strasbourg. M. d'Autigny, "head of the magistrature," stepped forward and began a speech in German. The Princess graciously interrupted him. "Do not speak German, gentlemen; from today I understand no language but French."

It is not known whether as a reward for her amiability she was spared the rest of the speech. In any case it is quite possible that this was a "saying" handed down from one foreign princess arriving in France to the next, but certainly no one can have uttered it as charmingly as Marie Antoinette.

In the unanimous opinion of witnesses, and from the first moment of her entry into France, Marie Antoinette's smile charmed and attracted, her "light step," her "archduchess's bearing" and "the somewhat proud carriage of her head and shoulders" made their effect. "As one watches the princess it is difficult to refrain from feeling a respect mingled with tenderness." And in all the accounts one finds the same astonishment of her contemporaries at Marie Antoinette's complexion, a complexion "literally a blend of lilies and roses . . . which can spare her the use of rouge," noted one woman, not without envy. Marie Antoinette's arrival among this decaying monarchy, this cankered age, this unhealthy society had the effect of a fresh bouquet of wild flowers.

"She is like the perfume of spring!" Burke exclaimed.

The spectacle given at Strasbourg was as fresh as the little Dauphine's smile. Children dressed as shepherds and shepherdesses offered her bouquets, girls threw flowers under the horses' hooves and little boys dressed as Swiss Guards lined the route. Marie Antoinette was charmed by this idea and asked that the guard at the Bishop's palace, where she was to stay, should be mounted by this miniature regiment. The request was made so graciously that it was granted with pleasure.

She continued to smile. She smiled at the presentation of the gouty Cardinal de Rohan, the dyspeptic counts forming the cathedral council, and the deputations from the guilds, who were followed by thirty-six ladies of the Alsatian nobility with serious and severe countenances. After an endless dinner, "not being at all tired," she consented, as though it were merely a dessert, to receive the deputies from the grand chapter.

She was not allowed to rest after this heavy day. A feast of Bacchus had been arranged, performed by coopers dancing with their hoops. She smiled, and the elderly Maréchal de Contades, commander of the province, escorted her to the theatre, where she watched performances of *Dupuis et Desronais* and *La servante-maîtresse*. She continued to smile when the Marshal led her back to the bishop's palace, showed her the illuminated town, gave her supper and displayed the garlanded barges on the River Ill which drew alongside the terrace so that, after swallowing her last mouthful, the Dauphine was able to cross the river and see the decorations from the park. The shrubs decorating the barges burst into flame, the fireworks were reflected in the Ill, from which sprang jets of water, while a choir sang "Long Live the King." Hardly had the entwined initials of the Dauphin and Dauphine faded in the sky than the indefatigable Marshal (it was now after midnight) led the little girl to the theatre which was now transformed into a ballroom. It was not until she had watched several dances that Marie Antoinette was allowed to go to bed. She was still smiling and her complexion was as brilliant as ever.

"If one can judge of the Dauphine's constitution from her outward appearance," Noailles wrote that evening to Choiseul, "I do not think one need be uneasy about her health."

The next morning, in the absence of the old Cardinal de Rohan, a strange prelate in a gold mitre received the girl in the porch of the cathedral. He was young, slender, elegant, and bowed gracefully. This was the Bishop Coadjutor of the diocese, Prince Louis de Rohan, later Cardinal de Rohan and one day to be "Cardinal Necklace." "As pleasant as it is possible to be"—and in those days they were good judges—he lived in a coterie of pretty women, gave a banquet every day or hunted the stag and the fox. He sometimes interrupted this princely and oriental existence to assist his uncle, while waiting to succeed him. But this prelate-cum-satrap did not forget that he was an Academician and addressed Marie Antoinette in terms befitting the illustrious company.

"For us, Madame, you will be the living image of that dear Empress, for so long the admiration of Europe, as she will be in ages to come. The soul of Maria Theresa will be united to the soul of the Bourbons."

Into "Madame's" eyes there sprang "two tears" which fell on to her cheeks "heightened in colour" and under the high, Gothic arches the soft, caressing voice came to the peroration: "The golden age will be born from such a union and under the happy rule of Antoinette and Louis-Auguste our nephews will see the continuation of the happiness we enjoy under the reign of Louis the Beloved!"

A questionable happiness, no doubt, but the speech was so well written and nobly spoken that the audience asked for nothing more. Before the Mass began the man who through ignorance and stupidity was to bear a heavy share of responsibility in the coming tragedy blessed "the child's bowed head" with an elegant gesture.

For a whole week, whether at Saverne, Lunéville, Nancy, Commercy, Bar-le-Duc, Saint-Dizier, Rheims, Châlons or Soissons, Marie Antoinette had to endure a terrible avalanche of speeches, poems and compliments. She stoically bore successive comparisons with Venus, Hebe, Psyche, Antiope, Flora and Minerva. She bravely submitted to triumphal arches, military honours, gala balls, peals of artillery, deputations, dinners, speeches, shows, entertainments, interminable presentations, bell-ringing. *Te Deum*, illuminations, endless whirling suns, "sheets of Chinese fire," Pyrrhic columns, cavalcades of horses "all alight," temples of conjugal love and betrothal, temporary buildings topped by spirits with trumpets announcing to France the arrival of her future sovereign. Sometimes, indeed, the programme seemed not to be full enough. At one stage "as it was very early the Comtesse de Noailles suggested that the Dauphine might dance," and she consented. A regimental band was sent for "and she danced in the antechamber with the ladies and gentlemen of her suite." Everywhere she went she seemed happy, and yet, apart from Mercy, Starhemberg and the Abbé de Vermond, she was surrounded by strangers.

The vast procession, preceded by fifty guards, wound its way slowly along the dusty road, which had been remade especially for this journey. Each stage required 386 horses. Reinforcements had to be sent by the posts of Périgueux, Pont-Saint-Esprit and Angoulême. Even the foot servants had been chosen for their physique. The reasons for which some of them were turned down are preserved in the Archives: "not good-looking," "too small," or both "ill-looking and coarse."

Two great wagons, each containing all the furnishings for a bedroom, went in front of the procession. They proceeded in relays so that at each stopping place the Dauphine would find one of the two bedrooms with its armchairs, screens and folding stools in crimson damask "enriched with fringes, gold braid and gold embroidered cushions." Her two beds were both covered with scarlet satin together with a white satin coverlet. In these beds she must have dreamed about the man whose wife she had been for three weeks and whom she knew only by miniatures and an engraving. Could the Dauphin, who was not yet sixteen, do anything besides guiding a plough? Had not Mlle Cosson de la Cressonière exaggerated slightly in the verses published in the Mercure:

> Bearing the wishes of her court,
> She comes, by noble marriage led:
> 'Tis Psyche in the bloom of youth
> Conducted here to Cupid's bed.

"Are you very anxious to see the Dauphin?" one of her ladies asked her.

With her charming smile, she replied mischievously: "Madame, in five days I shall be at Versailles, and on the sixth I shall more easily be able to answer you."

It was not at Versailles that "Psyche in the bloom of youth" was to meet "Cupid," but in the Forest of Compiègne.

2

❖

"Priceless" Festivities

ON THE EVENING of 14 May, not far from the Pont de Berne, on the outskirts of the Forest of Compiègne, lifeguards, light horse musketeers, and gendarmes were drawn up in battle formation keeping back the crowd.

The King was waiting for "my granddaughter," as he called her.

In spite of his sixty years he was still the handsomest man in his kingdom. His reign of half-a-century had not bowed him down. Surfeited with pleasure, he found a distraction in the arrival of the little girl with whom the dispatches of Ministers and Ambassadors had been occupied for the last three years. A few days earlier he had received Bouret, who after reading the official Act in the *salle de remise* had set off hot foot to carry the documents to the King.

"What did you think of the Dauphine?" the elderly libertine asked. "Has she any bosom?"

Marie Antoinette was to make up for it later, but at the moment—as can be seen in Ducreux's portrait—the little Princess's bust was only just developing. M. Bouret confined himself to replying that "the Dauphine had a charming face and very beautiful eyes."

"That is not what I was talking about," Louis XV interrupted. "I asked you if she had any bosom."

Bouret extricated himself gallantly. "Sire, I did not take the liberty of carrying my eyes so far."

The King burst out laughing. "You are a fool! It's the first thing one looks at in a woman."

The King was waiting. . . . He had forgotten to be bored and to

24

think of death. However, he was, if not anxious, somewhat pre-occupied. How would the Dauphine greet Mme du Barry? A fort-night earlier "the King's passion triumphed over his sense of shame," as Mercy wrote to Maria Theresa, and Jeanne Bécu, the illegitimate daughter of a little seamstress of Vaucouleurs, Jeanne Bécu, "the prosti-tute," as Choiseul said, Jeanne Bécu, called *la Bourbonnaise* by the pamphleteers, had been presented at court, presented to Mesdames, the King's daughters, presented to the Dauphin!

"She is very pretty, she attracts me, that should be enough," the King had written to Choiseul, and to Richelieu, with whom he was more intimate, "the old love-making machine" confided: "She has given me delights I did not know existed."

These were arguments which it would not seem easy to put to the young Archduchess, particularly as Maria Theresa had not thought fit to mention "the creature" to her daughter.

Mesdames, the daughters of Louis XV—a group of crabbed old maids—stood near the King. For some days now they had been feeling very disturbed; their number was now reduced to three. Madame Louise had just entered the poorest Carmelite convent in France, at Saint-Denis. And this decision, which had been hidden from Mesdames Adelaide, Victoire and Sophie, had astounded them. Now merely Sister Thérèse Augustine, and writing to the King only "by permission of our good Mother Superior," she had formerly been an intrepid horsewoman, loving fine clothes and, according to Mme de Boigne, "having a marked inclination for flirting." Indeed, when the King went to his eldest daughter's room to tell her that her sister Louise had left during the night, Madame Adelaide's first exclamation was, "With whom?"

Madame Adelaide, once enchantingly pretty, had withered up and become "as cross as two sticks." Her father called her "rag" or "dishcloth," according to his mood. She played the horn and the Jew's harp and made napkin rings, but in spite of these homely nicknames and simple tastes a haughtier being, more imbued with a sense of ancestry, could not be imagined. She was so proud of her title of "Daughter of France" that any union, even with the son of a reigning prince, seemed to her to be a misalliance and she had preferred to shrivel up at Versailles. Her sister Madame Victoire, plump and pious, retained some faint traces of beauty. Her kindness made one forget her stupidity. It was she, according to Mme de Boigne, who said "with tears in her eyes, during a period of scarcity, when someone was talking of the sufferings of the unfortunate people who lacked bread: 'But if only they could resign themselves to eating piecrust!'" It is only fair to explain that piecrust lay very heavy on her own stomach.

As for Madame Sophie, her "exceptional ugliness" astounded everyone, except the enormous Duc de Luynes, who considered she had "an air of beauty." "I never saw anyone so shy," said Mme Campan. "She walked extremely quickly, and so as to recognise the people she passed without looking at them she had formed the habit of glancing sideways, as hares do." Like Madame Victoire she was "passive"; it was Madame Adelaide who gave orders with the voice of an old sergeant-major. On that day her watchword was: try to get Choiseul and the du Barry dismissed and get the Dauphine on our side. For all that they had done everything possible to avert the marriage. Not only did Madame Adelaide not like Austria, but she would have liked herself to choose her nephew's wife so as to be able to control her. One of the officers of the future Dauphine, who came to ask for Madame Adelaide's orders before leaving for Strasbourg, drew on himself this reply: "If I had any order to give it would not be to fetch an Austrian!"

And this Austrian was now to take from her the first place at court which she had occupied since the death of her sister-in-law, the Dauphin's mother. This child of fourteen would shortly sit at the back of the coach with the King.

Suddenly a great murmur arose. The Dauphine's procession was approaching. The people applauded. The musketeers' drums, trumpets and hautboys sounded. The gold flowered carriage had hardly stopped when the little Dauphine jumped out. She made a few rapid, almost running, steps ahead of the radiant Choiseul, who by the King's special favour had gone to meet her a few leagues off. The girl threw herself at the King's feet; he raised her up and embraced her. He was smiling, for the young Dauphine was charming and beautifully formed. Of her own accord she kissed a great booby of fifteen who was stuck there beside the King, shifting from one foot to the other. This was the Dauphin.

Once seated in the King's carriage Marie Antoinette had plenty of opportunity for looking at her husband, who sat opposite her and did not even turn his vague, short-sighted eyes on his "wife." And yet she was very fresh and charming. It was obvious that this shy, awkward boy wished himself elsewhere. Naturally the fourteen-year-old girl could not guess that the sullen temperament and heavy, uncouth body concealed qualities of mind, heart and judgement which made him, if not a brilliant prince, at least a "good young man" and later a "worthy man." Besides, there was some excuse for his "lubberliness." His father had died when he was eleven and his mother just as he reached his thirteenth year, and he had been very badly brought up by that conceited windbag, the Duc de la Vauguyon. As for his grandfather, he had more frivolous or more serious preoccupations than concerning himself with the mind of an apathetic boy who was a mystery to him. Later he was to say to Mercy: "He is not an ordinary man!"

Fancy stuffing oneself regularly with cakes until one was ill! Fancy having a taste for manual labour, enjoying locksmith's work, or being so fond of mixing plaster that a workman could not enter the castle without the Dauphin hurrying up, lending a hand in the work and going back to his apartments dirty and exhausted!

However, Marie Antoinette knew nothing of all this. Yet although she said nothing and continued to smile, we can imagine her disappointment. She was a long way from the Dauphin of her dreams spouting flame through his nostrils!

And what did the bridegroom think of this blonde girl with the pink complexion who in two days would be brought to his bed? Did he already fear the irony in those somewhat prominent eyes? Did he know that she was given to mockery? Did he guess that the full, pretty lip, now ready to pout, would become very disdainful? But this would attribute to the lout of fifteen years and nine months a perspicacity he did not possess!

Louis XV was progressively more "enchanted." He was shortly to say so to Mercy, who hastened to send a messenger to Vienna, adding that "the whole royal family is infatuated with the Archduchess." Already, in the clearing on the outskirts of the forest, by winningly presenting her cheek she had almost softened the withered hearts of Mesdames and on her arrival at Compiègne she was to make the conquest of her cousins Orléans, Condé and Conti.

In Louis XV's apartments, "in spite of the King's presence," Marie Antoinette greeted the Princes of the Blood, who bowed to her in turn. Although the Duc d'Orléans, grandson of the Regent, the Duc de Penthièvre, grandson of Louis XIV and la Montespan, and the Princes of Condé and Conti seemed old in the Dauphine's eyes, her cousins Chartres and Bourbon, on the other hand, were almost her own age. One of them, the son of the Prince de Condé, was even a few months younger and was already married to Louise Bathilde d'Orléans, sister of the Duc de Chartres, who was nineteen. The son of the Duc d'Orléans, the future Philippe Egalité, was 23 and his wife, the Duchesse de Chartres, daughter of the Duc de Penthièvre, four years younger. The last princess to "salute on the cheek"—a young woman with a sad smile—was Marie-Thérèse de Carignan-Savoie, Princesse de Lamballe. Already two years a widow, she was only twenty-one. Her husband, only son of the Duc de Penthièvre, had died, after a wild life, from the results of a love affair. Since then she had lived a sad existence with her father-in-law, the inconsolable Duc de Penthièvre, who trailed his neurasthenia and his collection of watches from castle to castle.

The Dauphine was conducted to her apartments, where the ladies and gentlemen who had accompanied Louis XV to Compiègne were presented to her. Then, after supper with the King and the royal family, the Master of Ceremonies was ushered into the Princess's room, bearing twelve wedding rings provided by M. Papillon de la Ferté, the *Intendant des Menus Plaisirs*. One of the rings fitted her finger perfectly. It was then taken off, for she was not to wear it until the wedding ceremony.

The Dauphine then went to bed while the Dauphin, in accordance with etiquette, spent the night under a different roof. He was taken to the house of the Comte de Saint-Florentin, Minister and Secretary of State of the King's Household.

Marie Antoinette had nothing to fear. Louis-Auguste was not the kind of person to force his way into his wife's bedroom, as 36 years later, also at Compiègne, Napoleon was to do, after his marriage by proxy to a blonde archduchess.

At M. de Saint-Florentin's house the future Louis XVI, yawning, for he had eaten voraciously, opened his diary—a little notebook bound in grey cloth—and in his fine, small writing entered these five words under the date of 14 May 1770: "Interview with Madame la Dauphine."

For the last month M. de Mercy's life had been a burden to him. It was said that Mme du Barry was to be one of the 39 "ladies of quality" to be invited to supper with the royal family on the next day at the Château de la Muette, the last stage before Versailles. "It seems inconceivable," he wrote to Maria Theresa, "that the King should choose this moment to grant his favourite an honour which has hitherto been refused her."

And all day, as the carriages rolled towards Paris, the Ambassador quaked with apprehension. A ray of hope came to him when they halted at the Carmelite convent of Saint-Denis to present the Dauphine to "Sister Thérèse-Augustine." It would be impossible for the King to let his granddaughter become acquainted on one and the same day with his mistress and with the woman who, it was said, had entered into religion in order, by her sacrifice, to redeem her father's misconduct!

M. de Mercy was barely able to appreciate the applause of the Parisians, who cheered the Dauphine as her procession wound its way round Paris. The King, who had not been cheered for a long time, had preferred to go on ahead, and met his granddaughter at La Muette. On descending from her carriage she met the Dauphin's two brothers, Provence and Artois, the future Louis XVIII and Charles X. The Comte de Mercy began to breathe again. Surely the King would not make these two children of 13 and 14 dine with "the creature"! But suddenly the Ambassador turned pale. Among the ladies of quality Mme du Barry, sparkling with jewels, was bowing to the Dauphine. A little later, at supper, the King asked his granddaughter what she thought of the lady who was smiling at her from the end of the table.

"Charming," Marie Antoinette replied.

Interested, the Dauphine leant over towards the Comtesse de Noailles and asked her what place at court was held by that blonde, black-eyed lady whose complexion was like a rose-petal dipped in milk. The Lady of Honour hesitated, then said: "Her office? . . . To amuse the King!" The little bride at once exclaimed: "In that case I proclaim myself her rival!"

From the other end of the table the Comtesse considered the little girl who on the next day would become the first lady in France. Perhaps it was on that evening that she declared, with the lisp which enchanted her royal lover, "She is a *tsarming* little thing!"

In a month's time the two ladies would be finding each other infinitely less charming.

Twenty-three years before, another German princess—Maria-Josepha of Saxony—had also come to France to marry a Dauphin. She had been handed over on the same island in the Rhine, had been acclaimed at Strasbourg, awaited by the King and her "husband" in the Forest of Compiègne, and had then arrived at a castle where she had met the royal favourite—it was then Mme de Pompadour. Finally, on the following day, her carriage, greeted by the trumpets of the bodyguards, had drawn up before the marble staircase at Versailles. There Louis XV and the Dauphin had conducted her to her room on the ground floor of the palace looking out on to the south lawn.

On Wednesday 16 May 1770 Marie Antoinette in her turn, having made the acquaintance of two little girls—Mesdames Clotilde and Elisabeth, her husband's sisters—was led to the bedroom which had belonged to the Princess of Saxony and where the future Louis XVI, Louis XVIII and Charles X had been born.

The memory of "poor Pepa," as Louis XV had called his daughter-in-law, still clung to this room, which was next to the Dauphin's apartments and had been painted by Martin "in green with a covering varnish." At the beginning of his marriage Louis XVI's father, the widower of a Spanish princess whom he adored, could not enter his new wife's bedroom without bursting into tears. The very furniture reminded him of the one he had lost. The little Saxon had behaved admirably. "Give free course to your tears, Monsieur, and do not be afraid that they will offend me. On the contrary, they show what I have a right to hope for for myself, if I am happy enough to win your esteem."

She did win it, beyond anything she could have hoped for, and an astonished Versailles witnessed a touching idyll of royal marriage.

Would this exceptional phenomenon be renewed?

Marie Antoinette had finally noticed the Dauphin's bad grace. Louis-Auguste was as gloomy as his father had been on his wedding morning, although not for the same reason.

While in their adjoining rooms the bride and groom were being dressed in gold cloth and silver brocade a more serious problem disturbed the great building; a mounting drama had finally assumed considerable proportions. The Dukes and Peers gathered; a bishop—Mgr de Broglie—dared to present to the King a memorandum written in almost insulting tones; and Louis XV, although usually quite indifferent, was "so annoyed" that he threw his hat on the ground and "the tears sprang to his eyes."

And this was all because of a minuet.

The whole affair had begun exactly 274 years before—in 1496. When Charles VIII was reigning in France the younger branch of the house of Lorraine had broken away from the reigning dukes. Since then the elder branch had ended, in the person of Marie Antoinette's father, by sitting on the throne of Austria, while the younger branch— which included the Guises—had continued to serve France.

A few months before the date fixed for the marriage, Mme de Brionne-Lorraine, mother of the Prince de Lambesq and of Mlle de Lorraine, had visited M. de Mercy, to ask him if he could obtain "a distinction" for Mlle de Lorraine on the occasion of the wedding of the Archduchess, who was her cousin in the ninth degree.

The Ambassador considered the request a normal one and referred it to his sovereign, who was of the same opinion, so that one fine day Mercy went to Versailles to speak to the King about this "distinction." Louis XV agreed, and decided that on the day of the ball Mlle de Lorraine should dance the first minuet *after* the Princesses of the Blood and *before* the French Duchesses.

The news had run like wildfire through the palace. The Duchesses nearly fainted. Would not the Lorrainers, "those foreign princes," as they were contemptuously called, take advantage of this precedent to obtain a separate rank, half-way between the Princes of the Blood and the Dukes? The Dukes and Peers promptly got together under the presidency of the Bishop of Noyon and sent the King a petition signed by members of even the high nobility. Louis XV, extremely annoyed and unable to make up his mind, had been evasive. The Duchesses, who were furious, had then decided not to go to the ball. This was how matters stood on this bright spring morning in 1770.

The bride was now ready to make her entrance, for Versailles was like an enormous theatre presenting the spectacle of royalty at home. Everyone could enter to gape admiringly in the Hall of Mirrors at the King on his way to Mass, or to watch the principal characters eating. Louis XV, for example, had a way of slicing the top off his boiled egg which was worth going to see. Only "dogs, mendicant friars and people newly marked with smallpox" could not cross the threshold of the Salon of Hercules. Sightseers with no hat or sword were also turned back, but to get round this one had only to hire a hat and a rapier from the concierge, who did a trade in these accessories. Versailles was an anonymous mob, a public square. "Loose women" were admitted, on condition that they did not ply their "shameful trade" in the apartments. Even managers of performing animals were allowed. Cows went up to the first floor and were milked at the foot of the princesses' beds. If you had been "presented" you might watch the royal family rise, go to bed and have their hair dressed, and if your birth gave you a right to the *grandes entrées* you would have the honour of seeing the master of the house on his close-stool. The unfortunate people enjoyed a little privacy only back-stage, that is in their private apartments.

Since early morning the equipages of princes and dukes had been entering the royal courtyard. The harnesses were of tooled leather ornamented with ormolu plaques. Plumes and crimson or blue cockades adorned the tall horses, whose manes were plaited with coloured ribbon. The coachmen wore gold or silver hats with feathers and lace. Four lackeys in full livery hung on as best they could behind the coach and two pages sat next to the coachman.

The selected public—for gala first nights—crowded together in the Hall of Mirrors and the Chapel. For their better convenience and so that they might lose nothing of the spectacle balustrades and tiered seats had been installed by servants of the wardrobe. In principle only ladies in full dress, wearers of the blue ribbon and the many holders of invitation cards were allowed in—making over five thousand. But the order was not rigid and the commandant of the guard was told to allow ladies of quality into the castle "if they are followed by two lackeys or if they are escorted." The "best dressed" ladies were placed in the second gallery.

The curtain rose at one o'clock.

The Grand Master of the Ceremonies, full of his own importance, preceded the bride and groom, who were hand in hand. Marie Antoinette—a symphony in rose, gold and silver sparkling with diamonds—was like a ray of sunshine. As she passed through the Hall of Mirrors and the Grand Apartments she still kept her enchanting smile. She advanced with her "caressing walk," and some erudite courtiers quoted Virgil: *Incessu patuit dea.* At her side, with the rolling

gait which was typical of so many of the Bourbons, walked Louis-
Auguste, scowling in his gold clothes, which had cost 12,322 livres.

The Swiss Guards lined up in the Chapel beat their enormous drums
and blew their fifes to proclaim the King's arrival. The nave and the
galleries with their tiered seats were packed and many of the ladies
sighed on seeing their panniered dresses squashed as flat as pancakes.
It was an extraordinary sight. One seemed to be in a drawing-room
rather than in the house of God. The white and gold décor was so
pagan! The half-naked angels bearing the instruments of the Passion
resembled the disturbed dreams of adolescents, the cherubim of the
"heavenly glory" were like cupids and Judah was symbolised, naturally,
by a seraph. As for the Eternal Father, who hovered over the nave,
he was reminiscent of a bearded and indulgent Saturn.

The bride and groom knelt on squares of red velvet fringed with
gold. The King and the Princes stepped forward. The Grand
Almoner, Mgr de la Roche-Aymon, Archbishop of Rheims,
blessed the thirteen pieces of gold—a reminder of the purchase of the
wife—and the wedding rings. Before placing the ring on Marie
Antoinette's fourth finger Louis-Auguste glanced at his grandfather,
who nodded his head. The Archbishop gave his blessing to the two
children kneeling before him and Louis XV returned to his chair.
The Mass began, while the King's orchestra, placed behind the altar,
played a motet composed by Abbé Ganzargues. The court crowded
the transepts. "Members of the bodyguards, stationed at intervals, saw
to it that silence was observed and even that people who were
inattentive knelt down."

After the *Pater Noster* the Bishop of Senlis, the King's First Almoner,
and the Bishop of Chartres, the Dauphine's First Almoner, placed a
canopy of silver brocade above the pair. This canopy had been
provided by the King's privy purse, but after the ceremony it was
claimed by the eight almoners of the district to be sold for their
benefit, and this proceeding gave rise to a great deal of argument.

Ordinarily the Dauphin liked to accompany the divine service by
singing in a voice both loud and off key. Also, when the blessed
bread was distributed, he used to bring out a pocket-knife and cut
himself a slice or even bite off a piece. It would appear that on this
occasion he did not engage in any eccentricity, for the chroniclers—
dazzled, perhaps, by the spectacle—have recorded no picturesque details.

The parish priest of Versailles brought the marriage register. The King signed, followed by Marie Antoinette, whose hand trembled a little, making a blot.

On returning to her apartments Madame la Dauphine received the officers of her household. They took the oath of fidelity to her in the presence of the Comte de Saint-Florentin. After the Lady of Honour and the twelve ladies who accompanied her—the new ones were fortunately younger than those sent to Strasbourg—came the *Chevalier d'Honneur*, the First Maître d'Hôtel, the First Almoner, the Intendants, the serving gentlemen, the First Equerry, the Controllers-General, who had themselves received the oath from an army of employees: fourteen waiting women, two preachers, four almoners, five chaplains, a *Chevalier d'Honneur*, one maître d'hôtel in ordinary, four maîtres d'hôtel, two equerries in ordinary, four equerries, nineteen valets de chambre, five ushers of the bedchamber, two of the antechamber and two of the *cabinet*, two doctors, two apothecaries, four surgeons, a clock-maker, a tapestry-maker, eighteen lackeys, a stable equerry, a fencing-master, two muleteers of the *litière du corps*, a wig-maker, who was also attendant for the bath and Turkish bath, and a bearer of the close-stool, a post also held by a man. A further 168 servants were occupied with her food. For since the morning Marie Antoinette had become the mistress of her own kitchen gardens, cellarmen, *coureurs de vin, hâteurs*, scullery-boys, master cooks, butlers, pantlers, cooks, wine-bearers and fruiterers.

Had she any idea, as she saw these officers bow before her, that any encroachment on their prerogatives would provoke a drama? To use their own expression, it would destroy "all the splendour of their office."

It was a pity—for it would have opened the girl's eyes a little—that her Gentleman of Honour did not tell her about the dreadful struggle in which he was engaged with her maître d'hôtel. The former considered that he had a right to certain functions fulfilled by his colleague which concerned "parts of the Mouth of Madame la Dauphine." He wanted the honour not of drawing some of Marie Antoinette's irregular teeth, but of being able, on the days of the *Grand Couvert*, to give orders to the butlers for serving the wine. And these gentlemen disputed hotly, recalling precedents in force in the time of Queen Marie, wife of Charles VII.

These conflicts had not arisen on the creation of a new household. The King's servants, those of Mesdames, as well as those of His Majesty's grandsons and granddaughters, argued, complained and fought, while continuing to salute each other with elegance and courtesy. For example, the life of His Majesty's wardrobe master was a martyrdom. On Palm Sunday of 1728 a wardrobe boy had taken away "without orders" the folding stool on which that officer was allowed to sit behind the King in chapel. Since that ill-fated day the successive wardrobe masters had remained standing. In vain they sent in petitions, proposals and voluminous memoranda—the stool never returned. And for 42 years they searched their consciences. No! they were innocent! They "had done nothing to draw on themselves such a painful humiliation." Such is the conclusion of their report, which can still be read in the National Archives.

The state furniture—from the Salon de Paix to the Salon of Hercules —was ready. This evening the King was holding a reception. In the Hall of Mirrors the gilded wood furniture—which had replaced the massive silver furniture sent by Louis XIV to the Mint in 1689—had for the first time been taken away and replaced by candelabra of carved and gilded wood each bearing 32 chandeliers. It was as bright as day. Sitting at a table covered by a new cloth of green velvet with gold braid and fringes, the King and the newly married couple played the boring game of *cavagnole*. The ushers, the Swiss Guards and the King's *valets de chambre* received the 6,000 guests at the doors and saw them seated on the benches of the Grand Apartments. If one wanted to see the King play one had to walk along behind the railings in the Hall of Mirrors and go out by the Salon de Paix and the Queen's apartments. Many interested people joined this procession without being invited: they were the "common people." They had been chased from the park by the storm which broke during the afternoon. The barriers were forced and the dripping sightseers mingled with the guests and watched the spectacle.

A second storm broke. Madame Louise trembled with fright. "She was so scared," Madame Campan wrote, "that she approached quite insignificant people. She asked them all sorts of kind questions. If she saw a flash of lightning she pressed their hands. At a peal of thunder she would have thrown her arms round them."

The storm died down. Madame Louise "resumed her rigidity, her silence and her air of reserve" and the royal family moved to the new opera house, where the feast was to take place. Strange sounds of music were heard: they came from the French and Swiss Guards massed in the gallery of the north wing. They had left off their red, white and blue uniforms and were disguised as Turks, making "a great uproar with some music from that country." Along the way the salute was given by the bodyguards in blue coats with silver braid, red breeches and stockings and the Hundred-Swiss in slashed trunks, starched ruffs and plumed caps.

On entering the Opera House, which was being opened for the first time that evening, the guests did not feel that they were in a theatre. The stage was so deep that it had been possible to reproduce on it the balconies of the auditorium, thus forming a perfect oval of green-veined grey marble. On the false floor, which covered the seats and was on a level with the stage, was set up a table 26 feet long and 13 feet wide. The guests took their places in the order prescribed by etiquette:

Louis XV

The Dauphin	The Dauphine
Comte de Provence	Comte d'Artois
Madame Clotilde	Madame Adelaide
Madame Victoire	Madame Sophie
Duc d'Orléans	Duc de Chartres
Duchesse de Chartres	Prince de Condé
Duc de Bourbon	Duchesse de Bourbon
Comte de Clermont	Princesse de Conti
Prince de Conti	Comte de la Marche
Comtesse de la Marche	Duc de Penthièvre
Princesse de Lamballe	

The rest of the Court looked on admiringly with empty stomachs.

Escorted by the bodyguards and by a crowd of waiting gentlemen accompanied by maîtres d'hôtel with their silver-gilt batons, hailed by the rolling of drums, the "King's Meat"—that is, the hundreds of dishes making up the feast—arrived from the Great Offices 600 metres away.

Marie Antoinette ate hardly anything, but the Dauphin, who seemed pleased for the first time since the morning, devoured his food. The

King leant anxiously towards him and murmured: "Don't overload your stomach tonight."

The astonished bridegroom laughed and exclaimed: "Why not? I always sleep better after a good supper!"

The King did not insist and looked at Marie Antoinette rather sadly.

The programme included a gigantic show of fireworks, but the storm had drenched the preparations made by Ruggieri, the pyrotechnist, and the spectacle was postponed until the Saturday evening, to the great disappointment of the people, "who were very wet and said nothing."

All that remained was to put the couple to bed and here too the doors of the "Theatre Royal" were open. Everyone in the court was crushed together on the ground floor to see the Archbishop of Rheims bless the bed, the King hand the shirt to the Dauphin, who seemed progressively more bored and sleepy, and the Duchesse de Chartres help the blushing Marie Antoinette put on her nightgown.

The bride and groom lay down behind the hangings and then suddenly—as was the etiquette—the bed-curtains were drawn aside. All present bowed deeply and followed the King out.

Twenty-four years ago, in the same bed and after an evening of similar festivities, Maria Josepha of Saxony had spent her wedding night consoling her husband who was weeping bitterly as he thought of his first wife. On this evening Marie Antoinette had no one to console. In the bed where he was born the Dauphin, his stomach full, fell into a noisy sleep.

On the next day Louis-Auguste wrote his famous "Nothing," in his private notebook—a "nothing" which was to become distressingly symbolic. However, Marie Antoinette displayed no anxiety so far. Thursday 17 May was too full for the little bride to have time to dream of love. She had to receive the whole court and "present the cheek" to those entitled. In the evening she was taken to see "Perseus," the old opera by Quinault and Lulli, brought up to date for the occasion by a certain Joliveau, who, so as to insert a ballet of his own invention, had had the odd idea of "reinforcing Lulli's music" and of compressing the opera into four acts.

Once the curtain had risen Marie Antoinette had difficulty in stifling her yawns. The chronicler Bachaumon admitted frankly: "The Dauphine was bored to death by an unbearable recitative." She might have been diverted by the machinery, but it worked badly. Arnould, who was responsible, had unfortunately broken his leg just before the rehearsals. He dragged himself to the theatre, but fell a second time. He was there this evening, confined to a stretcher and quite unable to go everywhere in the enormous theatre. He could only watch helplessly the collapse of his work. Even the Eagle—symbol of the House of Austria and the highlight of the spectacle—flopped heavily on to the altar of Hymen, instead of perching nobly, and Arnould contemplated suicide.

At one moment Marie Antoinette seemed to get some pleasure from the spectacle. Perseus, having caught his foot in a floorboard, fell heavily at the feet of Andromeda at the very moment when he should have been freeing his future wife. But when Perseus got up the poor Dauphine relapsed into apathy.

After this soporific play Marie Antoinette had no difficulty in getting to sleep and imitating her husband, who once in bed had fallen into a heavy slumber. At dawn on Friday the 18th he left the conjugal bed to go hunting.

"He is leaving very early," the courtiers murmured.

He came back exhausted and remembered that he had a wife. He found Marie Antoinette playing with a little dog.

"Have you slept well?"

"Yes."

Their badinage went no further. Louis-Auguste went out and, according to the Abbé Vermond, who was present, "the Dauphine played with her little dog. He served as a diversion for a moment, then she fell to musing. My heart was wrung."

On the evening of the third day of marriage again "nothing" happened and the musings became more frequent. Mercy, who was at once informed, told Maria Theresa. He prided himself on possessing some medical knowledge and tried to explain to her that "the Dauphin's development is late probably because his constitution has been weakened by his sudden and rapid growth."

This absence of marital prowess did not alarm Louis XV. He was much more preoccupied by the tiresome business of the minuet, which was becoming serious. Duchesses with the right to a *tabouret* and bearing some of the finest names in France were threatening to leave the court if Mlle de Lorraine danced on the Saturday before they did.

Louis XV humbled himself so far as to write to the Dukes explaining that "the dance at the ball was the one thing which could not form a precedent, since the choice of dancers depended only on his will, without distinction of place, rank or dignity." The King ended his letter by declaring: "I trust that the princes and nobility of my realm, in virtue of the fidelity, submission, attachment and even friendship which they have always shown me and my predecessors, will never occasion anything which might displease me, particularly in the present circumstances."

These lines, judged "hardly worthy of a great monarch," did not settle the dispute, and Louis XV decided to send each lady a personal note enjoining her to appear at the ball.

At five o'clock on Saturday the 19th only the ladies of Lorraine were in the ballroom—once more a perfect oval. Finally a few dancers appeared, though very late. It was not the King's letter, or his personal note, which had made them change their minds, but regret, if they stayed at home, at not being able to show off their new gala dresses. However, the absence of many indomitable duchesses was noticed. In spite of these defections the ball took place as arranged.

After bowing to their grandfather the Dauphin and Dauphine opened the ball by dancing a minuet alone. The Dauphin was as clumsy as his wife was charming and accomplished. Then, still very prettily, she danced a quadrille with the Duc de Chartres, who was the best dancer at court. Then came the minuets in which Mlle de Lorraine and the Prince de Lambesq took part in the place the King had granted them. Did Marie Antoinette observe in the seventh minuet a delightful dancer with large, clear eyes, slender, pretty and shy, who was none other than the Comtesse Jules de Polignac?

When night fell everyone moved to the great gallery and the terrace to see the famous fireworks which had been prepared for the 16th. The bride and groom, the King and Mercy stood at the central window of the Hall of Mirrors, at which a grille had been put up in case of accidents. Then began the most beautiful firework display ever shown in France. Thousands of rockets painted on the sky the arms of the Dauphin and the Dauphine and the inevitable temple of Hymen. While the catherine wheels, the windmills, the spheres and the suns turned, while the pyramids of fire sparkled and the shining cascades flowed, while mortars and "rolling fires" exploded, imitating "the sounds of war," hundreds of musicians could be heard on the Grand Canal.

Only the bouquet "in gold and brilliants" misfired. While they were waiting for it it was already over. The two storms had soaked the fireworks, which gave off a thick smoke. Thousands of people from Paris and Versailles danced until six o'clock in the morning in the illuminated park. The soldiers on duty—700 Swiss Guards and French Guards with a white plume in their hats—did not have to intervene. Everything went quite well.

By the time the festivities ended Marie Antoinette had long since begun her fourth night as a married woman. Louis-Auguste snored at her side. Had she resigned herself to this strange situation? Since according to Mercy's diagnosis her husband's rapid growth had stopped everything, there was, perhaps, nothing to do but wait. This was what her mother was to advise. "You are both so young! As far as your health is concerned it is all for the best. You will both gain strength."

The festivities during May prevented the bride from falling too often into musing. One of the entertainments offered her was a performance of Racine's *Athalie* with additional music and choruses "especially written or taken from operas." Athalie was played by the famous Mlle Clairon, who had left her retirement for the occasion, much to the annoyance of Mme du Barry, who was a supporter of Mlle de Mesnil. Unfortunately the latter could act only after drinking a bottle of red wine, and another bottle placed in the wings went the same way during the performance. Perhaps it was feared that the emotion caused by the Dauphine's presence would cause the actress to exceed the usual amount. For whatever reason Mlle Clairon was chosen. Lekain, as ugly as he was talented, played the part of Abner in a costume of maroon velvet with gold frogging and a braided three-cornered hat. This was the tradition. Mlle Clairon wore a farthingale and chopines—very high pointed shoes. It was in similar shoes that she once fell down when playing Camilla fleeing from Horace's dagger, and Horace was seen to sheath his knife, put on his gloves, help his partner up politely and kill her in the wings.

A few days later the Dauphine saw the famous ballet *The Enchanted Tower*. This was a "mechanical drama" from an original idea by the Duchesse de Villeroy. It was about a princess held prisoner by a wicked spirit. She was, of course, freed by a handsome knight who killed the monster. The "very mediocre" words were by Joliveau and the music was a hotch-potch from various operas "arranged" by a certain Dauvergene. The finale was to be the crumbling of the tower which, full of chariots and knights, was to sink beneath the stage. But the racehorses from the King's stables were upset by the unexpected business and "disturbed the order of the spectacle." Marie Antoinette yawned gracefully behind her fan.

The festivities were over, but who was to pay the bill: the 30,385 rockets for the fireworks, the 90,000 lamps and the 603,611 vases for illuminating the park, the 4,492 roman candles, the 14,444 cartridges fired, the 6,820 pots of fire; the 1,841 costumes made for the theatrical performances—in short the nine millions (nearly 2,000 million francs of our money) spent on the marriage festivities?

"What do you think of my festivities at Versailles?" the King had asked his Controller of Finances.

"Sire, I think they are . . . *priceless!*"

So, as regards many of the expenses, the example was followed of M. de Marigny, who had decided not to settle the bills of the carpet manufacturers who had built the new theatre. Poor Arnould was ruined, having got nothing from the affair but a broken leg. A whole file of the National Archives is filled with the pathetic pleas of tradesmen in want who at the beginning of the Revolution were still asking to be paid at least something on account of what they had spent twenty years before for Marie Antoinette's wedding.

The Dauphine had come triumphantly through the test. She had conquered Versailles. "Her politeness embellished her countenance," we are told by a witness. "She had such a graceful word for everyone and curtsied so prettily that in a few days she delighted everyone . . . There is a charm in her manner which will turn all our heads." "She is all smiles," the stern Mercy admitted.

While waiting to wear the crown of France she wore that of charm and grace. Everyone crowded round her and flattered her. When she did not think of Louis-Auguste's sulkiness she was completely happy.

On Wednesday 30 May, at eight o'clock in the evening, the Dauphine entered her carriage with Madame Adelaide. The Dauphin was heaven knows where, but for all that Marie Antoinette was smiling. For the first time she was going—incognito—to Paris, where there was to be a great evening festivity.

On 28 April Louis XV had commanded the city of Paris to offer gifts to Marie Antoinette. "Do not fail in this," he had advised, "for such is our pleasure."

The Mayor, M. Bignon, and the magistrates had not failed, and gifts had been transported to Versailles on carts. On the wedding day the inhabitants had been enjoined "to shut their shops and illuminate their houses." On the old rampart—the present Boulevard des Capucines —a fair had been permitted where it was "forbidden for anyone to draw his sword, to blaspheme and to swear on God's name."

Furthermore the town had decided that on 30 May a great festival should be held at night in the Place Louis XV—now the Place de la Concorde. On the uneven ground in front of the new houses built by Gabriel and near the King's statue a Corinthian temple had been erected flanked by dolphins and crowned with the ciphers of Marie Antoinette and Louis-Auguste together with "a medallion in their likeness." It was on this that the fireworks were to be let off. Since the early morning essence of bergamot had been poured on the banks of the Seine. At five o'clock fountains of wine began to flow. When evening fell the façades of the two palaces were illuminated and the yews in the square and the trees of the Champs-Elysées were adorned with lamps and vases.

As Marie Antoinette drove towards Paris she was eager to arrive. The carriage had scarcely crossed the Pont de Sèvres when the sky was filled with light and the exploding fireworks could be heard in the distance. The Dauphine had not reached the Porte de la Conférence —the present Place de l'Alma—when the set piece, which was the perennial temple of Hymen, could be seen in the clear May sky. But suddenly the six carriages horses and the escort of bodyguards halted in the Cours-la-Reine. A great clamour arose from the square. People were running in terror. And little by little the Princess learned the details of the disaster. The set piece had hardly gone out when a crowd of 300,000 people, coming simultaneously from the square, the quays and the Champs-Elysées, rushed towards the Rue Royale to see the fair. The pressure was so great that a firemen's cart, which was moving towards the Corinthian temple to put out the beginnings of a fire, was overturned. The flood of people, which was divided into several streams by the carriages leaving the square, clashed with another crowd coming from the Boulevard to see the illuminations in the

Champs-Elysées. In a few moments 400,000 people—according to the report of the Hôtel de Ville—were jammed in the Rue Royale, the Rue Saint-Florentine and the Rue de la Bonne-Morue, now the Rue Boissy-d'Anglas. Men, women and children stumbled over the gutters and were trodden underfoot. Other unfortunates tripped over them and fell. A wafer-seller collapsed with his stall; carriages were overturned. People tried to climb on the carriages, but they gave way under the weight and the horses were suffocated. Soon people were walking on piles of corpses. It was like a scene from Dante: the dead, emptied of blood through the nose and mouth, stayed upright, and were carried along by the crowd. They toppled over only when they were no longer supported.

By the time Marie Antoinette was returning in tears to Versailles in her carriage drawn by six white horses, the panic had died down. The wounded were cared for and the dead taken away.

In the morning the Dauphin, overcome, wrote to the Hôtel de Ville: "I have learned of the disaster which came upon Paris on my account. I am deeply distressed. I have been brought the sum which the King sends me every month for my private expenses. It is all I have to give. I send it to you. Give aid to the most unfortunate." Marie Antoinette, shedding her first tears, followed his example.

On the same morning 132 labelled corpses were laid out in the Cemetery of the Madeleine, in the same grass enclosure where 23 years later the body of Marie Antoinette, the head placed between the legs, would be thrown on the bare ground.

3

※

One Word

THE FESTIVITIES WERE over. Versailles had relapsed into calm, pending the annual exodus of the court to Marly, Choisy, Fontainebleau and Compiègne. Etiquette held sway, but in between the performances —the *levers*, the *couchers*, midday mass, meals and games—ordinary life was able to go on. At 10 o'clock in the morning and 3 o'clock in the afternoon the King went down to see his daughters in Madame Victoire's great sitting-room on the ground floor under the Salon de la Guerre. Marie Antoinette would be there "in a light dress of gauze or taffeta." She had stopped wearing her sparkling diamonds and looked even more exquisite. But Louis XV did not stay long. He soon left his daughters to their intrigues against Choiseul and their quarrels over etiquette, and went to find his dear, blonde Comtesse, whom he had installed temporarily above his own apartments until the court's absence in the summer, when Gabriel (the architect) would be able to prepare the charming rooms which still exist. Louis XV would often come down again to his daughters' room a little before eleven, after supping in private. Marie Antoinette would be there too, having fallen asleep on a large sofa while waiting for him. She had spent her day embroidering a waistcoat for the King.

"I hope that with God's help it will be finished in a few years," she confessed, smiling.

The Dauphine had as much leisure as ever. Louis-Auguste exhausted himself hunting and in the evenings thought only of repose so as to be able to continue his sporting exploits on the morrow. "I am preaching patience to my daughter," Maria Theresa wrote to Mercy, "and assure her that she will not lose by it." It would seem that one night, after seven weeks of marriage, Marie Antoinette forgot her mother's advice and complained to her husband, for on Sunday 8 July the Dauphin, for the first time, discussed the problem with his wife.

"Rest assured that I am not ignorant of what is involved in the state of marriage. From the earliest days I imposed on myself a rule of conduct which I wished to observe, but the time limit I set myself has been reached. You will find that at Compiègne I shall live with you in the fullest intimacy you could wish."

The Dauphin would be 16 on 13 August. Was this the time limit he had set himself? At Compiègne, on 23 August, however, "nothing" happened.

The whole court was soon informed. Oddly enough, those most alarmed were the King's daughters, who, according to Mercy, "upset Madame le Dauphine and cause her anxiety." The King in his turn was surprised. Marie Antoinette once more gave her husband to understand that she too was "not ignorant of what was involved in the state of marriage" and the Dauphin promised to come to her room on 20 September. Marie Antoinette was so happy that she imparted this piece of news to her aunts who, like all old maids, announced the event to everyone. Madame Adelaide, who could not in fact have known much about it, felt it necessary to "exhort" the Dauphin to give him courage, as Mercy informed his sovereign. The 20 September arrived, and the Dauphin, "scared," remained in his own room. Marie Antoinette sighed and from 400 leagues' distance Maria Theresa advised her daughter "to be prodigal of her caresses." The Dauphine obeyed and her husband weakened, promising to come to his wife on 10 October. The court would then be at Fontainebleau and the Dauphin was convinced that the bracing air of the forest would have a good influence on his behaviour. But the same scene repeated itself: Marie Antoinette confiding in her aunts, Madame Adelaide gossiping and exhorting, and the husband taking fright. The King then decided to intervene and questioned his grandson on his "frigid condition."

"I find my wife charming," the young man replied. "I love her, but I still need a little time to overcome my timidity."

It was decided to wait.

But his "insensibility," as Mercy called it, continued and worried Maria Theresa, who was anxious to have a grandson whose mere existence would consolidate the alliance. "If a girl as pretty as the Dauphine cannot stir the Dauphin," she wrote in despair, "every remedy will be useless."

There was one, however.

Louis-Auguste's "strange behaviour" was to have such repercussions that it is worth dwelling on and listening to the opinion of a doctor. Dr. Paul Ganière, the excellent biographer of Corvisart, wrote to me on the subject: "What was the matter? Did the Dauphin feel physically repelled by the young Archduchess? Not at all. She was charming and expressed her satisfaction in being his wife. Although not very expansive he did not mind revealing his happiness on many occasions. Then was the heir to the throne abnormal? Everyone was soon convinced of it, particularly since rumours and indiscretions whose origin it is very difficult to trace have left the impression that nature had unfortunately endowed him with an anatomical abnormality which, although slight, required surgical treatment at an early age so as not to interfere with his future development. This malformation, which was either ignored or deliberately neglected when action should have been taken, through fear of responsibility, played a serious part in the difficulties surrounding the consummation of the marriage. But this was not all. The descriptions of the Dauphin which have come down to us present him as a boy heavy of mind and body, showing definite backwardness in various features, particularly in the glands to which doctors nowadays attach so much importance. Therefore, together with the physical peculiarity I have just mentioned, or more probably as a result of it, a kind of indifference due to this sluggishness of the genital functions had turned this 15-year-old adolescent into someone completely calm, just when he should have been thanking heaven for giving him a charming wife, quite ready to yield to his desires. Strong principles, natural timidity and an awkwardness increased by bad eyesight do not in themselves explain the marital conduct of Louis XV's grandson. Nature had made him what he was and if the scalpel had been used earlier he might have been different. Tormented by an inferiority complex and vaguely aware of being ridiculous, he yielded to the advice of the doctors who assured him that with the help of a healthy diet and violent physical exercise all would be well. This advice, which in its optimism and simplicity suited his temperament, seemed very sensible and he let weeks go by without thinking that Marie Antoinette, for all her innocence, might experience an indefinable uneasiness, or even a wound to her self-esteem, in having unwillingly to play the part of a wife in name only."

In order to follow his diet the Dauphin ate enormously. Nothing spoiled his appetite, neither the presence of 20 Officers of the Mouth busying themselves round his table, nor the armed guards protecting his "Meat," nor the hundred or so people who, in profound silence, watched him eat.

Marie Antoinette merely nibbled. The Dauphine already had a sense of the ridiculous and could not bring herself to follow the example of Maria Leczinska, who never hesitated to call on one of those standing by.

"Madame?" the spectator would say, coming forward and bowing.

"I think this stew is a fricassee of chicken," the Queen would declare solemnly.

"I am of the same opinion, Madame," the person addressed would reply proudly, walking backwards to his place.

Marie Antoinette preferred to observe the people standing in front of her table. She could not keep her thoughts to herself and would burst into laughter with her young Ladies of Honour. Mercy was soon warning Maria Theresa. "Madame la Dauphine is careless of outward appearances. . . . She makes fun of people who appear to her ridiculous." This was all the more serious because Marie Antoinette "knows how to infuse into her remarks just the amount of wit to make them more telling." The Ambassador often noticed her "whispering in the ears of the young ladies" and then "laughing with them." Maria Theresa scolded her: "It is said that you have begun to make fun of everyone and to burst out laughing in people's faces. . . . By amusing five or six young ladies or gentlemen you will lose the rest." On several occasions the Empress insisted: "Do not give way to an inclination to make fun of others." But the Dauphine shrugged her shoulders.

When Louis XV was informed of his granddaughter's mockery he did not hide his displeasure and sent for the Comtesse de Noailles.

"It is quite right that in private Madame la Dauphine should give way to her natural gaiety, but in public, when she is holding her court, her behaviour must be more reserved."

Marie Antoinette listened inattentively to the lecture brought to her by her Lady of Honour. She considered that she was no longer a child and that her education was complete.

So the smiling Archduchess became the mocking, lively Dauphine, who had only one idea: to amuse herself. She decided she would like to ride. Mercy, whom this idea frightened "in view of the Dauphine's extreme youth," warned Choiseul, who went to tell Louis XV. The King, who was bored by the whole affair, found a compromise and permitted the use of a donkey, which after several happy expeditions to Compiègne became a pony and then a real horse. Mercy proposed a middle course: "that the Archduchess should go only at a walking pace and rarely trot." Maria Theresa protested: "Riding spoils the complexion." Marie Antoinette looked in her mirror, and, reassured, galloped the harder. The Empress sighed: "The donkeys and horses will have occupied the time needed for reading." But at least let her daughter not go hunting! The girl promised, but at the beginning of May 1771, when she was fifteen-and-a-half, she disobeyed on the pretext of having "accidentally met the hunt." Then she repeated the offence, following the hunt on horseback or in a cabriolet, which frightened Maria Theresa still more but has given us a charming scene. One day the postillion fell and was trampled by the horses. The Princess refused to go on, had the wounded man tended in her presence and wrote to her mother: "I told everyone they were my friends, pages, grooms, postillions. I said: 'My friend, go and fetch the surgeons. My friend, run quickly for a stretcher, see if he can speak, if he is conscious!' "

The spoiled child, less felicitously, played the part of a caterer. "Her Royal Highness," Mercy reported, "has the habit of bringing in her carriages all kind of cold meats and refreshments which she likes to distribute to the courtiers following the hunt." Soon "all the young people in the King's suite" neglected the stag, not for the cold meats and the refreshments, but to cluster round the carriage in which the pretty young Princess laughed at the replies of those whom Mercy called "scatterbrains."

The Empress had to console herself with her one victory. Not without difficulty she had managed to get her daughter once more to wear the corset which she had decided to do without at Compiègne. After serious discussions between Mme de Noailles, the Abbé de Vermond and the Comte de Mercy, after the exchange of numerous letters on the subject between Vienna and Paris the Ambassador could at last utter a cry of victory: "Madame la Dauphine is again wearing her whalebone corset."

In spite of this brilliant result Maria Theresa lamented: "Her carelessness, her lack of pleasure in any serious concentration and her indiscretion provide me with many occasions of anxiety."

One evil came from her intimacy with her aunts. At the beginning, when she was neglected by her husband, whose marital failures had plunged him further into awkwardness and misanthropy, the little girl had no other resources than to go four or five times a day to see Mesdames. The Empress herself had advised this. "The Princesses are full of virtue and talent; this is very fortunate for you; I hope you will deserve their friendship." Mercy was of a different opinion. According to him—and he was right—these old maids "had never had the gift of behaving in a way befitting the circumstances." The ground-floor apartments of Mesdames were a hotbed of intrigue and gossip. Even among themselves there was jealousy and almost hatred, and Mercy noted that "Madame Adelaide and Madame Sophie are engaged in inspiring in the Archduchess a coldness for Madame Victoire."

The influence of Mesdames soon became disastrous. Marie Antoinette allowed herself "to be led into sharp remarks in which she indulges only when she is provoked by bad example. I have unfortunately learned," Mercy added, "that of all the ideas which Madame Adelaide contrives to teach Madame la Dauphine there is not one which is not either false or prejudicial to Her Imperial Highness."

It does not appear to have been Madame Adelaide, however, who first revealed to her niece what precisely were the "amusements" of Mme du Barry and the King. It was the Dauphin, and the Dauphine was sickened by the thought that her grandfather had a mistress—and such a mistress! She at once wrote to her mother: "It is pitiful to see the King's partiality for Mme du Barry, who is the most stupid and impertinent creature you can imagine." Fearing her mother's reactions to this outburst, she added: "You can be well assured that I shall commit no fault either for her or against her."

In fact she treated her grandfather's mistress "correctly," but Mesdames were gradually to force her from the line of conduct she had wisely set herself. A trivial incident came to help them.

It began by a women's quarrel. In the little drawing room of the

Château at Choisy the ladies attending court occupied the front benches. Madame du Barry arrived very late with two members of her following, the Maréchale de Mirepoix and the Comtesse de Valentinois. The favourite looked at the occupiers of the benches who showed clearly that they had no intention of giving up their places. No one moved and on both sides the fans fluttered. It was not known who spoke first, but in a few seconds remarks were exchanged, sharp, lively and full of innuendo. One of the Dauphine's ladies, Mme de Grammont, a sister-in-law of the Duchesse de Choiseul and "a leader in this dispute," strongly attacked Mme du Barry, who was forced to retreat and take her place at the back of the room.

On the following day Mme de Grammont received a *lettre de cachet* exiling her 15 leagues from the court, and she begged Marie Antoinette to intervene. The Choiseul family protested, Mesdames became agitated and the Dauphine prepared to act. Fortunately Mercy arrived, calmed the Dauphine and advised her to attack the King in his one weak spot. Marie Antoinette should show that she was "somewhat hurt that a person in her service should have been exiled without anyone mentioning it to her." The Dauphine followed this advice and the King could only murmur a kind of embarrassed apology. But Mme du Barry was on the watch—Mme de Grammont belonging to the clan of her greatest enemy Choiseul—and Louis XV did not rescind the order of exile. At Fontainebleau, a little later on, the young girl, all smiles, returned to the attack. Mme de Grammont was seriously ill and wanted to return to Paris "to receive treatment." The Dauphine became coaxing, and tried out the influence of her fifteen years.

"What a grief it would be to me, papa, if a woman in my service should die while under your displeasure!"

Mme du Barry was the stronger and the King did not yield until a medical examination had been held, but the culprit was still forbidden the court.

The Dauphine's pride had been seriously wounded by this affront. She was soon to suffer another victory by the favourite—the Choiseul affair.

The Minister had approved his sister-in-law's attitude at Choisy, all the more because he himself had undergone something similar at the grand theatre in Rome. He was then French Ambassador and as such regularly occupied a box of honour on the right of that occupied by the Governor. One day it was decided to award this box by lot, as well as the other seats. Choiseul nearly fainted, and on recovering himself threatened to ask for his passport. Apologies were made and the box was given back to him. But the Ambassador demanded reparation. Henceforth he insisted on having the Governor's own box surmounted by the papal arms. It was now Benedict XIV who nearly fainted, but Choiseul would not yield. He declared that he would leave Rome, and finally the Pope, less powerful in his own domain than Mme du Barry at Versailles, had to give way.

One may imagine how Choiseul's pride was offended by Mme de Grammont's exile. His attitude to Mme du Barry became more hostile and the Comtesse persuaded her royal lover to dismiss the Minister.

A pretext was soon found. The King and his Minister were in disagreement because Choiseul was urging war against England in order to support Spain in a complicated affair about an island off St. Malo occupied by English sailors. Louis XV averted the imminent conflict, but his Minister's warlike instincts were a good excuse for exiling him on 24 December and thus offering his pretty mistress the Christmas present she had been angling for for months.

What was Marie Antoinette to do when the man to whom she owed everything was exiled to the provinces? Mercy was on the watch and sent the Abbé de Vermond to this *enfant terrible*. The Dauphine should simply express "a little displeasure," no more. On 6 January Maria Theresa sent her an urgent letter enjoining her "never to forget the gratitude she owed to Choiseul," but also advising her not to "let herself be drawn into any faction" and to "remain completely neutral."

Marie Antoinette thought to obey her mother's wishes by ignoring the favourite's presence and according her not a word or a look. Mme du Barry might have been invisible. Her aunts and the Dauphin encouraged her in this course of action. The whole of Versailles watched the struggle with delight. They almost applauded. Under Mme du Barry's prompting the King spoke to Mme de Noailles about this attitude, but without daring to tackle the problem frankly.

"The Dauphine allows herself to speak too freely about what she sees or thinks she sees," he said. "Thoughtless remarks might produce bad effects within the family."

Louis XV thus placed his Comtesse "within the family." On the evening of this rebuke Marie Antoinette spoke to her "dear papa," who felt very ill at ease, said nothing and confined himself to coaxing and kissing his granddaughter. Everything was settled, or rather nothing was settled. The Dauphine continued to refuse even to look at Mme du Barry, who, however, reigned more securely than ever. It was not Maria Leczinska's room on the first floor, where Marie Antoinette now lived, which was "the Queen's apartment," but the little low-ceilinged but exquisite rooms in which the Comtesse was installed in December 1770. The seat of the Government was there, and d'Aiguillon, who through the favour of Mme du Barry had succeeded Choiseul, worked with the King in the favourite's new home. It became difficult, not to say impossible, for Ministers from abroad to avoid the uncrowned queen. Poor Mercy knew something about this. He found himself in the presence of the Comtesse for the first time at a dinner attended by the Duc d'Aiguillon, the Nuncio and the Sardinian Ambassador. The last-named was speaking to the favourite "as to a person with whom one is acquainted." The representative of His Holiness likewise made a leg. Mme du Barry was more charming to the Austrian Ambassador than to his Roman and Sardinian colleagues. Instead of sitting down to table they chatted like old friends.

Two days later Marie Antoinette, who had learned all about it—nothing being secret at Versailles—could not help saying to the Ambassador in a low voice: "I congratulate you on the fine company with whom you took supper on Sunday."

Mercy bowed. "Today, Madame, an even more remarkable event is to take place on which I shall have the honour to report to Your Royal Highness tomorrow."

That evening, indeed, Mercy consented to go and see the King in Mme du Barry's room. Needless to say, Louis XV was late and the Ambassador was alone with the beautiful woman, to whose charm he quickly succumbed. "She bears herself well," he wrote to Vienna. "She does not appear to have any tendency to malice." Fearing, however, that his report might offend his sovereign he added: "But her speech smacks strongly of her former condition." What she wanted was to persuade Mercy that she had a profound respect for the Dauphine and that she was in despair at the "kind of contempt" shown her by Her Royal Highness. The King arrived at last by the little staircase which linked his room to that of his mistress. The Comtesse rose. "Shall I leave, Monsieur?"

The word *monsieur* astonished Mercy, but left Louis XV unmoved. That was nothing! Yes, he wished to be alone, and at once moved into the attack.

"Until now you have been the Empress's Ambassador. I beg you to be mine, at least for a short time. I love Madame la Dauphine dearly. I think she is charming, but as she is lively and has a husband who is not in a position to guide her she cannot possibly avoid the traps set for her by intrigue."

As was his wont Louis XV did not go straight to his goal. For some time he beat about the question before asking Mercy to use his influence to get the Dauphine "to grant to every person presented the treatment which the latter has the right to expect."

The person presented told the Ambassador what she wanted. "All she wishes is that Madame la Dauphine should speak to her just once." Mercy added an observation on Mme du Barry which caused the Empress to ponder. "If one knows how to go about it it is very easy to make her talk and one might very often gain advantage from this."

Without daring to admit it Mercy was subjugated. He now had to persuade Marie Antoinette. As he had promised, he went to report on the interview and summed it up in the following alternatives: "If the Archduchess wishes to show by her behaviour in public that she understands the part played at court by the Comtesse du Barry, her dignity requires that she should ask the King to forbid the woman to appear henceforth in her circle. If, on the other hand, she prefers to appear to ignore the favourite's real position she must then, without any affectation, treat her as she would any woman presented and, when the occasion offers, speak to her, if only once, so as to put an end to any trumped-up pretext for recriminations."

Her mother's Minister might if he chose imitate the Nuncio and flutter round Mme du Barry in the second-floor attics of the palace— did not M. de Mercy himself live in concubinage with an opera girl?—but she would refuse to speak a single word to this "creature" whose body, before giving pleasure to the Well-Beloved, had been "leased out to anyone who was in a position to pay."

Madame Adelaide supported her niece's good resolutions. Mercy played his last card: policy. He explained to the girl that her attitude was so displeasing to Louis XV that the Franco-Austrian alliance was endangered by it. The Abbé, too, insisted and on 10 July 1771, not without reluctance, the spoilt child gave way. She agreed to say a few words "to la Barry," but in Mercy's presence. The Ambassador would simply have to come with her to the gathering. The Dauphine would stop, speak to Mercy and say a word "as though by chance" to the Comtesse. The Ambassador, delighted, sent word of his success to the woman who was now his "protégée": if she would come on Sunday to the Dauphine's she would be satisfied. On the 11th Marie Antoinette sent a note to Mercy, telling him of her anxiety, but assuring him that "the arrangement still stood." On Sunday, at the beginning of the evening, Marie Antoinette summoned the diplomat and murmured: "I am very nervous, but do not fear, I shall speak."

The play was over. Marie Antoinette began her usual tour of the room, uttering a banality to each person and listening to the banality returned to her with a deep bow. She was only a step away from the favourite and had already opened her mouth when Madame Adelaide broke in, in her sergeant's voice: "It is time to leave! Come, we are going to wait for the King with my sister Victoire."

The Dauphine turned round. She had made the mistake of telling her aunts about her promise. Cut to the quick, Mme du Barry returned to her apartments.

The story spread through Versailles and through Europe. The couriers whipped up their horses to carry the news to Madrid, St. Petersburg and Vienna. But, surprisingly enough, Maria Theresa, who in her own dominions had prostitutes whipped, immediately took the "stupid creature's" part. Austria's interests demanded it. The Empire had now more than ever need of French friendship. If the Alliance should fall apart France would not let Austria draw nearer to Prussia with a view to dividing Poland. In fact, if the "little girl," as Kaunitz called her, refused to speak one word to Mme du Barry the Austrian Empire might say goodbye to its share of the Polish cake which Catherine II and Frederick were getting ready to devour. East Galicia, Russia and two-and-a-half million inhabitants were in the balance. Marie Antoinette would have to sacrifice herself.

"Does one word about a dress or any trifle cost you so much fuss?" the Empress asked. "I can no longer be silent. After Mercy's conversation and all he told you about what the King wanted and what your duty required you dared fail him! What good reason can you put forward? None! You should not know or see the Barry in any other light than that of a lady admitted to the court and to the King's society. You are his first subject, you owe an example to the court and to the courtiers of executing the wishes of your master. If low actions or familiarities were required of you, neither I nor anyone else would advise you to them—but a non-committal word, a few glances, and not for the lady but for your grandfather, your master, your benefactor!"

Maria Theresa had gone rather far and the "little girl" rebelled. "You can be assured that I have no need to be guided by anyone in everything that is honest. If you were able to see as I do everything that happens here you would understand that this woman and her clique will not be content with a word and the whole thing will begin again."

"You made me laugh," Maria Theresa replied, "by imagining that I or my Minister would ever advise you anything against honour or even against the simplest propriety." In the Empress's view the aunts were alone responsible and the cause of all her daughter's *faux pas*. "I can see that you are in great subjection and you need to be quickly and firmly freed from it."

On 2 November 1771 Marie Antoinette was 16. Would she still oppose her mother and Mercy? She was proud and obstinate, as Maria Theresa was constantly repeating, and to yield caused her real suffering. But Austria's interests had spoken.

For the sake of the country which had never ceased to be a little her own—"I shall always glory in belonging to it," she wrote—she gave way. She promised Mercy to speak to Mme du Barry "but not at a fixed day and hour, so that she can let it be known in advance and make a triumph of it."

On the first day of January 1772 Mme du Barry, with the Duchesse d'Aiguillon and the Maréchale de Mirepoix, bowed before the Dauphine. Marie Antoinette said something to the Duchesse then paused for a second in front of the "creature" and remarked: "There are a great many people at Versailles today."

The whole palace heard of it. The aunts, who were furious, sulked, but the King wept with joy. He greeted the Dauphine "with demonstrations of tenderness." Maria Theresa and in particular Joseph II

4

❧

Madame la Dauphine

THE TRAGI-COMIC STRUGGLE between the two most important women at court—a child and a courtesan—had one advantage. It separated the Dauphine from her aunts. She herself confessed frankly: "I was too young and thoughtless. Now I know where I stand."

In consequence Marie Antoinette became more intimate with her husband. "As for my dear husband," she wrote to her mother, "he is greatly changed, and all for the better. He shows much friendship towards me and has even begun to repose confidence in me." Mercy was soon able to inform his sovereign that "the Dauphin is entirely captivated by his wife." He became almost gallant.

"She is so full of grace," he said, "that she does everything well. It must be admitted that she is charming."

The Dauphine could, of course, do nothing to remedy the "fatal object," as Mercy called it, but she was too much of a coquette not to try her power and at least "smarten up" her husband. At Compiègne, one day after the Dauphin had suffered from indigestion, she stopped him eating so many cakes, and even forbade them to be served to him until further orders. The greedy young man gave way smiling, and seemed very touched.

Emboldened by this Marie Antoinette tried to "wean the young prince from his extraordinary taste for all work connected with building." He would return from his labours covered with plaster. Here, however, the Dauphine, who was "extremely displeased by this conduct," obtained less success. In spite of her forceful complaints she did not succeed in preventing her husband from lending a hand to any workmen he happened to meet.

When he came back from hunting—always very late and often long after the King—the Dauphin sometimes staggered with exhaustion. So on 1 July 1771 Marie Antoinette gave her husband "a lecture on this excessive liking for the hunt which spoiled his health, and on the unkempt and rough appearance resulting from this exercise." Shamed by this explosion, Louis-Auguste retreated to his apartments, but the Dauphine pursued him and "continued to point out, somewhat strongly, all the drawbacks of his way of life. This language," Mercy continued, "so upset M. le Dauphin that he began to weep." Faced with his tears, the girl was affected and wept too.

An incident helped to weaken the influence which the Duc de la Vauguyon still had over his former pupil. "Something very odd has just happened," Marie Antoinette told her mother. "I was alone with my husband when M. de la Vauguyon hurried up to the door to listen. One of the *valets de chambre,* who is either a fool or a very honest man, opened the door and M. le Duc was left standing there like a post without being able to escape. So I mentioned to my husband the disadvantage there was in letting people listen at doors and he took it very well."

Like all Marie Antoinette's letters to her mother, this is written in French and the style is charming.

The Dauphin now consented to join his wife's circle. During these years preceding her reign it consisted principally of the young couples of Provence, Chartres and Bourbon. It was on 14 May 1771 that the future Louis XVIII had married Marie-Josèphe of Savoy, who was very ugly. It was even pretended that she had hair on her chest.

"What do you think of your sister-in-law?" the Comte de Provence asked the Dauphin on the day after his wedding.

"I don't like her very much. I should not care to have her as my wife."

"I am very glad that you have found someone more to your taste," the bridegroom replied, annoyed. "We are both satisfied, for my wife pleases me immensely."

The Comte de Provence began to flaunt bourgeois tastes and declared that he would like to remain by the fire in the winter with his better half. It was soon reported at court that the Comtesse de Provence was expecting a child.

"Is there any foundation for it?" Marie Antoinette asked her brother-in-law.

"A great deal, Madame. There is not a day when it might not be true!"

"Ah! since you reply so well I shall not ask you any more questions!"

The two families were never separated. "We two and my sister and brother get on very well together," wrote Marie Antoinette to her mother on 21 June 1771.

The two families were soon joined by the Comte d'Artois. The future Charles X was certainly to become a cheerful friend to the Dauphine and a gallant companion—even too gallant. But for the present he displayed nothing but "honourable sentiments." In November 1773 he married the Comtesse de Provence's sister, Marie-Thérèse of Savoy, whose appearance was not spared by Mercy. "She has a thin face, a very long nose with an ugly tip, crossed eyes and a large mouth, which all go to make up an irregular face with no charm and very common." She refused to utter a word and had only one wish, to be unnoticed. Her husband was quick to satisfy her on this point and hastened to Paris to his mistress, the beautiful Rosalie Duthé, who had a fancy for his family, having initiated the Duc de Chartres in 1766. Once the Comte d'Artois's escapade was known a jest ran round Versailles: "Having been given indigestion by a sponge cake (*gâteau de Savoie*), the Prince has gone to take tea (*du thé*) at Paris."

No one pitied the neglected wife, who seemed "to take no interest in anything" and was "very repellent." The Dauphine charitably "showed her every kindness" and tried to "rouse her from her apathy." She drew her into the quartet she had formed with the Provences and the Dauphin. The Comte d'Artois was obliged to follow. When there was no public dinner the three families took their meals together and then, unknown to the King, acted plays with Louis-Auguste as the only spectator. In an entresol room in the Dauphin's apartments the young people had fixed up a kind of small folding stage which could be hidden in a cupboard. The Comte de Provence was the most brilliant actor; the Comte d'Artois was graceful; Marie Antoinette was passable; and the two Savoyards extremely bad.

Campan, the father-in-law of Marie Antoinette's future *femme de chambre*, was the producer, prompter and principal actor. But one day, when he was dressed as Crispino, he was surprised behind a door by a servant of the wardrobe, who was so frightened that he fell down backwards with a loud cry. This was M. Campan's most successful part. But they were afraid that this incident might reveal the secret of the performances and the theatre closed its doors, much to the disappointment of the Dauphin, who laughed until he cried.

"It was from the period of these diversions," Mme Campan tells us, "that he was seen to lose his timid childhood air and take pleasure in the Dauphine's society." After a year's intimacy with her two brothers-in-law Marie Antoinette cared less for them. She admitted that she had been mistaken about them and, as Mercy noted with visible satisfaction, these new feelings provided "motives for comparison very favourable to M. le Dauphin."

"I am more and more convinced," she admitted, "that if I had to choose a husband from the three I should prefer the one heaven has given me. Although he is awkward he shows me every possible attention and kindness."

This letter is dated 1775, but these were already the Dauphine's feelings for her husband. Being obviously liked by the girl who was to become the most attractive woman in the court, the Dauphin seemed less clumsy. He began to acquire self-confidence and gave proof of it on the day of his joyful entry into Paris: if he did not succeed in pleasing the Parisians at least he did not go unnoticed.

It seems hardly credible that after living for more than three years in the Ile de France Marie Antoinette knew no more of Paris than the Porte de la Conférence, of which she had just had a glimpse on the evening of the accident of 30 May 1770. This was the fault of Louis XV, who did not at all care to see his grandchildren win the applause he had not received for a long time.

Finally, not without frequent requests from the city, the Entry was fixed for Tuesday, 8 June 1773. At half-past eight in the morning a procession left the Hôtel de Ville to fetch Maréchal de Brissac, the Governor of Paris, who lived in the Rue Cassette. From there it proceeded to welcome the Dauphin and the Dauphine at the Porte de la Conférence.

The horsemen of the watch, the guards and the town orchestra preceded the carriages of the city—that is, of the Prévôt, M. de la Michodière, and of the first and second councillors. But these important personages, who were at that time called the "Gentlemen" of the city, were not in their carriages: they were represented by the *huissiers*. It was the same with the Governor: it was his officers who occupied his four carriages attended by servants in livery holding the doors. The Maréchal, the Prévôt and his two magistrates were seated in the same carriage—called the *carrosse du corps*—preceded by officers on horseback and followed by "the livery of the Governor." Only the third and fourth councillors occupied their own coaches and brought up the rear of the procession with another squadron of horsemen and guards.

The trumpets sounded and at half-past eleven the cannon at the Invalides began to thunder. Everyone gathered at the entrance to the Cours la Reine, and soon the procession of the Dauphin and Dauphine appeared on the hill of Chaillot escorted by His Majesty's bodyguards. After three coaches filled with ladies came the carriage of the old Maréchal de Richelieu. In his capacity of First Gentleman of the Chamber for the year, he had the duty of accompanying the guests of Paris. The Dauphin, who did not care for him, called him a "desiccated mummy." Marie Antoinette blamed him equally for his amorous exploits, which began under Louis XIV and continued until the eve of the Revolution, and for the bad taste he showed in choosing the spectacles for the court, which was part of his office.

"At last, M. le Maréchal, your spectacles are ended," she said to him when his reign finished at the end of the year. "Now we shall be able to amuse ourselves!"

On this particular day the old libertine had nothing to do with the organisation and Marie Antoinette prepared to enjoy herself. She wore the same smile as at Strasbourg and came to conquer Paris. After the presentations the two processions continued along the quays until Notre Dame, while in the Place Louis-XV the *"boêtes d'artillerie"* fired a salute.

After the service in Notre Dame, and after being harangued at the entrance to the college of Louis le Grand and received in front of Sainte Geneviève by the Abbot and his chapter, Marie Antoinette and her husband took a round-about route to the Tuileries for dinner. All along the way the pretty Dauphine and Louis-Auguste himself were wildly cheered. The crowd in the Tuileries gardens were in transports. The young couple had to show themselves to the people ten times, amid cries, shouts and excitement.

"Madame," said Brissac, "there you have two hundred thousand adorers!"

"Tears of emotion mingled with the cries of joy," wrote the clerk of the Hôtel de Ville in his report.

A few days later the Dauphine wrote to her mother, "Last Tuesday I was fêted in a way I shall never forget as long as I live. We received every imaginable honour. But that, although it was very well, was not what touched me the most, but the tenderness and the eagerness of the poor people who, in spite of the taxes which oppress them, were transported with joy on seeing us. When we went to walk in the Tuileries there was such a great crowd that we remained for three-quarters of an hour without being able to go forward or back. The Dauphin and I several times ordered the guards not to strike anyone, which made a very good impression. There was such good order during the whole day that in spite of the enormous number of people who followed us around everywhere no one was hurt. On returning from our walk we went on to an open terrace and remained there for half an hour. I cannot tell you, my dear mother, what transports of joy and affection were shown us in that time. Before retiring we waved to the people, which pleased them very much. How happy we are, in our position, to win the friendship of a people so easily. And yet there is nothing so precious. I was well aware of that and I shall never forget it."

The people of Paris wanted to make it clear that they put their hope in their future sovereigns. They did not confuse them with "the old gallant" and his Bourbonnaise. In order to lessen the slight to her grandfather Marie Antoinette said to him as they returned to Versailles: "Sire, Your Majesty must be greatly loved by the Parisians, for they have fêted us well!"

From now on the Dauphine had but one wish: to return to Paris. On 16 June she went with her husband to the Opera. Louis was applauded, in spite of "two rather awkward little bows" which he made on entering his box. Disconcerted, he stepped back to give way to Marie Antoinette, who was cheered. She was cheered again on 23 June at the Comédie Française, where they were performing *Le Legs* and *Le Siège de Calais,* and she gave permission for the public to applaud the actors in her presence, which was contrary to etiquette. On 30 June it was the turn of the audience in the Théâtre des Italiens to fête the young woman. Clairval played the part of Montauciel in *Le Déserteur* by Sedaine, and at one point in the text had to cry "Long live the King!" and throw his hat in the air. With great presence of mind—well-thought-out beforehand—he added: "And long live his dear children!"

"All this is addressed to Madame la Dauphine," Mercy wrote. "One could fill volumes with the moving remarks which were made, the comments on the appearance, charm and gracious, kindly air of the Archduchess."

The Ambassador was moved and was ready to shout with the Parisians. Marie Antoinette often managed to disarm him. He was touched when the little coquette said to him with an angelic air: "I shall make as few mistakes as I can. When I do make any I shall always admit it."

But Maria Theresa was not blinded. She replied that she knew how much her daughter liked to get her own way and how well she could "turn round and about in order to reach her goal. She is compliant only when it is a question of something which does not particularly affect her. She did not hide it from you when latterly she said to you, on two separate occasions, that 'when one has adopted a line of conduct it is very difficult and painful to change it.' Her behaviour towards the favourite, her excursions on horseback and what is even more dangerous, her rides in the cabriolet, furnish enough proofs of a character which is impetuous and too closely wedded to its own ideas. In spite of her good qualities and her intelligence I always fear the consequences of her frivolity and obstinacy."

Mercy tried to defend his pupil by guaranteeing that the Dauphine was "in good faith when she confessed her little faults of the past and the one or two opinions which H.R.H. finds it difficult to renounce. But in so doing she does but give proof of the candour and truth of her mind."

The Ambassador was all the more moved by this candour, which in his opinion compensated for many faults, since it had "softened" the Dauphin. From the end of 1773 the latter hardly ever left his wife.

One morning he gaily entered his wife's room and eagerly announced that he had just inherited 2,000 crowns through the death of someone to whom he paid a pension from his privy purse. Marie Antoinette calmly asked him: "But have you found out if the dead man has not left a widow, children or relatives in need?"

Louis was startled for a moment and then replied cheerfully: "As to that, I must admit that you are quite right to remind me." He at once went "to make inquiries and did not fail openly to give Mme la Dauphine the credit for his charitable intentions." His wife's charm and charitable disposition and her extraordinary popularity, which all reflected on him, had combined to transform Louis-Auguste. "H.R.H. shows in the best possible light," wrote Mercy, "and M. le Dauphin fills this position much better than his physical and moral constitution would have led one to hope."

The booby of Compiègne was no more than a memory. Marie Antoinette said so herself. "M. le Dauphin has been wonderful every time he has been to Paris and if I may say so he has won the good opinion of the people on account of the air of perfect understanding between us. This is perhaps what has given rise to the rumour that he has kissed me in public, although it is not true." And she concluded: "For a long time everyone has noticed his attentions to me." "There is, however, no sign of pregnancy," Mercy observed, "but one may hope every day for this longed-for event."

They might indeed "hope every day," but we must hear again what Dr. Ganière has to say.

"The phase of waiting could not last indefinitely. As he grew older, his fortifying diet and particularly the presence of this fresh, tender girl ended by awakening the Dauphin's sluggish senses, but on account of the pain caused at certain moments by his malformation he had to give up his attempts. The doctors had to admit that only surgery could put an end to the real torture, both physical and mental, resulting from these fruitless and exhausting experiences. But he had not the courage to submit to it. Nature had already allowed him to make some progress, since now he did not immediately fall asleep on reaching the marriage bed; surely it would allow him to make more, and to be able to avoid the scalpel he relied on a spontaneous cure."

This drama often brought tears to Marie Antoinette's eyes. Shy and touched, the Dauphin embraced her. "Do you really love me?"

"Yes, you cannot doubt it. I love you sincerely and I respect you even more."

"The young Prince seemed very moved by this remark," Mercy reported. "He tenderly caressed the Archduchess and told her that when they returned to Versailles he would continue with his régime and hoped that all would go well."

But on 18 December, when the court had returned to Versailles, Mercy again sighed: "By the most incredible misfortune our hopes in that direction, instead of increasing, seem to have become more remote."

As a consolation Marie Antoinette went in for amusement. As often as she could she went to Paris. Nothing was more delightful than the masked balls during carnival time in 1774. There were so many people to mystify. On Sunday 30 January she arrived shortly after midnight, wearing a domino and a black mask, and recognised in the crowd a young foreigner who had been presented to her on Friday 19 November and whom she had again seen in the following month at two of her Monday balls. In true carnival spirit she went up to him and spoke to him for a long time without his recognising her. He was tall, handsome, well made and pleasant, but not at all foppish. They laughed together until the Dauphine, who was beginning to be recognised by the crowd, was obliged to move away. She soon left the ball, enchanted by her evening.

He was the son of a field-marshal and a member of the Royal Council of Sweden. He was making the tour of Europe for his education; would be 20 years old in a few months and was called Axel Fersen. "A masked ball, a domino, a mask, two hearts," wrote the last biographer of Marie Antoinette and the handsome Swede. This is all very pretty, but the two hearts were not yet beating in unison. Whereas his meeting with the Dauphine takes 10 words in Fersen's private diary, two other carnival adventures occupy two pages.

At Versailles the balls, held on Mondays at Marie Antoinette's and on Wednesdays at Madame de Noailles', went on until six o'clock in the morning. To please the Dauphine more festivities and more balls were organised and everywhere the Dauphine laughed, danced, made fun, enjoyed herself and, in the words of the Goncourts, bounding and fluttering "passed by like a song."

"At the end of Louis XV's reign," writes Pierre de Nolhac, "the most serious fault with which Marie Antoinette could be reproached was excused by her age: an excessive love of pleasure. With her health and youthful eagerness she found there a natural compensation for the strict and tedious court duties to which she had to submit." This is true, but there was something else which the most recent adorer of the Queen did not dare to touch upon.

The marital drama was becoming more serious: the "indolent husband" went to visit his wife with increasing frequency. A staircase had been built just behind his room on the ground floor which came out on the first floor quite near the Dauphine's bedchamber, at the spot where later Marie Antoinette's *Méridienne* was to be established. Before climbing these stairs this semi-invalid would have been wise to wait until he had the courage to undergo an operation. But Louis-Auguste, as conscientious as he was awkwardly embarrassed, persisted in his unfortunate attempts. In the words of Dr. Ganière: "Night after night, in the silence of the nuptial chamber, this clumsy and well-meaning young husband inflicted moments of real nightmare on his companion without ever attaining the desired result, except no doubt for some defilements on her flesh which these two innocents might believe would result in a pregnancy that would put an end to all the court's gibes."

This young girl, thus awakened but not satisfied, had no other palliative than to amuse herself, throw off all constraint and seek after every possible pleasure except—and this is to her credit—that of deceiving her husband. Melancholy, frivolous whims, mad gaiety and bad temper followed each other, to the terror of Maria Theresa, who did not guess the cause of the trouble. In those days there was no science of neurology.

Yet for the moment this thirst for pleasure did not go beyond the bounds permitted to an eighteen-year-old Dauphine. Her popularity was as great as ever. The Parisians, indeed, were glad to see that their future Queen could laugh as well as a Bécu or a Poisson. To please her the public was ready to abuse the King and his Bourbonnaise and even to adopt her tastes. "Paris is completely charmed by the Arch-duchess in a way that cannot be described," wrote Mercy.

This was to enable Marie Antoinette to get Gluck accepted.

Marie Antoinette was happy to welcome Gluck when he arrived from Vienna at the end of the autumn of 1773. Her former clavichord teacher seemed to bring a breath of her youth with him into the little rooms behind her bedroom where she received him. She remembered the *Parnasso Confuso*, a poem by Metastasio which Gluck had set to music and to which she and her brothers and sisters had danced at Schoenbrunn for the marriage of Joseph II, when she was eleven. Leopold had played the clavichord. She had indeed been brought up on music. And since her arrival at Versailles, in spite of the donkeys and the cabriolet, she had not neglected the clavichord and particularly her "dear harp." She sang Mozart and Gluck in a voice which, although only just true, was pleasant. She was therefore very disappointed when she had to listen to French operas. Rameau was no longer alive and to arouse the apathetic audiences whole operas were composed of potpourris of popular works. And there were the never-ending overtures. Lulli had once and for all set the pattern: "A slow passage, called serious, which was generally played twice, and a quick return of the subject, called gay, which was usually in the form of a fugue."

When Gluck had sent the Paris Academy the first act of his *Iphigenia*, inspired by Racine's tragedy, the director had frankly declared "that such a work would only kill all the old French operas" and with the same frankness had done everything he could to prevent "M. le Chevalier Gluck" from coming to Paris. But Mercy, who was on extremely good terms with Rosalie Levasseur of the Opera, had connections with the theatre and *Iphigenia* was accepted.

On his arrival Gluck was to play his opera on Marie Antoinette's clavichord. He explained what he had tried to do: "Reduce music to its real function, that of aiding the poetry so as to reinforce the expressions of feeling and the interest of the situations without interrupting the action of holding it up by superfluous ornamentation."

This music "with no other adornment than its own beauty" delighted Marie Antoinette and the rehearsals began, not without difficulty, however, for the cast were somewhat out of their depth. They were used to "seeking the model for the singing voice in the voice of declamation" and were astonished by Gluck's profession of faith: "I have taken great care not to interrupt an actor in the heat of a dialogue in order to make him listen to a tedious *ritornello* nor to stop him in the middle of his speech at a favourable vowel."

Not to be interrupted or stopped upset the French singers. The rehearsals went all the more badly since everything on the stage was at sixes and sevens. Faced with this anarchy, Gluck went into terrible rages.

"I am here, ladies, to put on *Iphigenia*. If you want to sing, so much the better; if not, it is as you please! I shall go to Mme la Dauphine and say to her: 'I find it impossible to get my opera performed.' Then I shall get in my carriage and take the road to Vienna."

On leaving the Opera House he was sometimes so excited—singing every part in the opera to himself—that one day a crowd followed him in the Tuileries, taking him for a madman, and warned the Swiss Guards, who arrested the composer.

He went into similar rages in Vienna and the Emperor Francis soothed the orchestra, who wanted to leave everything and go, by saying kindly to them: "You know what he is like, my children! But at heart he is a good man."

Like her father, Marie Antoinette calmed the cast, through the agency of Mercy, and herself took charge of the composer. She wanted "her" musician to have a triumph. She wanted this all the more since Mme du Barry appears to have declared that she detested Gluck and preferred Piccini. Versailles promptly divided into two parties: the Gluckists, partisans of clarity and truth of expression, and the Piccinists, who extolled the charm and sweetness of melody. The opinion of Gluckists such as Jean-Jacques Rousseau or Grimm, or of Piccinists such as Marmontel or d'Alembert, no doubt had its value, but the majority of the Versailles weathercocks either defended Gluck through hatred of the favourite or attacked him to please her. M. de Breteuil, French Minister at Naples, was even ordered to "buy" Piccini and bring him to Paris. Incidentally, the two rivals became the best possible friends and took their meals together, while their partisans devoured each other, until the day when Piccini began to write like Gluck.

But that had not yet happened and all Paris was getting ready to go to the first performance of *Iphigenia* on 13 April 1774, when Legros, who was to sing the part of Achilles, fell ill. Gluck announced calmly that the tenor would not be replaced and that the first performance would be put off for a few days. Everyone was scandalised. The royal family had reserved their evening and this would show a grave lack of respect. But Gluck declared that he would rather tear up the score and take his carriage back to Vienna. Marie Antoinette supported him and the performance was postponed until 19 April— an unprecedented event.

The Dauphine went with her husband, the Comte and Comtesse de Provence, the Duchesse de Bourbon, the Duchesse de Chartres

and the Princesse de Lamballe. The French audience were somewhat
taken aback by the long recitatives and the absence of trills. Certain
passages seemed flat and even mediocre but the majority of the spectators were "very much struck by the many new beauties, grand,
strong and simple, which burst forth in passionate, moving and
dramatic music."

"Since one can have such great pleasure for two hours," Rousseau
exclaimed, "I feel that life has some advantages."

The Dauphine never ceased applauding. "The Princess seems to
have joined a plot," remarked a contemporary chronicler, and the
sulky spectators clapped too, "in order to please Madame la Dauphine."

On the following day the throng was enormous and there were
no more criticisms. Guards had to be called out to restrain the crowds.
The call for the composer went on for ten minutes. The Dauphine
had triumphed. "In Paris no one thinks or dreams of anything but
music," wrote Grimm. "It is the subject of all our disputes and all our
conversations, and the preoccupation of our suppers, and it would
even seem ridiculous if one were to be interested in anything else."

German music—"music, simply"—took its place thanks to Marie
Antoinette. Her success and the clever way she had managed it proved
to Mercy what a great part his "pupil" would later be able to play. "I
see approaching the time when the great destiny of the Archduchess
will be fulfilled. The King is growing old . . ."

It would surely be she who would govern. "M. le Dauphin will
never have the strength or the will to reign by himself," Mercy
declared. "If the Archduchess does not govern him he will be governed
by others." Now the Archduchess cared nothing for affairs of state.
"She is very much afraid of them . . . The result is that her character
tends towards passivity and dependence." Mercy concluded: "It is most
important that the Archduchess should learn better to know and
appreciate her own strength."

The Empress replied with wisdom: "I confess frankly that I do not
wish my daughter to have a decided influence in affairs. I have learned
only too well from my own experience how crushing a burden is the
government of a vast kingdom. Moreover, I know my daughter's
youth and frivolity and her dislike of concentration—and she knows
nothing!—all of which makes me fear for her success in governing
a kingdom as dilapidated as France is at present."

Marie Antoinette may have felt that her mother was right. On the evening of 27 April 1774, eight days after the first performance of *Iphigenia*, her heart beat fast as she approached the bed of the sick King, who had been brought back from the Trianon wrapped in his dressing-gown. Had the moment come for those two children to take up the dishonoured crown? That evening the King's condition did not appear serious. He had a fever and a bad headache and asked his children to leave him alone: he only wanted Mme du Barry.

When the Dauphine saw the invalid again towards five o'clock on the following day he had become worse. He had already been bled twice. Around his bed were six doctors, five surgeons and three apothecaries. But the King thought there were too few. "He would have liked to have the number increased," a witness relates. "He had his pulse taken by all fourteen six times an hour and when this large faculty were not all in his bedroom he called the one who was missing so as to be constantly surrounded."

"Sire," said Le Monnier, the first doctor, "Your Majesty must show your tongue."

The King put it right out, left it there for more than five minutes and drew it in again only to say: "Your turn, Lassone!"

The second doctor stepped forward, looked, felt, bowed. The King put his tongue in. "Your turn, Bourdeau!" Again the King put out his tongue. The business was repeated. "Your turn, Lorry!"

The fourteen filed past one after the other "each showing in his own way his pleasure at seeing the beauty and colour of this precious royal organ." Next it was the turn of the stomach. "He made each doctor, each surgeon and each apothecary come past, calling each by turn and in their proper order." But to Marie Antoinette, the Dauphin and his daughters the King said nothing.

Around the bed were a crowd of useless people who were thinking only of the "third bleeding."

"A third bleeding," the King had exclaimed. "I am really ill, then!"

There was a tradition at court: "A third bleeding entails the reception of the last sacraments," and consequently, in the present case, it would decide the King to dismiss Mme du Barry.

"A third bleeding would reduce my strength," Louis XV had sighed. "I should very much prefer not to be bled a third time!"

The whole court were on tenterhooks. They cared nothing for the invalid; the only thing that mattered was the Comtesse's position.

The doctors were torn in two directions. If they ordered a third bleeding they would make a mortal enemy of Mme du Barry and M. d'Aiguillon, for no one doubted that the King would be on his feet again in a week. But if the favourite was dismissed would she return? "It is worth taking the chance!" declared the clique of Mesdames.

At 10 o'clock in the evening the Dauphine returned to the bedroom. The King had been placed on a small camp bed. He had sunk a good deal. In default of a third bleeding the Master Apothecary, M. Fargeau, and his assistant had given the King an enema. The fourteen doctors were still busy about him. The room was almost in darkness for the patient's eyes were hurt by the slightest light. Suddenly a servant of the bedchamber accidentally raised a torch. The King's face appeared in full light: his forehead and cheeks were covered with little red spots. The doctors looked at each other. The King had smallpox.

Marie Antoinette, who had been inoculated at Vienna, hastily led away the Dauphin, who had never had the terrible illness. But she was not to enter the King's room again.

However, she saw her "dear papa" again at dawn on 7 May. That night she had been awakened at five o'clock. The King wished to receive Communion. The dying man had just summoned the Abbé Maudoux and for the first time in 38 years was making his confession to the priest. This decision put an end to all the intrigues which had been disturbing Versailles for a week. When the doctors appeared hopeful the shadow of confession faded and everyone hurried up Mme du Barry's staircase. When the King's condition grew worse she was abandoned and M. de Beaumont, the Archbishop of Paris, went to see the dying man. But, having been lectured by Richelieu and Aumont, he did not dare mention confession.

"Archbishop," the Duc de Richelieu had said, "if you are so anxious to hear confessions come into a corner; I shall make my confession and I swear that it will interest you as much as the King's!"

But this time all was over. The night before the King had asked his mistress, who came down every evening, not to come again, and at four o'clock in the afternoon she had left for Rueil in a hired carriage, having wept for a long time in the arms of M. d'Aiguillon, whom she was to drag down in her fall.

On the eve of her reign Marie Antoinette was trembling. Had not

Mercy repeated that "to assure her own happiness" she should "take over the authority which in the Dauphin's hands would never be anything but precarious"? Was she capable of reigning?

It was six o'clock. In the *cour royale* the drums beat a ruffle. Mgr de la Roche-Aymon, Grand Almoner of France, left the chapel bearing the ciborium between a double row of bodyguards and Hundred Swiss. The Dauphin walked behind the canopy. He was very pale. For three days he had been repeating: "I feel as though the universe were falling on me!"

He stopped at the foot of the marble staircase, which owing to the infection he could not mount. On the top landing Marie Antoinette had come with the Princes to meet the Holy Sacrament. In her turn she walked through the state rooms following the canopy, which was borne by four gentlemen of the bedchamber. As they approached the King's room a dreadful odour became more pronounced. In the anteroom, whose door led into the apartments, the infection took one by the throat and was suffocating, in spite of the windows open on to the Marble Court. Here the Queen of tomorrow knelt down. Through the open door she could see the dying man holding the crucifix which Madame Louise had sent him from the Carmelites. His face, blackened, swollen enormously and covered with suppurating sores, was unrecognisable. The countenance of the Well-Beloved to which so many women had bent their lips was now only a carnival mask with bituminous reflections.

La Roche-Aymon had finished. He was about to leave, but the Abbé Maudoux plucked him by the rochet and whispered in his ear: the King wished to make a public confession. This was the price exacted by the Abbé for absolution. The Cardinal, who had promised Richelieu and d'Aiguillon that everything would go off without incident, was obliged to obey the confessor. He advanced towards the Cabinet Room, where the court was massed behind Marie Antoinette, and cried in a loud voice: "Gentlemen, the King has charged me to tell you that he asks pardon of God for having offended him and for the scandal he has caused his people."

There was a silence. Then from the thick, blackened and deformed lips in the Negro-like countenance ten words escaped: "I wish I had the strength to say it myself."

On 10 May, at a quarter past three in the afternoon, the flame of a lighted candle in one of the windows of the royal bedroom was extinguished. The appalling agony was ended.

Marie Antoinette was in her own apartments. The Dauphin was there, striding about the room. Suddenly, in the words of a witness, "a terrible noise, exactly like that of thunder, was heard": it was the crowd of courtiers running through the Hall of Mirrors to salute the new King. At this strange sound Marie Antoinette and Louis XVI started. They had understood, and the first comers to the room saw the young Queen of eighteen and the King of nineteen on their knees, weeping bitterly.

"Oh God," they repeated, embracing each other. "Oh God, protect us, we are too young to reign!"

5

❧

A Fashionable Little Queen

OWING TO THE infection the new King could communicate with his grandfather's Ministers only by letter. The all-important question was: "Will dispatches and commands be signed Louis or Louis-Auguste?" For the first time, in the margin of the same letter, Louis XVI wrote the five letters of the name he had chosen. He wrote them again, on the same day, at the foot of the documents concerning his grandfather's burial.

When a King of France died his body was opened and the heart taken out and sent to one of the churches of Paris. But on 11 May the Archbishop of Paris received word from Versailles that the putrefaction of the late King's body was so far advanced that there was no question of opening it and that consequently it was impossible to send him "in trust the entrails of that prince."

Louis XV was therefore the only King of France to be buried at Saint Denis with his heart. This special treatment, incidentally, resulted in the viscera of the Well-Beloved not being used, twenty years later, by Martin Drolling in painting his famous "Interior of a Kitchen." During the Revolution Drolling bought the royal hearts—which owing to the spices used had become mummified—to put into tubes and thence on to the canvas, to which they imparted "a wonderful shine."

No prayers were said at the deathbed. The monks, who could no longer stand the air of the bedroom, moved into the council room. Furthermore—as a last privilege—the body was transferred to Saint Denis in the middle of the night at full gallop in a "coloured coach," surrounded by forty bodyguards and thirty pages of the Great and Little Stables carrying torches. Along the route the inns were full of drinkers, crying out in a head voice: "Tally-ho! tally-ho!" in imitation of the rather ridiculous tones used by the King to urge on his hounds after the game.

Fun was made of the Abbé of the Church of St. Geneviève, who had brought the famous relic in order to obtain the King's cure. His patron saint must have very little credit in heaven! "Well, what are you complaining about?" answered the Abbé, laughing. "He's dead, isn't he?"

Only one person wept—Mme du Barry, who was "entrusted to the police." She was made a prisoner of the State and taken the same evening to the Abbey of Pont-aux-Dames.

In spite of the hard times the great mourning machine was set in motion. Whereas the equipages of princes and those having "the honours of the Louvre" were draped in black, the King and Queen rode only in carriages covered with violet cloth. It cost 322,650 livres— 64 million francs—for this one item alone. For the same sum were furnished the headstalls for the horses and the helm, coat of mail, gauntlets and spurs to be thrown into the tomb with the coffin. But the furniture and beds had to be covered with dark drapery, and all the officers and livery servants dressed in black, which cost nearly 300,000 livres. The mourning required 1,365 new suits for the Great Stable alone. No more gaudy liveries. Only large shoulder-knots of blue, fringed with gold or silver, according to the wearer's position, lightened the vast sepulchre that Versailles had become.

Although the décor was funereal, hearts were joyful. Everything was hoped for from the new reign and *resurrexit* was written on the pedestal of Henri IV's statue. Abundance would come again. The women wore in their hair nothing but ears of corn, and the dandies bought mourning snuff boxes adorned with portraits of the King and Queen and lined with shagreen. This signified "consolation in the midst of grief" (*chagrin*). Everyone wept. Eyes "wet with tears" were fashionable and indicated not grief but tenderness—tenderness towards the nineteen-year-old King who admittedly possessed no grace, no gallantry, but who seemed so simple and natural and such a "good fellow" in spite of his youth. Had he not commanded M. d'Estissac, the Grand Master of the Wardrobe, who had come to take his orders for the first time, to make him eight suits of frieze cloth? Had he not been seen at Choisy walking around the château like any bourgeois? And on returning from his walk had he not sat down on a park bench with his wife and sisters-in-law, who were eating strawberries and drinking milk? Was this not just like a picture by Greuze, "divine" and of an "indescribable grace"? And at this point in the story it was fashionable to shed "a torrent of tears."

There was tenderness, too, for the pretty eighteen-year-old Queen who so charmingly took her husband's arm when walking in the alleys at Choisy, the little Queen of whom Walpole wrote: "Hebes and Floras, Helens and Graces are streetwalkers to her." She had refused to touch the *"droit de ceinture,"* which went back to the distant times when queens carried their purse at the waist and was an additional tax raised after "joyful events" and levied in Paris on wine and coal.

At this refusal the tears flowed faster. "How I love the French at this moment!" exclaimed Maria Theresa. "What depths there are in a nation with such good feelings!"

Marie Antoinette was moved, and having recovered from her first anxiety she was intoxicated by the three words: Queen of France. "Although God caused me to be born into the rank I occupy today," she wrote to her mother, "I cannot refrain from admiring the disposition of Providence which has chosen me, the youngest of your children, for the finest kingdom in Europe."

But although Maria Theresa was full of emotion she faced the reality, and sighed: "My daughter's destiny can only be either completely great or very unhappy. . . . Her palmy days are over." On 18 May she wrote to the new sovereigns: "You are both very young and your burden is a heavy one. I am distressed, truly distressed by it." Although 400 leagues distant from the Ile de France, she seemed already to have guessed that now that her "Antonia" was her own mistress she would ride over Versailles and its customs like an escaped colt.

In fact she did not even wait to return to Versailles. After a short stay at Choisy the new court went to La Muette, a royal house originally intended for the erection of mews for the stags. Here Marie Antoinette received the "mourning respects." The women, in plain dresses of black *raz de Saint Maur,* coifs, black stockings and gloves, and carrying crêpe fans came to bow to the new Queen. The ceremony was endless and there was nothing cheerful in the dark scene. One of the young ladies of the palace, the Marquise de Clermont-Tonnerre, declared that she was tired and sat down on the floor, hiding behind the screen formed by the dresses of the Queen and her Ladies of Honour. This should have been enough to have her sent away from court, but Marie Antoinette said nothing. Indeed, when the Marquise began to play "all sorts of pranks" Marie Antoinette could not keep her countenance and "put her fan to her face to conceal an involuntary smile," Mme Campan reports. Other witnesses declare that "the Queen most improperly burst out laughing in the faces of the sexagenarian Duchesses and Princesses who had thought it their duty to appear at the ceremony."

This last description appears to be the more truthful since on the following day some ladies announced that they would never again set foot in the court of "this mocking little thing." Marie Antoinette shrugged her shoulders and called them "strait-laced" (*collets montés*). This nickname was her own invention. Similarly she described as "centenarians" ladies who were not necessarily very old. "When one has passed thirty," she remarked, "I cannot understand how one dares appear at court."

There were, too, the "bundles"—also so-called by Marie Antoinette, heavy, ill-dressed women at whom the Dauphine had formerly laughed behind her fan but at whom the Queen now laughed without any restraint. Belleval realised this: "She unfortunately makes fun of everybody without putting the least restraint on herself."

She was not able to restrain herself either during these "mourning respects" when the Duchesse d'Aiguillon made her bow. Not only did Marie Antoinette not speak to her, but "she looked down her nose contemptuously," a witness reports. On the next day the "Aiguillon clique" —formerly the coterie of Mme du Barry—was singing:

> Little Queen, have a care;
> If you behave with such an air
> You'll be sent back over there.

And she had only been reigning for a month!

The Abbé Baudeau, a contemporary, asserted that the first pamphlets against Marie Antoinette came from "the Chancellor's Jesuitical cabal." There is no serious proof in support of the serious accusation that d'Aiguillon was the organiser of this "shower of red bullets," to quote

the Abbé's expression. But there is one disturbing hint. A dossier in
the Archives of the Bastille proves that the Chevalier d'Abrieu, the
Chancellor's private secretary and friend, had made an agreement
with the pamphleteer Dubec for the elaboration of the well-known
Nouvelles à la main. Shortly afterwards, on 28 July, Dubec was arrested
for being one of the presumed authors of *Lever de l'Aurore,* an abominable pamphlet which described as an orgy an innocent vigil spent by
Marie Antoinette at Marly to watch the sun rise. It is unfortunate,
to say the least, that the name of M. d'Aiguillon's secretary should be
coupled with that of the scribbler.

Marie Antoinette had not even noticed the discordant note in the
symphony of praise surrounding her. She was intoxicated by the
clouds of incense about her.

On the day after his predecessor's death Louis XVI asked his aunts'
advice on how he should govern. They had no hesitation: the Dauphin
their brother would have called on M. de Machault. The King
consented. Then he asked them a further question: what should be
decided about the funeral celebrations held a month after the death;
who should be approached? Madame Adelaide's reply was: "No one
is more fitted, by his recollections and traditions, to take care of these
details than M. de Maurepas."

The same courier took the two summonses. In spite of his 73 years
M. de Maurepas made haste and arrived first at Versailles. He had been
forbidden to come to court ever since the reign of the Pompadour,
when, so it was said, he had sung at supper a song stigmatising "the
low-born whore who turned the court into a hovel."

Clever and insinuating, he paid his respects to the King and when
the usher came to tell Louis XVI that the Council was assembled the
old courtier bowed as though the news concerned him also. The
King was confused and left his companion without daring to take his
leave. M. de Maurepas followed and sat down at the Council table.

"Does Your Majesty wish to nominate me Prime Minister?" he asked.

The King gathered up his courage. "No, that is not my intention."

"I quite understand," Maurepas replied, smiling. "Your Majesty
wishes me to teach him how to proceed without one."

M. de Machault was forced to return home and Maurepas, who
in fact was virtually the Prime Minister, governed together with his

nephew d'Aiguillon, who, to everyone's astonishment, retained his portfolios and his title of Chancellor.

> Maurepas was impotent;
> The King restored his power anew.
> The grateful Minister then went
> To see the King and told him: "Sire,
> The only thing that I desire,
> Would be to do the same for you."

The rhymester did not realise how accurate he was. The new Minister
feared that the "separation" between husband and wife would give Maria
Theresa more influence over her daughter. But Maurepas had no need
to worry. Marie Antoinette could stand on her own feet. "I was very
struck by her behaviour in the d'Aiguillon affair," the Empress was able
to say.

In less than a month, indeed, the Queen was able to obtain her chief
wish: the dismissal of the "creature's" friend. She importuned her
husband every day. The Queen of France could not forget the injuries
done to the Dauphine, and Maurepas, who was secretly delighted at
being able to keep the power to himself, advised his nephew to give
up the unequal struggle. At the beginning of June the Chancellor sent
the King his double designation. "Being unable to restrain her animosity," wrote Mercy, "the Queen brought about by herself the dismissal of the Duc d'Aiguillon, who but for her would have retained his
position."

But Louis XVI, who had taken one step forward, now took two back
and granted the ex-Chancellor a gift of 500,000 livres, or 100 million
francs, which caused Marie Antoinette to sigh, as she was not concerned:
"I am afraid the King is too kind and easy-going."

The "horrid man's" disgrace should automatically have entailed the return of M. de Choiseul to be Minister of Foreign Affairs, for during
the first few months of the new reign this enemy of Mme du Barry was
still cooling his heels at Chanteloup with Mme de Choiseul. And he
cared "neither for his wife nor for the country." But Louis XVI did not
wish for his return; he did not want to play the part of Louis XII either.
Choiseul had unfortunately once said to him: "I may one day have the
misfortune, Monseigneur, to be your subject, but I shall never be
your servant."

The young King had not forgotten this. Choiseul would not be his servant; he would not return to Versailles for two months. Marie Antoinette then played her last card. According to Mercy she "demanded this concession from the King, and without delay." And Louis yielded, but when he saw Choiseul again on 15 June he confined himself to saying: "You have lost a lot of hair since I last saw you, M. le Duc."

What would Vienna say on seeing the "champion of the Alliance" so badly received? However, the Empress seemed satisfied by this partial success. She did not wish Choiseul to return to power. "In the present state of affairs a Minister of Choiseul's character would not suit us," she informed Mercy. This being her mother's opinion, Marie Antoinette asked for nothing more. She was content with the dismissal of M. d'Aiguillon.

Something much more important weighed on her and forced her to constant restraint: etiquette. In extenuation of the Queen's desire to throw off this perpetual yoke one should remember how tyrannical were these outworn customs, some of which dated from the time of Francis I. When she woke Marie Antoinette could not take her breakfast in peace: those with the right of the *petites entrées* were present. Perhaps it was all very well for the First Physician, the First Surgeon, a physician in ordinary and the Reader, the Abbé de Vermond, but why should the King's four first valets de chambre, their reversioners, and his First Physicians and Surgeons also come to see the young woman drink her morning chocolate? Admittedly she had a short respite afterwards in order to take her bath—a tub which was wheeled into her room. Only women were present. But towards mid-day the Queen, who had gone to bed again, had to rise. She sat at her toilet table in the middle of a circle of folding stools reserved for women of high office while the men with a right to the *grandes entrées* remained standing and watched Marie Antoinette do her hair and put on her rouge. Gentlemen were constantly entering the room and bowing. Marie Antoinette interrupted her toilette to incline her head and smile. In the case of Princes and Princesses of the Blood etiquette required her to put her hands on the arms of her chair as though she were about to rise, but to remain seated.

Then the men retired, jostling each other, for the most polite went out first so as to give others the happiness of contemplating their sovereign for as long as possible. She began to dress. One would do well to re-read the celebrated passage by Mme Campan: "The dressing of the Queen was a masterpiece of etiquette; everything went by rule. The Lady of Honour and the Mistress of the Robes, both taking part if they were there together, aided by the first waiting woman and two ordinary waiting women, performed the main functions, but there were distinctions between them. The Mistress of the Robes handed the petticoat and presented the dress. The Lady of Honour poured water for washing the hands and handed the chemise. When a Princess of the Royal family was present the Lady of Honour yielded her this latter office, but did not yield it directly to Princesses of the Blood. In their case the Lady of Honour handed the chemise to the first waiting woman, who presented it to the Princess of the Blood. Each of these ladies observed these customs scrupulously, as they were privileges. One winter day the Queen, who was quite undressed, was about to put on her chemise. I was holding it unfolded; the Lady of Honour entered, hastily took off her gloves and took the chemise. There was a knock at the door, which was opened; it was the Duchesse de Chartres. She took off her gloves and came forward to take the chemise, but the Lady of Honour could not present it to her. She gave it back to me and I gave it to the Princess. Another knock: it was the Comtesse de Provence; the Duchesse de Chartres handed her the chemise. The Queen held her arms across her chest and seemed to be cold. Madame noticed her discomfort and merely throwing aside her handkerchief kept on her gloves and in putting on the chemise disarranged the hair of the Queen, who began to laugh to conceal her impatience, but not without having muttered several times: 'How odious! what importunity!' "

When the King had spent the night with the Queen a mixed service began its ballet. Towards eight o'clock the menservants, to whom the Queen's women had opened the door, extinguished the torch which had been burning all night in a silver basin, drew open the bed curtains on the side on which Louis XVI was, and presented him with his slippers and dressing gown. The King left his wife to continue her night's sleep. He retired to his apartments followed by a manservant bearing the short sword which on the previous evening had been placed on a chair "within reach of His Majesty's hand."

Therefore when the ceremony of the royal *lever* began at half-past eleven, Louis XVI had already been up and dressed for over three hours. He had paid a visit to his little forge, asked his chief locksmith Gamin all sorts of questions, shot at the cats on the terraces of the château or, seated in an armchair on the roof, had watched through a telescope the people arriving at the château to be present at his *lever*. And he now had to take off his suit of plain cloth and put on his night clothes. During the long ceremony Louis XVI did not sigh like Marie Antoinette. He played games and dodged, and they had to run after him to put on his shirt or breeches. In summer he liked to edge his visitors on to the balcony, which was covered by canvas continuously watered by hoses. Laroche, the guardian of the Menagerie and the dirtiest of his pensioners, was often the butt of the royal jokes. The King guffawed when his pages succeeded in snatching off Laroche's wig. If the Duc de Villequier was present Laroche was left in peace, for he was distantly related to the First Gentleman of the Bedchamber. Louis XVI then made up for it by tickling an elderly valet de chambre, who was so sensitive that he fled in fear, pursued by the King's loud laugh.

Often, too, he would lift at arm's length a page sitting on a fire shovel. His strength was famous; he was the only man in the court who did not fall down when he used an arquebus belonging to one of the Swiss Guards which kicked like a little cannon.

But the strong man side of him did not make him forget what was due to etiquette. He knew well that if the Queen came to see him in the morning it was the Grand Chamberlain or the First Gentleman of the Bedchamber who must "take the dressing gown at the first door," whereas, no one knew why, the first valet de chambre had the privilege of carrying it as far as the bed railing.

At the least step Marie Antoinette was accompanied by an armed battalion.

"For whom is the detachment of warriors I found in the courtyard intended?" the Abbé de Vermond asked her ironically one day. "Is some general going out to inspect his army?"

Her Reader extolled the simplicity of the court of the House of Lorraine. When one of Marie Antoinette's ancestors had to levy a tax he went alone to the church, stood up after the sermon and, waving his hat in the air, stated the sum he needed. Marie Antoinette, who could not take two steps by herself, loved to tell this story. The smallest of her actions set in motion a cohort of officers, employees and servants, of whom she now had more than five hundred.

One might well think that Marie Antoinette could console herself by thinking that thanks to this antique pageant she was the best served woman in France. But the Queen was not surrounded by professionals and the holders of the great posts were only clumsy amateurs, fixtures imbued with a strong sense of their prerogatives. If Marie Antoinette saw dust on the counterpane and, with the help of several intermediaries, summoned the servants of the bedchamber, the latter replied that the dust did not fall within their jurisdiction, "the Queen's bed being considered furniture when Her Majesty was not lying in it." It was therefore the first upholsterer of the bedchamber who should be approached. When the Lady of Honour and the first waiting-woman were absent Marie Antoinette could not drink if she was thirsty, as these ladies alone had the right to present their mistress with a glass of water—a glass of tepid water, incidentally, on account of the number of hands through which it had passed.

When Marie Antoinette opened the windows of her little apartments a terrible stench rose from the courtyard of the *Œil-de-Bœuf,* for the château was a veritable sink. "The passages, the courtyards, the wings and the corridors," reports a contemporary witness, "were full of urine and faecal matter. The park, the gardens and the château made one retch with their bad smell." Viollet-le-Duc tells how in 1830 he visited the château with an old Marquise who had lived at the court of Marie Antoinette. She seemed bewildered and could not find her way in the unfurnished rooms. Suddenly the two visitors found themselves at a place where "a waste plug, which had burst owing to the frost, had covered the floor with filth." The smell drove them back. The old Marquise cried out with joy: "Ah! I know where I am now! That was Versailles in my day. . . . It was like that every-where!"

To these smells was joined a harsh odour of the soot with which the walls were impregnated; it lasted until August, for the chimneys drew very badly. An inventor did indeed try to create a "capnebalic" and "capnephaltic" apparatus which, according to him, would absorb all the smoke. A trial was made at the Château de Saint-Hubert, but the machine—a turret with valves—creaked so much that no one could sleep a wink and it was considered preferable to keep the smoke which had filled Versailles since the days of the Great King and which was borne with as an old acquaintance.

It was impossible to alter the château. Marie Antoinette had to be content with modernising the most out-dated customs. "The most ancient custom," Mme Campan tells us, "required that in the eyes of the public the Queens of France should appear surrounded only by women; the absence of servants of the other sex obtained even at meal times for the service of the table. Although the King ate publicly with the Queen he too was served by women with all the objects directly presented to him at table. The Lady of Honour, kneeling with a napkin on her arm, and four women in full dress presented the dishes to the King and the Queen. The Lady of Honour poured their drink. This service was formerly performed by girls of honour. On her accession the Queen abolished this custom. She also freed herself from the necessity of being followed everywhere in the Palace of Versailles by two of her women in court dress at those times when her ladies were not with her. From then on she was followed only by a single valet de chambre and two foot servants. All Marie Antoinette's faults were of the kind I have just mentioned. Her wish gradually to substitute the simplicity of the Viennese customs for those of Versailles did her more harm than she could possibly have imagined."

It was no good submitting problems of etiquette to her or reminding her of what Maria Leczinska used or used not to do, unless one wanted to draw on oneself such replies as: "Madame, manage these matters as you wish, but do not imagine that a Queen, born an Archduchess of Austria, can give so much interest and enthusiasm to them as a Polish Princess who became Queen of France."

"Her Majesty dislikes constraint," wrote a chronicler of the time, "and will not submit herself to an etiquette she had already thrown off when she was Dauphine."

Her first care, indeed, was to simplify the famous *lever*. Once her hair was dressed she left her ladies in their full court dress—their annoyance can be imagined—and followed only by her women returned to her private rooms, where, with no spectators, she could quietly get dressed and undertake the serious business of looking over her wardrobe. In any case she could not possibly do all this in the bedchamber, for the "artists" who took care of her—Mlle Bertin and the three Léonards—had no right of *entrée*.

Custom forbade any "underling" with a post at court to exercise his "art" outside. But Marie Antoinette feared lest the imaginations of Rose Bertin and the "Physiogonomist," as Léonard was called, should become provincialised among the "centenarians" of Versailles. The Queen therefore insisted that her favourite artists should continue to look after the dresses and the hair of the ladies of Paris. The devotees of etiquette shuddered.

It was scarcely two months after the death of Louis XV that the Duchesse de Chartres had presented Rose Bertin to the young Queen, and as soon as the blue and black of the "little mourning" ended in November Mlle Bertin threw herself into what she called "her work with Her Majesty." Several times a week, at the peep of day, the pretty Rose would arrive at Versailles followed by a graceful troupe of blushing girls bearing enormous boxes from which the dressmaker brought out dresses called "Indiscreet pleasures," "Stifled sighs" or "Masked desire." With each visit the boxes became larger, for panniers were soon to be two or three yards in circumference.

One morning the Queen hesitated in what shade to order the dress which Rose called "Honest compromise." Perhaps in this brown taffeta? At this point the King entered. "That's the colour of fleas!" he declared contemptuously. And so puce became fashionable. Distinctions were soon drawn between *ventre de puce* and *cuisse de puce*. But a few days later Marie Antoinette chose an ash-blonde silk. "It is the colour of the Queen's hair," said the Comte de Provence, who was more gallant than his brother.

That too became the rage. A fashionable woman was obliged to wear this "divine" colour. Couriers were sent to the Gobelins and to Lyons with a lock of Marie Antoinette's hair, so that the weavers could reproduce the colour exactly.

From the boxes there also came shoes whose heels were adorned with a row of emeralds—the *venez-y voir*. But Mlle Bertin's triumph was her *poufs aux sentiments,* coiffures designed in collaboration with the "Physiognomist." The day after Louis XV's death elegant women wore a cypress and a horn of plenty in their hair—mourning for the King and hope for the new reign, or a rising sun symbolising Louis XVI (they did not know him very well) and an olive tree, emblem of peace and plenty. "More simply" one saw fields of corn being harvested by Hope. One morning the Queen bore lightly on her head a whole English garden, with its lawns, hills and silver streams.

The Duchesse de Lauzun, who was not afraid of headaches, arrived one day at Mme du Deffand's house with a built-up *pouf* representing a whole countryside in relief. One could see a hunter aiming at the ducks flapping at the edge of a lake ruffled by the wind. On the heights was a mill with the miller's wife being courted by a sprightly curate, while the miller, who knew how to behave, went off with his donkey in the direction of the Duchesse's ear.

Mlle Bertin was once nearly dethroned by a certain Beaulard, who invented mechanical coiffures. One pressed a spring and a rose flowered. There was also a real piece of machinery, called "The good miller's wife," which with the aid of a winch hidden in the chignon could be lowered or raised when an old lady with retrograde ideas entered or left the room. Mlle Bertin went pale with jealousy. But Marie Antoinette remained faithful to Rose, who in collaboration with Léonard invented for the Queen coiffures *au Lever de la Reine*, *à la puce*—naturally! *à l'Iphigénie*, *à l'Eurydice*—to please Gluck, *à la Modestie* and *à la Frivolité*. But above all Marie Antoinette liked feathers. The coiffure *à la Minerve* had as many as ten, which were so tall that one day she found it impossible to enter her coach to go to a ball given by the Duchesse de Chartres. At the beginning of February 1775 Maria Theresa sharply criticised her daughter's "plumage" and when the Queen sent her a portrait of herself with her head covered in feathers the Empress sent it back, feigning to imagine that there had been a mistake in the destination of the present. "I did not see the portrait of a Queen of France but that of an actress."

Mercy, while admitting that "the feather head-dresses were somewhat exaggerated," pointed out that "in this matter the Queen is merely following a fashion that has become general." But the Empress would have none of it. "A young and pretty Queen, full of charm, has no need of all this nonsense."

Marie Theresa was not aware of the other disadvantages of Marie Antoinette's craze for Mlle Bertin. Mme Campan, an impartial witness, tells us: "The Queen was naturally imitated by all the other women. Everyone immediately wanted to have the same head-dresses as the Queen, to wear the plumes and garlands which were made infinitely charming by her beauty, which was then at its height. The young ladies' expenses were enormously increased; mothers and husbands grumbled; a few scatterbrains contracted debts; there were unpleasant family scenes and coldness or quarrels in several homes. And it was widely said that the Queen would ruin all the French ladies."

Rivarol observed justly: "Always more of a woman than a Queen, she forgot that she was born to live and die on a real throne." For Marie Antoinette, in the words of another witness, "the title she most desired was that of the most fashionable pretty woman."

To be fashionable one had to please—please oneself and please others. To be fashionable was to be constantly surrounded by a court of adorers. The Queen could not imitate the elegant woman of the day, the Parisienne of 1775, who in the mornings, dressed in her "night mantle" held together by a pink *désespoir*, smiled at the folly of her friends, while a sprightly abbé fanned himself in his armchair and hummed a popular tune. But just like a "belle" she could always be surrounded by crowds of young or not quite so young people.

At this time her favourite companion was her brother-in-law. In the eyes of the Comte d'Artois, who according to Mercy was interested in nothing but frivolity and whose behaviour was very much that of a libertine, "there was only one King of France: the Queen." When he met his brother he crowded him, "almost treading on his toes," never called him "Your Majesty" and considered that he lowered himself by paying his daily court. As for his sister-in-law, paying court to her consisted in amusing her. He asked her to distribute the prizes to the winners of the tilting at the ring, took her driving in a *diable*— an open two-wheeled carriage—or with his cousin, the Duc de Chartres, organised horse races. This was a novelty. Until then racing was carried on only at Newmarket. Now, on 9 March 1775, the two Princes invited the Queen to preside over the first races, at the gates of Paris on the outskirts of the Bois de Boulogne. In spite of the rain and the wind which tugged at her skirts, Marie Antoinette remained stoically on the uncovered platform to which she had mounted by a shaky ladder. The horse of one of her friends, the Duc de Lauzun, won the race, but died of its victory.

A large crowd was present at this "meagre spectacle" but, significantly, Marie Antoinette was very much less applauded than usual. She hardly noticed, thinking only of her next outing. During this first winter of her reign she was chiefly preoccupied by her balls, and the papers of Papillon de La Ferté, Keeper of the Privy Purse, reflect the Queen's frequent requests "which never cease to entail rather heavy expenses, in view of the large number of plumes and fine gilding ordered by H.M." Marie Antoinette paid no attention to Papillon's sighs; her main desire was to amuse herself with her friends. The carnival of 1775 "gave the young people too easy an access to the Queen," Mercy complained, but Easter did not restore calm. The Queen was constantly surrounded by a whole troupe of thoughtless, gilded youth. For all these "feather brains," to use a contemporary expression, who had very little in their powdered heads, Marie Antoinette was truly "their Queen." For them the faults which distressed Maria Theresa and Mercy—"hostile impulses," "remarks on her superior rank," "grudges," "feelings of revenge"—did not exist. She was just a pretty, fashionable woman who laughed delightfully and wanted to please her dear friends. With them she was exquisitely charming and kind. "It is always the same when she is given the opportunity of amusing herself," Mercy noticed bitterly. And her set was adept at doing this.

There was the Comte d'Adhémar, whose real name was Montfalcon. His dubious nobility was forgiven, for he was "very fashionable" and could sing while accompanying himself on the harp. Vaudreuil had presented him. Some people thought that the latter had a "charming" face; others found him "frankly ugly." The former were probably women and the latter men, for the Princesse d'Hénin said: "I know only two men who know how to speak to women: Lekain and M. de Vaudreuil."

"The Comte de Vaudreuil, who governs the Queen," said Tilly, "does not always know how to govern himself." This man, so exquisitely polite, went into dreadful rages. He was not a man but a weathercock: he changed his opinions as he changed his wig.

There was Esterhazy, a Hungarian who had just arrived at court. This officer was possessed of "brutal good looks" and was surrounded by legend: his line could be traced to Attila and his family owned 60 townships and 414 villages. But this did not satisfy him. He wanted to have his debts paid and asked for a regiment. The Queen hastened to satisfy him on both points and even occupied herself with garrisoning his hussars. "Is it enough for him to be one of my friends," she said to the Minister of War, "for you to persecute him? Why have you sent Esterhazy's regiment to Montmédy, which is a bad garrison? See that it is sent somewhere else! Let M. d'Esterhazy be satisfied! You will report to me on the matter."

The Hungarian obtained Rocroy—a much-sought-after garrison—where he occupied his leisure moments in receiving and writing a great many letters to the Queen.

Another foreigner was a member of the coterie: the Prince de Ligne, "an Austrian in France and a Frenchman in Austria," who adored Versailles. "The love of pleasure first brought me here; gratitude brings me back." At the slightest pretext he covered the distance between Beloeil and Versailles in 24 hours. He was the most disinterested of Marie Antoinette's friends and his love for the Queen was respectful and noble. For him "her soul was as beautiful and white as her face."

Another friend was the Duc de Coigny. In 1774, he was 38 years old. At the moment he was "simple and temperate," but he was soon to change. The friend with the most influence was Besenval, pronounced *Baiseval*. Polish on his mother's side—she was the Comtesse Bielinska —the Baron de Besenval was Swiss on his father's side and for this reason bore the rank in France of lieutenant-colonel of the Swiss Guards. His 53 years enabled this "old Celadon" to proclaim himself the young Queen's counsellor and to pay respectful court to her. He amused her. According to him, Marie Antoinette "with no fund of personal gaiety" was interested only in "the gossip of the day, little carefully veiled familiarities" and "in particular the kind of scandal heard at court." Besenval was king in that line, having, it is said, an excellent style of bad manners and "being able to risk impertinences which suited him perfectly." One has only to see his portraits, of which his descendant, the present Prince Amédée de Broglie, has a whole series, to realise that one is in the presence of a witty man. When he was away Marie Antoinette was bored—that perpetual disease of the great.

The most dangerous of them all was undoubtedly Lauzun, towards whom the Queen was much too friendly. It was a pity that she did not listen to Mercy when he declared that this irresponsible man was "very dangerous on account of his restless mind and his collection of all kinds of bad qualities." But for two years Marie Antoinette refused to take notice of the evidence. Like Besenval, Lauzun amused her. He too knew how to talk the "nonsense" which was popular in Marie Antoinette's circle.

"Tell me, Monsieur," she said one day to an old marshal who could talk of nothing but his two war horses, "which of your two horses do you prefer?"

"Madame," replied the Marshal with "comic gravity," "if on a day of battle I were mounted on my piebald I should not dismount to mount my bay; and if I were mounted on my bay, I should not dismount to mount my piebald."

A moment later the conversation turned on two pretty women at court.

"Monsieur," said the Queen, turning to one of her "associates"— Lauzun or Vaudreuil—"which do you prefer?"

"Madame," he replied, as gravely as the Marshal, "if on a day of battle I were mounted on—"

"That will do!" the Queen exclaimed, laughing.

Such was the prevailing tone.

Sometimes a spoilsport would come to spend the evening with the Princesse de Guéménée, with whom the coterie gathered: it was the King. Luckily he liked to go to bed early and retired at eleven. Then the conversation became much freer. So one evening, in order to hasten his departure, someone risked putting the clock forward, and the King disappeared, leaving the field clear. All Versailles got to know about it. The "centenarians" and "strait-laced" ladies were very severe on this joke, but the Queen shrugged her pretty shoulders. The important thing was to be among friends and chatter.

What did they talk about? According to Mme Campan, who cannot be accused of severity, these pretty scatterbrains in furbelows thought of nothing but trivialities. "To be childish" was the mode and it showed itself in a profound ignorance. Marshals of France or infantry lieutenants, cardinals or curates just leaving the seminary—all were ignorant! The Prince de Ligne confirmed this. And in this sphere Marie Antoinette was the most fashionable. She never opened a book, unless it were a licentious work, which caused Joseph II once to reproach her with "the trashy reading she filled her mind with."

It was all the more difficult for the Queen to fix "her attention on interesting objects," as Maria Theresa said, since her conversation was "inconsequent and sprightly, flitting from one thing to another." We learn this from Besenval, who knew what he was talking about. Now the Swiss colonel and the Queen's "associates" were ambitious. The rôle of clown must be made to pay off. In April 1775 the coterie urged the Queen to demand a marshalship for the Duc de Fitz-James. Marie Antoinette, who liked the Duchesse, undertook this and the King agreed. The Minister for War was horrified. "No one knows anything of M. de Fitz-James' actions in war!"

Louis XVI tried to go back on his promise, but the Queen had already informed the new Marshal, who was waiting in the ante-chamber to present his thanks. Nothing could be done. All Paris laughed at the nomination. So in order to mitigate this incredible promotion the King nominated seven other Marshals, who were hardly better qualified than M. de Fitz-James, and Paris sang:

> Rejoice, ye happy French, break forth and sing!
> The Marshals who have been made by the King
> Will bless us with eternal peace, for sure,
> Since not a single one is made for war!

But the Queen had had her way and Besenval now considered that they could go further. He had formed a scheme: to persuade Marie Antoinette that her pride would no longer tolerate the presence of M. d'Aiguillon a few leagues from Versailles. He must be exiled, not to his château of Veretz in Touraine, but to Aiguillon itself, on the Garonne. After all, was not the former Chancellor the instigator of the libels and pamphlets which were poured out on Marie Antoinette daily? Besenval and Mercy were convinced of it. The Ambassador declared: "As a result of extensive research and observations I daily receive more indications that it is the Duc d'Aiguillon who is the principal actor in all the little intrigues formed against the Queen."

The Ambassador reported his discoveries to Marie Antoinette. The Queen seemed indifferent to the steps taken by her mother's councillor; nevertheless she asked the King to exile d'Aiguillon to his lands in the country. "Somewhat embarrassed," the King first consented and then, after consulting Maurepas, withdrew under some vague pretext. The Queen made no comment and, said Mercy, "the matter stayed there."

Now it was Besenval's turn. The Swiss had one gift which the diplomat would never possess: he could get what he wanted out of Marie Antoinette by pulling a long face, and so he sulked. For the sake of peace and to make her entertainer resume his rôle the Queen yielded to his importunities, as she was later to yield to Mme de Polignac, who used the same technique.

M. de Besenval belonged to the "Choiseul party." "The Queen's concern in the matter would have sufficed to make me attack M. d'Aiguillon," the Baron confessed unashamedly in his memoirs, "but I was led to it by other considerations. He was responsible for the fall of M. de Choiseul. It suited my personal feelings to punish him. I could not flatter myself that there was any hope of M. de Choiseul's return as long as M. d'Aiguillon was in a position to wield any power." Soon, thanks to M. de Besenval, the Queen "felt how important it was to be rid of M. d'Aiguillon." "There was not much reason for exiling him," wrote Besenval. "I advised the Queen to stress his audacity in attacking the Comte de Guines."

Guines, a "fashionable man" of whom Marie Antoinette was really fond, was French Ambassador in England, but he stayed at Versailles as often as he could. The little time he spent in London did not prevent his enjoying the pleasures of smuggling by means of the diplomatic bag. Unmasked, Guines had protested loudly and thrown all the blame on his secretary, Tort de la Sonde. The two men were confronted in a trial. The Ambassador's guilt quickly became obvious and in order to defend himself Guines declared that it was all sheer calumny and accused M. d'Aiguillon of trying to ruin him.

When the Minister fell Guines attacked him with redoubled violence. Maurepas supported his nephew and Marie Antoinette the Ambassador. It was a cut-and-thrust fight, said Besenval, who was delighted by the turn things had taken. "One cannot hold out against a queen," sighed Maurepas, and left the field clear for Marie Antoinette. She persuaded the King to intervene and Guines was acquitted. He remained Ambassador. However, the Duc d'Aiguillon had to be punished for daring to attack Marie Antoinette's friend. "I have spoken to the King," she announced to Besenval, who was managing the intrigue alone. "He is at last beginning to suspect that M. d'Aiguillon is flouting him, and I think that he will settle matters."

Whatever the Queen might say, Louis XVI, like Mercy, had the idea that Besenval had "with treacherous cunning made the Queen discover in the protection she accorded the Comte de Guines a means of vengeance against the Duc d'Aiguillon." The King therefore tried again to temporise. Marie Antoinette was furious, and when the Duc d'Aiguillon came to receive her orders for the annual review of the King's Household, in which he was to ride at the head of his company, she exclaimed harshly: "My orders? Why do you not go and seek those of Mme du Barry?"

On 30 May, at Marly, when the light horse commanded by the Duc d'Aiguillon rode past, Marie Antoinette drew down sharply the blinds of her carriage. The ex-Minister asserted even that she put out her tongue at him. That evening she insisted that the King exile "the creature's" friend.

"My hair stands on end every time I see that man!"

Louis XVI sighed and allowed his wife to settle the matter. The Queen promptly summoned Maurepas. "What new offences has my nephew committed?" he asked. Naturally, there was nothing new. "No matter!" retorted the Queen. "The measure is full to the brim; the vase must overflow."

"But Madame, it seems to be that if the King must harm someone it should not be through you."

"You may be right, and I shall not do it again, but I wish to do it this time."

The "Prime Minister" could only give way. "My nephew is too obedient a subject to do anything which might displease the Queen. He will leave in a few days."

Marie Antoinette confessed: "This departure is entirely my doing. The measure was full to overflowing. This wretched man was carrying on all kinds of espionage and evil designs. He tried to defy me more than once in the affair of M. de Guines. I asked the King to exile him. It is true that I did not want a *lettre de cachet,* but nothing was lost by this, for instead of remaining in Touraine, as he wished, he was asked to continue as far as Aiguillon, which is in Gascony."

Now that the ex-Minister had been relegated to a half-ruined château in the heart of the Agenois, Marie Antoinette would have liked to continue with no more worries in what Maria Theresa called "her dissipations." But Louis XVI's coronation at Rheims had been fixed for Sunday, 11 June 1775, and it would interrupt the fashionable little Queen's happy existence.

She yawned as she listened to the Abbé de Vermond reminding her, on Mercy's behalf, that formerly "it was a fairly frequent custom that when kings were consecrated at Rheims their queens were consecrated at the same time." According to the Ambassador and his messenger, Marie Antoinette would have to take part in the great ceremony being prepared. But once again the Abbé returned empty-handed to the Petit Luxembourg, where Mercy lived. "He found the Queen completely indifferent in this connection." Maria Theresa's two confidants were hardly surprised. They well knew that these presentation days brought no amusement to their royal pupil. She much preferred to be queen of her coterie than Queen of France. The public were already beginning to be aware of this. And yet, once again—perhaps for the last time—her charm and the impulses of her heart would provoke enthusiasm and recall the first hours of her reign.

6

"The Feather-head"

IN RHEIMS CATHEDRAL, decorated in "the antique style" and brilliant with lights, the King was stretched before the altar on a fleur-de-lis covered carpet. At his side, in the same posture, was the Archbishop of Rheims. This was the only moment of the very wearing day when the two principal actors could draw breath, particularly needed by the Archbishop, who was 78 years old and already exhausted by the first two hours of the ceremony.

The anointings began. There were nine of them, accompanied by prayers which the Archbishop chanted in a trembling voice. Those who were following the ceremony could hear a sentence which was almost a thousand years old: "May he not abandon his rights over the king-doms of the Saxons, the Mercians, the people of the north and the Cimbrians." The Cimbrians were the English.

Before the final anointing the King was clothed with the tunic, dalmatic and mantle covered with fleurs-de-lis. The Keeper of the Seals, M. de Miromesnil, raised his voice: "Monsieur, you who represent the Duc de Bourgogne, present yourself at this act!"

The Comte de Provence stepped forward. Miromesnil turned towards the future Charles X, who in 50 years' time was to come there on his own account.

"Monseigneur, you who represent the Duc de Normandie, present yourself at this act!"

Then one by one, wearing the great ducal mantles of violet cloth edged and lined with ermine, their coronets on their heads, the collar of the Order of the Holy Ghost round their necks, the Ducs d'Orléans,

Chartres, Condé and Bourbon represented the other lay peers—Aquitaine, Toulouse, Flanders, and Champagne, and surrounded the King together with the six ecclesiastical peers. The Archbishop intoned further prayers, one of which has a curiously Oriental flavour: "May the King possess the strength of the rhinoceros, and may he drive the enemy nations before him, like a raging wind, to the uttermost ends of the earth."

The King had need of such strength to support the heavy crown of Charlemagne, studded with rubies and emeralds, which the Archbishop placed on his forehead with the help of the twelve peers, who laid their hands on it symbolically—a remnant of the elevation on the shield of the Frankish kings.

A hinge in the crown was unobtrusively opened and it was fastened on the forehead of the King, who bent under its weight. Those around him heard him sigh: "It hurts me!"

But Marie Antoinette did not hear. When from her seat she saw her husband holding the sceptre bearing the lily of enamelled gold and the hand of justice made from the horn of a unicorn, when she saw him looking just like the crowned kings adorning the manual from which the Abbé de Vermond used to teach her French history tears of emotion rolled down her fair cheeks.

The Constable, M. de Clermont-Tonnerre, who was 84, had difficulty in holding "Joyeuse," Charlemagne's heavy sword, in his wrinkled hands. He preceded the King, who walked slowly towards the rood-loft. This was the Enthronement.

The Archbishop and the peers kissed the King and cried three times: "*Vivat rex in aeternum!*" The doors of the cathedral were opened. The crowd filled the nave, crying: "Long live the King! Noel! Noel!" The fowlers freed hundreds of birds which, dazzled by the light, fluttered among the crystal chandeliers. Outside, salvos of musketry were fired and all the bells in the town answered the great bell of the cathedral.

"Noel! Noel!"

The applause, the clapping and the shouts increased. The Queen could not bear it and burst into tears. When she was seen to take her place again a few moments later the whole church, Mercy reported, in spite of the sacred character of the building "rang with shouts, claps and demonstrations difficult to convey." During the long ceremony which was only just beginning, the King, who was deeply moved, frequently turned his eyes towards the Queen "with a look of adoration impossible to describe." As though in a dream Marie Antoinette saw Louis receive a loaf of gold and one of silver, give the kiss of peace to the twelve peers and communicate in both kinds.

Husband and wife were both so moved that perhaps they did not notice that the sword of Charlemagne fell from Clermont-Tonnerre's trembling hands and that the Comte d'Artois, whose "careless attitude" shocked everyone, had thrown down his coronet, exclaiming: "Oh, to the devil with it!"

A little later, still as a spectator, the Queen was present at the interminable royal banquet. To the sound of hautboys, flutes and trumpets a whole crowd watched hundreds of dishes borne along, to be eaten under their eyes by about thirty privileged persons.

In the evening, the King, who had put off his stifling robes and heavy accessories, took the Queen's arm and without guards, like honest bourgeois, they went to walk among the crowd in the garden of the Archbishop's palace. Their reception was almost hysterical. People pointed out the envoy from Tripoli, "that barbarian," who was also weeping with emotion.

With admirable stoicism Louis then underwent the exhausting ceremony of the Order of Saint Sulpice—about a hundred bows to be received and returned. On the following day, riding his horse *Vainqueur* with silver trappings which had cost 27,543 livres, followed by all the nobility on horseback and preceded by trumpets, Louis XVI went to the Abbey of Saint-Rémy. Behind him were led two other horses, *Fier* and *Monarque*, in case the King should take a wish to change his mount. After Mass, surrounded by doctors and surgeons, he touched 2,400 persons afflicted with scrofula. "May God heal you, the King touches you," the Prince de Beauvau repeated 2,400 times, while the King "rested his hand on the head of each sick person."

In the evening Louis XVI went for a walk, on the arm of the Queen, in the Bois d'Amour outside the town. The applause was unceasing. The crowd pressed in from all sides. There was even a boy of fifteen there, who was not very good-looking. He had come from Troyes and his name was Danton.

On 16 June the Queen drove towards Compiègne, with the cries of admiration and affection still ringing in her ears. She repeated that if she lived until a hundred she would never forget the day of the coronation. Why were Mercy and the Abbé constantly scolding her? Was she not loved, adulated? Was she not acclaimed in spite of her "dissipations" and "mistakes"? As the Ambassador wrote to her mother on 23 June, she did not realise that all this was merely "a momentary success which should not dazzle" since "there is not sufficient foundation for it."

The diplomat may have been farsighted, but the Queen was not. "I did my best to respond to the eagerness of the people," she wrote to her mother. "It is at once amazing and gratifying to be so well received, in spite of the dearness of bread. . . . It is a remarkable trait in the French character to be carried away by evil suggestions and then to return at once to the right road. What is certain is, that seeing the people who in the midst of their unhappiness treat us so well, we have an even stronger obligation to work for their happiness. The King seemed to me to be struck by this truth."

The King was struck by it and would do what he could, but would she? Bread was not merely dear; there was a shortage. Did she know that as the carriages went along the road to Rheims the labourers making up the road "knelt down, raising their hands to heaven and brought them back to their mouths to ask for bread"? In the same year, 1775, at the time of the "flour wars," the rioters talked of going to "shake up" the Queen—and this was only one year after her accession, and fourteen years before the Revolution. That was indeed a warning. But once the Queen was back in Versailles she resumed her life of pleasure. For her "the happiness of the people" had nothing to do with her amusements. Maria Theresa, speaking of the inevitable consequences of this "endless dissipation," exclaimed: "I cannot put it too strongly to you so as to save you from the abyss towards which you are rushing."

Mercy was about to discover the reason, and the excuse, for this "thirst for pleasure" which had such "a mysterious power" over the Queen and wrought "such havoc" in her character. One day, when the Ambassador was repeating his reproaches, Marie Antoinette became "sad and thoughtful" and with a heavy sigh "went into a few details of the distress caused to her by her situation" as a "married" woman. "I must have some distraction and I can find it only in increased amusements."

Louis XVI was now undoubtedly in love with his wife "in every sense of the word," but the "fatal object" was still in the same condition. At the end of 1774 he discussed this subject with his doctor, Lassonne, who earnestly recommended an "incision." As Marie Antoinette told her mother on 17 December, the King was very favourably disposed, but a little later, when the surgeon showed the King all his tools, which were real instruments of torture, "His Majesty wished to put it off once again," as a chronicler relates. This did not stop him from visiting his wife. In the spring of 1775 a small, secret corridor was built between the bedrooms of the King and the Queen, passing under the Hall of Mirrors and emerging behind Marie Antoinette's bedroom. "The King's passage," of which only fragments remain today, enabled Louis to avoid the *Œil-de-Bœuf*, which was like a public square, and thus continue his too conscientious and vain attempts.

"The old Roman proverb, *Tota mulier in utero*, throws a striking light on this conjugal drama," writes Dr. Ganière. "If it is true, and daily instances prove it to doctors, that the uncertain female equilibrium is often based on the satisfaction of the senses, how can one be surprised if the young Queen, undoubtedly endowed with the impetuous temperament which has characterised so many members of the Hapsburg family, appeared to the eyes of her intimates and through them to her whole people as frivolous and capricious? Nearly every night she had to submit to her husband's demands, which, although they might not yet have any real result, aroused without appeasing her senses. 'There is certainly no indifference on my side,' she wrote to the Empress, 'but my dear mother must understand that mine is a difficult situation.' She did not fully understand the unfortunate effects of these unavailing onslaughts, but had ended by instinctively shunning them after having for months lamented her husband's indifference. She stayed up as long as possible in the hope of finding her husband asleep, when formerly that peaceful sleep had seemed an insult to her youth. By day she tried to lose herself in a whirl of sometimes questionable pleasures. She sought, certainly in no unhealthy spirit, friendships which would appease her ardent need of affection."

The reign of the favourites was about to begin.

It was the fashion of the times. In 1775 it was the accepted custom to have a woman friend—a completely respectable relationship, one must emphasise—of whom one said with a sigh: "She has such an attraction for me! There is such conformity in our way of life!"

Such a friend was "inseparable" until "a caprice or a trifling dispute brought about a rupture." This was called "friendship's flirting." It was so much in vogue that the Sèvres factory had to make groups "of a passionate sensibility" representing "The tender friends" or "Confidences between two young persons."

The first "young person" to whom the Queen "confided" was the Princess de Lamballe.

Marie-Thérèse of Savoy, Princesse de Lamballe, was not pretty "but seemed so at a little distance." The young woman had suffered so much and was so "naïve" that Marie Antoinette had a kind of protective feeling for her. She was emotional to the point of fainting when she saw a lobster in a painting. Were these faintings, which were then very fashionable, sincere? The Empress considered these swoonings to be "affectations" and for his part Mercy had every reservation about "the appearance of this Principal Lady in Waiting." During 1775, in which Madame de Lamballe rose to the height of her favour, Marie Antoinette had the Princess from Savoy appointed Principal Lady in Waiting in her Household.

"Picture my happiness," the Queen wrote on 13 July. "I shall make my dearest friend happy and I shall benefit even more than she will."

The nomination was not brought about without trouble. It had been necessary to plead with Louis XVI. On Marie Antoinette's assuring him that it "would be the greatest pleasure of her life," he yielded—as he always did. Faced with the extra expense entailed by the creation of this post, the Controller General protested loudly. But in spite of her father-in-law's huge fortune the Princess protested even more loudly, and she was able to enter on her duties "with the wages, pensions, lodging allowance, liveries and other rights" formerly granted to Maria Leczinska's Principal Lady in Waiting, Mlle de Clermont, who had had no personal fortune. Moreover, Mme de Lamballe received an extra 50,000 livres "to provide her with the means to maintain herself in this important post"—so important, indeed, that the two first Ladies of Honour resigned, considering their prerogatives attacked.

Marie Antoinette consoled herself by spending hours alone with the Princess and, as a chronicler tells us ingenuously, "appreciates her even more and enjoys herself immensely."

This friendship and these long *tête-à-têtes* did not suit M. de Besenval, who wanted the Queen to "create Ministers on whom she could rely." The Chevalier de Vergennes had been nominated "without the

Queen's being informed and without her paying the slightest attention." She took no interest either in the nomination of the upright, honest Turgot. Besenval thought this situation should change. Seeing her entertainer become gloomy, Marie Antoinette set about the dismissal of La Vrillière, Minister of the King's Household, whom Besenval did not like, and she succeeded without too much difficulty.

This victory was followed by a defeat. To succeed La Vrillière Marie Antoinette and her friends put forward Sartines, who was Minister of the Marine, although he had never seen a ship in his life, and intended to put in his place M. d'Ennery, another friend of the coterie. But the question was, how to bring about this general post, for Maurepas, whom the Aiguillon affair had placed firmly among the Queen's enemies, had other plans.

"What is to be done?" Marie Antoinette asked Besenval.

"Use the occasion to be on good terms with M. de Maurepas, so as to obtain the Ministry you want. You must therefore send for him and tell him you will make no recriminations about the past and have decided to forget it and in future to have a good understanding with him, and that you imagine he will be sufficiently aware of the advantages for public affairs, for the King, himself and you resulting from such an understanding, to strive to deserve your friendship and trust; that you ask nothing better than to grant him both, but that you must have proof of his good intentions so as to destroy even your slightest distrust; and that this proof would be the placing of M. d'Ennery in the Ministry of the Marine."

Marie Antoinette strongly approved but, complained Besenval, "I had no sooner left her room than everything was forgotten. A hunt succeeding a walk, a spectacle, caused it to be four days before the Queen held the conversation she had promised."

The conversation was a failure. Maurepas was sorry, but it was too late. M. de Malesherbes had been chosen for M. de la Vrillière's post. Consequently, M. de Sartines would remain at the Ministry of the Marine and there would be no portfolio free for M. d'Ennery. But unexpectedly Malesherbes refused. Maurepas insisted, but Malesherbes stood firm, in spite of two urgent notes sent to him in one night. The third letter was a real cry of alarm: "If the Queen prevails on this occasion, all is lost!" wrote Maurepas and Malesherbes finally accepted. "The Queen," wrote Besenval, "received what in the language of intrigue is called a rebuff." Marie Antoinette took it very badly. The King bore the blow courageously, but for all that advised Maurepas, who wanted to make his apologies, not to go and see the Queen. "Don't go, it is not very fine there today."

Besenval had made an error in tactics. It was not towards Maurepas he should have directed his scheming but towards the King "in love with his wife in the fullest sense of the word." When she applied to her husband Marie Antoinette was rarely refused. Indeed, at Rheims the Queen had obtained the King's permission to meet M. de Choiseul, although Louis XVI had an increasing aversion for him. It was true that on that occasion the Queen had been really artful. By recounting this to her childhood friend, the Comte de Rosemberg, Marie Antoinette caused a sensation. "You can be sure," she wrote, "that I did not see M. de Choiseul without mentioning it to the King, but you could never guess the skill I exercised so as not to appear to be asking permission. I told him that I wished to see M. de Choiseul and that I was only in difficulty about the day. I managed so well that *the poor man* fixed the most convenient time for me to see him. I think I made good use of a wife's privileges at that time."

"The poor man!"

Also to the Comte de Rosemberg she wrote: "My tastes are not the same as those of the King, who cares only for hunting and machinery. You must admit that I would be somewhat out of place in a forge!"

"The poor man!"

Here again Marie Antoinette was very fashionable. It was extremely bad taste to love one's husband. An affectionate husband who begged his wife to call him *tu* was thought ridiculous, but everyone was charmed by her reply: *"Eh bien! va-t'en."*

Unconcern and indifference were the two rules of the day. Men gave as good as they got to their wives. Métra tells us of this dialogue between two of the Queen's friends, the Duc de Coigny and the Marquis de Conflans.

"You know, I am very embarrassed."

"Why is that?"

"I have never once had supper at your wife's."

"Well, neither have I. Let us go together and back each other up."

Marie Antoinette had adopted the prevailing tone and in Paris they sang:

> The Queen imprudently let out
> To Besenval, her friend, one day:
> "My husband is a sorry lout."
> The other answered, winking,
> " 'Tis what all think, but do not say,
> You say it without thinking."

These three words, "the poor man," horrified the Empress when Rosemberg showed her the letter. Marie Theresa, who was unaware of what constituted a fashionable Frenchwoman, was shocked and wrote to Mercy: "My daughter is simply hurrying to her destruction. . . . What a style, what a way to think! This does but confirm my forebodings: she is hastening to her ruin and will be fortunate if, when she is lost, she retains the virtues owing to her rank!"

Rosemberg also showed the letter to the Emperor. Joseph II did not spare his sister: "You meddle in a great many matters which first of all do not concern you, which you know nothing about and in regard to which the cabals and associates who flatter you and know how to arouse your *amour propre* or desire to shine, or even foster a certain hatred or rancour, cause you to take one step after another calculated to spoil the happiness of your life and certain to bring *extreme unpleasantness* upon you sooner or later, and, by diminishing the King's friendship and esteem, to lose you the good opinion of the public and all the consideration which, with the aid of that opinion, you might acquire, and have acquired, astonishingly enough, until now. Why do you think it your business, my dear sister, to transfer Ministers, to send one to his estates, to have a particular office given to this man or that, to help another to win his lawsuit, to create a new and expensive post at your court, and finally, to talk about public affairs and even to use expressions by no means suited to your position? Have you ever asked yourself by what right you interfere in the affairs of the government and the French kingdom? What studies have you ever made? What knowledge have you acquired that you dare to imagine that your advice or opinion can be of any use, particularly in affairs which require wide knowledge? You are a pleasant young woman who all day thinks of nothing but frivolity, your appearance and your amusements. You never spend more than a quarter of an hour a month in reading or hearing anything intelligent. I am sure you never ponder or think out anything or reflect on the consequences of what you do or say. You act only from the impulse of the moment, and the words and arguments of the people you are protecting and in whom you trust are your only guides. Could anything more rash, unreasonable and improper be written than what you observed to the Comte de Rosemberg concerning the way in which you arranged a conversation at Rheims with the Duc de Choiseul? If such a letter ever went astray, if, as I have no doubt, you let slip similar words and observations to your intimate friends, I can only *foretell great unhappiness for you*, and I confess that on account of my attachment for you this distresses me very much."

Maria Theresa begged Joseph II to soften his letter. However, the expurgated text which Marie Antoinette received sent her into a passion. She made a scene to Mercy. After "an agitation lasting half-an-hour," the Queen, astonished by the Austrian Ambassador's silence, stopped. "In all conscience, what do you think of it?"

With great frankness Mercy replied that "his respectful observations" having so far been without result, he no longer knew what to say. "I therefore give myself up in silence to painful ideas which depress me by showing an unhappy future for the Queen . . . It must be admitted in good faith that everything is going badly, that Your Majesty does not trouble to examine any question, acting solely from the prompting and the passions of her associates. By engaging only in futile or dangerous dissipations Your Majesty risks losing all the trust, respect and love of the public."

Marie Antoinette looked at her mother's friend with astonishment. For the first time she seemed uneasy. The Comte de Mercy believed that she had understood the cry of alarm uttered by the Empress and Joseph II.

As usual the court went to Fontainebleau in the autumn. It was an incredible removal. Actors, singers, dancers and wigmakers all took the road to Fontainebleau. All these had to be lodged, as well as "people who have neither post nor service, but who constantly come to pay their court and who have to be lodged." The château had only 172 apartments, and only the four walls were provided. When the château was full lodgings were taken in the town and the guests found their names written in chalk on the doors as at a halting-place. Only Princes had the right to yellow chalk.

In 1775 it rained at Fontainebleau nearly every day and Marie

Antoinette, who had caught cold, hardly ever went out. She was present at several spectacles, which were not very good, but which, for all that, cost no less than 100 million francs. For reasons of economy the dresses of some of the actors had been made from the coronation robes and in spite of his short sight the King noticed it.

This more peaceful life allowed Mercy and the Abbé to continue with their exhortations. Their task was the harder and more delicate in that Marie Antoinette was at that time a victim to one of those "changes of affection" from which, according to Mercy, "there result only trouble and inconvenience." If one can believe what Lauzun says in his Memoirs, or if, to be more exact, one can believe Lauzun's Memoirs, which were possibly embellished by their first publisher, it was at Fontainebleau in 1775 that the favour of the future Biron rose to its highest peak—to such a peak indeed that people made transparent allusions in the presence of the favourite. According to himself Lauzun one day hastened to Marie Antoinette.

"I feel I must inform Your Majesty that some people are so bold as to blame her for the kindness with which she honours me. I take the liberty of begging her to demonstrate it less frequently and to allow me not to present myself before her so often."

Marie Antoinette refused. "I must beg Your Majesty," Lauzun insisted, "I must even demand, as the only reward of my complete devotion, that you do not compromise yourself by supporting me."

"What! You would wish me to be so cowardly! No, M. de Lauzun, our cause is inseparable; they will not ruin you without ruining me."

"I threw myself at her feet. She held out her hand, which I kissed ardently several times without altering my position. She leant towards me with great tenderness; she was in my arms when I rose. I was tempted to grasp the happiness which seemed to be offered to me."

Was this scene entirely invented? Did the Gascon's habitual complacency cause him to interpret as a yielding what was perhaps only a feeling of affection? One fact is certain: a few days later the Queen admired a white heron's plume adorning her favourite's military head-dress. Lauzun gave it to her and she wore it one evening.

According to Mme Campan "his conceit exaggerated the worth of the favour which had been granted him. Shortly after the gift of the heron's plume he asked for an audience. The Queen accorded it, as she would have done for any other courtier of his high rank. I was in the next room to the one in which he was received. A few moments after his arrival the Queen reopened the door and said in a loud, angry voice: 'Begone, Monsieur.' M. de Lauzun bowed deeply and disappeared. The Queen was very upset. She said to me: 'That man will never enter my doors again.'"

The "handsome Lauzun" makes no mention of this incident. But it is possible that the stories of the courtier and the waiting-woman are both true. Having misunderstood the Queen's affectionate gesture a few days earlier, Lauzun might on this occasion have tried "to grasp the happiness which seemed to be offered." Later on, when he had certainly lost favour, he followed Marie Antoinette all one day, disguised as a foot servant, in order to attract her attention. The Queen did not even notice him. "He seemed to have given his services for nothing," wrote Mme d'Oberkirch, "when, just as the Queen was to return in her carriage from a walk in the Trianon, he had the idea of kneeling on one knee so that she might place her foot on the other, instead of using the velvet step. Astonished, Her Majesty looked at him for the first time, but, like the witty and sensible woman she was, she pretended not to recognise him and called to a page: 'Please see that this servant is dismissed. He is very clumsy and does not even know how to open a carriage door.'"

"It is said," adds Mme d'Oberkirch, "that M. de Lauzun was deeply wounded by this rebuke and that afterwards he hardly ever presented himself to Her Majesty."

For this conceited fool the Queen's behaviour and her perpetual "changes of affection" may have been somewhat of an excuse. Marie Antoinette was already reaping what she had sown.

The Princesse de Lamballe had only just been nominated to her new post when, at Fontainebleau, Mme de Polignac came into favour. Mercy told his sovereign that "the Queen has an even stronger affection for her than for any who have gone before."

Mme de Polignac's reign was to last, with a few breaks, for fourteen years. For some people her face bore the marks of "her shameful villainy"; for others "no face ever expressed more charm and sweetness. . . . One of those countenances to which Raphael knew how to impart an expression of intelligence and infinite kindness."

"Her character," said Besenval, "was even more perfect than her face." She possessed "a calm which no situation, circumstance or object could shake." One might conclude that she had not a very open disposition. Mercy certainly asserted it.

In 1775 Mme de Polignac was 26 years old. She was married to a colonel, the Comte Jules, who had very little money. According to the best traditions the Comtesse's lover was her husband's best friend, the Comte de Vaudreuil, a tyrannical lover, who made very violent scenes. The family was completed by her sister-in-law Diane, née Polastron, who was ugly and hunchbacked, but a real live-wire and far and away the most intelligent, and the most full of intrigue, of the four.

It was at a concert at which "Comtesse Jules" was singing that Marie Antoinette had been touched by the young woman's charm and by her sweet, tender voice. Then she was attracted by her candour, her "careless grace" and the sensibility which constantly melted into tears. Soon she was to explain: "When I am alone with her I am no longer a queen, I am myself!"

According to Diane de Polignac the Comtesse first responded to the Queen's advances without enthusiasm, but cleverly: she had no fortune and informed her sovereign that it would be best if she retired from court. Marie Antoinette, much affected, strongly opposed this. Was she not there to help her friend? At Fontainebleau, feeling that the "Lamballe clan," especially the Chevalier de Luxembourg, was preparing to give her a hard time, the Comtesse burst prettily into tears and declared to Marie Antoinette: "We do not yet love each other so much that we will be unhappy if we are separated. I can feel it coming, and I shall soon be unable to leave the Queen. Let us anticipate this and let Your Majesty permit me to leave Fontainebleau."

This scene, which was reported by the Prince de Ligne, ended in a general outburst of emotion. The Queen mingled her tears with those of her pretty friend and then took her away to the park.

But a Queen of France had no more the right to laugh at the follies of a Lauzun than to put her arm round the waist of a Lamballe or a Polignac. The pamphlets and songs increased. It was "an epidemic," the Queen exclaimed, adding lightly: "I was not spared. Both tastes were freely attributed to me: for women and for lovers."

The people were easily "carried away by evil insinuations," particularly as these came from Versailles. As a pamphleteer said at the time: "A despicable courtier hatches them in the dark; another courtier puts them into verse or couplets and with the help of the flunkeys distributes them to the Halles and the herb markets."

Marie Antoinette's exaggerated and demonstrative affection for Mme de Polignac set all Paris talking and at court unleashed a positive drama. The astonished Mercy related that "the two favourites, mutually very jealous, are constantly complaining about each other and quarrelling." Fontainebleau was a battlefield for these ladies, who had each her partisans, enemies, jealousies and intrigues. The Queen suffered from these perpetual disputes. She would have liked her two friends to get on together and love each other, and she would then have been quite happy. "I should enjoy the pleasures of private life which do not exist for us if we have not the intelligence to secure them."

The evening was "the most critical moment of the day," the Austrian Ambassador assures us. After supper Marie Antoinette went to see the Princesse de Guéménée, where she found Mme de Polignac, Coigny, Vaudreuil, Besenval and a number of young people who were the terror of poor Mercy. Mme de Guéménée, Governess of the Children of France, now governed only Madame Elisabeth (Madame Clotilde had just married the heir to the Prince of Piedmont) and her office gave her a great deal of leisure. She busied herself with her many dogs, with whom she claimed "to be in communication, thanks to mediating spirits." Sometimes the Princess stopped dead in the middle of a conversation and fell into a trance: a "mediating spirit" was informing her of the wishes of her pack. When the Governess was receiving her spirits and her dogs the Queen preferred to visit Mme de Lamballe, to whom came the Duc de Chartres and "everyone connected with the Palais Royal," that is, with the younger branch of the family. "Guéménists" and "Lamballists" insulted, slandered and dragged each other elegantly in the mud. They agreed only on two points: backbiting and begging. "Every day," continued Mercy, "there come from both these sources so many insinuations and requests that it would be impossible to explain even part of them to Your Majesty without entering into endless details."

During the greater part of the stay at Fontainebleau Besenval and his friends were seething with excitement about the nomination of a new Minister for War. Besenval's candidate was the Comte du Châtelet, son of "the divine Emilie." Mme de Polignac and Vaudreuil preferred the Marquis de Castries. But prompted by Maurepas and Malesherbes, the King chose a Minister unconnected with any court intrigue. He was sent for from Alsace, where he was cultivating his pear trees. It was

M. de Saint-Germain who was appointed "to the applause of the whole army." The clan was greatly disappointed. M. de Saint-Germain—"a Jean-Jacques Rousseau in boots and a helmet"—cut down the parade establishment. Henceforth the gendarmes and the light horse would number only 88.

"I suppose they are to escort the King to the *lits de justice?*" the Queen asked ironically.

"No, Madame, they are to accompany him when the *Te Deum* is to be sung."

A more serious grievance was that he was not a courtier. One evening Marie Antoinette was bombarding her husband across the table with bread pellets.

"What would you do, brave soldier, if you were fired on like this?" Louis XVI asked the new Minister.

"Sire, I should spike the gun!"

There was a chilly silence.

Another drama, that of expenses, was unfolding. The end of 1775 saw the purchase of a pair of diamond earrings for 100 million francs of present-day money, to buy which Marie Antoinette got into debt. A little later she bought for 250,000 livres bracelets which "loaded her with debts." When Maria Theresa wrote that this "filled her with anguish for the future," she replied lightheartedly: "I would not have believed that anyone would have tried to occupy my dear mother's kind attention with such trifles." The trifles were bracelets worth 50,000,000 francs.

Marie Antoinette had soon forgotten her brother's lecture and during the winter her "taste for dissipation" revived strongly. On 11 February she went to a ball at the Opera, stayed there until five o'clock in the morning, came back to Versailles at half-past six and left again at ten to attend the races in the Bois de Boulogne. Conforming to the prevailing fashion of anglomania, the Queen had developed a passion for horse-racing. The Comte d'Artois and the Duc de Chartres organised a race every Tuesday in the Bois de Boulogne. On that day the Queen should have received the Ambassadors. The diplomats waited in vain, and one may imagine their acid remarks on leaving Versailles after their fruitless journey.

It was terribly cold in January 1776. Wrapped up in furs, the Queen went by sledge along the boulevards. Louis XVI put on an old overcoat and walked in the country, where he paid poor people to break the ice or pardoned wood-stealers arrested by the guards in the forest of Ville-d'Avray. One morning, on his return, he met the Queen, who was coming back from a ball at the Opera.

"Did the public applaud you? How did you find them?"

"Cold."

"Apparently, Madame, you were not wearing enough plumes."

"I should like to see you there, with your Turgot. I think you would be well and truly hissed."

Like "the lords and the grocers" Marie Antoinette did not care for Turgot. It was not because the Controller-General could not "come to terms with human weaknesses," nor because he treated Parliament, industry, finance and the nobility roughly, nor because, like Sully, he was kind only to the farmers, nor because he behaved more like a brutal vivisectionist than a careful surgeon. It was because M. Turgot had dared to recall M. le Comte de Guines from his Embassy in London.

This recall was to cost Turgot his portfolio. The Controller's sudden departure, willed and planned by Marie Antoinette, put an end to the famous economic reforms, which might perhaps have saved the monarchy and avoided the clash in 1789.

The pretty "feather-head," as Joseph II called her, might protest to her mother that she had had nothing to do with her enemy's dismissal (for she sometimes told a lie), but in fact her responsibility was equalled only by the King's weakness. Marie Antoinette made her husband rewrite three times a letter according de Guines, in exchange for the loss of his Embassy, "permission to bear the title of Duc." "The Queen's scheme," wrote Mercy, "was to demand that the King should dismiss Turgot, and even send him to the Bastille, on the same day that the Comte de Guines was declared a Duc." Not without difficulty the Austrian Ambassador managed to avert "the results of the Queen's anger" against a man "who enjoyed a great reputation for honesty and was loved by the people." But Turgot had to leave without even having been able to complete and submit to the King his plan for reorganising the finances.

Further, Vergennes, whose policy was successful, nearly lost his Ministry of Foreign Affairs, also "on account of the Comte de Guines." Mercy realised how astonished Maria Theresa would be and he explained: "The key to this enigma can be found in the Queen's associates, who are banded together in favour of the Comte de Guines. Her Majesty is *obsessed* and wants to be clear of it all. They manage to arouse her *amour-propre*, to irritate her, to blacken those who, for the sake of the general good, might resist her wishes. All this goes on during the races or other pleasure parties and in evening conversations with the Princesse de Guéménée. In fact, they are so successful in putting the Queen beside herself and in intoxicating her with dissipation that, given also the King's extreme compliance, there are times when it is quite impossible for reason to break through."

The Abbé de Vermond, entrusted by Mercy with the task of helping reason to break through, was so discouraged that he wanted to leave court. The Ambassador made him stay, but he too was in despair. During the summer of 1776 Mercy admitted that there existed "no active authority capable of opposing the Queen's wishes."

The Ambassador considered as particularly harmful the Queen's recent decision to appoint Madame de Polignac's husband "reversioner" of the Comte de Tessé, her First Equerry. "H.M. imagines that she has paid tribute to friendship, but the public sees in it only blind infatuation for the Comtesse de Polignac, who at the moment is completely in the ascendant." Again, he complained: "The late Queen had only 150 horses. When M. de Polignac has bought those he has to have as reversioner, the Queen's stable will have 300 horses and the expenses will be 200,000 livres more than in the time of the late Queen."

The poor man thought that was all, but he did not know everything. He knew nothing of the positive looting the Comte de Polignac was to engage in and which is revealed by a file in the National Archives whose contents have been overlooked until now.

It must first of all be noted that as the reversioner—that is, successor —to the Queen's First Equerry the Comte de Polignac had the right to horses and carriages which, according to a document, "are destined solely for the personal use of M. le Comte Jules and not for his service with the Queen, since every time he has the honour to follow H.M., whether in town, on an excursion or at the hunt, he is in a carriage of the Queen's suite and not in his own."

A staff had to be formed. The Comte was given fourteen "liveried servants"—footmen, coachmen, ostlers and postillions. He not only doubled this number but decided, using the King's money, to give his grooms a salary of 1,143 livres instead of the usual 756. His footmen's wages were raised from 503 livres to 759 and those of his chairmen from 596 livres to 893.

M. de Polignac thought that his servants, animals and carriages would be rather cramped in the King's stables. He therefore hired a house at Versailles, one at Compiègne and another at Fontainebleau. And "M. le Comte Jules, so as to have no difficulty in getting what he wants, has taken all the workmen from the Queen's stables," sighs an anonymous controller.

This was not all, however. The Queen granted the new reversioner two teams of seven horses and four saddle-horses—in all eighteen horses, which the Comte soon increased to 25. In the Little, as in the Great, Stable it was customary to spend 1 livre 12 sols per day per animal for the horses' upkeep and food. Comte Jules demanded 9 livres 6 sols a day for each horse. This useless post of reversioner consequently cost the State, in present-day francs, 13 millions in 1777, 15 in 1778, 19 in 1779 and nearly 23 in 1780. This was not surprising, since the reversioner's horses ate nine times more oats than those of the First Equerry.

An amusing and unpublished text, emanating from some discouraged controller, can be seen among these fabulous accounts. "If M. le Comte de Tessé refuses to pay, M. le Comte Jules will complain to the Queen, who will get the increases from the King, and M. le Comte de Tessé will simply appear to be acting with a bad grace."

A year after M. de Polignac's appointment the bitterness between the Grand Equerry and his successor became so violent that a duel was feared. M. de Tessé, who like his father and predecessor was completely absorbed by his profession (he said of a woman: "She is gentle— as gentle as a well-made carriage"), could not understand the careless frivolity with which his reversioner undertook the duties of his post. He decided to make a journey to Italy and asked for 15 months' leave to get over his irritation. Comte Jules replaced him and ran the stables in accordance with his own calculations. One set of figures will be a sufficient indication. Until now shoeing had cost 6,000 livres a year; henceforth it would cost 20,000.

Although he was unaware of these details, Mirabeau was in the right when he exclaimed: "One thousand crowns to the Assas family for having saved the State, one million to the Polignac family for having lost it!"

In the summer of 1776 Mme de Lamballe was in semi-disgrace, which did not prevent her "from causing annoyance and expense in connection with lodgings at Versailles, Compiègne and Fontainebleau." But worst of all, continued Mercy, "are the favours which the Principal Lady in Waiting manages to extract." Her brother, Prince Eugène de Carignan, who had entered the French service, received 40,000 livres as pension, together with 14,000 livres for his colonelcy, although the allowance for colonels was only 4,000 livres. These expenses, Mercy pointed out, were entirely the Queen's doing.

Marie Antoinette was incapable of refusing. She was too afraid that her coterie would imitate Besenval's procedure by sulking and giving her a hard time, for these bandits imagined that they could do what they liked and they played on their mistress's emotions. "The Queen is impulsive," wrote Mercy, "and nearly always accepts what her petitioners report. Before making requests she ought to find out their importance and extent, together with the services and rights of the petitioner. The Queen's credit is considered so high that most of the Ministers can only obey her without venturing to remonstrate. The Queen takes it upon herself to make requests as much from a dislike of refusing as from a real desire."

When Maria Theresa received this letter, which was sent to Vienna on 17 September 1776, she wished that her "dear daughter" might have a few setbacks to put her on the right road again. For some months she had taken the line of not scolding "Antonia," for she had lost her influence, but she now changed her mind. "I can no longer be silent, as I love you for your own good, not to flatter you. Do not lose by frivolity the credit you gained to begin with. The King is known to be very easy-going, and you would get all the blame. I hope I do not live to see such a change."

Marie Antoinette's credit with the public was already much diminished. In the preceding spring she had not managed to get Gluck's *Alcestis* accepted by the Parisians. The opera was a failure and Marie Antoinette's lavish "signs of approval" did not, as before, carry the public with them. At the beginning of the autumn of 1776 the cheers were much less enthusiastic and they became even fainter after the stay at Fontainebleau in October and November 1776 when the notorious races organised by the Comte d'Artois and the Duc de Chartres took place.

The lack of constraint shown at these race meetings horrified Mercy.

Marie Antoinette installed herself with her suite in a salon prepared at the top of a wooden grandstand. She was surrounded by "a swarm of young people in boots and *chenilles*" who shouted and yelled. "There was such a mob and so much noise one could not hear oneself speak." Between races they plundered the buffet. The most excited was the Comte d'Artois, who ran down the stand, hurried through the spectators to go and encourage his jockeys, returned to the "mob," presented the winner to the Queen, insulted the loser, whom he wanted to thrash if he had betted on him. He whined if he lost, indulged in "pitiful exhibitions of joy" if he won. Amid all this "pell-mell"—Mercy's word—the Queen managed to keep "her air of graciousness and grandeur," but the crowd of spectators were "unable to notice this difference" and were dumbfounded. They were even more so on 13 November.

The Comte d'Artois had bought in England the famous racehorse King Pepin, belonging to the Marquess of Rockingham, and the Duc de Chartres had acquired Glow-worm, a son of the celebrated Eclipse. The King had promised to watch this "futile" spectacle and risked three livres either on his brother's horse or on that of the future Philippe-Egalité—the reports do not agree. The Comte d'Artois wagered a fortune. Many English had crossed the Channel and one of them bet 10,000 louis against King Pepin. In fact 5,000 of these belonged to the Marquess of Rockingham, who knew that his former horse's legs were too long and would trip him up at the turnings. Glow-worm, indeed, was the winner. The Comte d'Artois flew into a rage, wanted to kill his jockey and, to the surprise of the King, who did not suffer from hippomania, was very harsh on the Duc de Chartres. "I am tired," he exclaimed, "of being continually cheated, either at the races or at play."

On the occasion of the performance of *Don Japhet d'Arménie* by Scarron, after the return to Versailles from Fontainebleau, the King asked the leaders of the troupe "to imitate the behaviour, poses and grimaces of the Queen and the Comte d'Artois at the famous Fontainebleau race meeting." The parody was so successful that Marie Antoinette recognised herself and her anger was appeased only by the King's loud laughter. These details seem to indicate that perhaps Marie Antoinette had not always kept an "air of graciousness and grandeur" during the race between King Pepin and Glow-worm.

Although Louis XVI disapproved of his wife's passion for horse-racing, he tolerated gambling, although it was forbidden elsewhere.

In the evening, after their visit to the Turf, the Queen and her friends sat round another, clandestine, green carpet, but the King did not play.

"I can understand your playing heavily," he said to one of the gamblers, "you are playing with your own money, but I should be playing with other people's."

Marie Antoinette did not grasp this distinction and plunged recklessly. She even persuaded her weak husband to get someone from Paris to hold the bank at faro.

"It will not matter as long as you play for only one evening," the King conceded.

The banker, M. de Chalabre, arrived on 30 October. Somewhat intimidated by the crowd of gamblers, he asked for an assistant. A M. Poinçot, a Knight of the Order of Saint Louis, volunteered, but he had not the right to sit down to the game as he was only a captain. The rank of colonel was the "lowest grade giving this right." Moreover, he was there *"en polisson"*—a recognised expression signifying that the captain's nobility did not go back beyond 1400 and that consequently he had not been presented at court.

This made no difference. "A chair for M. Poinçot!" the Queen ordered. This chair was to cost the *polisson* several months' pay.

They played all night and into the morning. The Queen left at four o'clock, having lost only 90 louis, about 430,000 francs, whereas the Comte d'Artois had won six times as much. The game was continued on the evening of 31 November at Mme de Lamballe's house. Marie Antoinette went to bed at three o'clock, but the game went on well into the morning of All Saints' Day. Louis XVI was displeased.

"You allowed one gambling session, without fixing its length," Marie Antoinette explained, "so we had a perfect right to prolong it for 36 hours!"

"Really!" exclaimed the King, laughing, "you are all a worthless lot!"

But his weak nature was not very admirable either, for on 11 December he proposed of his own accord to bring back the bankers. Once more the session lasted all night at Mme de Lamballe's house.

Inevitably, Mercy one day found the Queen anxious and "worried about the state of her debts, of whose total she was not herself aware." The diplomat turned into an accountant and, although the Queen's allowance had recently been doubled, found a tidy deficit of 487,272 livres—100 million francs. The Queen was "somewhat surprised" but showed no signs of panic.

Marie Antoinette's insensibility in this matter was more excusable. The expenditure all around her appeared to have been instituted and regulated by a madman. On opening some of the files in the National Archives one feels obliged to read every item twice, for fear of having misunderstood. The Queen's personal apothecary received the sum of 2,000 livres a year for his drugs, whether Marie Antoinette was ill or not. The army of domestic servants was given a yearly travelling allowance even if no moves were made. One also notes that when the gentlemen of the watch were on guard they were reimbursed their outlay for "straw and mattresses," although this rule was two centuries old and the watch had for a long time been provided with mattresses from the furniture store. To illuminate the suppers the ushers received every three days a torch of yellow wax which was never used. Leakage was a recognised thing. For example, the Queen's victualler received no salary, "the profit he makes on his supplies standing in its stead." The story is well known of the scullery boy whose task was to keep up a roaring fire in the furnace every night "to make ashes," which ashes were sold the next day for the benefit of the chief cook.

One of the files in the Archives proves how insincere were the complaints made by Papillon de La Ferté in his *Journal*. His outlays were very profitable. Ferté, "who had a good understanding with his contractors," simultaneously authorised and checked the expenses. This is why, to take one example out of many, one sees invoiced, for *Athalie,* shepherds' crooks and straw hats, but further on we learn "that there was no occasion to make use of them," which in the case of *Athalie* is not surprising. And the clerk to the Privy Purse sighed as he bent over his accounts: "I should never finish if I went into all the details of the waste and useless expenditure I see every day, for the underlings, taking their example from the master, think they can do as they please and are not supervised."

There were very strange customs, too. Why did the Queen's dentist receive six dozen handkerchiefs? Why did the chief footmen yearly draw a mysterious "parasol allowance"?

"Tipping" was universal. The Queen's servants of the bedchamber collected a toll for the oaths of senior officers and for the stools of duchesses and grandees of Spain, apart from their salary, New Year's gift and the "charge on the replacement of candles."

Oh, those candles! The moment the Queen left her bedroom for her private apartments the candles were extinguished. Even if they had burned for only a few moments they were not used again and fell to various privileged people who resold them for their own account. The candles in the antechamber, the *grand cabinet* and the corridors were given to the servants of the bedchamber; those in the private rooms, the gambling room and the Queen's bedroom were presented to Marie Antoinette's women. One evening when the chandeliers and standard lamps were not lit the servants collected an indemnity of 80 livres. This "right to the candles" brought in yearly to each of the Queen's four waiting-women 50,000 livres, or 10 million present-day francs. There were burned, or to be more exact, there were *lit,* 109 livres' worth of candles on summer evenings and 145 on winter days. If, for reasons of economy, it was decided to cut down the festivities the women demanded an extra payment.

"Charities, gifts and pensions" for Marie Antoinette's Household alone amounted to 867,383 livres, 18 sols, 11 deniers—or 175 million francs. The Queen's unpublished accounts reveal some curious obligations. Marie Antoinette had to give 252 livres a year to the Recollect Friars "instead of a carp on abstinence days." By a reverse process she had to give 120 livres to the nuns of "Pique-puce" "on account of the herb salads which they customarily present to the Queen," and which they never presented.

These accounts are amusing, but they did not help settle the Queen's affairs. Somewhat embarrassed, Marie Antoinette decided, on Mercy's advice, to speak to her husband about her 487,272 livres of debts. Just as he had allowed faro, tolerated the "swarm of young people," permitted the dissipations and granted the Ministerial portfolios, Louis XVI now declared to the Queen "without hesitation and with the best possible grace," that he would pay her debts out of his own pocket. There was not a complaint or a word of reproach. "This indulgence of the King's, which covers everything, is extremely unfortunate," Mercy declared, "since it makes it impossible to divert the Queen from things which cannot be for her real good."

But Louis XVI had an excuse, and it was Maria Theresa who guessed it from afar. The King preferred to shut his eyes so that his wife—who was still not yet his wife—"may not become attached to other, less suitable, pleasures." Louis XVI may have realised that his wife's dissipations were a necessary palliative and prevented the worst.

The courtiers might make jests and the rhymers verses about this paradoxical situation, but the "fatal object" obsessed some people's minds. On New Year's Eve 1777, when Marie Antoinette and Louis XVI were returning from the chapel, an Abbé rushed forward, knelt down on one knee and presented the King with a "Memoir giving the secret of perpetuating his august race." This was the root of mandragora "to be eaten or applied." The Abbé and his "memoir" were politely shown the door. The King laughed loudly, but Marie Antoinette had to force herself to smile.

Having so much to be forgiven, Louis XVI became more and more indulgent. He ordered the number of balls, entertainments, games and spectacles to be doubled. During carnival time in 1777, as Marie Antoinette realised and Mercy confirmed, he urged his wife to go as often as possible to the Opera, although she behaved there "with an air of familiarity to which the public would never be accustomed." Neither did it become accustomed to see its sovereign indulge, under the walls of Paris this time, in the "pell mell" and rowdiness of the Fontainebleau races. Parisian society, too, did not become accustomed to travelling fruitlessly to Versailles to pay court. The reception days were unchanged, but Marie Antoinette, whose moods were very uncertain, would change her mind at the last minute, and Paris began to hold aloof from its sovereign's invitations. "The small number of people who make up what the Queen calls her 'coterie' keep away the majority of courtiers of both sexes," wrote Mercy, "and deprive the latter of any occasion and possibility of paying their court."

But Joseph II was about to break in on their enjoyment and try to restore order. It was to be seen if he would succeed.

It was not the first time that Marie Antoinette had once more seen one of her brothers. At the beginning of 1775 the Archduke Maximilian had come to Versailles accompanied by the Comte de Rosemberg and this visit had caused a great deal of trouble. Since the fourteen-year-old Archduke was there incognito, under the name of the Comte de Burgau, the Princes of the houses of Orléans, Condé, Conti and Penthièvre considered that the Queen's brother should visit them first. They awaited his arrival, but in vain. Marie Antoinette showed "excessive warmth" and remarked haughtily: "My brother will be sorry not to see the Princes, but he is spending only a short time in Paris and has many things to see. He will do without it."

The affair grew considerably and Paris applauded the Duc de Chartres, who refused to appear at Versailles during the "Comte de Burgau's" stay.

This time, with the arrival of Joseph II, it was an Emperor who wanted to shelter behind an incognito. He wished to be known only as the "Comte de Falkenstein." The Princes were in great anxiety. They wished to behave correctly, but there were so many problems. Should they provide an armchair for the Emperor if he came to see them? Should they themselves sit on a folding stool or allow themselves a chair with a back? Should they reconduct the Comte de Falkenstein to the door of the salon or as far as the antechamber?

Joseph II, indeed, was very eccentric. When he was dictating his orders he took pleasure in snipping off the ends of his secretaries' pigtails. An unpublished text in the Archives recounts that he would amuse himself by firing from his window at the dogs passing along the ramparts and that he would drive away "with blows from his whip the girls bringing petitions." This anonymous report declares that the Emperor's greatest enjoyment was to go and watch the women in labour in the great hospital in Vienna or to spend hours at the top of a tower overlooking a courtyard full of shrieking madmen.

Marie Antoinette was very nervous about her brother's visit. She expected criticisms and, according to Mercy, was prepared "to sidetrack him on a good many subjects."

On 18 April, at 7:30 in the evening, the Emperor's sedan chair entered the courtyard of the Petit Luxembourg, where Mercy, who was kept in bed by a painful attack of rheumatism, was waiting for him. For nearly two hours the Ambassador discussed with his master the different aspects his first interview with Marie Antoinette might take. Mercy need not have been anxious. On the following morning the first meeting between the brother and sister in the Queen's private room went off extremely well. The Emperor remarked jestingly: "If you were not my sister I should not hesitate to marry again in order to have such a charming companion."

Marie Antoinette was softened and confided her deep distress to the Emperor. Of course she felt nothing for the King, as Joseph II wrote to his brother, but the "fatal object" was the cause of real tragedies. When the Comtesse d'Artois's son was born, the fishwives who had come to congratulate the King's brother had followed the Queen "right to the door of her private room, shouting in the coarsest terms that it was for her to provide heirs." She still wept at the thought. The Emperor promised to speak to the King and meanwhile took advantage of his incognito to see, and criticise, everything.

He mingled with the public. "Yesterday," he wrote to his brother on 29 April, "I saw Sunday celebrated *in publico* at Versailles: the *lever*, the mass, the formal dinner. I mixed with the crowd so as to watch everything. I must admit that I enjoyed it, and having to act a part so often myself I now take the opportunity of seeing other people do so." The public was in ecstasies over his simplicity. He had refused to sit at the back of the King's carriage and had taken his seat "on the front." He was lodging with a simple bath-attendant of Versailles, who had rented him two rooms. He slept only on a bearskin. He drove around in the rain in a "mean little open carriage."

> Majesty without pomp our eyes have seen,
> Amazed at Falkenstein's simplicity.
> But here how shameful has the contrast been,
> He has found only pomp, no majesty.

What first astonished him was the "strange spectacle" of Louis XVI and his two brothers. "Their behaviour was so free and easy that on rising from table they amused themselves with childish jokes, ran about the room and threw themselves on the sofas."

Through these "incongruities" Joseph II made rapid judgements: Artois was only a fop, his wife "a complete idiot," Provence "nondescript and very frigid" and Madame, "ugly, coarse and full of intrigue, is not a Piedmontese for nothing."

The King made a better impression. "He is rather weak, but no fool. He has ideas and good judgement, but his body and mind are apathetic . . . The *fiat lux* has not yet been spoken, the matter is still in a lump." The Emperor was particularly anxious for the *fiat lux* regarding the "fatal object" and Louis XVI, who had explained the position to his brother-in-law, promised that he would no longer put off the operation advised by his surgeon.

The Emperor thought his sister more and more enchanting and was the first to applaud at the Opera when, in Gluck's *Iphigenia*, the chorus sang on seeing Clytemnestra: "Let us extol our Queen." "She is good natured and charming," he wrote. "I have spent hour after hour with her and not noticed their passing . . . Her virtue is unassailed and indeed she is austere by nature rather than by reasoning . . . With all this she has wit and a penetrating judgement that has often amazed me. Her first impulse is always correct." He was dazzled, like everyone who approached the Queen, but this did not prevent him from criticising her. "The Queen is a very pretty and good-natured woman, but she thinks of nothing but enjoying herself!" To the actor Clairval he said: "Your Queen is very giddy, but fortunately you French do not dislike that!"

On the fourth day of his arrival at Trianon, after a dinner in private, the Emperor took his sister into the garden and began to lecture her on her "everlasting dissipation." "He developed his ideas," wrote Mercy, "and drew a striking picture of the Queen's position, of the pitfalls surrounding her, of the ease with which she let herself be seduced by the deceptive allure of dissipation. He showed the *infallible and terrifying* consequences of this for the future. Under this heading were included neglect of the King, the Queen's companions, the absence of all serious occupation and the passion for gambling."

Joseph II was particularly shocked by "the bad tone of society" and by the air of license prevailing at Mme de Guéménée's house as a result of the games of faro. "That house is simply a gambling den!" he declared.

The Queen was full of good intentions. She promised to reform, but only after the Emperor's departure. "I do not wish to appear to be managed."

Joseph II was full of emotion on leaving Versailles. "It was all I could do to drag myself away." France, too, had affected him. "A government could lead it anywhere at the touch of a finger. I beat my Germans and they never move an inch!"

Marie Antoinette was very grieved by this separation. In the evening of 31 May she had a violent nervous attack. "It is true," she wrote to her mother, "that the Emperor's departure has left a gap I cannot fill. I was so happy during that short time that now everything seems like a dream. But what will never be a dream for me is all the good counsel and advice he gave me, which is engraved on my heart for ever. I will confess to my dear mamma that one thing he left me, which I begged for, gives me particular pleasure. This is the written advice he left me. At present this is my principal reading, and if ever I should forget what he told me (which I doubt), I should always have before me this paper which would soon recall me to my duty."

This "recall to duty" did not mince its words. "You are getting older and no longer have youth as an excuse. What will you become, if you delay any longer? An unhappy woman and a still more unhappy Princess!" He then entered on a lengthy criticism of the Queen's behaviour towards the King. "When he caresses you, when he speaks to you do you not show irritation, even repugnance?" He then attacked her "associates." "Have you ever thought what effect your intimacies and friendships, if not bestowed on people in every way irreproachable and reliable, may and must have on the public, since you will seem to share in them and to authorise vice? Have you weighed the terrible consequences of games of chance, the company they bring together and the tone they set?"

He then spoke of the masked balls at the Opera of which the Queen was fond and of the adventures, or rather misadventures, in which she was involved there. "In itself the place has a bad reputation. What do you go there for—respectable conversation? You cannot have this with your friends, for the masks prevent it. Nor can you dance. Why, then, all these adventures and dubious behaviour? Why mingle with a crowd of libertines, prostitutes and strangers, listening to their remarks and perhaps making similar ones? How indecent! . . . I must confess that I could see that this was what most shocked those who love you and who have a proper way of thinking. The King is left alone all night at Versailles and you mix in society and mingle with the riff-raff of Paris! . . . I really tremble for your happiness, for it cannot turn out well in the long run and there will be a cruel upheaval (*révolution*) unless you take steps against it."

"You will have a fall unless you are careful," was what the Emperor meant, but one's mind cannot help pondering on that *révolution cruelle* mentioned here 11 years before the fall of the Bastille.

The effect of these reproaches did not remain long with the Queen and Mercy confessed his amazement. "I cannot get over my astonishment over the short duration of the impression made by H.M. the Emperor on the Queen's mind. When one has for *two months* seen this august Princess imbued with the useful truths which were presented to her it seems unbelievable that everything should return to a state which is really worse than it was before the Emperor's stay in this country. I have reason to believe that the rule of conduct written by H.M. has been torn up and thrown on the fire."

The favourites reigned as never before. Mme de Polignac and M. de Coigny were at the height of their power. "These two persons," Mercy complained, "extort from the Queen favours which give rise to continual complaints by the public. The protégés of the Duc de Coigny snap up the financial posts and the Comtesse de Polignac's satellites constantly receive pecuniary favours to the detriment of those whose right it should be to have them. No Minister dares resist the Queen's wishes."

In the summer of 1777 there began the famous walks on the terraces of Versailles which, as Mme Campan wrote, "absorbed the attention of Paris, France and even Europe in a way very detrimental to Marie Antoinette's character." Mme Campan and Mercy both say that in order to profit by the cool of the evening Marie Antoinette would walk on the terrace of the château arm-in-arm with one of her sisters-in-law or one of her ladies. Soon, at the suggestion of the Comte d'Artois, the musicians from the chapel were summoned and installed on a rostrum, where they played far into the night. The inhabitants of Versailles "wanted to enjoy these serenades" and there was soon a crowd, with which the Queen imprudently mingled. There is a well-known story of Marie Antoinette, thinking herself unrecognised and sitting on a bench with a clerk from a Ministry and then with one of Monsieur's bodyguards and striking up a conversation with them. These two innocent little scenes were embellished and ended up as a veritable saturnalia.

"How many times," wrote the author of the pamphlet, *A Reprimand to the Queen,* "have you left the nuptial bed and the caresses of your husband to abandon yourself to bacchantes or satyrs and to become one with them through their brutal pleasures?"

This torrent of filth would fill more than a hundred volumes. Shortly after the famous promenade concerts a whole collection of songs against the Queen was thrown into the *Œil-de-Bœuf*. Joseph II scolded from Vienna, but the Queen "brushed it all aside and replied merely by evasions which seemed almost like jesting."

Joseph II had more success with his brother-in-law. In July Louis XVI finally made up his mind. "No doubt his self-esteem conquered," writes

Dr. Ganière, "and enabled the King to overcome his repugnance for the knife." It was a mild enough operation in itself, but very cruel when one thinks that it was carried out with no help from anaesthetics. A few incisions—a kind of anatomical retouching, in fact—and the job would be done, as long as the operation did not leave a painful impression for a few days. Louis XVI, proud of his endurance, bravely overcame these discomforts, and looked forward to achievements of which he had merely dreamed for the last seven years. The revelation took place. In spite of the long delay neither of the two partners seemed disappointed. Louis XVI confessed to his aunts: "I very much enjoy this pleasure and I am sorry to have been deprived of it for so long." And Marie Antoinette confided to Mme Campan: "I am now experiencing the most important happiness of my life." And yet, when one thinks of it, although during an August night in 1777 Marie Antoinette at last became true Queen of France, one is free to imagine that the reality must have been very different from what her thoughts had idealised during that hopeless period of chastity.

One has no need to imagine, for Marie Antoinette soon admitted it to one of her "associates": "I should be neither grieved nor very annoyed if the King were to develop a passing and temporary attachment, as he might thereby acquire more vitality and energy."

As a result of the King's lack of skill and experience the operation, which should also have appeased the Queen's thirst for pleasure, brought about no change in her behaviour. Three months after the beginning of this "most important happiness" she was already shunning the conjugal bed, and explained to her mother "that the King does not like sleeping two in a bed." Mercy explained matters more correctly. The King had never felt this dislike, but during their stay at Fontainebleau Marie Antoinette's passion for gambling caused her to return home at an ever later hour. Consequently, the King, who retired early so as to rise early, preferred to remain in his own room rather than have his night's rest interrupted by his wife's noisy return.

Once again faro was all the rage in the evening at the Princesse de Guéménée's house. The passion for gambling had become sheer madness: "The Duc de Chartres has lost 30,000 louis"—that is, 44 million present-day francs. In vain Mercy told the Queen that "as the government recognised the danger of games of chance and was attempting to check their spread, it was unheard of and scandalous that these very games should be admitted by the Queen, particularly when they occupied those moments which should be given to etiquette." The only reply he obtained was: "I am afraid of being bored."

And play continued. "It is the one subject," wrote Mercy, "on which she will admit no protest. On 25 October 1777 H.M. had lost her last crown. On the next day she ordered her treasurer to bring her her November allowance, which was also consumed in a few days, without counting a debt of 500 louis which is still not paid." Marie Antoinette was enjoying herself more than ever and would not listen to any cries of alarm. She made a wager of 100,000 francs, which would be 20 millions today, that the Comte d'Artois would not manage to have a château built in the Bois de Boulogne in six weeks, during the stay at Fontainebleau. The future Charles X accepted the challenge and declared that he would give a feast in the Queen's honour at Bagatelle —as the little château was called—before the return to Versailles. He won his wager thanks to 900 labourers who worked day and night. "The most extraordinary thing was," Mercy sighed, "that as there was a lack of building materials, particularly freestone, lime and plaster, and no time could be lost in looking for them, M. le Comte d'Artois gave orders that patrols of the Swiss Guards should search the high roads and seize all the carts they found loaded with the above-mentioned materials. The price of the materials was paid right away, but as the goods had already been sold to other individuals, there was a kind of compulsion in this method which revolted public opinion. No one can understand how the King can allow such flightiness and unfortunately it is also supposed that it would not be tolerated without the protection accorded by the Queen. H.M. often deigns to assure me that she is very far from approving the rashness of the Prince her brother-in-law, but that she has no means of stopping his misconduct. The Queen speaks truly on the first point, of which I have had many proofs, but as regards the second point, the one way of preventing the Comte d'Artois's disorderly conduct would be to refuse to attend the pleasure parties which cause it."

But Marie Antoinette did not refuse. She visited the little château. We do not know if her brother-in-law showed her the entresol adorned with frescoes and high-reliefs among which the Marquis de Sade would have been quite at home, but the public was convinced of it.

After one incident the Queen became involved in the Comte d'Artois's unpopularity. On Shrove Tuesday of 1778 Marie Antoinette spent the whole night at the Opera in the company of her brother-in-law and Monsieur. During the masked ball Artois, as usual, mixed with "the worst company," and a little later on was seen walking arm-in-arm with Mme de Canillac, the companion to the Duchesse de Bourbon, who had just dismissed her as she was also companion to that Princess's husband. The Duchesse was not a model of virtue, far from it, but she was as jealous as a tigress. Recognising her rival, she uttered a few acid remarks in an audible tone. The Comte d'Artois, who was also masked, came forward and replied sharply.

"Only M. d'Artois or a rascal could speak to me like that!" exclaimed Mme de Bourbon. On this gracious remark she tore off the mask of the King's brother. One can guess the scandal. The excitement increased the next day, when it was learnt that the Comte d'Artois had boasted to Mme de Polignac of having hit the Duchesse right in the face with his fist. Mme de Bourbon promptly styled her aggressor an insolent personage. Although her husband thought very little of his wife, he considered it his duty to intervene and challenge his cousin to a duel.

"Do your duty and fear nothing," his father ordered. The Prince de Condé then ordered relays of horses to be set up along the road to Belgium in case his son killed the King's brother. Vaudreuil and Besenval organised a meeting and on 16 March, in spite of Louis XVI's orders and Marie Antoinette's attempts to prevent the duel, the two opponents took up their position in the Bois de Boulogne. After a few minutes' fencing the Comte d'Artois's sword slid under his adversary's arm, scratching him slightly.

"That is more than is needed to settle the question," exclaimed Crussol, the Captain of the Prince's guards.

Artois raised his sword. "It is not for me to have an opinion, but for M. le Duc to say what he wishes. I am at his orders."

"Monsieur," replied the Duke, lowering the point of his sword, "I am deeply conscious of your goodness. I shall never forget the honour you have done me." Whereupon the two adversaries embraced.

Nevertheless, the affair had two victims, who were not the combatants: the Duc de Chartres, brother of the Duchesse de Bourbon, who was reproached with not having taken the quarrel seriously, and Marie Antoinette, who, it was asserted, had taken sides with her "insolent" brother-in-law. This was certainly false, but the Queen was now reaping what she had sown.

Whereas the future Philippe-Egalité prudently refrained from appearing at the Comédie Française on the evening of the duel, the Queen rashly went there with her brother-in-law. The Prince de Condé and the Duc and Duchesse de Bourbon were applauded at length, but Marie Antoinette and the Comte d'Artois were accorded only a few handclaps, so sparse that they appeared ironical.

This dispute in the Carnival season gave the Queen her first opportunity of measuring the road she had travelled in five years, since the time when the Parisians in tears showed her their "tenderness and attention."

At dawn on Thursday before Ash Wednesday 1778, at a time when there was once more a shortage of bread, the Queen travelled along the boulevards in her sleigh which had cost 10,000 crowns, followed by 21 coaches. Marie Antoinette had just left the Opera ball and was still laughing uncontrollably. The evening had been full of surprises. For a few minutes the Queen had mingled with the prostitutes and then a masked man, disguised as a fishwife, had approached her box, called her "Antoinette" and scolded her for not being with her husband, who "must at that moment be snoring in the conjugal bed." In a cascade of laughter Marie Antoinette leant over to speak to the stranger "until he could nearly touch her breast."

And while the sleigh crunched over the icy road in the direction of Versailles, she exclaimed with disarming unconsciousness: "Ah! I have never enjoyed myself so much!"

7

*

Less Conspicuous Amusements

AT THE BEGINNING of 1778 France, which had for a long time
fought for the King of Prussia, very nearly had to fight for the Emperor of Austria. The Elector of Bavaria, Maximilian Joseph, had died
on 30 December 1777 and Joseph II, who saw in this the long-awaited
opportunity to seize Bavaria, made great play with rights going back to
the fifteenth century. These rights over certain districts had been confirmed by a secret convention between Austria and Charles Theodore,
the Elector Palatine and successor to the deceased.

The Queen's first fear on hearing of the death of the Elector was,
as she wrote to Comtesse Jules, that her brother would be "up to his
tricks." He soon was, and 12,000 men were sent to occupy Lower
Bavaria, a "district" claimed by Austria.

"This rounding off of territory is of inestimable value," declared
Joseph II, much to the dismay of Maria Theresa. "We may be able to
bring it off without a war!" He meant without a war against Prussia,
which would acquiesce in the "rounding off" *if* France showed itself
"firm in the Alliance" and *if* Marie Antoinette were willing to support
the Austrian view. Now a letter written by the Queen to Mme de
Polignac shows that Marie Antoinette shared French opinion concerning Joseph II's ambition. Besides France had taken sides with the
English colonies in America and was preparing for war with England.
Would it have to fight simultaneously against the English in America
and against Prussia in Europe?

Seeing that Marie Antoinette had no concern for the interests of
Austria, Mercy acted, and spoke decisively: the Queen of France must

remember the Archduchess. Maria Theresa went further: "I have need of all your feeling for me, for your house and for your country."

"Your country!" "My two countries," Marie Antoinette said. By yielding to her mother's wishes she became the first Queen of France to act in such a way. The Empress did not care, and brought a kind of blackmail to bear on her daughter's feelings: the King of Prussia would certainly do everything he could to upset the Alliance to his own advantage. "And this would be my death," sighed Maria Theresa.

Mercy, who was present, saw Marie Antoinette pale as she read these words. The Ambassador pressed the Queen. She must act and speak to the King. The Abbé de Vermond seconded him. The Queen's Reader was a Frenchman, and paid by the Treasury, but as always he acted as an Austrian agent. Marie Antoinette decided to see the King and spoke sharply to him. Louis XVI replied unexpectedly: "Your relations' ambition will upset everything. They began with Poland and now Bavaria will be the second chapter. I am sorry on your account."

"But, Sir, you cannot deny that you were informed about the Bavarian affair and were in agreement."

Apparently Louis XVI had no recollection of the allusions which Joseph II was supposed to have made, for he replied: "I was so little in agreement that the French Ministers have just been ordered to inform the courts to which they are accredited that this dismemberment of Bavaria takes place against our wishes and that we disapprove of it."

This was a failure. Marie Theresa, who at the bottom of her heart did not approve of her son's action, acknowledged her daughter's "critical position." The Queen, she repeated, must act "with all prudence and skill" so as not to be accused of betraying French interests. "If the Ministers ever became aware of it many of them would not hesitate to take advantage of it to weaken her credit and counteract her influence in public affairs."

But events moved fast. In March the King of Prussia made an official protest against the Hapsburg claims and demanded the withdrawal of the Austrian troops from the Bavarian districts. Maria Theresa, frightened by the gravity of the situation, no longer recommended prudence to her daughter and begged her openly to support Mercy, who was to ask France to fulfill the treaty of 1765: in the event of aggression the King was to supply the Emperor with 24,000 men or with money.

To begin with, Marie Antoinette, "much occupied with the dissipations and long evenings of the Carnival of 1778," gave little help to her mother's Ambassador, who complained: "If the Queen would only put some method into her proceedings and into the use of her power everything would go off here without a hitch, but I am very far from obtaining such a desirable state of affairs and Your Majesty need not fear that her noble daughter will interfere in affairs of state in such a way as to compromise herself. I am disturbed only by her lack of action in this respect."

However, between 20 and 25 March, as a result of the urgent and almost daily prompting of Mercy, Marie Antoinette decided to take action and summoned Maurepas and Vergennes. "They responded very well on the subject of the Alliance," she wrote to Maria Theresa, "and seem strongly attached to it, but they are so afraid of a land war that when I pressed on them the hypothesis of the King of Prussia commencing hostilities I could not get a clear answer from them."

The Empress considered her daughter's action insufficiently vigorous. She received this letter on 31 March, the courier having taken only six days, and two days later she wrote to Mercy: "In fact my daughter does not change. She is so taken up by her dissipations that she is hardly capable of reflecting coherently on major matters. We will have to be satisfied by what can be wrung from her by remonstrances."

Following another letter from her mother and another conversation with Mercy, Marie Antoinette interfered a second time in the middle of April. She again summoned Maurepas and Vergennes. "I spoke to them with some force and I think I made an impression on them, particularly the latter. I was not very pleased with the arguments of these gentlemen, who are only trying to compromise and to accustom the King to do the same."

The "arguments of these gentlemen" in reply to her pro-Austrian language had been clear: France could consider intervention only in the event of the King of Prussia threatening the Low Countries. This was also the King's opinion. The treaty did not guarantee new "acquisitions" by Austria in Poland and Bavaria which were nothing but thefts accomplished by the House of Hapsburg since the agreement of 1756.

But a "long-awaited, long hoped-for" event was to enable Marie Antoinette to act with new authority and to oblige the royal Government to take up its attitude in accordance with the wishes of Vienna.

Marie Antoinette was at last expecting a child. Mercy wrote: "The Queen's pregnancy has so greatly increased her credit from what it was in the past that there would be very advantageous changes here in every direction if this noble Princess could properly estimate her position and realise the profit to be gained from it, in view of the King's turn of mind and character and the disposition of his present Ministers. I am doing all I can to enlighten the Queen in this respect."

On 20 April 1778 Maurepas and Vergennes sent a rather "sharp" dispatch to Vienna, informing Austria that it could not count on France. Strong in her "increased credit" Marie Antoinette spoke out strongly. "I indicated my displeasure as soon as I heard of it. It is extraordinary what a gift the Ministers here have for drowning affairs in a flood of words. Nevertheless, after everything Mercy had told me, and as a result of the reflections which I cannot help constantly making on the most important event of my life, I pressed them so hard that they were obliged to alter their tone somewhat. They have sufficiently admitted their mistake as regards this wretched dispatch."

"As a result of the fear instilled in them by the Queen" the Ministers reversed their position on 26 April and formally guaranteed the safety of the Low Countries. If Frederick should attack Austria in the Belgian Provinces he would find the French troops at the side of Joseph II's army.

Maria Theresa was delighted with this success and henceforth considered her daughter as a real agent of Austrian policy. "As you have entered with so much affection and zeal into our interests and situation," she wrote from Schoenbrunn on 17 May, "I feel I must continue to keep you informed." Marie Antoinette approved her mother's decisions all the more since, without telling her, the King and his Ministers were explaining everything to the King of Prussia and revealing their real sentiments. In other words they gave him to understand that his hands were free in the south, towards Bohemia, but not in the west, towards France. It was through Mercy and not through the King's Ministers that the Queen learned of this secret warning. "I objected very forcibly to such a neglect of the Queen," he wrote, "and I made her see how disrespectful it was to her and added that if she overlooked such liberties she would no longer be able to maintain her influence and her credit. The Queen was struck by my remarks and decided to speak to the King."

This time there was a violent scene between husband and wife. Louis XVI, who was much annoyed, remained silent during the lecture and then sighed: "You see that I am so much to blame that I have not a word in reply." And Marie Antoinette concluded: "I would ask you to speak to your Ministers about the incivility of their silence towards me. It seems to me extremely important that they should not get into the habit of it."

Frederick II was not a man to postpone his schemes indefinitely. In the certainty that France would not move he turned his back on the Rhine, crossed the Bohemian frontier and at the beginning of July entered Nachod. The Queen's distress was so great that the King declared "he could not bear to see her so anxious, that he would do anything in the world to appease her grief, that he had always wished to do so but that his Ministers had prevented him." "The welfare of my kingdom does not allow me to do more than I have done."

As her husband claimed to have been prevented by his Ministers, Marie Antoinette attacked Maurepas, who evaded the storm by having recourse "to his usual subterfuges." Marie Antoinette raised her voice: "This is the fourth or fifth time, sir, that I have spoken to you on affairs and you have always given me the same reply. Until now I have been patient, but matters are becoming too serious and I will no longer put up with such defeats." She described how, in her opinion, "France had yielded to the coaxing of the King of Prussia and instead of holding him back had, if possible, made him more obstinate."

This was perfectly true, but it was in France's interest. The Austrian Alliance ought not to have been diverted from its principal aim, which was to maintain the balance between Prussia and Austria intended by the Treaty of Westphalia.

Marie Antoinette was launched, and continued to worry her husband and the Ministers. Even Maria Theresa exclaimed on 2 November: "I am grateful for the interest my daughter is taking in our affairs. I only hope she is not being too impetuous, with the sole effect of making herself importunate to the King, suspect to the Ministers and odious to the nation."

"Odious to the nation!" One would think one was suddenly in the year 1792.

But French policy was to meet the wishes of Austria. The weakness of the Hapsburgs and the new strength of the Hohenzollerns threatened to upset the balance of Europe. Consequently when in August the Queen, urged by Mercy, suggested "as though of her own account and without any appearance of prompting," that France should mediate, this was all the more welcomed since the Hanoverians might well take a hand and create a second front. Negotiations were begun and thanks to France and Russia, both powerful mediators, culminated in the following spring in the Peace of Teschen.

This war, in which three of her brothers risked their lives and which in the summer of 1778 threatened the road to Vienna, had a very good effect on the Queen. Mercy related that he had never seen the Queen so oppressed. "In a burst of confidence and kindness she deigned to tell me that she wished to make a general confession and went on to speak of her amusements and her friends and all the details of her private life generally, commanding me to give my humble opinion on each point and on each individual. I acquitted myself with zeal and did not omit a single point bearing on the Queen's interest. She deigned to listen to me with every mark of kindness and added that her present sadness made it a favourable time for her to reflect seriously on her future conduct and that she really felt the necessity of coming to a decision."

Once more Mercy trembled with hope.

Shortly after midnight on 19 December 1778 the Queen awoke with a start: her first pains were beginning. Once more Marie Antoinette was to be a victim to the tyranny of etiquette. At the end of the morning, when the accoucheur Vermond cried: "The Queen is about to give birth!" the crowd of curious people who poured into the room was so unruly, as is related by Mme Campan and confirmed by Mercy, "that it nearly caused the death of the Queen." Marie Antoinette's waiting-woman draws a picture of this public delivery which is not without its picturesque side. "During the night the King had taken the precaution of having the enormous tapestry screens around Her Majesty's bed fastened with cords; without this precaution they would certainly have fallen down on her. It was impossible to move in the bedroom, which was full of such a mixed crowd that one might have been in a public square. Two Savoyards climbed on the furniture to get a better view of the Queen, who was lying facing the fireplace on a bed erected at the time of her confinement. Either all this noise, or the sex of the child, which the Queen was able to learn by a sign agreed on, it was said, with the Princesse de Lamballe, or an error of the accoucheur, temporarily obstructed the natural consequences of the confinement. The blood went to her head, her mouth twisted and the accoucheur cried: 'Air, warm water, she must be bled in the foot!' The windows had been stopped up. The King opened them with a force that can have been derived only from his affection for the Queen, as they were extremely high and stuck down their entire length with bands of paper. As the basin of warm water did not arrive quickly enough the accoucheur told the Queen's First Surgeon to make a dry incision. He did so, the blood gushed forth and the Queen opened her eyes. It was difficult to restrain the joy which so quickly followed the liveliest alarm. The Princesse de Lamballe had been carried unconscious through the crowd. The valets and ushers seized the indiscreet sightseers, who were not in a hurry to leave, in order to clear the room."

The couriers immediately hurried off in all directions. The Paris municipality, which had been assembled since five o'clock in the morning, received the news of the birth of Madame Royale at half-past twelve from one of M. le Gouverneur's pages and at five past one from the Comte de Bevi, representing the King. As a reward the Comte received a snuff-box of gold and enamel worth 1,440 livres.

In the evening Paris was given up to rejoicing "for the opening of H.M.'s womb." The "Gentlemen" of the city, in their red and black robes and with bouquets in their hands—they wore garlands and bracelets of flowers only for a prince—came down into the square in front of the Hôtel de Ville. To the sound of drums and trumpets the Gentlemen, the ushers in livery, the foot-servants bearing torches, the Swiss guards shouldering their partisans, all walked three times round the square, in the middle of which was a bonfire of 500 faggots which the Mayor lit. An hour later the fireworks were set off and all the "*boetes*" and guns of the city pealed forth.

Admittedly a Dauphin had been hoped for, but the rejoicing was not diminished. The event proved that Marie Antoinette and Louis could have children, and this was all that mattered. A Parisian dairywoman—they were poets in those days—hung these verses under her sign:

> The Nation had from heaven a Cupid sought:
> A Grace comes to announce him to the court.

On the following morning a bulletin, of which 800 copies were printed, announced that "the Grace" was in good health. "The lochia were abundant" and "the Queen's condition is as satisfactory as can be expected." It was a Sunday and the rejoicings continued in Paris. The Gentlemen did not strain their imagination. They organised another procession around another fire, which was lit as on the day before.

On Monday a second printed bulletin informed that "the belly is supple and not at all painful," that "last night the Queen had a very peaceful sleep" and that "the perspiration is maintained," a point on which Lassonne and Vermond were particularly satisfied.

Two further bulletins were published, giving details in the crude terminology of the age which I will spare the reader. Everything was going well, "the lacteal matter is arriving normally." The Queen was taking nourishment, eating "cream of rice with biscuit" and on the 26th she ate some chicken and was "extremely gay during dinner."

On Monday, 8 February, Paris was in a ferment from early morning. The city was to receive the King and Queen. Previously 100 poor girls were married to whom Marie Antoinette gave a dowry corresponding to 100,000 present-day francs. The betrothed, with their hair "curled and arranged," went to their parish priest. The wedding parties then piled into the city coaches and drove to Notre Dame.

While the wedding ceremonies were taking place the city corporation, accompanied by the guards, waited for their sovereigns at the Porte de la Conférence. When the long procession of coaches appeared, surrounded by bodyguards, light horse and pages, the Gentlemen advanced towards the Queen's carriage, which was occupied merely by her Grand Equerry, M. de Tessé. Marie Antoinette had taken her seat with the King in the *"voiture du corps,"* which was preceded by "trumpeters in ordinary" and accompanied by twenty-four footmen and six pages on horseback. The Prévôt came to the door of the carriage and declared: "May this first fruit of your mutual tenderness and those destined by heaven for the future unite to the graces of their illustrious mother the virtues which Your Majesty will transmit to them by example and inheritance."

The King grasped only the intention of this verbose speech and replied "in the most gracious manner." The procession continued by the Quai des Tuileries to Notre Dame, where the hundred couples "lined up in order formed a very touching and moving sight."

But in spite of this sight, in spite of the monthly bonus of 15 livres to be given to the brides if they themselves suckled their future off-spring, in spite of the liberation of 132 prisoners sentenced for not having paid their child's monthly nurse, in spite of the buffets of cold meat, in spite of the curtseys of Mlle Bertin and her 30 assistants from a balcony in the Rue Saint Honoré, in spite of the fireworks let off on the Ile de la Cité and the illuminated fountain in the middle of the Pont Neuf, Paris's welcome was icy. From Notre Dame to Sainte Geneviève, from Sainte-Geneviève to the Place Louis XV, by way of the Rue des Francs-Bourgeois and the Pont Neuf, there were only a few shouts. In certain quarters the gilded procession passed through a double rank of completely silent idlers.

Marie Antoinette was furious. Mercy tried to explain to her that "the idea of her dissipation and the expense she caused, and finally the appearance of an excessive love of amusement in a time of calamity and war might combine to estrange people's minds and required a little tact."

The Queen agreed. She promised once more to change her way of life and "to renounce too conspicuous amusements."

But the evil had been done. Henceforth Marie Antoinette would be the victim of her slightest actions. Whatever she did would be turned against her.

On Shrove Tuesday 1779 she decided to go to the masked ball at the Opera in the strictest incognito. She left Versailles accompanied by the Princesse d'Hénin and drove in a coach to the house of the Duc de Coigny, the King's Grand Equerry. There, in order not to be recognised on her arrival at the ball, she changed into a plainer carriage without any coat of arms and so old that it broke down during the journey. The ladies got out. They could not remain in the street and, laughing over the adventure, the Queen and her companion, both masked, entered the first house they came to, which was that of a cloth merchant. The carriage could not be mended and the Duc de Coigny's footman went to look for a cab, and it was in this unexpected vehicle that the Queen arrived at the Opera.

"It is I in a cab! Isn't it amusing?" she said, laughing to her friends.

The story is well known. "All Paris soon knew of this adventure with the cab," wrote Mme Campan. "It was said that there was something mysterious about this evening adventure, and that the Queen had had a rendezvous in a private house with a gentleman honoured with her favours. The Duc de Coigny was openly named. . . . Once these ideas of light conduct had been awakened there were no limits to the calumnies about the Queen which were rife in Paris." Mme Campan adds that as a result of the "affair of the cab" every time the Queen spoke to any young men either at play or at the hunt they were "so many favoured lovers."

How could it have been otherwise when, in the following month, the public learned that Marie Antoinette, who had measles, was remaining at Trianon for three weeks, with Coigny, Guines, Esterhazy and Besenval? These gentlemen announced their intention of not leaving the Queen all night.

"I strongly opposed this ridiculous idea," said Mercy. "I called in the doctor, Lassonne, who was always weak and undecided and did not dare oppose things which his position gave him the right to forbid. Finally the Abbé de Vermond and I made so much fuss that it was decided that the gentlemen would leave the Queen's bedchamber at 11 in the evening and would not come back until the morning."

The court roared with laughter and amused itself by choosing the four ladies who would watch over the King if he fell ill. Neither Louis XVI nor the usual servants had the right to enter the bedchamber. An exception was made for the Abbé de Vermond, who on Mercy's orders begged the Queen "to write a few friendly lines to the King." Marie Antoinette rejected the suggestion "with great warmth." Not without difficulty the Abbé finally extracted a short note which "the poor man" received with emotion.

One may imagine the gossip of the town about this little Queen going disguised to the Opera in a cab or shutting herself up in her bedroom for three weeks with four men. Two of these nurses, Coigny and Guines, were named as the Queen's lovers. Had the former, while "extorting" numberless favours from Marie Antoinette, gone so far as to obtain the ultimate favour? Letters exist, it is said, but their present owner refuses to part with them out of respect for the Queen's memory. We are therefore reduced to conjecture.

According to public rumour, when the Duc de Coigny fell in love with Mme de Châlons, Marie Antoinette accorded her favour to the Duc de Guines. This is a calumny. The former Ambassador was far from being an Adonis. He had become enormously fat and for each of his suits had two pairs of breeches, one normal pair for the days when he would have to sit down and the other tightened as much as possible to make him look slimmer. In the morning, before helping him to dress, his valet would ask: "Will M. le Duc be sitting down today?" "When he was to remain standing," the Duc de Levis recounts, "he climbed on to two chairs and descended into his breeches, which were held by two of his servants."

He was not the Queen's lover, but he amused her better than anyone and his favour was so high that Mercy revealed his anxiety in a letter written during the summer of 1779. In order to get rid of this fat man, "as intriguing as he is ambitious," Mercy suggested that Maria Theresa should write to her daughter "that it is generally rumoured that the Queen is so much under the influence of the Duc de Guines that she makes no decisions without consulting him." The Empress followed this advice and the Queen, annoyed, claimed that these were slanders, "which are the usual thing in this country"; but the ruse was successful and gradually the Queen treated her favourite more coldly. Soon, in the autumn of 1779, Mercy, enchanted with his stratagem, was able to write that "the falling off of the Duc de Guines's favour" was complete.

In 1779 the danger, if there were a danger, did not come from that direction.

In August of the preceding year Axel Fersen had arrived at Versailles. Marie Antoinette had recognised him at once: "Ah! Here is an old acquaintance!"

In spite of this flattering welcome the Swedish officer had visited the château only at very irregular intervals. Surprised, perhaps even intrigued, by a reserve to which she was hardly accustomed, Marie Antoinette had displayed some astonishment and had questioned Creutz, the Swedish Ambassador in Paris. "The Queen, who is the prettiest and most amiable Princess I know," Axel wrote to his father, "was so kind as to ask after me often. She asked Creutz why I did not come to her card games on Sundays, and learning that I had come one day when there was no play she took that as a kind of excuse."

Although naturally modest, Axel was obliged to realise that he pleased the Queen, and every Sunday he went to Marie Antoinette's card games, where she treated him "with kindness" and "always spoke" to him. One day she expressed a great wish to see him in his uniform of a Swedish Light Dragoon. The young man complied and for the first time was received in the Queen's private apartments. Very carefully, according to a witness, Marie Antoinette studied the blue doublet, over which was a white tunic, the tight-fitting chamois breeches, the black shako topped with a blue and yellow plume—and admired.

During the spring and summer of 1779 Fersen, "without intrigue and without seeking notoriety," as the Comte de Tilly recounted, became an intimate of Versailles and Trianon. And the inevitable happened: he fell in love with the Queen. For her part Marie Antoinette felt drawn to this rather melancholy young man of 23, who perhaps possessed none of the French levity or brilliance, but whose grave masculinity charmed all the women. She was not yet in love with him, but expressed a lively affection for him. Axel's favour increased. "If there were anything which might cause it to be thought excessive," wrote the Queen's page, "it was a more restrained and respectful attitude which perhaps partook somewhat of the affectation of a courtier. . . . But M. de Fersen is not at all affected and all his art is in simplicity."

The feeling which he thus carefully concealed within his heart became so violent that Fersen decided to flee and signed an engagement with one of the expeditions which were then being prepared for America.

Versailles was thunderstruck. "What! sir, are you deserting your conquest?" Axel replied simply: "If I had made one, I should not desert it, but I am going without leaving any regrets behind me."

The announcement of this forthcoming departure made Marie Antoinette realise that, according to the expression of the time, she had an "inclination" towards the Swedish officer. When he came to take his leave "she could not take her eyes off him," a witness recounts, and "as she watched him they filled with tears."

But it was a false alarm. After a long wait at Le Havre the expedition was postponed and Fersen was obliged to return to Versailles. Although he did not ask for any post, thanks to the Queen he was appointed supernumerary officer to the regiment of the Royal Deux Ponts. Some of Marie Antoinette's associates began to find the Swede's attitude much less "restrained" and the officer wrote to his father: "The kindness she has shown me and this post of colonel have won me the jealousy of all the young men at court."

At Trianon Axel was invited to the intimate receptions. One evening the Queen, with obvious meaning, sang verses from the opera *Dido*, which was not performed in France until 1783:

> Ah! I was well inspired
> When I received you at my court.

Twenty-six years later, on hearing *Dido* performed at the Opera in Stockholm, Axel exclaimed: "How many memories and painful regrets does this opera recall to my heart!"

According to the Comte de Saint-Priest, "Mme de Polignac did not oppose her friend's preference. No doubt Vaudreuil and Besenval schemed for her because an isolated foreigner who was not very enterprising suited them much better than would a Frenchman, surrounded by relatives, who might win all the favours instead of themselves and perhaps end as head of a clique which would eclipse them all. The Queen was thus encouraged to follow her inclination, and she indulged in it without much prudence."

So as not to compromise the Queen any further Axel once more did all he could to go and fight in America. Finally, in March 1780, thanks to Breteuil and Vergennes, he was appointed aide-de-camp to General Rochambeau and left for Brest, where he embarked on 13 April in the *Jason*, a ship of 16 guns.

The Swedish Ambassador, boasting to Gustavus III of this "wisdom and prudence beyond his years," added: "Incidentally, the Queen is behaving with much more circumspection and wisdom than formerly."

Marie Antoinette had given Mercy her promise and this time she kept it. Two things helped her: the birth of Madame Royale and her inclination for Axel Fersen. The years 1779 and 1780 were certainly a decisive turning-point in Marie Antoinette's life. The whirlwind ceased and the classic countenance of the Queen of Trianon so dear to her later admirers appeared. It was at this time that Marie Antoinette left off feathers and wore instead "shepherdess hats" of simple straw. During this year she ordered 93 dresses, 41 formal dresses and 56 coats, but for all that everything was in "the simple style" for which Trianon was the ideal setting.

The year 1780 "marks the most interesting period in the history of Trianon," according to Pierre de Nolhac. Life went on in the "simplest" possible way. When the Queen entered the drawing-room the piano did not stop playing, the ladies' tapestry frames continued to work and the men did not break off their game of billiards or backgammon. The women wore dresses of white muslin with gauze fichus and straw hats. The men wore dress coats or long coats of cloth, the colour of "London soot," and lightened only by a collar of scarlet velvet.

Unfortunately Marie Antoinette was reproached for playing at the lady of the manor. Too many people were excluded. In June the only person staying at the château was Mme de Polignac, who shortly before had been made a Duchesse after giving birth on 14 May to Charles X's future Minister. Marie Antoinette had been so upset by her friend's confinement that the whole court had had to move to La Muette, so that the Queen could go every day to see Mme de Polignac, who lived at Passy. In this same month of May the new Duchesse had married her daughter, who was still an adolescent, to the Duc de Guiche. The girl, who henceforth was always called "Guichette," received a dowry of 800,000 livres (160 million francs) from Louis XVI, although dowries given by the King were usually not more than 6,000 livres. As a reward for having established her daughter so well the Duchesse received 400,000 livres (80 million francs), a duchy for the new-born son and the promise of lands with an income of 35,000 livres. Her lover, M. de Vaudreuil, was given an allowance of 30,000 livres (6 million francs) under the pretext that as his possessions were "in the islands" he was drawing no revenue, on account of the war.

One may imagine the disgraceful tone of the books and pamphlets. There was a jest current in Versailles: "Is Mme de Polignac's child the Queen's or M. de Vaudreuil's, since M. de Polignac has been in the country for a year?"

Marie Antoinette merely shrugged her shoulders. She was so glad to have the Duchesse in her little château of Trianon, that nothing else counted. On the second floor was "Guichette," whose husband, in view of his wife's youth, had been asked to stay at home. For the same reason a third guest, the young "Bichette," who had been married on 5 June to the Vicomte de Polastron, the brother of the Duchesse Jules, was also without her husband, who had been dispatched to his regiment the day after the wedding. Two cousins of the Polignacs made up the party: the beautiful Comtesse de Châlons, née d'Andlau, more than ever loved by the Duc de Coigny, and the brilliant Comtesse d'Andlau, daughter of Helvétius.

Even the ladies of honour remained at Versailles. As for the King, he occasionally came to dinner, when four entrées and two roasts were added to the menu. Louis XVI would not have had enough to eat with the meal served to the Queen and her guests—three soups, two main dishes, twelve entrées, four roasts, two medium entremets, fourteen little entremets and two dishes of pastries.

After the meal the coterie maintained a certain reserve for fear of a harsh remark from the King. "With the best intention of being polite to someone," writes Mme de Boigne, "he advanced towards them until they were against a wall. If he could think of nothing to say, which often happened, he gave a loud laugh, turned on his heel and went away." Five years of reign had not polished him, and he still possessed "no more gallantry in his manner," which was a great grievance to this dying society. Sometimes he would sit on the lap of young Narbonne and imitate a baby wanting to be nursed. Admittedly he was good, simple and natural, but these qualities were not greatly prized by Marie Antoinette's friends, for whom the possession of wit was the most important thing.

Sometimes, after dinner, the Queen gave a party in her own rooms and received a few privileged persons. But people slipped in uninvited and the porter asked the architect for double locks to all the doors.

The guests wandered in the famous garden of which all Europe was talking. The Hamlet was not built until later, but in the summer of 1780 the gardens were nearly finished. Marie Antoinette's own part had been important. It was she who had influenced the development of the final stage of the art of gardening in the 18th century. Neat rows, trim scalloped flower-beds, embroidered hedges, yews shaped like dragons, and "well-turned" bowers all seemed the height of boredom, melancholy and ugliness.

"Nature plants nothing in a line!" exclaimed M. de Wolmar in the *Nouvelle Héloïse,* and he added that it was amusing to see men "as though they were already tired of their walk on beginning it, construct it in a straight line so as to arrive at the end more quickly."

Marie Antoinette considered that Le Nôtre had massacred nature "by subjecting everything to the standard of architecture." But, as the Marquis de Girardin said, it is not enough, under the pretext of realism, "to substitute a winding garden for a square garden," one must "compose landscapes to interest the eye and the mind at the same time."

Marie Antoinette, fortunately, was concerned only with the eye and not with the mind. Away with those gardens Laborde speaks of, "containing a moral lesson," where "each tree has its sentimental motto," where "every rock utters something tender." Having "a thirst for rusticity," she wanted to "create reality." She intelligently rejected both the "turco-chinoiserie" of Antoine Richard and the artificial ruins advocated by Gabriel. She would have none of the fallen temples which so enthralled the Prince de Ligne. The Queen settled on the plan conceived by the Comte de Caraman. The former Lieutenant-General of Louis XV's armies proposed an uncultivated hillock covered with yews and box, a grotto and waterfall—this was the "Montagne de l'Escargot" —a "Swiss" rock, and a belvedere surmounted by a pavilion mirrored in a lake. The lake fed a river which meandered through the garden and after winding round a Temple of Love died away in two branches in front of the château.

Everything had to be constructed in record time, "for you know your mistress," we read in a report in the Archives, "she wishes to enjoy her garden very soon." In spite of the cost—352,275 livres in a single year—the garden rapidly took shape. A whole forest was transported from the royal nurseries of La Rochette, near Melun, to Versailles.

In 1780, too, Mique was working on the Queen's dwelling. In Marie Antoinette's boudoir there was a mechanism permitting mirrors to be moved to cover the windows in the evening: this was "the room of the moving mirrors." In the same year the library was painted in off-white and adorned with apple-green taffeta curtains. A lot of space on the shelves was given up to collections of plays—*French Drama* in fourteen volumes, *Bourgeois Drama, Dramatic Proverbs, Italian Plays, Society Plays, Country Plays*. These last two volumes were the favourites in 1780, for this year saw Marie Antoinette's début on the stage of the papier-mâché theatre at Trianon, which was completed that summer. Marie Antoinette was the leader of a "troupe" composed of Madame Elisabeth, her young sister-in-law, who was now one of her friends, the Comte d'Artois and the coterie—the new Duchesse de Polignac, her daughter "Guichette," her sister-in-law Comtesse Diane de Polignac, the Comte Esterhazy, Adhémar, Crussol and Vaudreuil, who was reputed to be "the best actor in Paris society." In the balcony there were only the King and the royal family. The Comtesse de Provence had been asked to join the troupe, but she was shocked and had refused. "It is beneath me!"

Astonished, the Queen remarked: "But if I, the Queen of France, act, you should not have any scruples."

"I may not be a Queen, but I am the stuff of which they are made."

This was the only memorable saying of her life and Madame remained a spectator, together with the King and the other members of the royal family. Even the Princes of the Blood were not admitted. In the boxes and the pit were those in service at Trianon. Campan had resumed his role of prompter, much to the fury of the First Gentleman of the Chamber, the Duc de Fronsac, son of the Maréchal de Richelieu, who, as one of the prerogatives of his position, should have had the ordering of "Her Majesty's amusements."

"You cannot be the First Gentleman when we are actors," explained the Queen. "Besides, I have already told you my wishes concerning Trianon. I hold no court here. I live here as a private person."

The troupe performed comic operas, or comedies with music: *L'Anglais à Bordeaux* by Favart, *Le Sorcier* by Poinsinet, *Rose et Colas* and *La Gageure Imprévue* by Sedaine. In the latter Marie Antoinette played the maid Gotte, who exclaimed: "We servants. . . ."

In Berthe's *Les Fausses Infidélités* Marie Antoinette chose the part of the charming Angélique, betrothed to the choleric Dormilly, played by Vaudreuil, whose temperament was far from placid.

"It's lifelike" declared the King, not without malice.

Louis XVI was delighted and applauded wildly, "particularly when the Queen performed her part of the play." During the interval he went on the stage, watched Marie Antoinette's "toilette" and congratulated her with tears in his eyes. And yet, it is said, it was "royally ill-played."

Marie Antoinette was an accomplished actress compared with the Comte d'Adhémar. In *Le Devin du Village* by J. J. Rousseau, in which he played Colin, his voice was so trembling that Marie Antoinette as Colette had difficulty in keeping a straight face when she saw him, disguised as a shepherd, on his knees declaring his love.

"Malice would be hard put to it to criticise the choice of such a lover," she said when the curtain fell.

But malice had something to go on with *Le Sabot Perdu*, a play with songs by Piis and Barré, which was staged a little later. It was the

Queen who, in the part of Babet, lost the famous sabot after having long resisted her suitor. The latter ended by kissing her and Babet sang:

> Dans l'plaisir où ton coeur s'épanche
> C'n'est pas agir d'une magnière franche
>   Comment te pardonnerai
> De m'prendre ainsi c'que jallions donnai?

It was true that the scene was supposed to be taking place in the snow—hardly an exhilarating spot—and that the lover Colin was played by the Comte d'Artois. As Pierre de Nolhac has said "it was a kiss given in the family," but the pamphleteers did not see it that way.

When there was no performance, they played at *tire en jambe*—you mounted astride a stick and fought in that position. The King took part, but without amusement. There was also the famous *Descampativos*. This was the blindman's buff in reverse. The players were all covered with a large white sheet, except for the one who was "it," whom each in turn touched with a napkin and who had to guess the name of his assailant. There were forfeits, which had "to be redeemed by some odd penance, and the bustle occasioned by this often continued far into the night," according to Mercy. Needless to say, under the acid pen of the pamphleteers *Descampativos* became a veritable orgy.

In September the diversions at Trianon were somewhat overshadowed by the economies of Necker, Turgot's successor. The coterie was furious. Four hundred "principal idlers" and twelve hundred "subordinate idlers" of the King's household were dismissed.

"I want to bring order and economy into every part of my household," Louis XVI had declared. "If anyone has any objections I shall break them!"

Marie Antoinette was one of those who had objections. She is said to have warned Necker "that she did not care to manage her house in the style of the Rue Saint-Denis and to carry the keys of the cellar in her pocket."

Necker realised that his task would not be easy—in the following spring he abandoned it—but meanwhile, in default of large savings, he launched his famous loans, the interest on which encumbered the Treasury with a heavy burden which finally crushed it once and for all.

The coterie plucked up courage—it was not much affected by the plans of the Director-General of Finances—but the spectacles at the

Trianon were interrupted in October by the death of the Duchesse de Polignac's uncle, who was also a relative of M. de Vaudreuil, and the troupe rested. As the favourite and her lover were prevented by their mourning from treading the boards they consoled themselves, at the beginning of the winter of 1780, by taking on the role Besenval had asked them to play with the Queen. It was simply a question of "creating a Minister for War."

On 18 October 1780, after rather confused intrigues on the part of Marie Antoinette, Sartines had been replaced at the Ministry of the Marine by the Marquis de Castries.

"Is the Queen going to stop there?" Besenval asked Mme de Polignac. "Now she has the prestige of having created a Minister of the Marine, would she not also like to make a Minister for War?"

"Indeed, we should now turn our attention quickly and seriously to M. de Ségur."

It was a scheme dear to Besenval—to have the Prince de Montbarrey dismissed and his portfolio given to the Maréchal de Ségur. But, knowing the female mind, he had managed it so that Mme de Polignac should take an interest in this appointment and now the pretty scatterbrain thought that the idea had come from her. "I never stopped urging Mme de Polignac," relates Besenval, "so that she would stir up the Queen, who always replied that she was persisting with her plan, but that matters could not be hurried."

Maurepas certainly considered that Montbarrey should no longer remain in his post, but he, too, had his candidate: M. de Puységur. He therefore cleverly succeeded in persuading Marie Antoinette that "Mme de Polignac had taken advantage of the influence she had over her." Mercy had on several occasions tried out the worth of this argument with the Queen. Marie Antoinette was really angry and addressed bitter reproaches to her friend: "You wanted to sacrifice me to your personal wishes."

The Duchesse burst into tears and declared that she would leave the court. Marie Antoinette was in despair, "tears streamed down her face and she finally threw herself at Mme de Polignac's feet, imploring her to forgive her." The Duchesse's tears flowed faster, but they were tears of affection. The two friends fell into each other's arms, embraced—and Marie Antoinette promised to protect the Maréchal. Then the scene was forgotten and the appointment was delayed. Besenval returned to the attack, and "strongly urged" Mme de Polignac, reproaching her with not employing "the necessary energy."

With dramatic suddenness the Queen announced to her friend on 30 December that Puységur had been appointed. The coterie was amazed. On instructions from Besenval Mme de Polignac sent a note to Marie Antoinette, asking to see her urgently. The Queen obeyed and arrived at her friend's house at 11 o'clock in the evening. Well coached by the Baron, the favourite "represented forcibly to her how humiliating it was for her that M. de Maurepas should triumph on this occasion."

"Everyone is on the watch to see who will win—you or M. de Maurepas. It will be a shocking rebuff for the one who loses."

Marie Antoinette saw the distress in her friend's face and promised to see the King the next day. At seven in the morning she went to the King and did not mince her words. Maurepas, who lived above the King, in the apartments of Louis XV's mistresses, was called and put forward rather weak arguments against the appointment of Marie Antoinette's candidate. Louis XVI, who had just put up with a violent scene, yielded to his wife's wishes and agreed with all she said. Maurepas, unconvinced, looked at the King.

"Monsieur," pronounced the Queen, "you have heard the King's wishes. Go at once and send to M. de Ségur."

Maurepas bowed. "It was the severest blow of my life," he said later.

However, the choice was not a bad one, and the Maréchal would have been a worthy successor to Saint-Germain, were it not for his ruling of 22 May 1781, forbidding promotion to officers not possessing four quarterings.

Maria Theresa was not to know of her daughter's victory over Maurepas. Since mid-November the great Empress had been seriously ill with "a hardening of the lungs." She retained consciousness until the end. On 29 November she sighed: "This is my last day!"

At eight o'clock in the evening she was seized with choking, rose and supported by her son went to the window. Joseph II, seeing her terribly oppressed, asked: "Are you ill?"

"Ill enough to die."

Turning to her doctor she ordered: "Light the mortuary candle and close my eyes."

A minute later she expired in the arms of her son before the still-open window.

At Versailles the Abbé Vermond was entrusted by Louis XVI with breaking the news to Marie Antoinette. The Queen was overwhelmed. On 8 December the court went into mourning, the liveries became black and the court coaches were draped in violet and black. On the 10th Marie Antoinette tried to write to her brother, but could only trace a few lines while she shed tears. "I can no longer see what I am writing."

Her tears flowed faster when she learned that 48 hours before her death her mother had given her blessing to her absent children. Raising her hands to heaven, she had named each in turn: Leopold, Grand Duke of Tuscany, Maria-Cristina, Duchess of Saxe-Teschen, Amelia, Duchess of Parma, Maria-Carolina, Queen of Sicily and Naples. Then, after a moment's silence, she had almost shouted the last name: "Marie Antoinette, Queen of France!" And she had burst into sobs.

Since 31 July 1775, when the Empress had written to Mercy from Schoenbrunn: "My daughter is hastening to her ruin," she knew there was no hope. Marie Antoinette, in the Empress's own expression, was "hurrying to destruction." Maria Theresa had not complained about the amusements at Trianon—"I regard them as transient," she said to Mercy—but with her astonishing clear-sightedness she had not concealed her anxiety at the dangerous void Marie Antoinette had brought about at court so as to remain with her dear friends. In her last letter to Mercy, on 3 November, she had approved and judged "very sound" the observations the Ambassador had thought it his duty to make to Marie Antoinette on her return from Trianon: "A great court must be accessible to many people, otherwise hatred and jealousy turn everyone's heads and give rise to complaints, dislike and a kind of estrangement."

In the calm of her private apartments, where she had shut herself up with the Duchesse de Polignac, Marie Antoinette could re-read the last letter sent to her by her mother: "I am very glad that you intend to resume your state at Versailles. I know how tedious and empty it is, but believe me, if there is none the disadvantages that result are much greater than the little inconveniences of holding state, particularly in your country, with such an impetuous nation."

Marie Antoinette had in fact promised her mother to stop being merely "Queen of Trianon." But, unfortunately, it was too late and the "kind of estrangement" Mercy had spoken of had taken place. At the end of the previous year she had made an effort to be in her apartments three days a week, but no greater number of people came to Versailles.

Her coterie had finally kept at a distance all who might surround the throne in case of danger. Marie Antoinette did not yet realise this isolation. The great machine was still in motion and its wheels hardly creaked. But during ten years at Versailles and six years of reign the Queen had succeeded in estranging for ever all those she had ignored, those she had despised, those she had mocked, those who were not among her beloved "associates," those who seemed to her too old, those who had come so many times to Versailles without getting a glimpse of their sovereign, those to whom she refused to speak and above all those who had been her friends, her companions of pleasure and whom she now ignored, such as the Duc de Chartres, who was already the centre of a group. The sister-in-law of the future regicide, the Princesse de Lamballe, who was barely tolerated at court in 1779, was also excluded from the gatherings of 1780, and in the autumn she left court to take refuge with the Duc de Penthièvre. She had yielded, but the Duc de Chartres was far from being resigned to his disgrace. Marie Antoinette had not even defended him after the Battle of Ouessant, where his conduct as commodore had been despicable. It was even said that she had sided with the jesters who did not spare the Duke with jokes about his "cowardice." Moreover, in July 1779, in order to spare him "the severity of an order from the King," the Queen had written to him advising him to leave the army, which was threatening England from Saint Malo, and return to the Palais Royal. Louis XVI did not like his cousin and had no intention of running the risk of seeing the man who was to become head of the younger branch be more successful on land than on sea. The Duc de Chartres obeyed and returned to the Palais Royal, where, at a distance from the court, he retired into private life while waiting to throw himself into the opposition. But in 1780 the Palais Royal clan was already attracting the malcontents and opposing itself to that of Trianon.

While waiting to send each other to the scaffold they continued to wage war with pinpricks. Marie Antoinette did not seem to attach much importance to it. In this she resembled the Duc de Chartres, who when faced with the attacks of his enemies—for he also had a great many—merely repeated his famous: "Je m'en f. . ."

With her eyes shut to all this, Marie Antoinette asked M. de Boufflers

to compose a song "in which he would successively enumerate all the
faults with which she was reproached in libellous publications." The
Chevalier did so, and drew a picture of the Queen under the name of
Thémire.

Air: "Phyllis asks for her portrait"
> Are you concerned to hear
> What's said about Thémire?
> At moments, it is said,
> You'd think she'd lost her head.
> Is that really so?
> Yes, but you must know
> She can so fashion it
> That her strange lack of wit
> Would even captivate
> A mind of Cato's weight.
>
> Too much good sense, 'tis said,
> Has never plagued her head,
> But incense, so they say,
> Enchants her all the day.
> Is that really so?
> Yes, but you must know
> So full of skill is she
> That every deity
> Would come down to adore her
> And burn incense before her.
>
> If she has promised you
> A private rendezvous
> Or business talk, they say,
> She soon forgets the day.
> Is that really so?
> Yes, but you must know
> That when you meet once more
> Her faults fly through the door,
> And time itself will fly
> Only too quickly by.
>
> Self-centredness supreme—
> That is her guiding theme.
> She loves herself, they say,

As dearly as she may.
Is that really so?
Yes, but you must know
She must be left her creed.
Can she be blamed, indeed,
For loving as she does
What everybody loves?

The Queen was not angry. On the contrary, the author of the *Mémoires secrets* goes so far as to assert that "Her Majesty deigned to sing it herself to her court." It must be admitted that Marie Antoinette's lively intelligence, mentioned by certain historians, is no more than a pious legend!

When she finally opened her eyes and understood, she was in a cell in the Conciergerie and the executioner was binding her hands.

8

❧

The Pure Soul

IN 1781 MARIE ANTOINETTE was pregnant for the second time. She would be 26 on 2 November. What had become of the little Archduchess with the slender bosom and childish eyes? She now possessed what, on a throne, is better than flawless beauty—the bearing of a Queen.

"If I were not a Queen," she said to Mme Vigée-Lebrun, "one would almost say I looked insolent, don't you think?"

They said so, in spite of her position. How many of her contemporaries, from the Comte de Séneffe to the young Camille Desmoulins, seeing her behind the windows of her coach, were struck by her "haughty air" and her "arrogant look."

Her page, the Baron de Tilly, who did not like her, drew this portrait of her: "She had eyes which were not beautiful, but could assume every expression. Kindness or dislike were mirrored in this look more strikingly than I have ever seen elsewhere. I am not sure that her nose matched the rest of her face. Her mouth was decidedly unattractive; that thick, prominent and sometimes drooping lip has been quoted as giving her countenance a mark of nobility and distinction, but it could only be used to indicate anger and indignation, and that is not the habitual expression of beauty. Her skin was admirable and so were her shoulders and neck. Her bosom seemed rather too full and her waist might have been more elegant. I have never seen such beautiful arms and hands. She had two ways of walking: one decided, rather hurried and always noble; the other more relaxed and swaying, I would almost say caressing, but without provoking any loss of respect. No one ever curtsied with

152

so much grace, saluting ten people in one single bend and giving each his due in look and inclination of the head. In a word, unless I am mistaken, just as one offers a chair to other women, one would almost always have been inclined to draw up her throne."

Looking at her portraits we can realise the defects in this face, which was yet so attractive: a forehead too broad, a rather thick nose, short-sighted eyes and a heavy chin. With age the famous Austrian lip had become more pronounced. Burgundian lip would be more accurate, for Charles the Bold was the first to have it. But what would mar another face is hardly noticeable here. One sees only that dazzling colouring of a blonde, the incomparable texture of the skin, that Greek neck, that long waist, the somewhat heavy but beautiful breasts and the body that seemed made for love.

"She was then at the height of her youth and beauty," wrote Mme Vigée-Lebrun, who had watched her for many hours as she painted her. "Marie Antoinette was tall, beautifully made, rather plump, but not too much so. Her arms were superb, her hands small and perfectly shaped and her feet charming. She walked better than any woman in France, holding her head high with a majesty which made one recognise the sovereign among all her court. . . . Her features were not regular. She had inherited from her family the long, narrow oval, peculiar to the Austrians. But what was most remarkable in her face was the radiance of her complexion.

"I have never seen any so brilliant, and brilliant is the word, for her skin was so transparent that it held no shadows. For this reason I could never reproduce it as I wished. I had no colours to paint that freshness, those fine shades which could be seen only in that charming face and which I have never found in any other woman."

Mme Vigée-Lebrun has painted another picture of Marie Antoinette which, though not on canvas, is still charmingly coloured. Suffering from an advanced pregnancy, Mme Vigée-Lebrun missed an appointment the Queen had given her, and on the following day, distressed and confused, she arrived at the château at the very moment when Marie Antoinette was about to enter her carriage.

"My heart was beating, for I was all the more afraid since I was in the wrong. The Queen turned towards me and said gently: 'I waited for you yesterday all the morning. What happened to you?'

" 'Alas! Madame,' I replied, 'I was so unwell that I was not able to obey Your Majesty's orders. I have come today to receive them and I am leaving again at once.'

" 'No, no! Do not go,' replied the Queen. 'I would not like you to have made the journey for nothing.' She dismissed her carriage and gave me a sitting.

"I remember that in my eagerness to respond to her kindness I seized my paint-box so quickly that it was upset. My brushes and pencils fell on the floor and I stooped to repair my clumsiness.

" 'Leave them,' said the Queen. 'In your condition you should not bend down.' And in spite of my protests she picked everything up herself."

Another thing that emerges from the portraits of Marie Antoinette is a great purity. Joseph II, who made a short stay at Versailles in 1781, several times expressed his astonishment, in view of the Queen's "associates" and "the prevailing licentious tone," at seeing his sister's virtue untouched. According to the Prince de Ligne, "her discretion inspired as much respect as her majesty. One could no more forget it than forget oneself. In her presence no one dared venture an indelicate remark, a ribald story or a marked piece of spite." It had certainly not been so before 1780, during the "reign" of the Comte d'Artois, but the Prince de Ligne was gallant and remembered only the Queen's "pure soul." Prudery had come with the birth of Madame Royale.

"I do not meet women separated from their husbands," she declared, when refusing to receive the Princesse de Monaco.

When in 1781 young Tilly wrote a comedy taken from a story by Marmontel and entitled *Laurette, or Virtue Rewarded By Love*—a "delightful play in the best of taste," if the author is to be believed—Marie Antoinette forbade her page to give it to the actors.

"But, Madame, is there any harm in having it staged?"

"No harm, no, but it is not seemly. A gentleman should not advertise himself."

And when the young man persisted and quoted the example of M. de Boufflers and the Cardinal de Bernis, she interrupted him: "You will oblige me by giving no more thought to it."

Tilly, incidentally, behaved badly, spent too much and went in for amusements. Having read Mercy's letters one is surprised to find this lecture from the Queen: "Behave according to your duty and you will get from me all the support you would wish to receive. You should dress more simply. In the last two days you have had two embroidered suits. Although you have a sufficient fortune it will not be enough if your tastes outrun it. Why this hair style and these curls? Are you going on the stage? Simplicity will not make you noticed, but it will bring you esteem."

Reading Tilly's *Memoirs*, edited by Christian Melchior-Bonnet, we can almost hear the sound of Marie Antoinette's voice. The scene begins one morning in the Hall of Mirrors, when the Queen was on her way to chapel. "Having noticed me, she did me the honour to greet me and to speak to me as she walked, so that I followed her. After putting several questions she was silent for a moment, and I seized the opportunity to take the liberty of telling her that I very much wished to throw myself at her feet and that I begged Her Majesty to hear me for a minute. 'Come to see me before five o'clock,' was her answer."

Tilly presented himself at the appointed hour. "An usher informed me that the Queen was not in her room but that she would soon return. In fact before five minutes had elapsed she came back.

" 'Good day. Where did you dine?'

" 'With Mme de Beauvilliers, Madame.'

" 'My Mme de Beauvilliers?'

" 'No, Madame, Madame Adelaide's.'

" 'Does she give dinners?'

" 'Yes, Madame, at least she does for me, whom she knew as a child and with whom she makes no ceremony.'

" 'If M. de Champcenetz had been at Versailles you would have dined with him. There is someone who is good company!'

" 'Madame, he has some wit and much gaiety.'

" 'Oh! he is charming. He will go far! Well, Monsieur, what do you want? Come in.'

" 'I beg the Queen to listen to me with indulgence, because I may take longer than I should.'

" 'But of course I shall listen to you.'

" 'Madame, there is a gentleman arrived here, a sort of magistrate, to whom my parents wish well, as I do also. He would like to obtain a post at Alençon, it is vacant—here it is written on a piece of paper—it all depends on M. de Miromesnil. My friend is a very worthy man and I should be happy if he had this post. One word from the Queen to the Keeper of the Seals and it is clear . . .'

" 'Well, it is clear . . .'

" 'Yes, Madame, that he could not refuse . . .'

" 'Is that all?'

" 'Yes, Madame.'

" 'I shall write. Give me that paper.'

" 'Madame, it is very crumpled.'

" 'Give me that paper. Come back tomorrow at half-past three. The letter will be ready. Goodbye.'

" 'I do not know how to express all my gratitude to the Queen.'

" 'By behaving well.' "

Let us follow the affair and see how posts were "wangled" in those days. The page went to see Miromesnil and explained the "gentleman's" wishes. The Keeper of the Seals leapt: "My God! your head's been turned, bold youth! You ask for a post which is the reward of the highest services and demands a degree of competence of which you have given no proof!"

Smiling and triumphant Tilly showed Marie Antoinette's letter. Miromesnil was taken aback and stammered: "Monsieur, I am sure that Her Majesty did not know what difficulty . . . How it is, I should say *almost* impossible . . . However . . . All my happiness is in obeying the Queen's orders."

When Joseph II made his second journey to Versailles in July 1781 Marie Antoinette gave an evening party for her brother in her beloved Trianon. The Comte de Liedekerque-Beaufort, page to the Comte de Provence, gives an account of it in his *Souvenirs*, of which only a few fragments have appeared in the *Revue de Paris*. "We arrived at the château, where all was confusion and freedom. In our gold livery we had no difficulty in entering. We passed one antechamber and were making our way towards the smell of food in the dining room. We were very surprised and embarrassed, although we were pages, to find ourselves in the salon where coffee was laid out for the royal party. As we were about to leave through one of the doors the two sides opened and we were face to face with the Queen and Joseph II, who was handing her out before the rest of the company into the coffee room. You may imagine our fright. It did not last long. The Queen was amused and said with gaiety and kindness: 'Well, where are you going, my little friends?' Her gentle smile reassured us and we confessed that as we were dying of hunger in the garden, her beautiful feast would be rather depressing for us unless someone gave us a piece of cake, which we had come to ask for in the pantry, but had mistaken the door.

" 'Well,' she said to her brother, 'they are very nice, they are not afraid to speak the truth.'

"She made us come back with her into the coffee room and made us sit down in a corner and help ourselves to cakes, brioches, etc., and there we were taking our coffee together with all the distinguished people, to whose teasing, including that of Joseph II, we replied gaily, without losing a bite. We were delighted to be told afterwards that we could follow the royal party all through the gardens, as for the moment we were part of Monseigneur's suite. We followed, as may be imagined, at a respectful distance. Soon a trellised door was opened leading to a private alley, in which, however, there were already a great many distinguished people who had come in beforehand by means of private tickets, so that there was already a great crowd of strollers. They were needed, too, to give a better idea of a crowd at a fair. To this end stalls had been erected on either side of the alley, as in a real fair. Ladies attached to the court, and elegantly disguised as vendors, invited the purchase of lottery tickets at their stalls, offering them on credit. No one waited to be asked twice. They knew that that meant that the number they received corresponded to one of the little things on show, which were thus intended as gifts, and everyone seized their little prize."

Where can Marie Antoinette be better evoked? Perhaps in that salon at Trianon "where coffee was laid out for the royal party," in which garlands of wild flowers adorned the wood panelling, that salon upholstered in green velvet with gold braid "*à la Bourgogne*," where one can still see on the marble violet chimneypiece the two vases of petrified wood sent from Vienna in 1780 by Joseph II. Better still, in her bedroom next door. It was indeed *her* bedroom, for the King never slept in this mezzanine room whose walls were covered with muslin and embroidered silk in bright colours. In the adjoining boudoir doves, incense-burners, crowns, quivers and rose trees adorned the delicate woodwork. Is it here that her presence can still be felt by lovers of the past? Either here or at Versailles in her little apartments looking out on the courtyard of the *Œil-de-Bœuf*. In spite of the lack of light in these delightful little rooms, one can understand that Marie Antoinette preferred to live in these charming jewel boxes which suited her so well, rather than in her sumptuous bedroom shimmering with gold and silver brocade on a background of crimson, or in her marble and stucco salon looking out on the south lawn.

She liked best to stay in her "inner room," the most modern room in the château, whose winged sphinx and smoking antique tripods presaged the Empire style, where she sat on a couch in an alcove of mirrors draped in silk. There were her writing desk, her workbasket and her clavichord, on which she often played Mozart's music.

It was in this room that she received the famous singer P. J. Garat, "the Bordeaux wonder," who was presented by his father, a magistrate in Parliament, and accompanied by the musician Salieri.

"How is this, M. Garat," she reproached him, "you have brought your son to Paris, an excellent musician and an accomplished singer, and you have not presented him!"

The younger Garat defended himself, explaining that he knew only dialect songs of Aquitaine.

" 'Well, let us hear your Gascon songs.' "

Salieri sat down at the piano. Marie Antoinette was delighted, particularly as Garat took care to translate each poem into French.

"But, M. Garat, do you know no music from the French operas?"

"I have not learnt any, Madame, as my father has allowed me to waste my time only in studying law."

The Queen laughed, and the magistrate was enough of a courtier to follow her example.

"What, nothing at all?"

"Well, Madame, I went to the Opera yesterday and heard *Armide*. I might be able to remember some of it."

"Ah! good! M. Salieri, would you take the music and accompany M. Garat?"

His memory did not betray him and young Garat sang all the solos from the famous opera. Marie Antoinette was overjoyed and applauded.

"We shall meet again, Monsieur," she said, giving him her hand to kiss.

When she rested after dinner during her second pregnancy, which in September 1781 was entering its eighth month, Marie Antoinette deserted her bedroom dominated by the vast bed with its great arched canopy surmounted by a "coping richly sculptured with flowers and garlands." She opened the door of the alcove and entered the little passage she had asked Mique to arrange for her, "Her Majesty wishing to be alone whenever she thinks necessary, without disturbing her suite or being disturbed by them." Only too rarely did she open the door on the right leading to her library, which had just been completed and where that very year Campan had arranged the Queen's books, which she never opened. Sometimes she would pull open one of the drawers by its handle in the form of a two-headed Austrian eagle and turn the pages of a book of engravings. But after dinner she preferred to retire to her new *Méridienne*, which Mique had finished in September 1781, and lie down in the mirrored alcove in which from a certain angle one could see oneself without a head. How many times must her blue eyes have wandered over the admirable frames—gems chiselled by Forestier—which surrounded the plate glass and repeated the design of the admirable woodwork, by the Rousseau brothers: branches and crowns of roses, royal lilies, cupids, hearts pierced with an arrow, Austrian eagles and dolphins. An allegory of the love and power of the Dauphin she was awaiting with so much impatience, the Dauphin who was stirring within her, for this time she was sure she would give birth to a king.

No one could have been more maternal. How she had trembled at the beginning of October in the previous year, and how distressed she had been at the sight of Madame Royale's "great pain," when "several of her teeth were coming through at once." On 11 October, in her last letter to the Empress, she had described how touched she had been "by the sweetness and patience of the poor little thing in her suffering." Then there was the day, not so long ago, when someone had asked the little Princess where her mother was. "Without anyone telling her, the poor little thing smiled at me and held out her arms. This was the first time she had shown that she recognised me. I confess that it gave me great joy, and I believe that I now love her even more."

Louis XVI, in the whole of his lifetime, wrote two narratives: one page concerning the birth of Madame Royale and two sheets recounting the Queen's confinement on 22 October 1781. Let us have it in his words: "The Queen had a very good night from 21 to 22 October. She had a few small pains when she woke, but they did not prevent her from taking her bath. She left it at half-past ten. The pains continued slight. I gave orders for the shoot I was to have held at Saclé only at midday. Between noon and half-past the pains increased. She lay down on her delivery bed and at exactly a quarter-past one by my watch she was successfully delivered of a boy. During her labour there were in the room only Mme de Lamballe, Monsieur, the Comte d'Artois, my aunts, Mme de Chimay, Mme de Mailly, Mme d'Ossun, Mme de Tavannes and Mme de Guéménée, who took turns to go into the Salon de la Paix, which had been left empty. In the *Grand Cabinet* were my Household and the Queen's, the *grandes entrées,* and the sub-governors, who entered when the final pains began and stood at the back of the room so as not to impede the air."

Infinitely preferable to this official report is the extract from a letter to King Gustavus of Sweden from M. de Stedingk, Fersen's friend: "After a quarter of an hour's suspense one of the Queen's women, all dishevelled and excited, entered and cried: 'A Dauphin! But you must not mention it yet.'

"Our joy was too great to be suppressed. We hurried out of the apartment, which led into the hall of the Queen's Guards. The first person I met there was Madame, who was rushing to the Queen's room. I called out to her: 'A Dauphin, Madame! What happiness!' It was only the effect of chance and my extreme joy, but this seemed amusing and it is retold in so many ways that I am very much afraid that it will not make me liked by Madame. . . .

"The Queen's antechamber presented a charming sight. Everyone's joy was at its height and all heads were turned. People who hardly knew each other laughed and wept by turns. Men and women fell on each other's necks and even those who cared least for the Queen were carried away by the general rejoicing. But it was very different an hour after the birth, when the two doors of the Queen's room were opened and M. le Dauphin was announced. Mme de Guéménée, beaming with joy, held him in her arms and was wheeled across the apartments in her armchair to take him to her rooms. Everyone wanted to touch the child, or even just the chair. A crowd followed him, adoring. When he had arrived in his apartments, an Archbishop wanted to decorate him with a blue ribbon, but the King said he should first of all be a Christian. The baptism took place at three o'clock in the afternoon.

"At first no one had dared tell the Queen it was a Dauphin, for fear of arousing too strong an emotion. Everyone around her held in their feelings so well that the Queen, seeing only constraint about her, thought it was a daughter. She said: 'You see how reasonable I am. I have asked no questions.'

"Seeing her anxiety, the King thought it was time to reassure her. With tears in his eyes he said: 'M. le Dauphin begs to enter.'

"They brought her the child and those who witnessed the scene say they have never seen anything so touching. She said to Mme de Guéménée, who took the child: 'Take him, he belongs to the State, but I now take back my daughter.'"

In Paris the "Gentlemen," the ushers and the Governor took part in the traditional ceremonies and in full procession walked three times round the bonfire. This time they wore garlands and bracelets of flowers, artificial flowers, "in view of the season." The tocsin rang without ceasing for three days and nights, money was distributed to the people, buffets were set out under the wind and for two days all work in Paris was stopped. The women replaced their gold cross by a dolphin; the locksmiths presented the King with a mysterious lock which he could not manage to open; the chimney-sweeps brought to Versailles a chimney "large enough for one of them to hide in it"; the bakers made bread "in the Queen's vestibule" which "Her Majesty found delicious"; and finally the fruiterers presented a charming silver cauldron for the newborn child's food.

The Parisians dispatched verses and songs. Even a certain Collot d'Herbois sent the Queen an ode which ended with the lines:

> O sheltering heaven, protect
> The life of Antoinette!

This was the future regicide Collot d'Herbois!

Another poet preferred to make fun of his colleagues and sent this quatrain to the château:

> O Monseigneur, you are indeed in luck,
> Not for being born to govern France,
> But on account of your total ignorance
> Of all we're grinding out in the way of poetic muck.

The fishwives came from Paris and recited to the King a song whose verses made a point of being, in the words of those ladies, "broad and unkempt," so unkempt, indeed, that we can transcribe only the first three lines:

> *Notre charmante Antoinette*
> *Vient de faire un petit bout*
> *Et j'avais vu la croquette. . . .*

The description of the said "croquette" apparently delighted Louis XVI and he laughingly demanded an encore. The ladies did not wait to be asked twice and began again "with contortions, grimaces and gestures" to help. Side by side with its beribboned graces the 18th century offers us these surprises reminiscent of the Middle Ages.

On Friday 26 October the "Gentlemen" went in ceremonial dress to Notre Dame, where a *Te Deum* was sung in the King's presence. Two days later they again put on their robes and went by carriage to Versailles to inform His Majesty of their wish to admire the Dauphin. Louis XVI granted them this favour, but, according to the report, "ordered the Mayor to use the title of Monseigneur" to the child who was not yet a week old. The "Gentlemen" bowed and "advanced towards Monseigneur, who was in his cradle, and the Mayor offered congratulations on behalf of the city." At his side stood his appropriately-named nurse, Mme Poitrine, superintended by a *"gardienne du Ventre,"* who never left her "so as to report to the Faculty on her state of health."

On Tuesday 31 October the city authorities returned to congratulate Marie Antoinette, who received the city clerk and told him that she was "as well as could be wished."

Paris then considered it had done enough. Times were hard and the capital would have preferred to postpone the festivities, *Te Deum* and entries until the fine weather. The city's finances were in a bad state. During the preceding year seven Princes or Princesses allied to the royal family had died: Louise of Brunswick, the Comte of Modena, the Duke of Wolfenbüttel, the Duchess of Württemberg, the Electress Dowager of Saxony, Prince Charles of Lorraine, Marie Antoinette's uncle and finally Maria Theresa. Admittedly, the King was generous enough each time to present the "Gentlemen" with a "mourning robe" with weepers, but all this mourning had cost the city a great deal, 2,700 to 3,000 livres for each death. On the preceding 30 May Paris had been obliged to have a solemn service celebrated at Notre Dame for Maria Theresa and to dress the heralds in a violet velvet dalmatic, and the king-at-arms and the official crier in a black robe with the Empress's arms on the front—not to mention the church, which had to be draped in black, and the costly allegories which were constructed above the portico and around the catafalque.

M. de Caumartin, the Mayor, in view of the frequent and costly journeys of the city council each time a member of the royal family had a "tertian fever," was of the opinion that on this occasion the rejoicings could be postponed until later. Feasts in the middle of winter were twice as expensive, and besides there was already a shortage of bread. But Marie Antoinette asked laughingly if they were waiting until Monseigneur was old enough to dance at the ball to be given in the Hôtel de Ville and the "Gentlemen" obeyed. The feast would take place on the 21 and 23 January. But the citizens, who were at close quarters with the poverty in the city, grumbled, and the rejoicings started badly.

Some precautions were therefore taken. The simplest consisted in increasing the number of charcoal braziers, buffets and orchestras so as to disperse the ordinary people and prevent them from gathering in a mass before the Hôtel de Ville, where the fireworks were to be set off. So that the King and Queen could see better, a long wooden gallery was built at the site of the display. Although Marie Antoinette was to stay only a few hours at the Hôtel de Ville, a room was fitted up in blue damask with the ceiling "mingled with flowers," as well as a wardrobe room draped with crimson material. In order that the sovereigns would not have to bring their own Officers of the Mouth, the "Gentlemen" created the post of "city maître d'hôtel."

M. de Caumartin might well sigh. A contributory cause was that the Princes of the Blood, who had been invited only to the reception after the banquet, had told the King that "being unable to be of any use to him on this occasion," when they would be "mixed up with everyone else," they preferred to remain at home. A great deal of trouble was caused by this princely bad humour.

The Dukes, too, were discontented. They had actually been invited with the same formula as that used for the nobility. The Mayor did not know what to do, for if there had been two formulas the nobility would have been offended.

By the morning of 21 January everything was ready. The weather was superb. During the night the mud under which Paris was submerged had been cleared away and the inhabitants had carefully swept before their doors and prepared the "fire pots" to illuminate their houses in the evening. For their part the city authorities had 6,201 fire pots and 3,141 lamps placed on the public monuments, and M. de Caumartin sighed again at the thought of the bill.

The Queen arrived from La Muette alone at nine o'clock. As it was her churching she had the right to a special entry. In her carriage were Madame Elisabeth, who now attended all the ceremonies, Madame Adelaide, the Duchesse de Bourbon, the Princesse de Chimay and Mme de Lamballe, who now came to court only to carry out the duties of her post.

At the Porte de la Conférence the Governor, according to custom, knelt on one knee to make his speech to the Queen, and Marie Antoinette "replied with all her own particular grace."

This time Paris's welcome was as it should be. It was, of course, far from the wild applause at the beginning of the reign, but as the Queen had assured the succession people wanted to show their joy.

After the ceremony in Notre Dame, where she knelt on the flagstones to say the prayers for her churching, and after the visit to Sainte Geneviève, Marie Antoinette proceeded to the Pont au Bled, to the sound of the tocsin and the city artillery. In front of the old Hôtel de Ville she descended from her carriage, not without having to hear another speech, and went to wait for the King in her blue damask room.

Louis XVI, who had left La Muette in grand array at a quarter-to-one, arrived in the Place de l'Hôtel de Ville an hour later, accompanied by his two brothers, the Grand Equerry, Prince de Lambesq, the First Equerry, Duc de Coigny and the Captain of the Guards, Duc d'Ayen.

Only Provence and Artois were to sit at the royal table, in company with 76 women. M. de Caumartin presented the King's napkin and tasted each dish by putting a small piece of bread to the food. Mme de la Porte, the Mayor's sister, served the Queen. The other "Gentlemen" bustled round the Princes and Princesses, while the ladies were served by 70 valets in scarlet uniform with gold frogging. The other tables were served by 230 valets dressed in the same way—and M. de Caumartin's sighs were by now innumerable. The dishes were brought by 150 city guards in uniform but without rifle or hat.

Tiers had been built on either side for the "people of the highest consideration," but this consideration did not go so far as to offer them anything to eat. There was an endless file of people behind the railings which had been set up "to give everyone the opportunity of enjoying a noble and magnificent spectacle." The meal, which began at a quarter-to-three, ended at five, but only for the royal table, for there had been a certain amount of disorganisation in the kitchens. The Dukes' table, among others, had only reached the *hors-d'oeuvre,* and according to the clerk's report: "MM. les Ducs had only radishes and butter to eat, as His Majesty rose from the table." One can imagine their ill humour, particularly as "MM. les Ducs" had to be turned out in order to clear the large room. It was from here that after the reception the sovereigns would watch the fireworks being let off from a Temple of Hymen adorned with dolphins. "The fireworks," the clerk reported frankly, "did not come up to expectations, either because of the bad management of the artificer, Master La Varinière, or because of the bad weather."

The city officials then all went back with the King and Queen to La Muette. In the Rue Saint-Honoré the Queen stopped her carriage in front of the Hôtel de Noailles, where stood, bare-headed, the Marquis de Lafayette, who had just returned from America covered with glory and had not yet been able to present himself at Versailles. He came to the door of the coach to bow, and Marie Antoinette gave the hero of the day her hand to kiss.

The coaches then resumed their way towards the Cours la Reine and, the clerk concluded briefly, "the Governor went away and the Gentlemen also."

Two days later the masked ball took place. It was the last great festivity of the old régime. Thirteen thousand people had been invited. More than twice as many came and complete confusion reigned over the evening. Marie Antoinette, who came although she was not expected, was nearly suffocated. The buffets were rifled and every corner of the Hôtel de Ville invaded, although places had been set aside "where people who were tired or who wished to leave could rest and more conveniently wait for their carriages." Marie Antoinette left at two o'clock, but the ball went on until seven in the morning. On the same day the indefatigable Mayor and four magistrates went to Versailles to thank the King and Queen, and much to M. de Caumartin's relief, they received 30,000 livres to cover part of the expenses.

The "Gentlemen" were touched by this gesture and when, a little later, Marie Antoinette was suffering from erysipelas a city officer went every day to inquire after her health. And when, at Pont Notre Dame, a Parisian fisherman caught a sturgeon six-and-a-half feet long (times have changed somewhat), the magistrates hastened to buy the fish and to have a "bath" made to carry the monster to Versailles to be presented alive to the King and Queen. They arranged for a whole cavalcade of mules with barrels "to refresh and change the water from time to time," but the sturgeon died and was taken by coach to Versailles, where it was admired by everyone before being sent to the kitchens.

On 30 January M. de Caumartin was again at Versailles to "stroll about" at the ball given to the Queen in the opera house of the château by the bodyguards, still in honour of the Dauphin's birth.

"Have you come to learn how to give a party?" a masked figure asked him, bursting into laughter.

It had to be admitted that the evening was particularly successful. Marie Antoinette opened the ball at five in the afternoon with M. de Moret, the oldest bodyguard. Artois danced with Mme de Condé and "Guichette" with the Duc de Bourbon.

At six o'clock the guards let in the common people and showed them to the buffet "which contributed not a little to their applause expressed by cries of 'Ah! that's good!' and clinkings of glasses accompanied by 'Long live the King! Long live the Queen! Long live M. le Dauphin and all the family!'" During a silence a voice was even heard to cry: "Long live the wine and pie the Guards have given me!"

At eight o'clock the people were shown out and the bodyguards sat down to eat. The French Guards, "who had been keeping order indoors," succeeded them.

The evening was not yet over, for the masked ball was yet to come. The King came back at about eleven, "but His Majesty was overcome by sleep and went to bed at half-past eleven." Marie Antoinette stayed, and enjoyed herself. She had come in a black domino, but as she was soon recognised she changed her disguise three times during the night.

She was still fond of balls but considered that at her age—she was not yet thirty—she ought not to dance as much as she used. In three or four years she would allow herself no more than a quadrille or a *colonne anglaise* in an evening. When the King was present etiquette required him to dance without ever turning his back on his wife. Hampered by this acrobatic feat, he was sometimes overtaken by the music, "but then," Horace Walpole declared gallantly, "it is wrong to dance in time!"

Ah! those balls given by the Queen! In fifty years' time the last supporters of Charles X, exiled in Prague with the former Comte d'Artois, would speak of them with emotion. In those days they had been pages "charged with doing the honours." At a gracious smile from Marie

Antoinette, who supervised everything, they would accompany the ladies "with the easy manner of their age and the politeness of their rank," to give them refreshments and return them to their places. The ballroom was on the left of the royal courtyard, on the spot where there is now a passage leading to the park by the princes' courtyard.

In a few hours the department of the *Menus Plaisirs* would enlarge the pillared hall by means of wooden pavilions. "One entered first into a leafy grove adorned with statues and rose trees and ending in an open temple, where the billiard room was," related one of the Queen's pages. "On the right little paths led to the ballroom and to the gaming room, and so that those who were playing could see the dancing without losing the warmth of this fine room one of the doors had been made of an enormous piece of plate glass, so transparent that a Swiss Guard had to be placed as a sentinel to prevent careless people from trying to walk through it. The ballroom was a rectangle, to which one descended by a few steps. All around was a gallery, which allowed people to walk about without interrupting the dancing, which could be watched between the pillars. It was from here that people not presented and admitted to the boxes surrounding the ballroom could see the dancing."

In winter heating pipes warmed the apartments and in summer cascades of water falling into vast marble shells brought a pleasing freshness to the ballroom. From the gallery one could watch the dancers, whose black suits embroidered with jet and plumed hats shimmered and sparkled in the light.

Newcomers were watched with particular attention. Woe betide anyone who might commit a gaffe, like the "almost fashionable" M. de Chabannes, who had the misfortune to fall during a quadrille, exclaiming "Jesus Maria!" The nickname stuck. "He went to fight in America," Mme de Boigne tells us, "and gained some distinction, but he came back 'Jesus Maria' as he had left." The Duc de Guines had reason to tell his daughters on the day of their presentation at court: "Remember that here vices are without importance, but ridicule can be fatal."

Certain "elderly young men" danced bare-headed, for, by a characteristic quibble of the age, "they were supposed not to have come to dance and consequently were not dressed for it." Refreshments could be found nearby in a semi-circular hall, where there were enormous baskets of fruit and pastries and large urns full of wine. In some small rooms there were maids to repair the dresses disarranged in dancing.

The Queen supervised everything and, like a hostess of today, prevented the young men from remaining together to talk about horses and politics. At midnight supper was served at tables with twelve places each, waited on by footmen of the King and Queen in red and silver livery. The King would arrive after supper, play a game of billiards, risk a crown at backgammon, send back to their regiment those who were playing too heavily, and then watch the dancing from the gallery before going to bed.

"Once Louis XVI had left one could laugh and enjoy oneself," the Queen's page related much later. Dawn put an end to the ball, which finished with the farandole of the *colonne anglaise* in which Marie Antoinette took part, laughing. Then the most wide-awake pages conducted the ladies to their carriages, having first given them soup and "restoratives," while others slept in corners, overcome with exhaustion.

Those who were staying at the château would meet the Swiss Guards in the corridors or on the stairs, patrolling with their spaniels, which had been trained to search in corners. Without this precaution the château would have been a playground for prostitutes and a haunt of thieves.

Late in the evening, or early in the morning, the patrols would sometimes meet a pale, haggard man "like one whose mind is wandering." But the Swiss Guards said nothing. It was M. de Castelnaux, Marie Antoinette's elderly adorer, whose life consisted in gazing from afar at the woman he loved. "Always alone, he would calculate the moments when he might find himself in the Queen's presence." He would stay for hours in the Hall of Mirrors, and never missed a state dinner. "Did he hear wheels? He was at once at the foot of the stairs." Even the cold did not put him off. "While the Queen was staying at the Little Trianon," relates Mme Campan, "this unhappy man's passion became even more importunate. He would snatch a bite of food with one of the Swiss Guards and would spend the whole day, even when it rained, walking round the garden, always walking at the edge of the ditches. The Queen often met him when she was strolling alone or with her children." One day she asked M. de Sèze to try to make the unhappy man see reason. After agreeing to "retire to his estates," he recanted. To withdraw seemed to him beyond his powers.

"Ah well!" sighed the Queen. "Let him vex me, but let no one take away from him the happiness of being at liberty."

At the beginning of the summer of 1782 Versailles and Trianon were enlivened by fresh festivities. The Comte and Comtesse du Nord, otherwise the future Tsar Paul I and his wife, born a Princess of Württemberg, were in Paris. Marie Antoinette was not aware of the Tsarina Catherine II's dislike for her, but she gave a very courteous reception to "those Norths," as she rather contemptuously called them, and organised a feast for them at Trianon. The Comtesse du Nord proudly wore on her head a little jewelled bird which "at her slightest movement sways on a spring above a rose." Marie Antoinette thought it so pretty that she wanted one like it. Scaffoldings of hair were now out of date and instead flowers were worn with their stems "in little, flat bottles, curved to fit the head." "When one finally managed it," recounts Mme d'Oberkirch, who wore just such a headdress on 6 June at Trianon, "it was charming. The spring flowers on the head in the midst of the snowy powder produced a unique effect." But one hardly dared move one's head, for fear of being drenched.

Dresses and hair styles were in garden or wild flower fashion. One dressed as a lavender seller or country girl, and Marie Antoinette was soon to ask Mique to construct a simple, unpretentious hamlet at the bottom of the park. Like an ordinary, artless shepherdess, she enjoined, her simplicity should be her sole ornament.

But we must hear again from the Baroness d'Oberkirch, who had been invited to the formal ball given by the Queen in honour of "those Norths." "I still cannot get over the difficulty of managing one's dress and one's hair in the carriage from Paris to Versailles. One was extremely uncomfortable, and the women who follow this postillion's calling several times a week must be very tired. The ball was wonderful. The Queen danced with the Grand Duke and no one could display more grace and nobility than our august sovereign. Her figure and bearing are wonderful. At one moment I was standing behind her and the Grand Duchess. 'Madame d'Oberkirch,' said the Queen, 'say something to me in German, so that I can see if I remember it. I now know only the language of my present country.'

"I said a few words in German and she mused for a moment without replying. 'Ah!' she said at last, 'I am charmed by the sound of the old German. You speak like a Saxon, Madame, without any Alsatian accent, which surprises me. German is a beautiful language, but French!

On the lips of my children it seems to me the sweetest tongue in the world.' "

She instilled similar sentiments into her children. When Mme d'Oberkirch went to see little Madame Royale, the child asked her name.

"You are a German then, Madame?" she said.

"No, Madame, I am French—from Alsace."

"Ah! I am glad of that, for I should not wish to love foreigners."

At the end of the summer of 1782 her children's education caused Marie Antoinette a great deal of worry, M. de Guéménée's startling insolvency—33 million livres—forced the Princesse to give in her resignation. Who should replace her? Marie Antoinette thought of the pious Princesse de Chimay or the learned Duchesse de Duras. But Besenval was on the watch—the Queen must nominate Mme de Polignac.

"Any other nomination would give the idea that Your Majesty no longer had enough influence to have the post given to her best friend."

"I should have thought you knew the Duchesse better. She would not want this post."

But the Swiss was clever, and he had touched the Queen on a sensitive spot. She interceded and, naturally, the King yielded. One can imagine the murmurs of the public. The Polignac family's revenues were to become even larger, and even Joseph II, in Vienna, declared himself "shocked" by this choice. Marie Antoinette was to be very much blamed for this appointment, but she consoled herself by saying that she would have "the opportunity to supervise her children's education—in particular that of her daughter—without the risk of wounding the governess's vanity."

The little Marie Thérèse—Madame Royale—never left her mother's rooms, and every "important or serious business," as Mercy wrote to Joseph II on 28 December 1782, "is interrupted by the little incidents of the royal child's games, and this inconvenience so chimes with the Queen's natural disposition to be superficial and inattentive that she hardly listens to what is said to her, and understands even less! . . . Consequently I find myself kept more at arm's length than ever."

With all respect to the Ambassador, that was a good thing. To draw Marie Antoinette into the question of the free navigation of the Scheldt, so dear to Joseph II, or into the eternal Austro-Prussian quarrels, would have harmed the Queen a great deal in public opinion. We shall see this later.

"One can no longer calculate the effects of the Queen's vacillating ideas," wrote Mercy in the same letter. But this vacillation had its good side, for in spite of the new favour granted to the "clan," the great "passion" had lessened somewhat. Mme de Polignac was still Marie Antoinette's "most tender friend," but sometimes her credit waned. She wearied the Queen with her perpetual demands. Recently she had taken it into her head to ask for the post of Minister of the King's household for the Comte d'Adhémar, who with his quavering voice had played Marie Antoinette's lover in the *Devin du village*. The Queen refused. Mme de Polignac, annoyed, had sulked. Marie Antoinette consoled herself more easily, perhaps, than she would have done two years before, for she had found a new friend—Geneviève de Gramont, Comtesse d'Ossun, her Mistress of the Robes since the previous year.

This time one may be thankful for Marie Antoinette's "vagaries of affection," which always upset Mercy. Mme d'Ossun was not an intriguer and never asked for money. She received 600 livres salary, 4,000 living allowance, 3,600 for *plat* (?) and 886 for her "coaches and hackneys," in all less than 10,000 livres. And she asked for nothing more. Marie Antoinette, who often invited herself to dinner with her Mistress of the Robes, together with four or five other people, had difficulty in getting her to accept a few thousand crowns in recompense.

Marie Antoinette's wardrobe was a real Ministry, and Mme d'Ossun had a large staff under her. "Everything was under her authority," wrote Mme Campan, "and nothing was released without her signature, from shoes to suits embroidered at Lyons. . . . The Mistress of the Robes had under her a first tiring-woman, entrusted with the care and upkeep of all the Queen's clothes; two women to fold and press anything that needed it; two valets of the wardrobe and one wardrobe boy. This last had to bring to the apartment every morning baskets covered with taffeta which contained everything the Queen was to wear during the day, and large dress-covers of green taffeta, in which were wrapped the ball and other dresses. Every morning the wardrobe valet on duty gave the first woman of the bedchamber a book containing patterns of the dresses, ball dresses, négligées, etc. A little portion of the trimming indicated what kind it was. The woman of the bedchamber presented the book to the Queen when she awoke, together with a pincushion. Her Majesty marked with pins everything she wanted for the day: one for the ball dress she wanted, one for the formal dress, for gambling or for supper in the small apartments. The book was taken back to the wardrobe and soon everything needed for the day arrived in the taffeta covers."

One of these daily "gazettes," in which one can still see the marks of Marie Antoinette's pins, has been preserved for us in the Archives. One cannot help musing over these patterns of "spotted green" or "white braid on a lilac ground." In the spring of 1782 she wore dresses of "white spots on a lavender ground," or of "striped satin," or a dressing-gown of "gosling-green figured with white spots." The ball dress at the head of the list, perhaps the one she wore for the feast given at Versailles to the "Norths," is of "mottled lilac," and the "paniered dress," perhaps for Trianon, was made of "gold-embroidered muslin, *présence de l'Impératrice*."

According to Mme Campan, Marie Antoinette "usually had for the winter 12 ball dresses, 12 small, so-called fancy, dresses, 12 rich hooped dresses for when she played or for supper in the small apartments. The same number for summer. The spring dresses served for autumn. All these dresses were scrapped at the end of the year, unless she kept back one or two she preferred." The Queen's devoted waiting-woman tried to hide part of the truth from us, and indeed, she succeeded, for the figure of 100 new dresses a year is that usually given by historians. Now, by consulting the files of the Archives and taking the year 1782, which was a year below the average, we arrive at a total of 170 dresses. "On being cast off, the dresses were given, by order of the Mistress of the Robes, to the waiting-women." Mme Campan skates over this question. In reality, still according to the Archives, the first women of the bed-chamber each received in 1782, apart from their candle rights, 12 coats, 22 wrappers and at the beginning of each season "a ball dress or a day dress," not to mention all the little taffeta underskirts, shoes, silk stockings, gloves and mittens. And it was not a question of worn clothes. A note points out that the "outfits were so numerous that they could not all be used and that many are cast off without having been worn." It must also be mentioned that the remainder, principally dresses and ball gowns, came to Mme d'Ossun, who might sell them for her own profit. This was only fair, for the Mistress of the Robes was the only one of the Queen's women who, apart from her titular rôle, did any real work.

The unfortunate Comtesse d'Ossun was scared by her mistress's expenditure. Marie Antoinette received between three and four million livres a year—between 600 and 800 million present-day francs—for all the expenses of her household and privy purse, the latter post totaling 300,000 livres in 1780. For clothes there was a budget of 120,000 livres, which was never enough. In 1776 a supplement of 28,000 livres was required, in 1780 one of 74,118. In 1783 Mme d'Ossun had to ask the treasurer for 73,067.

And Mme Campan dares tell us that Marie Antoinette's love of adornment, after "the first years of her reign, had given way to a love of simplicity, which was carried to unwise lengths." The truth can be more accurately found in the accounts of Mme d'Ossun, who when asking for the payment of these "truly excessive" sums, to use her own expression, added: "In bringing these statements to the King's notice, I would ask you to express to him my regret at having to request such a large supplement."

Incidentally, the treasury was not able to pay at once and it was not until February 1784 that the Mistress of the Robes received the money for the excess expenditure of 1782. "This deficit is the work of Mlle Bertin, among others," wrote Mme d'Ossun, when she sent in her accounts. The Queen's dressmaker was the Comtesse's *bête noire*. Rose Bertin, indeed, delivered directly to the Queen, instead of to the wardrobe. She sent in her bill three or four months later and "no one could remember anything about it . . . which means that one is often forced to agree in her invoices to things which one has neither seen nor used, and to pay for them without even being sure that they were furnished." Mlle Bertin's prices were "exorbitant." She actually asked 6,000 livres for a ball gown for New Year's Day—1,200,000 francs for a dress. "A sum as large as this might well have been given in some detail," sighed the secretary of the wardrobe, and he suggested "the employment of a specialist to review Mlle Bertin's invoices." But, he went on, "it would seem much more desirable to make Mlle Bertin give these details herself in her invoices, under pain of having those articles crossed out which are given without explanation. She has been asked to do this for a long time, and she cannot be brought to do it." And without consulting anyone he cut down one of the bills by 9,000 livres.

Rose Bertin was not the Queen's only dressmaker. Besides the "outside sewing-women" there was at the château a whole staff of "ordinary sewing-women," twelve of them, sewing-women for extraordinary dresses, sewing-women who specialised in dressing-gowns, tailors for riding-habits, not to mention the "manufacturers of hoops and collarettes," bonnet-makers and even a certain Demoiselle Brisemiche, whose job was "to construct the flounces on the Queen's petticoats." This troupe, which was paid on a different budget from the one managed by Mme d'Ossun, could not have been overworked, since the mending was done outside, by among others Mme Eloff, who repaired dresses and shoes. She also provided Marie Antoinette with her basques, brocade dresses and her bodices.

The Queen did not feel in the least guilty about this prodigality which distressed her new friend. Her disbursements were as nothing compared to those of the Comte d'Artois, who had debts of 21 million "as a result of heavy expenditure and much dishonesty on the part of his business men," says Mercy. But Marie Antoinette was no more anxious than her brother-in-law. In 1783 the new Controller of Finances, Calonne, appeared, who refused them nothing, in accordance with his famous principle: spend a great deal in order to appear rich. Meanwhile Marie Antoinette did not observe that her extravagance was as harmful to her as her past follies. A contemporary, the Abbé de Véri, wrote at the beginning of 1783: "The people of Paris are attached to the King merely because they cast on the Queen all the reproaches they might make to Louis XVI. The continual changes in the fashion of adornments, hairdressing and clothes, together with a few small showy expenses, are the real reason for popular feeling against the Queen. The middle-class man says he is ruined by the fancies of his wife and daughters, who want to imitate all the Queen's changes of taste. The merchant and the manufacturer have no fixed standard for predicting what will sell. And as these people know that the King has none of these tastes and that his way of life is simple, he is loved for the contrast between his taste and the Queen's."

How should she feel guilty, since when she wished a simple way of life she was reproached with that too? Witness Mme Vigée-Lebrun's picture of the Queen in a *gaulle,* a kind of blouse made fashionable by the creoles of Santo Domingo, which was exhibited in the Salon of 1783. People gathered before the picture to see Marie Antoinette "dressed as a chamber-maid." She wanted to ruin the silk merchants and weavers of Lyons in favour of the Flemish drapers, her brother's subjects.

The picture was given a title: "France, under the features of Austria, reduced to covering herself with a rag."

The Queen, annoyed, had the portrait withdrawn. Since, on the one hand, Calonne asked it of her and, on the other, the public thought she was ruining the country's textile industry by dressing in batiste and muslin, why should she worry? And the wardrobe expenses mounted sharply from 199,957 livres in 1783 to 217,652 in 1784 and 258,002 in 1785.

Although "less conspicuous," her amusements were none the less ruinous.

9

✣

"Limited Lovers"

ONE AFTERNOON TOWARDS the end of June 1783 Marie Antoinette was playing the harp in her gilded drawing-room when an usher scratched at the door. A moment later Axel Fersen stood before her. How changed he was! "As handsome as an angel" when he left for America, he had "aged by ten years." The Queen stopped playing and gave him her hand to kiss.

It was certainly not grief at being separated from Marie Antoinette that had preyed upon the "supernumerary" colonel, but the fatigues of war. During these three years spent in America he had certainly not forgotten his "conquest," but it would be ridiculous to try to make an inconsolable lover out of him. Before embarking for France he had even considered renewing, on his return, his plans for marriage with an Englishwoman, Miss Leijel, whom he had once known, and he wrote to his father: "After taking care for my promotion and satisfying my self-esteem, I must now think of a more solid establishment. I am now at an age when marriage becomes necessary, however little vocation I may have for that sacrament. A marriage with Miss Leijel would have many advantages. I have not lost sight of her and during my stay in America I continued to correspond with her. I wrote her five or six letters, but have had no reply. . . . If she failed me and persisted in her rejection I have my eyes on someone else. This plan will depend entirely on your wishes. I have no other influences except what you would exert: it is the daughter of M. Necker."

But then he met Marie Antoinette again. A month after his return, hearing that Miss Leijel had married during his absence, Axel wrote to his sister Sophie and confessed his love for the Queen. "I am very glad that Miss Leijel is married. She will not be mentioned to me again, and I hope no one else will be found. I have made up my mind. *I cannot belong to the one person to whom I should wish to belong, the one who really loves me,* and so I wish to belong to no one." His scheme for marrying Mlle Necker was also abandoned—Staël had just entered the lists.

Marie Antoinette seemed to have renewed her "inclination" and soon Axel had but one wish: to remain in France and obtain from Louis XVI the command of a foreign regiment. The proprietor of the Royal Swedish, Comte Alexandre de Sparre, was ready to sell it to him for 100,000 livres. Axel spoke to his father, asking him to help pay this sum, which would allow him to remain for part of the year at Versailles, and begging him to consent to "the one thing which can make me happy for ever" and for which, he said, "there were a thousand other reasons I dare not put on paper."

Senator Fersen replied in a stern letter: "I would willingly consent to your scheme, if I did not see in it a physical impossibility. Neither you nor I have the necessary capital."

Fortunately King Gustavus intervened and asked Louis XVI to grant a commission to Count Fersen "who has served in Your Majesty's armies in America to the approbation of all and has thus rendered himself worthy of your benevolence." On 12 September Axel handed the letter to the King and on the same day reported to Gustavus III: "The King consented at once and displayed the strongest desire to do something to please Your Majesty. The Queen also wished to take a hand in it." On 20 September Marie Antoinette also wrote to the King of Sweden to assure him that she would "omit nothing to second the wishes of her brother and cousin." And on the following day, 21 September, Louis XVI appointed "M. le Comte de Fersen commanding officer and proprietor of the Royal Swedish." Axel paid the Comte de Sparre the 100,000 livres, which he had borrowed, but "His Majesty, on this same 21st day of September, granted the Comte de Fersen a *brevet de retenue* for the said 100,000 livres," which would enable him to discharge his debt.

Axel had by that time left Paris and was on his way to join King Gustavus, who was travelling in Germany under the name of Count de Haga and had asked Axel to accompany him. On 9 November he noted in his correspondence book: "(Wrote) to the Queen to thank her for the regiment."

Did he also express his regrets for the accident which had befallen her nine days before at Fontainebleau? Marie Antoinette had then "given birth, without much pain, to what is commonly called a false germ." No complications arose and the Queen was quite well again when on 29 November peace with England was solemnly proclaimed. Twelve trumpets, 12 hautboys and eight drums of the Great Stables marched through the streets of Paris and at each crossroads an officer announced the news.

Fersen was then in Italy. He was not a man to play at the faithful lover—he never would be. In Florence he made the conquest of Lord Cowper's stepsister, "the fair Emily." In Naples he consoled Lady Elizabeth Foster, daughter of the Duke of Bristol and unhappily married to John Thomas Foster. The pretty Englishwoman found Axel the most charming of consolers and considered a separation from her husband, and when Fersen left Naples a correspondence was carried on between the lovers.

On 7 June 1784 Count de Haga and his suite arrived at Versailles. Louis XVI, who had not been forewarned, was hunting at Rambouillet and returned in a hurry. His servants were not there; he dressed as best he could and presented himself before the King of Sweden with two different shoes.

"Have you been dressing for a masked ball?" asked Marie Antoinette laughing.

The visit lasted six weeks. "We are in a whirl of feasts, pleasures and entertainments of every kind," Axel wrote to his father. "We are constantly occupied and always in a hurry. We never have time to do everything arranged for us. This giddy life suits the Count de Haga very well. It does not suit me nearly so well and I am exhausted. We have already had a grand opera at Versailles and a state ball, not to mention numerous dinners and suppers. Tomorrow there is a feast in the Queen's large garden at Trianon. This will be the last, but there are still many suppers and spectacles in Paris. We never miss any of them, and we would rather go without drinking, eating and sleeping than not be present at the spectacle from the beginning right to the end. It is a mania!"

We know what the feast at Trianon was like through Gustavus III, who wrote to his brother: "In the little theatre they performed the

Dormeur réveillé by M. de Marmontel, music by Grétry [it was the *Dormeur réveillé* with music by Piccini] with the whole ballet company from the Opera, together with the Comédie Italienne. The spectacle ended with the diamond transformation scene. Supper was served in the garden pavilions and after supper the English garden was illuminated. It was perfectly enchanting. The Queen had opened the gardens to respectable people who had not come to the supper and who had been warned that they must dress in white, which really provided an elysian sight. The Queen would not sit down at table, but did the honours like any mistress of the house. She spoke to all the Swedes and entertained them with great care and attention." Marie Antoinette seemed transfigured. "She is miraculously beautiful," writes the Baroness d'Oberkirch.

The "inclination" was to become a "passion." But feasts and distractions did not make Marie Antoinette forget that Fersen had no fortune and before he left for Sweden Axel was given 20,000 livres a year income in his capacity as colonel of a French regiment.

At each stage of the long journey Axel wrote to a mysterious "Josephine." "Under this name," wrote the admirable archivist Alma Söderjhelm, "Fersen kept up a secret correspondence with Marie Antoinette." Doubt has recently been cast on this interpretation by M. Henry Valloton. Now, from Luneberg, on 27 July, and from Vernamynde, on 29 July, Axel wrote to "Josephine," as he notes in his correspondence book, to ask her "what name should be given to the dog" she had asked him to buy and "if any secret should be made of it." Josephine presumably replied that the purchase need not be secret, for on 9 November he wrote from Stockholm to M. de Boye and summarised his letter in his correspondence book: "Asked him to send me a dog, not small, the size of those owned by M. Pollett. Said it was for the Queen of France."

Much later, during the Revolution, we read in his private diary: "I went to see Mercy to ask him if he had taken care of Josephine's diamonds. He had the face to tell me that he did not know if there were any, that he had received a box, but that he had given the key to the Archduchess [Christina] on his arrival." Now we know that when the Queen was about to leave for Varennes she had her diamonds taken to Mercy so that he could give them to her sister. Marie Antoinette, then, was definitely "Josephine."

However—and it is this which gives rise to M. Henry Valloton's mistake—there must have been a second Josephine. The correspondence book shows that he wrote "to Josephine" to ask her to make "a straw hive." Obviously this could not be the Queen. Mrs. Sullivan, one of the Swede's mistresses, had a chambermaid called Josephine. Fersen sometimes lived on the same floor as the servant in the house belonging to Craufurd, Mrs. Sullivan's protector. What was this Josephine to Axel? Apparently no more than "the obliging friend" who even undertook to deliver letters from Fersen to her master, witness these words in the private diary: "Wrote to Craufurd by Josephine."

Axel, then, was in continuous correspondence with Marie Antoinette. These letters have disappeared. About sixty letters addressed to Fersen by Marie Antoinette had been preserved at the castle of Stafsund in Sweden. A grand-nephew of Axel, the Baron Klinckowström, published them in 1878, but the letters were incomplete, whole sentences being replaced by dots. According to the Baron, Fersen himself, or else his brother Fabian, had crossed out certain lines to make them illegible.

According to Fersen's grand-nephew, "when the Comte de Fersen had answered these letters they were sent to the King of Sweden so that from the Queen's remarks he could judge of the political situation and its dangers. But so that the King of Sweden might not be tempted to challenge some of the Queen's expressions on delicate points Fersen, through his erasures, rendered all indiscretion impossible. These are perfectly adequate reasons for Fersen to have concealed by erasures certain sentences in the Queen of France's letters. The friends of that noble martyr will find them quite sufficient to dispel all malicious conjecture . . ."

Very few friends of "that noble martyr" found them sufficient. The famous rows of dots indicating erased passages have been closely studied. For example, would Marie Antoinette talk of political questions at the beginning or end of the letters, in between affectionate phrases? When she writes: "How is your health? I am sure you are not looking after yourself and you are wrong . . . (erased passage) . . .; as for myself I am bearing up better than I ought," would she have slipped in remarks likely to offend Gustavus III? And when, later, Marie Antoinette wrote: "Farewell . . . (erased passage) . . . I shall not be able to write to you again . . . (erased passage)" would the King of Sweden, on reading the complete text of the letter, have been annoyed by "some of the Queen's expressions" on political affairs placed among affectionate sentiments?

Baron Klinckowström realised how improbable his explanation was. He was afraid that modern science might succeed in deciphering the erased passages and one evening, feeling death approaching, he called to his bedside an elderly woman friend and a faithful servant—this is historical fact and not a scene out of an old melodrama—and under the Baron's eyes the faithful servant lit a fire and the old friend consigned Marie Antoinette's letters one by one to the flames.

"Now let the world know what it will, it will never know more."

Fortunately, in the house of Countess Nordenfalk, née Sophie Piper and a descendant of Axel's favourite sister, Mme Alma Söderjhelm discovered a mass of documents: the end of the private diary, the correspondence book, letters from Axel to his father, a letter from Sophie to her brother, etc. These enable one to realise that, contrary to the opinion of the historian Heidenstam, the love of Marie Antoinette and Fersen was something other than a feeling of all purity "worthy of the troubadours and the Knights of the Round Table."

Moreover, Lucien Maury had the luck to discover in the castle of Stafsund an important letter which escaped the old Baron's holocaust. It is in cipher, and Baron Klinckowström probably thought it without interest. This letter is from Marie Antoinette. It dates from the return from Varennes and has been deciphered by M. Maury. There is no erasure, and it begins: "I can tell you that I love you and indeed that is all I have time for." It ends: "Let me know to whom I should address the news I may write to you, for I cannot live without that. Farewell, most loved and loving of men. I kiss you with all my heart." These kisses are not an exception. "Farewell, my dear Rignon," she ended on another occasion—this was her name for him—"I kiss you tenderly."

M. Henry Valloton, for whom Fersen is "the pattern of the discreet knight deeply devoted to his lady," writes in this connection that "epistolary embraces were customary at that time. The Baron Stedingk, Swedish Ambassador in Moscow, sends kisses to Fersen, his old friend and comrade of the American war; Fersen kisses von Taube; Louis XV gives the accolade to the future King of Sweden at their first meeting in Paris; the Comte de Provence kisses Gustavus III; Lafayette 'kisses with all his heart' General Bouillé, whom in fact he cordially detested. It is needless to insist," he concludes, "on the poverty of such a 'proof.'"

M. Valloton merely gives examples of embraces between men—men kissed each other easily by letter—but "I kiss you tenderly," when it is a question of a Queen of France writing to a colonel in the Light Dragoons is, if not a proof, at least an indication all the more disturbing as it is coupled with other presumptions.

Alma Söderjhelm wrote: "The way in which Fersen received the rumours which circulated about Marie Antoinette is very significant. Would he in 1791 have noted that 'it is said the Q. sleeps with Barnave' as being something in itself quite possible unless he had reasons which forced him to admit this possibility?" Mme Söderjhelm further relates that "when, after Marie Antoinette's death, he went to one of his estates in Sweden, which, in its time, had been given by Queen Hedvig Eleonora to her lover, Count Gyllenstierna, he made a note of this fact and added that 'the parallel' made him even more attached to this estate."

There is, too, the famous *resté là* (stayed there).

On the evening of Monday, 13 February 1792, the Swede, disguised, managed to gain entrance to the Tuileries, where the Queen was a prisoner of the Revolution. One can read in his diary: "*Allé chez elle, passé par mon chemin ordinaire; peur des gard(es) nat (ionnaux) son logement à merveille, pas vu le Roi.*" (Went to her by my usual road; afraid of the National Guards, her room wonderful, did not see the King.) There follow two words crossed out. Mme Alma Söderjhelm considers that "in spite of the erasure one can see that the crossed out words are *resté là*" and that, indeed, it emerges from the context that the Swede did not leave the Tuileries until the following evening. M. Valloton was able to submit the page of the diary to experts. "For the sake of clarity," he writes, "let us summarise the conclusions: the Swedish Institute admits, without prejudice, that the erased text *appears* to be *resté là* and the Director of the Swedish Institute *has the impression* that this reconstruction of the text *might well* correspond to the reality." At all events, I am of the same opinion as my eminent colleague when he writes that this "*resté là*" in no way constitutes a proof of adultery. Fersen may have spent the night in the château through fear of the National Guards, but elsewhere than in Marie Antoinette's bed.

Of course the morning ballet laid down by etiquette had never found Axel Fersen in the Queen's bedroom, but at Trianon, as at Versailles, Marie Antoinette was able to escape from her "cloud of enemies." In Besenval's memoirs we read that one March morning in 1778 Marie Antoinette summoned the Swiss Baron to discuss with him the duel between the Comte d'Artois and the Duc de Bourbon. "I began by going to the King's *lever*. I had hardly entered his cabinet when I saw Campan, the Queen's secretary, who motioned to me with his head. I went to him and he said, without appearing to speak to me: 'Follow me, but at a distance, and let no one notice.'

"He made me pass through several doors and by staircases which were quite unknown to me and when we were out of sight and hearing he said: 'You must admit, Monsieur, that this looks odd, but it is not what it seems, for the husband is in the secret.' 'My dear Campan,' I replied, 'when one has grey hair and wrinkles one does not expect a young and pretty Queen of twenty to have one brought through the back ways for anything but business.' 'She is waiting for you,' he replied very impatiently. 'I have already sent twice to your house and I looked for you in all the places I thought I might find you.'

"As he finished speaking we were under the roofs, in a dirty corridor and opposite a mean little door. He inserted a key and having pushed vainly several times, exclaimed: 'Oh heavens! the bolt is shot on the other side. Wait for me here. I shall have to go round.'

"He returned shortly and said that the Queen was very annoyed, that she could not see me at that moment because it was nearly time for Mass, but that she asked me to come back to the same place at three o'clock.

"I did so and Campan introduced me by a side entrance into a room with a billiard table, which I knew from having often played there with the Queen, then into another room, which I did not know, simply but comfortably furnished. I was astonished, not that the Queen should have wanted these facilities, but that she had dared to procure them."

In her Memoirs Mme Campan, while trying to defend the Queen's virtue, confirms the accuracy of this account and gives details of the use of this lodging, which was intended for Her Majesty's Lady of Honour "in case of confinement or sickness." When Marie Antoinette was not unwell she appropriated "this very small antechamber, this bedroom and this sitting room, situated above her private apartments."

We must not leave Mme Campan without reproducing the "confession" of Georges Laguerre, which appeared in the *Intermédiaire* in March 1906: "My family was very friendly with M. Jean-François Barrière. François Barrière, publicist and man of letters, born in 1786, had published Mme Campan's Memoirs in 1823. M. Barrière died in

August 1868 in the Rue de Monceau, where he lived opposite my parents. My father, Léon Laguerre, a doctor of law and an enthusiast for *belles-lettres* and history, often used to go and talk with M. Barrière and explore his very fine library.

"One day, about 1867 (my father has often told me of it), François Barrière lent him, on his promising to return it the same evening, a small manuscript, a few pages only, by Mme Campan, which was not included in the Memoirs. My father read it with great interest. Mme Campan said that horrible calumnies had attributed many lovers to Queen Marie Antoinette, that they were pure invention, against which she protested, but that, since she was on this delicate subject, she had to admit that she was aware that the Queen had had a partiality for the young Chevalier de Fersen. She pleaded extenuating circumstances on behalf of her unhappy mistress. . . .

"Faithful to his word, my father returned the precious pages that same evening. Shortly afterwards François Barrière died at the age of 82. My father made the inventory of his papers and set about winding up his estate. He had not forgotten the famous unpublished fragment of Mme Campan's Memoirs and not finding it, he asked Mme Barrière, who was a very distinguished woman and an inspector of schools in the city of Paris, what had become of the manuscript. Pointing to the fireplace of the study, she replied that shortly before her husband's death they had together burned it there 'out of respect for the memory of Queen Marie Antoinette.' "

After reading all that has been written on this delicate question can one really come to a decision? Can one, without any reservation, believe Saint-Priest when he affirms that Marie Antoinette and Axel were lovers? Their amours must certainly have been rather limited, and as a result of this "limitation" we need hardly dwell on the hypothesis that Fersen was the father of the future Louis XVII, who was born on 27 March 1785, nine months after Axel's stay at Versailles. In any case, even had their love affair been more "extensive," "the risk of committing the crime of *lèse-dynastie*," as Pierre Audiat has very justly remarked, "would have been enough to confine Fersen, who was an ardent royalist, to his role of a limited lover."

Limited as was his love affair, Axel none the less considered himself bound to Marie Antoinette. This "burning spirit in a shell of ice" would undoubtedly have many more adventures, but Axel always refused to commit his life. His two conquests in Italy, Emily and Elizabeth, whiled away their time far from the man who had crossed their life. Both Englishwomen would have liked their Italian adventure to end in marriage, but Fersen refused. He dealt first of all with Emily and wrote to her "that it could never be and must no longer be thought of." He charged Lord Cowper to console his sister. During the winter, from the castle of Gripsholm, where the Swedish court was, he replied to Elizabeth Foster, stating the reason for his refusal, in his notebook, in two words, which he himself underlined: "Declared everything."

Axel thought only of returning to France. During the winter of 1784-5 the talk was all of a possible war with the Low Countries, a war in which France, and consequently Axel's regiment, would be involved. Moreover, the fighting would have been against Austria, and from a distance he could imagine Marie Antoinette's distress.

Once more it was the Mouths of the Scheldt which threatened to set Europe aflame. In the previous year Joseph II had drawn nearer to Catherine II, with a view to planning the dismemberment of the Ottoman Empire: this year he wanted to let some air into Antwerp. The Netherlands had been in possession of the Mouths of the Scheldt since 1460—in fact they still are—and they kept the estuary closed, much to the fury of the Emperor, who would have liked France to intervene with the Dutch. Louis XVI and Vergennes, having been at peace with England for a year, knew perfectly well that to make the Scheldt an Austrian river would displease both London and Berlin. So when on 1 September 1784 Marie Antoinette, at Mercy's instigation, brought up the question of the Scheldt with Vergennes, the Minister prudently replied that "the court of Versailles could not lay down the law for the Dutch." Learning of this, Joseph II was extremely annoyed and wrote to his sister: "It is quite certain that M. de Vergennes' conduct is hardly calculated to strengthen, or indeed even to maintain, the bonds of alliance and policy which united us."

Not maintain the Alliance! All Maria Theresa's work would crumble, and consequently Marie Antoinette began a campaign against Vergennes. "I spoke openly to the King about it more than once. Occasionally he replied with anger, and as he is incapable of discussion I was not able to persuade him that his Minister was deceived or was deceiving him."

An event took place which enabled Marie Antoinette to revive the affair. As the Dutch continued to refuse to free the Scheldt estuary, Joseph II ordered one of his ships to leave Antwerp and to force a passage. On 4 October the Austrian ship, a brigantine called *Le Louis*, was fired on not far from the mouth of the river, opposite Saftingen.

The Emperor mobilised an army of 80,000 men to avenge the outrage, and to complete matters the United Provinces asked for Louis XVI's protection. Mercy and Joseph II insisted that the Queen should act "energetically," and the events at the time of the Bavarian affair were to be repeated, with all the more serious results as the King, according to Mercy, no longer had "any credit in the affairs of State, as he brings to them no energy and very little knowledge." Consequently we have the spectacle of Vergennes dictating to Louis XVI a letter for Joseph II in which the King seemed to be trying to make excuses for the Dutch. Marie Antoinette considered the letter "impossible," and did all she could to obtain another letter from her husband which he would write by himself. Louis XVI, who had a horror of scenes, gave way and made his brother-in-law an offer of mediation in a letter which was delivered to the Emperor on 6 November. Without waiting for the reply Vergennes, backed up by the Council of Ministers, decided on 12 November to send a "very stiff note" to Vienna. This time France put all the blame on Joseph II and announced a concentration of troops on the Netherlands frontier. The King signed the note on 15 November. Marie Antoinette made her husband another scene and succeeded in having the "odious dispatch" delayed for five days.

Joseph II was no less furious, but proposed a curious peace offer: the Elector of Bavaria should cede his State to Austria; in exchange he would receive the Netherlands, and the quarrel over the Mouths of the Scheldt would end.

Louis XVI and Vergennes distrusted this scheme. The Minister was faithful to the old principle of Henri II: "Keep Germany's affairs in as much difficulty as possible." They did not care for the idea of seeing Germany installed all the way from Dunkirk to Bâle, and so they found a compromise. They would agree to the scheme on condition that Joseph II obtained the consent of the King of Prussia. This was to condemn the scheme to failure, for Frederick II would never accept.

Discussions began again and the threat of war became more urgent. Two army corps under the command of the Prince de Condé encamped in Flanders and on the Rhine. Marie Antoinette redoubled her activity.

During all this time, it must be sadly admitted, she was much more her brother's Minister than Queen of France. Joseph II sent her two letters by the same courier—one she would show to her husband and one she must keep secret. In the latter, dated 19 November, he urgently advised her "to take no step without the authorisation of the Comte de Mercy," and Marie Antoinette obeyed. She even ran counter to the French point of view, which was in favour of gaining some advantage from the affair. Breteuil talked of the cession to France of Luxembourg and Namur; "the Queen gave him a rough handling," writes Mercy, and the Minister held his peace.

It is somewhat embarrassing to read the congratulations Mercy bestowed on his master's sister for her "true zeal" in the service of His Austrian Majesty. Almost condescendingly he acknowledged that "in the present situation the Queen has been less unsuccessful than in any other, in her attempt to be of use to her august brother." Urged by her monitor, who was quite shameless about it, Marie Antoinette kept Ambassador Mercy informed about what went on in the King's Council and continued to hold up the courier. "All things considered," she wrote to Mercy, "I shall not give the King his letter [from Joseph II] until late this evening or tomorrow morning." She would then see her husband before he had time to confer with Vergennes. She thus obtained promises from Louis XVI which were in contradiction with the Council's decisions.

The following day there was a violent scene between Marie Antoinette and Vergennes in the presence of the King, who was very vexed at the turn taken by the discussion. The Queen, moreover, was only half successful and on the 31st she made her excuses to Joseph II: "M. de Vergennes's delays and difficulties would make you impatient, my dear brother. They would be much worse if I had not spoken to him in a way that had its effect."

Joseph II was impatient, in fact, and demanded a solution. A month later he wrote to his sister: "I insist on it and shall not cease my requests."

The Emperor's courier crossed that of the Queen. He carried a letter in which Marie Antoinette declared: "You certainly have a right to complain about the methods of this country. Remember what you have seen and what you know of it." "This country" is indeed the language of an Archduchess. Marie Antoinette finally obtained what she wanted: in a note France promised not to declare war on Austria in the event of a conflict between Joseph II and the United Provinces and to confine itself to sending "an army to watch the frontier."

The Dutch, feeling themselves abandoned, gave in. They would send an embassy to Vienna and apologise for firing on the brigantine. They would also pay a reasonable indemnity, and France, which had had nothing to do with the firing, promised to pay a share.

This was the beginning of the legend of the cases of gold crossing the frontier and of the famous 200 million sent by Marie Antoinette to her brother to enable him to make war against the Turks.

The Parisians knew that France's disgraceful attitude in the affair of the Netherlands and the tithe paid to the Emperor were both the Queen's doing. Henceforth they always called her the "Austrian," a nickname she was to keep right up to the scaffold.

In the spring of 1785 it was quite usual to hear the public say: "We are going to Saint Cloud to see the waters and the Austrian." For since 20 February Marie Antoinette was the owner of the château of Saint Cloud, which the King had bought from the Duc d'Orléans for the attractive sum of six million. One may guess the cries and murmurs of the opposition—for one can already use that term: "So the mania for English gardens is beginning again!" "M. Mique is preparing plans for enlarging it, estimated at several millions!"

And a councillor exclaimed in Parliament: "It is both impolitic and immoral for palaces to belong to a Queen of France."

When, on 24 May, Marie Antoinette made her entry into Paris after giving birth to her second son, she received no applause whatsoever. Fersen, who had just arrived in Paris, wrote sadly to King Gustavus: "The Queen was received very coldly. There was not a single cry of welcome, but a complete silence."

On returning to Versailles she wept for a long time in Louis XVI's arms. For the first time she realised how deep was the gulf separating her from the French, but the motives for this icy reception escaped her.

"What have I done to them? What have I done to them?" she asked through her sobs.

10

❦

The First Thunderclap

MARIE ANTOINETTE WEPT, but a very important event soon absorbed her attention and dried her tears—she was to rehearse the part of Rosina in *The Barber of Seville*. With complete lack of intelligence she deliberately chose a play by the author of the *Marriage of Figaro*, which had been prohibited by the King, a play by M. Caron de Beaumarchais, of whom Louis XVI said: "That man undermines everything that should be respected in a government."

But the Queen's coterie, who loved to scoff, had had the *Marriage* performed at Vaudreuil's, and thanks to Marie Antoinette the play was given on 27 April 1784 in Paris, where its triumph is well known.

"There is only one thing madder than my play," said Beaumarchais himself, "and that is its success!" There was something madder still— the delight of the great lords at seeing themselves castigated, and the Queen's intervention in the affair.

At Trianon Marie Antoinette was to be Rosina, "the prettiest and most provoking little thing," Vaudreuil was to play Almaviva and Artois Figaro. There were rehearsals every day and the performance was fixed for 19 August.

On 12 July 1785 the Queen was at Versailles when the crown jeweller, Böhmer, arrived, bringing her a diamond epaulette and buckles, a gift of the King on the occasion of the baptism of the Duc d'Angoulême. At the same time the jeweller gave Marie Antoinette a note from his partner Bassenge.

Madame,

We are filled with happiness and venture to think that the last arrangements proposed to us, which we have carried out with zeal and respect, are a further proof of our submission and devotion to Your Majesty's orders, and we have real satisfaction in thinking that the most beautiful set of diamonds in existence will belong to the greatest and best of Queens.

Marie Antoinette looked up from her reading. She seemed not to understand a word of this jumble. What was it all about? But Böhmer had vanished. The arrival of the Controller General had caused the jeweller to disappear. Marie Antoinette ordered him to be sent for so that he might give her the key to the mystery. Perhaps he was still in the Gallery—but he could not be found. The Queen read the note to Mme Campan, who could not understand it either. And yet, said the Queen laughing, she was so good at solving the riddles in the *Mercure*. This Böhmer must certainly be mad. In 1774 and on several other occasions he had begged Marie Antoinette to buy an extraordinary necklace *"en esclavage,"* which incidentally was rather ugly, like a collar for a circus horse, made up of 540 admirable diamonds. The Queen had refused to buy this 1,600,000-livre breastplate, and Böhmer, who had sunk all his fortune in the necklace, had even thrown himself at her feet and made a ridiculous scene, threatening to "go and throw himself into the river." Marie Antoinette had told him sharply to stand up and not to give way to these "despairing contortions."

This affair of the unsold necklace had evidently deranged poor Böhmer's mind. "That man exists to torture me. He has always some mad scheme in mind! I do not think I shall make use of him any more. If I want my diamonds reset I shall use my valet-jeweller, who will have no ambition to sell me a carat."

A lighted candle stood near, and Marie Antoinette put the note to it. "It is not worth keeping!"

This apparently insignificant gesture is dramatic and was to have terrible consequences. For this brief moment, the most poignant of the drama, as Funck-Brentano has remarked, was the only instant when the Queen was in contact with the intrigue of the necklace.

On 1 August Madame Campan left for her country house, where she had a visit from Böhmer, who was "very worried at having no reply to his note." The waiting-woman tried to make him understand that there was no hope of the Queen changing her mind. She did not want to buy any more diamonds.

"If I had any money to spend," Marie Antoinette had told her recently, "I would much rather enlarge my estate at Saint Cloud." And she had even asked Mme Campan to take the first opportunity of telling the jewellers so.

"But," exclaimed Böhmer, who seemed astounded, "to whom should I address myself for a reply to the letter I presented the Queen?"

"To no one! Her Majesty burned your petition without even having understood what you were trying to say."

"Ah! Madame, that is not possible. The Queen knows that she must give me some money."

"Money, M. Böhmer? But we settled your last accounts for the Queen some time ago."

"Are you not in the secret, Madame? It is not a settlement if one ruins a man by not paying him when one owes him more than 1,500,000 francs."

"Have you lost your wits? For what object could the Queen possibly owe you such an exorbitant amount?"

"For my necklace, Madame," replied Böhmer coldly.

"What!" said Madame Campan. "That necklace you vainly worried the Queen about for several years?"

"But the Queen wanted to have it and caused it to be purchased by the Cardinal de Rohan."

"You are quite wrong," exclaimed Madame Campan. "The Queen has not spoken once to the Cardinal since he returned from Vienna. There is no man less in favour at court."

"It is you who are wrong, Madame," retorted Böhmer. "She so well receives him in private that she handed His Eminence 30,000 francs, which were given to me on account and which she took, in his presence, from the little Sèvres porcelain desk near the fireplace in her boudoir."

"Was it the Cardinal who told you that?"

"Yes, Madame, the Cardinal himself."

On Madame Campan's advice Böhmer hastened to Trianon, but Marie Antoinette was rehearsing her rôle as Rosina.

"He is mad. I have nothing to say to him and do not wish to see him."

But two or three days later, when she learned from Madame Campan exactly what Böhmer wanted, she was stupefied. "The whole thing was a mystery to her. She could not see her way through it." She quickly summoned the jeweller, who came at once and began his extravagant and incredible tale.

The jeweller's confused remarks involved only Cardinal Louis de Rohan. After the blessing at Strasbourg Marie Antoinette had often heard about this curious Eminence, who knew women so well—even too well. His tastes had driven the Empress Maria Theresa to despair when he had been sent to her as Ambassador at the time of Mme du Barry's reign. In nearly every one of her letters to her daughter and to Mercy she had mentioned the licentious prelate. "All our young and plain women are bewitched by him," sighed the Empress and she remarked that the court ladies went eagerly to the dinners given at small tables in the Embassy.

Scandalised, Marie Antoinette's mother saw the "young and plain women" dance and flirt with this priest, who frequented masked balls, or went hunting in lay dress and fired 1,328 shots from his gun in one day. "He is stuffed with extremely improper remarks, which ill beseem his position as an ecclesiastic and a Minister, and which he impudently lets out to everyone he meets . . . His turbulent suite is exactly the same, a mixed lot of people without merit or morals." After two years of his Embassy Maria Theresa could no longer put up with this "incorrigible" man.

At Versailles Rohan was supported by d'Aiguillon and at Vienna by Joseph II, whom the prelate amused "by his follies, chatter and buffoonery." Even Kaunitz got on very well with this Ambassador, who "did not disturb him and was submissive to him in every way." Maria Theresa had to wait for her son-in-law's accession to see an end put to this "horrible and shameful embassy." She then dreaded the possible havoc which might be wreaked on her daughter by this man who was so "supple, flattering and eternally amusing." In fact, all through 1776 Rohan had tried to find "opportunities to ingratiate himself with the Queen," but Marie Antoinette had refused to receive the Cardinal, for whom she had a pronounced antipathy.

When he was still at Vienna he had written to d'Aiguillon: "I did indeed see Maria Theresa weep over the misfortunes of oppressed Poland, but this Princess, who is a past mistress of the art of concealing her thoughts, seems to me to be able to cry at will. In one hand she holds a handkerchief to dry her tears and with the other she seizes the sword, so as to be the third sharer." The Minister had given the letter to the du Barry, who had read it aloud at one of her suppers. Marie Antoinette had heard of this and had been all the more wounded since the epigram was true. Would Rohan ever manage to get that unfortunate letter forgotten?

"Although my daughter holds the Coadjutor of Strasbourg at a distance, I think her quite capable of changing her mind, either as a result of her incapacity for reflection or from her habit of yielding to the whims of her favourites of both sexes."

Fortunately Prince Louis had had to go back to Strasbourg, where he had succeeded his uncle. But he might be returning to court, as he was certain to succeed Cardinal de la Roche-Aymon, the Grand Almoner of France, who had one foot in the grave. Louis XVI had let this promise be forced from him by the Comtesse de Marsan, Rohan's cousin. When at the request of Marie Antoinette, who had been well coached by Mercy, the King wanted to take back this stupid promise, Mme de Marsan had protested loudly and reminded the King of his word.

"My cousin," sighed Louis XVI, "I know I promised to make your cousin Grand Almoner, but it is now impossible."

The discussion became bitter. The Comtesse would not give up her point.

"I cannot do it now," Louis XVI almost implored. "I have given the Queen my word."

"I respect the Queen's wishes, Sire, but Your Majesty cannot have two words. The Queen would not wish that the King, in order to please her, should do what the threat of death would not force from the meanest gentleman! I therefore take the respectful liberty of assuring Your Majesty that having published the promise he gave me I should find myself urgently compelled also to make known that the King has broken it merely to please the Queen."

He had to give way. And so, on the death of Mgr de la Roche-Aymon, M. le Prince de Rohan, Bishop of Strasbourg, Cardinal of the Holy Church and member of the Académie Française, became Grand Almoner of France. He was present at the King's *lever*, officiated at all the great feasts at court, and had just baptised the little Duc de Normandie, but Marie Antoinette never addressed one word to him. It was hardly likely, then, that the Queen would have asked this man to be her intermediary in the purchase of a necklace.

Another name kept on coming up in Böhmer's story, that of "Mme la Comtesse de la Motte-Valois," who claimed to be descended from Henry II. Marie Antoinette sat up. There were no more princes of the Valois family and no lady at court with that illustrious name. She had never heard of this woman. But Böhmer explained how he and his partner had been put in touch with Mme de la Motte. He knew a certain Louis-François Achet, attorney in the court of appeal, whose son-in-law, the lawyer Laporte, was friendly with the Comtesse. According to the attorney the lady was in favour with the Queen, and she had even shown the lawyer letters written to her by Marie Antoinette.

"We would willingly give 1,000 louis to anyone who could sell the necklace," the jewellers had said, seeing a ray of hope.

This was at the end of November 1784. Urged on by his father-in-law, M. Laporte, who was riddled with debts, had spoken to Mme de la Motte about the necklace and the difficulty the jewellers were in. If they did not sell this regal piece they would be ruined, as they had borrowed heavily in order to assemble the stones. Since the Comtesse was in favour with the Queen why should she not intercede for them?

"Have you seen this necklace?" Mme de la Motte had asked Laporte.

"It is a marvel, Madame! The crown jewellers have worked on it for years and from the value of the stones alone it is a treasure."

Yet Mme de la Motte did not seem in a hurry to admire the treasure. It was not until 29 December that she went to see "the Böhmers," as they were called, and appeared to think the necklace very fine, in spite of the ungraceful heaviness of its setting. On 21 January the Comtesse arrived with Maître Achet. She had come to inform the jewellers that a "very great nobleman," acting "in the Queen's name," would perhaps acquire the necklace.

The jewellers nearly fell over themselves thanking her, and offered her a trinket, which she refused. On 24 January the Comtesse reappeared at seven o'clock in the morning to announce a visit from the Cardinal de Rohan, the "very great nobleman" mentioned four days earlier.

A few hours later His Eminence arrived at the Böhmers' house, saw the necklace, asked the price, which was 320 million present-day francs, and "did not conceal his intention to negotiate, not for himself, but for a person whose name he might get permission to mention."

On 29 January the Cardinal proposed to buy the necklace from the Böhmers for the agreed price of 1,600,000 livres, to be settled in four payments spread over two years. The necklace was to be delivered on 1 February and the first payment made on 1 August. The Cardinal wrote out these conditions himself and they were signed by Charles Böhmer and Paul Bassenge. On 1 February the two jewellers received a hurried note from the Grand Almoner, asking them to bring him the necklace. Carrying the case, the Böhmers hastened to the Hôtel de Rohan.

"The jewels are for the Queen," the Cardinal told them and showed them a sheet containing details of the transaction signed on 29 January by the jewellers and written by the Cardinal. At the side of each article was the word "approved" and at the bottom was the signature "Marie Antoinette of France."

"Take a copy of it."

The jewellers copied the sheet "without the peculiarity of the signature raising any doubt in their minds" and they left the Cardinal the jewel case to be presented to the Queen.

After that they had again met Mme la Comtesse, had invited her to dinner to show their gratitude and had themselves gone to the Rue Neuve Saintes Filles to a meal given to them by "the Queen's friend" in her house.

On 1 August Böhmer and his partner had received a visit from the Cardinal. His Eminence did not bring the first payment of 400,000 livres, but on behalf of the Queen asked them to grant a delay of three months. Mme de la Motte had on the previous day brought the Cardinal a letter signed Marie Antoinette and telling him of her financial difficulties. The Queen promised to pay 700,000 livres on 1 October and meanwhile paid 35,000 livres as interest on the debt. This sum had been given to the Cardinal by Mme de la Motte, and His Eminence had the money on him. The jewellers had taken the matter rather badly, as they had obligations to pay their creditors, among them M. de Saint-James, who was pressing them. The Cardinal had promised to take the matter up with the Queen and on this 1 August things had gone no further.

Two days later, to the astonishment of the jewellers, Mme de la Motte had summoned Bassenge.

"You have been deceived. The written guarantee the Cardinal possesses bears a forged signature, but the Prince is rich enough and will pay."

Böhmer had then seen Mme Campan, who had opened his eyes, and then, with beating heart, had gone to see the Cardinal and told him of his interview with Marie Antoinette's waiting-woman.

"The Queen said she did not know what we were talking about and that the whole thing confused her." In his distress the jeweller had added: "Are you sure your intermediary has not deceived you both?"

The Cardinal had hesitated and then replied: "If I hesitate to answer, it is not because my answer is not ready. I am merely wondering if I ought to tell you everything." And after a silence he had added: "I ought and I can. If I tell you that I have dealt directly with the Queen will you be satisfied?"

"Yes, Monseigneur."

"Well then, I assure you that I have dealt directly with the Queen and I affirm it by raising my right arm as a sign of affirmation."

The Grand Almoner had then claimed to have seen Marie Antoinette take the money out of a "small desk of Sèvres porcelain." Moreover, the Cardinal had given a similar assurance to M. de Saint-James, asking him to wait before exacting payment from Böhmer of the money due to him.

On hearing this tale Marie Antoinette was thunderstruck by this monstrous audacity. Even if she had wanted to buy the necklace, were not the jewellers made suspicious by the purchase being carried out without the King's knowledge? They were not, for in June 1776, without telling His Majesty, the Queen had had two bracelets made for 300,000 livres in exchange for which the jewellers had bought back some stones cheaply. Moreover, this had not been enough, particularly as there were also earrings to be paid for, and Marie Antoinette had been obliged to confess her purchase to the King. Mercy had told Maria Theresa about it: "The monarch received this proposal with his habitual equanimity, merely permitting himself to say kindly that he was not surprised that the Queen had no money, in view of her taste for diamonds. After this remark the 2,000 louis were given to her the following day." The Empress had declared that this event "filled her with alarm for the future," but the "madcap" was not frightened, and had said lightly to the Abbé de Vermond: "Now my bracelets have got as far as Vienna!"

"Does the Empress sound angry?"

"A bit. See for yourself," Marie Antoinette had contented herself with replying as she handed the letter to the Abbé, and she had not given it another thought.

The jeweller remembered very well, too, that in the same year the Queen had bought chandelier earrings for 600,000 livres, also without the King's knowledge, and that she had finally had to speak to her husband, who had once more paid the debt by four annual instalments from his own purse.

Marie Antoinette felt the ground giving way under her. But only a few days ago she had said to Mme Campan: "I do not like diamonds any more. I shall never buy another."

That might be, but she had liked them very much. The jewellers were still living in the time when the Queen adored them. And so Böhmer and Bassenge had been no more surprised than the Cardinal when Mme de la Motte had told them that the Queen wanted secretly to buy the necklace she had officially refused.

When her first emotion was over Marie Antoinette must have thought that the affair was no more serious than that of Mme Cahuet de Villers, wife of a treasurer of the King's Household, who in 1777 had made use of her name to get money out of various people. She too had claimed to be frequently received by the Queen. She too had written, or caused to be written, what claimed to be a request from the Queen for 200,000 livres, and she had found a farmer-general, one Béranger, who was delighted to render a service to Marie Antoinette so as to obtain "the honours of the court."

But was the Cardinal another Béranger, or had he appropriated the necklace himself? Was he a fool or a swindler?

According to Marie Antoinette, who wrote of it to her brother, the Cardinal, "who had an urgent need for money, had thought he would be able to pay the jewellers at the appointed time without anything being discovered."

On 9 August 1785 Marie Antoinette still knew nothing of the notorious story of the grove where she was supposed to have given Rohan a secret interview, and so she wanted this "strange romance," as she called it, to be cleared up as soon as possible. She asked Böhmer to draw up an account of it, which the jeweller brought on 12 August. It was at once made known to the King, and on 15 August, Assumption Day and the Queen's feast day, Marie Antoinette, Louis XVI, the Baron de Breteuil, Minister of the King's Household, and M. de Miromesnil, Keeper of the Seals, met in conference in the King's cabinet room. The Queen wanted the Cardinal arrested. "He has used my name like a vile and clumsy forgerer." It was a swindle. The strongest proof was in the flagrant lie made by the Cardinal to the Böhmers and Saint-James, that solemn oath which the Prince of the Church had dared take to them. How had he dared to raise his arm and affirm that he had dealt directly with the Queen?

Miromesnil counselled prudence, but Breteuil supported Marie Antoinette. He detested the Cardinal, whom he had replaced in Vienna and who since then had never stopped making fun of him. According to Breteuil, the Cardinal was riddled with debts and had invented the whole plot in order to lay hands on the necklace. Like Miromesnil Louis XVI considered that "Rohan's rank and family entitled him to be heard before being arrested," but Marie Antoinette displayed such exasperation that he sent immediately for the Cardinal, who was with the *grandes entrées* in the Council Room while waiting to go to the chapel.

It was eleven o'clock. Wearing a scarlet watered silk soutane and lace rochet, the Cardinal entered the room. The King questioned him.

"My cousin, did you buy diamonds from Böhmer?"

"Yes, Sire."

"What did you do with them?"

"I thought that they had been given to the Queen."

"Who gave you this commission?"

"A lady called the Comtesse de la Motte-Valois, who had handed me a letter from the Queen, and I thought that by carrying out this commission I was paying my court to Her Majesty."

Here the Queen interrupted him. "How could you believe, Monsieur, you to whom I have not spoken for eight years, that I had chosen you for these negotiations, and through the intermediary of such a woman?"

"I can see that I have been cruelly deceived," replied the Cardinal. "I shall pay for the necklace. My desire to please Your Majesty blinded my eyes. I saw no trick and I am very sorry."

The Cardinal did not dare look at the Queen, who was red with anger. He took a wallet from his pocket; it contained the contract signed "Marie Antoinette of France."

"This is neither the Queen's writing nor her signature," exclaimed the King. "How could a Prince of the House of Rohan and a Grand

Almoner of France think that the Queen would sign 'Marie Antoinette of France'? Everyone knows that Queens sign only their Christian names. Explain all this mystery to me," continued the King. "I do not want to find you guilty; I should like you to be justified. Tell me the meaning of all these negotiations with Böhmer, these assurances and these notes."

The Cardinal was as pale as death; they thought he would fall. He clung to the table. "Sire, I am too distressed to reply to Your Majesty in a way which . . ."

"Calm yourself, M. le Cardinal, and go into my room. You will find paper, pen and ink there. Write down what you have to tell me."

The report he handed the King a quarter-of-an-hour later was as confused as it could be. One thing was clear: "A woman called De Valois had persuaded him that the necklace was to be acquired for the Queen, and that woman had deceived him."

"Where is this woman?" asked the King.

"Sire, I do not know."

"Have you the necklace?"

"It is in the hands of that woman."

The Baron de Breteuil read the report written by the Böhmers, and then the King asked: "Where are the alleged authorisations written and signed by the Queen and which are mentioned in the report?"

"Sire, I have them; they are forged."

"I know quite well they are forged!"

"I will bring them to Your Majesty."

The King looked at him with contempt. "I must warn you that you are to be arrested."

The Grand Almoner paled. "Ah! Sire, I shall always obey Your Majesty's orders, but let him spare me the pain of being arrested in my pontifical robes in the eyes of the whole court."

"It must be so!"

Rohan persisted, and recalled that his cousin, Mme de Marsan, had brought up the King. At this recollection Louis XVI was about to weaken, but Marie Antoinette's eyes were full of tears, and he made up his mind.

"Monsieur, I shall try to console your relatives as best I may. I should be glad if you could exculpate yourself. I am doing my duty as a King and a husband."

Pushing the Cardinal in front of him, Breteuil went to the door opening on to the Salon de la Pendule. All the *grandes entrées* were there, while the rest of the court were massed in the Council Room, the State Room, the *Œil-de-Bœuf* and the Long Gallery. A voice—that of Breteuil addressing the captain of the Bodyguards—made everyone jump.

"Arrest M. le Cardinal!"

If a bomb had exploded in the Hall of Mirrors it would not have caused more fright and stupefaction. Only the Cardinal retained his calm, and standing at the entrance to the gallery, he wrote a note to his *alter ego,* the Abbé Georgel, asking him to burn all the letters contained in the "red portfolio."

These were the notes which the Grand Almoner had imagined were written to him by the Queen and which had been delivered to him by Mme de la Motte.

There was a considerable scandal. "Only in France," wrote the Archduke Leopold to his brother Joseph II, "could one see a Cardinal-Archbishop, Grand Almoner to the King, without religion or morals arrested as a forger of letters, a swindler and a cheat." "It is incredible!" he also exclaimed. The Emperor was of the same opinion. "I should not have thought him capable of such roguery and such a sinister trick as he is accused of." One can see that Marie Antoinette's two brothers had doubts about the Cardinal's guilt. They did not dare ask if their sister was entirely unconnected with the intrigue, but in Paris they had no such reticence.

All unconscious, Marie Antoinette heaved a sigh of relief. "As far as I am concerned," she wrote to her brother, "I am delighted at the thought of not having to hear this wretched business talked of any more."

For her everything was finished, and on the day after the accusation, while the Cardinal, who had spent the night at home, was on his way to the Bastille, Marie Antoinette took the road to Trianon, where the final rehearsals of the *Barber* were awaiting her.

As she listened to her partner, Don Basilio, repeating his famous speech on calumny, did she realise that the scene might be a dramatic representation of her own case? Yesterday, as the Comtesse de la Marck said, "the Queen was going to the Opera and to the Comédie, piling up debts, canvassing for lawsuits, covering herself with feathers and pompoms and caring nothing for anybody." Yesterday calumny had been no more than a "faint noise, skimming the ground like a swallow before the storm." But today the Queen's name was to be dragged in the mud, coupled with those of a prelate "without religion or morals," a forger, a cheat and a prostitute. Calumny then would be seen to "raise its head, hiss, swell and grow before one's eyes." And this chorus of hate was to attribute the Grand Almoner of France to Marie Antoinette as a lover.

The principal accused, the Comtesse de la Motte-Valois, was at Bar-sur-Aube, where before her arrest she was given plenty of time, with the help of her friend Beugnot, Louis XVIII's future Minister, to burn the passionate letters written by the Cardinal to the Queen of France.

On the next day, 18 August, she was arrested and taken to the Bastille. It was then discovered that the prisoner was not entirely an adventuress. She really was descended from the Valois and her arms were "argent, one fess azure charged with three fleurs-de-lis or." Four generations separated her from Henry de Saint-Rémy, acknowledged son of King Henri II, and Nicole de Savigny, Dame de Saint-Rémy, but from a misalliance to misalliance the family had sunk into poverty. Jeanne's father, Baron Jacques de Saint-Rémy, had died in the poorhouse. She herself had had an unhappy childhood. Her mother, a peasant, had set up with a soldier and both of them beat the child and forced her to beg, imploring passers-by "for the sake of an orphan of the blood of the Valois." It was in this condition that a noble lady, the Marquise de Boulainvilliers, had discovered her by the side of the road leading to Passy. She was moved, and taking the child and her sister brought them up in her house, then apprenticed them and finally sent them to the convent of the Abbey of Longchamp, where only daughters of the nobility were taken. Mme de Boulainvilliers had had her protégées' genealogy established by the famous Hozier. From the end of 1776 the King granted a pension of 800 livres to his distant cousins. The two little "Princesses," as they called themselves, rewarded the Marquise for her kindness by running away from their convent to finish up in an inn at Bar-sur-Aube. A second protector, Mme de Surmont, took charge of the runaways and it was in her house that Jeanne, now a very pretty young woman, met an officer of the gendarmes called Marc-Antoine Nicolas de la Motte. The marriage was celebrated at Bar-sur-Aube on 6 June 1780 and the couple, who on their own authority had become "Comte and Comtesse de la Motte-Valois," set out to seek their fortune. The young Comtesse decided she had found it the day when Mme de Boulainvilliers, who did not bear grudges, presented her to the Cardinal de Rohan on the way from Saverne to Strasbourg.

A few months later, the "Comte," now a "supernumerary captain in Monsieur's dragoons," came with his wife to Paris. The first months were very difficult, in spite of the frequent charity of the Grand Almoner, and in spite of the visits of "military men and men of the gown," whom Mme de la Motte received while, like a well-behaved husband, the "supernumerary captain" disappeared. "The inheritor of the blood of the Valois" decided to use cunning and to faint from inanition in the antechambers of Versailles. Twice she fell in a swoon in the presence of the Queen, who did not even notice. She was no more successful in the apartments of the Comtesse d'Artois. Only Madame Elisabeth was moved when she saw this pretty girl with clear eyes sink to the ground in her "servants' hall." She had the royal pension increased to 1,500 livres, but after another swoon, possibly less well counterfeited, Louis XVI's sister suspected the truth. Mme de la Motte then transformed herself into "a promoter of business in the offices of Ministers and at court," which was almost a recognised profession. This occupation was much more paying than syncopes, as Jeanne succeeded in making people, including even the Cardinal, believe that she frequently saw the Queen, and soon affluence was reigning in the la Motte home.

The two principal accused were now behind bars. The Cardinal's defence was that he had bought the necklace in the Queen's name and that the Comtesse de la Motte had been the link between Marie Antoinette and himself. On the evening of 1 February he had gone to Versailles, where Mme de la Motte had a small property. He took with him the large case containing the necklace. Mme de la Motte was alone. "The Queen is waiting; this necklace will be given to her this evening."

A few minutes later someone announced "coming from the Queen." "From discretion" the Cardinal retired into a "half-opened" alcove and had seen a man dressed in black hand over a note and then leave the room. Mme de la Motte approached the alcove and showed the letter. It was a word from the Queen "giving orders for the box to be handed

to the bearer." The man was brought back, the jewel case handed to
him and he disappeared into the night.

"Who was that?" asked the Cardinal.

"He is attached to the Queen's Bedchamber and Music."

To these details the Comtesse de la Motte replied that the story of
the handing over of the jewel case was pure invention. "By way of
conversation" with the Cardinal she might, one day, have made allusion
to the necklace, but the prelate had replied to her "with the same indifference." "The next day, or two days later, M. de Rohan had asked
her for the address of the Böhmers." She knew nothing more. The
paper signed "Marie Antoinette of France" was in the hands of the
Cardinal, who had written it in the presence of the jewellers. It was
the Cardinal who had dealt with the Böhmers. According to her, "it
was without the Queen's knowledge that the Cardinal negotiated."
Prince Louis was in straitened circumstances as a result of the fire at
his château of Saverne and as a result of his extravagance. Everyone
knew that. Then suddenly the prisoner made an accusation: the chief
culprit was Cagliostro.

What had the brilliant alchemist to do with it? He was not concerned
in the swindle, but Mme de la Motte considered that by dragging the
famous charlatan into an affair which was already pretty much confused she would do herself no harm, but on the contrary distract everyone's attention. In Paris no one talked of anything but this Comte de
Cagliostro, who claimed to be two thousand years old, to have been
present at the Marriage of Cana and to have walked with Christ on the
shores of Lake Tiberias. When a disbeliever pushed him further, he
answered arrogantly: "I am who am!"

In reality his name was Joseph Balsamo and he was no more a
Comte than Jeanne was a Comtesse. He had managed to gain the
Cardinal's confidence, to become intimate with him and to make gold
and diamonds for him. The Cardinal had said to the "Comtesse": "He
is a great man, a god! He should be spoken of with the greatest respect.
He is going to make me a Minister!" He had also promised to reconcile
the Cardinal and the Queen. The Cardinal, as he was fond of proclaiming, was inconsolable "at having incurred his sovereign's hate." "It
brings a bitterness to my heart which poisons my happiest days."

In order to console His Eminence Cagliostro made Marie Antoinette
appear in a carafe. Of course the Cardinal saw nothing by himself,

but through the intermediary of a child who must be "as pure as an angel." The latter was dressed in an apron woven in silver and with "a large sun in the middle," and wore the blue ribbon. He was the child the Queen was to give birth to in March, the future Louis XVII. Cagliostro then drew his sword, placed his hand on the child's head and blew on his hair as he waved his rapier. Then he drew him behind a screen, where there was a carafe of clear water on a table.

"I command you," cried Cagliostro, "to make me see everything I wish. What do you see, child?"

With beating heart the Cardinal held his breath.

"Nothing," replied the "seer."

"Strike with your foot, child. What do you see?"

"Nothing."

"Strike again! What do you see?"

"I see a tall, beautiful pregnant woman dressed in white. I see her in her bed."

"Do you know the Queen? Have you seen her? Do you recognise her?"

"Yes, Monsieur, I see the Queen."

"The Cardinal was in ecstasies," related Mme de la Motte. "He crawled at the magician's feet and kissed his hands."

The "Comtesse" detested the alchemist, who where swindling was concerned was a dangerous rival. So at her first interrogation, on 20 August, she accused Cagliostro. It was he who had helped the Cardinal steal the necklace. This mountebank was the accomplice of the Prince of the Church.

But there was too much evidence involving the "Comtesse" for the lieutenant of police to believe this version. How was it that since 1 February the La Mottes had been living like princes? Forty-two carriages had brought sumptuous furniture to Bar-sur-Aube. They had bought six coaches and twelve horses and engaged a large staff—cooks, lackeys, kitchen maids, a coachman and even "a Negro covered with silver from head to foot." It was nothing but feasts and receptions, and to defray the expenses they were constantly selling diamonds. The "Comte" had even gone to London to negotiate the sale of 240,000 livres' worth of stones, "some of which were damaged as though they had been hastily and carelessly prised from a piece of jewellery with a knife." These must have been the diamonds from the necklace.

"Perhaps," replied Mme de la Motte, when she was interrogated on 26 August, "but it was the Cardinal who had told me to sell them to pay the instalments. On two occasions he gave me a large quantity of diamonds."

On Monday 25 August she began to write her defence. Her arguments were skilful: "If I were guilty, I should not have stayed in France. I should have fled to rejoin my husband, who is at present in England."

In spite of this argument the lieutenant of police was convinced that Breteuil and the Queen were mistaken. The Cardinal was innocent. Mme de la Motte was not his accomplice but the instigator of the swindle. Rohan had been speaking the truth in his account of how the "Comtesse" had hoaxed and plucked him.

For the police officer the affair was now clear. For the Queen's enemies, reinforced by the tribe of Rohan, Marson, Brionne and Soubise, the Cardinal was not the victim of an adventuress but of the Queen. "In the town," relates the *Correspondance secrète*, "they accused Mme de la Motte and the Cardinal; but at court they accused the Queen."

The opposition members of Parliament were delighted. "What a great and fortunate affair!" cried one of them. "A swindling Cardinal, the Queen involved in an affair of forgery! . . . What mud on the crozier and sceptre! What a triumph for the ideas of liberty! How useful for Parliament!" and from hatred of the Queen these gentlemen began immediately to campaign for the "illustrious victim."

But suddenly a story pre-dating the theft emerged from the first interrogations and explained the Cardinal's hitherto incomprehensible credulity.

This was the affair of the grove, more serious perhaps than that of the necklace and already a year old. And, like us today, Marie Antoinette, by studying the memoranda and documents of the case, could reconstruct "this horror," as she henceforth called the affair.

Mme de la Motte had formed a plan to take advantage of the stupidity of the Cardinal, that great fool in purple. She claimed to have spoken to the Queen about the Grand Almoner and his grief with "such enthusiasm that she had gradually dispelled her prejudices." One day the "Comtesse" declared joyfully to the prelate: "I am authorised by the Queen to ask you for a written defence to the faults imputed to you."

The Cardinal, moved to tears by gratitude, wrote. The Queen

answered, and soon a correspondence was carried on through Mme de la Motte. The Queen's letters were written by a friend of the "Comte," a former gendarme called Marc-Antoine Rétaux de Villette. To his talent as a forger he joined that of a singer, and when he sang Rameau's music or recited his own verses his voice was so captivating that the "Comtesse" had allowed herself to be captivated.

Needless to say, consoling the Cardinal was of no interest to the triangle unless there was money in it, and so Mme de la Motte began to dictate to her lover letters in which Marie Antoinette, on various pretexts, asked His Eminence to lend her money. The Grand Almoner found this quite natural. At that time everyone was talking about the Queen's reckless expenditure and debts.

Meanwhile, in exchange for services he was delighted to render, and which permitted the trio to live in luxury, the Cardinal wished to have an audience with Marie Antoinette. This was where matters became complicated. Unlike Cagliostro, Mme de la Motte had no means of summoning the Queen to her house in a carafe. Some other way had to be found, and Jeanne had an idea. Everyone was aware that Marie Antoinette walked in the park in the evenings—there were countless stories about these walks. Why should not the Cardinal be granted an audience at night in the gardens? All that had to be done was to find a woman who in the darkness could play the part of the Queen. This bold project did not daunt the Comte de la Motte, who began to search. Soon he found in the gardens of the Palais-Royal a fair young woman who was astonishingly like the Queen. This was Mlle Oliva, the "street walker." He entered into conversation with her, seduced her and after nine visits brought her to the Comtesse, and then faded away.

Jeanne did not beat about the bush. She called Oliva "dear heart" and declared: "I have the Queen's complete confidence. She and I are hand in glove. She has just given me further proof by ordering me to find a person to do something which will be explained in due course. If you wish to undertake it I shall make you a present of the sum of 15,000 livres."

The girl was dazzled. "I should be very flattered by doing anything that might please the Queen."

"M. le Comte de la Motte will come to fetch you tomorrow evening in a carriage and will take you to Versailles," ended Jeanne, leaving the young woman, in her own words, "intoxicated with joy and hope."

The next day the "Comte" took the girl to Versailles. When the carriage drew near the gates of the château it was stopped by the "Comtesse," who ordered her husband: "Take Madame to my house." La Motte obeyed, left the girl in the Rue Dauphine and disappeared. Two hours later he came back with Mme de la Motte. "Their faces were alive with gaiety."

"I have told the Queen of your arrival," Jeanne announced, "and she was very pleased at it. She is impatient to be there tomorrow to see how things will go."

Mlle Oliva was surprised. "But what is it, then, that you want me to do?"

"Oh! it is nothing at all. You will soon know."

On the next day Mme de la Motte dressed the young woman. "I was dressed in a white robe of spotted linen; as far as I can remember, it was a *robe à l'enfant* or a *gaulle*." This was the dress the Queen was wearing in Mme Vigée-Lebrun's portrait, which was exhibited in the Salon in the same year, 1784.

The "Comtesse" then gave the girl a letter with no name on it. "I shall take you into the park this evening and you will give this letter to a very great nobleman you will meet there."

On 11 August 1784, between 11 o'clock and midnight, M. and Mme de la Motte came to fetch Oliva, who had a white tippet round her shoulders and a *Thérèse* on her head. When they came to the grille of the Orangerie the "Comtesse" handed her companion a rose. "You will give this rose with the letter to the person who presents himself before you and you will say to him only this: 'You know what this means.' The Queen will be there to see how the interview goes off. She will speak to you, she will be behind you."

Oliva, seized "with trembling all over," began to stammer with emotion. She was only a poor girl and did not know what title she should give the Queen.

"You must always say 'Your Majesty,'" declared the former gendarme.

The "Dame de la Motte" stationed the young woman in an arbour. "Stay there. I am going to fetch the great nobleman."

She went away, and the girl's heart beat fast. The "great nobleman"— it was the Cardinal—arrived and bowed, while Jeanne remained at a short distance. "I was trembling so much that I cannot even now imagine how I was able to do even half of what I had been commanded." In fact the young woman merely handed the rose to the Cardinal, uttering the agreed phrase, and forgot the letter. The Grand Almoner had scarcely taken the rose when one of the Queen's valets—it was Rétaux in disguise—ran up, saying: "Here are Madame and Madame la Comtesse d'Artois!"

Madame de la Motte hurried up, took the girl's arm and led her away, saying "urgently": "Quick, come quickly!"

She handed the young woman over to M. de la Motte and returned to the Cardinal, who was intoxicated with joy. He thought he had heard the "Queen" say to him: "You may hope that the past will be forgotten."

His Eminence was dazzled and not in the least surprised. It was currently said that Marie Antoinette received her lovers in the park. The court and the town had mentioned the names of Guines, Coigny, Lauzun and Fersen.

Henceforth Mme de la Motte could make all kinds of demands on him "in the name of the Queen" and they would be received with "a deep sentiment of respect and gratitude." August 1784 was not over when Jeanne asked the Grand Almoner for 60,000 livres "for some poor people in whom she knew the Queen was interested." Until the end of the year demands for money and passionate letters written by the former gendarme Rétaux de Villette succeeded each other. As for the Cardinal, he replied by letters "which no man with any self-respect could read right through," related Beugnot, who was able to read them before the holocaust at Bar-sur-Aube.

The Cardinal was all the less suspicious since Jeanne, in order to deceive him, continued to ask him for a few louis to help her to live. Faced with such an outstanding example of imbecility, Mme de la Motte did not hesitate for a moment when Maître Laporte asked her, on behalf of the jewellers, to intercede with the Queen. Her mind was soon made up: she would have the Cardinal buy the necklace and would keep it for herself.

Everything seems clear to us today, but at the time it was not so.

"It is impossible," cried the Archbishop of Tours, "that the Cardinal should be guilty of being involved in such a gross swindle!"

Fersen, who was with his regiment, noted these rumours. "It is said that the whole thing was only a game between the Queen and the Cardinal, that he was on very good terms with her, that she had in fact commissioned him to buy the necklace, that the Queen pretended not to be able to bear him in order to conceal her aims, that the King had been informed of it, that he had reproached her with it, that she had been made very ill by this and had pretended to be pregnant."

In the opinion of her enemies Marie Antoinette must have been mixed up in the affair one way or the other. The most tolerant assumed that the scene in the grove had been stage-managed to amuse the Queen, who was hidden in an arbour. With the complicity of Breteuil —some even said of Jeanne de la Motte—Marie Antoinette had wanted to fool His Eminence. After that Jeanne had gone on with the intrigue on her own account. Everything then appeared more normal: the Cardinal was no longer an imbecile and Mme de la Motte was no longer the moving spirit in the intrigue. Others were surprised that Rétaux de Villette, who was arrested at the same time as Oliva, should confess everything, the forgeries as well as the scene in the grove, give all the required details and yet deny having played the part of the man in black who came to fetch the necklace from Mme de la Motte in the night of 1 February. Others were surprised that a special messenger had not been sent to Bar-sur-Aube on 15 August to arrest the "Comtesse." Why wait three days? Finally, everyone was astonished at Jeanne's calm, having left for Bar-sur-Aube on 5 August, receiving and paying visits there, living like a Princess and making no attempt to escape. Was someone trying to protect her?

And so Mme de la Motte's consummate cunning, the mistakes made by the investigators and the accused, and the details which did not come to light all turned against Marie Antoinette. The victim of her reputation, was she now to see opening before her feet that "abyss" of which Maria Theresa had once spoken?

As unconcerned as ever, and instead of avoiding the Parisians, who were dragging her in the mud, she showed herself—and in great array. On 5 October, having made up her mind to go to Fontainebleau by the Seine, she decided to embark "at the beginning of the plain of Issy" and to cross Paris on board a *hyac*. On the bank 15 horses drew the little boat, which sailed up the Seine as the cannon of the Invalides thundered. Marie Antoinette came on deck and took care "to be seen by all the assembled people."

Soon all the actors in the drama, even those with only walking-on parts, were in the Bastille, with the exception of La Motte, who having taken refuge in England was selling off the rest of the diamonds. The truth was becoming clear. Everyone confessed, but Jeanne, although overwhelmed by detailed proofs, refused to speak the truth.

"It was M. de Rohan who stole the necklace. It was by your orders that my husband and myself had the diamonds from it mounted or sold."

When she was urged to give up this ridiculous line of defence, she declared: "There is a secret which I shall confide only in private to the Minister of the King's Household." But when she felt that Breteuil might well decide to accept this interview she simulated madness and also indulged in exhibitionism by remaining naked in her cell for hours on end.

Finally she grew tired, and at her last interview burst into tears. But she would admit only to having instigated the scene in the grove. As for everything else, Jeanne declared that she "threw herself into the arms of Providence."

Before the Cardinal took up residence in the Bastille he had worn secular clothes as often as possible. Now he never put off his ceremonial robes. He appeared in a rochet of Malines lace and a purple cape. While he confessed his error his slender hand on which the ring sparkled played with the pale blue ribbon of the Order of the Holy Ghost. His attitude was noble, dignified and even humble when necessary. His greatest anxiety was to absolve Cagliostro and his wife. We possess the secret correspondence he managed to keep up with his lawyer, Maître Target. Only twice did he ask for news of Marie Antoinette. "Tell me if it is true that the Queen continues to be sad," he wrote.

When the preliminary investigation was over Maître Target, according to custom, published a voluminous "Memorial," showing his client's defence. And the rhymers said:

> Target in his Memorial
> Has told as best he can
> The story of the Cardinal,
> That most unhappy man.
> And all his arguments set out,
> His wordy eloquence,
> Prove clearly without any doubt
> His client's innocence.

Rohan then sent a letter to the King asking if he might appear before Parliament to be judged, but he added these very important lines: "However, if I might hope that the explanations which may have been given, and of which I know nothing, might have led Your Majesty to judge that I am guilty only of having been deceived, I should venture to beg you, Sire, to pronounce sentence in accordance with your justice and your goodness."

In other words, Louis XVI need only declare that the Cardinal was completely innocent and send him, by means of a *lettre de cachet,* to a house where he would be kept under surveillance. A public trial would thus be avoided. But Marie Antoinette had other views. "I want this horror and all its details to be brought into the open before the eyes of all the world." Blinded by a desire for vengeance, she thought the Cardinal was guilty, if not of having stolen the necklace at least of having dared to believe she loved him, and she urged the King to send the affair to the Parliament. By so doing she was to make everyone believe that she was guilty.

So the Queen did not hesitate to entrust her honour to the discontented gentlemen of the robe, who detested her and whose only aim was to humiliate the crown and abase the Queen. It was no longer the Cardinal's trial which was about to begin, but Marie Antoinette's. In Goethe's words, the affair of the necklace was in fact to become the preface to the Revolution.

Being innocent of the theft for which he had been arrested, the Prince de Rohan was to be judged on one point only: was the Grand Almoner of France justified or not in believing that the Queen could give him an amatory interview, write him passionate letters and commission him, without the King's knowledge, to buy a necklace worth 1,600,000 livres?

But could a Prince of the Church be brought before a tribunal? Some people went so far as to evoke the Councils of Antioch and Nicaea, where "it was laid down that Bishops were the sole judges of Bishops."

"No doubt," replied the supporters of a trial, "but at that time Gaul was not Christian."

"But from the time of Clovis to the 10th century one can find judgments proving that the Bishops were judged by Councils." And they recalled the case of the Cardinal de la Balue, whom Louis XI had had arrested and condemned on his own authority.

"But His Holiness censured King Louis XI, who acknowledged his error and asked for a Bull of absolution."

"Did not Henri III have Cardinal de Guise assassinated?"

"Yes, but he was excommunicated."

A decision had to be made, and so "ancient Bulls" were evoked, without any more specific detail, which had formerly warned Bishops and Cardinals "that in temporal matters even their souls were subject to the laws of the sovereign princes." And the trial was fixed for 22 May 1786.

> Oliva says that he was victimised.
> Lamotte says that his crime is undisguised.
> He says himself that he was mesmerised.
> Alleluia!

> The Holy Father dressed him up in red.
> The King and Queen have blackened him instead.
> The Court will sprinkle whitewash on his head.
> Alleluia!

The Cardinal whitewashed? It was impossible that the Government would allow such a verdict, which would be an affront to the Queen.

Before the pleadings had been opened the battle had started. The women were the most enthusiastic. The Prelate's supporters wore headdresses in which sparkled a rivière of diamonds fastened by red ribbons lined with yellow: this was called "Cardinal on the straw." Even in the Polignac clan Marie Antoinette found partisans of her enemy, for example Vaudreuil. "The great ladies of the court," wrote Hardy in his *Journal*, "undertook the defence of the Cardinal with great warmth, for they were greatly touched by and grateful for the delicacy he had displayed at the moment of his arrest in ordering the Abbé Georgel, his confidential agent, to destroy or hide from general view his correspondence with a great many of them."

On 22 May 1786 the Parliament assembled, without the Princes of the Blood and the Peers. The judges—the *Grand'Chambre* and the *Tournelle* together—numbered 64. It took six days to read the documents, and then the Procureur Général, Joly de Fleury, was called on. He asked "that the document signed *Marie Antoinette de France*" should be "declared fraudulently falsified." According to him, the Cardinal ought to come "to the *Grand'Chambre* to declare out loud that he had audaciously believed in the meeting in the grove, that he had helped to deceive the merchants by giving them to believe that the Queen knew of the transaction, to declare that he repented and to ask pardon of the King and the Queen; and that furthermore he should be condemned to resign his positions, to give alms to the poor, to spend his whole life at a distance from the royal residences and finally to remain in prison until the execution of the judgement."

And the Procureur concluded: "The Cardinal puts forward what happened in the garden at Versailles as being of a nature to encourage his delusion. But could he allow himself to believe in a false and pretended meeting at night on the terrace at Versailles, could he allow himself to go there, and in going there did he not commit an offence towards the Queen worthy of the highest punishment?"

Hatred for Marie Antoinette was so lively among the lawyers that this wise and just peroration touched off a violent scene. Séguier, the Advocate-General, rose, red with anger. He exclaimed loudly: "The Cardinal should be acquitted!" and turning to Joly de Fleury, he cried: "You are about to descend into the tomb and will leave your ashes covered with ignominy which will be shared by the magistrates!"

"Your anger does not surprise me, Monsieur," replied the Procureur Général calmly. "A man as devoted to licentiousness as yourself was bound to defend the Cardinal's cause."

"I sometimes visit prostitutes," Séguier admitted, amid smiles. "I even leave my carriage at their door. That is my affair. But no one has ever known me basely sell my opinion to fortune."

On 30 August the examination began. Rétaux de Villette, who came first, extricated himself very well, "even anticipating the questions before they were finished, with an air and tone of the greatest precision."

When Mme de la Motte, who came next, saw the ignominious seat she recoiled. "Sit there, Madame," said the usher coldly.

"In less than two minutes," related an observer, "she managed things so well, and her countenance was so assured that she seemed to be in her own apartments seated in her best armchair."

With "intrepidity" and "without the least appearance of embarrassment," "she replied to the questions," we are told, "making herself heard and paying more attention to probabilities than to facts and fastening particularly on the court's inability to show any of the letters, writings and material proofs they would have liked to see." When the alleged

letters from Marie Antoinette to Rohan were mentioned she refused
to reply "so as not to offend the Queen." But the President insisted, and
she went so far as to declare that the Cardinal had shown her "two
hundred letters written by the Queen in which she called him *tu*."

There was an uproar. In private all these gentlemen were willing to
speak every possible ill of "the Austrian," but in public they owed it
to themselves to be scandalised by such ignominy.

When Jeanne had left, President d'Aligre sent word to the Cardinal
"that as the accused's stool had been removed he could now come
into court." Rohan entered wearing violet robes—the mourning of
Cardinals. He looked so pale, as he had just had an attack of food
poisoning in the Bastille from drinking whey prepared in a verdigrised
pot, and he trembled so much that the President said: "M. le Cardinal
is at liberty to sit, if he wishes."

Rohan obeyed, recovered himself and for half-an-hour "spoke from
the fullness of his heart," telling his pitiable tale and succeeding perfectly in making himself appear even more stupid than he had been.
On ending his speech "he saluted the chief bench and the other magistrates." All returned his salute and the chief bench even rose, "which
was a marked distinction."

Oliva made the judges wait, which touched them, for she was
occupied in suckling her child by her future husband, the Sieur de
Beausire; it had been born in the Bastille. "Rousseaumania" was then
prevalent and the occurrence seemed charming. Pathos was followed
by laughter with Cagliostro, who expressed himself in a jargon composed of Latin, Greek, Italian and Arabic. The court relaxed.

"Who are you?" asked the President.

"A noble voyager!"

On Wednesday 31 May, judgement was given.

It was five o'clock in the morning. All the Rohans, Brionnes, Soubises,
Montlasons and Marsans stationed themselves in deep mourning at
the entrance to the *Grand'Chambre* and bowed as the 62 magistrates
passed in slow procession before them.

"At two o'clock the voting magistrates interrupted their work to dine
at a table laid for forty which the First President had had set up in the
Salle Saint-Louis, but most of them ate standing and at half-past three
they were in session again."

Two magistrates asked for the death sentence. This was a manoeuvre, for a punishment involving death obliged the thirteen *conseillers-clercs*, who were churchmen, to retire. Among them were eleven of the Cardinal's enemies. Once the priests had left the battle began. There was no question of inflicting a penalty on Rohan, since there had not even been "the beginning of any proof," but according to the friends of the court a formula must be found to punish the "offence."

The President proposed that at least "the Cardinal should be obliged to abstain from carrying out the functions pertaining to the post of Grand Almoner until it should be otherwise ordered by the King." In fact, this judgement would have recalled the fact that "one did not leave the Bastille without being exiled." Other magistrates were in favour of making the accused publicly admit "that he had, as a result of an abuse of the Queen's name, made to the said Böhmer and Bassenge a payment of 30,000 livres for which he received a receipt in the name of the Queen; that he had dared to be lacking in respect for the sacred persons of the King and the Queen; that it was from audacity that he had permitted himself to believe in an alleged nocturnal meeting on the terrace at Versailles; that it was from audacity that, unbeknown to the King and Queen and without having himself made sure of their intentions, he opened and carried on negotiations with the said Böhmer and Bassenge."

Fifteen councillors agreed with these stern but just conclusions. Others, who were wiser, felt that the majority would never come round to this point of view, and simply suggested a nonsuit, which did not completely whitewash an accused, holding him responsible but not guilty of the facts as indicted. This sentence would also have given the Queen some slight satisfaction.

But the majority was stronger. By 26 votes to 22 the Cardinal was entirely "discharged from every species of accusation." Cagliostro was similarly treated and Oliva's case was nonsuited, Rétaux was banished from the realm and Jeanne de la Motte was condemned to perpetual imprisonment after being marked on both shoulders with the letter V given to thieves.

Paris wanted illuminations, but the police intervened. That evening 10,000 people gathered round the Bastille to shout their enthusiasm and in acclaiming the Cardinal demonstrated their joy at seeing the Austrian humiliated. It was in fact the Queen's defeat which was being celebrated.

At Versailles Marie Antoinette wept long and bitterly. "Condole with me," she said to Mme Campan. "The intriguer who wanted to ruin me or to get money by making use of my name and my signature has just been completely acquitted."

The King, too, still considered Rohan guilty both of the "offence" and of swindling. Instead of bowing to the judgement, which would have been the more sensible course, he wrote to Breteuil: "The Keeper of the Seals has informed me of the judgement by which all the indictments are withdrawn. In consequence you will give orders to M. de Launay to let Cardinal de Rohan and Cagliostro leave the Bastille, but as the Queen has been particularly compromised by the affair of the necklace and the diamonds, in which he was greatly involved, you will order the Cardinal to hand in his resignation from his position as First Almoner and the decoration attached to it. You will order him to leave Paris in three days, to see only his family and his advisers, to betake himself to his abbey at Chaise-Dieu, where I hope he will receive only a few persons. You will order Cagliostro to leave Paris in eight days and the kingdom in three weeks."

Mme de Marsan threw herself at the Queen's feet to implore pardon for her cousin. Marie Antoinette looked at her coldly. "The Cardinal must submit to the King's orders."

"This refusal makes me realise how disagreeable my presence must be to Your Majesty. This is the last time I shall have the honour of presenting myself to her."

"Madame, I shall be very sorry."

And the affair ended with the inevitable pun, just as the Archduke Leopold had foretold on the day after the arrest:

> *Le Parlement l'a purgé*
> *Le Roi l'a envoyé à la Chaise!*

The execution on Wednesday 21 June of the sentence pronounced on Jeanne de Valois was a dreadful scene. In the Cour de Mai six executioners were needed to hold her down on her knees while the clerk read the sentence. She struggled, bit, shrieked, howled. Then she refused to undress. "She fought like a tigress with her feet, hands and teeth, in such a way that they were obliged to cut her garments right down to the chemise, which was of the greatest indecency before all the spectators."

She rolled on the ground and reached the foot of the great staircase, pursued by the executioners. She was held down, face to the ground, with her skirts turned up. The red-hot iron was applied to her shoulder and sizzled on the skin. The condemned woman made such a sudden bound that she turned over and the second V was applied on her breast. Before falling in the faint she had time to bite one of the executioners right through his jacket.

A minute later a cab left the courtyard and set off for the prison of the Salpêtrière. The two watchmen "in short robes" who accompanied Mme de la Motte had great difficulty in preventing her from throwing herself out of the window.

Ten months later she managed to escape and of course it was said, as an added calumny, that the Queen had facilitated her flight, for La Motte, who was still in London, was threatening to publish "documents whose publication was feared, unless his wife were restored to him."

"Goodbye, Madame," the nun who opened the secret door for her was supposed to have said. "Take care that nobody *remarks* you."

In three years the storm was to break, but the first thunderclap had already been heard. "This event fills me with as much terror as the head of the Medusa," wrote Goethe.

11

Madame Deficit

ON 1 JUNE 1786, the day after the Parliament's judgement, Marie Antoinette wrote to Mme de Polignac: "Come and weep with me, come and console your friend. The judgement that has just been pronounced is an atrocious insult. I am bathed in tears of grief and despair. . . . Come to me, my dear heart."

The Duchesse must have found the right words to say, for on 4 June the Queen, who had to write to Mercy to tell him about a dinner at Trianon, added, merely as a postscript: "What do you think of the judgement?" Mercy wrote to Kaunitz that the Queen had been "affected" by the judgement but that she had soon regained her "calm."

A few years earlier Marie Antoinette would have hurried to Mme de Polignac's house, instead of asking her to come and weep with her. But she no longer cared very much for her friend's home, where Vaudreuil was always lolling about on the sofas. During this painful year he had openly displayed his sympathy for Cardinal de Rohan. "Four years before the Revolution," an observer remarks, "matters had come to the point where before leaving her apartments to go to Mme de Polignac the Queen would always send one of her valets de chambre to find out the names of the people there, and on receiving the reply she often stayed away." The former Comtesse Jules was in no hurry to change the list of her guests. She went so far as to exclaim: "I think that because Your Majesty is kind enough to come to my drawing room that is no reason for her to try to exclude my friends."

Marie Antoinette sighed, but bore her no grudge for her boldness. "I am not angry with Mme de Polignac on that account," she said one

218

day to La Marck. "At bottom she is good and she loves me, but her associates have subjugated her."

After the affair of the necklace the monarchy was rapidly approaching the abyss, but there was a short period of calm during the last six months of 1786. Astonished by their unbelievable victory, the Queen's enemies seemed to have paused to take breath, and at Trianon the summer had never seemed so pleasant.

At the beginning of June Marie Antoinette, who was now eight months pregnant, went in her carriage to visit the hamlet, which was now finished. In spite of the artificial cracks, the artificially crumbled stones and the artificial old bricks, it really was a village. There were sheep which were sheared, cows which were milked and hens whose eggs were carefully collected. In the porcelain churns and milk pails bearing Marie Antoinette's cipher, and on the marble tables of the clean dairy, butter and cheese were made—the best in the Ile de France, it was asserted, particularly when the Queen and her friends amused themselves at making them under the somewhat anxious eye of the farmer's wife. For there were a farmer and his wife, the Valy-Busard, who came from Touraine and had a small staff under their command.

The Queen had had a little house built, whose walls are still standing and where the floors were made of straw coloured to imitate marquetry work. From the windows of the "Queen's house" Marie Antoinette, exhausted by her advanced pregnancy, could, as she drank milk from one of the famous breast-bowls (but were they ever really used at Trianon?), watch the farmer's wife and her servant washing their linen at the edge of the lake, or follow the work of the gardener's boys as they picked vegetables in the little gardens surrounding each house. On the lawn the hens scuttled about in their enclosure; the cowman led his troop out to pasture; and the farmer fished in the little lake into which 27 pike and 2,000 carp had been placed.

Surrounded by what she thought of as, if not "an agricultural enterprise," at least the "happy village" demanded by Bernardin de Saint-Pierre, Marie Antoinette forgot the lawyers' insult during this month of June, but the King's journey to Cherbourg helped especially to bring a little comfort to her heart.

On Tuesday, 20 June, Louis XVI had left Trianon for Rambouillet and at the end of the week he wrote to Marie Antoinette from Cherbourg to tell her how happy he was. He had been wildly acclaimed.

"My people's love for me found its echo in my heart. You may think of me as the happiest King in the world."

Marie Antoinette began to hope again; perhaps the monarchy was not detested after all. But when the King left Normandy the acclamations diminished. "I can see I am approaching Versailles!" he sighed. Paris's hate for Marie Antoinette was reflected on the "poor man," whom everyone considered too tolerant a husband,

> Who's never jealous.
> He's indifferent. The thing at which he's able
> Is stuffing himself like a swine
> And swilling down his wine
> With his elbows on the table.

When Marie Antoinette gave birth to her fourth child, Princesse Sophie, on 9 July 1786, the only people who rejoiced were those Parisians who had free drinks at the expense of the "Gentlemen."

The people often suffered from hunger and knew that at Versailles the money was still flying. Calonne was reigning as Minister. During this year—the year of the necklace—Marie Antoinette spent 272,000 livres on dress, 60 million present-day francs and 150,000 livres in excess of her budget. And yet the Queen was wearing so-called "milkmaids" or "shirt" dresses. Admittedly Mlle Bertin made up for it with the hats, which were enormous bonnets, big enough for ten heads, or hats resembling by their size hatters' shop signs and costing a small fortune.

Since the beginning of the reign Monsieur had extracted 3,000 million present-day francs and the Comte d'Artois 2,400 million. When these figures were shown to M. de Calonne he was delighted. He borrowed "to spend," he borrowed again, he went on borrowing. He was called "The Wizard."

"How could I have suspected that the finances were in such a bad state?" Marie Antoinette was later to ask. "When I asked for 50,000 livres I was brought 100,000."

> 'Tis not Calonne himself I love,
> But gold, which he's not sparing of.
> If there's no more for me
> I quickly send to him by name,
> My favourite does just the same,
> And then we laugh with glee.

At the end of 1786 the "Wizard," who had come to the end of his tricks, collapsed. There was only one solution left—to summon an assembly of notables and ask them to find a way to fill the coffers without spending other people's money. The monarchy had gone bankrupt and filed its petition.

Calonne showed his books to all the Marshals, Dukes, Peers, magistrates and Princes, and now all France knew what Versailles was costing the nation. Poor devils who earned barely one livre a day learned that Madame Elisabeth alone ate each year 100 million francs' worth of meat and fish. A scapegoat was needed. It could not be the King, who was so good natured and so simple. It was not the costly and outdated ceremonial demanded by etiquette, nor the posts surviving from another age, the 2,111 servants and 4,000 members of the King's Household. One person alone, it was shouted and written, was responsible—the Queen. The deficit was due to her wild expenditure, her pleasures, her reckless gambling, the greed and thefts of her favourites. Already Marie Antoinette's enemies—and she had made a great many—were covertly accusing her "of having in a shocking manner squandered the finances of France, fruit of the people's sweat, to satisfy her irregular pleasures." Now it was merely whispered, but soon a magistrate would cry it aloud from the floor of the court, for the sentence is an extract from Fouquier-Tinville's indictment.

Henceforth she was always known as "Madame Deficit." In her own person she was held to be the incarnation of the bankruptcy of the monarchy. In February 1787, the month in which the Notables met, Marie Antoinette went to the Comédie, where *Athalie* was being given. Joad's speech was madly applauded:

> Confonds dans ses conseils cette reine cruelle;
> Daigne, daigne, mon Dieu, sur Mathan et sur elle
> Répandre cet esprit d'imprudence et d'erreur
> De la chute des rois funeste avant-coureur.

At this applause the Queen left her box. A few days earlier she had been hissed at the Opera.

She admitted only one responsibility—her friendship for Mme de Polignac, "who had made herself loathed by her rapacity," as Mercy said on 14 August 1787. In the Queen's mind her favourite was the only reason for this "odious and unjust outburst in which the public obstinately persists." And yet she continued to be friends with the Duchesse merely "from habit, from fear of boredom and from the need for dissipation," as Mercy, not without satisfaction, announced to Vienna.

Marie Antoinette retained her incomprehension in the face of the tide of hatred she felt rising towards her, and which was soon to engulf her. "I shall conquer the malicious by trebling the good I have always tried to do," she sighed.

As Louis XVI had been obliged to let Calonne go, Marie Antoinette suggested the Archbishop of Toulouse, Loménie de Brienne, who was supported by Vermond. The Abbé had first of all wanted to have him made Archbishop of Paris, but the King had opposed it. "The Archbishop of Paris ought at least to believe in God!"

This might also have been a condition for a Controller of Finances in 1787, who needed a miracle to save him!

Louis XVI gave way and accepted Loménie de Brienne. The Queen rejoiced. "Make no mistake, Messieurs," she said as she left the Council Chamber, "he is a real Prime Minister."

Those with privileges were soon to be aware of it, but to their cost. As Brienne had not been able to obtain from the 144 Notables permission to reform the financial structure of the country completely, and consequently to increase certain taxes, he fell back on the court and decided to make economies. It was decided to abolish for the next year 173 posts in the Queen's Household alone. The serving gentlemen, sergeants and their assistants and ordinary messengers said nothing, but those with high posts protested. The Duc de Coigny, who had to give up his title of Grand Equerry—the Great Stable being amalgamated with the Little Stable—made a scene to the King, although his salary still remained. Vaudreuil resigned himself to giving up his post as chief falconer, but Besenval, although he kept his Swiss Guards, was deeply wounded.

"Madame," he dared to say to Marie Antoinette, "it is terrible to live in a country where one is not sure of possessing one day what one had the day before. That used to happen only in Turkey!"

The Duc de Polignac was one of the few to keep quiet when the post of director general of the post-horses was taken away from him, but then he still kept the reversion of the Little Stable.

Marie Antoinette cut down her style of living; there were few feasts or balls. In any case she had no heart for dancing, for in the summer of 1787 she was in mourning. Princesse Sophie was dead, "the pulmonary organ being in a very bad state," according to the "report of the opening" made at Trianon.

In spite of the dismissal of 600 guards and light horse, these economies did not fill the gap and Loménie de Brienne was obliged to come before the Parliament. But the lawyers revolted and refused to register two edicts concerned with the imposition of a stamp duty and making all nobles and commoners who owned property pay the King a land tax. According to the magistrates only the States General could avert bankruptcy and they began to set in motion their customary procedure of "remonstrances," "protests" and "reiterated remonstrances." Urged on by Marie Antoinette, Loménie de Brienne had the two edicts registered at a *Lit de Justice* held at Versailles on 6 August, and the King exiled the Parliament to Troyes.

Paris flared up at once. The carriages were stopped, processions were held and Loménie de Brienne was burned in effigy. Paris was practising for the great combat. The capital was aware that since the death of Vergennes the Queen was taking an active part in the Government and in exiling "the Fathers of the country." If the police had not intervened they would have burned her in effigy too. The lieutenant of police advised the Queen not to show herself in Paris.

The situation was becoming worse, the coffers were empty and a compromise had to be made. The Parliamentarians grew tired of Champagne and agreed to vote a "twentieth part." But on 19 November the conflict started again. The King held another *Lit de Justice* in the great chamber of the Palais de Justice in order to register another edict permitting him to issue successive loans of 420 million. "I order that the edict be transcribed in the registers of my Parliament to be executed according to its form and purport."

In order to spare the magistrates' susceptibility Louis XVI had omitted to add "by my express command," which was the obligatory formula for *Lits de Justice*. On this occasion, therefore, Justice was only half asleep on the bed and it was not forbidden to express an opinion. The tumult grew louder. Through the noise new words were heard for the first time: "arbitrary power," "despotism." The uproar increased, and then suddenly died down. The former Duc de Chartres, who had been Duc d'Orléans for two years now, rose. The head of the younger branch stood up before Louis XVI for the first time. He was heard to say calmly: "If the King is holding a session of Parliament the votes should be collected and counted; if it is a *Lit de Justice* we should be silent." He then added: "This registration is illegal."

This remark does not seem very unpleasant to us, but in the 18th century it constituted an "insolence" which made the King stammer: "Yes, it is legal! It is legal because I wish it!"

While the future Philippe-Egalité was being applauded the King returned to Versailles. Marie Antoinette had a great deal to do with the measures which were now to be taken and which ended in the virtual suppression of the Parliaments. It would appear that until the return of Necker hardly anything was done without her consent. Moreover, after the arrest of the two ringleaders, d'Eprémesnil and Monsabert, and after the Duc d'Orléans had been sent to Villers-Cotterets, the magistrates wrote to the King, assuring him that "such steps are not in his nature, such examples do not stem from his principles: *they have another source.*" They could not have indicated the Queen more clearly.

For his part Fersen wrote to King Gustavus on 27 December 1787: "The King is still weak and suspicious. He trusts only the Queen and it appears that it is she who does everything. The Ministers often go to see her and keep her informed of all business. It was often said by the public that the King was beginning to drink, that the Queen encouraged this passion and took advantage of his condition to make him sign anything she wanted. Nothing could be more untrue. He has no liking for drink and, granting the general supposition, it would be far too dangerous a vice by its consequences, since other people besides the Queen could extract a signature."

If anyone was well informed it was Axel Fersen. According to Saint-Priest, Fersen used to go "on horseback in the park, near the Trianon, three or four times a week; on her side the Queen did the same alone, and these meetings caused a great deal of public scandal, in spite of the favourite's modesty and restraint, for he never showed anything outwardly and was the most discreet of all the Queen's friends."

Axel was obliged to leave for Sweden, since Gustavus III was at war with Russia. During his absence Louis XVI received a packet of letters one day, while he was hunting. He sat down on the grass to read them and his equerries went away. On their return they found the King weeping bitterly. So great was his grief that he could not mount his horse and was brought back to Versailles in a carriage. He revealed to Marie Antoinette that the letter contained horrible accusations concerning the Queen and Fersen.

"They want to take from us the only friend we can rely on," sighed Marie Antoinette, and she proposed to her husband that they should not receive the Swede when he returned. The King dissuaded her, however, and when Fersen came back to France he resumed his almost daily visits to the château.

In spite of the ominous rumbling of the thunder the sky was still clear. The storm might have rolled away, but by an irremediable error the monarchy declared itself powerless: it called on the help of the Nation and set in motion the formidable machine which was to crush everything in its way. The initiative would pass to Moloch.

At the time of the suppression of the Parliaments a few disturbances had broken out here and there and degenerated into riots. At Grenoble the royal troops had been beaten back with a shower of tiles. In all France there was but one cry: "The States General and the return of Necker!" Louis XVI vacillated for six months and finally, realising that the Notables had also failed, he yielded and promised to summon the deputies of the States in the following year at Versailles. An inevitable consequence was that on 26 August 1788—check to the Queen—he dismissed the Archbishop, to whom Marie Antoinette had a Cardinal's hat given in compensation. Loménie de Birenne was replaced by Necker. "I tremble—excuse this weakness," wrote Marie Antoinette to Mercy on the same day, "because it is I who have caused him to be recalled. My fate is to bring misfortune. And if as a result of devilish schemes he fails again or if he extends the King's authority I shall be even more detested." She was seeing clearly now, but it was too late.

Necker no doubt did what he could—he even lent the Treasury two millions of his own money—but he, too, trembled. "I can see the great wave advancing. Will it engulf me?"

The "great wave" was the States General. The public was so occupied by the convening of the deputies that the deficit took second place. Thousands of pamphlets appeared. Public opinion was at fever-heat. The women were the most impassioned. "You know as well as I do," Fersen wrote to a friend, "to what extent women set the tone here and how they like to take part in everything. At present they are only interested in the constitution and to please them, and to be in the swim, the young men talk of nothing but States General and Governments, although their waistcoats, cabriolets and jackets often cause a diversion. I do not know if the kingdom will profit by all these changes, but society is the loser." If Mercy is to be believed, Marie Antoinette was also the loser. "H.M. now seems entirely occupied with the arrangements regarding the interior, the economies, the reforms, the parliamentary discussions. All these affairs are treated without any method or prearranged plan . . . and the result is a confusion which aggravates the evil instead of lessening it. Complaints and disgust follow, and the resulting ill-will falls partly on the Queen, who is so acutely distressed that her temperament is much affected by it."

The Ambassador was not very indulgent towards the woman who at the same time was writing to him: "My confidence in you does not permit me to let you remain in ignorance, Monsieur, of the result of the conversations I have had with several of the Ministers."

On 1 January 1788 Paris learned that the Third Estate was to have as many deputies as the two others put together. The houses were illuminated.

The last day of the Versailles year unfolded with the ceremonies unchanged since the time of the Roi Soleil. It had never been so cold. All the windows were covered with a thick layer of ice. The wood smoked, but did not burn. It was impossible to find in the whole château a log that was not damp, but the *lever* went on at its customary deliberate pace. Indeed, it was slower than usual for the "Gentlemen" of the town had come in a grand procession to present the King with their traditional gift of silver coins. It was so icy in the chapel that the Mass was shortened. During the formal dinner the water froze in the jugs, but that did not prevent the Duchesses *à tabouret* in their low-cut dresses and the crowd of courtiers from watching the King eat. He was the only one to swallow anything. Marie Antoinette did not even unfold her napkin and sat stoically through the interminable procession of fifty dishes.

Her political anxieties were coupled with a great personal grief: the ill-health of her elder son. The Dauphin, who had grown very thin, had a fever every evening. His vertebrae were "displaced and projecting." At that time the good effects of mountain air were unknown and, faced with the child's "state of weakness and languor," the doctors argued fiercely about the salubriousness of the air of La Muette compared with that of Versailles.

"The air at La Muette has more motion than that at Versailles," declared Le Monier. "The river which washes it helps to provide this motion."

"Neither Mont Valérien nor the heights of Montmartre protect La Muette from the cold winds," replied Portal, "and besides, the garden faces due north."

"But the north wind sweeps the air clean!"

Dessaut was in favour of Versailles. "The soil is fertile and suitable for vegetation, whereas the soil at La Muette is sandy. Moreover, Versailles is Monseigneur's native air!"

"But Monseigneur's apartment at Versailles is damp and unhealthy," declared Sabatier. "The walls drink water like a sponge. One of the windows looks on to the Swiss lake, which is stagnant, and the other looks on to the grand canal, which has no outlet."

"Not at all," replied Dessaut. "The air is healthy there and the marshes have been drained! I have lived in Versailles for forty years and I am convinced there are no epidemics there. It is sheltered from the north, whereas the Bois de Boulogne is damp."

There was no end to it! In order to prevent the medical staff from coming to blows the little Dauphin was sent to the château of Meudon. When Louis XVI was a child he too had been sickly and the air at Meudon had done him good; one had only to look at him now. But the invalid's condition grew daily worse. "It is heartrending," wrote the young Comtesse de Laage, who visited the little Prince with the Princess de Lamballe. "His suffering, reasonableness and patience are touching! When we arrived he was being read to. He had taken a whim to lie on a billiard table and a mattress had been put there for him. The Princesse and I watched him, and it occurred to both of us that it looked like a lying-in-state. Mme de Lamballe asked him what he was reading.

" 'A very interesting period of our history, Madame, the reign of Charles VII. There are a great many heroes.'

"I took the liberty of asking if Monseigneur read continuously or merely the most striking passages.

" 'Continuously, Madame. I do not know enough about it to choose, and it is all interesting.'

"He turned his beautiful, dying eyes to me as he spoke."

Marie Antoinette often went to see her son. "Everything the poor little child says is amazing; he breaks the Queen's heart. He shows the greatest affection for her. The other day he begged her to dine in his room. Alas! she swallowed more tears than bread."

The Queen remembered the day he had amused her so much as he sat on his father's knee during a performance in the little theatre at Trianon. She had dried up during a scene and Campan, in his prompter's box, tried to find the page, but in spite of his large spectacles did not succeed. The Dauphin's little voice was heard in the tense silence: "Monsieur Campan, take off your large spectacles, Mamma cannot hear you."

She remembered too the child's joy when, on 22 August of the preceding year, the "Gentlemen" of the town had brought him two pistols, a gold sword and a gun whose stock was charmingly decorated with little dolphins and lilies—a gun he would never shoulder.

He left his bed on 4 May 1789 to lie on the balcony of the Little Stable at Versailles and watch the procession of the States General going from the church of Notre Dame to the church of Saint-Louis.

The Revolution started with a procession.

And what a procession! A procession in which walked the last Kings of France: Louis XVI, Louis XVIII, Charles X, Louis-Philippe, then Duc de Chartres, and the young Duc d'Angoulême who, one day at Rambouillet in 1830, was for three minutes to be the King least known to schoolboys of the future—King Louis XIX of France.

The Duc d'Orléans, who was to send Louis XVI to the scaffold, and whose son would at one blow dethrone Charles X, Louis XIX and Henri V, walked with the deputies of the Nobility. He was the hero of the day. And among all the deputies of the Third Estate there was even the future master of France, M. Maximilien de Robespierre, in a black woollen suit with a black silk cloak and a white muslin cravat.

Everyone carried a candle, except for the standard bearers and the King's falconers, who carried their birds on their fists.

The King, in full dress, wearing a mantle of cloth of gold and with the "Regent" diamond in his hat, was surrounded by the high officers of the crown. He was wildly applauded. But when Marie Antoinette appeared in her dress sprinkled with gold and silver there was silence, a contemptuous silence. In the Place d'Armes, just as she was passing under the balcony where her little Dauphin was dying, a single cry stung her: "Long live the Duc d'Orléans!"

She tottered and grew pale. Would she fall on having the name of the former companion of her pleasures, now her enemy, thus thrown into her face? She wavered, and the Princesse de Lamballe hurried up, but the Queen raised her head, with its bunch of white feathers, and murmured: "It is nothing . . . nothing."

A few minutes later, in the church of Saint-Louis, the Bishop of Nancy, Mgr de la Fare, mounted into the pulpit and dared to say: "Sire, the people over whom you rule have given clear proofs of their patience. They are a martyred people, whose life seems to have been spared only that they may suffer the longer."

The deputies of the Third Estate, who up to this moment imagined that they merely represented over-harassed taxpayers, raised their heads. They would not lower them again.

The Bishop now attacked the luxury of the court. All eyes turned towards the Queen.

"It is in the name of a good King, a just and feeling monarch, that these wretched people practise their barbarities."

For the first time in a French church, and with the Blessed Sacrament exposed, there was applause. On returning to the château Marie Antoinette had such a violent attack of nerves that she broke her diamond bracelets.

At the formal session on the next day the Queen listened to Necker's interminable and blundering speech and anxiously watched the 1,165 deputies. They were taken aback, to say the least, on learning that "it is not to the absolute necessity for pecuniary assistance" that they owed "the great privilege of being summoned by His Majesty as the States General." In his monotonous voice Necker declared that the regular deficit was no more than 56 million. Nothing was easier than to cover it: for example, could not "the sale of ground tobacco be extended to Brittany"?

"What a country is this, where without taxes and with the aid of everyday, insignificant objects one can dispose of a deficit which has made such a stir in Europe!"

Such was the conclusion of the "Magician." The deputies looked at each other, stupefied. It was hardly worth while to have come so far to learn that henceforth, by taking snuff instead of chewing, the Bretons would save France. If the deficit could be covered by "insignificant objects," why could they not turn their attention to uniting the kingdom so that, in Voltaire's phrase, one did not have a change of laws with each change of horses? This was not what Louis XVI had summoned them for, but the King seemed full of good intentions—he had just called himself "the first friend of his peoples"—and he would certainly be glad to see a little order and unity brought about in the patchwork of his *pays d'état* and *pays d'élection*, or even in such provinces as Alsace and Trois-Evêchés, which, although part of France, were not able to trade freely with her.

"The battle is on," wrote a deputy of the Third Estate that evening, and by that he meant not the battle against the King, but with the King to save the kingdom. It was significant that when the King rose he was greeted with applause. To please him they also shouted "Long live the Queen!" They were rather sorry for her "look of sadness and depression." Startled, Marie Antoinette gave a pale smile and sank to the ground in one of the graceful curtseys of which she held the secret and which earned her an immense ovation.

It was with a slight smile on her lips that she returned to the château. As soon as the King had taken off his heavy ceremonial cloak they both hurried to a carriage and went to Meudon, where the Dauphin's condition was growing steadily worse.

It is painful to read the laconic entries in the King's private journal during the next few months. The three words, "Visit to Meudon," appear nearly every day like a *leitmotiv*. Between two audiences given to the deputies, between two hunts, the King hastened to join Marie Antoinette, who hardly left the dying boy's bedside.

On 2 June, at 10 o'clock in the evening, the great bell of Notre Dame sounded for the Forty Hours' Prayer. On the 3rd the Blessed Sacrament was exposed in all the churches in Paris. The King arrived at Meudon at four o'clock and left in his carriage at 10 o'clock in the evening. The Queen remained at her son's bedside. At one o'clock in the morning the child breathed his last. But, in accordance with etiquette, Marie Antoinette had not the right to weep by the little corpse, which was already surrounded by twelve candles. She had to return to Versailles.

The autopsy, which was carried out at once, showed that the child's "vertebrae were decayed, bulging and out of place, the ribs curved and the lungs adhering."

It was not the Queen who placed the body in its white velvet coffin with silver nails, but her "service"; it was not the King who accompanied his son to Saint-Denis, but the Prince de Condé, flanked by bodyguards, soldiers of the Hundred-Swiss and valets bearing torches. As for the little boy's heart, it was the Duc d'Orléans's son, the future Louis-Philippe, who conveyed it by coach to Val-de-Grâce. Slaves of ceremonial, the parents remained at Versailles. "Mass at eight o'clock," wrote the King. "Benediction. I saw no one. My son's funeral." They were allowed one thing: they went to spend a week at Marly—the last Marly —and asked the Archbishop of Paris to have a thousand masses said. Before giving the order the Archbishop made inquiries. How would payment be made, since the State coffers were empty? What was His Majesty's decision? Louis XVI replied: "Have the sum paid by M. de la Ferté and recover it from the expenses on the silver plate." Matters had reached this point.

It was at Marly, on 19 June, that the King received "his councils." It was a crucial moment. Two days earlier the deputies of the Third Estate, together with a few members of the Clergy, had set themselves up as a "national assembly," as they represented "ninety-six per cent of the nation." Without further delay they pronounced illegal any tax raised without their consent, and they invited the two other Orders to take counsel with them. On 18 June part of the Clergy joined them. The "advanced" nobles had not been able to win over the Nobility, who still wished to discuss by themselves—but for how long? The Archbishop of Paris, Cardinal de la Rochefoucauld, and the Duc de Luxembourg, who was President of the Nobility, exhorted the King to resistance. His crown was in peril; he should dissolve the States General, who were exceeding their rights.

Necker arrived at Marly. Received first of all by Marie Antoinette, who called the deputies "a pack of madmen," the Genevan tried to advocate conciliation. The Privy Council began its meeting and the Minister outlined his plan, which was that the King should allow the three Orders to join together and should authorise modifications to the constitution of the kingdom, but on condition that two Chambers were formed. Necker was also in favour of allowing all Frenchmen to have access to all civil and military posts.

After two hours of discussion in the Council Louis XVI began to be influenced by Necker's arguments. Suddenly the door opened and an officer came and spoke in a low voice to the King, who hurried out.

"The Queen has sent for him," murmured Necker. "We've got nowhere!" He was quite right. When Louis XVI came back into the council room he had changed his mind. Marie Antoinette had won her point. There must be no treating with the "rebels."

But on the next day, 20 June, while the King was hunting the stag at Le Butard, the "rebels," finding the Salle des Menus Plaisirs shut, assembled in the Jeu de Paume and the famous Oath followed. As Mirabeau's secretary, Dumont, wrote later, the Third Estate was henceforth "in league against the power of the Throne."

The King and Queen returned to Versailles. Necker, Saint-Priest and Montmorin begged them not to "embitter the Third Estate, the mouthpiece of public opinion." But Marie Antoinette, backed up by Provence, Artois and three Ministers out of six, advocated the use of authority. Louis XVI, only a sawdust puppet who could be made to take up any position, agreed to play the authoritarian. The three Orders would deliberate separately; he had not summoned a national assembly but the States General, and these gentlemen should hold no meeting apart from the royal sessions just as their predecessors of 1588 had done when they had been neatly drawn up at Blois by the Baron d'Oignon.

On 22 June the order of deputies was not made according to the *"rang d'oignon."* Young Dreux-Brézé, all rustling with plumes, introduced the members of the Nobility and Clergy by the main door, while the deputies of the Third Estate floundered in the mud (for it was pouring with rain) while awaiting their turn to enter the hall by the side door conceded to them.

Necker, who had made his opinions publicly known, did not attend the session. Surrounded by his wife and the Princes, Louis XVI played the part of a blind despot. The decrees on taxes of 17 June had no force; the manorial tithes and rights would be maintained.

"If, by a misfortune far from my mind," the King concluded, "you were to forsake me in such a great enterprise, I should work alone for the good of the people and I should consider myself as being its only true representative." In other words: I should not hesitate to dissolve the States General.

Before leaving the hall, followed by the triumphant Queen, Louis XVI commanded the three Orders to separate and take counsel in their respective rooms, but no one moved. The Marquis de Dreux-Brézé, putting on his hat, went over to Bailly and said: "Did you hear the King's orders?"

Most historic remarks have been made up after the event. Mirabeau doubtless refused to leave his place and doubtless spoke of the bayonets which alone could make him rise, but very probably did not utter his famous exclamation which has made the fortune of generations of print-sellers.

When Dreux-Brézé reported his failure to the King, Louis XVI sighed: "They want to stay? Well, to hell with them, let them stay!"

The King seemed to take no interest in the matter. His private Journal reveals what may have been one of the reasons for this strange attitude. On 23 June, after the "royal session with the States," one can read these unexpected and incomprehensible words: "Journey to Marly at quarter-past seven to do the packing." Had the King, then, left possessions and papers at Marly which he was anxious to pack up on that day? It would seem hardly worth while having several hundred servants!

While the King was busy with his "packing" Mirabeau had had the immunity of the representatives decreed. Henceforth to arrest a deputy —such as d'Eprémesnil—would be a "capital crime" for the King. The deputies looked on the royal message as a "challenge" and Mirabeau talked of "denouncing the Queen," who according to him was the cause of all the evil.

"What, the Queen?" asked the youngest son of the Duc d'Orléans.

"And why not?" exclaimed his brother, the future Louis-Philippe. Absolute monarchy, so many centuries old, was dying.

During the days that followed Louis XVI wrote his famous "Nothing" each day in his Journal. On 25 June "Nothing" was accompanied by this sigh: "The stag was hunted at Saint-Appoline," the implication being: "and I was not there." He no longer galloped with the hunt, for he was trying to win the race for the revolution. Having forbidden the Three Orders to meet together, he now commanded them to. The Nobles thereupon declared "that the monarchy must be protected from the King." Marie Antoinette was of the same opinion, but, overwhelmed, she wept and let her husband act.

"Monsieur," the King declared to the President of the Nobility, "I beg your Order to join with the two others. If begging is not enough, I wish it!"

On 27 June "the family was complete," in Bailly's words, and Paris was illuminated. Marie Antoinette could not understand this popular rejoicing. How could France be happy when the monarchy had been degraded by a pack of clodhoppers and lawyers? They must regain the power snatched from them. Louis XVI, who like a bubble obeyed the least breath, hastened to resume his rôle of despot, which he had abandoned on 23 June. He approved the idea of a *coup d'état*. But to dissolve the Assembly he needed troops. The regiments converged on Paris by forced marches. Soon the *Royal-Cravate* was garrisoned at Charenton, *Salis-Samade* at Issy, the Hussars at the Ecole Militaire and the Royal German at La Muette. Besenval, whose job was to "control" Paris, was responsible for them all.

The Assembly was frightened and on 9 July sent a deputation to the King, who replied on the following day: "Only the ill-disposed could mislead my people about the precautionary measures I am taking."

What followed is well known: on 11 July Necker's dismissal was like the crack of a whip. It became known in the town on 12 July and Camille Desmoulins at the Palais Royal cried: "I have just come from Versailles. M. Necker is dismissed. This is the signal for a St. Bartholomew's Day of the patriots. This evening the Swiss and German battalions will cut our throats. We have but one resource—to take to arms."

And two days later, in "searching for arms," they were to take the Bastille.

That evening the King went to bed, after writing in his notebook: "14, nothing." And yet that afternoon a deputation had again come from the Assembly to ask him to withdraw the troops encamped in the Champ de Mars, so as to calm Paris. He had agreed. He risked nothing, for Versailles and the suburbs of Paris were full of soldiers, and the bodyguards had been ready for two days. That very afternoon Mme de Polignac had taken biscuits to the two German regiments encamped in the Orangerie. The deputation had also announced that the Parisians were marching on the Bastille. All right, it would defend itself. After all, M. de Launay had cannons and at the first shot the attackers would disappear. Tomorrow he would go to the Assembly and dissolve the States General.

The King fell peacefully asleep. He awoke with a start. The Grand Master of the Wardrobe, the Duc de la Rochefoucauld-Liancourt, was at his bedside.

"The Bastille has been taken! The governor has been assassinated! His head is being borne on a pike through the town."

The King was now wide awake.

"But . . . but then it is a revolt?"

"No, Sire, it is a revolution."

They consulted together. Should they go to Metz, as Marie Antoinette advised? Maréchal de Broglie remarked sensibly: "It is easy to go to Metz, but what should we do when we got there?"

The King decided to abdicate. Just when nothing prevented him from carrying out his *coup d'état*, for which he now had an excuse, he preferred to change his mind again. On the next day he went to the Assembly with his brothers and announced to the deputies the withdrawal of all troops. But although a weathercock he was none the less a worthy man and he uttered from his heart a sentence which provoked enthusiasm: "I am one with the Nation, I entrust myself to you."

There was wild applause. Hand in hand the deputies accompanied the King, who returned slowly on foot to the château. The crowd which had gathered followed them, crying: "Long live the King!" And one of them added, looking at the Comte d'Artois: "In spite of you, Monseigneur, and your opinions."

The courtyards of the château were filled with an immense crowd who called for the King, the Queen and the new Dauphin to appear on the balcony. Marie Antoinette told Mme Campan to go and find the future Louis XVII and to ask Mme de Polignac not to accompany the little Prince.

"Ah! Madame," said the Duchesse when she heard the Queen's order, "what a blow this is!"

Having carried out her orders, Mme Campan went down into the courtyard just as the King and Queen, with Mme Royale and the Dauphin, appeared on the balcony.

"Ah!" said one woman, disappointed, "the Duchesse is not with her."

"No," a man replied, "but she is still at Versailles. She is like a mole! She is working underground, but we shall be able to dig her out."

Terrified, Mme Campan reported this conversation to Marie Antoinette. The Queen had received many warnings of the same kind that morning and she summoned the Duchesse.

"I fear the worst. In the name of our friendship leave me. You still have time to avoid the fury of my enemies. When they attack you they are more incensed against me than against you."

Mme de Polignac resisted. How could she leave her whole life?

"Do not become a victim to your affection and my friendship."

At that moment Louis XVI entered the room.

"Come, Monsieur," the Queen exclaimed, "come and help me persuade these faithful subjects that they must leave us."

Louis XVI, who had just decided to recall Necker, sighed.

"My cruel fate forces me to send from me all those I love and esteem. I have just ordered the Comte d'Artois to leave, and I give you the same order. Pity me, but do not lose a single moment."

The Duc and Duchesse yielded. At midnight, just as Mme de Polignac, her husband, daughter and sister-in-law were entering their carriage, the Duchesse was handed a note from the Queen: "Farewell, dearest of friends, the word is a dreadful one. Here is the order for the horses. Farewell, I have only the strength to embrace you."

Not without difficulty, for at Sens they were nearly recognised, M. and Mme de Polignac arrived at Basle. Soon they received a letter from Marie Antoinette: "I can only venture to write a word, my dear love . . . I cannot express all my regret at being separated from you; I hope you feel as I do. We are surrounded with nothing but grief, misfortune and unfortunates . . . Everyone is fleeing and I am only too happy to think that all those I care for are far from me."

Fersen was at Valenciennes, where he saw passing through the Comte d'Artois, the Prince de Condé, the Duc de Bourbon, the Duc d'Enghien, Vaudreuil and the Marquis de Polignac. All the Queen's friends left Versailles: Coigny, Calonne, Lambesq, Luxembourg, the Marsans, the Rohans, the Castries, Breteuil, and even the Abbé de Vermond. They left her to face the storm alone.

"My sole resource is in my children," she wrote to Mme de Polignac. "I have them with me as much as possible. You have certainly heard of the appointment of Mme de Tourzel. It gave me great pain."

Mme de Tourzel, indeed, had been appointed Governess to the two Children of France and it was for her benefit that, while the tempest raged and grumbled, the Queen prepared a report on 24 July. It is worth reading some extracts from it, for it shows us an unknown Marie Antoinette, hitherto concealed from us by her frivolity.

"My son is four years and four months old, less two days," Marie Antoinette wrote to Mme de Tourzel. "I will not speak of his build or appearance, for you have only to see him. His health has always been good, but even when he was in the cradle it was noticed that his nerves were very delicate and that the slightest unexpected noise affected him. He was late with his first teeth, but they came through without illness or accident. It was only with the last, and I think with the sixth, that he had a convulsion at Fontainebleau. He has had two since, one in the winter of '87 or '88 and the other after his inoculation, but the latter was very slight. As a result of his delicate nerves he is always frightened by any noise to which he is not accustomed, for example, he is frightened of dogs because he heard one bark near him. I have never forced him to see them because I think that as he gains in reasoning power his fears will disappear. Like all strong, healthy children, he is very thoughtless, very frivolous and violent in his anger, but he is good-natured, gentle and even affectionate when he is not carried away by his thoughtlessness. He has an exaggerated sense of self-esteem which, by good guidance, might one day be turned to his advantage. Until he is at ease with anyone, he knows how to control himself and even conquer his impatience and anger so as to appear gentle and amiable. He keeps his word faithfully once he has given it, but he is very indiscreet and easily repeats what he has heard and often, without meaning to lie, he adds things suggested by his own imagination. This is his greatest fault and it must be firmly corrected. Apart from that, I repeat, he is good-natured and by using kindness and firmness, but without being too severe, one can do what one likes with him, but severity would make him rebel, for he has a strong character for his age. For example, even when he was very small, the word "Pardon" always shocked him. He will do and say whatever one likes when he is in the wrong but he will pronounce the word "Pardon" only with great difficulty and many tears. My children have always been taught to have complete trust in me and when they have done wrong to tell me so themselves. By this means, when I scold them, I appear more hurt and sorry at what they have done than angry. I have accustomed them to accepting a yes or no from me as being irrevocable, but I always give them a reason suited to their age, so that they do not think it is merely a whim on my part. My son cannot read and has great difficulty in learning, but he is too scatterbrained to concentrate. He has no ideas of grandeur and I should wish that to continue. Our children learn only too quickly what they are.

"He is very fond of his sister and has a good heart. Every time some-

thing pleases him, like going somewhere, or if someone gives him something, his first impulse is to ask for the same thing for his sister. He was
born gay. His health requires plenty of air and I think the best thing
is to let him play and work outside on the terrace rather than take him
farther. The exercise taken by little children as they run and play in
the open air is much healthier for them than being made to take walks,
which often tires their backs."

The tragic events of this first month of the Revolution were to bring
Marie Antoinette closer to her husband. When the Assembly and the
town of Paris, wishing simultaneously to humiliate Louis XVI and make
him sanction the massacre, asked him to visit his "good town," Louis
XVI agreed. Marie Antoinette protested that it was folly. But the King,
having been to communion and appointed Provence Lieutenant General of the kingdom "in the event of his not returning," left for Paris
like a man going to the scaffold. The Queen trembled for him. This
poor man, this cork on the water, had at last moved her. She suppressed
her tears and retired to her private rooms with her children. "A silence
of death reigns over all the palace," wrote Mme Campan. Marie
Antoinette was convinced that her husband would not return, and she
ordered the stables to get horses ready, not for flight, but to go as a
sovereign to the Assembly. She even wrote out a declaration:

"Gentlemen, I come to deliver to you the wife and family of your
sovereign. Do not permit what was joined in heaven to be sundered
on earth."

"As she repeated this speech," wrote Mme Campan, "her voice was
broken by tears and by these sorrowing words: 'They will never let him
return!' "

When he came back, after being humiliated and wearing in his hat
the tricolour cockade he had been forced to display, Marie Antoinette
threw herself in his arms, weeping with joy. It cannot be true that,
as Mercy asserted, she then drew away from him, on seeing the three
colours he wore, and said: "I did not know I had married a commoner."
The insult is not in keeping with this day of tears and anguish and one
finds it difficult to believe in it.

Versailles then resumed its calm. Mercy, who went to the château on
23 July, saw "nothing but confusion." "Chance is relied on for everything," he wrote. He returned to Versailles on 11 August and reported:
"The Queen bears her troubles with the greatest courage, and a great

deal is needed not to be overwhelmed or revolted by the injustice and the horrors against which this noble Princess has to fight." Marie Antoinette even began to hope. "These last few days things seem to have taken a better turn," she wrote to Mme de Polignac at the end of the month, "but one cannot rely on anything. The wicked have great power and the means to frustrate or prevent the most just actions . . . But you can always be sure that adversity has not lessened my strength and my courage." True devotion was being revealed. "I am discovering all kinds of truly and sincerely attached people of whom I had never even thought." Such a one was Grétry, who one day came to present to Marie Antoinette his future son-in-law, Bouilly, author of the libretto of *Peter the Great*, an opera by Grétry which had just been performed.

The young dramatist, incidentally, wore a sword knot embroidered by his beloved Antoinette Grétry, the Queen's goddaughter. But let the charming and simple Jean-Nicolas Bouilly speak for himself.

"About half-past twelve we were shown into the Queen's private apartments. She had just been hearing mass in the chapel and as she entered her music-room she took off the black velvet *pouf* she was wearing on her head and her large black lace mantilla and called us forward. Grétry had not finished introducing me when Marie Antoinette, trying to account for the surprise my face occasioned her, suddenly exclaimed: 'I am not mistaken, Monsieur. This is not the first time I have seen you.'

"I replied smiling: 'Your Majesty, I see, deigns to remember the young scamp who on the terrace of the Orangerie dared to take a seat. . . .'

" 'Yes, yes, on one of the marble benches where I was sitting. I remember you perfectly. Grétry,' she added very graciously, 'you can congratulate yourself on having for a colleague a most faithful champion of ladies.'

"So saying, she congratulated us on our success and, looking keenly at me, she deigned to thank me for the devotion I had displayed in the King's cause.

" 'I was all the more delighted,' she added with a slightly mischievous smile, 'as I hear, Monsieur, that you are the son of a deputy of the Third Estate.'

"In this tone of enchanting gaiety and displaying her patronage for the arts and letters, she put several questions to me full of charm and

interest on the sweet illusions of a first success. I replied that it was
not enough to gain it, one must also be able to deserve it. She again
examined me with close attention and I distinctly heard her say to
Grétry, who was standing near her sofa: 'He is very pleasing, your
collaborator, very pleasing indeed.'

"I was intoxicated. I shook the chains which were already beginning
to bind me.

"Marie Antoinette produced a particularly strong impression on me
as she spoke of Antoinette Grétry with the affectionate interest of a
godmother. Oh! how those kindly words which escaped her lips penetrated deep into my heart! Until then she had dazzled me by her beauty
and charmed me by her grace. How moved I was by that penetrating
goodness, by that encouraging and majestic familiarity which conquered
all who heard it!

" 'How old is my goddaughter now?' she asked her father in truly
maternal accents.

" 'Seventeen,' replied Grétry, 'and since then she has been clothed and
adorned only with Your Majesty's gifts.'

" 'I hope,' the Queen added, 'that she will always be so. She has
everything that will one day make of her a distinguished and accomplished woman, and I shall take it on myself to choose her a husband.'

" 'I think,' replied Grétry, with his accustomed subtle smile, 'that
we would do better to let her choose for herself.'

" 'I am strongly in favour of that system,' replied Marie Antoinette.

"Thus speaking, she held out her beautiful hand to the celebrated
composer and he hastened to impress a most respectful kiss on it. In-
voluntarily I exclaimed with enthusiasm: 'Ah! who would not envy the
prerogatives of fame?'

" 'Yours is just beginning, Monsieur, under such favourable auspices
that I must be eager to encourage it.'

"So saying, Marie Antoinette held out her royal hand to me also.
Surprised and confused, I sank on one knee and brushed that noble
hand with my trembling lips.

" 'Your Majesty must excuse him,' said Grétry, pressing my arm
and signing to me to take hold of myself, 'it is the first time he has
drunk ambrosia.'

"This charming remark completely restored me."

It is a pretty scene. And before the collapse of this delightful epoch—

so delightful that for many years it concealed the stench rising from the decaying heart of the age—before this whole world crumbles for ever, let us evoke one last image of the Queen of Trianon.

During these months of August and September she often went to her beloved Trianon, which was visited nearly every day by the deputies of the Assembly, who were quite surprised not to find the famous drawing-room carpeted with precious stones, which was mentioned in the pamphlets. They seemed almost disappointed when they were told that it was only a stage setting and that the jewels were nothing but glass.

After dining in the little château Marie Antoinette went to her musical-comedy dairy. It was there that one day she was nearly taken unawares by three young Lorrainers, who were visiting Trianon. One of them, François Cognel, has given a description which affords us yet another, and very charming, picture of the Queen. "Just as we were about to leave, Marie Antoinette's arrival was announced and as we had no time to reach the garden gate our guide made us go into the stable. The Queen, who was accompanied by a lady of the court, then dismissed her and came on alone towards the dairy. She was wearing a plain linen dress with a scarf and a lace cap. In these simple clothes she seemed more full of majesty than in the grand robes in which we had seen her at Versailles. Her way of walking is peculiar to her. One cannot distinguish her steps; she glides with incomparable grace. She bears her head much more proudly when, as when we were watching her, she believes herself to be alone. Our Queen passed quite close to where we were standing and all three of us had an impulse to bend the knee as she passed."

Her walk was still "caressing," in spite of her generous proportions. Thanks to the journal of Mme Eloff, her dressmaker, we know that at that time the Queen measured about $23\frac{1}{2}''$ round the waist and $43\frac{1}{2}''$ round the bust. This latter figure may seem somewhat large, but was admirably suited to the fashion of the time.

Very often, in the morning, when she had drunk a glass of milk from "her" cows, she would rest on the bed of dry moss arranged in the little grotto behind the box-covered hill. Lulled by the sound of the little spring which rose out of the sand of the grotto, she would fall to musing.

She was musing thus on the afternoon of 5 October.

For the last few days things seemed to have been going better. Of
course the taxes were still not coming in, but the King had sent to
the Mint 13,000 livres' weight of silver plate, and on her side the Queen
had sent 386 dishes, a large quantity of torches and cutlery in silver
gilt and silver. She had even wished to make a personal sacrifice and
had deprived herself of her patch-boxes, her *crachoirs à manche,* her
toothpick cases and the large silver bucket in which she was accustomed
to wash her feet.

On Monday 5 October, Marie Antoinette plucked up courage.

"I was delighted with my day on Thursday," she had once more told
a deputation the evening before.

Thursday had been the banquet given by the officers of the Versailles
garrison on 1 October to their comrades of the Flanders regiment, which
had just arrived from Douai to protect the royal family. The latter, indeed, were somewhat isolated since the desertion of the French Guards,
who had left for Paris during the night of 30-31 July with all their
arms and baggage. Admittedly a National Guard had been formed
at Versailles, but there was not much to be said for these shopkeepers
disguised as soldiers and commanded by an Admiral, the Comte
d'Estaing. "Flanders," of course, had hardly 1,100 men, but they could
still count on the Provost of the King's Household and on the detachment of Chasseurs Lorrains encamped at Rambouillet. Moreover the
300 bodyguards of the "July barracks" had been retained, thus doubling
the usual numbers of that somewhat undisciplined troop composed
undoubtedly of "warm partisans of the Third Estate"—who on the
preceding Thursday, however, had demonstrated their warm loyalty to
the crown.

At first Marie Antoinette had not wished to attend the banquet
given in the Opera Theatre, but one of her ladies, Mme de Tessé, came
to ask her at least to have a look. The guests, numbering 206, ate at a
horseshoe-shaped table on the stage. After the second service the Duc
de Villeroi, Captain of the first company of guards, had invited all the
grenadiers, cavalrymen and Swiss Guards who were drinking in
the pit to bring their glasses up to the horseshoe and drink four
healths: to the King, to the Queen, to the Dauphin and to the royal
family. As each health was drunk the trumpets sounded the charge.
One of the guests, it appeared, had murmured "To the health of the
Nation," but no one had paid any attention. On hearing this report

Marie Antoinette hesitated, but at that moment the King came back
from the hunt and the Queen bore him off with their two children to
the railed-in box facing the stage. The guests had already done justice to
the wines and the meal prepared by the chef Deharmes, and when the
royal family appeared they were given a wildly enthusiastic reception.
The applause and the welcoming cries still rang in the Queen's ears
after five days. She had entrusted the Dauphin to an officer of the Swiss
Guards and the smiling child, who was placed on the table, walked all
round the horseshoe without upsetting a glass. The orchestra had played
Grétry's *O Richard, ô mon Roi*, and everyone sang together:

> *O Richard, ô mon Roi*
> *L'univers t'abandonne.*
> *Sur la terre il n'est donc que moi*
> *Qui m'intéresse à ta personne.*

This was followed by one of Sedaine's songs: *Peut-on affliger ce
qu'on aime?* The applause grew so loud that the royal family came down
on to the stage. Marie Antoinette had found the subsequent cries,
dances and applause in the marble hall somewhat excessive and she
doubtless disapproved of M. d'Estaing's aide-de-camp, a certain Perceval,
who went so far as to climb up on to the balcony, shouting: "The posts
are ours. From now on we must be called the royal guards." But these
young hotheads could be forgiven some excesses due to the wine.

As was to be expected, however, on Sunday the Paris pamphleteers—
the Marats, Desmoulins and Loustalots—had transformed this happy
evening into an orgy. They had actually written that the guests had
drunkenly trampled on the tricolour cockade. The Queen had seen
nothing of the sort. At the most, perhaps, some young men of the Versailles National Guard had reversed their tricolour cockades, thus displaying the white worn by "Flanders" and the Chasseurs. Perhaps, too,
white cockades had been given to some of the guests at the horseshoe
and they had taken them. Perhaps, again, when the evening was well
advanced, some young men excited by drink had cried: "Down with
the Assembly!" under the Queen's windows. So it was said, but Marie
Antoinette had heard nothing.

Besides, all these imaginative and exaggerated details came from
absentees, such as Lecointre, the Lieutenant General of the Notre
Dame barracks of the National Guard, who had not been invited to

the banquet. Eye-witnesses were either unaware of them or denied them.

During the meal the guests had shouted so much that many of the dishes and nearly 400 bottles were left over. And so on Saturday the leavings had been finished off at the royal riding-school, and there were fresh cries of "Long live the King!" and "Long live the Queen!" but this time the Nation and the Assembly were not forgotten.

Marie Antoinette thought the trouble would die down. In the words of a contemporary: "the moment there was a lull and an appearance of security she quickly resumed all her illusions." And now, on Monday 5 October, her illusions prevented her from realising that since Thursday's "orgy" Paris was in a ferment. There was no bread in Paris, whereas, according to the pamphleteers, flour was being hoarded at Versailles, where, to make matters worse, they were insulting the Nation. In the streets there were cries of: "It is time to cut the Queen's throat."

How far away all this seemed at Trianon! Through the narrow crack in the rock the Queen gazed at the ravine, where the trees were already changing colour. The sky was dark and the rain began to fall. Suddenly Marie Antoinette saw a page hurrying towards the grotto. In a moment he was before her, panting.

He was sent by M. de Saint-Priest. Paris was marching on Versailles.

12

✤

The Entry into History

IT WAS POURING with rain. The first horde of 6,000 women marched towards Versailles preceded by ten drummers, four cannon and Maillard, the conqueror of the Bastille. Covered with mud and soaked to the skin, they called to the onlookers: "See what a state we are in, but the jade will pay us dearly!"

They were armed with broom handles, pitchforks, swords, skewers and old pistols. There were even some enormous kitchen knives, which the termagants sharpened on the milestones.

"How glad I should be if I could open her belly with this knife and tear out her heart by thrusting my arm in up to the elbow!"

"We each want to bring back part of Marie Antoinette."

"I shall have a thigh!"

"I shall have the entrails!"

"As they said these things," reports a witness, the lawyer Antoine Périn, "many of them held out their aprons, as though they already carried in them what they had promised themselves, and in that attitude they danced." The lawyer also reported other remarks and revolting gestures relating to Mme de Polignac and the Queen which it is impossible to repeat.

Here and there a few muskets were seen, but they were carried by men disguised as women. This is not a legend; there exist 392 depositions for these two days in October which are unanimous on the point. A contemporary observer gives us the reason for this masquerade: "They were less likely to decide to repel women by force of arms." So the men who wanted to follow had had to place themselves at the rear of the column or wear a disguise. However, they were not behind in crying: "We will take the Queen dead or alive!"

And the women replied: "You will take charge of the King! It is we who will take the Queen dead or alive!"

"Her throat must be cut! We will make cockades of her guts!"

At half-past three the van of the terrifying crowd reached Versailles. At the entrance of the Avenue de Paris some of the women were almost knocked down by a group of riders. It was the King, who having heard of the march from Paris was returning hurriedly from the hunt. When he arrived at the château the tocsin sounded and the gates, which had not moved on their hinges since the time of the Roi Soleil, were closed. The bodyguards, the Flanders regiment and 200 men of the Versailles National Guard were drawn up in battle array in the Place d'Armes. Not a single cartridge had been distributed.

Behind the hedge of troops the château was seething. The King was in council with the Queen. What was to be done? The Captain of the Guards came to ask for orders.

"What! For a crowd of women? You are jesting!"

Marie Antoinette was quite calm. Saint-Priest explained his plan. "I described the danger of awaiting this multitude at Versailles and I suggested measures to be taken in this event. They consisted in having the bridges over the Seine guarded by a battalion of the Flanders regiment at Sèvres, by another at Saint Cloud, and by the Swiss Guards at Neuilly, and finally in the King's sending the Queen and the royal family to Rambouillet, where the Chasseurs of the Lorraine regiment were stationed, while His Majesty went to meet the Parisians with 200 Chasseurs des Evêchés and his 800 bodyguards. Once the thousand horse were drawn up on the other side of the Pont de Sèvres the King would order the crowd from Paris to retire and, if they did not obey, would order several cavalry charges to disperse them. Finally, if this did not succeed, the King would have time to regain Versailles at the head of his troops and then to march to Rambouillet."

Louis XVI was tempted, but Marie Antoinette did not want to be separated from her husband.

"I do not wish the King to incur a danger which I cannot share."

While hours went by in waiting and inaction at the château the fishwives, covered with mud from head to foot, infiltrated into Versailles. Maillard, at the head of a group, invaded the Assembly.

"The people have no bread," he cried. "They are in despair, their arms are raised and they will certainly be led into some excesses. We ask permission to search the houses suspected of holding flour. It is for the Assembly to avert the shedding of blood, but the Assembly contains enemies of the people, who are the cause of the famine. Wicked men are giving money and bonds to the millers to ensure that they do not grind."

"The names? The names? Name them!" was cried on all sides.

In all seriousness Maillard replied: "The Archbishop of Paris has given 200 livres to a miller to stop him grinding!"

Those on the right were angry, but Robespierre, in one of his first interventions, approved this absurdity. Disorder crept in, grew and became indescribable. The women howled: "Bread, bread, bread!"

They climbed over the benches, embraced the President—the Bishop of Langres—took off their skirts to dry, booed the deputies, and soon "the most indecent joy filled the sanctuary of the representatives of the leading people of the world."

One harridan, with a "sharpened dagger" in her hand, went up to Maître Thomas de Frondeville, *Président à mortier* of the Normandy Parliament, and asked him in a low voice: "Is the Queen's apartment as well guarded as they say? Isn't there some way of getting in?"

A fishwife brandished a piece of black bread: "I want to make the Austrian woman swallow it before I wring her neck!"

Other women came up against the troops who were still arrayed in the Place d'Armes. Some of them "offered to pull up their skirts in front of the cavalry." The same theme recurred incessantly: "Ah! The bitch! If I could get hold of her I would tear her apart!"

A thick mist fell on the town. Behind the cavalry gleaming with rain a few windows in the château lit up. The King was receiving a delegation of five women of Paris escorted by several deputies. One of them, Louison Chabry, a "worker in sculpture," aged twenty, fainted with emotion on finding herself in Louis XVI's presence and the King made her smell spirits. While he was speaking kindly to the delegation the cries of the viragos reached the *Œil-de-Bœuf* and could be distinctly heard: "We will bring back the Queen's head on the end of a pike."

The King sighed and asked Louison: "Have you come to harm my wife?"

But one of Lafayette's aides-de-camp brought serious news. The commanding officer of the Paris National Guards was marching on Versailles with 30,000 men, including the former French Guards. Saint-Priest immediately recommended a general removal to Rambouillet and even Normandy. The King would not decide before taking Marie Antoinette's advice. She agreed, since there was no longer any question of leaving her husband, and hurried into the children's apartments, where she informed the sub-governesses: "We are leaving in a quarter-of-an-hour, get your things together and hurry!"

But it was too late. What had been possible at four o'clock was no longer possible at eight. The crowd prevented the carriage from leaving the Stables. Force would have been needed and the King refused to employ it. Marie Antoinette sighed: "Go and tell those ladies that everything is changed. We are staying."

There was consternation in the whole court, but Marie Antoinette reassured those about her. During this night of 5 to 6 October she remained astonishingly calm. She entered into history. "Her countenance was noble and dignified," reports an observer, "and her face was calm, and although she could have had no illusions as to what there was to fear, no one could perceive the least trace of anxiety. She reassured everyone, thought of everything and was far more preoccupied by all that was dear to her than with her own person. During this evening of 5 October she was seen to receive a great many people in her drawing-room, to speak with firmness and dignity to all who came near her and to communicate her confidence to those who could not conceal their alarm."

"I know they have come from Paris to demand my head, but I learned from my mother not to fear death and I shall await it with firmness."

This evening, for the first time, she seemed to realise her terrible responsibilities.

A few gentlemen and a handful of officers surrounded her. Among them was Fersen. They begged for an order authorising them to take horses from the stable, so that they might defend the royal family if it were attacked.

"I shall consent to give the order on one condition," replied Marie Antoinette. "If the King's life is in danger you will use it promptly; if I alone am in danger you will not use it."

Meanwhile, Louis XVI, at the urging of the deputy Mounier, gave, weeping, his "pure and simple" consent to the Declaration of the Rights of Man. Still weeping he ordered the bodyguards and the Flanders Regiment to leave their posts and to bivouac, the former in the park, on the "Green Carpet," and the latter in the courtyard of the Little Stables. As Louis XVI no longer wanted these men as defenders he could not let them become victims. Only the Versailles National Guard remained on parade.

"As wet as ducks, floundering and stumbling in the mud," the army of Parisians arrived half-an-hour after midnight. Lafayette left his men in the Place d'Armes and entered the château. The General always seemed to be taking part in a scene intended for coloured reproduction. With a telling gesture of his arm he exclaimed: "Sire, I bring you my head to save that of Your Majesty. If my blood must flow, let it be in the service of my King rather than in the shameful light of the torches of the Place de la Grève."

"Monsieur de Lafayette," replied Louis XVI, "you must never doubt that I always have pleasure in seeing you and your good Parisians. Go and let them know my feelings."

In words that have not come down to us, Lafayette then asked the King to let the former French Guards take over the posts they had deserted a month before and to be entrusted with guarding the château. Louis XVI—in his second abdication of the evening—accepted, "trusting in *everything* a General who was sure of *nothing*," in Rivarol's words.

"Go to the Queen," he ordered his valet. "Tell her to go to bed. I shall do so also."

It was then two o'clock in the morning. Marie Antoinette dismissed her servants, refused the protection of several gentlemen who wished to spend the night outside her door, and went to bed. The sound of drums mounted from the courtyard. It was the Versailles National Guard handing over the passwords to the French Guards. In the distance the Queen heard horses' hooves dying away in the night. The bodyguard were retiring to Rambouillet, while the Swiss Guards regained their barracks at Rueil.

Only a handful of bodyguards were guarding the inner doors. The French Guards were at their posts—the gates and openings on to the park—but in accordance with old orders they left all the doors open to facilitate the changing of sentries.

The Queen slept. Lafayette retired to the Hôtel de Noailles, a short distance from the chapel gate, went to bed and sank into slumber.

"I had no anxiety," this heroic donkey was to say later. "The people had promised me they would remain calm."

Tuesday, 6 October, dawned. The Queen's wonderful musical clock tinkled delicately the notes of "_Il pleut, bergère._" It was six o'clock. At that moment Marie Antoinette heard a noise under her windows. She rang. Her first waiting-woman, Marie Elisabeth Nolle, informed her that it was "the women of Paris who, not having found anywhere to sleep, were walking on the terrace." Relieved, Marie Antoinette dozed off. A quarter of an hour later she was suddenly awakened. Two of her women, Mmes Thiébaut and Augié, were before her. The château was invaded, and some of the guards had been massacred. Not far off Marie Antoinette heard the immense clamour of the people looking for the entrance to her apartments. They caught phrases: "This way! This way! . . . Kill! Kill! . . . No quarter! . . . Death . . . We must have the Queen's heart! . . . Where is the damned bitch?"

Aided by her two women, Marie Antoinette put on her stockings and a petticoat and fled by the little corridor behind her bed. But the door leading to the _Œil-de-Bœuf_ was closed. Behind her Marie Antoinette heard the rioters enter her bedroom. With all the shouts filling the palace it was several minutes before a boy heard the fugitives. Weeping, the Queen ran across the room to get to the King's apartments. They heard her beg: "My friends, my dear friends, save me!"

She took breath again in the old dining room, but the King was not there. A minute before he had left by the secret passage to help the Queen. Learning from a guard that she was in safety, he went to find the Dauphin, while Marie Antoinette hurried to little Madame Royale. Finally, five minutes later, they were all four reunited in Louis XVI's bedroom. They could hear the attackers' axes on the very door of the _Œil-de-Bœuf_. The panels flew in pieces. Suddenly the noise was stilled. What was happening? The French Guards charged and cleared the château.

But the Cour de Marbre and the Cour Royale were black with people. "A crowd of almost naked women," reports an observer, "and men armed with pikes threatened the windows with terrifying cries." Marie Antoinette looked out.

"There she is, the damned whore!"

"We don't need her body, we only want to take her head to Paris!"

"The trollop!" yelled a tall, red-headed woman, showing a sickle held by one of her companions. "This will take her head off!"

Another cry kept on recurring: "Long live the Duc d'Orléans!"

The future Philippe-Egalité arrived at Versailles when everything was over, but in the opinion of the people and the royal family, as well as the historians, it was he who had decided, planned and organised everything. Some people were even to claim to have seen him at the head of the marble staircase showing the attackers the way to the Queen's apartments. But at that time he was still at the Palais Royal.[1]

"They will kill my son!"

Marie Antoinette did not retire from the window embrasure. Madame Elisabeth was at her side, Madame Royale in front of her and standing on a chair, the Dauphin watched uncomprehendingly.

"Mamma, I'm hungry!"

The Queen kissed him with tears in her eyes.

"Be patient."

Other shouts now came from the courtyard.

"Let the King come to the balcony!"

Lafayette, who had finally been got out of bed, retained his disarming optimism and dragged Louis XVI to the casement of the state bedroom.

"To Paris! To Paris!"

Lafayette incessantly begged the crowd to retire. Not a man moved. Suddenly a voice demanded: "The Queen on the balcony!"

All went pale and begged Marie Antoinette not to expose herself. Maria Theresa's daughter looked at the surging crowd brandishing its arms.

"I shall appear."

She came forward, holding by the hand her children, who burst into tears.

"No children!"

"The Queen alone!"

With a movement of her arms she pushed back the Dauphin and Madame Royale and appeared alone on the balcony. Thousands of

---

[1] On this subject see the author's *Philippe-Egalité, le Prince rouge* (Amiot-Dumont).

eyes gazed at this woman, with her hair disordered, who crossed her hands on her yellow and white striped wrapper.

"Shoot! Shoot!"

Marie Antoinette bowed her head and curtsied.

At this gallantry a great shout of "Long live the Queen!" rang from end to end of the great parade ground.

The Queen re-entered her bedroom, covering her children with tears and kisses. But the cries of "To Paris! To Paris!" grew louder, swelled and became so menacing that there was no drawing back. For the tenth time Louis XVI returned to the balcony with Lafayette. Not without difficulty they obtained a moment of silence.

"My friends," cried the King in a loud voice, "I shall go to Paris with my wife and children. I entrust what is most precious to me to the love of my good and faithful subjects."

There was a thunder of applause, punctuated with shots and even cannon-fire.

"Madame," Lafayette asked Marie Antoinette, "what are the Queen's personal intentions?"

"I know the fate that awaits me, but my duty is to die at the King's feet and in the arms of my children."

"All right, Madame. Come with me."

He led her on to the balcony. But there were such howls that at first Lafayette could not make himself heard. He kissed the Queen's hand. There was applause, and shouts of "Long live the General, long live the Queen!"

Lafayette then made this extraordinary speech: "The Queen has been deceived. She promises that she will be so no longer. She promises to love her people, to be attached to them, like Jesus Christ to his Church!"

Through her tears—tears of shame—she looked at the crowd which was now applauding her loudly.

At twenty-five past one the procession of the fallen monarchy left Versailles for ever, on their first stage towards the scaffold.

As the great guardroom was full of blood the royal family went down by a small staircase and entered their carriages with the Comte and Comtesse of Provence and Mme de Tourzel. After waiting for half an hour the long procession set off, preceded by a vanguard carrying the bloody heads of the two bodyguards massacred at the invasion of the château. The weather was mild and clear.

After the "tragic masquerade of the soldiers," after the troupe of "drunken women astride the cannons," came the royal coach. Marie Antoinette bore in her face "the marks of violent grief." From time to time the King covered his face with his handkerchief "to hide his tears." Women danced around the coach, crying: "We are bringing back the baker, the baker's wife and the little baker's boy. They'll give us bread or we'll know why!"

Some of Lafayette's officers also uttered remarks which, an observer held to be "hardly proper."

Behind the royal coach marched the disarmed guards, then 2,000 court carriages. In one of them was Fersen.

The journey lasted seven hours, and the Dauphin wept with hunger. At the Chaillot barrier Bailly, the Mayor of Paris who had succeeded the *Prévôt des marchands*, made so bold as to say to the King: "What a wonderful day, Sire, on which the Parisians hold Your Majesty and his family in their city."

But the "wonderful day" was not yet over. Bailly led his prisoners to the Hôtel de Ville. "As the National Guard were not sufficient to line the whole of the processional route," relates Dom Leclercq, "a battalion had been made up of Franciscans, Recollects, Capuchins, Picpusians, etc. It was a battalion of mendicant friars commanded with jealous care and irreproachable skill by a certain Corbeau, captain of artillery. With a large tricolour tassel on their chests by way of a cockade and a naked sabre on their shoulders these reverend gentlemen affected a martial bearing behind their chief, who in his regimentals displayed a conquering air. Passing before this group, which did its best to present arms and attract his attention, Louis XVI turned away his head and furtively wiped away a tear."

In the Place de l'Hôtel de Ville a dense crowd greeted the sovereigns. These were no riff-raff or fishwives but honest folk who were glad to cry: "Long live the King, long live the Queen, long live the Dauphin, long live us all!" Everyone wept with joy and embraced. The Revolution was over!

Fersen had gone to await Marie Antoinette at the Tuileries, but Saint-Priest asked him to withdraw. "His liaison with the Queen being well known," he might put Marie Antoinette in danger merely by his presence. Axel obeyed.

It was nearly ten o'clock when the royal family finally arrived at the Tuileries, which had been abandoned by the monarchy since Louis

XV's minority. The château was unfurnished and since noon a crowd of people who had installed themselves there of their own accord had been chased away. The court camped as well as it could in this lumber room. The Dauphin's door would not shut and Mme de Tourzel, not daring to go to bed, watched all night by the child's little bed.

In the morning there was a ray of hope. A good-humoured crowd surrounded the castle, continually acclaiming the King, the Dauphin and even the Queen. Marie Antoinette appeared at a window and declared "that she loved the inhabitants of her good city of Paris."

"Yes, yes," cried a voice, "but on 14 July you wanted to besiege the city and bombard it and on 5 October you were going to flee to the frontier."

This was no more than a laughing reproach and the applause thundered again. "If we forget where we are and how we came here," Marie Antoinette wrote to Mercy, who had been advised not to show himself too much, "we should be pleased with the people's mood, particularly this morning. I hope that if there is no lack of bread a great many things will settle down. I speak to the people. The militia, the fishwives—all give me their hand and I give them mine. . . . No one would believe all that has happened in the last 24 hours and yet whatever one imagined would be less than what we have had to endure."

"All hate must cease," she had said that morning to the fishwives. But with her, in spite of her good intentions, hate did not leave her heart. Marie Antoinette had difficulty in not feeling some contempt for her husband, who waddled about being hearty. It would be impossible for Maria Theresa's daughter to forget the terrible awakening of 6 October and the insults thrown in her face. Although she was to claim to have "known everything, seen everything, forgotten everything," there would always be present to her memory those two heads stuck on two pikes, the shameful trophies dripping with blood which had preceded her carriage. She would always hear the cries of the dregs of humanity who had come to tear her from her palace. Like her son she would pronounce "the word Pardon only with great difficulty and many tears." Even more, she would never pronounce it with sincerity. Lafayette was to observe very justly: "She has all that is needed to win the hearts of the Parisians, but an ingrained arrogance and a temper which she is not able sufficiently to conceal more often alienates them. I wish she would bring more good will to it."

Even if Marie Antoinette wished it, and perhaps she did, she would never succeed. It is enough to spend a few hours in the "Inferno" of the Bibliothèque Nationale, where they keep the nauseating pamphlets illustrated with licentious engravings which were written to attack Marie Antoinette from 1788 to 1793, to be no longer able to reproach her with her attitude. The Queen was probably aware of only a small part of this heap of filth and obscenity, but what had come to her eyes had wounded her "pure soul" as much as the people's cries for her death.

"Calumny kills people better than anything," she said to Mme Campan, "and it is by calumny that they will kill me."

Her whole energy was bent to a single end. Once more Lafayette revealed it: "To think how to be beautiful in the midst of danger rather than try to avert it."

Marie Antoinette received the Parliament of Paris in her private apartments. "Her grief had acquired a shade of firmness and her indignation could be seen. She held her son on her knees and, in spite of the courage of which she had given so many heroic proofs, one could not help feeling that her son was a bodyguard whose protection she accepted."

Her children—*Mousseline* and *Chou d'amour,* as she called them—were now her only joy. "We lodge all three in the same apartment," she wrote to Mme de Polignac. "They are nearly always with me and are my consolation. If I could be happy I should be so by reason of these two little creatures. *Chou d'amour* is charming and I love him madly. He loves me very much, too, in his way. . . . He is well, grows strong and no longer becomes angry. He goes for a walk every day, which does him much good."

Axel also brought her consolation. For the first time, as we learn from one of the letters Fersen wrote to his sister at the end of 1789, he spent "a whole day with Her." "Imagine my joy!" he added.

During the whole of the spring of 1790 he was to see Marie Antoinette "freely in her own house" and he sighed, touched: "Poor woman, she is like an angel in her behaviour, courage and feeling. No one has ever been able to love like that." A few days later he wrote: "She is extremely unhappy, but very brave. I try to console her as best I can. I owe her that; she has been so perfect to me!"

It seems that without his dear presence Marie Antoinette would not have been able to bear her burdens. There was nothing to be got from the King. Admittedly, when Louis XVI spoke to her "he revealed in his eyes and behaviour a devotion rarely inspired by the most beloved mistress"; admittedly he constantly consulted her and asked her advice, but the poor man, victim of his perpetual hesitations, was no help or support. He had been completely overtaken by events and by the total disruption of his life.

"When one discusses business with him," said one of his Ministers, "one feels as if one were talking of matters concerning the Emperor of China."

By an outstanding error he let the *Moniteur* publish the famous "red book" showing the expenses of the court. Needless to say, all that was noticed was the sums squandered by the Queen on her protégés. There was not a single village in France that did not know now how much the Polignacs and Marie Antoinette's friends had received.

During this twilight of the monarchy Marie Antoinette, deeply offended, refused to take part in any business at all.

"I am not interfering!"

"The vessel of State is buffeted by a violent storm and there is no one at the helm," Mirabeau was to say.

Gradually, urged by Mercy, Marie Antoinette agreed to alter her decision and soon the tribune exclaimed, not without admiration: "The King has only one man with him—his wife!"

It was of Mirabeau that Mercy was thinking. He was the only man who could restrain the Revolution. At the Ambassador's request La Marck undertook to persuade Marie Antoinette. It was not easy. The Queen had too many memories.

"I think we shall never be so unfortunate as to be reduced to the painful extremity of having recourse to Mirabeau," Marie Antoinette had exclaimed after those days in October.

Mirabeau, to whom this remark was reported, had prophesied: "The King and Queen will perish and the populace will batter their corpses!"

Marie Antoinette felt that the tribune was in the right and so she gave way. Mercy and La Marck could try to win over Mirabeau. This was not very difficult. The plebeian Count, now disillusioned, had veered strongly to the right and he accepted the offers of the court. As Lafayette, who was sometimes witty, remarked: "He is only betraying in the direction of his convictions." Besides, Mirabeau saw that his "treachery" was well paid for—6,000 livres a month (1,200,000 francs), plus the payment of his 208,000 livres of debts and, as a "premium," one million payable on the closure of the Assembly. On 10 May he sent Louis XVI an actual undertaking: "I promise the King loyalty, zeal, activity, energy and a courage which, perhaps, no one can really imagine. Indeed I promise him everything except the success which never depends on one person alone and which only a rash presumption would guarantee amid the terrible sickness which undermines the State and threatens its head."

"When one undertakes to direct a Revolution," said Mirabeau on 10 October 1789, "the difficulty is not to spur it on but to restrain it."

Six months later this observation had never been more accurate. Mirabeau, who on concluding his agreement tried to give back to Louis XVI a few scraps of the power the King's clumsy hands had let slip, came up against the triumvirate of the left: Barnave, Lameth and Duport. He was only partly successful. He might perhaps have succeeded better if he had been willing to join with Lafayette, but the two men hated each other.

Marie Antoinette had not yet received Mirabeau. Like Axel she thought he was a "fine rascal" and that he was "not to be trusted." However, she finally agreed to receive him in the park at Saint Cloud, where the royal family had "permission" to spend the summer. He saw the Queen's eyes veiled with tears, he guessed at the suffering concealed by her pride, and he was conquered. He was so humble, so respectful, and seemed so sincere in regretting his excesses—the thousands of livres had something to do with it—that the Queen, too, was moved and gave him her hand, which he kissed kneeling.

"Madame," said the Comte as he rose, "the monarchy is saved!"

And he wrote to La Marck: "Nothing can stop me. I would die rather than not fulfil my promises!"

This interview was on 3 July 1790. Marie Antoinette was to have a month of hope. The monarchy's last "holidays" were for her an almost happy pause. Axel was staying with friends at Auteuil and "in the gloaming" went to Saint Cloud. He spent his days there. "I write to you from Her house," he told his sister. "My only grief is not to be able completely to console her for all her misfortunes and not to be able to make her as happy as She deserves."

There was gossip, of course, but Marie Antoinette did not mind. "I was informed," wrote Saint-Priest, "that a soldier of the French

Guards, then paid guards, meeting Fersen coming out of the château at three in the morning, was about to arrest him. I thought I ought to speak of it to the Queen and mention that Comte de Fersen's presence and his visits to the château might put her in some danger. 'Tell him, if you think it necessary,' she replied. 'For myself I do not care.' And, in fact, the visits went on just as usual."

This state of well-being—the calm between two storms—was prolonged by the feast of the Federation, one of the finest days in the history of France. At the Champ de Mars, in front of the Ecole Militaire, the Queen attended this first, extraordinary "Fourteenth of July," wearing tricolour ribbons in her hair. In front of her 400,000 people she heard Mass celebrated by Talleyrand to the sound of trumpets and drums. This vast crowd was seated on stands which 200,000 Parisians had built themselves to receive the delegations from the National Guards from all over France. This communal work, carried out in an atmosphere of good humour, had created an amazing feeling of fraternity, which increased after the oath taken by the King. The hearts of all the French seemed to beat in unison. The Queen was carried away by the enthusiasm; her sad face lit up and she lifted the little Dauphin in her arms. For several minutes the air was filled with cries of "Long live the Queen!" and "Long live the Dauphin!"

In the evening everyone danced and embraced. The Revolution was over! As Octave Aubry has so justly remarked; this 14 July was "the first day of patriotism!"

"If Louis XVI had known how to take advantage of the Federation, we would have been lost," Barnave was to admit.

When they returned to Saint Cloud life resumed its slow course. The epoch of the jewellers, of Rose Bertin, of Léonard, of the happy bursts of laughter was now only a pleasant memory. Marie Antoinette now stayed for hours in her room, embroidering or watching her children play. "When I am sad I have my little boy with me." A game of billiards with the King, a walk in the Bois de Boulogne or to the Chaussée d'Antin and the evening suppers were her only distractions.

But the Jacobin revolt of the garrison at Nancy, which was followed by the harsh repression of the General Marquis de Bouillé, set the Revolution moving again. Paris accused the Queen of having encouraged the executions ordered by the General. She certainly approved them, and at the Opera the chorus from *Iphigenia*, "Let us praise our Queen," was booed.

13

*

Varennes...or the Hand of Fate!

WITH A HEARTBROKEN sigh Louis XVI had brought himself to sign the decree concerning the civil constitution of the clergy. "I would rather be King of Metz," he had said to Fersen, "than remain King of France in such conditions."

When on 10 March 1791, after several months' delay, the Pope finally condemned the civil constitution of the clergy voted by the Assembly, the Queen realised that there remained only one solution for the King—flight. They could reach Montmédy, the headquarters of M. de Bouillé. There Louis XVI could assemble troops "and those of his subjects who were still faithful to him, and could try to win back the rest of his people led astray by seditious leaders." If order could not be re-established, the King would rely on "the help of his allies," that is, on Austria. For six months Marie Antoinette's one idea had been flight. Mirabeau himself was of the same opinion.

"But what are these people thinking of?" he exclaimed. "Cannot they see the abyss opening before their feet?"

According to him, as we learn from La Marck, "the King had only to announce *quite firmly* that he wished to leave Paris, fix the day for leaving and persist energetically in his decision. They would have to let him do what he wanted."

Mirabeau was deceiving himself, and a serious incident proved it. On 25 February, under the pretext of a popular rising at Vincennes, five or six hundred nobles armed with sword-sticks and hunting-knives gathered at the Tuileries, apparently to protect the King and the Queen, but in fact to try to "surround them" and carry them off to Metz. Warned in time, Lafayette hurried from Vincennes and forced the King to order the gentlemen to lay down their arms. Amid a dead silence the "knights of the poniard," as they had been called, placed their inadequate weapons on the chests and tables in the antechamber and left the château between two rows of National Guards, some of them never to return.

After this painful scene Louis XVI was overcome and was still more so when at the end of March Mirabeau took to his bed to die. "In my heart I wear mourning for the monarchy, whose remnants will become the prey of the factious," he sighed. On 2 April he was dead.

To convince her husband of the necessity for leaving was a difficult task for Marie Antoinette, all the more difficult since on 19 February 1791 Louis XV's daughters, Mesdames Adelaide and Victoire, had secretly left Paris. They were arrested at Moret, then at Saulieu and finally at Arnay-le-Duc, and a decree of the Assembly was needed to allow the King's aunts to proceed. The various National Guards had shown themselves the most eager in pursuit all along the route taken by the two old maids' berlin.

This near-failure was not very encouraging. But 15 days later a serious event, which assailed Louis XVI both in his conscience and in his Christian faith, was to force him to decide. Would the King agree to receive Easter communion from the hands of a constitutional curé of St. Germain l'Auxerrois?

Louis XVI adopted a plan which succeeded in putting everyone against him. On Palm Sunday he heard Mass said by Cardinal de Montmorency, a non-juring priest, but refrained from receiving communion. The reply was not long in coming. On his return from the chapel the grenadiers of the National Guard refused to line the King's route. The city immediately became stormy. On the next day, 18 April, Louis XVI decided to leave for Saint Cloud, as he had done the year before. At once the Revolution began to rumble. The King was undoubtedly leaving Paris to fulfil his Easter duties *unconstitutionally!*

Towards noon the King, the Queen, Madame Royale, Madame Elisabeth and the Dauphin entered their coach. The Place du Carrousel was packed with people. The carriages had barely left the courtyard of the Tuileries when men seized the bridles. The National Guard made no attempt to interfere, in fact the grenadiers threatened the postillions with their sabres. The coaches were surrounded by a howling mob. Lafayette and Bailly ordered the National Guards to clear a passage.

"We do not want him to leave!" they replied. "We swear that he shall not leave!"

The King put his head through the window and exclaimed: "It would be extraordinary if, having given the Nation its liberty, I should not be free myself!"

The shouts were like a slap in the face: "F—ing aristocrat! Fat pig!"

Lafayette suggested that Louis XVI should proclaim martial law and resort to force.

"I do not wish blood to be shed for me."

For two terrible hours the royal family remained thus besieged. Finally the carriage door opened and Louis XVI descended calmly.

"So you do not wish me to leave?"

There was dead silence. The King's voice resumed: "It is not possible for me to leave? . . . Very well, I shall stay." And with his rolling gait Louis XVI went back to the château.

"You must admit now that we are no longer free," remarked the Queen sharply as she mounted the steps.

This time Louis XVI agreed to leave for Montmédy. "The event which has just taken place," Marie Antoinette wrote two days later to Mercy, who had taken refuge in Brussels, "confirms us more than ever in our plans. . . . We are in a dreadful position! We absolutely must flee from it during the next month. The King wishes this even more strongly than I."

Axel Fersen had undertaken to arrange the departure. At the Queen's request he had ordered, at the end of December, a far too luxurious berlin painted outside in green and yellow and upholstered in white Utrecht velvet. The carriage contained "two iron cooking-stoves, one canteen to hold eight bottles, two chamber pots of tanned leather, two iron-fitted forks to steady the berlin in the mountains. . . ," not to mention "precautionary objects," such as "bolts, axle-nuts, clamps for the swingle-bars, buckles, nails, rivets, washers, etc."

During the two months before the great adventure Axel overflowed with activity to save the woman he loved. Nearly every day he entered the Tuileries by an unguarded door, kept Marie Antoinette informed on his steps to obtain a false passport in the name of Mme de Korff and brought her Bouillé's ciphered dispatches.

Gradually the plan became organised. The royal family would leave with Mme Elisabeth, Mme de Tourzel and three bodyguards disguised as couriers. They would also take two waiting-women, who would travel in a cabriolet. With the six occupants of the berlin this would bring the number to eleven. At each stage they would have to order six draught-horses for the berlin, three horses for the cabriolet and two post-horses for the couriers. This was a large number.

Bouillé came himself to Paris and had long discussions with Fersen. "The most difficult point seems to me to be getting out of the Tuileries where all the exits are guarded." How, indeed, were the royal family to leave their caravanserai? In the summer of 1791 the Tuileries resembled a nomads' camp. Indeed, one has only to read the interrogations of the under servants of the palace, who were closely questioned after the escape.

Pierre-Joseph Brown, guard of the apartments, passed the night on two mattresses placed on the floor of the Grand Gallery looking out on the Cour des Princes. "In the gallery where I sleep," he explained, "there also sleep two little boys, whose names I do not know, who are the messengers of the _garçons du château_." In the evening the latter also set up their beds in the same room, as did the servants of the _garçons de la chambre_. Quite a dormitory!

Pierre Hubert, a _garçon du château_, preferred to place his mattress in the billiard room, because his friend Péradon "usually slept there."

Each night a footman of the guard slept "on a mattress placed across the door" of Madame Elisabeth's bedroom, while a _garçon de la chambre_ set up his bed in "a little room on the right of the said apartment."

But it would be tedious to pursue the list. Not only were the state rooms and the royal apartments packed each night with servants sleeping on camp beds, but a whole population of valets, _garçons de chambre_, male and female wardrobe servants and waiting-women were crowded from eleven onwards in the attics and the garrets between floors. Could the royal family leave the château without being noticed by all these people? And once in the courtyard, could they avoid the sentinels and patrols which surrounded the royal home as though Paris were besieging a fortress?

Axel promised Bouillé to "be responsible for this delicate operation." On the evening of the flight it would be impossible to park the berlin near the château, for it would attract the passers-by. Fersen therefore bought a _citadine_—a kind of omnibus—which would take the fugitives to the barrier. He himself, disguised as a hired coachman, would take the reins.

It was decided that the travellers would then be left to themselves until Châlons. After Pont-de-Somme-Vesle, the first post after Châlons, the fugitives would find detachments of cavalry at each post who would escort them to Montmédy by way of Sainte-Menehould, Clermont, Varennes, Dun and Stenay.

Axel agreed to Bouillé's scheme only very reluctantly. He concurred with the General on the precautions to be taken from Paris to Châlons, for, as he wrote, "the best precaution is to take none at all; all must depend on speed and secrecy." But after that? "If you are not very sure of your detachments," the Swede continued wisely, "it would be better not to have any until after Varennes, so as not to arouse notice in the countryside. The King will then get by easily." He frequently came back to this point. "Be quite sure of your detachments, or do not station any until after Varennes," he repeated. If only they had listened to him!

The departure was fixed for the evening of Monday, 20 June. Axel's private Journal enables us to relive the last days before the adventure.

"Thursday, 16. With the Queen at 9.30. Took the things myself; nothing is suspected here or in town."

"Friday, 17. To Bondy and Bourget" (to reconnoitre the first part of the route).

"Saturday, 18. With the Queen from 2.30 until 6."

"Sunday, 19. Took 800 livres and the Seals. Remained in the château from 11 to midnight."

"Monday, 20 June, arrived."

"Monday, 20. Nothing," wrote Louis XVI in the Journal.

It was a quarter-to-ten. Marie Antoinette, the King, Madame Elisabeth, and the Comte and Comtesse de Provence were together in the Queen's reception room on the ground floor of the palace, whose windows led on to the garden. The future Louis XVIII and his wife, each by a different route, were also to escape that night.

"Take care not to make me moved," the Queen had said to her brother-in-law as they sat down at the table. "I do not want anyone to see I have been crying."

Supper was soon over, the ceremonies having for some time been cut down, and since half-past nine the King and his family had been conversing in low tones. Ten o'clock struck.

"Now we are approaching the worst moment," Marie Antoinette sighed in distress.

The Queen left the drawing room, went into her bedroom and passed through the corridor and up the little staircase to the first floor, where Madame Royale's bedroom was. She had to knock for a few moments before Mme Brunier, alerted by little Marie-Thérèse, opened the door to her. The waiting-woman was informed of the situation in a few words: she was to make the journey; she was to leave with Mme de Neuville, the Dauphin's waiting-woman; in a few minutes they would leave the château and wait for the royal family at Claye, the second stage on the road to Metz.

"Someone will take you to the cabriolet which is already waiting at the Pont-Royal."

But she must hurry. The Queen ordered her to get Madame Royale out of bed and dress her in the little dress she had brought. It was a simple cotton dress "with little blue flowers on a gosling-green ground."

The Queen next went to the Dauphin's apartments. On Mme de Tourzel's orders the future Louis XVII had already been awoken by Mme de Neuville.

"We are going to a place of battle, where there will be many soldiers," the Queen told him.

The child, delighted, asked for his boots and sword. "Quick, quick! Hurry up! Let's go!"

But, alas! he was not brought his French Guards' uniform but a girl's dress. He seems to have been quickly consoled, for a few moments later, in the Queen's entresol, when his sister asked him "what he thought they were going to do," he replied happily: "We are going to act a play, for we are in disguise!"

It was already a quarter-to-eleven. Following Fersen's carefully arranged plan it had been decided that the Children of France would leave the château first. The Queen, followed by Madame Royale and Mme de Tourzel carrying the Dauphin, left her apartments, entered the corridor which ran the whole length of the palace and went towards the apartments of M. de Villequier, First Gentleman of the Bedchamber, who had emigrated. Marie Antoinette opened the door with the key she had provided herself with and the little group entered an unfurnished room. They crossed it to reach an antechamber which led on to the Cour des Princes by an unguarded glass door. The Queen first of all looked into the courtyard. A silhouette could be seen behind the window lit by the carriage lamps and the torches in the courtyard. It was Fersen dressed in his coachman's greatcoat.

Axel entered and took the Dauphin's hand. Madame de Tourzel took the hand of Madame Royale and followed, most rashly, by the Queen, the little group went down the steps leading to the courtyard noisy with National Guards, coachmen and servants.

Following the shadows of the carriages of courtiers who had come for the King's *coucher*, the fugitives reached the *citadine*, which was almost in the middle of the courtyard. Mme de Tourzel and the children got in. Fersen climbed on the driver's seat, cracked his whip at the hired nags and quietly drove out of the courtyard. The Queen, whose emotion and anguish may be imagined, watched the departure of the ramshackle vehicle, which after making a detour by the quays and the Place Louis XV, would wait in the Rue de l'Echelle, at the corner of the Place du Petit-Carrousel. By a miracle Marie Antoinette returned unnoticed to the drawing room. The Comte de Provence was saying goodbye. "We embraced tenderly and separated," he related.

While the King, still slave to a persistent etiquette, had now to play his usual part in the ceremony of the *coucher*, Marie Antoinette went to her bedroom and calmly gave her orders for her walk the next day. One can imagine how her heart beat as she thought of her children, from whom she had never been separated, wandering about in a cab at the mercy of suspicious patrols in that dreadful Paris. If Axel had not been with them she would never have agreed to such a dangerous plan. Her women undressed her, while the servants fastened the bolts and the inside shutters. Marie Antoinette went to bed and was left alone.

It was a quarter-past eleven.

A few minutes later Mme Thiébaut, who was in the secret, came to help her mistress put on a grey dress and black mantle and a large hat with a veil falling from it. Marie Antoinette slipped the bolt and opened the door giving on to the long corridor. She drew back, terrified.

There was a sentry pacing up and down. After ten minutes of hesitation and suspense she took advantage of a moment when the man's back was turned, leaped across the passage, reached the staircase and was soon in M. de Villequier's apartment. One of the bodyguards, M. de Malden, was there, disguised as a courier. Marie Antoinette took his arm and they went down into the courtyard, calmly crossing the guard-room, where the National Guards were chatting. As they walked to the Place du Petit-Carrousel Malden soothed the Queen. Everything had gone well. Madame Elisabeth had reached the meeting place first, but they had had to wait for the King. His *coucher,* at which Lafay-ette had been present, had been longer than usual. A carriage escorted by cavalry men bearing torches brushed past the Queen and her com-panion. Marie Antoinette recognised Lafayette's coach and lashed the wheels with her switch. But now Malden had lost his way in the maze of little streets between the Place du Petit-Carrousel and the Louvre and could not find the Rue de l'Echelle. It was midnight before they finally found the *citadine* with Axel pacing up and down before it.

Everyone embraced the latecomer. Fersen whipped up his two horses and they set off.

But suddenly Louis XVI became anxious. Fersen was taking a curious route for the Saint-Martin barrier; he was going in the direction of the Chaussée d'Antin. The King, who knew Paris very well, did not dare put his head out to question the "coachman." Much to the fugitives' astonishment the *citadine* stopped in the Rue de Clichy, where the berlin had been kept. Fersen got down, knocked on the door and asked the porter if the carriage had indeed left. On receiving an affirmative answer, he quickly resumed his seat and at last drove off towards the barrier, doubtless by the boulevards and the Porte Saint Martin.

It was 1.30 in the morning when they finally came in sight of the round customs house. Another half-hour was lost in looking for the berlin, which was stowed away on the lower side of the Metz road. Fersen's coachman and the second guard, M. de Moustier, had hidden it too well. The *citadine* drew up alongside the berlin so that the royal family passed from one carriage to the other without setting foot on the ground. Fersen turned the *citadine* over in the ditch, entangled the two horses in their harness and mounted the box.

It must have been nearly two o'clock. It was the shortest night of the year and day would begin to break in an hour. They galloped along and in less than half-an-hour the berlin reached Bondy. The six draught-horses ordered by the third guard, M. de Valory, were waiting in their harness before the posthouse. While the grooms unharnessed the horses belonging to Fersen, Axel got down from the box. The King had been opposed to the idea of the officer's going any further. Perhaps he did not think it proper to travel under the protection of a man whom everyone thought to be his wife's lover.

Her eyes filled with tears, Marie Antoinette saw the Swede open the door and bow to her.

"Goodbye, Madame de Korff!"

According to Moustier, "the King embraced Fersen with all his heart and thanked him with touching kindness." If one remembers that Axel was disguised as a Parisian coachman, the grooms and postillions, who were already in the saddle, must have been slightly surprised.

The relay was quickly carried out and soon Fersen, standing in the middle of the road, saw the heavy coach disappear, escorted by Malden, who had mounted a post-horse. Valory had already left to get the horses ready at Claye.

The noise of the iron-bound wheels of the berlin faded and died away in the night. Fersen looked at his watch.

The fugitives were already two hours behind their scheduled time.

Specialists say that at the centre of a typhoon, or at the heart of a whirlwind, is a zone where not a breath of wind disturbs the surface of the sea. During the twenty hours' journey separating Bondy and Varennes—the first and last stages—the royal family will always seem to be in this "dead calm," while all about them the storm rose and burst forth.

Six o'clock

The heavy yellow and green berlin, preceded by the cabriolet with the two waiting-women, left Meaux. The relay had gone off without incident. The two carriages drove towards Trilport on a road bordered by four rows of trees. The worst was over! Marie Antoinette plucked up courage and smiled as she heard her husband exclaim: "Believe me, when I have my backside on a saddle I shall be very different from what you have seen hitherto!"

The Argonne was swarming with detachments going to take up their positions. The disposition of troops arranged by Bouillé and Fersen was being put into action.

At Sainte-Menehould, half-way between Châlons and Varennes, the call to boot and saddle was sounded. Forty hussars, who had been stationed in the little town, set off. They were to occupy the stage of Pont-de-Somme-Vesle, which the royal berlin was to reach at about two o'clock. The inhabitants grumbled at this "detachment of aristocrats."

Eight o'clock

The berlin was not going very fast. The fugitives, their appetites sharpened by the previous night's emotions, "attacked the canteen" prepared by Fersen: bœuf à la mode and cold veal. They ate "without plates or forks," Moustier recounted, "like hunters or economical travellers." The Queen called to Malden, who trotted to the carriage, offered him something to eat and drink and said: "Perhaps at this moment M. de Lafayette's head is no longer on his shoulders."

In Paris Lafayette jumped out of bed and put on his uniform. The astonishing news spread from the royal apartments, reached the attics and descended to the kitchens and like a trail of powder ran all through Paris: "The King has left! The Queen has escaped!"

As he buckled on his belt in his room Lafayette could hear an approaching "murmur like the roar of a wave driven by the storm." By the time he reached the château a "stormy sea" greeted him. All Paris, "intoxicated at being for the first time without a master," was filling the streets.

At Clermont-en-Argonne, the last post before Varennes, the population was uneasy at the presence of 180 dragoons. The head of the detachment announced that he was expecting "a convoy of silver," but all through the morning the rumour went round: "This so-called treasure is none other than the Queen!"

Ten o'clock

The berlin changed horses at Vieils-Maisons, a little village in a hollow between La Ferté-sous-Jouarre and Montmirail. Louis XVI got out "to make water." At the following relay station Marie Antoinette was not able to prevent him leaving the carriage again "to talk to the peasants about the harvest."

At Sainte-Menehould the people, who were already made uneasy by the passage of the hussars, watched the arrival of 30 dragoons, commanded by Captain Dandoins, who took over the little town to protect "the passage of the treasure" intended for paying Bouillé's army.

Anxious townsmen stopped the newcomers: "My friends, these troop movements are not natural. Look out for yourselves!"

Indeed, money usually travelled by coach with an escort of two gendarmes.

In Paris the crowd was in a ferment. The Tuileries were invaded. A cherry seller had installed herself on Marie Antoinette's bed and cried: "Come on! Cherries, fine cherries at 6 sous the livre!"

Of his own authority Lafayete sent out volunteer couriers, mostly National Guards, in all directions, with orders to "run down" Louis XVI and Marie Antoinette.

Noon

The royal berlin rolled peacefully towards Fromentières. On arriving at the relay station the King got out once more "to gossip with individuals of the people who came to see the travellers." Moustier, who was rightly anxious, wanted "to shield him with his person from the gaze of the curious," but Louis XVI prevented him.

"Don't bother! I do not think this precaution necessary. . . . I feel my journey is safe from all accident."

At the Saint-Martin barrier one of the messengers sent by Lafayette went by at a gallop. He took the Metz road, not knowing he was going in the right direction. The fugitives were ten hours ahead of him.

At Sainte-Menehould the Municipality, alarmed by the passage of troops, distributed 300 new muskets to the National Guard.

At Clermont the dragoons were ordered to stay in the stables near their saddled horses. The population guessed "something" was happening.

At Pont-de-Somme-Vesle the young Duc de Choiseul, Colonel of the Royal Dragoons, a friend of Marie Antoinette and nephew of the Minister, came to a halt before the post-house isolated in the middle of the chalky plain. He had come from Paris with Léonard, whom Marie Antoinette had sent out travelling so as not to be deprived of her favourite hairdresser. At the same time the 40 hussars who had spent the night at Sainte-Menehould dismounted before the relay station. At their head was Goguelas, another of the Queen's friends. The officers hastened to dine while waiting for the berlin to pass.

One o'clock

The royal excursion was taking on the appearance of a country outing. Before reaching Etoges Marie Antoinette got out of the carriage at the bottom of a hill "in order to refresh herself," took her husband's arm and both followed the berlin, which slowed to walking pace. Madame Royale and her brother, so it is said, chased after butterflies.

In Paris the Jacobin Club voted a resolution: "Louis has abdicated from the monarchy; henceforth Louis is nothing to us. We are now free and without a King. It remains to be seen whether it is worthwhile appointing another."

A second horseman passed the Saint-Martin barrier. This was Romeuf, Lafayette's aide-de-camp, who carried a decree of the Assembly ordering the King's arrest. A second wave of couriers had been sent out on the high roads. At Bondy Romeuf picked up the trail of the fugitives. This officer had a knightly attachment to Marie Antoinette and spurred on his horses merely to catch up Bayon, whom he knew to be before him, and hold up the pursuit.

Two o'clock

The fugitives reached the relay station of Chaintrix, the last halt before Châlons. It was stifling. The low, heavy sky weighed on men and beasts. The post-master came forward. Stupefied, he recognised Louis XVI and Marie Antoinette. There was no need of explanations. All France knew that the King wished to flee to Paris. With emotion and respect he suggested that the travellers should get out "in order to refresh themselves." The children were dead tired. The Queen accepted and they sat down to table in the large room of the post-house. They were now nearly three hours behind their timetable.

Romeuf passed through Claye. Although he urged his horse on he realised that Bayon was going faster.

At Pont-de-Somme-Vesle, Choiseul, Goguelas and Léonard paced up and down the road. They listened. Surely they would soon hear the clatter of hoofs and the crack of whips announcing the arrival of the fugitives.

Twenty-past two •

At Chaintrix the carriages left the relay station, but barely a minute later one of the berlin's wheels struck against a little bridge, the horses fell and the harness broke. It would have to be repaired.

At Pont-de-Somme-Vesle, Choiseul and his companions began to be anxious about this prolonged delay.

At Meaux, Bayon, the first pursuer, changed horses. The post-master, Petit, informed him that that morning, about five o'clock, he had provided 11 horses for a large berlin coming from Paris accompanied by a cabriolet and two couriers. A man, three women and two children were in the coach. Bayon gave a shout of joy—he was undoubtedly on the right road.

Three o'clock

At Chaintrix the accident was repaired and the berlin set off, driven fast by the son of the post-master.

At Pont-de-Somme-Vesle the officers became even more anxious as the peasants of the district gathered round the relay station. They had not paid their taxes and imagined that the "hussars had come to take action against them." Their attitude became almost menacing and, in spite of his forty horsemen, Choiseul was frightened.

At Sainte-Menehould the agitation grew. Why did not Dandoins have the horses saddled? The commander of the detachment had definite orders: he was to be warned of the King's imminent arrival by a courier sent by Choiseul from Pont-de-Somme-Vesle. Therefore no order was meanwhile to be given to the horsemen.

In Paris the fleurs-de-lis were scratched off the fronts of buildings and the portraits of Louis XVI and Marie Antoinette in the print sellers' displays were torn up. Some cried: "A King and Queen have been lost. A good reward will be paid to whoever does not find them!"

Four o'clock

The carriage, rapidly driven, entered the suburbs of Châlons. It was to change horses at the other end of the town, and in spite of the crowd assembled at the post-house everything went off without incident.

Bayon, his horse covered with foam, changed mounts at La Ferté. Romeuf had just left Meaux, having covered 11 leagues in two-and-a-half hours.

At Clermont the dragoons were alert. They had received orders to be ready to mount at five o'clock.

At Pont-de-Somme-Vesle, Choiseul, taking as his excuse the King's delay and the excitement around the relay station, decided to abandon his post of "advance sentry." He ordered Léonard to warn the detachments at Sainte-Menehould and Clermont "that there was no sign of the treasure passing today." Then, followed by his horsemen, he went at walking pace by a short cut which would enable him to avoid passing through the towns and would lead him directly to Varennes through the Argonne forest.

Six o'clock

The berlin arrived at Pont-de-Somme-Vesle. Marie Antoinette looked through the window. The plain was deserted; no sign of a horseman. Yet all was calm. Since the detachment had left the peasants had gone back to their villages.

At Chaintrix, Bayon dismounted before the relay station. He learned from the post-master himself—who in three hours had become considerably less royalist—that the fugitives were now only a short way ahead of him. But he was exhausted. He had ridden 35 leagues in six hours and changed horses ten times. Someone—it is not known who—offered to go on in front and the officer scribbled an order: "On behalf of the National Assembly, all good citizens are ordered to stop the berlin with six horses in which the King and Queen are suspected of being . . . I am dispatching the bearer with the recommendation to call on the public force."

At Sainte-Menehould Captain Dandoins, after Léonard had gone through, dismissed his dragoons. The men began wandering through streets "in police caps and stable dress." Some sat down to table with the townsfolk.

Eight o'clock

The berlin went down the main street of Sainte-Menehould. For the first time since they left Marie Antoinette saw horsemen who automatically brought their hand to their police caps and saluted. As though it were a "joyful entry," the Queen bowed her head "with that air of benevolent and majestic kindness which she never loses." The carriages stopped before Drouet's posthouse. The relay went off without incident, in spite of the presence of a few dragoons and of a group of inhabitants who came to look at these travellers going by in "such grand style." Did the fugitives notice the arrival of Drouet, who at that moment came in from the fields and, seeing the heavy coach, ordered his postillions "not to kill the horses"? Ten minutes later the berlin, flanked by its two horsemen and preceded by the cabriolet, entered the forest road.

At Clermont, Léonard left the relay-station. He had just given the commander of the detachment Choiseul's orders. The horsemen were ordered to return to their billets, but to hold themselves ready to mount.

Romeuf arrived, in his turn, at Chaintrix. Bayon, who had taken some rest and refreshment, had left hardly half-an-hour before.

The next two-and-a-half hours were the most tragic of the whole journey. Nothing is more dramatic than the calm of these poor people who thought themselves safe and the ferment which immediately followed their passing.

The pincers were closing.

Nine o'clock

The berlin rolled slowly over the Argonne hills.

At Sainte-Menehould the rumour ran from house to house "that the King and Queen had just passed." The tocsin sounded, the dragoons were disarmed, and when Bayon's messenger arrived Drouet and his friend Guillaume leaped into the saddle. They rushed off down the road taken by the berlin an hour before.

At Châlons Bayon arrived at the Hôtel de Ville, where he showed his orders. The tocsin sounded at Saint-Alpin. Nearly the whole of the population of Châlons crowded into the streets.

Half-past nine

At Clermont the six horses had just been harnessed to the berlin. The town seemed somewhat excited but the travellers were able to pursue their journey without any incident. They left the main Metz road and took the road on the left to Varennes. On leaving the town Marie Antoinette listened. Surely the commander of the detachment would sound to boot and saddle.

At Châlons there was a great clamour: "Room for the messenger from the Assembly!" It was Romeuf. On arriving at the Hôtel de Ville he announced that he wanted to go quickly on his way. Bayon appeared. He had intended to go to bed, but "begged for the honour" of accompanying Lafayette's aide-de-camp. Against his will Romeuf agreed.

At Varennes, in the lower town, Léonard's cabriolet stopped in front of the Hôtel du Grand Monarque, where two young officers, the

Chevalier de Bouillé, son of the General, and Captain de Raigecourt were guarding the relay horses in the hotel stables. The horses belonged to the conspirators, for there was no posthouse.

"I am Léonard," he called out to them, without getting down from his carriage. "I know all! The King has left Paris but there is no sign of his having continued his journey."

Five minutes later the hairdresser disappeared towards Stenay. The Chevalier de Bouillé decided not to go and inform Lieutenant Röhrig, who was commanding the 60 hussars billeted at Varennes. Besides, he was not in the secret.

Ten o'clock

With its lamps lit, the berlin rolled along the road to Varennes. Rocked by the slow trot of the horses, and convinced that the detachments of Sainte-Menehould and Clermont were galloping behind the carriage, Marie Antoinette fell asleep.

Two leagues behind the carriage two horsemen galloped at full speed. They were Drouet and Guillaume, who, thanks to a short cut, had avoided the bend at Clermont. Meeting his postillions on their return journey, the post-master had learned that the large berlin had left the main road.

At Châlons, Romeuf and Bayon passed through the Porte Saint-Jacques and rode quickly on to the Metz road.

At Clermont the townspeople opposed the dragoons' departure.

At Varennes young Bouillé and his companion went to bed. Lieutenant Röhrig, not seeing the "treasure" arrive, let his men drink "more than was reasonable."

In the Argonne forest Choiseul and his exhausted horsemen wandered hopelessly about. They had lost their way and had not yet found the path leading to Varennes.

Half-past ten

Marie Antoinette was awakened by a "fearful shock." The carriage had stopped at the first houses of the "upper town" of Varennes. The road was deserted and not a hussar was to be seen. The relay horses they had expected to see at the entrance to the town were not there. Marie Antoinette got out and took a few steps. With the King she knocked at the door of an isolated house. A sleepy voice replied: "Go on your way!"

While one of the bodyguards went into the town in search of the horses they got back into the carriage and waited.

Quarter-to-eleven

The berlin was still halted at the top of the little town. The bodyguard who had gone to look for the horses had not yet returned. None of the occupants of the carriage seems to have noticed two horsemen, Drouet and Guillaume, who passed the fugitives and descended into the "lower town." A little farther on, outside the Bras d'Or inn, they dismounted.

Ten minutes later the trap was ready. A cart full of furniture barred the little bridge over the Aire. The *Procureur* of the district, the grocer Sauce, was awakened and with several National Guards took up his position at the end of a vaulted passage, a real death-trap which could even be closed by a carriage-gate. Standing against the walls, they waited for the berlin, which could take no other road.

Eleven o'clock

For thirty minutes the berlin had been waiting by the first houses of the "upper town." They could not stay there for ever. The bodyguard had found nothing. Perhaps Bouillé had got the horses ready on the other side of the river. The Clermont postillions agreed to drive that far. Everything seemed so calm that there was no anxiety in the heart of the fugitives. The heavy coach, with its brakes on for the hill, proceeded towards the vaulted passage which spanned the road.

Suddenly there were cries: "Stop! Stop!"

On the previous evening, at the same time, Marie Antoinette had been pretending to go to bed in her bedroom at the Tuileries.

The escapade had lasted exactly 24 hours.

The Queen and her family were once more prisoners of the Revolution.

The Chevalier de Bouillé and Captain de Raigecourt were the last people in Varennes to hear of the King's arrest. Together with Lieutenant Röhrig, who was horrified at learning what had been the "treasure" he had to protect, they leaped to horse and disappeared in the direction of Montmédy to warn General de Bouillé, who was at Stenay with the Royal German regiment.

The tocsin rang urgently. All Varennes had been awakened and was now in front of the grocery run by the Procureur of the district, a plain wooden house to which the royal family had been conducted. Suddenly the Queen started. She could hear in the distance the sound of a troop of horsemen. They were the 40 hussars from Pont-de-Somme-Vesle, who had finally left their woods and swamps. With Choiseul at their head they galloped quickly down the main street, clearing the approaches to the grocery. But Louis XVI refused to order the use of force to snatch him from the hands of the municipality.

"One must have the soul of a monster to shed the blood of one's subjects."

Marie Antoinette had only one hope: the arrival of General Bouillé, whom his son had gone to warn. She heard the King explain: "There are only eight leagues from here to Stenay. On horseback a man could cover the distance in two-and-a-half hours. M. de Bouillé will be here about four or five in the morning and we shall leave here in safety without any danger or violence."

Meanwhile the National Guard from five leagues around marched on the little town which was making its entry into History. Varennes soon took on the appearance of a vast pleasure-garden or an enormous fair. Everywhere bread was being baked and bacon cooked and wine flowed like water. The crowd pressed so closely against the house that they finally entered. The most daring managed to climb to the first floor and gaze boldly at the "Austrian."

The hours passed, filled with anguish. Seated on cane chairs, the prisoners waited for their rescue, which could come only through Bouillé.

Suddenly, at five in the morning, the door of the little room opened. It was Bayon, with his coat unbuttoned and staggering with exhaustion. He could hardly speak and murmured disconnected phrases: "Sire . . . They are slaughtering each other in Paris! Our wives and children may be threatened. You will go no farther . . ."

Marie Antoinette came forward, took the officer's hand "with a forceful gesture" and pointed to the grocer's bed, where the Dauphin and his sister were sleeping.

"Am I not also a mother?"

Suddenly she saw Romeuf, white with dust. He was holding a paper.

"What, Sir!" cried the Queen, who saw the aide-de-camp every day at the Tuileries. "What! Is it you? Ah! I should never have believed it!"

Weeping, he handed the King the Assembly's decree. Louis XVI read aloud: "Order to all functionaries to arrest all the members of the royal family. . . ."

He looked at the Queen and said dully: "There is no longer a King in France."

Then he put the decree down on the bed. Marie Antoinette lost her self-control. She snatched the sheet of paper and flung it violently to the ground. "I will not have it contaminating my children!"

Ten thousand people had flocked into Varennes and howled under the windows: "To Paris! To Paris!"

They, too, were thinking of Bouillé. The cries grew louder. "We will drag them by the feet into their carriage! To Paris! To Paris!" The King tried to gain time and asked for some supper, but the crowd threatened to invade the house. Marie Antoinette lowered herself so far as to entreat Mme Sauce.

"Well, Madame," replied the grocer's wife, "you are in a very unpleasant position, but my husband is responsible. I don't want any trouble to come to him."

Finally Louis XVI left the little room and gave orders to harness the carriage. The tocsin was still ringing; the steeple of Varennes seemed to be sounding the knell of the monarchy.

"At about half-past seven," wrote an under-officer of dragoons, who was stationed at the entrance to the town, "I saw the royal carriage coming surrounded by a troop of armed men. It passed close to me and moved so slowly that I could see the Queen returning my salute. The King made a gesture which revealed his deep grief and prostration. The Queen appeared even more distressed. . . . I have never in my life experienced such a sensation and this poignant scene was never effaced from my mind."

A quarter-of-an-hour later General de Bouillé arrived at the little town at the head of the Royal German regiment. From the farther side of the river, which was too deep to be forded, he could still see the berlin driving away with its guard of 4,000 men. By a refinement of misfortune he was unaware that a little farther on the road crossed to the right bank of the Aire. The regiment would only have had to gallop for a few minutes in order to overthrow the escort and rescue the King. From the hamlet of Ratantout Bouillé ordered the retreat to be sounded.

The berlin, which seemed to be borne along by a large crowd, rolled slowly along the road to Paris. The procession gave so much the impression of a mob that towards eight o'clock the magistrates of Châlons, who had ridden out to meet the King, could not get near and retired, horrified, to their town.

At half-past eleven, when they had been travelling for 16 hours, Marie Antoinette finally saw at the entrance to Châlons the silhouette against the sky of the triumphal arch erected in her honour when she arrived in France. It was adorned with an inscription:

> *Aeternum stet, ut amor!*
> May it stand as long as our love!

It was thus that Châlons had paid honour to the

> Princess, whose every charm and grace
> Bring new adornment to our race.

Now, on 22 June 1791, Marie Antoinette was not surrounded by a brilliant cavalcade, but by four or five thousand men, dishevelled, yelling, drunk and brandishing the bloody remains of Comte de Dampierre, who had just been massacred for having dared to salute the Queen. Marie Antoinette, "in a state of prostration hardly to be conceived," watched the appalling spectacle. The procession stopped before the former "Intendancy" of Châlons, where the Dauphine had spent the night 21 years before.

It was two o'clock in the morning when the unfortunate people, who had not been to bed since they left the Tuileries, finally retired. But a wild hope kept them awake. Mme de Tourzel informs us that certain of the town's authorities showed the King a secret passage leading from the room where the Dauphin was sleeping and suggested that he should flee and ride to join Bouillé's army. But he would have had to leave the royal family, and Louis XVI refused. Why should they not try to remain at Châlons? The National Guard of Rheims would arrive at dawn and Louis XVI, remembering the cheers at his Coronation, trusted to the feelings of "his good Rémois." Perhaps with their help he could surround himself with defensive forces.

At dawn Marie Antoinette fell asleep. It was the dawn of 23 June, a terrible day for Fersen, who on his arrival at Arlon learnt of the catastrophe from Bouillé himself. "All is lost," he wrote, "and I am in despair. Imagine my grief and pity me." Marie Antoinette had guessed what would be the extent of the despair of the man she loved. During the night at Varennes she had asked Choiseul with tears in her voice: "Do you think M. de Fersen is safe?"

On Thursday, 23 June, the King and Queen were awakened at nine o'clock by an immense outcry. It was the "good Rémois" entering Châlons. As a serenade they shouted under Marie Antoinette's windows: "We will eat her heart and liver!"

The dregs of Rheims now took charge of the procession. There are no words to describe that appalling day.

A little before four o'clock the inhabitants of Chouilly saw the berlin slowly descend the slope of Haute-Borne and halt at the entrance to the village. The heat was suffocating. The National Guards rushed to the inns to refresh themselves. During this time men crowded round the carriage and hooted the King and Queen, shaking their fists. One of them climbed on the step and spat in the face of Louis XVI, who without saying a word wiped himself with a trembling hand. At half-past four, having roasted under a burning sun for half-an-hour, the carriage set off again.

The arrival at Epernay is past belief. An enormous crowd filled the courtyard in front of the Hôtel de Rohan. A meal had been prepared. It was impossible to get the berlin as far as the steps. The royal family hesitated before venturing through all those people armed with pikes and shouting insults and threats of death. A witness of the scene relates that he distinctly heard a man say to one of his companions: "Hide me so that I can fire on the Queen without anyone knowing where the shot comes from."

They had to get out, however, and all arrived safe and sound in a room at the inn, where Marie Antoinette, her dress having been torn by the crowd, asked if anyone could find a seamstress. The innkeeper's daughter, "a young and very pretty person," knelt down and tried to repair the damage as best she could.

"That's what you get by travelling!" remarked one of the members of the Epernay council.

Going back to the berlin was another ordeal. Amid a storm of booing the Queen, insulted, threatened, jostled, was pushed by the crowd to the carriage door. "Get along, my girl, you'll get worse than that!" a Sparnacienne shouted in farewell.

An hour later the mob, drunk with shouts, exhaustion and exasperation, were at a halt before the farm of Chêne-Fendu on the bank of the Marne. A great shout arose. The carriage of three deputies of the Assembly, come to meet the prisoners, was in sight and soon stopped at the head of the procession. Preceded by an usher, the two "advanced" deputies, Pétion and Barnave, together with their colleague of the right, Latour-Maubourg, advanced towards the berlin.

"We came up to the carriage door," Pétion related. "It opened at once. Confused noises could be heard. The Queen and Madame Elisabeth appeared, profoundly moved and in tears.

" 'Gentlemen,' they said, eagerly and breathlessly, with tears in their eyes, 'Gentlemen, ah! Monsieur Maubourg!' taking his hand, 'for pity's sake! Ah! Monsieur!' taking Barnave's hand also, 'Ah! Monsieur! Let there be no misfortune, let not the people who accompanied us be victimised, let no attempt be made on their lives. The King did not wish to leave France.' "

Latour-Maubourg took his seat in the cabriolet with the waiting-women, while Pétion and Barnave squeezed themselves as best they could into the berlin. Barnave, the Dauphinois, who had so often attacked the Queen in the Assembly and who had in the Tribune denounced Mirabeau's "treachery," was at first very embarrassed at finding himself seated between Marie Antoinette and the King. This strict Protestant, although not so far to the "left" as Pétion, hated the monarchy and the nobility. He was quite surprised by the royal family's "air of simplicity." He had pictured royalty in coronation robes and was taken aback by "the easy ways and family good-humour" of the travellers. Marie Antoinette and Madame Elisabeth called each other "my little sister"; the King dandled his son on his knees. The child then installed himself on Barnave's knees. He looked at the young deputy's engraved buttons and spelled out the letters on them. "Look, Mamma, do you see? 'Live free or die!' "

Marie Antoinette did not reply. Barnave felt his convictions weaken. He was moved by the tear-filled eyes of this woman, still young and pretty, who spoke to him with trust and friendship. With the Chevalier de Rougeville, Barnave would be Marie Antoinette's last conquest. He would listen to her, be won over and would soon be scandalised by the cries of the populace, who insulted the King and Marie Antoinette at each town they passed. On his orders, when they left Château-Thierry, the berlin out-distanced its sweating, yelling escort.

The next day saw the last stage. It took 13 hours from Meaux to Paris. All during the journey the heat was dreadful. "The dust raised by the people surrounding the carriage," recounted Mme de Tourzel, "was as thick as the worst fog."

In spite of this stifling atmosphere, the "free, cheerful" conversation, at least at the beginning of the day, went on "with the ease one has with friends." From time to time the King handed out a little tepid orangeade to drink. Marie Antoinette teased Barnave, asking him questions which were very embarrassing for an almost republican deputy. Ill at ease, he turned away his eyes.

"Please tell M. Barnave," she said laughingly to Pétion, "not to keep on looking out of the window when I ask him a question."

And they all laughed. They were very young. Louis XVI was the oldest, and he was only 36. Marie Antoinette was a year younger, Madame Elisabeth was 27, Barnave 30 and Pétion 32.

The first clash with the Parisians who had come to meet the prisoners took place in the forest of Bondy. "A crowd of madmen," in the words of a witness, issued from the wood and threw themselves on the National Guards. "In vain were they driven back, they slipped under the horses and between the wheels," in their attack on the carriage. There were nothing but yells and in all the noise the Queen was the most often attacked. "Harridans uttered dreadful cries: 'The bitch, the slut, the whore!'"

To calm the crowd that besieged the berlin Marie Antoinette lifted up the little Dauphin, who was crying. A voice lashed out: "It's no good her showing us her son, we know very well it's not fat Louis's."

The King heard the insult, turned pale, but said nothing. Tears rolled down from the Queen's eyes. The Dauphin uttered "cries of terror."

The berlin moved forward again, laden with men and *tricoteuses*. They were everywhere, on the seats, on the shaft, on the mudguards and even on the box. It was a "hideous and sinister spectacle." A little farther on there was another incident. The National Guards on horseback, who had accompanied the carriage since Meaux, and the grenadiers on foot, commanded by Captain Lefebvre, the future Marshal, began to fight. Each side claimed that the "post of honour" near the berlin was due to them. "The fray grew lively, and bayonets flashed around the carriage." Mathieu Dumas, who commanded the escort, could no longer make himself heard. Barnave then leant right out of the window, shouting above the tumult: "Remember, Colonel, you must answer with your head for the safety of the royal family!"

Spurred on by the young deputy's voice, Dumas managed to free the carriage.

They skirted Paris by the boulevards. Apart from the sound of drums beating in funereal time there was a crushing, insulting silence. The National Guard lined the road with their muskets reversed, as for a funeral. Still hung with groups of "patriots," the berlin reached the Etoile barrier and went down the Champs-Elysées.

Marie Antoinette seemed to be suffering deeply. The Dauphin "stood at the window, looking at the people," and as for Louis XVI, who seemed to have a mantle of lead on his shoulders, he looked at the multitudes with a dazed eye, "the look of a drunken man," reported a witness. The three bodyguards were chained together on the seat; one of them was weeping. "Before the carriage went eight cannons, and as many behind, with the fuse lit. . . . The only radiant face was that of M. de Lafayette, who was riding a superb battle-horse. A large white plume in his hat marked him out from a distance. He commanded the whole crowd with the dignity of a hero. He really appeared like a demi-god." And the bitter, thick, whirling dust still entered by the lowered windows, covering the women's dresses and the King's brown plush clothes with a layer of white, mingling with the sweat and painting black lines on the faces of those poor people, who were a thousand miles from understanding the reasons for all this hate.

The King entered the Tuileries and Lafayette came forward with "affection and respect," as he himself asserted.

"Sire, Your Majesty knows my attachment to you, but I did not leave you unaware that if you separated your cause from that of the people I would remain on the side of the people."

"It is true," admitted the King. "You have followed your principles. It is a party affair. Now, here I am. I shall tell you frankly I thought I was surrounded by a crowd of people of your opinion whom you had put around me, but that that was not the opinion of France. During this journey I have come to see that I was mistaken and that it is the general opinion."

Lafayette was modest in his triumph. "Has Your Majesty any orders to give me?" he asked, bowing.

The King gave a loud laugh. "It seems to me I am more at your orders than you are at mine!"

The Queen did not conceal her "irritation" and went to her rooms. She took off her hat. Her hair, ash-blonde five days before, was now quite white "like that of a woman of seventy."

Two days later she wrote to Fersen: "I exist. . . . How anxious I have been about you and how I pity you. . . . I shall not be able to write to you again. . . ."

That same day Louis XVI wrote in his Journal: "I took some whey."[1]

---

[1] For further details on the royal escapade see the author's *Souverains en fuite* (Amiot-Dumont) and *Varennes, le roi trahi* (André Bonne).

14

*

Lost Opportunities

THE KING AND QUEEN were prisoners. Sentries were posted everywhere, even on the roofs of the château. Marie Antoinette informed Fersen of this and the latter noted in his Journal: "The officers wished to sleep in the Queen's bedroom. The most she could obtain was that they should remain between the two doors. They came two or three times during the night to see if she was in her bed."

The King accepted everything. When a parliamentary committee came to question him on the details of his "abduction"—for they pretended to believe in this childish version—Louis XVI replied politely and then turned to his sister, who at that moment entered the room.

"Elisabeth, go and see if the Queen can receive these gentlemen. See that she does not keep them waiting."

Marie Antoinette sent a message that she "had just entered her bath" and that she would receive the "gentlemen" the following day. Not without irony she then offered them armchairs and herself sat on an ordinary chair.

How was this drifting kingdom to be governed? Louis XVI was less capable than ever of "acting like a King," as he was advised by Rivarol. He took advantage of his enforced leisure to indulge in the pleasures of statistics. "From 1775 to 1791," he wrote in his private Journal, "I went out 2,636 times." This calculation filled him with satisfaction.

Marie Antoinette had probably never been so much aware of the unfortunate man's incapacity as at that time. After the deep prostration into which she had fallen after the insult of her entry into the capital and after the dull despair which had seized her when her dream crumbled, she suddenly took hold of herself. She cast about for the best thing to do. There was no King left in France. She took a decision which was to have unlimited consequences: she decided to replace the sovereign who was no more than a royal ghost. But where could she find support? There was no hope on the right; 256 deputies declared that since the King was a prisoner they would take no further part in the work of the Assembly. This "emigration to the interior," as it were, left the Constitutionals, such as Barnave, facing the Jacobins. A compromise had to be made with the "lukewarm." Through the intermediary of the husband of one of her waiting-women, General de Jarjayes, Marie Antoinette got in touch with Barnave. At the beginning of July she wrote to Jarjayes: "I would like you to try to see 2-1 [a cipher indicating Barnave] on my behalf and tell him that I was struck with his personality, which I recognised during the two days we spent together, and that I should very much like to know from him what there is for us to do in our present position. . . . Having thought a great deal, since my return, about the strength, capacity and intelligence of the man I spoke to, I felt that it could not but be advantageous to begin a kind of correspondence with him, always on condition, however, that I should frankly let him know what was in my mind."

Barnave read the note several times "with delight." He promised to save the Queen with the help of his friends. But Lameth and Duport were more reticent. In their eyes Marie Antoinette was "very frivolous" and incapable "of any continuity of thought." However, events were to force them to give her "her chance." The Republicans—a party born as a result of the catastrophe of Varennes—wanted to depose Louis XVI. The Triumvirs knew that once the King was suppressed the whole edifice built by the Constituent Assembly would crumble. The Moderates would have to stand with the threatened King.

"Once the Nation is free," Barnave declared in the Tribune, "and once all French are equal, to wish for more is to wish the beginning of a cessation of freedom and to become guilty."

There was applause and Robespierre was not even able to get a hearing.

Thanks to Barnave's speech the King was "maintained," but he was "suspended" until he should be presented with the new constitution on which the Assembly was working. Barnave had unfortunately been unable to prevent the arrest of all those who had taken part in the flight, including Mme de Tourzel, who in view of her state of health was allowed to remain at the Tuileries. This outcome was a success, however. The worst might have been feared, for indeed one has only to read the press of the extreme left, which called Marie Antoinette "a criminal prostitute" and demanded that her friends in the Assembly should be "impaled alive."

Barnave ignored these attacks. Moved by the good intentions displayed by Marie Antoinette and with his friends' authorisation, he took up his rôle of teacher. Everything must be altered. "The King has for long been deceived. He has allowed himself to be led into a succession of steps the last of which threatens to lose him his crown." But all could yet be saved if the King and Queen would "take their stand" on what they had seen during their journey. Was not the "general wish" of the country for the new constitution then being discussed article by article? The Queen must let her "present intentions" be publicly known. This could be done by working on her brother Leopold and on the Emigrés, even more numerous, who were stirred up and spoke of invading France and rescuing the prisoners of the Tuileries. It was for Marie Antoinette to make them understand that in all loyalty the King and Queen wished to become constitutional monarchs. Provence—who had crossed the frontier without incident—and Artois must return to the kingdom and the Emperor of Austria must recognise the future constitution. Barnave declared that Marie Antoinette "can neither adopt other ideas nor leave this path without being ruined."

The young deputy saw clearly. Either Louis XVI accepted the constitution without reservations and asked his brother-in-law Leopold not to meddle in his affairs, or he abdicated. By refusing to adopt one or other of these two positions the King and Queen hastened to their doom.

On 9 July Marie Antoinette sent her second secret letter to the Triumvirs. She seemed a little more reticent. Perhaps she had been somewhat ruffled by the clear-cut tone of Barnave's reply. On the same day the Assembly voted a decree against the Emigrés, providing for the sequestration and subsequent seizure of their property if they did not return to the kingdom. Marie Antoinette was therefore in a good position to tell Barnave that it "seemed impossible to her that people who had voluntarily left their country two years before should take part in negotiations at a time when a large part of their fortune had been taken from them." As for the Emperor, although the Queen thought she had no influence on Leopold II she "did not refuse to write to him." But she was anxious on one point: would the constitution declare Louis XVI to be "inviolable"?

On the next day Barnave calmed her fears on this subject. "Success is certain. If the King and Queen have as much confidence as they on their side will have constancy and courage, they will answer for everything." In the lines that follow one can perceive the suspicions of Lameth and de Duport. If the King and Queen are not sincere, if Marie Antoinette should fall under "the influence of any adviser," if the sovereigns should "diverge from the plan of conduct," the Triumvirs "could see safety for themselves and for the public weal only in throwing themselves into a completely opposing party." The problem was set and the threat was definite: Marie Antoinette would have to assume her responsibilities.

On Sunday, 17 July, a serious occurrence showed the path the King and Queen would have to take. The extreme left had summoned their supporters to the altar in the Champ de Mars to sign a Republican petition. The affair began as a farce: two citizens had hidden themselves under the altar and spied on the concealed charms of the petitioning ladies. The two *voyeurs* were taken for spies and with sudden brutality the tragedy began. They were massacred and their heads carried through the city. Bailly, Lafayette and Charles de Lameth, who was the brother of Alexandre and, so to speak, the fourth Triumvir, decided to re-establish order. The troops invaded the Champ de Mars, but by an irreparable stroke, the guards fired as a result of an incident, which remains obscure, and fifty corpses were left on the ground.

The "massacre of the Champ de Mars" dug a trench of blood between the constitutional and the advanced deputies. The latter—Danton, Marat, Desmoulins and Santerre—went into hiding. Louis XVI and Marie Antoinette ought now to have had no hesitation in going forward blindly with the moderates. Barnave's speeches at the Tribune were of prime importance for the monarchy and Marie Antoinette seems to have understood this. "I saw with pleasure the force and courage with which the people to whom I write have supported the monarchy. This force cannot but inspire me with confidence on all other points."

On 20 July, with patent goodwill, she asked for more frequent contacts with the Triumvirs. Feeling "isolated and being unable to see anyone," she even expressed the following wish: "I should like to be given a few points to consider, either concerning present events or concerning those of even more importance in the future, and in my retreat I shall always reply with care and truth."

Full of joy, Barnave wrote on the following day to Marie Antoinette to say: "The Revolution must be ended." He emphasised the rôle which the Queen "can and must play" to make her brother abandon the idea of war and to persuade the Emigrés "to return to the great family of Frenchmen." Barnave declared that these madmen must be left "without help." If the King and Queen and the allies abandoned them, "they will be forced to renounce all their rash ideas."

Marie Antoinette seemed to be entirely in agreement with him and asked both for an interview with the Triumvirs and for the draft of a letter to be sent to the Emperor.

When he sent the draft, Barnave—and here one feels the anxiety of his two colleagues—felt it necessary to repeat once more the point of view of those in whom Marie Antoinette "revealed her confidence." The Queen was now about to act, but before doing so she should "question herself" and "be sure that she will never retreat from or vary the line of conduct she is going to adopt." The advice given by Barnave and his friends was "good" and "success was certain," but Marie Antoinette should *"above all be resolved to follow it steadfastly."* She had, of course, "aroused profound resentment against herself, but she had suffered" and the French, who had been moved by this, were ready to forget the past and to love their sovereign. Marie Antoinette could once more become Queen of France. Perhaps she would never more see, "as before, everything bow to her sovereign and absolute will, but she could again see herself surrounded by the attentions of a numerous society and the homage of an immense people." She must, then, hasten to act for the good of the country. And he concluded: "The Queen still has a moment and has no more than a moment."

On 26 July Marie Antoinette replied. One can see that she was somewhat shocked by this summons, although she declared that she was touched by the "frank way" in which he had spoken to her. She thought the draft of the letter to Leopold "very good" and she promised to copy it and to send it to Brussels, where Mercy would send it on to Vienna.

This exchange of letters, Marie Antoinette's good intentions and the noble enthusiasm displayed by Barnave could be very moving. But, unfortunately, only the Triumvirs were sincere. Marie Antoinette was lying to them.

She had not the slightest wish to follow these "exaggerated ideas," which would never "suit her." Furthermore, she had entered into the correspondence merely in order to "temporise." She admitted this to Mercy on 29 July and asked him to warn her brother to pay no attention to the letter dictated by the Triumvirs. In Marie Antoinette's view, as she explained to Mercy, to Breteuil and to the Emperor, it was necessary that "at least for some time to come" *they* should think that she was "of their opinion." For some time to come—until the Allies could intervene and come to save her. "The army is lost," she wrote to Mercy on 4 August. "There is no more money and no bond or hindrance can hold back the armed populace from all sides."

Marie Antoinette was all the more at a loss as, since her return, she was without news of Axel. She wrote to Esterhazy: "If you write to him tell HIM that many miles and many countries can never separate hearts. I feel this truth more strongly every day." She sent the same friend of happier days two rings of a kind which "are sold everywhere here." Outside each ring were engraved three fleurs-de-lis and inside this inscription: *"Lâche qui les abandonne."* "The one wrapped in paper is for HIM. Ask HIM to wear it for me. It is just his size. I wore it for two days before packing it. Tell HIM it comes from me. I do not know where he is. It is torture to have no news and not even to know where the people one loves are living."

Marie Antoinette remained without news until the end of September. Axel certainly wrote to her but the letters went astray. He was then in Vienna trying, not without difficulty, to interest Leopold II in his sister's fate and to prevent the Emigrés from doing harm. Marie Antoinette also feared what might come of that "noisy, confused and inconsiderate" opposition, who, with the King's brothers, were agitating in Coblenz. "You know yourself," she wrote to Mercy, "the Emigrés' evil talk and evil intentions. After abandoning us, the cowards want to insist that we alone should expose ourselves and that we alone should serve their interests." She constantly spoke of "that wicked race of men, who profess themselves attached to us and do us nothing but harm." Without the assistance of the Allies they could do nothing. The Queen reiterated this to Esterhazy: "Their arrival in this country would mean the loss of everything."

The heroics of the Emigrés were all the more dangerous as during

August the Assembly was occupied with the future constitution. Only Barnave and his friends could make what the Queen called "the charter" acceptable, and so she continued her "double game." "The moment has now come," she wrote to Barnave on 4 August, "when I can fully judge those who have bravely come out in favour of the monarchy. It is not words that are needed, but the preservation of the monarch's real rights, giving him the necessary dignity, in a word, giving him the strength and the means to govern." Finally she threatened the Triumvirs that she would "withdraw" if they did not maintain "with all their courage the monarch's just and lawful rights."

Barnave, Duport and Lameth were stupefied. Why did she speak to them in that tone "when for the past month we have influenced opinion and the direction of affairs in a way that no one but us would even have dared to try?" Besides, was it not the Queen who had sought them out?

Marie Antoinette realised that she had been unjust and hastened to retreat. Finally, thanks to Barnave and his friends, the constitution was voted. It gave the King powers which were undoubtedly limited but which were infinitely more extensive than the practically non-existent powers which the extreme left wished to grant him. Louis XVI could exercise his "veto" if he did not like a law. He would continue to nominate the Ministers, the Ambassadors and the military chiefs. He no longer had the right to make war, but the future legislative assembly could start a conflict only if the King asked it of them. Elsewhere it was laid down that only those could vote who had a landed revenue of 200 francs in the towns and 75 francs in the country. It was the triumph of the bourgeoisie.

But what was considered by the advanced deputies as "a step backwards" and resulted in Barnave's being described by Robespierre and Pétion as "an infamous cheat sold to the Austrian party," what seems to us today extremely moderate, appeared to Marie Antoinette, as she wrote to Mercy on 7 August, "a tissue of insolence and impractical absurdities." Now Barnave and his friends saw in this "absurdity," which they considered "very monarchical," the only means of saving the royalty. Louis XVI would have the title of "representative of the Nation, the most majestic that the King can bear." Marie Antoinette pretended to be convinced by Barnave's arguments. "Certainly," she wrote on 31 August, "there are advantages to be gained from the constitution both for the King and for the monarchy. . . . My trust in the courage, firmness and intelligence of those who wish for what is good reassures me." But three days before she had written to Mercy: "It is not possible to go on existing like this. All we have to do is to hoodwink them and make them trust us so as better to defeat them afterwards."

One would very much like to be able to tear this page from the Queen's life!

"Our only resource now is in the foreign powers," wrote the Queen on 26 August. "At all costs they must come to our aid."

Like most rulers of the time, Marie Antoinette had no feeling of "patriotism." For them the country was a possession, just as a landowner possesses farms. In their eyes all sovereigns formed one large family and it was not betraying the nation to want to correct it when it was unfaithful. After all, a family council was summoned when a child needed to be set on the right path.

Marie Antoinette was more excusable in calling on the help of foreigners than in deceiving loyal, honest, and sincere people who because they had believed in her and had tried to save her would one day mount Sanson's ladder.

The comedy went on. In order to give his consent Louis XVI had to make a speech to the Assembly, which was soon to disperse. "We will answer for everything," Barnave wrote, "if the King's speech is as it should be," and Marie Antoinette hastily asked her "friends" to revise the text carefully. They worked on it and one can imagine Marie Antoinette's feelings once the speech was drawn up. "I would have liked the acceptation to have been simpler and shorter," she wrote to Axel, from whom she had at last heard, "but it is our misfortune to be surrounded only by villains."

The session of 14 September was a series of rebuffs for Louis XVI. From one of the benches Marie Antoinette could see the Assembly sit down when the King pronounced his oath. The deputies did not rise either when Louis XVI began his speech and "disconcerted and annoyed," he sat down in his turn. On his return to the Tuileries he sank into an armchair and burst into tears.

"And you were a witness to this humiliation!" he sighed to Marie Antoinette. "You came to France to see that!"

The Queen knelt down and folded him in her arms and the husband

and wife, brought closer to each other by misfortune, embraced weeping.

The orders which had turned the château into a citadel were lifted, the "artisans of the flight" were liberated and on 18 September Marie Antoinette was applauded at the Opera, where *Psyché* was being performed. She smiled. Amid acclamations the sovereigns drove to the Champs-Elysées in their carriage.

The deputies dispersed to their provinces, convinced yet again that the Revolution was over. Barnave was triumphant. "The King is re-established, and the most difficult, the most critical and, we may even say, the most painful times are over." Marie Antoinette agreed and received the Triumvirs in the Tuileries, but she wrote to Axel: "You would never believe how much it costs me to do all I have to at present!"

As one reads the letters of Barnave and his friends one can perceive the latent drama and feel these honest men's weariness when faced with "the langour and apathy" of Louis XVI and with what they called "the Queen's uncertain and irresolute conduct." It is quite certain that Marie Antoinette's double game created an indefinable state of uneasiness. Marie Antoinette confirmed her good intentions by writing a letter to Barnave on 20 October which, for the sake of the Queen's memory, one would prefer not to have survived. "When I began my correspondence with those gentlemen I was completely frank and I always shall be in everything, for such is my character. I have always sacrificed my prejudices. . . . My approaches were made without any mental reservations. I said to myself 'This is my duty,' and that idea was enough for me."

The day before she had written to Axel: "Set your mind at rest, I am not going over to the madmen, and if I have relations with some of them it is merely to make use of them. They revolt me too much for me ever to go over to their side."

Axel calmed down and approved. Presumably before receiving this letter he had been somewhat anxious. He doubted whether the Queen would ever succeed in "winning over the factious." "You would be disgraced in the eyes of Europe," he wrote. But a few days later he was quite reassured on receiving a note from Marie Antoinette: "How wonderful if I could one day be again [powerful] enough to show all these wretches that I was not their dupe."

One cannot read these lines without feeling uncomfortable.

Every day, with the help of invisible ink and lemon juice, she wrote letters, sometimes 30 pages long, which were sent to Brussels hidden in hats or biscuit boxes. "I am exhausted with writing," she sighed. "I have never worked so hard!"

To start off with, the new Legislative Assembly, a somewhat mediocre gathering, voted two decrees, one demanding the famous civic oath for priests, in default of which they would be imprisoned, and the other condemning the Emigrés to death if they did not return to France within two months.

Encouraged by Marie Antoinette and Barnave, who was no longer a deputy, the King refused to approve the two decrees.

"I do what everyone desires often enough for them to do what I want for once," he declared. And he persisted in his veto. This unaccustomed obstinacy amazed everyone. The "poor man's" obduracy is in keeping with Louis XVI's character, however. When a weak man is given the means to be strong he becomes wilful. For the King this right of veto granted by the Assembly was the plank to which he clung and from which, as he thought, he could peacefully manifest his wishes in virtue of the very principles of his adversaries. The latter took it badly and were already thinking of stirring up the people so that "Monsieur Veto" would be forced to yield. The calm of September was forgotten, the gulf yawned again and the Revolution began to move once more.

At the end of 1791 the Duc d'Orléans came to offer himself to help save the monarchy.

"He returns to us in all sincerity," admitted Louis XVI after receiving his cousin, "and he will do all he can to repair the evil done in his name and in which his share may not have been as great as we imagined."

Marie Antoinette was not so easily convinced and in the Queen's drawing-room Philippe was insulted by the sovereign's remaining supporters. Some of them spat in his face. Convinced that Marie Antoinette had inspired the indignities he received, he left the château never to return. The Queen, who had never known how to make friends with those whose help she needed, did not recall him and threw him back on the mob.

At Coblenz, Provence and Artois were still agitating. They had but one aim: to return to the old régime. In Paris they were supported by Madame Elisabeth, who dreamed of absolutism. Louis XVI knew that such a plan could be realised "only by shedding seas of blood." "You make me shudder with horror," he is said to have written to his brothers on learning of their wild talk. "I would rather the monarchy crumbled than that it should ever agree to such schemes!" The letter may not be authentic, but those were certainly the King's feelings. In his will he was to speak of those who by their "false zeal," or by "misunderstood zeal," had done him "much harm." Marie Antoinette was of the same opinion.

"Cain! Cain!" she was to call her brothers-in-law.

While, in spite of his veto, Louis XVI honestly imagined he could become King of the Revolution, Marie Antoinette had only one hope—Austria.

And yet Leopold repeated: "There can be no question of expending our gold and our blood in order to re-establish France in its former powerful state."

What did Marie Antoinette, in whom the Archduchess was always latent, care if France was diminished by her liberation in the future? Louis XVI, on the other hand, knew his brother-in-law's greedy disposition. These ideas were constantly in conflict and the Queen, her husband and her sister-in-law were constantly opposed in violent arguments. "Our home is a hell," Marie Antoinette wrote to Axel.

Fersen knew that the interests of the Emigrés, the Austrians and the Fanatics were irreconcilable, and he therefore suggested a fourth solution—flight. In order to defend his proposition he decided to come to Paris. It was madness, for as a foreigner, with a warrant out for his arrest, he risked his life in order to rescue Marie Antoinette from her agony. Furnished with forged papers and disguised as a courier, he managed to enter Paris on Monday, 13 February 1792.

Without being recognised he entered the château "by his usual route" and did not leave the Queen's apartment during the whole of the following day. At six o'clock in the evening he finally saw Louis XVI. The delay of a day may have been due to the Queen concealing Axel's presence from her husband in order to remain alone with him.

The King refused to repeat the Varennes adventure. The National Guards were closely stationed not only round the château but also round the apartments. "In fact," wrote Axel, "he feels scrupulous about it, having so often promised to remain, for he is an honest man."

"Well now," continued the King, "among ourselves we can speak frankly. I know I am taxed with weakness and irresolution, but no one has ever been in my position. I know I missed the right moment. I missed it on 15 July. Then was the time to go. . . . Since then I have never found it. I have been deserted by everyone."

At half-past nine, without arousing attention, Axel slipped out of the Tuileries. For a whole week he lived in hiding at the house of one of his mistresses, Eleonore Sullivan, without her official lover, Craufurd, ever noticing. In the evening, when the Englishman was out, Eleonore ordered supper as though it were for herself. Half-an-hour after midnight Craufurd returned and, wrote Fersen in his Journal, "ate what I had left, believing that it was she who had been eating."

On 23 February Axel left Paris, apparently without having seen Marie Antoinette again. During the following night, in extremely cold weather—"the wheels crunched as they do in Sweden"—he crossed the frontier without trouble. Would he succeed in persuading the Allies to fly to the help of the prisoners of the Tuileries? Unfortunately his strongest supports gave way: King Gustavus was wounded by Captain Anckarström during a ball at the Stockholm Opera House and died a fortnight later on 30 March.

"This blow will rejoice your Jacobins in Paris," sighed the dying man.

Deprived of Sweden's help, would Austria and Prussia still enter into a war with France? It was France which took the first step.

At that time Louis XVI had a constitutional Ministry, the Feuillant Ministry, as the moderate deputies were called. They wanted peace, whereas the Girondins wanted to fight Austria. Lessart, the Minister for War, concealed from the Assembly certain news which might have touched off a conflict. He was impeached and the Ministry fell.

The monarchy now had only four more months to live, and these four months would see the birth and death of the last of the lost opportunities—that of Dumouriez. The Gironde had forced Louis XVI to have the General as Prime Minister. Dumouriez wanted to be a second Mirabeau and save the monarchy. This was reckoning without Marie Antoinette, who could not bring herself to consent to the monarchy's being put under guardianship. He had asked for an audience, but the Queen did not give him a good reception.

"Monsieur, at present you are all-powerful, but this is through the favour of the people, who soon break their idols. Your existence is dependent on your conduct."

And as Dumouriez seemed somewhat abashed by this reception, she added: "Neither the King nor I can bear all these innovations in the constitution. I tell you frankly: you must make the best of it!"

At least this was frank. Dumouriez would not be put off and tried persuasion.

"Believe me, Madame, I detest anarchy and crime as much as you do. I am in a better position than Your Majesty to judge events. This is not a passing popular movement, but the almost unanimous insurrection of a great nation against inveterate abuses. Everything that tends to separate the King from the Nation leads to the ruin of both. I am working to reunite them; it is for you to help me."

Like Mirabeau 18 months before, he threw himself at her feet and kissed her hand. "Allow yourself to be saved!"

Would she faithfully trust the man who was bringing her her last chance? No.

"One cannot believe in the protestations of a traitor," she was to say to Madame Campan.

She had let the last opportunity slip. Henceforth, with her eyes bandaged, the poor woman walked towards the scaffold.

For her, help could come only from abroad. In any case, everyone wanted war, but for different reasons, from the Girondins and Marie Antoinette to Francis of Austria, son of Leopold, who had just succeeded his father and saw in the Revolution an enemy to be struck down.

There was a pretext ready, for Austria had authorised Condé's army to assemble on its territory.

War—a war which, with truces, was to last for 23 years—was imminent. Dumouriez explained his clever plan to the Council held at the Tuileries on 25 March. Marie Antoinette wrote to Mercy the next day: "M. Dumouriez, no longer in doubt as to the agreement between the Powers, owing to the troop movements, has formed the scheme of being the first to start with an attack in Savoy and another by the Liége country. M. de Lafayette's army would be used in the second attack. This is the result of yesterday's Council."

One cannot help starting as one reads what for us is clear and definite treachery. But we should try to understand. Marie Antoinette did not in any way consider herself to be Queen of the France of 1792. Admittedly, when she formerly busied herself with the affairs of Bavaria, so dear to Marie Theresa, or the problem of the Mouths of the Scheldt, in which Joseph II was so interested, Marie Antoinette had behaved more like an Austrian Archduchess than the wife of Louis XVI. But would she, in the event of war, have gone so far as to communicate to her mother or brother the French army's plans of campaign? Nothing is less certain! But now she felt she was in danger. The woman who, to save her life and that of her children, calls her family to help her has the right to plead extenuating circumstances, especially if she has not the soul of a Camilla. Let us not forget that in the Tribune Vergniaud had just threatened Marie Antoinette with the gallows, with a violence that sent a shudder of terror over the Assembly: "From here I can see the windows of a palace where counter-revolution is being plotted, where they are working out ways to plunge us once more into the horrors of slavery. . . . Let all those who live there know that our Constitution grants inviolability only to the King. Let them know that the law will reach without distinction all who are guilty, and that there is not *one single head* which, once convicted, can escape its sword!"

The speech terrified Marie Antoinette. There must be a war, as she wrote to Mercy, "so that one may finally be revenged for all the outrages inflicted in this country."

Finally, on 20 April, Louis XVI "formally proposed" to the Assembly "a war against the King of Hungary and Bohemia." Five days later Marie Antoinette revealed to Brussels the negotiations begun by Dumouriez in an attempt to detach Prussia from Austria.

As was to be expected, when the French offensive began—the offensive whose plans the Queen had sent to Austria and Prussia—there was a rout. Naturally, Marie Antoinette and "the Austrian committee" were accused.

This accusation enabled the Girondins to pass a series of important measures. The constitutional guard given to Louis XVI some months before was dismissed; the non-juring priests were to be deported; and a camp of 20,000 Federates was set up in front of the walls of Paris. The King yielded only on the first measure, although the monarchy was henceforth practically undefended, but exercised his veto with regard to the two others, in spite of Dumouriez's urging. No longer in agreement with his Girondin Ministers, Louis XVI dismissed them, with the exception of Dumouriez, whom he tried to keep. But on 16

15

❧

Madame Veto

ON THE EVENING of Tuesday, 19 June, Paris was in a ferment. On the next day it was to celebrate the anniversary of the oath of the Jeu de Paume (it was also a year since the King had tried to escape), and Louis XVI had chosen the eve of the Republican festivities to declare to the Assembly that he definitely opposed his veto to the decrees. The suburbs seethed with faces only seen in Paris on sinister occasions. Here and there armed groups formed. There was a rumour that 18,000 "knights of the poniard" had gathered at the château and that the King "had been to confession and made his will." There was one dominating cry: they must go to the Assembly and insist on the suppression of the vetoes. The Directory of the Department—a body somewhat like the present Prefecture of the Seine—had pronounced "all assemblies against the law." Roederer, the *Procureur Général Syndic* (or Prefect), reminded the municipal officers of this, but they, being completely overtaken by events, "agreed in saying that the citizens seemed to them to have the most peaceful intentions, but that they insisted with the greatest stubbornness in going armed" (to the Assembly).

Pétion, who was still Mayor of Paris, alleged that he had "insisted" to the municipality. "They replied," he told his friend Roederer, "that they thought it impossible to overcome the general feeling on this matter. As you see, it is a very delicate position." It was so delicate that at the Hôtel de Ville, Pétion confined himself to ordering "the doors to be held," but paid no attention to the dangers to which the capital might be exposed by the "seditious gathering." Neither did he think of requisi-

299

tioning troops, as he was allowed to do by law and as the Directory advised him. Moreover, at midnight he wanted to "legalise the movement" which he could not check, and authorised the "gathering to march and to unite under its flags and under the command of its chiefs."

The Directory rejected this proposal and at five o'clock Pétion still persisted in his resolve. The gathering grew larger.

At eight o'clock on the Wednesday morning the Minister of the Interior, Terrier, asserted that "the night's news was not alarming," but at nine o'clock, his eyes having been opened, he sent a cry of alarm to the Directory, asking them "without delay" to "give the order to the troops to march to defend the château." Apparently no order was given and only the usual posts of the National Guard protected the Tuileries. All that was done was to close the gates.

An hour later the crowd began to gather. It did not approach the gates of the Tuileries, fearing "the treachery" of the court. The intention of the *"Piques,"* as they were called, was still merely to march to the Assembly. The meeting hall was the former riding school of the Tuileries, on the site of the present Rue de Rivoli, near the Place Vendôme. The hall abutted on the former Convent of the Feuillants.

Marie Antoinette was listening. The Princesse de Lamballe, who had come back to France now that her former friend was in danger, was standing near her. The two women could hear the murmuring of the petitioners moving about in front of the Manège as they waited for the deputies' decision. Would the "armed citizens" march up to the bar? In the Assembly they first of all heard "the orator of the troupe," who had come to present the wishes of the petitioners.

"We ask you to inquire into the causes of the inaction of our armies. If it results from the executive power then the latter should be abolished. The blood of patriots must not flow to satisfy the pride and ambition of the perfidious château of the Tuileries."

The results of a deliberation with 20,000 armed men at the door may be foreseen. At two o'clock, preceded by about ten musicians, according to an eye-witness, there began the procession "of citizens from all sections, mingled with detachments of the National Guard and led by Santerre and Saint-Huruge, who was half mad. The men were armed with pikes, axes, paring-knives, knives and sticks; some of the women carried sabres. Various emblems were displayed, on which could be read menacing inscriptions, such as 'Down with the veto! Warning to Louis

XVI: The people are tired of suffering. Liberty or death!' An old pair of black breeches was seen on the end of a pike, and above it the words: 'Long live the SANS-CULOTTES! Down with the veto.' "

The crowd penetrated into the Manège by what is now the Rue de Castiglione and flowed on through the Passage des Feuillants towards the Tuileries. From the windows of the château the Queen could see the *Piques* assembling outside the garden gates. As the crowd marched up the pressure against the gates grew stronger.

Three municipal officers were received by the King. "My colleagues and I, Sire, observed *with sorrow* that the Tuileries were closed just as the procession arrived. The people, confined in the Passage des Feuillants, are all the more annoyed as through the wicket they could see people in the garden. We ourselves, Sire, *were very strongly affected* on seeing cannon pointed against the people. Such steps *are more likely to irritate than to satisfy them.* It is urgently necessary that Your Majesty should give the order for the Tuileries gates to be opened."

"I agree to their being opened, but on condition that you make the procession move along the terrace and out by the door of the courtyard of the Manège, without going down into the garden."

At that moment there was a shout from the garden; the gates had given way. The tide of people rushed in across the garden, confining itself to yelling the usual threats. On arriving at the terrace, the head of the procession turned left and passing through the Louvre gates reached the Carrousel in front of the entrance to the château. It was four o'clock. Santerre, who had been the last to leave the Assembly, stood in front of the great door.

"Why have you not entered the château? We must enter; that is all we came for."

Behind him a group of citizens from the Val-de-Grâce section were dragging a cannon. Turning to the National Guards of the Petits-Pères battalion, who were drawn up in the Cour Royale, the "General" shouted: "If you refuse to open the doors we shall break them down with shot!"

"Then everything moved at once. . . ."

Marie Antoinette heard the clamour growing nearer. This time she was not the only one to be attacked. "To hell with the veto! Down with Monsieur Veto!"

There was a dull sound—the tramp of feet on the steps of the great staircase, then a crashing noise—the cannon being hoisted to the first floor. The rioters were massed in the great vestibule which took up the whole of the first floor of the central wing of the château, from the "courtyard side" of the Carrousel to the "garden side" of the Tuileries, in the phraseology of the actors of the King's theatre, whose stage ran the width of the château. Marie Antoinette, whose apartments were on the ground floor, could hear a door overhead being broken down with an axe. The rioters had just burst into an enormous room whose windows also looked out on to the "courtyard side" and the "garden side" and which, since it was used as an antechamber to the state bedroom, was called the *Œil-de-Bœuf*, as at Versailles. After this room, where the bed was, there were rooms on both sides of the château. Looking on the courtyard there were successively the Council Room and the Galerie de Diane, and looking on to the garden were the apartments of the King and the Children of France.

Other *Piques* had remained on the ground floor and were trying to find an entry into the Queen's apartments. A small band of National Guards were on duty in the antechamber, but they let the crowd pass in. One of them, the volunteer Jaladon, admitted that their muskets were not even taken from the racks. A man reached a door and broke down the panels with an axe. Marie Antoinette was only a step away and heard: "I shall take the Queen dead or alive."

The unhappy woman wanted to seek refuge with the King, who on the first floor had gone to meet the raging crowd, but the Princesse de Lamballe stopped her.

"What have I to fear? The worst would be to be killed!"

Her women dragged her in haste to the Dauphin's apartments. The child was no longer there, for his valet had taken him to Madame Royale. At last Marie Antoinette was able to press her two children in her arms. All three hid in a little passage separating the Dauphin's bedroom from the King's, the door of which was hidden in the woodwork and could not easily be seen. It was by this corridor that the King had escaped a year before.

They had to wait a long time. The tumult about them grew louder and the threats of death fiercer. "Marie Antoinette stifled her sobs," relates Mme de Tourzel. For a quarter-of-an-hour she knew nothing of the King's fate. Finally, someone came to tell her that Louis XVI and his sister, hemmed in by the rioters who milled about them, were in the

Œil-de-Bœuf. A "Chevalier de Saint-Louis" held the King's left hand and his right was grasped by Garland de Saint-Farre, director of the Théâtre de Minerve, formerly "Les Enfants Comiques."

The *Piques* were still looking for the Queen. The noise of doors being shattered by axes drew nearer. The first room of the Dauphin's apartments was forced open. Marie Antoinette had to leave her hiding-place.

"Let me go to the King, my duty calls me there!"

Weeping, she advanced towards the mass of armed men, who were coming to seek the coffer on which the King had finally taken refuge. Its appearance in the antechamber was apparently the signal for the rush for spoils. An habitué of the Tuileries, the Chevalier de Rouge-ville, one of the "knights of the poniard," stopped her.

"Where are you going, Madame?"

"To the King. I count on you, Monsieur, to help me to reach him."

The Chevalier would not allow her to pass.

"It is only with me that the people are angry," begged Marie Antoi-nette. "I am going to offer them their victim."

But Rougeville, paying no attention to the Queen, bore her off to the Council Room, which had not yet been invaded. The Chevalier asked Marie Antoinette to sit with her children and her ladies behind a heavy table, which was pushed into a corner of the room. The grenadiers of the royalist section of the *Filles Saint-Thomas* were drawn up in three rows in front of the table.

Meanwhile, the crowd was still pressing round the King, demanding that he withdraw his veto and threatening "to come back every day."

"Force will have no effect on me and I am above terror."

He was handed a red bonnet; he put it on, accepted everything, but refused to yield.

The butcher Legendre managed to make himself heard.

"Monsieur, listen to us. It is your business to listen to us. You are a traitor. You have always deceived us and you are still deceiving us. But take care; the measure is full to overflowing and the people are tired of being your plaything."

The deputies who were deliberating in the Manège did not go to the help of the "executive power."

"The King cannot be in danger, he is surrounded by the people," cried Thuriot.

"They are not the people, they are brigands!" retorted Beugnot.

Pétion finally appeared at the Tuileries. It was six o'clock. Since early afternoon he had been at the Hôtel de Ville, watching the crowd go by and sighing: "What a fine sight!"

He advanced towards the King.

"Sire, I have *this moment* heard of the situation you are in."

"That is very surprising," Louis XVI replied calmly. "This has been going on for two hours."

Pétion was hoisted on to the shoulders of two grenadiers. The King rang a bell and the Mayor began his speech.

"The people have done what they should. You have acted with the pride and dignity of free men. But this is enough. Let each man retire."

Louis XVI put forward a suggestion: "I have had the state apartments opened. If the people file past on the gallery side they will enjoy seeing them."

It was not easy to change the rioters into peaceful visitors, but curiosity won, and the crowd passed through the state bedroom. The door of the Council Room was then opened. Everyone halted, astonished. Marie Antoinette, whom they had been looking for everywhere, was there behind the table, on which the Dauphin was standing. Santerre came forward the first, calling to the grenadiers who were protecting the Queen and the little group of women around her.

"Make way for the people to enter and see the Queen!"

The soldiers obeyed. A certain M. de Wittergoff, Lieutenant-General of the 17th Division (some eye-witnesses also refer to him as M. de Wisquichef), placed a red bonnet on Marie Antoinette's head. The Queen took it off and put it on her son's head.

With anguish Marie Antoinette now saw Santerre approach the table and lean on it. "Fear nothing, Madame, I do not want to hurt you, but remember that you are in the wrong and that it is dangerous to deceive and try to dominate the people. However, I shall answer for everything and I shall make them file past."

He turned back towards the crowd, which, somewhat intimidated, had remained in the doorway, and shouted like a barker: "See the Queen and the Royal Prince!"

The people slowly walked past the table. Very pale and with blood-shot eyes, but holding her head erect, Marie Antoinette watched these men and women brandishing whips and carrying placards: "To the lantern with Marie Antoinette!" Did she also notice the man who, as he passed in front of the table, shook a gibbet with a cord from which hung a female doll?

One harridan shrieked: "You're a vile woman!"

"Have I ever done you any harm?" the Queen murmured quietly.

The crowd pressed in from the courtyards and the neighbouring streets, mounted the staircase and filed through. Gradually they became simply sightseers, following their leaders. One woman looked at Marie Antoinette and her two children and the group of frightened ladies. She burst into tears.

"She is drunk," explained Santerre.

In order to reach her sister-in-law Madame Elisabeth had to join the line. On arriving at the table she calmed the Queen, saying in a low voice: "The King is safe."

"Next time they will kill me," murmured Marie Antoinette, "and what will become of my children?"

At eight o'clock in the evening the masquerade was over. Shattered doors lay on the ground, and there was broken glass under foot. The cannon had staved in the floor-boards. Louis XVI was at last able to rejoin his wife. His sister and children threw themselves in his arms. The Queen looked at him, horrified. He had forgotten to take off the red bonnet the rioters had put on his head.

"I still exist, but it is by a miracle," wrote Marie Antoinette to Fersen. "The 20th was an appalling day. It is no longer against me that they are most enraged, but against my husband's very life, and they do not conceal it." The next day she again called for help. "Your friend is in the greatest danger. . . . Let his relatives know of his unhappy position."

Louis XVI had not yielded. He now seemed to have lost his apathy and did not hesitate to read a violent lecture to the Mayor of Paris. His manifesto of 22 June held a tone which the King was not to quit right up to the scaffold and which would have had its effect if the monarchy had not reached the end of its resources. "The French will learn not without grief that a mob, misled by a few malcontents, entered with arms into the King's dwelling. . . . He replied to threats and insults only with his conscience and his love for the public weal. . . . If those who wish to overthrow the monarchy need yet another crime they may commit it."

When Pétion's house was searched, later on, letters were found which are now preserved in the Archives and enable us to realise how terrified Roederer and the Mayor were at the serious situation which had arisen from their inertia and weakness. Pétion wrote to Santerre on 22 June, begging him "for pity's sake to calm the people's minds." There was already talk of another uprising and the Mayor, a veritable sorcerer's apprentice, implored the "General" to intervene. Into what "an abyss of evil a further and illegal action by the citizens of Paris" might plunge the city! As far as Pétion was concerned the principal evil would be to be dismissed for not having been able to keep order, and this soon happened. On 8 July he received a note from Roederer, addressed to "M. Pétion himself," and dated four o'clock in the morning, informing him of his dismissal, embracing him and congratulating him: "May I also find someone to suspend me, until they hang us!"

Lafayette would have liked to hang the members of the Paris Commune and of the Directory who cried with the pack. On learning of the behaviour of the Paris magistrates on 20 June, Lafayette left the army and hastened to the Tuileries. He was full of schemes for saving the King, but Marie Antoinette remarked sarcastically: "I can see that M. de Lafayette wishes to save us, but who will save us from M. de Lafayette?"

The château was no more than a tempest-tossed wreck. Louis XVI and Marie Antoinette lived there like castaways, their ears open to the sinister rumours that reached them. "The band of assassins grows constantly larger," wrote Marie Antoinette, whose tortures increased. Mme Campan had a bodice made for her mistress which would "resist knife-thrusts and bullets." Marie Antoinette refused to wear it.

"If the insurgents assassinate me it will be a blessing for me; they will deliver me from a most miserable existence."

The Queen sometimes longed for the final and immediate catastrophe. Anything seemed preferable to this protracted agony. In the galleries, as the sovereigns passed by, the National Guards cried: "Down with Veto!" The chapel orchestra played the "Ça ira!" when the King and Queen entered. The gardens were full of fanatics, who yelled when they saw a curtain drawn aside. Under the Queen's windows hawkers sold passers-by indecent engravings showing Marie Antoinette lying in the arms of Mme de Polignac, the Princesse de Lamballe, or the Comte d'Artois.

"They have taken everything, except my heart," the unhappy woman sighed.

One morning the château was alerted: the suburbs, it was said, were marching on the Tuileries. Mme Campan refused to wake the Queen, who had not fallen asleep until dawn. The King agreed with the waiting-woman.

"It is good to see her take a little rest. Her sufferings increase my own."

When the danger had passed the Queen awoke and "wept bitterly with regret."

"Elisabeth was with the King and I was sleeping, I, who wish to die at his side! I am his wife, I do not wish him to incur any danger without me."

Soon the poor woman did not even sleep. "She insisted that the shutters and blinds should not be closed," wrote Mme Campan, "so that her long, sleepless nights might be less trying."

Occasionally she had a moment of hope. It was not possible that her nephew Francis should leave her in this terrible situation and not do everything he could to overthrow the French troops and reach Paris. She constantly urged Fersen: "Ours is a dreadful situation . . . time presses and it is impossible to wait longer." And on 24 July: "Tell M. de Mercy that the lives of the King and Queen are in the greatest danger, that one day's delay may produce incalculable misfortune, that the manifesto must be sent at once, that it is awaited with extreme impatience."

It was on 25 July that the Duke of Brunswick proclaimed the Manifesto at Coblenz, threatening Paris with military force "if the least violence or the least outrage is committed against Their Majesties the King and Queen." The text was soon all over Paris and caused an explosion. The arrival on 30 July of the Confederates from Marseilles increased the tension. The final attack was imminent. The remaining adherents never left the Tuileries, which they tried, as well as they could, to prepare for resistance, for it must not be thought—following the example of some over-royalist historians—that those of the right prepared meekly to have their throats cut. Police reports and letters found in the Tuileries the day after the 10 August (documents which have remained for the most part unused and are preserved in the Archives) prove that the defenders armed and organised themselves.

It was hoped that the émigré bodyguards would return from Coblenz—their money was still being paid; it was said that barges brought arms and powder; the Swiss were dismissed to their barracks. On 25 July eight witnesses claimed to have seen pages of the King's Household, disguised as National Guards, mounting guard around the château. The son of a miller of Montmartre was sure he had noticed "three Knights of Saint-Louis" pacing the heights of the *Butte* in order to find the best place to set up the artillery. Other witnesses asserted that powder and arms were stored at Meudon and Montrouge.

"The King and Queen are preparing a counter-revolution," the agitators repeated.

In the King's mind it was only a question of defending himself; in that of the people it was a question of attacking the "patriots" once the Royalists had gathered strength.

Curiously enough, Pétion himself no longer believed in the danger. In a letter to Roederer on 1 August he asserted "that an attack on the château" was a "completely false and absurd rumour."

In spite of what many historians have said, there were no misgivings in the Tuileries on the evening of 9 August. To be convinced of this one has only to read the fragment of the unpublished diary written by the Abbé Gallois, the chapel sacristan, a diary which the revolutionaries found on 10 August on the table in his little bedroom in the attics of the Tuileries.

"It is nine o'clock and have just got ready for the night," wrote the Abbé before going to bed. In a neighbouring room François de la Rochefoucauld, who had been to the theatre, was drinking punch with his friend Tourzel, son of the governess. The latter was always well-informed through his mother.

"Nothing will happen, or at least not much."

The two young men gossiped peacefully, but at 11 o'clock they were disturbed by a message from Mme de Tourzel. There was to be no King's *coucher* that evening. Until now etiquette had been preserved aboard this leaking wreck. La Rochefoucauld and Tourzel were worried by the news. Undoubtedly His Majesty was going to try to reach Fontainebleau on horseback, and the two young men hurried to put on their boots.

The Abbé was still sleeping. At half-past two he awoke and wrote:

"I can hear the tocsin sounding and the alarm being beaten, which indicates that vigorous action is being prepared." The sacristan went to find out what was happening. On being told, he returned to his room and wrote: "The Confederates are assembling in the Champs-Elysées. Are they waiting for the Marseillais and the other *sansculottes*? I do not know. . . . All I know is that they are planning an attack on the château."

In fact the bells of Paris were giving the signal not for an attack on the château, but for an attack on the Hôtel de Ville. Commissioners appointed by the sections of Paris were occupied in dismissing a municipality which was too respectful of formalities and in replacing it by a "revolutionary *commune*."

The Abbé was a sound sleeper, for the tocsin had begun to sound just before one o'clock at the church of the Cordeliers. By half-past two all the churches in Paris were answering the signal given by Danton. Marie Antoinette, who had not gone to bed, listened to the alarming sound of the bells ringing through the stifling night. At that moment Paris was taking over power, but she did not know this. Standing at the windows, each one named the church whose bell he recognised. The abolition of the *coucher* had disorganised the life of the château. The bewildered court encamped in the drawing-rooms, to the despair of the ushers, who were horrified by these crimes of *lèse-etiquette*.

Roederer brought reassuring news. Undoubtedly, as Pétion had announced at midnight, the suburb of Saint-Antoine was "in a ferment"; "the citizens are stationed before their houses, armed and ready to march," but there were only 1,500 to 2,000 men assembled.

"The tocsin is having no results," someone came to inform them.

They were all the more reassured since this time the Swiss regiment of 900 men had been summoned from Courbevoie and was guarding the château. There was also the National Guard, not very reliable, it is true, but the royalist battalion of the Filles Saint-Thomas was also on guard. They could count on 1,500 faithful men, together with two or three hundred gentlemen who had arrived at the château.

The King went to lie down in his room fully clothed, but Marie Antoinette, followed by the Princesse de Lamballe, wandered from room to room. She was determined to face the rioters. Madame Elisabeth called her.

"My sister, come and watch the dawn break."

The sky was blood red. It was four o'clock.

Suddenly the tocsin ceased and everyone felt relieved. "I conclude that no one is coming," wrote the Abbé. In front of the window Marie Antoinette continued to look out over Paris. The heavy silence which followed the sound of the bells seemed even more menacing. Her presentiments had not deceived her; the Marquis de Mandat, commander of the National Guard, had been summoned to the Municipality and cut down on the steps of the Hôtel de Ville. His body was thrown into the Seine. In him the Tuileries lost its only defender.

Marie Antoinette went to look for Louis XVI. Woken from a heavy sleep he staggered into the *Œil-de-Bœuf*. His wig was flattened and unpowdered from where he had slept on it. Roederer proposed taking refuge in the Assembly. Marie Antoinette raised her head.

"Monsieur, there are troops here. It is time to find out who will be the stronger, the King and the Constitution or the factions."

And she ordered drinks to be taken to the Swiss Guards. Marie Antoinette was calm. There was no excitement, no anger, no despair, and no useless bravado either. Roederer was to say: "During this fatal night the Queen made no show of masculinity or heroics, was neither affected nor romantic; I saw no rage or despair in her, nor any spirit of revenge. She was a woman, a mother and a wife in danger. She feared, hoped, sorrowed and was reassured."

The suburb began to make its way towards the Tuileries. In the gardens and courtyards the troops who were to defend the château lined up. Three cannons were placed facing the Carrousel. Two more were put on the terrace. Urged by his wife, Louis XVI went down to review the defenders. The drums beat the general salute. From a window Marie Antoinette watched the scene. Nothing less royal could be imagined than the fat man in a grey suit and flattened wig, who with a gloomy look passed silently in front of the men who were to die for him. A great shout of "Long live the Nation!" drowned the applause of the Swiss Guards and royalist companies of the National Guards. Some gunners left their cannon and came to insult the King. Marie Antoinette could hear their cries: "Down with the veto! Down with the fat pig!"

The poor man stammered: "I love the National Guard."

Pale, "as though he had ceased to exist," according to a witness, he returned to the château. Some of the gunners were already leaving their posts to join the vanguard of the *Piques* approaching the château.

The Queen waited in the state bedroom for the King to return. She wept "without a groan, without a sigh, without a word." When she came back into the Council Room, where Roederer was, "the redness of her eyes and cheeks had passed" and she appeared "calm and even detached." Around her all were preparing to die. M. de Saint-Souplet, the King's Equerry, and a page were seen solemnly shouldering the fire-tongs which they had broken in two to use as weapons in place of muskets.

"Half-past seven," wrote the Abbé in his attic. "Word has just come that they have arrived and are at present in the Carrousel."

"Sire," said Roederer at the same moment, "Your Majesty has not five minutes to lose. You will find safety only in the National Assembly."

"But I did not see many people in the Carrousel," the unhappy man stammered.

"But Monsieur," asserted Marie Antoinette, "we have troops."

"Madame, all Paris is marching."

And turning to the bewildered Louis XVI, he added: "Sire, time presses. We are no longer begging you, we no longer take the liberty of giving you advice. There is only one thing for us to do at this moment; we ask your permission to take you away."

"What!" said Marie Antoinette, "are we alone, can no one do anything?"

"Yes, Madame, alone. Action is useless, resistance impossible."

"The King raised his head," wrote Roederer, "looked fixedly at me for a few seconds, then, turning to the Queen, he said: 'Let us go,' and rose."

At the top of the staircase Roederer cried: "The King and his family are going to the Assembly alone, with no other accompaniment than the Ministers and a guard. Make way for them!"

"But, Monsieur," replied Marie Antoinette, "we cannot abandon all these brave people who have come to the château to defend the King."

"If you oppose this move," Roederer declared, "you will have to answer for the King's life and those of your children."

Marie Antoinette gave way.

Surrounded by a body of National Guards, the King, who had put on the hat of one of the guards marching beside him, preceded the Queen, who, "red and weeping," held her son by the hand. Behind her came Madame Royale, Madame Elisabeth, the Princesse de Lamballe, Mme de Tourzel, the Ministers and a handful of faithful supporters.

Marie Antoinette called to M. de Jarjayes: "We shall soon be back."

And the little group moved slowly towards the garden sparkling in the sunshine.

"It seems as though it would end there," wrote the Abbé, but he resumed: "I am wrong. Voices from outside announce perseverance in the plan to attack . . ."

There, without a full stop, the sacristan's log-book ends. The defenders were also persevering. Now that the King had gone, the best thing for them would have been to go too, but old Maréchal de Mailly, who was 84, considered that for him the finest end would be to die with his sword in his hand and, taking the command on himself, he proceeded to transform the château into a fortress.

During the remaining fourteen months of her life Marie Antoinette was to hear herself accused of having, on that morning, "caused the people to be fired upon."

The Assembly, which had been in session since two o'clock in the morning—under the Revolution one slept when one had the time—was occupied with the report "concerning the gradual abolition of the slave trade," when it was announced that the Revolutionary Commune of Paris had arisen in opposition to them. Without being greatly disturbed the deputies referred "these details" to a committee and were about to go back to their negroes when the royal family entered the hall.

Did the King utter those dignified words attributed to him by the *Moniteur*? "I have come here to avoid a great crime and I believe that I cannot be safer than among you."

The President replied cautiously: "Sire, you may count on the firmness of the National Assembly."

This "firmness" consisted first of all in shutting the King and his family up in a little office behind the President's chair, which was used by the editors of the *Logographe*. They stayed squashed together in this tiny box until ten o'clock in the evening.

Whereas the King had recovered his good-humour and chatted with various deputies, Marie Antoinette, her head held high and wearing a fixed expression, watched the endless session without uttering one word. From this cupboard, which was unbearably hot, the Queen saw her last hopes crumble. Near by, the cannon and musket fire raged. Would the Swiss Guards succeed in holding the château, in spite of the order sent by Louis XVI to cease firing? Participants in the battle were constantly arriving to give news of its progress and of the "treachery" of the Swiss, who had greeted the assailants with shots.

"Is this how French citizens should be received in the palace of their King?" demanded a powder-blackened patriot.

But were the French citizens in the habit of presenting themselves with arms and munitions at the palace of their King?

The gunfire died away, and soon only a few shots could be heard. Finally there was silence: the château had surrendered.

Then, like a wreck thrown up on the shore after a tempest, the victorious rioters carried their trophies to the Manège. Marie Antoinette saw brought into the hall her jewels, her silver, letters found on her table, boxes of correspondence and even fragments of trunks found in her apartments. The looters interrupted their unpacking only to give way to the unfortunate and terrified Swiss Guards, who were being exhibited before being sent to the Abbaye Prison. There was a farcical interlude: a petitioner, "his heart wrung with anguish, all covered with blood and dust," in his own words, came to show a Swiss he had captured and for whom he had conceived a sudden affection. He embraced him and fainted with emotion. On being revived his first words were to ask that he be authorised to take the Swiss to his home "to have the honour of feeding him."

"That is how I wish to avenge myself on him."

The deputies were no longer the masters, in spite of their "firmness." The Commune, Robespierre, Marat and Danton were in command and insisted that matters be settled. At the beginning of the afternoon Marie Antoinette saw Vergniaud rise, refer to the "grief" with which his colleagues were filled and ask for the immediate adoption of two measures:

"The French people is invited to form a National Convention . . .

"The head of the Executive Power is provisionally suspended from his functions."

But there was still no question of the Temple prison. Once calm was re-established the royal family would be allowed to reside in the Luxembourg. Gradually the tone changed. By the end of the day no one paid any attention to "the grief of the colleagues." The Assembly was a passive herd, harassed by the delegations, who, incited by the Commune, continually demanded the deposition of the monarchy.

"It has been rendered incapable of doing any harm," Vergniaud promised. "The future Convention will make the decision."

Dazed, overcome with exhaustion and thirst, her fichu and handkerchief "wet with tears and sweat," supporting her son's nodding head in her hands, Marie Antoinette, apparently unmoved, received these rebuffs.

In the evening the royal family, the Princesse de Lamballe, Mme de Tourzel and one of the Queen's women, Mme Augié, were placed in the little cells of the Feuillants convent next to the Manège. For Marie Antoinette it was another sleepless night. At the end of the corridor, behind a grille, a mad crowd shouted threats of death. "When one of the ladies appeared at the door of the apartment," wrote an eye-witness, "she was obliged by the terrifying cries to return at once. Every time I looked at the grille I thought I was in a menagerie watching the fury of the wild beasts when someone approaches the bars."

The Queen's name constantly recurred in their insults.

"I fear she is lost," sighed Mme de Lamballe.

During the evening a few supporters—Choiseul, Goguelas, Nantouillet, Aubier and young Tourzel—managed to find their way to the "apartments."

"My handkerchief is soaked with tears," murmured Marie Antoinette.

Aubier offered his and the Queen thanked him "with a painful smile which wrung my heart," the officer reported.

At six o'clock in the morning an unknown man—a certain Dufour—managed to prepare a meal, but Marie Antoinette, who was "moaning," could not swallow a mouthful. At half-past seven on Saturday, 11 August, their martyrdom began again and they were once more led to the little press-box.

Throughout the day they were humiliated by speeches in which each man tried to show himself more republican than his neighbour and in which vexatious measures were proposed to prevent the King from being carried off.

On the 11th a traitor had improvised a meal, but on the 12th the service of the *Bouche* was resumed. Dinner consisted of two soups, eight entrées, four roasts and eight desserts and supper of two soups, two entrées (one of which was *noix de veau sauce Menehould*), a fowl, a rabbit, cold chicken and five desserts. In spite of the shouting which continued around the convent, Louis XVI ate heartily. Marie Antoinette, who hardly touched anything, was embarrassed. That morning, in her little green-papered cell in the Feuillants, seated on a poor chair, she had wept in the arms of Mme Campan, who had succeeded with some difficulty in joining her.

On Sunday, 12 August, the prisoners had to listen to long discussions on their future residence. Paris was opposed to the Luxembourg Palace, where "there are several concealed exits." The Assembly suggested the house of the Minister of Justice in the Place Vendôme. Manuel, speaking for the Commune, refused. "It is surrounded by houses through which it would be very easy to escape." Why should the Assembly not entrust the Commune with guarding the prisoners? In the evening Manuel suggested putting "the King with his wife and their sister" in the Temple, where "they will be conducted tomorrow with all the respect due to misfortune."

"All their correspondence will be intercepted, for they have only traitors for friends. The streets they will pass through will be lined with all those soldiers of the Revolution, who will make them blush for having imagined that there could be slaves among them willing to support despotism. Their greatest torture will be to hear the cries of 'Long live the Nation.' 'Long live Liberty!' "

The frightened deputies pretended to think that by the Temple was meant the former palace of the Comte d'Artois and they left "to the Commune of Paris the task of fixing the King's residence and entrusted them with guarding him."

It was the gesture of Pilate. The Queen, too, had no thought of the famous keep with its four towers of medieval appearance, which stood in the gardens of the Temple and which she had often asked her brother-in-law to pull down. But Artois liked this useless and gloomy fortress.

On the next day the prisoners were spared the session of the Assembly. The King argued with the Commune in order to obtain twelve servants. "By dint of insisting" he was allowed no more than two valets and four women. At six o'clock the royal family, the Princesse de Lamballe, Mme de Tourzel, her daughter Pauline, Manuel, the Procureur of the Commune, the magistrate Colonge and Pétion, "once more mayor by the people's choice," squeezed themselves into one of the large court coaches harnessed with only two horses. It took an hour to reach the brilliantly lighted palace by way of the boulevards. The Commune had done things well: the meal prepared by the *Bouche* was worthy of the Tuileries.

In the *Salle des Quatre Glaces,* where the Comte d'Artois had formerly received Marie Antoinette, they had to sit down and make a pretence of eating. This time there were no lackeys in powdered wigs; the table was surrounded by men "dressed in the dirtiest and most disgusting clothes." There was no clavichord, no violas d'amore or de gamba; in the gardens and courtyards the Marseillais attended to the musical side of the evening.

Pétion did not dare tell the King that he was not to reside in the palace but in the tower, which could be seen a hundred yards from the palace in the crude light of the *terrines.* Before the interminable meal was over the Mayor went to the Hôtel de Ville and declared that he "had not thought it right to comply with the decision of the previous day and had authorised residence in the palace." There was an uproar and the municipality decreed that "the decision concerning the tower was to be maintained."

The keep, about 60 feet high, was composed of four identical floors, four halls whose ogival vaults were supported on each floor by a heavy stone shaft. On each side two barred windows were set in embrasures so deep that there was ample room for a bed in them. The walls, in fact, were nearly ten feet thick.

To lodge the prisoners, ceilings would have to be built and the rooms divided by partitions. Meanwhile Manuel decided to confine the royal family in "the little tower," a more modern construction backing on the keep. It was here that the cultivated M. Berthélemy, the archivist of the Order of Templars, lodged. In a few minutes he was expelled from his apartment, in spite of his tears, complaints and vehement protests.

It is not known who had the courage to announce to the King and Queen, at the end of their meal, that they were not to reside in the palace. Towards one o'clock in the morning the municipal officers preceded Marie Antoinette to the medieval keep which was henceforth to be her dwelling. As she crossed the garden her ears were assailed by singing:

> Madame is mounting to her tower,
> Who knows when she'll descend?

Marie Antoinette seemed not to hear the coarse laughter which greeted each repetition of the refrain. She hurried across the damp garden—there had just been a storm—and towards the entrance to the tall tower which led to the Gothic Hall on the ground floor and thus to M. Berthélemy's lodgings. On the first floor she found her son, who had fallen asleep while drinking his soup and whom Mme de Tourzel had carried there a short while before. In front of the little trestle-bed, where her Dauphin was sleeping so peacefully, Marie Antoinette experienced a moment of weakness. Tears filled her eyes.

In the garden, and on each landing of the tower, the sentries continued to yell:

> Madame is mounting to her tower,
> Who knows when she'll descend?

16

✤

The Widow Capet

AFTER DINNER ON 3 September, at about three o'clock, Marie Antoinette and Louis XVI were playing backgammon in the Queen's room on the first floor of the small tower of the Temple. The room, which was upholstered in sky blue, looked almost elegant with its sofa and armchairs *à la reine* "in blue and white lampas." Madame Royale and her brother, seated on heart-shaped stools, watched their parents' game. Were it not for the presence of the two municipal officers in their hats with the tricolour feathers, one might have been in one of the *bourgeois* homes so dear to Chardin.

Marie Antoinette was at last able to breathe freely, after the terrible days of 20 June and 10 August and the anguished nights at the Tuileries and the Feuillants. Protected by a numerous guard, she enjoyed relative tranquillity. There was no risk now of waking with a start, to find her bed surrounded by murderers; the worst seemed to be over. Certainly there were many more humiliations in store for her. Already, during the night of 19-20 August, the Princesse de Lamballe, Mme de Tourzel, her daughter Pauline, the three waiting-women and the King's two valets had been snatched from their beds and taken God knew where.

What fresh danger could she fear? The only penalty contained in the constitution was deposition. But above all, Marie Antoinette clung desperately to the idea of an Austrian victory. Learning from her jailers the capture of Verdun and the threat to Longwy, she found it difficult to conceal her feeling of hope. These defeats had aroused a great deal of excitement around the prison. The alarm gun had been fired and the tocsin had rung sombrely. The day before, Cléry, the Dauphin's valet, had announced "that there was a commotion in Paris" and that "the people were going to the prisons." The municipal guards were shortly to refuse to allow the royal family to walk in the garden. During dinner the drums were still heard beating and a few cries came from the direction of the Rue de Temple.

Now there was calm. Only a confused murmur came from the garden —doubtless from the workmen who were building a wall around the tower.

Suddenly a piercing cry came from the little ground-floor dining room, where Cléry and the Tisons, the servants installed by the Commune, were beginning their dinner. A few seconds later Cléry appeared in the room, haggard, his eyes full of horror. He looked at the Queen and said nothing. He could not speak of what he had just seen on the end of a pike, framed in the window—the severed head of the Princesse de Lamballe. Her long fair hair, still curled, floated in the air. Seeing this appalling picture, Mme Tison gave a cry, which the frenzied crowd answered by "frantic laughter"; they thought they had recognised the Queen's voice.

The Princesse had been murdered during the night in the prison of La Force. She still wore on her finger a ring set with a blue stone and containing some white hairs plaited *"en lac d'amour,"* with the motto: "They were whitened by misfortune." It was the Queen's hair. The horribly mutilated body, cut open to the breast, was dragged by the legs to the Temple by a cabinet-maker of the Faubourg Saint-Antoine, a chess-board maker of the Rue Popincourt, a gunner from the Montreuil section and a young drummer from the Halles. In front of them other men brandished the head, waved a strip from a blood-stained vest and exhibited the head and genitals. The victim's private hair was worn as a moustache by one of the assassins.

The officers of the guard had not been able to prevent this bloody masquerade from yelling at the foot of the tower and shouting for the Queen to come to the window.

"As she doesn't show herself we must go up and make her kiss the head of her whore!"

On the first floor one of the municipal guards drew the blue taffeta curtains. Cléry could still not utter a word and Marie Antoinette did not know what was going on.

"They are spreading the rumour that you and your family are no longer in the tower," one of the officers explained. "They want you to appear at the window, but we will not allow it."

The cries grew louder. Other municipal guards appeared in the room; they were ghastly pale. Marie Antoinette, seized with anguish, asked what was being hidden from her. There was a tall fellow there, whose sword struck against the velvet chairs. Marie Antoinette looked at him and the man explained "in the coarsest possible tones: 'They want to hide from you the head of the Lamballe which has been brought here to show you how the people takes its revenge on tyrants. I advise you to appear.'"

But Marie Antoinette did not hear the end of the sentence. "Frozen with horror," without a cry, she fell in a faint.

Once more the storm moved away. For three months Marie Antoinette was to live in calm.

The Queen had arrived in the Temple with four chemises, four petticoats, a wrapper, a spare coat and a few bodices which had been ordered, on 12 August, from the Feuillants. Very little had been saved from the Tuileries, but the Commune was generous and Marie Antoinette ordered a wardrobe suitable for a pretty woman, who, in spite of her imprisonment, did not intend to abandon all elegance. Thirty dressmakers worked incessantly for "the former Queen," and one is somewhat surprised on reading, in the Archives, the bulky accounts of the tradesmen who delivered to the Temple coats of Florence taffeta in "Paris mud" colour, hundreds of fichus, lawn bonnets, shoes of puce, blue or grey, kerchiefs, *pierrots* of toile de Jouy or pink cambric, lawn sashes for "coat-dresses," Chinese sabots, jockey-caps in black beaver. One of the latter must have been particularly becoming, for Madame Elisabeth ordered for herself "the same as the Queen's." This is apart from the "*pâtes royales* for the use of the tyrants," invoiced by the perfumery of Prevost and Laboulée, whose bill amounted to 110,000 present-day francs.

The Commune was just as generous where food was concerned. The meals, whose menus have been preserved, were sometimes more abundant than at the Tuileries. At dinner there were three soups, four entrées, six roasts, and four or five desserts, not to mention fruits and jams. In the evening two of the entrées were withdrawn, but the number of roasts and desserts was the same.

At the beginning of the imprisonment the officers were often good people, as for example the former inspector of food at the Halles, who from the beginning of his guard duties was surprised and conquered by Marie Antoinette's simplicity.

"Come here, Monsieur," she said to him. "Where we are you will see better to read."

A little later she came to show her jailer the hair of the first Dauphin and of the little Sophie. "The Queen put them back where she had taken them," he related, "and came back to me rubbing scent into her hands and passing them before my face so that I could smell the scent, which had a very sweet perfume."

Thanks to Turgy, a serving-lad who had been in the kitchens at the Tuileries, Marie Antoinette was kept aware of events and the code she gave him shows how much hope she still had. From the way this faithful servant placed his fingers on his face the Queen would know if the Austrian troops had won a victory. "When they are fifteen leagues from Paris, the fingers will be carried to the mouth."

Poor people!

At the end of September the work on the great tower was ending. The Commune had brightened up the building by having blinds placed in the windows which let only a narrow band of light through.

No work of any importance had been done on the two lower rooms. That on the ground floor would be used as a Council Room, where the eight municipal officers, half of whom were relieved every evening, would sit, and the first floor would be a guard room. The second and third floors were each divided into four rooms by means of wooden partitions and false ceilings of canvas. The second floor, for the King and the Dauphin, comprised an antechamber, a bedroom for Louis XVI and his son, a dining room and a room for Cléry. Louis XVI moved in on 26 September. Marie Antoinette's floor, the third, was divided into four rooms and was not finished until 26 October. On that day Marie Antoinette climbed the winding-stair, interrupted by wicket gates, for the first time. There was an opening in the middle of each gate. It was large enough for a man to pass through by bending down and stepping over, but impossible to get through quickly. Such was the purpose of the obstacles, of which there were twelve between the ground floor and the third storey. On each landing two heavy doors, one of iron and the other of wood, covered with bolts, locks and chains, divided the staircase from the "apartments."

The Commune had a bath installed for the Queen—it was a luxury at that time—and hired "bath shirts." Furthermore, a clavichord was placed in Marie Antoinette's bedroom, just above the King's, and every day the Queen sang songs which were "nothing less than sad," as Cléry related. Without the presence of the Tisons, whom it was impossible to soften, life would have been bearable. Escorted by municipal guards, who never left them, the prisoners on the second and third floors met at meal times and for their daily walk. In the afternoon "the Queen and Madame Elisabeth," relates one of the officers, "busied themselves with a little work in their room and with the education of the young princess, as did the King with that of his son, which the Queen did not neglect either, for one day, when the young prince was leaving her to come into the room I had just entered and had passed in front of me, looking at me but not saluting me, the Queen, having noticed it, called him and said sternly: 'My son, go back, and salute Monsieur when you pass in front of him.'"

One morning after breakfast—it was Friday, 7 December—the King remained alone with Marie Antoinette and announced a piece of news which Cléry had learned the day before from his wife, who had come to see him in the parlour. In four days' time his trial before the Convention would begin.

At dawn on Tuesday, 11 December, Marie Antoinette heard the alarm sounded. The whole enclosure of the Temple was full of noise. Cannons were even placed in the garden. The King was fetched to be taken to the Convention. Marie Antoinette was not to see her husband for another six weeks. She tried to convince herself that as the constitution pronounced the King "irresponsible" the outcome of the trial, now that France was a Republic, would merely be to exile Louis and his family. Certain newspapers, indeed, argued: "An exiled King has no partisans; a King who has been killed arouses sympathy . . . Tarquin had no successors; Charles I still has."

Her illusions were short-lived. A few days earlier the "Commune of the 10 August" had been replaced by a "provisional Municipality," whose new officers allowed the guards to cover the walls with graffiti which the Queen could read as she went to take her walk: "The guillotine is permanent and waits for the tyrant Louis XVI. . . . Veto will tread the measure." The prisoner could even see caricatures showing her husband on the scaffold, with the caption: "Louis spitting into the sack." Each time the Queen passed before him the concierge amused himself by blowing smoke into her face, while the guards burst out laughing.

The unhappy woman grew thinner. We learn this from the bills of citizen Roussel, dressmaker, who "unstitched a corset to take it in all round." From 1 January onwards she drank a "medicinal soup" every day.

Through Cléry and Turgy she received news of the accused. Did she know that on Christmas morning, alone in the prison where he had been confined by his subjects, the King seemed to have been touched by Grace? Louis XVI wrote his will: "I commend my children to my wife. I have never doubted her maternal tenderness for them. I charge her particularly to make of them good Christians and honest men, to make them look on the grandeurs of this world (if they should be fated to experience them) merely as dangerous and transitory advantages, and to fix their eyes on the sole reliable and lasting glory of eternity. I beg my sister to continue in her tenderness for my children and to be a mother to them if they have the misfortune to lose their own."

Perhaps he had guessed that when he was gone Marie Antoinette could not hope for a pardon.

"I beg my wife to forgive me all the evil she is suffering for my sake and the grief I may have caused her during the course of our marriage, *as she may be sure that I hold nothing against her, if she should think she had anything with which to reproach herself.*"

The paper-sellers cried the news. One of them, a pedlar with a stentorian voice, had been paid by a friend of the Queen to shout out a summary of his paper in the Rue de la Cordonnerie, not far from the tower. On Sunday, 20 January, Marie Antoinette heard him cry: "The National Convention decrees that Louis Capet shall undergo the death penalty. . . . The execution shall take place within 24 hours of its notification to the prisoner."

The "notification" took place at two o'clock, so the execution was to take place the following day. Marie Antoinette passed the day in sobbing. In the evening, at about eight o'clock, the two landing doors burst open; she and her family had been sent for, as the Convention had given permission for the condemned man to see them.

The scene took place in the dining-room. The Queen appeared first, holding her son by the hand, and then came the two Princesses. All threw themselves into the King's arms. The Abbé Edgeworth de Firmont, who had come to help the condemned man, remained in a little room in one of the small towers. In spite of himself he was a witness of the scene. "No pen can ever describe how heartrending it was. For nearly a quarter-of-an-hour not a word was spoken." There were nothing but "cries so piercing as to be heard outside the tower. The King, the Queen, Madame Elisabeth, Monsieur le Dauphin and Madame lamented together and their voices were mingled. Finally the tears ceased, since no one had strength to shed any more. They spoke in low tones, and fairly calmly."

Louis related his trial at length, the questions put to him, which he had not expected and which had confounded him, and the presence among his "judges" of his cousin Orléans. Unconditional death had been voted for by 361 deputies, and since 361 was an absolute majority the King had been condemned by a majority of one vote. Without the vote of Philippe-Egalité Louis XVI would have escaped the scaffold. The former Duc de Chartres, the friend of Fontainebleau and of the excursions in the forest, the friend of the Opera balls, the man with whom Marie Antoinette had danced at her marriage had voted for the death penalty.

The little Dauphin, who in a few hours would be King, stood between his father's knees.

"My son, promise me never to think of avenging my death."

Taking the child in his arms, he added: "You heard what I just said? Lift your hand and swear that you will fulfill your father's last wishes."

At a quarter-past ten the King rose. When Cléry entered the room he saw Marie Antoinette holding her husband's arm and making a few steps towards the door "uttering cries of the deepest grief."

"I assure you," said the King, "that I shall see you tomorrow at eight o'clock."

"Why not at seven o'clock?" begged the Queen.

"Very well, yes, at seven o'clock," Louis replied.

Madame Royale fell in a faint, and the little Dauphin threw himself on his knees before the officers, begging them to let him go and ask for a pardon "from the gentlemen of the Paris sections, so that his Papa should not die."

After putting her son to bed Marie Antoinette did not herself undress. She threw herself in her clothes on her bed covered with green damask. "We heard her all through the night trembling with cold and grief," wrote Madame Royale.

How far they were now from the time when, in Mme de Polignac's house, the clock was put on so that the spoil-sport would go to bed earlier! Was remorse mingled with those tears? Marie Antoinette, indeed, had often blushed for her husband's blunders and coarseness. Not long ago, at the Feuillants, she had been distressed at seeing the fat man munching away peacefully while behind the bars in the corridor the crowd yelled for his death and insulted him. She could still hear the King's loud laugh, his "simple joy," when on 2 September he watched the houses in the Temple enclosure being pulled down. He had so often embarrassed her. But this King, who was soon to be executed by his subjects, lacked neither goodness nor greatness of soul.

"As long as I reign my first care will be to see that religion is respected and to watch over the maintenance of morality."

Did Marie Antoinette remember the remark of the Maréchal de Richelieu?

"Each of the three branches of the House of Bourbon has a dominating and pronounced taste: the eldest loves hunting, the d'Orléans pictures and the Condés war."

"And Louis XVI?" someone asked.

"Ah! he is different. He loves the people!"

This was meant to be ironical, but it was only too true. Louis XVI did indeed love the common people, whose representatives had voted his death. But all these qualities had been frustrated by his hesitation, his habit of "detaching himself," his perpetual weakness.

How he had loved her, too! He had loved her to the point of deferring to her feelings for Axel. This inadequate lover felt that perhaps he had no right, once the succession was assured, to prevent his wife from enjoying a few moments of happiness.

In default of passion, she gradually came to feel a great tenderness for him. This good man—this "honest man," as Fersen called him—finally moved her by all his "sincere and inert" virtues, in Mirabeau's words.

And now this calm in the face of death, this "martyr's courage," touched her in the very depths of her heart.

Perhaps, during that long night, she believed she loved him.

From Paris came the noise of cannons being continually moved about. In the distance the drums were beating, calling to arms those who were members of the armed sections. Horses' hooves clattered on the damp, greasy roads.

In the distance a clock struck five.

Marie Antoinette sat up—a noise could be heard in the King's room. It was Cléry lighting the fire. There were footsteps on the stone staircase. At six o'clock the heavy doors of the apartment opened noisily. They had not come to fetch her. It was only an officer asking for Madame Elisabeth's missal for the condemned man's Mass. The door shut again and the bolts were pulled to.

A misty day was dawning. Detachments of cavalry entered the enclosure, and then "a great rumour" was heard. "General" Santerre, followed by municipal officers and gendarmes, mounted the staircase. The Queen stood near the door. Why did they not come to take her to her husband?

"It costs me a great deal to go without receiving their last embrace," the King was sighing at that moment.

He then turned to Cléry. "I entrust you with my farewells to them."

Suddenly Marie Antoinette heard trumpets sound under her windows. Surrounded by gendarmes, Louis XVI crossed the garden and turned round twice to look at the keep. In the distance she could now hear a vast muffled beating of drums, which gradually faded away and became indistinct.

It was eight o'clock.

At ten o'clock the door opened. Turgy was bringing dinner: chicken, larks and a rabbit. The Queen wanted to make the Dauphin eat, but the child refused. Marie Antoinette's clock, which represented "Fortune and her wheel," showed half-past ten. In the distance salvos of artillery were heard.

Louis XVI's head had just rolled on the scaffold.

The drums of the Temple guards were beating. Under the windows of the keep the sentries cried: "Long live the Republic!"

The Queen understood. "She choked with grief," related Turgy. "The young Prince burst into tears, Madame Royale uttered piercing cries." Her body shaken with sobs, Marie Antoinette sank on to her bed. Suddenly she rose, went to kneel before her son and saluted him with the title of King.

The "widow Capet" was able to procure "full mourning" dresses, "waxed" shoes, underskirts of *histaly* and even a black taffeta fan.

She refused to go down to the garden, as she did not want to pass Louis XVI's door. She would remain for hours seated in her green and white damask chair and knitting by the window, which was still obstructed by the shutter. She had become "extremely emaciated," according to a witness, and preserved a gloomy silence.

This prostration touched one of the officers on duty, the Toulousain Toulan. This fanatical revolutionary, who had been at the taking of the Tuileries on 10 August, had become profoundly royalist soon after first going on guard at the Temple. It is said that he was in love with Marie Antoinette and it is quite possible. By her charm, her voice and her smile the Queen was always able to arouse extraordinary devotion, and moreover she was now unhappy. Toulan did a few small services for the prisoner, paid the pedlar with the stentorian voice and on 1 January transmitted Louis XVI's good wishes to his family, but on the day after the King's death he made a serious decision—to help Marie Antoinette escape from the Temple.

Was it, as has been affirmed, a mad, unrealisable scheme? Certainly not. The Templars' keep was far from being a model prison. One had only to wear a uniform to be able to reach the tower, and one could even go in. One day the municipal officers found themselves face to face with three gendarmes, who were walking about "from a curiosity to see the building."

The prize for assurance undoubtedly goes to a certain Christophe Va, who was a brother, or so he claimed, of a municipal officer. On 26 September 1792 he entered through the main door of the Temple Palace, declaring that he had come to see his brother, and he was allowed to pass. On the 27th he entered the little tower where Louis XVI was still living, contemplated the royal family at his leisure and then—incredible detail—invited himself to dinner at the officers' table! Having developed a liking for this, he presented himself at the wicket-gate on the 28th just as the prisoners were going for their walk in the garden. He was sent off by the concierge, Mathey, but reappeared a few minutes later with the guard going on duty. He had managed to replace a certain Liemberger of the section of *Cloître Saint-Jacques de la Boucherie*, who had lent him his uniform and musket. With the air of an *habitué* he showed his comrades round the prison and decided to mount guard in the tower from four to six in the evening. "I shall not do it any where else!"

The Commune was not unaware of this state of things and ordered "a visit to the cellars which may exist around the Temple." Then, to reassure its members, it detailed two of Palloy's aides to dig a 12-foot ditch around the keep.

These unpublished details show that at the beginning of the royal family's captivity the Temple tower was not, in spite of what has been said, a fortress completely cut off from the land of the living. One could enter with comparative ease—and consequently leave also.

Marie Antoinette knew this. When Toulan declared he could arrange for her to escape with her children and Madame Elisabeth her heart beat with hope. But she did not want to continue with the scheme before consulting with General de Jarjayes, who, it may be remembered, had been the intermediary between Barnave and the Queen. On the King's orders he had remained in Paris. One may imagine his stupefaction—and his fear—when on 2 February 1793, Toulan, all blazing with the tricolour, came to see him. The Commissaire had a friendly face—bright eyes, a broad forehead and a rather flat nose—but the General remained on the defensive. Toulan was armed with a note from the Queen: "You may trust the man who will speak to you on my behalf and will hand you this note. His sentiments are known to me. During the last five months he has never wavered."

Without wanting to go any further, Jarjayes asked Toulan if he could get him into the Temple. The municipal officer was full of daring and, in spite of the presence of the Tisons, informed the Queen that Jarjayes would very soon be coming to see her. Marie Antoinette became uneasy and wrote: "Now that you have decided to come here, it had better be soon. But, good heavens, take good care not to be recognised and in particular beware of the woman who is shut up here with us."

With all the southerner's power of invention Toulan managed to persuade the "Illuminator," who came every day to look after the lamps in the Temple, to lend him his clothes for a "patriotic" friend who wanted the pleasure of contemplating the Queen "in her fetters." The lamplighter agreed and Jarjayes was able to have his interview with Marie Antoinette without difficulty.

The plan of escape took shape, but for it to succeed Turgy, who was on their side, and a second officer had to be informed of the plot. The municipal officer Lepitre was chosen. He had not a very suitable name for a conspirator, but he took fire at Toulan's first words. This semi-cripple—he limped heavily—was delighted to take part in such a plot and protested his loyalty. Marie Antoinette sent him to Jarjayes. "You will see the new man. His appearance is not prepossessing but he is absolutely necessary and we must have him." In fact Lepitre was be-traying the Commune not from royalist conviction but from personal interest. He intended his help to be well paid for, but the main thing was that he agreed to help. The motives did not matter.

Mounting guard at the Temple had become a tiresome job for the municipal officers, and so Toulan and Lepitre frequently proposed replacing their colleagues. In this way the two conspirators managed to be on guard once or twice a week. "To be quite sure we were not separated," Lepitre related, "Toulan invented this scheme: three of us would arrive; generally the same number of tickets were made out, one of which said 'day' and the other two 'night.' Toulan wrote 'day' on all three and drew lots with our colleague, and when the latter opened his ticket with the word 'day' we both threw ours into the fire without looking at them and went to take up our posts. As we hardly ever came with the same person this ruse was always successful."

Toulan and Lepitre appeared very fat when they entered the Temple. Under their coats they concealed two jackets, or sometimes two quilted wraps. On occasion they entered the prison with hats on and left it bare-headed. They and Jarjayes had decided that Marie Antoinette and her sister-in-law should leave the tower dressed as municipal officers. "It was enough to show one's card from a distance not to be stopped by the sentries," Lepitre explained. The little King would be placed in a dirty linen basket covered with cloths such as Turgy regularly took out of the prison each week. As for Madame Royale, she would be dressed in rags like those worn by one of the two little boys who always came with the lamplighter. The royal family would thus escape in four groups after the Tisons had been put to sleep with a powerful narcotic.

Once they were out of the Temple Toulan was in favour of their fleeing in a large berlin, in which Jarjayes and Lepitre would also be seated, while he himself would precede them on horseback in order to arrange for the boat to take them across the Channel. Relays would be set up between Dieppe and Paris. But Marie Antoinette remembered

Varennes and preferred taking three cabriolets.

"Our plans were so laid," wrote Lepitre, "that no one could set out in our pursuit until five hours after we had left. We had calculated everything. First of all, no one went up into the tower until nine o'clock in the evening, to lay the table and serve supper. The Queen was to ask that it should not be served until half-past nine. Knocking several times and being surprised at not seeing the door open; inquiring from the sentry, who having relieved the guard at nine o'clock would not know what had happened; going down to the Council Room and telling the other members of the surprising occurrence; going back with them, knocking again, calling the preceding sentries and getting only vague answers from them; sending for a locksmith to open the doors, whose keys we would have left inside; succeeding only after much time and difficulty, as one of the doors was of oak and covered with large nails, and the other of iron, both with such strong locks that they would either have to be burst inwards or else part of the wall would have to be knocked down; searching the apartments and the towers; shaking Tison and his wife without being able to wake them; going down to the Council Room; drawing up a report and taking it to the Council of the Commune, who, even if they had not separated, would lose more time in futile discussion; sending for the police and the mayor, and to the committees of the Convention to find out what steps to take—all this delay would have helped our flight forward. Our passports were in order, since as a President of the Committee I had drawn them up myself, and gave us no anxiety for our journey, while we would have preserved our advantage in time."

Lepitre recounted all this with cheerful optimism—in 1817. In 1793 he was considerably more indecisive. Having received an advance of 200,000 francs from Jarjayes (20 million nowadays), he was so long in making out the passports that it was already 13 March. After Dunmouriez's treachery a state of semi-siege was proclaimed and the Passport Committee was ordered to deliver no more *laissez-passer*. Jarjayes became anxious and in these conditions thought the successive departure of the whole family a "chimera." The four disguises seemed too risky to him. Only the Queen's escape appeared "practicable."

But Marie Antoinette refused to leave her son. "We dreamed a beautiful dream, no more," she wrote to Jarjayes, "but we have gained much from it, as this occasion has provided further proofs of your total devotion to me. My confidence in you is unbounded. You will always find that I have character and courage but my son's interests are the only ones that guide me. However happy I should have been to escape from here I cannot consent to be separated from him. I could never enjoy anything without my children and this idea leaves me without any regret."

There was nothing more for Jarjayes to do in Paris. Marie Antoinette asked him to take to the "Regent"—the Comte de Provence—the seal with the arms of France and the King's wedding-ring, on which was engraved: "M.A.A.A. 19 aprilis 1770," the wedding-ring which had been blessed in the Augustines' Church in Vienna at the marriage by proxy and which Marie Antoinette had brought with her to France. Louis XVI had given it to Cléry on the morning of 21 January, telling him "to give it to his wife, and to tell her that it grieved him to part with it." Toulan had managed to get hold of these two relics, which were locked up in the Council Room, and to hand them to the Queen. Then he had cried out louder than anyone else when the "theft" was discovered.

With the wedding-ring and the seal, which were intended for the future Louis XVIII, Marie Antoinette sent an impression from a seal, intended for Fersen. "The impression I send is something quite different. I want you to give it to the person whom you know to have come to see me from Brussels last winter and to tell him at the same time that the motto has never been more true." It shows a pigeon in full flight, Axel's emblem which Marie Antoinette had adopted. The bird was surmounted by a motto: *Tutto a te me guida*—Everything leads me to you.

"The motto has never been more true."

A little later Baron de Batz, who had already tried to save the King between the Temple and the scaffold, conceived another plot. Together with 30 royalists he formed a troop of National Guards. With the complicity of the prison administrator, Citizen Michonis, he planned to enter the Temple, give the prisoners military hats and cloaks, put them in the midst of his patrol and so leave the prison. This improbable plot nearly succeeded in the night of 21-22 June. Michonis was already in the Queen's apartment. Batz and his men in the bodyguard, the other band of conspirators, were waiting in the street. Midnight struck.

Suddenly the entrance bell rang. It was the shoemaker Simon, one of the Commissaires of the Commune, who entered in indescribable excitement. He cried: "Call a roll of the men!"

He had just received an anonymous note: "Beware, Michonis will betray you tonight." Batz, who was disguised as a National Guard, managed to slip away into the night, and Michonis, during his interrogation, succeeded in giving the impression that a "joker" had played a trick on the "fool of a shoemaker."

After this fresh setback Marie Antoinette still retained some hope, and at the end of June Turgy was receiving notes in the following style: "Is it thought that we shall still be here in August? If yes, blow your nose without turning round. Are the men of Nantes at Orléans? Two fingers when they reach it."

The days went by, long and depressing. The two women played with "Republican cards," or sometimes the Queen worked at her embroidery. The Commune had not been ungenerous in giving her the silks she asked for.

The Toulan affair was to have its sequel. Furious because one day she had not been allowed to see her daughter, Tison's wife denounced the Toulousain, the terrified Lepitre and all the officers who had "truckled to the widow Capet." Furthermore she indicated that the prisoners were able to correspond with people outside the prison, thanks to Turgy. Having made her denunciation, the unhappy woman became a prey to remorse. It was even worse when, on the evening of 29 June, she learned that the Committee of Public Safety had decided to take the little King from his mother.

"I shall remove him from his family so that he may lose any idea of his rank," promised Chaumette.

Tison's wife was convinced that this terrible step was the result of her declaration. Realising how great the Queen's grief would be, she became frightened and threw herself at the prisoner's feet.

"Madame, I ask Your Majesty's pardon. I am very unhappy. I am the cause of your death and that of Madame Elisabeth."

She shrieked and fell into convulsions. The next day eight men had difficulty in carrying her out of the tower; she had gone mad.

In her ravings she had not revealed anything about the Committee's decision and when Marie Antoinette went to bed on 3 July she had not the slightest suspicion that anything was to happen.

At ten o'clock there was a knock on the door. A group of men with plumes in their hats entered the room. They were the officers of the relieving guard and included a stone-cutter, a painter, a perfumer, a lawyer and a "secretary-reader." The voice of the man who had to read the decree trembled.

Without at first understanding what it was about, Marie Antoinette looked at him. What! They were taking away her son?

"Never!"

The child had woken up. He understood, and uttered "loud cries," throwing himself into his mother's arms. The officers approached the bed and Marie Antoinette stepped between them. She would never consent to give up her child. Madame Royale, the only eye-witness, related: "The officers threatened to use violence and to summon the guard to take him away by force. An hour went by in discussions, in insults and threats from the officers, in pleading and tears from all of us. Finally my mother consented to give up her son. We got him up and when he was dressed my mother handed him over to the officers, bathing him in tears, as though she could see into the future and knew she would never see him again. The poor little boy embraced us all tenderly," concludes Madame Royale, "and went out weeping with the men." The cobbler, Simon, was waiting for him in Louis XVI's bedroom, where he was to live with his "ward."

For an hour Marie Antoinette had defended her son's bed. When, on the following day, she learned who was the "tutor" chosen by the Commune, she was overwhelmed. From her room she could hear her son's sobs, which went on for two days. The child's despair was so great that Simon did not dare take him down into the garden. Surprised at not seeing him, the soldiers of the guard murmured: "He is no longer in the Temple."

The Committee of General Security became alarmed and on 7 July sent four of its members, including Drouet, to the tower. They found the child somewhat calmer. "Capet's son was playing quietly at draughts with his mentor." His tears seemed dried and the members of the Convention decided to take him down into the garden. When they were in the chestnut walk the little boy stood firmly before the men and asked them "to show him the law which commanded that he should be separated from his Mamma."

For hours on end Marie Antoinette watched from a little window in one of the towers "to see her son pass at a distance when his guardian led him to the roof of the tower." She was now no more than a shadow. This time they had taken everything from her, even her heart.

Very soon little Louis would listen without flinching to his "tutor's" advice and would follow his directions with extraordinary diligence. Chaumette and Hébert had advised Simon to turn the "whelp" into a perfect *sans-culotte*. The cobbler was completely successful and in a few weeks the goal was reached. Pleased at behaving "like a man," at making the officers laugh, delighted to be able to indulge in everything he had hitherto been forbidden to do, the little King had become as badly brought-up as the lowest "patriot." With anguish Marie Antoinette heard him utter "dreadful oaths against God, his family and the aristocrats."

The poor woman would never know how far the cobbler's "education" had led her little King. "I was playing a game of bowls with him one day," related Daujon, a municipal officer. "It was after his father's death and he was separated from his mother and aunt by order of the Committee of Public Safety. The room where we were was below one of the family's rooms and we could hear a sound like jumping and chairs being moved over our heads, which made quite a lot of noise. The child thereupon said with an impatient gesture: 'Haven't those damned whores been guillotined yet?'"

Her *chou d'amour!*

17

※

The Conciergerie

SHORTLY AFTER NOON, on 1 August, through the windows, which were open on account of the stifling heat, the prisoners could hear a noise with which they were now familiar: a murmur interrupted by trumpets and orders being shouted in the palace courtyard.

A few minutes later footsteps sounded on the staircase, sabres clanked against the steps and the walls, the wicket-gates creaked as the jailers opened them loudly, the bolts grated and slid back heavily and all these noises reverberated in the tower as in an organ-pipe.

It was the usual inspection. This time Hanriot, commander of the armed forces of Paris, which were making all the noise, hardly glanced at the prisoners' apartments. He was much more anxious about the "lack of artillery" of the Temple garrison. He therefore ordered fresh measures of surveillance: the commanders of the guard would receive munitions and from that evening the gunners were to stand by their guns.

This decision to order a state of siege at the Temple was a result of the taking of Valenciennes, where Fersen's regiment had formerly been stationed. The road to the capital was open. In Brussels Axel was forming a plan "to drive with a large force of cavalry towards Paris, which would be all the easier since there was no army ahead and all the barns were full of provisions."

Once these security measures were taken the Committee decided, in order to avoid a surprise attack, to make the Allies believe that the Queen was about to be brought to trial. They might then be able to exchange Marie Antoinette's life for an advantageous peace treaty.

Still on 1 August Barère, in reply to the taking of Valenciennes, cried in the Tribune of the Convention: "Is it our forgetfulness of the Austrian woman's crimes, is it our indifference towards the Capet family that have thus deceived our enemies? Well then, it is time to root out every trace of the monarchy!"

Without further hesitation the Convention voted the decree referring "the widow Capet" to the Revolutionary Tribunal.

When the news reached Brussels both Allies and Emigrés were convinced that the Queen's last hour had struck. They simply did not understand that it was merely an offer to negotiate, and from fear of hastening the prisoner's end they even gave up Axel's scheme of invasion.

"There is nothing to do but wait," said Mercy philosophically.

He had never liked his "ward," and so his grief was slight. Fersen, on the other hand, was overcome.

"I am no longer living," he wrote to his sister Sophie, "for it is not living to exist as I do and to suffer such grief. . . . If I could only still act to deliver her I feel that I should suffer less, but to be able to do nothing but entreat is agony for me."

The government did not delay in carrying out its threat. A few hours after the Convention's vote, during the night of 1-2 August, four police administrators, headed by Michonis and surrounded by officers of the guard, read to Marie Antoinette the decree transferring her to the Conciergerie to be sent to the "Tribunal extraordinary." Without a word she rose. Henceforth the poor woman had no strength to react, and "without emotion," as Madame Royale was to relate, helped by her daughter and sister-in-law, she prepared a parcel of her clothes. Then, in the presence of the men who had invaded her room and who refused to leave her by herself, she dressed and on their request "showed her pockets." After searching her the officers left her only a handkerchief and a bottle of smelling-salts, "in case she felt ill." They took possession of the rest, which they packed up.

She was urged to hurry. She embraced her daughter, telling her to "take courage and care of her health," entrusted her children to her sister-in-law, and without looking at Madame Elisabeth and Marie-Thérèse left the room in which she had lived for more than nine months.

Twelve times she bent down and twelve times stepped through the wicket-gates. The procession halted on the ground floor in front of the Council Room. The officers drew up a report "handing over the person of the widow Capet." Marie Antoinette remained standing at the door, carrying her bundle and waiting for the officers and the representatives of the Commune to finish their paper work. Finally everything was completed and the Queen was urged on towards the garden. As she passed through the last wicket-gate, Marie Antoinette forgot to stoop and hit her forehead. Michonis was alarmed. "Did you hurt yourself?"

"Oh, no! Nothing now can hurt me any more."[1]

Half-past two sounded from a near-by clock. Like an automaton she walked towards the palace of the Temple, where she had not been for nearly a year, since the supper of 13 August. At the top of the flight of five steps she may perhaps have turned round to look for the last time at the tall outline of the sinister keep standing out in the bright August night—the keep where, on the second floor, her little King was sleeping and, on the third, her little blonde *Mousseline* was crying in her aunt's arms.

The little group quickly crossed the large salon and the billiard room and descended into the great courtyard by another flight of five steps. There were two or three cabs there, surrounded by about 20 gendarmes on horseback. Followed by Michonis, the Queen took her seat in the first carriage. The procession trotted rapidly through the palace gates, turned to the left and entered the Rue du Temple. Twenty minutes later the cab entered the Cour de Mai and stopped under the arcade, to the right of the main staircase of the Palais de Justice. The Queen went down four or five steps, crossed the little basement courtyard and stopped in front of the prison door. Ignoring the knocker, the soldiers of the guard beat on the door with the butts of their muskets. Larivière, one of the eight turnkeys, still full of sleep, for he had been dozing in the concierge's large winged armchair, opened the door and through the gloom perceived a "tall, beautiful woman," surrounded by men whose gilded uniforms glittered in the night. The prisoner bent down, stepped over the stone threshold between the two wickets and entered the hall, which became filled with lights. Amazed, Larivière then recognised the Queen "dressed in a long, black garment which made

[1] M. André Hurtret, keeper of the Château of Vincennes, has recently informed me that this door is now the entrance door to the keep at Vincennes.

her extraordinary whiteness even more dazzling." He had often seen her at Versailles, where he had been a pastry-cook's apprentice in the King's kitchens.

The prisoner was taken to the record office, a little room on the left, leading off the hall, where the search and the traditional committal were to take place, but Michonis then changed his mind and quickly pushed the Queen towards the third gate leading into "the black corridor." With a few steps the Queen reached her new prison, a cell dripping with damp and lit by a low window almost level with the ground of the women's courtyard. General de Custine had been occupying it a few hours before. During the afternoon the wife of the concierge, Mme Richard, assisted by her servant, pretty Rosalie Lamorlière, had sent to Bertrand, the upholsterer, who lived a short distance away, for a camp-bed, two mattresses, a bolster, a blanket, a cane armchair to put clothes on and a "red leather basin with its spray, all new, for the use of the said widow Capet." Mme Richard had added a table and two cane chairs.

Richard, the concierge, as the director of the prison was then called, put the large register on the table and made a note of the entry of his 280th prisoner "accused of having conspired against France," as the text shows. In August 1793, therefore, there were not thousands of prisoners in the Conciergerie as is usually stated. Then the packet of things taken from the Temple was opened. Richard counted them, noting them down in his stained book.

Still standing, dazed, treated with no more consideration than a thief or a prostitute arrested in the public street, Maria Theresa's daughter watched this degrading scene. It was hot in the small, low room filled with people, and Marie Antoinette frequently wiped the drops of sweat from her face. Richard collected the prisoner's possessions in his coarse hands and made a clumsy packet of them. Wax was heated and the Queen affixed her seal.

Now everything was over. The Queen of France was "committed." The prisoner was now alone with Mme Richard and Rosalie. Her shortsighted eyes took in the dreadful bareness of the cell, which daylight was beginning feebly to light up and whose walls were half covered by "hangings of paper nailed on to frames." In the Temple Berthélemy's furniture, the armchairs in lampas *à la reine*, the chairs of velvet *prune de monsieur* were certainly modest, but never in her life, except perhaps for the night of Varennes, had Marie Antoinette sat on such chairs as these or eaten from such a table. Thanks to Mme Richard the bed was made with fine linen and not coarse cloth. Rosalie had brought from her own room a little tapestry stool. The Queen looked about her. She was looking for somewhere to hang her watch, which had been left to her, the little watch she had brought from Austria twenty-three years before. There was a rusty nail in the wall, rather high up. She stood on Rosalie's stool, hung up her watch and began to undress. The servant came forward shyly and offered to help the prisoner.

"Thank you, my girl, but now that I have no one I serve myself."

The sun was now completely risen. The two women took the torch away.

Early in the morning Richard sent to her the turnkey Larivière's mother, who had formerly been a concierge at the Admiralty. The old woman—she was nearly 80—made a good impression on the Queen. For thirty years she had been attached to the household of the Duc de Penthièvre and "from her youth had lived with the nobility." On this morning she told her son to buy "half an ell of muslin" to patch the prisoner's dress, which was "in holes under the arms and worn at the hem" by contact with the stones of the Temple.

Four days later Michonis decided that the woman Larivière was too old—or at least that was the reason he gave—and replaced her by "Citizen Harel," aged 36, whose husband was a clerk at the town hall. The Queen does not seem to have cared much for her. On the day the woman Harel began her duties the Administrators confiscated the little gold watch from which Marie Antoinette had never been parted since her earliest youth. On being separated from this last remembrance of the Empress, the watch which had for thirty years told so many happy hours, Marie Antoinette wept bitterly.

Two other people were forced on her: Gilbert, a "National Gendarme," and his superior, Sergeant François Dufresne. Until 13 September they lived in the same little room, which was only $11\frac{1}{2}$ feet square. The room was divided into two by a screen, so that the Queen could undress without being seen by her two keepers. They were not bad men—they regularly brought flowers to their prisoner—but they were gendarmes just the same. When they were not sitting in their corner with their sabres and muskets they smoked and drank about four pints of wine a day and 2 livres 5 sols' worth of brandy, which is not bad for a sedentary job.

In the morning the Queen rose at seven, put on her little "turned-down" slippers and drank a cup of coffee or chocolate. She performed her toilet before a little mirror lent to her by Rosalie, which had cost the girl 25 sous. "Her hair was very simply dressed," the servant related. "She parted it in front, after putting on a little scented powder. Mme Harel bound the ends of her hair with a piece of white ribbon, about an ell in length, knotted it firmly and then handed the ends to Madame, who by tying them herself and pinning them on the top of her head arranged her hair in the form of a loose chignon." On top she wore her buckram mourning bonnet, which was so large that she was soon able to divide it "to have two informal bonnets." While Rosalie made the bed the Queen put on one of her two dresses, either the black or the white, and the hours passed by.

A few days after her arrival Marie Antoinette obtained pen and ink and wrote to her daughter. "I want to write to you, my dear child, to tell you that I am well. I am calm and would be at peace if I knew that my poor child was without anxiety. I embrace you and your aunt with all my heart. Send me some silk stockings, a dimity coat and an under-skirt."

The letter was confiscated by the Commissioners, but thanks to Michonis Marie Antoinette had sent from the Temple some chemises "trimmed with lace known as *mignonettes*," two pairs of black silk stockings, a mantle, three lawn fichus and, most important, a pair of shoes *à la Saint-Huberty*, of which she was "urgently in need," as she told Michonis. Those she already had were falling to pieces with the damp. She was also able to obtain a bottle of dentifrice, a box of powder and a puff. So that she could keep these treasures from getting dusty Rosalie lent her a cardboard box, which she received "with as much satisfaction as if she had been lent the most beautiful piece of furniture in the world."

Dinner was served at two or half-past two. Mme Richard laid the table, while Rosalie, Mme Harel and the gendarmes looked on. The food was ample: "Soup, boiled beef, a dish of vegetables, chicken or duck—her favourite dish—and a dessert." In the evening her supper comprised cutlets, beef, a fricassée of turkey or pigeon. The cost to the Treasury for the "74 days" was 1,110 livres. The Queen drank only Ville-d'Avray water—*Viledavré*, as Madame Royale wrote—which was sent every day from the Temple. "On account of the recent law Madame Richard had hidden all her silver," Rosalie recounts. "The Queen was served on pewter plates, which I kept as clean and polished as possible. Her Majesty had a fairly good appetite. She cut her fowl into two, that is, to last her two days. She cleaned the bones with incredible ease and care. She rarely left any of the vegetables, which formed the second dish. When she had finished she said her grace in a low voice, then rose and began to walk. That was a signal for us to leave."

After supper her only distraction was to lean on the back of a chair and watch the two gendarmes playing backgammon. "Overcome with boredom," she had asked for the work she had begun—a pair of stockings for her son—to be brought from the Temple, but this had been refused. She might perhaps have tried to kill herself with the needles. So from time to time she pulled out the coarse threads of the cloth covering the walls "and with these threads, which she smoothed with her hand, she made very plain lace, using her knee as a cushion."

She was also given some travel books: "The Travels of Captain Cook," "The Travels of Young Anarcharsis," "A Voyage to Venice," "A History of Famous Shipwrecks." Marie Antoinette confided to Richard "that she read with pleasure the most terrifying adventures."

They had forgotten to take away her two solitaire rings. "Without her realising it," wrote Rosalie, "these two jewels were a kind of toy for her. As she sat and mused she would take them off, put them on again, and pass them from one hand to another several times in one minute."

Motionless and with her gaze vague, she seemed haunted by memories. At the beginning of her imprisonment she saw Larivière enter in his uniform of a National Guard. Marie Antoinette turned to the turnkey's mother.

"Please ask your son, our former servant, not to wear that uniform in my presence as it reminds me of the 6 October and all the misfortunes of my family."

To distract her, Mme Richard one day brought her youngest child, "who was fair and had very pretty eyes." The poor woman, relates Rosalie, "seeing this handsome little boy, started visibly. She took him in her arms, covered him with kisses and caresses and began to cry, while she spoke to us of M. le Dauphin, who was about the same age. She thought of him day and night and constantly spoke of him. . . . Hidden in her bodice she wore the portrait of the young King and a lock of his hair wrapped in a little yellow leather glove, which had belonged to the child, and I noticed that she often concealed herself near her wretched camp-bed to kiss these objects as she wept. One could speak to her of her misfortunes and of her situation without her showing any emotion or depression, but her tears flowed unceasingly at the thought of her deserted children."

Sometimes, too, she spoke of the King.

"He is happy now," she sighed.

At the Conciergerie in 1793 the political prisoners were still mixed with the thieves and murderers awaiting their appearance before the criminal court, and the old lags quickly "initiated" the newcomers. At dawn the vast cells—the *Gaillote,* the *Taillerie,* the *Noviciat* and the *Bonbec*—were opened, and until the evening the prisoners could walk at will in a large covered courtyard. In the central corridor of the prison and in the famous "Rue de Paris" there was a continual coming and going of turnkeys, gendarmes, prisoners going to the registry or coming back, and visitors going to the parlour. In the women's courtyard, on to which the windows of the Queen's cell looked, a railing marked off a narrow strip of ground where the prisoners kept in what was known as the *Quartier des Douze* could walk. Through its bars men and women shared their meals or started romances. The prisoners seemed to have been able to communicate easily with the outside world, for at that time they were even able to have their dinner brought in by the caterer, Citizen Maire, who also furnished the meals for the Queen's gendarmes and "waiting-woman." It was child's play to get anything in or out of the Conciergerie if one is to believe letters written by a prisoner from the prison itself. "If I make my long journey shortly, and as one knows in advance the day one is to appear [before the Tribunal], I shall make up a parcel and have it delivered in town."

No objection can therefore be made to the story of the concierge Richard's protégée, Mlle Fouché, a young woman from Orléans, who in company with the Abbé Charles Magnin, Director of the Little Seminary of Autun, which had moved to Paris, often entered the Conciergerie at that time.

One day in August, probably about the 10th, Mlle Fouché, who had been visiting some prisoners, asked Richard "if it would not be permitted for her to see the Queen." After some persuasion the concierge agreed. At half-an-hour after midnight he showed the visitor into the Queen's cell. Marie Antoinette had not yet gone to bed. She silently gazed at the unknown woman, who bowed to her and placed some linen and "a little food" on the table.

Mlle Fouché's account was written at the end of the Restoration and this last detail seems a little exaggerated. The Queen's diet was more than sufficient, but no doubt in the reign of Charles X it was good form to have prevented the Queen from suffering hunger. The rest of Mlle Fouché's account appears more truthful. Marie Antoinette received the young woman "with icy coldness," refused even to speak to her and confined herself to giving her "an imposing look." The interview was therefore short, and before taking her leave Mlle Fouché asked if "Her Majesty [this was written in 1824] would permit her to return."

"As you will," the Queen replied indifferently.

It would seem that the prisoner must have made some inquiries with Richard, for at a second interview she greeted her visitor with "trust." Mlle Fouché became bolder and proposed "bringing a priest" to the Queen.

"But do you know one who is a non-juror?"

The existence of the Abbé Magnin was revealed and at the third visit Richard allowed the priest to remain with the Queen for an hour-and-a-half.

In order to give some credence to what is about to follow, it must be remembered that not far from the Queen's cell the Abbé Emery was hearing confessions, saying Mass and giving communion. A letter from Barthélemy de la Roche confirms that hosts "were procured from the town." Although the Abbé Emery, Superior of the Saint-Sulpice Seminary, was in prison, other refractory priests were not, and were able to enter the prison regularly to bring "the Almoner of the Conciergerie" the pyx full of hosts. The evidence is incontestable.

When those who had been condemned left the Tribunal, surrounded by gendarmes, and crossed the courtyard to the office, where the executioners were waiting for them, the Abbé did not dare to meet them and give them absolution, for there were always a few members of the Tribunal, judges or jurors, at the windows of the bar on the first floor to enjoy the spectacle. But the jailers could not resist the Abbé and allowed him to spend the night with those who were to die, in the "waiting room," a wretched hovel which can still be seen today.

If the Abbé had not been able to obtain this favour he would let the condemned persons know at what point on the route they would meet one of his former pupils to whom he had sent a message.

The Abbé Magnin helped the Abbé Emery and "continued to bring the prisoners the consecrated hosts in a box hung round his neck." In the light of these incredible, but historically correct, facts, there is no reason not to believe that the Abbé Magnin—as he himself wrote in 1824 and solemnly swore to in the pulpit and before the altar—"had the happiness of twice hearing the confession of the Queen of France and of taking holy communion to her at the time when Richard was still the concierge of the prison of the Conciergerie."

The Abbé Magnin and Mlle Fouché were not alone in being thus able to enter the prison. It is said that Richard also introduced into the Queen's cell a certain Mme Guyot, head nurse of the Archevêché hospital, the wife of the hairdresser Laboullée, who lived at 83 Rue de Richelieu, and even—Fersen tells us in his private Journal—an Englishman, who for 25 louis was able to enter the prisoner's cell "to bring a jug of water."

Why should Richard have minded, when the example was set by the police administrators, who came to see the prisoner "on different occasions with one, two and sometimes three women," according to Gilbert, not to mention the painter Prieur, who was granted several sittings?

Among the administrators the one most frequently seen was undoubtedly Michonis. During the first three weeks of the Queen's imprisonment the "citizen administrator of police in charge of prisons" transformed himself into a guide. Whenever he was asked he agreed to show the Queen. One would hardly believe this without having seen Michonis's interrogations and depositions. The administrator admitted readily having entered to see "the widow Capet."

"I went with several people who were moved by curiosity and whom I could not have refused to take with me."

When the Queen was asked about the faces of these visitors she was able to reply with a shrug: "So many of them come!"

18

❧

The Carnation

ON WEDNESDAY, 28 August, Michonis entered the cell as usual. He was accompanied by a visitor, a man about 36, rather short, with bright eyes and a round face marked with smallpox and framed by curled hair. He was dressed in a striped, somewhat dark suit, the "colour of Paris mud," and was wearing two carnations in his button-hole. The moment the Queen set eyes on him she started and "her face was aflame." She recognised Rougeville, the Chevalier de Saint-Louis, who when the Tuileries were invaded on 20 June of the previous year had prevented her from joining the King and had taken her to the Council Room.

Tears sprang to her eyes. Michonis's companion looked at her earnestly. He had difficulty in recognising the Queen in this old woman who looked like "a deformed spectre." Rougeville stepped forward, took the carnations from his buttonhole and threw them down by the stove. Marie Antoinette looked at him blankly, without understanding. The Chevalier then "gave her a meaning look," but the Queen still did not comprehend. The Chevalier drew closer and in a low voice told her to pick up the note. But Michonis was already moving towards the door.

The two men left the cell. A few seconds later, through the barred window, the prisoner saw Michonis taking his companion to visit the women's courtyard. With astonishing presence of mind she asked Gilbert to take a complaint to Michonis about her food. The gendarme meekly went to the window, called the Administrator and reported the complaint. The moment he turned round the Queen went towards her screen. She had had time to pick up the two flowers and to see that each contained a note. Her heart beat rapidly.

Born on 17 September 1761, Rougeville was really called Alexandre Gousse, or Gonsse, which he did not like at all. He had therefore chosen to adopt the name of a farm belonging to his father and bestowed on himself the more noble title of Chevalier de Rougeville.

Whatever Alexandre Gousse de Rougeville may have written and affirmed, he was never a gendarme of the King's Guard, nor an aide-de-camp to General Lee, nor to Washington, nor a lieutenant-colonel in America, nor a cavalry colonel in France, nor an equerry to Monsieur, the King's brother. Lenotre, carried away by his zeal, even declared that "Marquis" de Rougeville had never been a Chevalier de Saint-Louis and consequently had never worn a sword. Rougeville, who does not appear to have claimed to be a Marquis, was certainly a Chevalier de Saint-Louis, as witness the register of the Archives de la Guerre under the date of 6 October 1791.

Everything Rougeville wrote was not boasting, as some historians have asserted. "The great agitation on the face and in the limbs of the widow of Louis Capet" when she saw Rougeville in the Conciergerie, the tears which came to her eyes, prove that Marie Antoinette knew what the man was worth and what he was capable of. She remembered what he had already done for her. Not for one moment, when she saw him enter the prison with the Administrator, did she think that Rougeville had changed his opinions, as had so many others. If he was there it was to save her.

This rehabilitation is necessary if one is to try to understand this plot of the carnation, which has remained so obscure. If one tries to decipher it by giving some credence to the Chevalier's statements and by checking them with unpublished documents from the Archives,[1] many points, particularly the ending, become clear.

On the evening of 10 August 1792, Rougeville did not reappear at the Hôtel des Tuileries, 75 Rue Saint-Honoré, where he was living. This was not because he was afraid of being arrested as a frequenter of the château. A more serious danger threatened him: a woman with whom he was living, a certain Dame Lacouture, 33-year-old widow of a councillor of the Presidial of Coutances, who found consolation for

---

[1] See the chapter "Sources," pp. 417-418.

her loss in the arms of our conspirator. Rougeville, deciding that the massacre of the defenders of the monarchy was an excellent pretext, disappeared neatly from the life of Dame Lacouture, who not seeing her consoler reappear thought herself a widow for the second time. But one day, at the beginning of March 1793, the deserted woman learned that far from being dead her Chevalier was consoling in another hotel, in the Rue des Quatre-Fils, another widow called Sophie Dutilleul, who had the undoubted advantage over Dame Lacouture of being ten years younger and a Parisienne. In Rougeville's absence the two widows had a violent scene. The Rue des Quatre-Fils rang with their shrieks. The Norman soon realised that she could not fight her pretty young rival. Her lover being definitely lost to her she decided it would be as well if he were also lost to the seductive Sophie and she denounced the Chevalier de Rougeville to the Municipality as being a friend of the King and a combatant of 10 August.

On 3 June the police were able to lay their hands on the consoler of widows. He was hiding in a cupboard of a country house which Mme Dutilleul owned at Vaugirard.

To be arrested in the middle of the Jacobin uprising, under the accusation of having been a "knight of the poniard," was the equivalent of a ticket for the other world. And yet on 10 June Rougeville cheerfully left the Madelonettes prison. This was thanks to the administrators "whom I had suborned with money," he explained later, adding: "I had particularly noticed the director Michonis."

In reality Rougeville had been recommended to Michonis by a certain citizen Fontaine, who was possibly a friend of Batz. What is more certain is that during Rougeville's absence he had become the protector of the widow Dutilleul after a meeting "on the boulevard." Michonis therefore had the Chevalier released and the two men began to conspire feverishly. Later, in order to save his head, the administrator declared that he had not met Rougeville until 15 August 1793, but we know from the documents preserved in the Archives that the two conspirators met constantly during the months of June, July and August.

In asserting the contrary during his interrogation Michonis was lying, and if he was lying it was because he had something to hide. The administrator was quite simply Rougeville's accomplice. To deny this, as have so many historians, made the conspiracy of the carnation completely meaningless. Besides, Michonis had a previous history. In June 1793 he had helped Baron de Batz in his schemes for Marie Antoinette's escape from the Temple. If one refuses to admit Michonis's complicity how can one explain that a quarter-of-an-hour after throwing the carnations down in the Queen's cell Rougeville was able to come back alone to see the prisoner, while Michonis *was still in the courtyard,* and in spite of the presence of the gendarme? The Queen stated this definitely at her trial.

"He came back twice in the space of a quarter-of-an-hour."

During this quarter-of-an-hour the prisoner had had time to read the note behind her screen. "I shall never forget you, I shall always seek means to demonstrate my zeal. If you have need of three or four hundred louis for those about you I shall bring them next Friday."

As for the other note, which was not mentioned at any inquiry, it contained, according to Rougeville, "a safe and well thought-out plan for her escape, if she wished to lend herself to it."

One can guess at Marie Antoinette's emotion as she looked at her visitor. A rapid exchange took place between them.

"I tremble at your rashness."

"Do not worry about me. I have money, men, administrators, and sure means to get you out of here."

"I am not moved by the danger to my life. My children are the cause of all my anxiety."

"Is your courage low?"

"If I am weak and downcast, my heart is not."

"Take courage, we shall save you. I shall come back on Friday, the day after tomorrow, and shall bring you the money you need for your keepers."

Michonis came to fetch Rougeville. They had hardly left the room when the Queen, with beating heart, drew near to the gendarme Gilbert. They were alone. The woman Harel had gone to fetch water and Sergeant Dufresne had also gone out. Marie Antoinette decided to wait no longer to try to win over her keeper. He often brought her flowers and he had closed his eyes to the Abbé Magnin's visits.

"Monsieur Gilbert, you see how I tremble. The gentleman you have just seen is a Chevalier de Saint-Louis, employed in the army, to whom I owe much for not having abandoned me in trouble."

Through these words, which were related by Gilbert at his interrogation, one can feel the emotion which must have seized the unhappy woman. If she could move her keeper she was saved. Her voice became softer and her tone more confiding.

"You would never imagine how he managed to hand me this note. He gestured to me with his eyes and as I did not understand what he was trying to say, he came close to me and said in a low voice: 'Pick up the carnation on the ground which holds my most ardent wishes. I shall come back on Friday.' You know the rest. I stooped and picked up the carnation, in which I found the note."

The end of the gendarme's account is false. During this same conversation the Queen is supposed to have shown Gilbert a reply intended for Rougeville and consisted of a dozen words traced, or rather pricked with a pin, on a little piece of paper. When could she have done this? Let us hear from Gilbert.

"Michonis went out with the individual and it was then that she showed me a note she had pricked, in which the holes formed two or three lines of writing, saying to me: 'You see I do not need a pen to write with.' She added that it was her answer, to be given on Friday to the man who had handed her the note inside the carnation."

Still according to the gendarme, the woman Harel came back to the cell at precisely that moment. Gilbert alleged that he then snatched the note from the Queen's hand. "I went out *at once*," Gilbert continued, "to find the wife of the concierge and to tell her that I had something to give her. Taking her aside, I handed her the pricked note, relating what had just taken place."

It was not on Wednesday 28 August, *between Rougeville's two visits*, that the note was traced. In his report written in the morning of 3 September, the gendarme declared: "As her waiting-woman was playing a game of cards with me the woman Capet took advantage of this to write with a pin on paper."

The woman Harel was asked: "While Michonis and this individual were in the room were you not engaged in playing cards?"

"It was not on that day," she replied, "for on the day Michonis and the individual you are speaking of came *I was not playing, I was at work.*"

That is unambiguous!

The woman Richard alleged during her interrogation that "on the same day" as the gendarme brought her the note she handed it "in the same moment" to Michonis. The latter declared that the note was given to him *one or two days after the day he had come, Wednesday, the 28th, with the Chevalier*. The note was therefore given to him on the Thursday or, better still, the Friday, the day when Rougeville came back to the Conciergerie with Michonis and brought the money for the Queen. This fact, which seems not to have been noticed up to now, proves that at first Gilbert had readily agreed to enter the conspiracy.

For Gilbert lied in saying that he had taken the concierge's wife aside to give her "the pricked note"; it was the woman Richard who took it from him. Sergeant Dufresne revealed this. "In sport the wife of the concierge put her hands in his pockets and took his papers, among which was the note."

One can guess the Queen's terror. To whom would Mme Richard hand the note? All through the day she "persecuted" Gilbert—the word is his—asking him to go and get back the note which might cause everything to miscarry.

But what was in those three lines? The note—a narrow piece of grey, rather silky paper—is still pinned to the Queen's interrogation in the National Archives. It is completely illegible. An expert, M. Pilinski, claimed to have deciphered these words:

> I am closely watched.
> I speak to no one.
> I trust you. I shall come.

When the Queen was asked "what her writing contained," she declared: "With a pin I tried to write that I was closely watched, that the danger was too great to reappear there [for Rougeville to return] and that I could neither speak nor write."

Not a word, of course, about the last line deciphered by the writing expert. The Queen kept to the same line of defence during the interrogation she underwent on the eve of her trial.

"I tried, with a pin, not to reply to him but to tell him not to come back, in case he should once more present himself."

She could hardly reply otherwise. And it is curious that neither Fouquier-Tinville nor President Hermann replied: "Why incur such danger and run the risk of all being discovered in order to write to the man who wanted to free you what you had just said to him? You are hiding the most important fact!"

And, indeed, "I trust you. I shall come" is undoubtedly the one accurate line of the note. Influenced by the Queen's answers, M. Pilinski may have made a mistake in deciphering the beginning of the riddle. The first line told Rougeville nothing he did not know, and the second was manifestly untrue.

The note, traced by the Queen *after* her conversation with Gilbert, must have informed the conspirators that she had been able to win over the two gendarmes, thanks to the money brought by Rougeville that same day. In the various interrogations this third visit is not mentioned, but it seems probable that the Chevalier was not lying when he asserted that on the 30th, *in another dress,* he was able to return to the prison, bringing the Queen 400 louis d'or and 10,000 livres in promissory notes. "It was during this interview," Rougeville recounted, "that it was decided that, in spite of the Queen's state of extreme weakness, the escape would take place on the night of 2-3 September."

A letter preserved in the Archives shows that the Chevalier was right to speak of the prisoner's "extreme weakness." On the following evening, at ten o'clock, Lieutenant de Busne wrote to Fouquier-Tinville, informing him that the widow Capet had been taken ill twice during the evening. These swoons were certainly a result of the Queen's anguish at the confiscation of the famous note. Mme Richard had indeed handed the note to Michonis and the latter had pretended to treat the matter as unimportant and had advised the concierge's wife not to speak of the incident, but the Queen was unaware of these reassuring details and one may imagine the unhappy woman's anxiety as she waited for the time when Rougeville was to enter her cell. Would the conspirators go forward at the last minute? The Queen tried to calm herself with the signs before her: Gilbert had been in the secret since Wednesday, 28 August, and had said nothing to his superiors. The same was true of Sergeant Dufresne. The Queen had given him Rougeville's 50 louis d'or and there seemed to be nothing to worry about in that direction. There was one person unaccounted for: the woman Harel, who did not appear to be in the plot. If she had noticed anything would she keep silent? It was true that she had been brought into the Conciergerie by Michonis himself.

The night of 2-3 September closed over the prison. Through her two windows, which were open on account of the heat, the Queen could hear the yard bell ringing. It was the signal for the prisoners to return to their cells. But the prison did not go to sleep. Those who were due to "go up" to the Tribunal the next day had asked their cell companions to supper. There was much drinking and singing. The steps of the turnkeys on their rounds could be heard in the corridor.

Suddenly, just before eleven o'clock, the door opened. Michonis and Rougeville were there. On behalf of the Municipality the administrator had come to transfer Marie Antoinette to the Temple. At least, this was what he had said to the turnkeys and to Richard, who if he did not believe it pretended to do so. In reality the carriage waiting for the prisoner in the Cour de Mai was to take her to the Château de Livry, where Mme de Jarjayes lived, and thence to Germany.

Flanked by her two gendarmes the Queen walked quickly down the "black corridor."

At this point we must hear from Rougeville, for we have no other documents. "We had already passed through all the wicket-gates and only the street door remained to go through when one of the two guards to whom I had given 50 louis d'or came forward threateningly to prevent the Queen's leaving."

Which gendarme was it who took fright at the last moment and changed his mind? According to the turnkey Larivière and Rosalie Lamorlière it was the woman Harel who caused the escape to miscarry. But nothing is known for certain. However, on the next morning, in a report to Colonel Du Mesnil, Gilbert denounced Rougeville's visit of the week before, spoke of the carnation and of the "pricked note," but, obviously, concealed facts which would have established his and Dufresne's complicity.

While the colonel hurried to inform the Committee of General Safety, Michonis dined at Fontaine's house with Rougeville and Sophie Dutilleul. This was apparently in order to take the necessary decisions after the previous night's failure. Rougeville decided to disappear. On leaving Vaugirard he took with him "two shirts and several pairs of stockings." These precautions of the Chevalier confirm the truth of the night's events. If, like Lenotre and many other historians, one refuses to admit the complicity of Gilbert and Michonis and the conspirators' attempt to carry out their plan, then the attitude of all the actors in the drama becomes quite incomprehensible.

When dinner was over, and while Rougeville was escaping,

Michonis decided to go to the Conciergerie to see how the land lay. He still had the famous note in his pocket, but apparently, in order to make the matter of no importance, he had riddled the paper with pin-holes in order to make it illegible. On arriving at the prison, around half-past four in the afternoon, he learned that he was wanted by two deputies of the Convention, Amar from l'Isère and Sevestre from Ille-et-Vilaine, accompanied by citizen Aigron, aide-de-camp to the armed forces. They had been charged by the Convention's Committee of General Safety and Vigilance to inquire into Gilbert's denunciation. They had arrived at the office half-an-hour earlier and having "asked the officer on duty to give them six gendarmes," they had gone to the Queen's cell.

Both actors and supernumeraries were interrogated but they all concealed some part of the affair, either to exculpate themselves or to avoid compromising their accomplices. When Michonis arrived at the office the investigators were questioning the Queen in a "private room in the said house."

In spite of her anguish the Queen denied everything systematically. She could not remember anything.

"Did you not, a few days ago, see a former Chevalier de Saint-Louis?"

"It is possible that I may have seen a face I knew, as so many of them come."

"And the carnation?"

"No one gave me a carnation and no note fell to the ground that I could see. Something may have fallen, but I saw nothing."

The deputies pressed her hard.

"A few days ago a Chevalier de Saint-Louis entered your lodging and you started when you saw him. We ask you to say whether you knew him."

"It is quite possible that I saw faces I knew, as I said before and that, in the tense state of my nerves, I started, without knowing on what day, or on whose account, or why."

"We would mention to you, however, that it has been stated that you knew the former Chevalier de Saint-Louis and that you trembled lest he should be recognised. Those are the expressions you are reported to have used."

"One would think that if I trembled lest he should be recognised I would not have mentioned it, for I would have wanted to conceal it."

She skilfully denied having "written with a pin." One of the Commissaires then tried kindness.

"In your position it would be natural to take advantage of any means offered to you for your escape and for getting messages to those you thought you could trust. It would not be surprising, therefore, if this Chevalier de Saint-Louis were a person who might be an associate of yours and of whom you would consequently not wish to speak."

"It would be very sad if the people I were interested in made so little impression on me. If I were alone I should not hesitate to try every means to be reunited with my family, but as there are three people in my room, although I never knew them before I came here, I should never involve them in anything."

The investigators were hardly more successful with the woman Harel and with Michonis. If the first was to be believed, she was practically blind and deaf. As for the second, he presented the picture of a police administrator whose carelessness had outrun his understanding. He treated everything lightly and simply admitted to having been a "prisoner's showman." As regards the "Rougeville affair," he confessed to having shown him into the widow Capet's cell, but pretended that he had not known the Chevalier's name.

When it was Gilbert's turn there was a rush of details, but as we have already seen they were often in complete contradiction to the report the gendarme had sent that morning to his colonel. The woman Richard was then summoned. She too claimed to know nothing; she had handed the note to Michonis and that was all. Michonis was therefore recalled and he took from his pocket the note, which was completely unreadable. The Commissaires passed it from hand to hand, but with no result, and pinned it to the report, which made two holes more.

This time Michonis was interrogated at length. When one reads his clumsy and embarrassed answer it is impossible not to recognise in him an accomplice of Rougeville. He contradicted himself, and then confessed that he had advised the concierge's wife to keep quiet. He claimed not to know that the note handed to him by Mme Richard was intended for Rougeville, and then declared: "I considered the matter unlikely to have any consequences and so I did not give him the note."

The investigators were enabled to reply: "To the question first put to you, whether the note was intended for him, you replied in the negative and yet you have just said that among the reproaches you made him you had not forgotten to mention that the note might have been for him."

Michonis's position was quite indefensible and one of the Commissaires exclaimed: "You must have been either very blind or indifferent to your duties not to have had that man arrested the moment Mme Richard handed you that note!"

The deputies were not examining magistrates and were unaware of the first rule of the profession: not to leave witnesses and accused in the same room. Everyone appeared to be in Marie Antoinette's cell. Weeping, the Queen asked the two gendarmes "not to repeat what she had confided to them" and several times asked Gilbert if the Chevalier de Saint-Louis had been arrested. We learn this from Gilbert and Dufresne, who appear to have been indulging in an orgy of accusations. Admittedly, they had been holding their tongues for six days.

The Queen was now aware of the depositions of the two gendarmes. She also knew that Mme Richard and Michonis had admitted part of the truth. So when the investigators called her a second time she did not continue to deny. She recalled the part played by Rougeville on 20 June, admitted the visit on the preceding Wednesday, the handing over of the note in the carnation and confessed to having replied with the help of a pin. The most difficult part was to conceal Michonis's hand in the affair.

"Has the administrator Michonis ever made any proposals to you?"

"Never."

"Why do you show so much interest in seeing him again?"

"Because his honesty and humanity touched me."

"And yet this interest would seem to have another cause and to spring from the fact that he introduced into your room a man who offered to help you?"

"It would appear that Michonis did not know him himself."

Michonis had probably had time to inform her of his line of defence, otherwise how would she have thought of giving such an answer?

The interrogations continued far into the night. When she signed the report Maria Theresa's daughter had a movement of pride. She was ashamed of having previously lied to these boors and wished to explain that "if she did not tell the truth it was because she did not want to compromise that individual and preferred to harm herself."

"When I saw that all was discovered I did not hesitate to tell what I knew."

Before going to bed the investigators had Michonis arrested and imprisoned, at half-past seven, in the Conciergerie itself. Four days later they arrested Sophie Dutilleul, who declared she had "committed only one crime—that of having loved Rougeville."

On 4 September the Queen's cell was thoroughly searched. The investigators went so far as to "overturn the bed and the chairs." Bars and walls were carefully examined. The policemen themselves searched the prisoner, taking her two rings, confiscating her linen and leaving only her bonnets and fichus. Henceforth her chemises would be given to her one by one. There was a particular ban on giving her flowers. Even the food was reduced to a minimum.

From a distance, although without news, Fersen guessed the misery she was undergoing. On 4 September he wrote to his sister: "I often grudge myself the very air I breathe, when I think that she is shut up in a horrible prison. This thought pierces my heart and poisons my life and I am constantly torn between grief and rage."

Rosalie watched the unhappy woman, "anxious and abandoned," pacing for hours up and down her cell. She was quite broken. She was not even left in peace at night. The Commissaires forced her to rise so that they could search her bed. The accounts of Robert, the apothecary, reveal that on the 4th there was ordered for the widow Capet a soothing potion "composed of lime-flower water, orange-flower water, maidenhair syrup and Hofman's liquor." On the next day, and until the 16th, she was given a cooling and soothing soup "made in a bain-marie with lean veal, chicken and various plants."

The events of 11 September were not calculated to calm the sick woman. The investigators had doubtless discovered that the Richards were partly involved, for the concierge and his wife were arrested. On the same day six police officers arrived at the Conciergerie "to choose a place of detention for the widow Capet, other than the one where she is at present detained, which they consider to be too near the office," that is, too near the front door. After seeing "all the rooms," they chose "the one in which citizen Guillaume Lacour's pharmacy is situated." Between this room and the Cour de Mai there were six wicket-gates or grilles, three obstacles more than those passed by the Queen in the night of 2-3 September. But this room was not arranged as a cell. The police therefore ordered the window looking on to the women's courtyard "to be closed up to the fifth cross-bar." The rest of the window was to be grated with close-mesh wire. Another window looked on to the infirmary. This was to be entirely closed "by means of a sheet of iron." A third window looked on to the corridor; this was "to be entirely stopped with masonry." The administrators noticed that light came under the door, and they therefore ordered a piece of wood "three inches thick" to be placed there. A second door was installed.

The police worked quickly and summoned Lemoine, a mason from the Rue Vendôme, Leroy, a carpenter from the Rue des Capucines-Chaussée d'Antin, and the locksmith Gonvin from the Rue Antione. Citizen Gonvin's account includes iron bars, and the netting which had been ordered became a proper grille. The new door was two inches thick, "studded with big nails," and closed with "a strong lock." Two bolts and two "safety locks" were also placed on the first door. The cost to the State was 983 livres.

And so there was fulfilled the wish of the municipal officers of Chapelle-Gontier, who had demanded that "the Fury who had sworn their ruin should be imprisoned in the darkest dungeon."

On the 13th or 14th the cell was finished and the prisoner and her wretched belongings were transferred there. The woman Harel had disappeared; nothing more is heard of her. The two gendarmes had orders to remain, one of them in the corridor and the other in the women's courtyard. The latter was stationed just in front of the half-boarded window, where he could see everything that went on in the cell. The prisoner could not even go behind her screen without the gendarme hurrying forward.

The new concierge, citizen Bault, who had come from the prison of La Force with his wife, was answerable with his life for the Queen's person. Only he had keys to the cell and could enter only with an officer or under-officer of the gendarmerie. "When Bault came to the Queen for the first time," related Rosalie, who had been able to keep her post, "I was with him and I brought Madame her usual soup for breakfast. She looked at Bault, who in accordance with the fashion of those days was wearing an all-in-one jacket and trousers called a carmagnole. The collar of his shirt was open and turned down, but his head was bare. Holding his keys, he stood by the wall near the door. The Queen took off her nightcap, sat down and said to me pleasantly: 'Rosalie, you will do my hair today.'

"Hearing this, the concierge hurried forward, took the comb and said loudly, as he pushed me aside: 'Go away, I must do that.'

"Astonished, the Princess looked at Bault with an indescribable air of majesty.

" 'I thank you,' she replied, and rising immediately she rolled up her hair herself and put on her bonnet."

The Queen then took the white ribbon which Madame Richard had hitherto used for her hair.

"Rosalie, take this ribbon and keep it always in memory of me."

She wore a look "of sadness and dejection which went to my heart, and tears sprang to my eyes," Rosalie recounted.

Such was the end of the affair of the carnation.

Rougeville, whose head had a price on it, was hiding in the plaster quarry in Montmartre. He was writing a pamphlet: "The crimes of the Parisians towards their Queen, by the author of the carnations presented to the Queen in her prison." When he had finished he made a great many copies and before taking the road for Belgium went himself to place them in the bureau of the Convention and the Revolutionary Tribunal a few moments before the sessions opened.

When Alexandre Dumas wrote his famous *Chevalier de Maison-Rouge* he fell well short of the truth!

19

❧

The Anteroom to the Guillotine

IT IS DIFFICULT to pass by the Conciergerie without looking up at the first floor of Caesar's tower. There, at the beginning of year II, was the office of Antoine-Quentin Fouquier de Tinville, son of the "seigneur of Hérouël and other places," former prosecutor at the Châtelet and since March 1793 citizen Fouquier-Tinville, Public Prosecutor of the Revolutionary Tribunal.

From his window he could see the cartloads of condemned people crossing the Pont-au-Change. In this vaulted room, whose ogives and ribs date from Philippe le Bel and where formerly the gentlemen of Parliament came to take their refreshments, he carefully perfected his grinding machine during the months of July and August 1793. The Tribunal, which had been at work since 6 April, had already pronounced 63 death sentences in its first session, but at that time the judge still respected the formalities, and there were twice as many acquittals as condemnations. Moreover, for the past few weeks the magistrates and juries had been weary. They condemned "without zeal." On 17 July President Montané had tried to hold out "a safety plank" to Charlotte Corday, in the words of the scandalised Fouquier-Tinville. On 24 July the number of judges was raised to seven, and on the 30th to ten and on the same day Montané was sent to the prison of Sainte-Pélagie. On the next day Fouquier succeeded in having his tribunal divided into two sections, so as to provide more work.

The Convention's decree committing the widow Capet to his Tribunal had whetted his appetite. But he was greatly disappointed. Days passed and the Government seemed not to want to send him the prisoner. On 25 August he could bear it no longer and wrote to the Committee: "The Tribunal is attacked in the newspapers and in the public places because it has not yet dealt with the affair of the former Queen." On 2 September, therefore, just as Rougeville was leading the Queen to escape, the members of the Committee of Public Safety met in secret session at the house of Pache, the Mayor of Paris. There were present Cambon, Hérault, Barère, Jean Bon Saint-André, Hébert and a secretary. The secretary was a spy in the pay of England and on the next day he sent to the English Resident at Genoa a detailed report which was then sent to Lord Grenville in London.

Current business having been dealt with, Cambon opened the discussion of "the Queen's death" and informed his colleagues that one of the Committee's agents was at that moment trying to negotiate with Brussels, Vienna and Prussia.

"By postponing the judgement could we not turn this affair to great profit?"

There was a general uproar.

"The life of Louis XVII would answer exactly the same purpose."

"The Queen's blood is needed to bind the Revolutionary Tribunal to the Convention and to make the city of Paris a co-sharer in the destiny of the Convention!"

The editor of *Le Père Duchesne* could not be bothered with such subtleties; Hébert went straight to the point.

"I have promised Antoinette's head. I shall go and cut it off myself if there is any delay in giving it to me. I promised it on your behalf, to the *sans-culottes*, who have asked me for it and without whom you would cease to be. The instinct of the Republic leads them to wish to unite themselves with us by this expiatory sacrifice, and yet you are hesitating!"

Cambon pointed out that the Queen was a hostage whom it would be folly to get rid of, so Hébert promptly took on a prophetic tone.

"I know not if you still have any hopes for a Republic, a constitution and the safety of your persons, but I know that if you have you are greatly mistaken. You will all perish, anything else is impossible. I know not if it was well or ill done to bring matters to this point, but there they are. The Kings will harm themselves by wishing to annihilate us, who will annihilate them in twenty years. But we shall none the less perish. France will be in subjection. We shall all perish!"

But supposing the Queen's life could be used as a medium of exchange? Supposing that by using it an amnesty could be obtained?

"If we are promised an amnesty it will not be honoured, because it could not be. You will merely be knifed or poisoned instead of being torn in pieces. In these circumstances, therefore, we live only for vengeance, a vengeance which could be great. In perishing let us bequeath to our enemies the seeds of their own death and, in France, a destruction so great that its marks will never be effaced. To bring this about we must satisfy the *sans-culottes*. They will kill all our enemies, but their zeal must be nourished by the death of Antoinette. Remember that the way to make them dare everything is to persuade them of what I shout to them every day—that in this crisis, whatever the event, their obscurity is their safeguard and that we alone are answerable for everything. Thus they will give us every help, for the profits are for them and the danger for us. This is all I have to say to you to tell you of my opinion."

The secretary added: "So saying, he went out without staying a moment longer."

The debate went on all night, and finally Cambon was defeated. Dawn was breaking as Fouquier-Tinville was sent for, and asked what he intended to do and what was needed to be certain of the result.

"Renew the jurors."

They must have men on whom they could count. They must be permanently appointed and given a salary.

"A certain amount of rebellion is needed to overcome the fear of the Tribunal."

Some of the judges, indeed, were in favour of poisoning the Queen "so as to get rid of this thorn in our side."

Fouquier got his "certain amount of rebellion" two days later. The discovery of the conspiracy of the carnation having stirred up the half-hearted, the Convention decided on 5 September that the Tribunal would judge not only the nobles, priests and counter-revolutionaries, but all the "enemies of the people," that is, "the shopkeepers, rich merchants, former attorneys [Fouquier-Tinville was to be able to guillotine some of his old colleagues], ushers, insolent valets, intendants and men of business, men of private means, cheaters by nature, profession and education." It can be seen that no one was forgotten.

On 28 September the new judges and jurors demanded by Fouquier were permanently appointed by the Committee. The axe was ready to work.

After Rougeville's plot the number of petitions increased. The *Section de l'Unité* asked, nay begged, "that the widow Capet should be definitely judged." The Central Committee of the "Patriotic Society" demanded that "the modern Messalina, this woman who seems to be rejected by nature and society, should be delivered to the vengeance of the law." Letters flowed in to the Committees, the Convention and the Tribunal. Even children—the young citizens of the *Section des Piques*—took a hand, asking "if the crimes of Marie Antoinette, that impious woman ruled by a barbarous nature, need to become blacker still before her fate is pronounced?"

The provinces followed Paris's lead. Calais, Evreux, Riom, Pamiers, Laigle, Grignan, Louhans, Senlis, Sens, Charolles, Josselin, Orgelet, Mont-Terrible and even the fishermen of La Flotte-en-Ré asked for sentence on "the shameless and despotic woman," the "wretch Antoinette," guilty of the crime of *lèse-nation*. The town of Chantilly was even more impatient and begged simply "that the Austrian she-wolf should be delivered to it" without the formality of a trial. Crécy was of the same opinion. "Antoinette is a thousand times guiltier than Louis XVI and she must pay with her impure blood for the sea of generous blood she has spilled."

Finally, on 3 October, the Convention decreed that the Revolutionary Tribunal "shall deal immediately and uninterruptedly with the judgement": On 5 October Fouquier replied that the Tribunal wished to hold the trial, but that he still had no documents concerning Marie Antoinette.

Perhaps the Prosecutor informed Hébert and Chaumette of his lack, and was told that documents could be procured, for the two accomplices, together with Pache and some Commissaires, arrived at the Temple and went up to the apartment "occupied by Louis-Charles Capet to hear his declarations regarding conversations and events within his knowledge." This idea, admittedly, could spring only from the mind of a Chaumette or a Hébert—to make a child of eight give evidence against his mother.

The little boy was questioned about the Commissaires "who were in the habit of coming to his mother and his aunt and holding conversations with them." The child first accused Lepitre and Toulan and then those "who conversed with more familiarity than the others": Michonis, Jobert, Moëlle, Beugnot, Vincent and Lebœuf.

"During these conversations I was sent away."

With disarming seriousness Simon made his pupil say that "Pétion, Manuel, Bailly and Lafayette" had behaved "very mysteriously in the Tuileries, with his mother and aunt." In the Tuileries the child had been barely seven years old!

Hébert soon realised that gossip of this kind would not create a favourable "climate" for the trial. The two accomplices then began their revolting plot, "Louis-Charles Capet declares also that having several times been surprised on his bed by Simon and his wife, who were entrusted by the Commune with guarding him, while committing indecencies harmful to his health, he confessed to them . . ."

We need not publish any more; it is nauseating. The accusation may have appeared probable to these men, who for fifteen years had been hearing all sorts of calumnies against the Queen, but Fouquier was intelligent. It is surprising that he did not feel that he risked having everything "blow up in his hands," in his own words, by making use of such filth. But he noted his customary *hic* against the most odious passage of the report. "From the way in which the child expressed himself we gathered that on one occasion his mother called him to her and there resulted . . ."

Was it the Prosecutor who asked Hébert to have these declarations supported by the testimony of the sister and aunt? However that may be, the next day the little group, which had been joined by the painter David and the Commissaire Danjou, returned to the Temple and began by confronting the two children. "We immediately summoned Charles Capet and asked him to declare if what he had said yesterday relative to the attempts on his person was true. He persisted in his statement, repeated them and continued in them in the presence of his sister and persisted in saying that it was the truth. Asked a second time to declare if it was really true, he replied: 'Yes, that is true.' His sister said she had not seen it. It was pointed out to her that her brother appeared to us to have spoken the truth and that as they were nearly always together it was impossible that she had not noticed everything her brother had declared."

Madame Royale replied: "It might be that her brother had seen things she had not, in view of the fact she was occupied with her education."

Madame Elisabeth, summoned in her turn, was horrified and exclaimed: "Oh! the monster!"

Would Fouquier's prey escape him? Madame Royale's denials concerning her mother's conversations with Toulan and Lepitre admittedly lacked sincerity, but a wish to escape was merely a breach of the prison rules; it was not a crime against the Nation.

The Prosecutor again asked the Convention to send him the papers found in the Queen's apartments on the morning of the departure for Varennes, the documents of Louis XVI's trial and the interrogation of the accused after the failure of the conspiracy of the carnation.

On 11 October a letter from the Committee, signed by Robespierre, Hérault, Collot d'Herbois and Billaud-Varenne authorised the Keeper of the Archives to let the Prosecutor have the documents he required.

In the evening all that arrived in the office in Caesar's Tower were the two interrogations of the Queen on the night of 3-4 September. Fouquier opened the first one. The Queen's answers to Amar had been very skilful.

"Do you sympathise with the success of our enemies' forces?"

"I sympathise with the success of those of my son's country."

"What is your son's country?"

"Can you be in doubt? Is he not French?"

How cleverly she had avoided giving up her rights!

"As your son is only a private person do you declare that you have renounced all the privileges which formerly gave him the empty title of King?"

To reply "yes" or "no" was equally dangerous. She therefore replied: "There is none finer than the happiness of France."

The *hic* in the margin bit deeper. Another trap was set:

"You are glad, then, that there is no more King or monarchy?"

She exclaimed: "All we need is that France should be great and happy!"

There, again, she had not answered the question, and another *hic* marked the reply. She was now going to be asked to approve of regicide.

"You must therefore wish for the People to have no more oppressors and [that] all of your family who wield arbitrary power should undergo the fate undergone by the oppressor of France?"

"I can answer for my son and myself. I am not responsible for others!"

Hic, wrote Fouquier.

The Varennes episode enabled Sevestre and Amar to lay another trap.

"How was it that you showed such an eager desire to use every means to be united with your family at war with the French nation?"

Here was the only valid accusation. Marie Antoinette could have replied that in June 1791 France and Austria were not at war, but from her replies one can see that she had lost her footing.

"My family is my children. I can be happy only with them and without them in no place."

"You therefore consider as your enemies those who make war on France?"

She might have answered "yes," but she refused to lie. Fouquier was therefore able to write a victorious *hic* against these two lines:

"I regard as my enemies all who might do harm to my children."

"And what is the nature of the harm that might be done to your children?"

"Any harm . . . of whatever kind."

She was obviously confused, but was able to recover herself. When the two deputies spoke to her of the abolition of royalty "which she could not consider wrong," she cried: "If France is to be happy with a King I wish it to be my son. If she is to be happy without a King I shall share the happiness with him."

Corneille could not have found anything better, and this time there was no *hic* in the margin.

Fouquier took up the text of the second interrogation. Perhaps he would have more luck there. It must have been well on in the night of 3-4 September when the Queen came back for questioning, and so this time the Prosecutor might find what he wanted. Amar and Sevestre tried to make the accused assume her share in Louis XVI's "crimes."

"Did he inform you of his plans?"

"He told me what his trust in me prompted him to."

"Did you approve those plans?"

"Everything that might lead to the peace of all was his desire and mine . . . I felt his troubles keenly."

"How was it that if, as you say, the people's happiness was your one wish, the people were so unhappy and constantly harried and tyrannised over by the perfidy of the court and the treachery of the Ministry?"

"There was much treachery. I am not in a position to know it nor to speak of it. All I know is that his heart wished only for happiness."

Amar and Sevestre preferred to leave the matter there. Neither weariness, nor the anguish of that last week which had seen the birth and sudden death of the hope of freedom brought by Rougeville had managed to diminish the mental faculties of Maria Theresa's daughter.

Fouquier wrote no *hic*, but closed the dossier. An indictment should be supported by more solid documents. And so on that same evening, Saturday, the accused was to be questioned and the trial could begin two days later, Monday 14 October, or "23 Vendémiaire." The revolutionary calendar had just begun its poetic cycle, but unfortunately it was soon to evoke not rime, blossoms, prairies, mist and wind, but bloody days and murderous laws.

Had the Queen a presentiment of what was being plotted against her? Since 5 October she was no longer alone in her cell. An officer of the gendarmerie guarded her—Lieutenant Louis-François de Busne, who before the Revolution had worn the uniform of the *Royal-Dauphin* Regiment. Two sentries were stationed before the window, but by speaking very loudly the prisoners in the courtyard had managed to inform Marie Antoinette "that she was to go up."

On 12 October Marie Antoinette was suffering from the cold and from serious hæmorrhages. At dusk she put on her "night shirt," which Rosalie brought to her all warm from the kitchen, and went to bed. The pretty servant managed to drag out her "little evening tasks," in order, as she tells us, that the Queen should not yet be "in solitude and obscurity." Finally Rosalie went away and the cell was lit only by the lamp in the women's courtyard.

Marie Antoinette took a long time to get warm. She had indeed asked the concierge for an extra blanket, but without success. When he transmitted the accused's request Bault was sharply spoken to by Fouquier-Tinville.

"What's that you're daring to ask for? You deserve to be sent to the guillotine!"

The prisoner had been in bed for two hours when the two doors of her cell were noisily opened. An usher and four gendarmes had come to take her to be questioned. Behind the screen the Queen hastily put on her black dress and then, surrounded by her guards and preceded by a turnkey carrying a torch, she left the cell, turned to the left into a corridor where a lantern burned by day and by night, went through the two grilles of the parlour—a real animal's cage—and went down a short flight of steps into the men's courtyard, which at that late hour was empty. She crossed the court and mounted the "Bonbec staircase." The boots of her escort rang loudly on the narrow stone staircase. On reaching the first floor the group followed a winding corridor, interrupted by steps, and finally emerged in the former *Grand-Chambre* of Parliament, the "tabernacle" of the old régime where Louis XVI had held his *lits de justice,* that "basilica" of which a monarch had said: "It is in seeing such things that one is proud to be King of France!"

The vast room was now called the Hall of Liberty and had become the seat of the Revolutionary Tribunal. The tapestries with their fleurs-de-lis had disappeared and the Crucifixion by Albert Dürer or Van Eyck—it was not known which—had been replaced by a picture painted on paper and reproducing the Declaration of the Rights of Man. Coustou's bas-relief, "Louis XV between Truth and Justice," had given way to busts of Marat, Lepeletier and Lucius Junius Brutus, a man who at that time was generally held up as an example, since to show his love for the Republic he had condemned his own children to death for having conspired to restore the Tarquins.

The Queen was given a seat on a bench in front of Fouquier's desk. In the shadows behind the tall balustrade of the public gallery could be seen a few faces of privileged people invited by Fouquier. The Queen heard murmurs and looked towards the back of the hall, but her short-sighted eyes could distinguish nothing.

The enormous room was lit only by two candles on the desk of the clerk, Paris from Marseilles, who as a sacrifice to fashion called himself Fabricius. The *Grand-Chambre* appeared like a tomb and the Queen was already speaking of herself in the past tense.

"I was called Marie Antoinette de Lorraine d'Autriche."

The question had been put by the young President of the Revolutionary Tribunal, Hermann, who was to preside at the debates two days later and was this evening acting as examining magistrate and sat alone at his table. He affected an air of compassion, but he was a friend of

Robespierre, to whom he owed his promotion (four months earlier he had been only President of the Criminal Tribunal at Arras), and was entirely at the orders of his "chief," Fouquier-Tinville. The Prosecutor could count on him.

He went straight to the point. "Before the Revolution you carried on political relations with the King of Bohemia and Hungary and these relations were contrary to the interests of France, which was showering advantages on you."

Maria Theresa's daughter denied it, of course. But this was one of the points on which Marie Antoinette was terribly vulnerable. How Fouquier would have exulted if he could have taken from his dossier that letter of Mercy's of fifteen years before. There would have been a *hic* against every line: "The Queen has taken steps to bring the King round to her way of thinking and to set him in opposition, to some extent, to his Ministers. She deserves to be congratulated."

Without delay Hermann struck another blow. "Not content with squandering in an appalling way the finances of France, the fruit of the people's sweat, for your pleasures and intrigues . . ."

No proof was given. And yet it would have sufficed to open a few of the account books of the Queen's Household or to summon a few witnesses who in the old days at Fontainebleau had sat down at the faro table. This absence of proof enabled the accused to deny vehemently.

"Never! I know this argument has too often been used against me. I loved my husband too much to squander my country's money!"

Hermann continued: "Since the Revolution you have never for a moment ceased intriguing with foreign Powers and at home against liberty, when even now we have only the shadow of that liberty which the French people desires above everything."

"Since the Revolution I, personally, have forbidden myself all correspondence abroad and I have never meddled at home."

The accused denied what was a secret for no one in France. However, she did not feel in the least guilty. For her there was no State, there was only the King—it was the famous "*L'Etat, c'est moi!*" of Louis XIV. To call for help, to ask her brother to assist her in regaining the throne, to beg him "to put an end to the troubles of the Revolution," as she had asked him on 3 September 1791, was not in Marie Antoinette's eyes to behave like an Austrian. Far from committing a crime when she addressed herself to "the enemies of the Nation," she was saving the State!

Marie Antoinette was again to deny the evidence.

"Did you not employ secret agents to correspond with foreign Powers, in particular with your brother?"

"Never in my life!"

Hermann could exclaim quite honestly: "Your reply does not seem to us to be correct, for it is stated that at the former château of the Tuileries there were secret, nocturnal councils, over which you yourself presided, and where the replies to be sent to foreign Powers and to the Constituent and Legislative Assembles were discussed, debated and drafted."

She denied it. But did she know that in the iron chest at the Tuileries the Republic had discovered letters from Barnave alluding to his correspondence, to her interviews with the Triumvirs and to the notes sent to Brussels? Fortunately there was so much lack of order that Fouquier-Tinville had not been able to get hold of the documents.

Hermann and the other members of the Tribunal—and they were perfectly sincere—approved of the Convention's vote of regicide. Louis XVI was guilty—guilty of having supported the non-juring priests, guilty of having opposed his veto to the decrees, guilty, as was proved by Barnave's reports, of having played "a double game." If they could prove that the Queen had been the prime instigator of this wavering policy she would be more "criminal" than her husband, who was decreed "irresponsible." This was one of the Prosecutor's aims.

"It was you who taught Louis Capet the art of profound dissimulation by which he so long deceived the good French people, who did not imagine that rascality and perfidy could be carried to such lengths!"

Need we recall that letter from the Queen to Mercy, dated 26 August, 1791: "All we have to do is to hoodwink them and make them trust us so as better to defeat them afterwards"?

When Hermann reproached the accused with the advice she had given "Louis Capet," advice which had gone so far as "persecution," so that the King should "put himself at the head of the malcontents," how can one not remember the Queen's admission to Fersen, the "hell" their home had become, the "serious obstacles" she met in trying to make her point of view prevail and which she mentioned to Mercy, the "great struggles" she was forced to have with her too hesitant and changeable husband?

To recall these documents is not to accuse the Queen, but to try to explain, otherwise than through fear of the guillotine, the behaviour of the judges and jurors who were to send this woman to her death, in the persuasion that they were acting justly.

In guise of proof Fouquier had only the documents relating to the flight of June 1791.

"You opened the doors and made everyone leave. There is no doubt that it was you who ruled the actions of Louis Capet and persuaded him to flight."

She replied, reasonably: "I do not think that an open door proves that one is constantly ruling a person's acts."

She seems to have made her reply somewhat ironical. The President exclaimed violently: "Never for one moment have you ceased wanting to destroy liberty. You wanted to reign at any price and to reascend the throne over the bodies of patriots."

Still ironically she replied: "We had no need to reascend the throne; we were there!" More seriously, she added: "We have never wished for anything but France's happiness. As long as she was happy, as long as she is so, we shall always be satisfied."

It was a fine phrase, but it allowed Hermann to remark that if the Queen had really wished for France's happiness she would have prevented her brother from breaking the treaty signed with the King. It was then easy for Marie Antoinette to reply "that it was France who declared war."

Hermann admitted it. "But the accused cannot be unaware that this declaration of war came only through the intrigues of a liberticide faction."

"The Legislative Assembly repeated its request for a declaration of war and my husband consented only after receiving the unanimous assent of his Council."

Hermann was not well placed and preferred to attack the unhappy woman on more shifting ground: the banquet of the bodyguards at which, it was alleged, they had "trampled under foot the tricolour cockade so as to wear the white cockade." Here again she was skilful in her replies.

"That can have been no more than the mistake of one or two people

. . . It is not credible that such devoted people should have trampled on and changed the sign worn by the King himself."

Without transition Hermann asked: "What interest do you take in the forces of the Republic?"

"The happiness of France is what I wish for above everything."

Now the questions came thick and fast.

"Do you think that Kings are necessary for the people's happiness?"

"An individual cannot decide such matters."

"No doubt you regret that your son has lost a throne to which he might have mounted if the people, finally conscious of their rights, had not destroyed that throne?"

"I shall never regret anything for my son when his country is happy."

The moment her son was in question Marie Antoinette found the right answer. Hermann therefore hastened to change the subject.

"What is your opinion on the day of 10 August when, by order of the master of the château, the Swiss Guards fired on the people?"

"I was out of the château when the firing began. I do not know how it all happened. I only know that no order was ever given to fire."

After several traps about the Temple and a long interrogation on the conspiracy of the carnation, Hermann put his last question.

"Have you any counsel?"

"No. I do not know anyone."

"Would you like the Tribunal to appoint one or two?"

"I am quite willing."

"Upon which we appointed, as official counsel and defenders, citizens Tronson du Coudray and Chauveau-Lagarde."

Fabricius handed the Queen the pen. She signed, and then Hermann, Fouquier and the clerk wrote their initials.

As the prisoner and her escort returned to the Conciergerie, Fouquier shut himself up in his office in Caesar's Tower to prepare the indictment. Right at the beginning he committed an historical error in comparing Marie Antoinette to Messalina, Fredegonde and Brunehaut, whom he described as "Queens of France." He began by writing "Bruneau," then feeling something was wrong corrected it to "Brunechaut" and, finally, "Brunehault."

Sprinkling his text with such phrases as "scourge and bloodsucker of the French . . . full of intrigues of all kinds . . . disordered pleasures . . . criminal intrigues . . . excessive squandering . . . perfidious views," the Prosecutor repeated and amplified all the questions put to the Queen by Hermann.

Needless to say, he paid no attention to the accused's replies, except for one point regarding the journey to Varennes. "That the widow Capet admits in her interrogation that it was she who arranged and prepared everything for the carrying out of this escape and that it was she who opened and closed the door of the apartment through which all the fugitives passed."

As regards 10 August, he alleged that on the evening before, Marie Antoinette had gone "to the hall where the Swiss Guards and others devoted to her were working at making cartridges; that while she encouraged them to hasten the manufacture of the cartridges, and in order to spur them on still more, she took some cartridges and bit on the bullets (there are not words to paint such an atrocious act); that on the next day, the 10th, it is well known that she urged and begged Louis Capet to go to the Tuileries, at about half-past five in the morning, to review the true Swiss Guards and the other rascals who were wearing the uniform, and that on his return she handed him a pistol, saying: 'Now is the moment to reveal yourself,' and that on his refusal she called him a coward; that although during her interrogation the widow Capet persisted in denying that any order was given to fire on the people, her conduct on the 9th, her actions in the Swiss Guards' room, the discussions held all night, at which she was present, the matter of the pistol and her remark to Louis Capet, their sudden retreat from the Tuileries and the shots fired just as they were entering the hall of the Legislative Assembly—all these circumstances together leave no doubt that it was agreed, during the council which was held during the night, that the people must be fired on, and that Louis Capet and Marie Antoinette, who was the prime mover in this conspiracy, herself gave the order to fire."

Fouquier-Tinville now came to a serious matter, so serious indeed that it would be unnecessary to seek further, if the Prosecutor were able to prove it.

"That it was by her manoeuvres and intrigues, always fatal to France, that the first retreat of the French from Belgian territory came about. That it was the widow Capet who conveyed to the foreign Powers the plans of campaign and attack which had been agreed on in the Council, so that by this double treachery the enemy was always aware in advance of the movements of the armies of the Republic, from which it follows that the widow Capet is the cause of the reverses suffered at different times by the French armies."

Before finishing the Prosecutor actually made use of Hébert's plot. "That, finally, the widow Capet, immoral in every way and a new Agrippina, is so perverted and so familiar with every crime that, forgetting her position as a mother and the line drawn by the laws of nature, she did not recoil from indulging with Louis-Charles Capet, her son, as is confessed by the latter, in indecencies the mere idea and mention of which arouse a shudder of horror."

By uncovering this garbage in court and providing details which would be eschewed by a writer of cheap melodrama—the Queen calling Louis XVI a coward, or biting bullets on the eve of 10 August— Fouquier imagined he would make a good impression on the jurors.

He had chosen them carefully. First there were the zealots: the Pyrenean surgeon Souberville, the printer Nicolas, both of whom were friends of Robespierre, the former *procureur* Thoumin, the valuer Besnard and the former Marquis Antoinette, who had been a deputy from Bouches-du-Rhône in the Legislative Assembly. Fouquier could be as sure of them as of himself. The others were rather simple-minded men, who liked ready-made formulas and believed in enormities: the wig-maker Ganney, the cobbler Desboisseaux, the café-keeper Chrétien, the hatter Baron, the musician Lumière, a certain Fiévé and two carpenters, Devèse and Trinchard, the latter being a former dragoon of the Bourbon Regiment. On the following morning the Prosecutor was to summon them.

That same evening Fersen wrote in his Journal: "The news of the Queen is a little more reassuring. The Public Prosecutor is complaining that he has no documents. It has been decreed that he should have them and this at least means a delay."

At his country house not far from Paris Chauveau-Lagarde, aged 28, was informed by the clerk of the court that on the previous day he had been appointed to defend "the widow Capet" and that the trial was to begin at eight the next morning.

The lawyer hastened back to Paris and at two in the afternoon arrived at the Conciergerie, where he showed the order signed by Fouquier. Preceded by a concierge he passed through the wickets and went down the corridor. "With trembling knees and moist eyes," as he related afterwards, he entered the cell. On the left were two armed gendarmes; on the right, behind the screen, the bed, table and two cane chairs. The Queen greeted him with "majesty and kindness." She had not yet received the indictment and spoke to her defender about the interrogation of the day before. To find out more about it Chauveau-Lagarde went up to the clerk's office, which led out of the waiting-room. According to custom Fabricius's clerks were making as many copies of the indictment as there were to be judges and jurors. The lawyer was given a copy and then asked to see the accused's dossier. The documents had finally arrived and the defending counsel was taken aback by the mountain of paper.

"I cannot possibly become acquainted with the documents in such a short time!"

Discouraged, the lawyer returned to the prison. Citizen Eustache Nappier, the court usher, had just given the accused her copy of the indictment, "speaking personally to her between the two wickets of that house, as in a place of freedom." Marie Antoinette was "accused of having conspired against France."

Together with his client Chauveau-Lagarde read the eight pages. In order to be able to reply to this farrago he would need the dossier.

"But I cannot get to know the documents in such a short time."

"To whom must you apply?" asked the Queen.

"To the National Convention," Chauveau-Lagarde murmured.

To those who had voted for her husband's death. "No, no, never!" she cried, "turning her head away."

The lawyer insisted. The Queen might, in the name of her defenders, make "a complaint against a haste which by the terms of the law amounted to a real denial of justice."

Marie Antoinette gave way. Without uttering a word she took the pen held out to her by Chauveau-Lagarde, "let fall a sigh," and wrote to ask the President of the Assembly for a delay of three days, as she owed it to her children "to omit nothing necessary for their mother's entire justification."

When the letter was finished Chauveau-Lagarde went again to the Tribunal and gave the request to Fouquier, who promised to send it to the Assembly. He took care not to do so, however. One day he was to give the letter to Robespierre and after 9 Thermidor it was found under the Incorruptible's mattress, together with the Queen's will.

At Brussels, on this same 13 October, Fersen was once more in despair. "Although there are no proofs against this unfortunate Princess, how can one hope for anything with wretches who manufacture proofs when they have none and who condemn simply on vague assertions and on suspicion! No, let us not hope for anything. We must be resigned to the divine will. Her fate is certain. We must be prepared for it and summon strength to bear this terrible blow. I have for long been trying to prepare myself for it and I feel that I shall receive the news of it without great emotion. Only God can save her; let us implore His mercy and submit ourselves to His decrees."

That evening Gluck's *Armide* was being performed at the Opera. How often, seated at her clavichord in the Trianon, had Marie Antoinette sung the famous aria: "Ah! if my freedom should be taken from me!"

20

❧

The Trial

A FEW MINUTES before eight the usher of the Tribunal, Lieutenant de Busne, and the gendarmes opened the cell door. The Queen was ready. She had put on her worn black dress and had managed to give herself a widow's headdress by adding "weepers" to her lawn bonnet and fixing a crêpe veil under it.

When the crowd saw her enter "free and without fetters," a murmur rang round the *Grand-Chambre*. The public crowding behind the rails had difficulty in recognising the 37-year-old Queen in this woman with white hair and pallid complexion. "She is prodigiously altered," wrote the *Moniteur*. During the last few months Marie Antoinette had grown so thin and her face had become so sunken that she looked about sixty. She was led to a little platform, where there was an armchair so placed "that the accused could be seen by all." Chauveau-Lagarde and Tronson du Coudray stood near the Queen. In front of her were the tables adorned with gryphons at which President Hermann was enthroned together with the judges Coffinhal, former clerk, former doctor, former lawyer, former errand-boy, former police officer and still only 31, Antoine Maire, who pleaded in that same hall in the time of the Parliament and who was alleged to be a son of Louis XV, born in the Parc au Cerf, the former deputy Deliège, who wore a wig, and the doyen Donzé-Verteuil, a man of nearly 60, whose tiny mouth was lost in the middle of a large, round face. According to some documents there were also present, as alternates, Etienne Foucault, once a farmer, whose large nose stood out in a face marked with smallpox, and Marie-Joseph Lane.

Marie Antoinette remained standing while the witnesses took the oath.

"The accused may be seated . . . Your name, surname, age, position, place of birth and residence?"

"My name is Marie Antoinette Lorraine d'Autriche [the scribe wrote *dautriche*], aged about 38 [she would not be 38 for another 18 days], widow of the King of France, born in Vienna. At the time of my arrest I was in the session hall of the National Assembly."

The clerk Fabricius then read the eight long pages of the indictment. Did she listen to the text she had read the day before with Chauveau-Lagarde? Somewhat irritated, "with seeming inattention," she moved her fingers on the arm of her chair "as though over the keyboard of her pianoforte."

The usher finished mumbling.

"This is what you are accused of," the President announced. "Pay careful attention. You will now hear the charges to be brought against you."

The first witness, who was to testify for two hours, was Laurent Lecointre, formerly a linen-draper and now a deputy to the Convention. It will be remembered that he was second in command of the National Guard at Versailles. "The witness," says the report, "entered into the details of the feasts and orgies which took place in the town of Versailles from the year 1779 to the beginning of 1789, the result of which was an appalling dilapidation of French finances."

We do not know these "details," but the text is much more precise concerning the "orgy" of the bodyguards.

"Have you anything to say about the witness's testimony?" Hermann asked the Queen.

"I have no knowledge of the greater part of the facts mentioned by the witness. It is true that we visited the table on the day of the bodyguards' feast, but that is all."

"It is notorious that throughout France at that time the rumour was that you yourself visited the three armed corps at Versailles to urge them to defend what you called the prerogatives of the throne."

"I have nothing to reply."

Hermann now came to the famous royal session of 23 June 1789, which he pretended to call a *lit de justice.*

"It was in your apartment that the articles [of the King's speech] were prepared?"

"This affair was decided in the Council."

"Did your husband not read the speech to you half-an-hour before entering the hall of the people's representatives and did you not urge him to utter it with decision?"

"My husband had great confidence in me and it was for that reason that he read it to me, but I did not allow myself any observations."

"What were the decisions taken to surround the representatives of the people with bayonets and to assassinate half of them, if it had been possible?"

There had been bayonets only in Mirabeau's famous phrase, and so the Queen exclaimed in astonishment: "I have never heard such a thing mentioned."

She lost ground when the President recalled the troop movements on 12 July 1789, troops which were placed under the orders of Maréchal de Broglie and Besenval.

"You are doubtless aware that there were troops in the Champ de Mars, and you must know why they were assembled?"

"Yes, I knew at the time that they were there, but I am entirely unaware of the reason."

"But as you had your husband's confidence you cannot have been unaware of the cause?"

"It was to re-establish public tranquillity."

"But at that time everyone was tranquil; there was but one cry, that of liberty."

Hermann's second attack also had its effect. These were, incidentally, almost the only attacks to reach their target throughout the long trial.

"How did you use the immense sums given you by the various Controllers of Finance?"

"I was never given immense sums. What was given to me I used to pay the people in my service."

"Why were the Polignac family and several others gorged with gold from you?"

"They had places at court which procured riches for them."

The vague testimony of a certain Lapierre, Adjutant-General on duty at the Tuileries on the evening of 20 June 1791, enabled Hermann to put some questions about Varennes. Roussillon, "surgeon and gunner," came next and alleged "that on 10 August 1792, having entered the château of the Tuileries and into the accused's apartment," he had "found under the bed bottles, some full and some empty, which led him to believe that she had given drink either to the officers of the Swiss Guard or to the Knights of the Poniard who filled the château."

It would soon be said at the Jacobins Club that "the testimony of Roussillon had been a fire burning like a fuse."

There was another "fuse" from the gunner-surgeon. "The witness affirms that the accused helped to bring France within an inch of her ruin by sending enormous sums to her brother [the former King of Bohemia and Hungary] to help in his war against the Turks and to enable him later to make war against France, that is, against a generous nation which was nourishing her, her husband and her family. The witness observed that he had this fact from a good citizeness, an excellent patriot, who had served at Versailles under the old régime, and in whom a favourite of the former court had confided."

Fouquier-Tinville pricked up his ears and immediately dispatched a summons in the name of "the good citizeness."

The *tricoteuses,* who were crowded behind the rails, constantly insisted by their shouts that the accused should reply standing, so that they should not miss anything. She murmured: "Will the people soon be weary of my hardships?"

With Hébert's deposition Marie Antoinette entered a new phase of her agony. In order to give substance to Toulan's conspiracy the deputy Prosecutor recalled the life of the prisoners in the Temple and put forward the declarations of "little Capet." He then stated coolly: "Finally, young Capet, whose health was worsening each day, was surprised by Simon in indecent defilements, baneful to his constitution. When the latter asked him who had taught him this criminal behaviour he replied that he owed his knowledge of this baneful habit to his mother and aunt. From the declaration that young Capet made in the presence of the Mayor of Paris and the Prosecutor of the Commune it was revealed that these two women often made him lie down between them; that there then took place acts of the most uncontrolled debauchery; that there was no doubt, from what Capet's son said, that there had been an act of incest between the mother and son."

One may imagine the Queen's horror and suffering at hearing the ignominy contrived by the abominable Hébert and the part her son had been forced to play. But Hébert had not finished.

"There is reason to believe that this criminal intercourse was not dictated by pleasure but by the calculated hope of enervating the child, whom they still liked to think of as destined to occupy a throne and whom they wished to be sure of dominating morally as a result of this scheme. As a result of the efforts he was forced to make he suffered from a hernia, for which a bandage was needed. Since the child has been away from his mother his constitution has become robust and strong."

Hermann questioned the accused. "What reply have you to the witness's deposition?"

In a trembling voice she replied: "I have no knowledge of the incidents Hébert speaks of." She eagerly refuted the details concerning Toulan which Hébert had given, but after a few sentences he interrupted her.

"I omitted one important fact, which should be brought to the attention of the citizen jurors. It shows the characters of the accused and her sister-in-law. After the death of Capet these two women treated little Capet with the same deference as if he had been King. At table he always took precedence over his mother and his aunt. He was always served first and sat at the head of the table."

Marie Antoinette turned towards the witness and asked him calmly: "Did you see that?"

"I did not see it, but the whole of the Municipality will confirm it."

Hermann cut this conversation short and asked the Queen about Rougeville and Michonis. Suddenly one of the jurors—his name is not known—rose.

"Citizen President, would you kindly observe to the accused that she has not replied concerning the incident mentioned by citizen Hébert, regarding what happened between herself and her son."

The President, perhaps unwillingly, repeated the question. The Queen rose, "much moved," according to the report.

"If I did not reply it was because nature recoils from such an accusation against a mother." Turning to the crowd she cried: "I appeal to all those who may be here!"

"At this sublime cry," wrote two eye-witnesses, the brothers Humbert, "an electric shock ran through those present. The *tricoteuses* were moved in spite of themselves and they nearly applauded . . . Cries could be heard and the Tribunal had to threaten to call the disturbers to order."

For a few moments the session had to be suspended. The Queen called Chauveau-Lagarde and asked him in a low voice: "Was there too much dignity in my answer?"

"Madame," he replied, "be yourself and you will always do right, but why do you ask?"

"Because I heard a woman of the people remark to her neighbour: 'See how proud she is!'"

"This remark of the Queen's," wrote the lawyer, "shows that she still had hope. It also proves that with her pure conscience she was entirely mistress of herself, since amid the greatest agitation of mind she heard everything that was said around her and in order to prove her innocence she tried to regulate her silence and her words to suit the situation."

It was nearly two o'clock and the first session would soon be over. They were still hearing the trivial testimony of a certain Abraham Silly, "on duty in the château on the evening of 20 June 1791." However, this gave Hermann the opportunity to ask a series of questions about Varennes which were only remotely connected with the indictment.

"Who provided or caused to be provided the famous carriage in which you went away with your family?"

"It was a foreigner."

"Of what nation?"

"Swedish."

"Was it not Fersen, who was living in Paris in the Rue du Bacq?"

"Yes," murmured the accused.

At this name a tremor went through the public.

Followed by her lawyers and surrounded by gendarmes, the prisoner went down to her cell.

"The Queen asked me what I thought of the testimony we had just heard," wrote Chauveau-Lagarde, "summarising it quite correctly and complaining bitterly of the falsehood which filled most of it. I replied, as was true, that not only was there no proof of all the ridiculous calumnies of these witnesses, but there was not the slightest foundation for them and that they defeated themselves by their very grossness and by the vileness and meanness of their authors."

"In that case," replied the Queen, "I fear only Manuel!"

Marie Antoinette was wrong to fear him. When the session resumed, at about four or five, he opened fire. But as with the two succeeding witnesses, Bailly and Perceval, it was merely a matter of self-defence and personal questioning. They might have been in the office of an examining magistrate.

It was now Reine Millot's turn to appear in the *Grand-Chambre*. She was the "good citizeness" summoned by Fouquier, and had been fetched from the café of the Couronne-d'Or in the Rue du Bourdonnais. Formerly a servant in the château of Versailles, she alleged that she had "taken it on herself" to ask the former Comte de Coigny, whom she saw one day to be in "a good humour": "Will the Emperor go on making war against the Turks? Heavens, it will ruin France, on account of the great sums the Queen sends her brother, which must now amount to at least 200 millions."

"You are not mistaken," replied the "Comte" de Coigny (who in fact was a Duke). "Yes, it has already cost more than 200 millions and we have not finished yet."

"I would also mention," continued the witness, "that I was told by different people that as the accused had conceived the plan of assassinating the Duc d'Orléans, the King, having learned of it, ordered that she should be searched at once and that as a result two pistols were found on her. He then confined her to her apartments for a fortnight."

Marie Antoinette replied disdainfully: "It may be that my husband ordered me to remain in my apartments for a fortnight, but it was not for any such reason."[1]

The farce continued with J. - B. Lebenette, editor of the *Journal du Diable*, who declared with the utmost seriousness that "three individuals came to assassinate him on the orders of the accused." He did not explain how he had put them to flight.

With the gendarme Dufresne, the two Richards, the woman Harel and Gilbert they were back to the conspiracy of the carnation and, with that memory of the hope that had gleamed the month before, the first day's hearings ended at eleven o'clock.

Tuesday, 15 October, was the feast of Saint Teresa, her mother's feast-day and her daughter's. For the *sans-culottes*, who followed the new calendar, it was the feast of the Amaryllis.

[1] No mention of this punishment inflicted by the King is found either in Mercy's correspondence or in the memoirs of the time.

When Marie Antoinette crossed the courtyard at nine o'clock it was raining and the wind was blowing.

The session opened. The Queen listened, without interest, to the testimony, or rather the interrogation, of ex-Admiral d'Estaing, but her heart beat violently when she saw the approach of Simon, who must just have woken the little King. Louis XVII's "tutor" brought no serious accusations against the Queen. When the President asked him: "Is it within your knowledge that the little Capet was treated as a King, particularly at table?" he replied with restraint: "I know that at table his mother and aunt gave him precedence."

Fouquier was banking on vouchers signed "Marie Antoinette" which were said to have been discovered in the possession of Septeuil, the former Treasurer of the Civil List. Hermann began by asking the Queen: "Did you not sign vouchers to obtain money from the Treasurer of the Civil List?"

"No."

Fouquier rose and declared triumphantly: "I must tell you that your denial will soon be useless, seeing that among Septeuil's papers there were discovered two vouchers signed by you."

A little less boastfully he added: "As a matter of fact these two documents, which were deposited with the Comité des Vingt-Quatre, have temporarily gone astray, as the committee has been dissolved, but you will hear witnesses who have seen them."

There was only one witness—a common spy, who dignified himself with the title of "merchant." He was called François Tisset and recited the piece demanded by Fouquier.

"As an unsalaried employee, at the period of 10 August 1792, of the Vigilance Committee of the Municipality, I was sent on a mission to Septeuil, the Treasurer of the former Civil List. I was accompanied by armed forces of the Place Vendôme Section, now the *Piques*. I could not seize his person, as he was absent. Among Septeuil's papers were found two vouchers for the sum of 80,000 livres, signed 'Marie Antoinette,' which documents were all deposited with the Comité des Vingt-Quatre, which is now dissolved."

He was reciting a lesson, but he did not know it very well. The Queen, who was following attentively, asked very calmly: "I would like the witness to say what was the date of the vouchers he mentions."

"One was dated 10 August 1792; as for the other, I do not remember."

"I never signed any vouchers, and in any case how could I have done so on 10 August, the day on which we went to the National Assembly at about eight in the morning?"

The twentieth witness reminded the Queen of her "happy dream" of the preceding winter. It was Lepitre, who had been arrested the week before and brought from the prison of Sainte-Pélagie, and had been present at the trial since morning.

"Did you not procure means for the accused to learn the news by sending a pedlar every day to call out the evening paper near the Temple tower?"

"No."

Marie Antoinette explained: "I have never had any conversation with the witness. On the other hand, I had no need for pedlars to be hired to come to the tower. I could hear them well enough every day when they went through the Rue de la Corderie."

The Queen had then to submit to a painful experience: the opening by Hermann of the packet of possessions seized at the Temple on which the prisoner had put her seal when she was registered at the Conciergerie. In his Marseillais accent Fabricius read the inventory aloud.

"A packet of hair of various colours."

"They come from my dead and living children and from my husband."

"Another packet of hair."

"They belong to the same people."

"A paper with figures on it."

"It is a table for teaching my son to count."

"A hussif or little wallet fitted with scissors, needles, silk, thread, etc. A little mirror, a gold ring in which is some hair, a paper on which are two gold hearts with initials, another paper on which is written 'Prayer to the Sacred Heart of Jesus; prayer to the Immaculate Conception'; a portrait of a woman."

Hermann raised his head.

"Whose is that portrait?"

"Madame de Lamballe," replied the Queen.

"Two other portraits of women," cried the usher.

The President inquired: "Who are the people represented by these portraits?"

"They are two ladies with whom I was brought up in Vienna."

"What are their names?"

"Mesdames de Mecklembourg and de Hesse."

Fabricius continued: "A small piece of cloth on which is a heart in flames pierced by an arrow."

It was Fouquier's turn to intervene and to pretend not to know what a scapular was.

"I notice that among the accused who have been brought before the Tribunal as conspirators and whom the law has justly dealt with by striking them with its sword, it has been observed that most of them, or indeed the majority, wore this counter-revolutionary sign."

Under his judge's robes Fouquier himself wore a "counter-revolutionary sign." When the last surviving daughter of the Public Prosecutor died in 1856 at Saint Quentin there was found on her a paper enveloping a medal of the Virgin. On the paper was written: "He had it round his neck when he condemned the widow Capet."

The clerk rewrapped and carried away all those beloved and painful remembrances which recalled to the Queen so many well-loved ghosts.

The twenty-first witness was Philippe La Tour du Pin Gouvernet.

"Were you not present at the festivities at the château?"

"I practically never went to court."

"Were you not at the banquet of the former bodyguards?"

"I could not have been there, for at that time I was commanding in Burgundy."

"What! Were you not a Minister then?"

"I have never been a Minister and would not have wished for the post if those then in power had offered it to me."

The President, who thought the witness was lying, questioned Lecointre.

"Do you recognise the witness as having been, in 1789, Minister of War?"

Lecointre enlightened Hermann. Philippe La Tour du Pin had been summoned in error. The right one—Jean-Frédéric—was there and would appear. The former Minister came forward unmoved and made the Queen a respectful court bow. When he had finished his testimony he made another. Fouquier-Tinville would not forget these two greetings when on the following 28 April he sent La Tour du Pin to the scaffold.

There was another interrogation which stirred the audience. It concerned the King's departure for Rambouillet on 5 October and the disbanding of the army. Hermann finally came back to the trial.

"During your Ministry did the accused ask you to let her know the exact state of the French Army?"

"Yes."

"Did she say what use she wanted to make of it?"

"No."

"When you asked the witness for the state of the army," asked the President, turning to the Queen, "was it not to communicate it to the King of Bohemia and Hungary?"

"As it was publicly known there would have been no need for me to communicate it to him. The public papers would have told him all about it."

"What then was your motive in asking?"

"As there was a rumour that the Assembly wished for changes in the army, I wanted to know the state of the regiments to be suppressed."

Fouquier had scored a point.

It would be useless to look for the guiding thread in Hermann's conduct of the argument. He suddenly changed the subject and with three syllables reminded the Queen of her former happy life.

"Where did you get the money to have the little Trianon built and furnished, where you gave parties at which you were always the goddess?"

"There were funds especially for that purpose."

"These funds must have been large, for the little Trianon must have cost immense sums?"

"It is possible that the little Trianon cost immense sums, perhaps more than I would have wished. We were gradually involved in more and more expense. Besides I am more anxious than anyone that what happened there should be known."

"Was it not at the little Trianon that you knew the woman Lamotte?"

"I have never seen her."

"Was she not your victim in the famous affair of the necklace?"

"She cannot have been, since I did not know her."

"Do you persist in denying that you knew her?"

"I have no system of denial. It is the truth that I have told and will persist in telling."

The questions continued to rain down, and this time the accusations were just.

"Was it not you who appointed the Ministers and filled other civil and military posts?"

"No."

"Did you not have a list of persons you wanted places for?"

"No."

"Did you not compel various Ministers to accept the persons you indicated to them for vacant posts?"

"No."

"Did you not compel the Ministers of Finance to send you money and did you not threaten with your indignation those of them who refused?"

"Never."

"Did you not ask Vergennes to convey six millions to the King of Bohemia and Hungary?"

"No."

Fouquier, who had realised the bad effect made the day before by the testimony of the policy spy regarding the vouchers signed by the Queen, found at Septeuil's house and then mysteriously lost, summoned the former secretary of the Comité des Vingt-Quatre, a certain J. - B. Garnerin. There was no longer talk of two vouchers, but of one only "in favour of the former Polignac" which had come into the hands of citizen Valazé.

"Have you any remarks on the witness's testimony?" Hermann asked the Queen.

"I repeat that I never signed any vouchers."

On the same subject Valazé supported the Prosecutor. Among the papers that had been through his hands he had noticed two "which concerned the accused."

"The first was a voucher, or rather a receipt signed by her, for the sum of 15 or 20 thousand livres, as far as I can remember. The other document was a letter in which the Minister asked the King to be so good as to communicate to Marie Antoinette the plan of campaign which he had the honour to send him."

The latter document was obviously important and, if it had been produced at the trial, would have been a proof of great value for the prosecution.

"Do you know what has become of these two documents?" asked the President.

"The documents which were used in preparing the indictment of Louis Capet were claimed by the Paris Commune. I believe that now all these documents must have been returned to the Convention's Committee of General Safety."

Hermann avoided drawing attention to the confusion among the files of the young Republic and turned to the accused.

"What have you to say in reply to the witness's testimony?"

"I know nothing of the voucher or the letter he mentions."

Fouquier intervened. "It seems to be proved, in spite of your denials, that through your influence you made the former King, your husband, do whatever you wished."

"There is a great difference between advising that something should be done and having it carried out."

"You can see that it is shown by the witness's declaration that the Ministers were so well aware of your influence on Louis Capet that one of them asked him to inform you of the plan of campaign which had been presented to him a few days earlier, from which it follows that you made use of his weak character to make him carry out many evil deeds, for even supposing that he had followed only the best of your advice, you must admit that it was impossible to make use of worse means for leading France to the brink of the abyss which nearly swallowed her."

"I never knew him to have such a character as you describe," she said calmly.

But the blow had gone home. Admittedly Valazé did not produce the document, but he had seen it. He was, of course, a Girondin, and in prison, that is, a "counter-revolutionary," but to the jurors the former deputy to the Convention, the ex-member of the Committee of Vingt-Quatre, was the man who had drafted Louis XVI's indictment. He may have been suspect, but his testimony had the "official" ring of a man on oath, and it was with a certain feeling of anguish that the Queen left the court when the sitting was suspended.

When it was resumed a whole series of *commissaires* of the Commune and former municipal officers followed: Nicolas Lebœuf, August Jobert, Antoine Moëlle, J. - B. Vincent, Nicolas Beugnot. Their testimony concerning the life of prisoners in the Temple did not bring much for the prosecution. These "citizens" had "seen nothing," "noticed nothing," and had never had any conversation with the prisoners, or at least so they said. But some of their replies made the Queen's heart beat faster. On several occasions the names of "Thérèse Capet" and, in particular, "little Capet" were heard in the court.

"I would point out to you that as regards these facts your testimony is in opposition to your son's."

"It is easy to make a child of eight say whatever one wants."

"But there was not just one declaration. He was made to repeat it several times and on several occasions; he always said the same thing."

"Well, I deny the facts."

The testimony of Brunier, doctor to the little King and Madame Royale, once more reminded her of those from whom she was parted. Hébert, who had been silent for a long time, became excited and reproached the doctor "with having never approached the children of the accused without all the servility of the old régime."

"It was correct behaviour, not servility," exclaimed Brunier, whom Marie Antoinette had formerly blamed for his familiarity.

When Renée Sévin, Marie Antoinette's former "under waiting-woman," gave evidence there was laughter.

"In what part of the château did you sleep?"

"At the end of the Pavillion de Flore."

"In the night of the 9th-10th did you hear the tocsin ring and the alarum sound?"

"No, I slept in the attic."

"What! You slept in the attic and you did not hear the tocsin?"

"No, I was ill."

"And through what chance were you present at the royal review?"

"I was up at six o'clock."

"What! You were ill and you rose at six o'clock?"

"It was because I heard a noise."

"On the previous evening did you see the unusual mustering of the Swiss Guards and the rascals who had taken their uniform?"

"On that day I did not go down into the courtyard."

"But you must have gone down to take your meals?"

"I did not go out. A servant brought my meals."

"But this servant must have told you what was going on?"

"I never held any conversation with him."

"It would seem that you have passed all your life at court and have learned how to dissimulate."

Hermann then asked the Police Administrator Dangé some curious questions.

"What is your opinion of the accused?"

"If she is guilty she should be judged."

"Do you think she is a patriot?"

"No."

"Do you think she wants a republic?"

"No."

At half-past four the sitting was suspended. The Queen had eaten nothing since the morning.

"The accused is not coming down; they are asking for soup," Mme Bault informed her pretty servant.

"I immediately took some excellent soup which I was keeping ready on my stove," Rosalie recounted, "and I went up to the Princess. I was just about to enter the hall when one of the police officers called Labuzière, who was short and snub-nosed, snatched the soup-dish from my hands and, giving it to his mistress, who was young and covered with finery, he said to me: 'This young woman is very eager to see the widow Capet; it is a *charming* opportunity for her.' The woman went off at once, carrying the soup, which was half spilt. In vain I begged and prayed Labuzière. He was all-powerful and I had to obey. What must the Queen have thought when she received her soup from the hand of a person she did not know!"

It was nearly night when the sitting was resumed. Here and there in the large room a few candles were placed and behind the judges two wall-lamps with reflectors were lighted.

The interminable procession went on. The Queen followed the debates attentively. Michonis and Fontaine took her through the backstage events of the conspiracy of the carnation, about which she probably knew nothing. The trial dragged on with evidence of no interest: Tavernier, lieutenant on duty at the Tuileries on 20 June, who spoke of Lafayette; Jean Lebrasse, lieutenant of the gendarmerie, who again recalled "the carnation scene"; the painter Boze, who did a portrait "of the former King," but who had never spoken to the accused. For some unknown reason Fouquier had him arrested as he left the court. There was Michel Gointre, who accused the Queen of having had forged assignats made. Finally there was the usher Jourdeuil, who claimed to have found a letter from Marie Antoinette at the house of d'Affry, commander of the Swiss Guards. "Can one count on your Swiss?" the Queen was alleged to have asked the officer. "Will they make a good showing when the time comes?"

"I never wrote to d'Affry," Marie Antoinette exclaimed.

Faced with this new document, which was mentioned but not put in evidence, Fouquier felt obliged to bring himself into the matter.

"Last year, when I was leader of the prosecuting jury to the Tribunal of 10 August, I was entrusted with the preliminary examination of the trial of d'Affry and Cazotte. I well remember having seen the letter mentioned by the witness, but the Roland faction, having succeeded in abolishing the Tribunal, had the papers removed by means of a decree which they rushed through in spite of the protests of all good republicans."

With equal relevance Hermann asked: "At the time of your marriage to Louis Capet, did you not conceive the project of uniting Lorraine with Austria?"

"No."

"You bear its name?"

"Because one must bear the name of one's country."

Without any transition the President continued: "Did you not investigate feeling in the departments, districts and municipalities?"

"No."

Fouquier rose, triumphantly.

"There was found in your desk a document proving this fact conclusively, in which are written the names of the Vaublancs, Jaucourts, etc."

"The said document was read. The accused persisted in saying that she could not remember having written anything of the kind."

Hermann put his last question.

"Why, when you had promised to bring up your children in the principles of the Revolution, did you instil errors in them, for example by treating your son with a deference which made it appear that you still thought that one day you would see him succeed the former King, his father?"

"He was too young to be spoken to of that. I set him at the top of the table and myself gave him what he needed."

"Have you nothing more to add in your defence?"

Marie Antoinette rose.

"Yesterday," she declared with surprising cleverness, "I did not know the witnesses. I was ignorant of what they would testify. Well, no one has uttered anything positive against me. I end by remarking that I was only Louis XVI's wife and that I was bound to submit to his will."

The debates were over. The sitting was suspended. It was midnight.

When it was resumed Fouquier turned to the jurors. If the report is to be believed the Prosecutor attacked "the perverse conduct of the former court," rather than the Queen. Only at the end did he declare that he looked on the accused "as the declared enemy of the French nation, as one of the principal instigators of the disturbances in France during the past four years to which thousands of French had fallen victims."

Tronson du Coudray and Chauveau-Lagarde followed him. According to the report "they discharged this duty with as much zeal as eloquence." But Hébert has given us some details in his *Père Duchesne*.

"Is it possible that there should exist a rogue bold enough to defend her! And yet two babblers from the law-courts had that audacity. One of them carried his effrontery so far as to say that the Nation owed her too much to punish her and to assert that without her, without the crimes for which she is blamed, we should not be free! I cannot understand, damn it! how it can be endured that low-class pettifoggers, lured by the spoils of scoundrels, by a gold box, a watch, or diamonds, should betray their conscience and try to pull the wool over the jurors' eyes. I myself saw these two devil's advocates not only dance like cats on hot bricks to prove the slut's innocence, but actually dare to weep for the death of the traitor Capet and say to the judges that it was enough to have punished the fat pig and that at least his trollop of a wife should be pardoned!"

Chauveau-Lagarde pleaded for two hours regarding "the alleged conspiracy with foreign Powers." When he had finished the Queen murmured "in the most touching voice": "How tired you must be, Monsieur Chauveau-Lagarde! I am very sensible of all your trouble."

Fouquier suspended the sitting and called a gendarme. Chauveau-Lagarde was arrested in court. In spite of this warning, Tronson du Coudray pleaded with equal zeal "on the alleged conspiracy, on the enemies of the interior," and he underwent the same fate as his colleague. He was carefully searched, and on him were found two little gold rings and a lock of the Queen's hair, which she had asked her lawyer to give to a "citizen Mary or Maray," living at Ligny with citizen La Borde. This was Mme de Jarjayes.

Meanwhile the debates were resumed and Hermann pronounced an indictment.

"Today a great example is given to the universe and it will doubtless not be lost on the peoples inhabiting it. Nature and reason, so long outraged, are at last satisfied. Equality triumphs.

"A woman who was formerly surrounded with all the brilliant splendour that the pride of Kings and the servility of slaves could invent, now occupies in the Tribunal of the nation the place occupied two days ago by another woman, and this equality assures for her impartial justice. This affair, citizen jurors, is not one of those in which a single deed, a single crime is submitted to your conscience and your intelligence. You have to judge the accused's whole political life since she came to sit beside the last King of the French. But above all you must consider the manoeuvres which she has never for a moment ceased to employ to destroy the budding liberty, either at home, by her intimate connections with base Ministers, treacherous generals and faithless representatives of the people, or abroad, by negotiating that monstrous coalition of European despots which Europe will ridicule for its impotence and by her correspondence with the former émigré French Princes and their worthy agents."

Hermann had been a lawyer too long not to be obsessed by the absence of documents.

"The material proof," he explained, "is in the papers which were seized from Louis Capet and listed in a report made to the National Convention by Gohier, one of its members, in the collection of documents relevant to the indictment of Louis Capet by the Convention, and finally, and above all, citizen jurors, in the political events which you have all witnessed and judged."

In default of these absent documents, which should have proved "the accusation of high treason which lies heavily on Antoinette of Austria, widow of the former King," Hermann and Fouquier had only one resource—to assimilate the Queen's trial with the King's (a trial which in any case was only an elimination) and to affirm that she was "the instigator of most of the crimes of which the last tyrant of France was guilty."

"There is a general observation to be noted," Hermann went on, "which is that the accused agrees that she had the confidence of Louis Capet. It also emerges from the testimony of Valazé that Marie Antoinette was consulted on political matters, since the former King wished her to be consulted about a certain plan, whose object the witness either could not or would not declare."

He quickly tried to take from each witness's evidence one fact to illustrate his main accusation, but there was nothing to prove "intelligence with foreign Powers," or plots against the safety of the State. There was nothing but cockades distributed, empty bottles found under the Queen's bed on 10 August and "desires for vengeance" observed in the accused's expression. He shrank only from Hébert's plot, which he did not dare mention. He also slid prudently over the carnation affair.

"I shall not speak to you, citizen jurors, of the incident in the Conciergerie, the interview with the Chevalier de Saint-Louis, the carnation left in the accused's room and the paper pricked, or rather prepared for a reply. This incident is not more than a prison intrigue which can have no place in an indictment of such great importance."

In the final sentence of the indictment one can again feel the embarrassment of a lawyer confronted by an absence of documents.

"I end by a general reflection, which I have already made to you: it is the French people who accuse Antoinette. All the political events of the last five years testify against her."

The jurors were asked four questions:

(1) Is it established that there were intrigues and secret dealings with foreign Powers and other external enemies of the Republic, which intrigues and secret dealings aimed at giving them monetary assistance, enabling them to enter French territory and facilitating the progress of their armies there?

(2) Is Marie Antoinette d'Autriche, widow of Louis Capet, *convicted* of having co-operated in these intrigues and of having kept up these secret dealings?

(3) Is it established that there was a plot and conspiracy to start civil war within the Republic?

(4) Is Marie Antoinette d'Autriche, widow of Louis Capet, *con-*

victed of having taken part in this plot and conspiracy?

It was three o'clock in the morning.

When the jurors retired the judges remained in the *Grand-Chambre*. The public, who in spite of the cold had remained for the end of the pleadings, went into the waiting-room, which was almost in total darkness, to join the little groups of interested spectators, friends of the Queen, or Jacobins, striding up and down the room to get warm. Here and there in the darkness could be seen a few policemen, listening. Even Ducâtel, one of the murderers of the Princesse de Lamballe, was there, wandering from group to group. Outside there were not, as Hébert was to say, "two or three hundred thousand *sans-culottes* surrounding the Palace, and waiting in silence," but a few hundred sightseers.

Was she guilty? The trial had not proved it. Juridically she was innocent. Taking away the low gossip, the tittle-tattle of kitchens, backstairs, clubs and the Temple council room, what positive facts for the prosecution remained? The description of "orgies" at Versailles by witnesses who had not been there, the accusation—without any documents to support it—regarding the sums given to the Polignacs, the Queen's influence over her husband vouched for by people who had never been intimate with the royal family. Nothing, absolutely nothing, on what Fouquier called treason.

The trial had in no way shown that Marie Antoinette, more of an Austrian Princess than a Queen of France, obeyed orders from her mother and brother transmitted by Mercy. Nothing had been established, neither her culpable frivolity, her blind friendships, her fatal influence, her intrigues with foreign Powers, nor her vacillating policy, her over-tenacious rancour, her double game in 1791 and her "treachery" in 1792. But for everyone these were obvious facts. The way in which the second and fourth questions were worded, however, would have enabled the jurors to answer "no." Although guilty, the accused was not *convicted* of being so.

Such was the unanimous opinion. Mme Bault had just heard someone exclaim: "Marie Antoinette will get away with it. She gave her answers like an angel. They will only deport her."

This optimism was not blindness. It was still only the beginning of the Terror. The law on "suspects" was only a month old. The machine of death, prepared by Fouquier, started work with the Queen's trial.

In a room adjoining the *Grand-Chambre* Marie Antoinette waited in company with Lieutenant de Busne. The Queen, too, was full of hope. As she had said, no one had uttered anything positive against her. Her throat was dry from anxiety and she asked for something to drink. De Busne brought her a glass of water.

At four o'clock the Queen heard the President's bell in the distance. The minutes went slowly by. She could distinguish the voice of Hermann, who was exhorting the crowd "to the greatest possible calm" and reminding them "that the law forbade them any sign of approbation and that a person once overtaken by the law, with whatever crimes she might be covered, belonged only to unhappiness and humanity."

An usher came to fetch the accused. She was greeted by a menacing silence as she took her place on the platform. Chauveau-Lagarde and Tronson du Coudray, escorted by gendarmes, were also brought back into the hall. Hermann addressed the Queen with familiarity.

"Antoinette, here is the jury's declaration."

In dying Antonia was to return to her childhood's name.

As in a dream she heard: "Yes, to all the questions." Then Fouquier was heard, demanding "that the accused be condemned to death, in accordance with Article One of the first section of the first chapter of the second part of the penal code, which reads: 'All intrigue, all intelligence with the enemies of France tending either to facilitate their entry into the territories of the French Empire, or to deliver up to them towns, fortresses, ports, vessels, magazines or arsenals belonging to France, or to furnish them aid in soldiers, money, food or munitions, or to favour in any manner whatever the progress of their armies on French territory, or against our forces by land or sea, or to undermine the loyalty of officers, soldiers and other citizens towards the French Nation, shall be punished by death.'"

By death! Those must have been the only words she grasped from the text. These two syllables held the beginning and end of its pathos. But the dry, cutting voice continued: "And again, in Article Eleven of the first section of the first chapter of the second part of the same code it reads: 'All conspiracy and plots tending to disturb the State by civil war, by arming citizens one against the other or aimed against the exercise of the legitimate authority, shall be punished by death.'"

"Antoinette," resumed the President, "have you any objection to make to the application of the laws invoked by the Public Prosecutor?"

She had no strength to reply and merely shook her head.

Hermann then turned to the two defenders surrounded by their guards and put the same question.

"Citizen President," replied Tronson du Coudray, speaking as a lawyer attentive to formalities, "the jury's declaration being definite and the law in this respect clear, I announce that my services to the widow Capet are ended."

Hermann turned towards Douzé-Verteuil and Lane. The plumed heads bowed. For the last time Hermann spoke.

"The Tribunal, according to the unanimous declaration of the jury, which complied with the indictment of the Public Prosecutor, and according to the laws quoted by him, condemns the said Marie Antoinette, called Lorraine d'Autriche, widow of Louis Capet, to the pain of death; declares, in accordance with the law of 10 March last, that her possessions, if she has any within the territory of France, are acquired and confiscated for the benefit of the Republic and orders that, at the request of the Public Prosecutor, the present judgement shall be executed in the Place de la Révolution and printed and displayed throughout the Republic."

Overcome, she left the platform like an automaton. Without a gesture, her head down, "seeing and hearing nothing," according to Chauveau-Lagarde, she crossed the hall. When she arrived at the railings, where even the *tricoteuses* had fallen silent, she raised her head and left the hall. De Busne escorted her bareheaded. On arriving at the darkened Bonbec staircase which led to the courtyard, she murmured: "I can hardly see to walk."

The officer gave her his arm to the foot of the stairs. A few steps farther on she nearly slipped and de Busne helped her down the three steps leading to the courtyard. It was cold, barely 35 degrees, but the sky was clear. With their faces pressed against the bars of their cells the prisoners watched, in the feeble light of the yard lamp, the Queen of France go by with her hand on the arm of her last bodyguard.

Meanwhile the *Grand-Chambre* was slowly emptying.

It was an assembly of dying men who went their ways. Of the Prosecutor, the President and the six judges, only Douzé-Verteuil, Deliège and Maire would escape the guillotine, but the last-named was to slip one day on his hearth and perish with his head burned.

Chauveau-Lagarde survived, but Tronson du Coudray, a proscript of Fructidor, was deported and disappeared in Guiana.

Fourteen of the witnesses were to climb Sanson's ladder,[1] and three to perish by a violent death. Mme Richard was stabbed by a prisoner, the gendarme Gilbert blew his brains out for having embezzled his company's money, and the Girondin Valazé, hearing he was condemned to death, stabbed himself twelve days later in the same *Grand-Chambre*, and his body was carried to the foot of the scaffold.

Of the twelve jurors there were to escape only three, who when the trouble was over went to ground. Renaudin, Nicolas, Châtelet, Besnard and Deboisseaux mounted the scaffold. Trinchard, Antonelle, Jourdeuil and Chrétien were deported to Cayenne or "to the islands."

But during this night of 15-16 October they thought only of eating the lavish repast Fouquier had ordered to be prepared for them. They were convinced of having done their duty, as can be seen from the carpenter Trinchard, who proudly wrote the following note to his brother: "Je t'aprans, mon frerre, que jé été un des jurés qui ont jugé la bête féroche qui a dévoré un grande partie de la République, celle que lon califiait cideven de Raine." (I inform you, my brother, that I was one of the jurors who judged the mad beast who devoured a large part of the Republic, she who was formerly called Queen).

---

[1] Bailly, Manuel, Simon, Hébert, Jobert, Lebœuf, Michonis, Lecointre, Vincent, Dangé, Lebrasse, Estaing and the two La Tour du Pin.

21

✤

The Knife

"There is something worse than regicide there."

Napoleon.

SHE HAD BEEN able to obtain two candles, a sheet of paper, a pen and ink. While de Busne dozed in the corner of the cell, she sat down at her little white-wood table, and this woman who had lived through two days and one night of trial, this woman weakened by hæmorrhages, who had undergone a final session lasting more than twenty hours, was to write, while waiting for her executioner, the admirable letter which should be read yet once again.

"It is to you, my sister, that I write for the last time. I have just been condemned, not to a shameful death, for it is shameful only for criminals, but to rejoin your brother. Like him innocent, I hope to display the same firmness as he did in his last moments. I am calm, as one is when one's conscience holds no reproach. I regret deeply having to abandon my poor children. You know that I lived only for them and for you, my good and kind sister. In what a situation do I leave you, who from your affection sacrificed everything to be with us. I learned from the pleadings at the trial that my daughter was separated from you.[1] Alas! poor child, I dare not write to her, she would not receive it. I do not know even if this will reach you. Receive my blessing on them both. I hope that one day, when they are older, they will be able to join you again and profit to the full from your tender care

[1] Madame Elisabeth and Madame Royale were questioned *separately* in the apartment occupied by the Simons and the little King. Hence the Queen's misapprehension on hearing the report of the interrogations.

and that they both remember what I have always tried to instil in them: that the principles and the execution of their duty should be the chief foundation of their life, that their affection and mutual trust will make it happy. Let my daughter remember that in view of her age she should always help her brother with the advice that her greater experience and her affection may suggest, and let them both remember that in whatever situation they may find themselves they will never be truly happy unless united. Let them learn from our example how much consolation our affection brought us in the midst of our unhappiness and how happiness is doubled when one can share it with a friend—and where can one find a more loving and truer friend than in one's own family? Let my son never forget his father's last words, which I distinctly repeat to him, never to try to avenge our death. I have to mention something which pains my heart. I know how much distress this child must have given you. Forgive him, my dear sister, remember his age and how easy it is to make a child say anything you want, even something he does not understand. The day will come, I hope, when he will be all the more conscious of the worth of your goodness and tenderness towards them both. I now have only to confide in you my last thoughts. I would have liked to write them at the beginning of the trial, but apart from the fact that I was not allowed to write, everything went so quickly that I really would not have had the time.

"I die in the Catholic, Apostolic and Roman religion, in the religion of my father, in which I was brought up and which I have always professed, having no expectation of spiritual consolation, and not even knowing if there still exist any priests of that religion here, and in any case the place where I am would expose them to too much danger if they should enter. I sincerely beg pardon of God for all the faults I have committed during my life. I hope that in His goodness He will receive my last wishes, and those I have long since made, that He may receive my soul in His mercy and goodness. I ask pardon of all those I know, and of you my sister in particular, for all the distress I may, without wishing it, have caused them. I forgive all my enemies the harm they have done me. I say farewell here to my aunts and to all my brothers and sisters. I had friends. The idea of being separated for ever from them and their troubles forms one of my greatest regrets in dying. Let them know, at least, that up to my last moment I was thinking of them.

"Farewell, my good and loving sister. May this letter reach you! Think of me always. I embrace you with all my heart, together with those poor, dear children. My God! what agony it is to leave them for ever! Farewell! Farewell! I shall henceforth pay attention to nothing but my spiritual duties. As I am not free, they will perhaps bring me a [conformist] priest, but I protest here that I shall not say a word to him and that I shall treat him as a complete stranger."

At five o'clock the call to arms was sounded in Paris and cannons were placed "in strategic positions." At seven o'clock all the troops were mustered and patrols were scouring the streets. Day was just breaking when Rosalie entered the condemned woman's cell. The two candles had burned out.

A young officer of the gendarmes was standing in the left-hand corner of the room. It was no longer de Busne. He had just been arrested, on the denunciation of one of his men, who had seen him give the Queen a glass of water and walk back with her bareheaded.

Marie Antoinette had not undressed. Still wearing her black dress, she was stretched out on her bed. She wept quietly, facing the window, with her head resting on her hand.

"Madame," said Rosalie in a trembling voice, "you ate nothing yesterday evening and hardly anything all day. What would you like this morning?"

"My child, I need nothing. Everything is over for me."

Rosalie insisted. "Madame, I have been keeping some soup on my stove . . ."

Rosalie was weeping, too, and began to leave. The Queen called her back, fearing to have distressed her, and between two sobs whispered: "Well, Rosalie, bring me your soup."

She sat up, but could eat only a few spoonfuls.

"Come back at eight to help me dress."

She remained lying down for an hour, letting her mind wander among her memories. A pale light filtered through the barred windows. She watched her last day dawn. It was the feast of the Ox, which had replaced that of St. Gal, Priest.

Gradually the condemned woman pulled herself together, and when Rosalie returned trembling to the cell Marie Antoinette asked her to help in changing her chemise for the last time. She had lost much blood

since the previous day. The unhappy woman laid her clean chemise
out on the bed, slipped into the little passage between the camp bed
and the wall and let fall her black dress. At a gesture from the Queen
the young servant came and stood in front of her, but the officer of the
gendarmerie came forward, leaned over the bolster and watched.

"In the name of decency, Monsieur, allow me to change my linen
without witnesses."

"I could not permit it," the man replied shortly. "My orders are that
I must keep an eye on all your movements."

The Queen sighed, and "with all the precautions and modesty possible" took off her stained chemise. Over the clean one she put on the
white négligée she usually wore in the morning. She then took a large
muslin fichu, which she folded high under her chin, and put on a white
bonnet without a mourning veil. Rosalie then saw her "carefully roll
up her pitiful bloodstained chemise, tuck it in one of its own sleeves,
as in a sheath," and then "look anxiously around her as though seeking
some object she feared not to find." Suddenly, with "an expression of
ineffable satisfaction," she slipped the soiled linen into a hole she had
just noticed in the wall behind a torn part of the hangings.

Without daring to say goodbye, Rosalie left her and the dreadful
waiting began. In her thin white piqué négligée Marie Antoinette was
trembling with cold. The Abbé Girard, a conforming priest sent by the
Tribunal, advised her to put her pillow over her knees. He then offered
her "the services of his ministry." She refused.

"But Madame, what will be said when it is known that you refused
the help of religion in these final moments?"

"You will tell those who speak of it to you that God's mercy provided
for it."[1]

The priest asked timidly: "May I accompany you, Madame?"

"If you wish."

A few moments later she asked the gendarme: "Do you think the
people will let me go to the scaffold without tearing me in pieces?"

Larivière entered the cell and Marie Antoinette said to him in a small
voice: "Larivière, you know they are going to put me to death?"

At the same hour conspirators were going towards the Rue Saint-
Honoré, along which the condemned woman was to pass. As they went

[1] For the "Queen's communion," see the chapter "Sources," pp. 418-420.

to their posts they were full of hope. They would shortly number 500—1,500 even, some thought—and they would rush at the cart.

Who were these last defenders of Marie Antoinette, who were to lose their lives in trying to save that of the Queen? Former bodyguards? Former officers of the Queen's Household? Former friends from the Trianon, who would once have died to kiss their sovereign's rosy finger-tips?

No. At the head of the conspiracy was a former working-woman, who had lost her sight making lace—a hunchback from Auvergne, called Catherine Urgon, wife of Fournier. Her staff was composed of her son, a fourteen-year-old boot-black, and two barbers: Guillaume Lemille and Jean-Baptiste Basset. The latter, who was eighteen-and-a-half years old, had managed by himself to win over 460 men. Their headquarters were in a wine-shop in the Rue de la Vannerie, at the sign of *La Cave des Charbonniers.* The principal lieutenants were two locksmiths, three pastrycooks, two wine-sellers, two grocers, two butchers, two conveyors, two masons, a knife-grinder, a house painter, a gardener, a second-hand dealer, a lemonade-seller and four barbers. All lived in the *Section des Incorruptibles,* otherwise called the *Section des Arcis,* which lay to the north of the Place de Grève, a stone's throw from the Conciergerie. Their rallying-sign was a little round card bearing a heart in its centre, with all round the words "Long live Louis XVII, King of France."

Their main "forces" had been recruited from among the Volunteers barracked at Vanves and Courbevoie. There was talk of 1,500 men, and the blind, hunchbacked lace-maker knew how to speak to them.

"We do not want men who talk! We need brave men, people who can strike! They must all be Charlotte Cordays!"

At the beginning of the month they had wanted to storm the Conciergerie.

"We must act at once," cried one of the barbers. "Otherwise this unhappy woman will perish!"

Their arms consisted of 1,500 pistols. Their plan was ingenious, and came from young Basset. In the daytime they would light all the street lamps in the quarter so that, for lack of oil, they would go out during the night. Under cover of the darkness there would then have been a mass attack on the Conciergerie.

But six police spies got wind of the plan. Posing as ardent royalists, they managed to gain the barbers' confidence and have the attack on the prison postponed and held back for so long that the trial had already begun.

The hunchback then exhibited "a terrible despair." "There is not a moment to be lost in saving the poor Queen. It is absolutely essential that orders should be given to rally and kidnap the condemned woman on the way."

And the order was given to the conspirators to go to the Rue Saint-Honoré.

At the same time Hermann entered the cell with the judges Foucauld and Douzé-Verteuil. Fabricius followed them, holding a large sheet of paper. The condemned woman, who was kneeling by her bed, praying, rose.

"Pay attention," declared Hermann. "Your sentence will be read to you."

Contrary to custom the four men dressed in black took off their hats. They seemed "struck" by the majestic air of the condemned woman, who raised her voice to declare: "It is useless to read it; I know the sentence only too well."

"No matter," declared one of the judges. "It must be read to you a second time."

And the words as sharp as knives sounded in the low vaulted cell: ".... complied with . . . condemned . . . declares . . . orders . . . executed . . ."

The clerk had just uttered the word "Republic," which ended the decree, when, followed by Nappier, the usher to the Tribunal, a young man entered—the executioner.

He was Henri Sanson, son of the executioner who had guillotined Louis XVI and who since 21 January no longer exercised his duties. He came forward, seeming to fill the cell with his "enormous size."

"Hold out your hands."

The Queen recoiled two steps and asked in a frightened voice: "Are my hands to be bound?"

The executioner bowed his head. She exclaimed: "Louis XVI's hands were not bound!"

Sanson turned towards Hermann, who ordered: "Do your duty."

"Oh, my God!" cried the condemned woman, "all bewildered."

"At these words," Larivière recounted, "Henri brutally seized the poor Queen's hands and bound them too tightly behind her back. I saw that the Princess sighed, raising her eyes to heaven, but she held back her tears, which were ready to flow."

Then Sanson, who towered over Marie Antoinette, suddenly took off the bonnet she had arranged so carefully a short while before, and with a large pair of scissors cut off the wonderful hair which had gone white, but in which ash-blonde lights could still be seen.

The Queen thought she was to be executed there with an axe and she turned round, her eyes terrified. She saw the executioner putting in his pocket the hair, which was shortly to be burned. With his large hands he replaced the bonnet on the top of the Queen's head. Irregularly cut locks surrounded the freed nape.

It was nearly eleven o'clock.

The bystanders moved away from the door. In silence Marie Antoinette left the cell, followed by the executioner holding the ends of the rope, which pulled at her elbows. Walking between a double row of gendarmes, she reached the office and suddenly her eyes filled with horror. Beyond the rails of the little courtyard, beyond the two doors which had just been opened, she had caught sight of the ignominious cart. Louis XVI had gone to death in a coach. She would have to mount that garbage cart! A weakness seized her. She asked them to undo her hands and there, on the ground, in a corner of the office which was called the Mousetrap, she squatted down, then went and held out her hands again to Sanson.

The picture of the Archduchess, the features of that "charming and dangerous favourite of an old monarchy" become blurred and are effaced. Everything disappears—and should disappear—leaving to posterity only the picture of a woman in a white dress, walking to the guillotine like a true Queen of France.

The temperature was a little warmer—45 degrees at eleven o'clock. The weather was fine; a light mist, that indefinable Paris mist, blurred the horizon. In the Cour de Mai gendarmes on foot and on horseback, together with pikemen, surrounded the muddy cart. Here, in the happy years, the lawyers' clerks planted a beribboned may-tree each spring, a fine oak which the clerks went "in full battle array" to find in the forest of Bondy.

In the Rue de la Barillerie the crowd huddled in silence behind the beautiful gilt railings.

The white figure, which seemed to be held in leash by the executioner, appeared under the arcade, took a few steps and stopped by the cart. A small ladder of four or five steps had been placed there. The executioner showed the Queen where to put her foot and supported her with his hand while, holding her head high, she mounted the tail-board. It was noticed that she wore a black petticoat under her white dress. A narrow, uneven plank was fixed more or less securely to the sides, cutting the cart in two. She was about to step over it and sit down facing the two cart-horses, who were harnessed in tandem to the shafts. But the executioner and his assistant stopped her; she was to sit facing backwards.

The Abbé Girard climbed the ladder in his turn and sat down on the right of the condemned woman. Behind them, leaning on the rails, stood the executioner, holding the rope in one hand and his three-cornered hat in the other. His assistant, also bare-headed, was at the back.

It was a quarter-past eleven.

The cart set off noisily. The actor Grammont, on horseback and carrying a sword, preceded it; the gendarmes surrounded it; the pike-men followed.

The great gateway opened. The crowd was silent. Without a murmur or an insult they watched the passing of the woman whom they had acclaimed twenty years before. Marie Antoinette appeared unmoved and seemed to see nothing with her motionless, bloodshot eyes. As they crossed the bridge did she look at the towers of the Conciergerie, her last palace? Fouquier had no doubt left his files to watch the procession from his window.

Thirty thousand troops were lined along the route. At the entrance to the Rue Saint-Honoré the cries of hate could be heard. For a moment the cart stopped. Marie Antoinette looked round her. A smiling child, lifted up by its mother, blew her a kiss. The blood rushed into her cheeks and her eyes filled with tears.

At that moment the little King was laughing in the Temple with his municipal officers, while in the crypt of Saint-Denis the coffin of the first Dauphin, who had died at Meudon four years before, was being opened by order of the Convention and the body thrown into the common burying-ground.

The cart started with a jerk, amid cries. The Queen nearly lost her balance. A mocking voice shouted: "Ah! those aren't your cushions from Trianon!"

Cries of "Make way for the Austrian!" and "Long live the Republic!" broke out, but Marie Antoinette did not seem to hear. Her eyes rested unmoved on the narrow fronts of the houses, where tricolour flags and revolutionary signs waved gently.

The cart passed by the arcade over the passage leading to the Jacobins. A board carried the inscription—"Workshop of Republican arms to strike down the tyrants." She appeared not to have been able to read it, and for the first time turned to the priest and questioned him. The Abbé, who from the beginning had kept his eyes fixed on a small ivory crucifix, was about to reply, when suddenly Grammont "raised his sword, brandished it in all directions" and rising in his stirrups yelled: "Here she is, the wicked Antoinette! She is done for, my friends!"

He was answered by shouts. On the steps of the church of Saint Roch the *tricoteuses*, wearing red bonnets and carrying pikes, yelled.

The Rue Saint-Honoré seemed endless. And yet she knew it well. How many evenings had she gone down it in her carriage drawn by eight white horses! As she passed, the cannon in the Invalides fired a salvo and then, in the distance, that of the Bastille answered. Paris mobilised its guards and its cavalry of the watch to guard its sovereign. Paris placed twelve cannons in the Place Louis-XV which fired when twenty of the King's bodyguard galloped past surrounding the gold and silver carriage in which a young woman in evening dress and an extravagant headdress, almost lost in her glittering skirts, laughed so attractively.

The young Queen of twenty, the young Queen of the most beautiful kingdom in the world was going to the Opera.

On this October morning she was going to the scaffold.

The crowd became even thicker. Not far from Robespierre's house, and in front of the house numbered 404, a mother, hearing the procession approach, said to her daughter: "Above all, don't cry when you see her. You will have us guillotined."

The cart passed. "It bumped on the cobbles and could be heard to crack as though it would break." A woman's cry lashed the Queen.

"Death to the Austrian!"

She looked with an "expression of contempt," which faded at once. She had recognised a former waiting-woman from the château. Did she also perceive, at the corner of the street, a group of "honest folk," simply dressed? They were the defeated barbers. They numbered barely eighty: about thirty small shop-keepers and workmen from the Arcis quarter and 52 volunteers from Vanves. The spies had acted. The police had done their work and "infiltrated" the movement. In vain did the little boot-black cry out in despair: "We must go to the big merchants, who want nothing better than to snatch her from the executioners!"

The wig-makers realised that everything was over.

The cart had gone by.

They remained there, deserted, haggard, waiting for the police to pick them up.[1]

Noon struck.

Since eight in the morning the Place de la Révolution had been filling up. It was now black with people.

When the cart was seen coming from the former Rue Royale, the applause broke out and cries of "Long live the Republic!" were heard. "The aristocrats are easily recognized," wrote a police-agent, "by their closed lips and embarrassed faces."

It was a few minutes past noon.

The cart rattled over the uneven ground of the square. The Queen was still impassive. "The slut was audacious and insolent to the end," Hébert was to remark. She turned her head, saw the Tuileries on her right, changed colour and "became much paler." With a few more turns of the wheels the cart arrived at the place of execution. The cries and applause grew louder and hats flew in the air. The Queen was still looking to her right. Through the great alley she could now see the façade of the château. Twenty years ago, on the evening of her joyful entry, the crowd packed in the Place Louis-XV applauded just as today, and the men threw their hats in the air, when Marie Antoinette and her husband appeared on the terrace. "Tears of affection mingled with the cries of joy each time that M. le Dauphin and Mme la Dauphine had the goodness to give the citizens signs of their satisfaction."

"You have two thousand adorers there, Madame!"

The cart stopped.

Rapidly and without accepting any help, Marie Antoinette got down, turned round and saw the two raised arms holding the heavy triangle of steel. She hurried, climbed the steep ladder with such pre-

[1] The epilogue to the "Barbers' Conspiracy" was played out before the Tribunal. See the chapter, "Sources," p. 422.

cipitation, "in bravado" one witness wrote, that she lost one of her little purple shoes *à la Saint Huberty*. On reaching the platform she trod on the executioner's foot.

"Monsieur, I ask your pardon. I did not do it on purpose."

These were her last words.

Marie Antoinette looked at the vast square around her. The assistants came forward. With a movement she let fall the bonnet from her head. She shut her eyes and felt that she was being dragged to the upright plank. She was tied on. It took long—horribly long. Finally the plank tipped over and she felt the heavy wooden collar fixed round her bared neck.

A click.

It was a quarter-past twelve.

Between the moment she appeared on the platform and the moment the crowd heard the dull noise four minutes had passed. One of the assistants picked up the head dripping with blood, held it up by the white hair and, to applause, carried it round the scaffold.

Suddenly the gendarmes in the front rank were seen to rush forward and arrest a man who had come out from beneath the scaffold. His shoes were covered with blood, he held a white handkerchief in his hand which was also bloodstained and between his teeth was a carnation.[1]

While he was being taken to the Tuileries section the crowd parted to make way for the cart streaming with blood. Its path could be traced to the Madeleine cemetery. There the executioners noticed that no coffin or grave had been prepared.

Anxious to get their dinners, they threw the body on the grass, the head between the legs.

The mist had quite cleared away, but the wind rose and from the north there came heavy clouds which gradually covered the whole sky.[2]

[1] For further details on this strange affair see "Sources," pp. 421-422.
[2] Archives of the Observatory (National Meteorological Office).

Sources

Would one, on the eve of the Revolution, have found a thousand French people bearing the same sentiments towards Marie Antoinette as we do today? The Queen was then frankly detested. Her martyrdom did not disarm the hate which some people continued to feel for her. To realise this one need only go through the vast files preserved in the National Archives and containing letters and petitions congratulating the Convention and the Revolutionary Tribunal for having rid the world of that "tigress thirsting for blood," that "poisonous viper," that "cannibal woman," "the implacable harridan who for too long profaned the holy land of liberty with her pestilential breath."

In order to make the reasons for this execration understood I wanted to avoid as much as possible following the example of most of my predecessors, who divided the first part of their character's life into a series of subjects (the favourites, the marital drama, Marie Antoinette and her mother, the feasts, the friends, the expenses, etc.). It seemed to me that this procedure did not lead to the presentation of an accurate picture of Marie Antoinette. I preferred to bring the Queen to life by following the chronological order. But in trying to carry out such a plan it was necessary to go back to the sources.

I do not know if I have succeeded with this scheme, but at least it enabled me—in dealing with the Queen's life as well as with that of the "widow Capet"—to lay my hands on numerous documents which have hitherto gone unnoticed and to use these forgotten texts of which one might say that "they were as good as unpublished."

I

VIENNA

I was able to reconstruct this part of Marie Antoinette's life with the help of documents which have never yet been used and which are preserved in the *Minoritenplatz* of Vienna (*Haus-Hof und Staatsarchiv*). Unlike those of the Rue des Francs-Bourgeois these series have not been given a serial number but a title.

Zeremonialakten, Sonderreihe. Bd. 52 (Feast given at the Belvedere Palace on 17 April 1770 and feast given by Durfort at the Liechtenstein

411

Palace on 28 April 1770; *Hausarchiv. Familienakten Kart.* 50 (Documents concerning the marriage by proxy and the various ceremonies). Little Antonia's history exercise is filed in Box 55 of the *Familienakten* series.

All the correspondence of Mercy, Durfort, Kaunitz, Choiseul is pre-served in the archives of the Ministry of Foreign Affairs. I gleaned unpub-lished details in the collections *France 426, Vienne 285, 307, 308, 310, 311, 312*; and in the *Haus-Hof und Staatsarchiv,* dossier *St. K. Frankreich, Berichte (Fasz. 207, 208, 209, 210).*

Among printed sources the most important are the remarkable study by Maurice Boutry (*Le mariage de Marie-Antoinette*), the Comtesse d'Ar-maillé's book (*Marie-Thérèse et Marie-Antoinette*) and above all *La Correspondance secrète* between Mercy-Argenteau and Maria Theresa, Kaunitz and Joseph II, full collections published by Arneth, Flammermont and Geffroy, which form the basis of any study of Marie Antoinette. I mention these works here, but, as can be seen, I have obviously made use of them all through my work.

II

FROM VIENNA TO PARIS
and
THE MARRIAGE AT VERSAILLES

I have made use of numerous unpublished details from:

(1) Vienna Archives: *Familienakten Kart.* 50 (Formation of the proces-sion, suite, journey to Günzburg and *Remise*). *St. K. Provinzen, Vorder Osterreich, Fasz.* 10 (The journey, the procession, the stages, etc.).

(2) National Archives: 01.3254 (*Remise*, Strasbourg, marriage feasts), K.1715 (Route and marriage feasts), 01.3791, 01.3793, 01.3797, 01.3252, 01.3253, 01.3254 (Household of Madame la Dauphine), K.506 (Eti-quette, ceremonial), 01.1783 (Opera), K.1015 (Evening of 30 May 1770. Report on the accident).

(3) Foreign Affairs: *France 426, France 429, Vienne 285.*

(4) Manuscripts: *Nouvelles à la main* of the House of Penthièvre (Bibl. Mazarine), *Manuscrit de Hardy* (B.N.), *Registre de l'Intendant des Menus* (Mazarine), *Mémoire sinédits* by the Comte de Caraman (in the possession of Mme la Comtesse du Bouchage).

(5) Printed sources: *Mercure de France* (May, June, July and August 1770), *La Gazette* (same months), *Mémoires* by Weber, Goethe, Mme d'Oberkirch, Mme de Boigne, Mme Campan, Croy, etc. *Mémoires secrets, Correspondance* of Mme du Deffand, Mouffle d'Angerville (*Vie privée de Louis XV*) and: works by Pierre de Nolhac (*Marie-Antoinette, dauphine*),

Maurice Boutry (op. cit.), Funck-Brentano (*L'Affaire du collier*, 1st chapter), Lenotre (*Versailles*), L. Dussieux (*Le château de Versailles*), etc.

III

THE DAUPHINE

National Archives: Dossiers cited above and: K.1014, K.1016 (Ceremonial and etiquette), 01.3792, 01.3785, 01.3786, 01.3797 (The Dauphine's household), 01.1044, 01.903 (Death of Louis XV).

Private archives: *Mémoires* of the Comte de Caraman.

Printed sources: To the collections of Mercy's correspondence one must add, once for all, the *Correspondence* of Marie Antoinette edited by La Rocheterie and Beaucourt which is the only one which can be used without misgiving. The letters edited by Feuillet de Conches and by Hunolstein are, indeed, nearly all apocryphal.

Apart from the works already mentioned I used the *Mémoires* of Besenval, *La dernière maladie de Louis XV* by the Duc de Liancourt (published by Paul Cottin in the *Revue Rétrospective*), *Marie-Antoinette et l'art de son temps,* thesis by Jeanne-Armand Bouteloup, *Histoire de la Musique* by Jean Combarieu, *Gluck et Piccini* by Desnoiresterres, *Ch. von Gluck* by A Schmidt, *Histoire de Marie-Antoinette* by La Rocheterie, *Secret du Roi,* by the Duc de Broglie, *Madame du Barry* by Alfred Leroy, *Louis XV* by Pierre Lafue, etc.

IV

THE QUEEN

National Archives: 01.1044 and 01.903 (Accession of Louis XVI), K.1016 and K.1017 (Mourning ceremonial), K.1714, K.161, 01.3250 (Coronation of Louis XVI), K.505 (Accounts, expenses, voyage to Fontainebleau), 01.3791 (Mme de Lamballe, library, wardrobe, economies), 01.3194 (Candles), 01.3792 (Looting by Comte Jules de Polignac, the Queen's wardrobe), 01.3795, 01.3796, 01.3797 (Queen's Household), 01.3793 (Expenses), K.3796 (Saint Cloud), K.159 to K.164 (The King's papers), 01.1883, 01.1072, 01.1885 (Trianon), 01.3193 (*Menus Plaisirs* of Trianon), K.161 (Letter about Joseph II), K. 506 (Visit of Comte de Haga, Comte du Nord and Joseph II; etiquette, life at court), 01.1031, 01.1032 (Equipages), 01.903 (Carriages), 01.3798, 01.3799 (Household of the Children of France), 01.3469 and 01.3470 (Inventory of the château), etc. In the *Armoire de fer* of the Archives is the register containing the samples of Marie Antoinette's dresses. This folder bears the title: *Garde-robe des atours de la Reine. Gazette pour l'année* 1782.

In an important series of dossiers (K.1015 to K.1019) I discovered numerous unpublished details concerning the births of the Children of France, Marie Antoinette's lyings-in, the Dauphin's illness, the presents offered to him, his funeral, the mourning, the Queen's visits to Paris, her journey in a *hyac*, her evenings at the Opera, the feasts given in her honour, the gigantic fish brought to Versailles and, in general, the relations between the "Gentlemen" of the city and the royal family. These dossiers are supplemented by unpublished information coming from the King's Household or the Queen's: 01.3791 (entry into Paris), 01.3260 and K.161 (Births of the Children of France), K.903 (Illness and burial of the Dauphin).

Memoirs, Souvenirs, Diary: Works already mentioned, and: Tilly (edited by Christian Melchior-Bonnet), d'Hézèques, Ligne, Lauzun, Vigée-Lebrun, Saint-Priest (edited by Marcel Thiébaut), Levis, Augeard, Tourzel, La Marck, Papillon de La Ferté, Diane de Polignac, Luynes, Maurepas, Belleval, Richelieu, Liedekerque-Beaufort (published by the *Revue de Paris*, May 1952), Mme Eloff, Hanet-Cléry, Abbé de Veri (edited by Pierre de Nolhac), Talleyrand, Esterhazy, Stael-Holstein, Genlis, Volude, Lage, Frenilly, Aiguillon (Minister), *Mémoires* by Souslavie, Collé, Bachaumont, historical and anecdotal *Mémoires, Correspondance secrète*, correspondence of Métra, Grimm, Walpole, etc.

Several pages would be needed to give a complete bibliography of Marie Antoinette. We will merely mention the studies of P. de Nolhac (*La reine Marie-Antoinette, La Trianon de Marie-Antoinette, Autour de la Reine*), by M. Mauricheau-Beaupré (*Versailles*), Alméras (*Les Amoureux de la Reine*), by Stefan Zweig (*Marie-Antoinette*) and the works of Fleichmann, Maugras, Küntzler, Lescure, Serieys, Ségur, Viel-Castel, Otto Friedrich, Hilaire Belloc, Maurice de La Fuye, Jullien Kageneck, Paul Gruyer, Lenotre, Leroy, La Rocheterie, Baumann, Ed. Pilon, Robiquet, Renard, Geffroy, La Faye, etc., and the various books of the Goncourts.

V

FERSEN

The first place goes to Mme Alma Söderjhelm's book (*Fersen et Marie Antoinette*), written according to the private diary and correspondence of Axel preserved in the Archives of Stafsund, Sweden. Axel's letters to Sophie are at the castle of Lösta.

I have also consulted with profit *Le Comte de Fersen* by R. M. de Klinckowström, which is very incomplete, and the interesting books by Henry Valloton, *Marie Antoinette et Fersen*, Charles Kunstler, *Fersen et son secret*,

Paul Gaulot, *Un ami de la Reine*, P. de Witt, *Le comte de Fersen et la cour de France*, etc. The article by G. Laguerre on the *Mémoires* of Mme Campan appeared in the *Intermédiaire des Chercheurs et des Curieux* of 20 March 1906.

VI

THE AFFAIR OF THE NECKLACE

National Archives: K.162, K.163.

The accused and the lawyers published a mass of *Mémoires, Réponses, Précis* and *Exposés*. There is thus plenty to choose from when reconstructing the "affair." First place, however, must be given to the works of Campardon, remarkably well documented, and of Funck-Brentano. One may also mention the studies by Combes (very biased), G. Chaix d'Est-Ange and the *Mémoires* of Beugnot. Funck-Brentano has also published the *Rapport officiel* by the lieutenant of police at Crosne.

VII

THE REVOLUTION

National Archives: K.1719 (States General), K.506 (Plate sent to the Mint), K.164 (5 and 6 October), K.505 (Tuileries, Kitchens, wardrobe, installation), D. XXIX bis 31 to D. XXIX bis 38, F7.4385, F7.6762, M.664, AD.101, C.71, A.194, W.290 and W.33 (Varennes).

I also discovered in the Archives many unknown details concerning 20 June and 10 August.

In M.664 is the dossier No. 21, filed by error in a box containing documents concerning the King's flight. This unpublished and very important dossier provides us with many details on "the siege, invasion and sacking" of the château. I have also used documents from: ADI.101 (Eve of 20 June), ADI.102 (20 June), F7.4774,70 (Very important box containing the papers seized from Pétion), C.185 (Roederer's letters). To be noted also are: F7.3688, W.15, F7.4390, W.319.

In C.222 (Papers seized at the Tuileries) are many unpublished details, particularly the report Rougeville sent to the Queen and which was taken from the table of Mme Thiébault, the Queen's waiting-woman. It is quite certain that Rougeville would not have allowed himself to invent anything in a document intended to be read by Marie Antoinette. He therefore did play an important part on 20 June, whatever may have been said.

To reconstruct the period between these two dates, consult: C.222 (Papers found in Mme de Tourzel's possession), C.185 (Durathon's departure),

ADI.101 and F7.4387 (Defence measures, reports of eye witnesses, denunciations, "counter-revolution," etc.).

10 August. The short narrative by the Abbé Gallois, written during the night of 9 to 10 August, is also in C.222. Pétion's papers (F7.4774,70) give further important information. For lack of space I was not able to use the whole mass of unpublished documents in W.19, C.161, F7.4408, C.162, F7.4666, M.667, C.184, F7.4426, C.159, but I draw them to the attention of research workers.

Memoirs, Souvenirs and Correspondence: in addition to the works already cited: Roederer, Dumont, Mathieu, Dumas, Lafayette, Paroy, Gouverneur Morris, Mme de La Tour du Pin, Mercier, Mounier, Mme de Béarn, de Staël, La Rochefoucauld, Cubières, Rivarol, Mallet du Pan, Chastenay, Lindet, Mirabeau-Lamarck, *Journal d'un Garde Suisse,* published by A. Augustin-Thierry (*Revue des Deux-Mondes,* 1-VIII-1928), etc.

Printed works: For 5 and 6 October we possess a considerable number of depositions by eye witnesses published in the two volumes of *Procédure criminelle instruite au Châtelet de Paris.* Also on the same subject, the remarkable study by Dom. Leclercq, *Les journées d'octobre,* a work which is as full as one could wish. It is impossible to mention everything on the Revolution, but I should note: *La Révolution française,* by Pierre Gaxotte; *La Révolution française,* by Octave Aubry; *Crépuscule de la Monarchie* and *La Révolution* by Louis Madelin; *Les derniers mois de Versailles,* by Vte Fleury; *La Révolution française de 1789,* edited by P. Sagnac and J. Robiquet, etc. Also the *Moniteur* and the numerous newspapers and brochures of the time.

For the chapter "Lost Opportunities" I used Alma Söderjhelm's book, *Marie-Antoinette et Barnave,* based on their unpublished correspondence and, on the same subject, *Barnave,* by J. - J. Chevalier and *Marie-Antoinette et la politique,* by J. Arnaud Bouteloup. In *Varennes, le roi trahi* and in *Souverains en fuite* I was able to make use of many unpublished documents from the National Archives, from private archives and from inquiries made on the spot. This material helped me in writing the chapter "Varennes . . . or the Hand of Fate!"

Works to be consulted regarding the royal flight are *La Fuite de Louis XVI à Varennes, d'après les documents judiciaires,* by E. Bimbenet, and the many *Souvenirs, Relations* and *Récits* of the actors and witnesses.

VIII

THE FEUILLANTS AND THE TEMPLE

National Archives: F4.1310 (The Feuillants), AA.53.1486 and F4.1304 to F4.1314 (Supplies, accounts, corset-makers, mourning, etc.), F4.4390

(The furniture in the Temple), F4.1319 (Bath), W.400 (Toulan), F4.4391, F4.4392, F4.4393 (Life in the Temple).

Memoirs, Accounts, Souvenirs: Madame Royale, Pauline de Béarn, Mme de Tourzel, Cléry, Hüe, Turgy, Abbé Edgeworth de Firmont, Dufour (Feuillants), and the police officers, Danjon, Goret, Lepitre, Moëlle.

Newspapers: *Le Moniteur* (sessions of 10, 11 and 12 August), and the gazettes of the period.

Works by Paul Gaulot (*Un complot sous la Terreur*), La Morinerie (*Papiers du Temple*), Lenôtre (*La captivité de Marie Antoinette, Louis XVII*) and the works of Bord, Charles Kunstler, Louis Hastier, Viel-Castel, Reiset, Gautherot, Funck-Brentano, Maurice Garçon, etc.

IX

THE CONCIERGERIE

We possess a vast number of documents on the last nine weeks of the Queen's life. First of all there are accounts of eye witnesses. The most important is undoubtedly the *Déclaration de Rosalie Lamorlière, native de Breteuil en Picardie, servante à la Conciergerie durant la captivité de Marie-Antoinette,* and Mme Simon-Vouet's research, which supplements it. Next come the *Relation de Louis Larivière, porte-clef à la Conciergerie* and the *Souvenirs de Mlle Fouché.* The *Relation de la femme Bault, veuve du concierge de la prison de la Conciergerie,* I used with reserve, for it seems to me to be full of errors. Note also: *Clubs contre Révolutionnaires* by Challamel and *Marie-Antoinette* by Saint-Hugues, published in 1815.

Several boxes in the National Archives provide important details, some of which are unpublished or little known: W.15.534 (Prison register), F7.4392, W.296, F7.4393, Wia.112 (Accounts), F7.1319, and W.151 (Prisoner's state of health). The prison register and Wia.121 also give the list of objects possessed by Marie-Antoinette.

On the Conciergerie itself, on the topography of the district and on the Palais de Justice I consulted with profit: C.226, F13.1528, F13.1279, AF.11, 22.170,55, F16.580, F13.1279 and the following works: *Souvenirs* by Berryer, *Etude sur les Tribunaux de Paris,* by A. M. Cazenave, *Guide du voyageur et de l'étranger* (1787), by Thierry, *La Sainte-Chapelle et la Conciergerie,* by F. Gebelin and, in particular, *Mémoires d'un détenu,* by Riouffe.

X

THE CARNATION

Our information on the affair of the carnation comes from the interrogations, the originals of which are preserved in the Musée des Archives

(W.296 [No. 261], Armoire de fer). We possess two interrogations of the "widow Capet," two of Michonis, one of the woman Harel, two of the gendarme Gilbert (plus his report of the morning of the 3rd, which set matters off), two of citizen Fontaine, one of Sergeant Dufresne, two of citizeness Richard, one of Lieutenant Brasse and finally, two days later, that of the woman Dutilleul. Moreover, at her interrogation of 12 October and during her trial Marie Antoinette was again questioned on Rougeville's conspiracy and during the debates the principal actors—in particular Michonis—were in the box. Other important information is in the Archives, in the Rougeville's dossier (F7.6413), in particular his petition and the draft of his letter to Metternich. Also worthy of mention is Michonis' dossier *(W.296,261)*. In the Archives de la Guerre there is information on the military side, principally regarding Rougeville's Cross of St. Louis (Série E, Saint-Louis, 13 A,V° 197, No. 93). *Autour du Temple*, by Gustave Bord, and *Le vrai Chevalier de Maison-Rouge*, by Lenôtre (although our theory is quite different from that of the latter work) were of great use. Also the two little volumes by Pierre-Etienne Regnaud published at the beginning of 1795, which recount the events of 10 August and the role played by Rougeville during July and August 1792.

With regard to the changing of the Queen's cell, which ended the affair of the carnation, besides Rosalie's *Relation* and the report of the police officers published in the issue of 14 January 1883 of *La Révolution Française*, and besides the report preserved in W.296, I discovered in the dossier F7.4392 the bills for "the work carried out in the former dispensary," which appear to have remained unnoticed until now.

XI

THE QUEEN'S COMMUNION

For the Queen's confession and communion I consulted *Souvenirs* by Mlle Fouché, the *Déclaration* of the Abbé Magnin *(Le Monde*, 23 July 1864), *La Communion de la Reine à la Conciergerie (Le Monde*, 31 May 1863), *L'Eglise de Paris sous la Révolution*, by the Abbé Delare, *Vie de l'Abbé Emery*, by the Abbé Gosselin, *Un Episode de la Terreur* (1864), by A. de Ségur, *Revue des questions historiques* (1870), *Marie-Antoinette, la Captivité et la Mort*, by G. Lenôtre, and *Autour du Temple*, by Gustave Bord.

In her will Marie Antoinette wrote: "Having no expectation of spiritual consolation, and not even knowing if there still exist any priests of that religion here, and in any case the place where I am would expose them to too much danger if they should enter."

How can this sentence be reconciled with the confidence made by the

Abbé Emery, according to which he was able, shortly before the trial, to get a note passed to the prisoner: "Prepare yourself to receive absolution. Today, at midnight, I shall be before your door and I shall pronounce the sacramental words over you"? Still according to this account, the almoner of the Conciergerie went to the Queen's door at the hour fixed, heard "the sighs of that unfortunate Princess" and "spoke with her for several moments before giving her absolution." This scene can have taken place only before 14 September, when the Queen did not have two heavy doors separating her from the corridor.

The will can be reconciled with Abbé Magnin's account and that of Mlle Fouché. When Marie Antoinette wrote "if there still exist any priests here," she might have been implying "as there did formerly." Again, "the place where I am detained would expose them to too much danger" could imply "whereas where I was formerly imprisoned it was possible."

Yet Mlle Fouché and the Abbé Magnin asserted that Bault let them into the cell *after* 14 September. But the priest's own words must be heard:

"The memory of what happened when Louis XVI was in the Temple, in the same situation, and the sentiments which inspired the Queen caused me to suggest that I should say mass in the obscure cell she occupied and give her holy communion. I assured Her Majesty that it would be easy for us to bring all the objects for these august ceremonies. We had, indeed, for our use in those terrible days very small chalices which took to pieces, small 18mo missals, portable altar-stones a little longer than the base of a small chalice. All these articles fitted into a small work-bag and we could easily hide them in our pockets.

"The Queen accepted gratefully and thanked us. Among the gendarmes employed in guarding the cell we had noticed two who, by their respect for their Sovereign and the open display of their religious feelings, inspired us with complete confidence. As they were well known to the concierge I did not hesitate to tell them of the happiness that the Queen was about to enjoy, and these Frenchmen, good Christians and faithful subjects, revealed their desire to share in this glorious opportunity.

"The day for the holy work being fixed, the concierge came to fetch us during the night, at an appointed spot, and led us through the night. I heard the Queen's confession. Mlle Fouché had prepared herself to receive her God, and the two gendarmes told me that they also were prepared and that they ardently desired to communicate on this occasion, as fortunate as it was unexpected. Without losing a moment, we prepared everything needed on a little table.

"I celebrated the august sacrifice of our altars and I gave communion to the Queen, who by the nourishment of the eucharistic bread received from her God the courage to bear, without complaint, all the torments awaiting her. Mlle Fouché and the two gendarmes were also admitted at the time to the divine feast.

"The promise I have made to be brief in my narration does not allow me to depict the emotion caused by such a touching scene, which took place at the beginning of October 1793. I fell ill shortly afterwards and it was the last time that I had the honour of seeing Her Majesty. Mlle Fouché, more fortunate than myself, presented M. Cholet, a priest from the Vendée, to her. This priest gave the Queen communion during the night of 12-13 of the same month."

The Abbé Magnin explains the sentence in the Queen's "will" as follows: "Prudence and a desire to shield the priests who had helped her, as well as the persons who had helped to introduce them, were enough to give rise to the phrase in question, or to any similar phrase. However that may be, the facts speak."

What must one conclude? The presence of the two gendarmes seems all the more unusual since the Queen was alone in her cell from 4 September to 5 October. At the time of the Restoration did the fact that the Queen might have died without being in a state of grace determine the priest to utter a "pious untruth"? For myself I cannot believe it, particularly since the Abbé Magnin, on being violently attacked, entered the pulpit and, turning to the altar, "raised his hands and affirmed before God that everything he had said was the pure truth."

XII

THE TRIAL

First of all one must mention *Histoire du Tribunal Révolutionnaire,* by H. Wallon, *Le Tribunal Révolutionnaire de Paris,* by Campardon, and in particular *Le Tribunal Révolutionnaire,* by G. Lenôtre.

On the important question of the route taken by the Queen to or from the Revolutionary Tribunal I am in disagreement with G. Lenôtre and I owe the reader an explanation. This master of "little history" makes Marie Antoinette go by the chapel staircase, the foot of which was undoubtedly nearer her cell but which came out rather a long way from the *Grand-Chambre,* right at the end of the *Galerie des Peintres,* now the *Galerie Saint-Louis.* My opinion is supported by two texts written by eye-witnesses. The Lieutenant of gendarmes, de Busne, who was arrested the day after the trial for having brought the prisoner a glass of water and offered her his arm, wrote in his petition: "I offered her my right fore-arm and she descended the staircase in this way; she took it again in order to descend the *three slippery steps of the perron.*" And a prisoner wrote: "The Queen's trial began on Monday morning. *We saw her pass through the courtyard four or five times,* modestly dressed in black." (*Un épisode de la Terreur,* written by Barthélemy B. de La Roche and published by the Comte de Ségur.) On the evenings of the 14th and 15th, it was not from the courtyard that the prisoners saw the Queen pass but from the windows of their cells looking out on to the courtyard. On the mornings of the 14th and 15th and at four o'clock in the afternoon of the 14th she must have twice crossed the yard where the prisoners were free to walk between sunrise and sunset.

The text of the Queen's trial, the interrogations of 5 and 6 October (Louis XVII, Madame Royale and Madame Elisabeth), the interrogation of the Queen on 12 October and the indictment were published, from the originals, in *La Révolution Française* directed by August Dide (1883 and 1884). But the dossier W.290 gives us the report, the times of suspension of sessions, which are not in the document published by Dide, and the names of the judges and jurors, which differ from those given by *La Révolution Française.*

I also consulted with profit the *Souvenirs* of Chauveau-Lagarde, the dossier for Chauveau-Lagarde and Tronson du Coudray, *La Souveraine devant la Justice,* by Marcel Rousselet (F7.4774,94), the dossiers W.295, 296 and 297, AE.15, 18, F4.1319, Wia.121, F13.1279, etc., the *Déclaration* of the brothers Humbert discovered by Mme Siimon-Vouet, *Marie-Antoinette et la Révolution,* by Viel-Castel, etc. The dossiers C.166, C.271, 272, 276, 279 to 286 contain the petitions for the Queen's trial and the many congratulations from municipalities after her execution. Trinchard's famous note is in the Bibliothèque National *Mss. fr.* 12759, and the account of the secret session of the Committee of Public Safety was published by Francis Drake in *Historical Manuscripts Commission; The Manuscripts of J. B. Fortescue, Esq. preserved at Dropmore* (Vol. II).

XIII

THE EXECUTION

The details of the Queen's last hours are taken from the *Relation* of Rosalie and from accounts by eye-witnesses: Louis Larivière, the gendarme Léger, Desessarts, Charles Desfossés, Rouy, Hébert, Lapierre, Notelet (letters published by Jules Mazé), from the unpublished report of the police officer Roubaud (F7.3688,3) and of an unknown police officer (*Fic. III,* 13). The archives of the Observatoire (preserved at the O.N.M.) show the weather hour by hour on 14, 15 and 16 October. In the dossier W.291 (183) are the details of the curious affair of Maingot, the man who came out from under the scaffold all covered with blood after the execution. He was arrested by those standing in the front row. His name was Maingot and he was a second-hand dealer. The presence of a carnation aroused

interest. "Do you know Rougeville, the former Chevalier de Saint-Louis?"
He denied this, he was searched and on him were found two holy pictures,
"a rallying sign for the enemies of the Republic." Moreover, he was
curiously tattooed with a blue cord in a saltire, on top of which was a
cross, on the chest the letters G.B., on the right arm J.H.S. and on the
left arm a crucifix. There was enough there to have him sent to the guillotine the same day! Maingot appeared twice before the Tribunal—once for
the blood and the carnation and once for the tattooing and the holy pictures
—and was acquitted! He was even given back his bloodstained possessions.
He had succeeded in proving that "the stigmata on his skin" dated from
1787, when he was a soldier "in the regiment of Neustrie" and that he had
found the pictures on the ground. As for the blood, he claimed "to have
been pushed by the crowd" and to have "walked in the blood with the
intention of effacing it."

What was the end of the pitiful barbers' conspiracy, details of which are
in the dossier W.311 of the National Archives?

The day after the execution the heads of the conspiracy, numbering 29—
the Volunteers were left alone—were arrested and sent to the Conciergerie.

On 17 January 1794 Fouquier-Tinville brought the 29 to trial as "guilty
of having hatched a plot to kidnap the widow Capet in order to preserve
her from the vengeance of the Nation." There were 54 witnesses: hatters,
dyers, launderers, weavers, charcoal-burners—and barbers. Urged by fear,
they brought overwhelming evidence against the lace-maker, the Lemille
family, Basset and the little boot-black.

After three days' trial Basset and Lemille, together with his wife, and
the woman Fournier, the head of the conspiracy, were condemned to death.
Thirteen other conspirators were imprisoned "until the peace." The little
boot-black, "in view of his age," got off with 20 years' imprisonment. While
the verdict was being announced the poor blind lace-maker embraced her
child. "She was suffocated by sobs," a witness said. All during her journey
in the cart she was heard to repeat, weeping, *"Pobré pitit! . . . Pobré pitit!"*

The barbers died bravely. The lace-maker struggled so violently that the
knife took off only part of her head.

Two days later, on the same spot where his mother had died, the little
boot-black was placed on the scaffold and tied to a post on which were
written his name, his age, his profession and the text of the verdict.

Such, in Nivôse of the Year II, was the end of the last defenders of the
Queen of France.

In the registry of the Conciergerie (W15.534 [11]) is the inventory of
the widow Capet's effects made after her death (chemises of fine linen,
mantle of *raz de St.-Marc*, two pairs of black stockings, a lawn headdress,

Sources

423

a crêpe sash, etc.). All these clothes were given, according to custom, to the Salpêtrière, to be distributed among the prisoners. The legacies of the two people the Queen most detested are also inscribed in the registry not far from hers. After reading of "the swansdown puff and the little tin pomade box" which end the inventory of the widow Capet, one has only to turn two pages. There, after Bailly, who left only a gold watch and a key, is the legacy of Philippe-Egalité. It is a real dandy's wardrobe, the most luxurious of all the prisoners. There is a long list of breeches, waistcoats, cravats and dressing-gowns. There are even sets of silver plate, a picnic basket and a travelling suitcase. Turning another two pages, one can see, under the date of 19 Frimaire, the inventory of the du Barry's effects. After she left for the scaffold there was found in her cell only a white wood box containing two teapots and two cups—nothing else.

When did the grave-digger Joly bury Marie Antoinette's body? How long did the corpse remain lying on the grass? We do not know exactly. It was not until 1 November that the grave-digger sent in his bill.

> The widow Capet, for the coffin   ..   6 livres
> For the grave and grave-diggers ..   ..   15 livres, 35s.

The authorities waited nearly four years to be reimbursed. Only in the Year V did the Commissaire Dardoize put up for auction the objects seized in the Temple and unpacked during the trial. There remained only the little green morocco hussif, which reached 5 fr. 75, and the three little portraits in shagreen cases, which reached 4 fr. 40. The rest had disappeared, stolen, nobody knew by whom.

"This being done, and seeing that there remains nothing to say, do or sell, we have closed the account of the said objects at the sum of 10 fr. 15 centimes." (Archives de la Seine.)

This was the sum produced by "the goods acquired and confiscated for the profit of the Republic."

To end with, we reproduce the Queen's death certificate.

"Death certificate of *Marie-Antoinette Lorraine d'Autriche*, on 25 of last month, *aged* 38 *years, widow of Louis Capet*. On a declaration made to the Commune by ...., aged .... years, profession ...., living at ....
The said declarant said ....
Dated ...."

No one had dared to go to the Hôtel de Ville to declare the death of the daughter of the Empress Maria Theresa of Austria, widow of the King of France.

Index

wilfulness, 63; popularity, 64; meeting with Fersen, 65; love of pleasure,
65-66, 88, 98, 104, 109, 118, 121,
128-151; love of music, 67; accession
to the throne, 73, 74, 76; pam-
phleteering against, 77-78, 91, 107,
123, 145, 150, 255; opposition to
court etiquette, 80-85; etiquette of
dressing, 81; friends, 87-90; conversation, 90; reading of licentious
works, 90; consecration at Rheims,
93, 96-97; "dissipations," 93;
"feather-head," 95-127; failure of
King to consummate marriage ("fatal
object"), 46, 57, 64, 66, 98-99, 117-
118, 120, 124, 131; favorites, 99;
advice from brother, 103, 121-123;
extravagance, 109, 174, 256; loss of
favor with the public, 113-114;
gambling, 114-115, 124-125; debts,
115-117; walks on Versailles terraces, 123; action against Prussia,
128-130; first pregnancy, 131; birth
of Mme Royale, 133-136; coldness
in Paris toward Queen, 136; adventure in a cab, and calumnies in
Paris, 136-137; début as an actress,
143-144; isolation, 149; poem by
Boufflers, 150-151; second pregnancy,
152, 158, 159; pure soul, 152-175;
birth of the Dauphin (first), 159-
166; education of children, 170;
wardrobe, 171-175; "limited lovers,"
176-188; abortion, 178; "Josephine"
of Fersen, and love for Fersen, 179-
180; scandal about Barnave, 182;
defense by Mme Campan, 183-184;
birth of second son (Dauphin, second; Louis XVII), 188; "The Austrian," 188; legend of gold shipment
to Joseph II, 188; as an actress, 189;
"Mme Deficit," 218-244; dairy at
Trianon, 219, 241; birth of fourth
child, 220; children, 237; entry into
history, 245-258; arrest at Varennes,
275-278; prisoner, 284 *et seq.*;
double dealing, 291, 292; "Mme
Veto," 299-317; Widow Capet, 318-
334; wardrobe, and meals in the
Temple, 320; plots for escape, 327-
332; imprisonment in the Conciergerie, 335-344; trial, 335-398; Plot

of the Carnation, 345-358; interro-
gation before trial, 364-372; counsel,
jury, and judges, 371, 373, 376, 398;
last letter, to sister, 399-401; execu-
tion, 399-409; attempt at rescue, 403-
404, 407-408
Marie-Caroline, Queen of Naples, 2
Marie-Christine, Princess of Saxe-
Teschen, 2
Marie-Elisabeth, Abbess, 2
Marie Louise, Queen of Spain, 7
Marie Thérèse of Savoy. *See* Provence,
Comtesse de
Marie Thérèse Charlotte. *See* Mme
Royale
Marigny, M. de, 41
Marmontel, Jean François, 68, 154, 179
Marsan, Comtesse de, 193, 199, 205,
216, 236
Maudoux, Abbé, 71, 72
Maurepas, Comte Jean, 78-79, 91-93,
101, 102, 108, 130-132, 146, 147
Maury, Lucien, 181
Maximilian, Archduke, 118-119
Maximilian-Joseph, Elector of Bavaria,
16, 128
Melchior-Bonnet, Christian, 155
Mercy d'Argentau, Count Florimond,
3-9, 17, 23, 27, 29, 31, 38, 40, 41,
44, 45, 48-55, 57-60, 63, 64, 66-69,
72, 79, 80, 86, 88, 89, 91, 93, 96,
98, 104-108, 110, 111, 113-115, 117-
119, 121, 122, 124, 125, 128-131,
133, 136-138, 140, 145, 146, 148,
154, 170, 171, 174, 179, 185-187,
192, 196, 218, 221, 222, 225, 226,
238, 254, 256, 261, 288-291, 296,
307, 336, 368, 369, 395
Meridienne of Queen, 66
Mesdames, daughters of Louis XV, 25,
49, 50, 57, 78. *See also* names
Mesnil, Mlle de, 40
Metastasio, 5, 66-67
Michodière, M. de la, 60
Michonis, Citizen, 331-332, 336-340,
344-356, 363, 380, 390, 398 n.
Migazzi, Cardinal, 12, 13
Minuet, Affair of, 31, 38-39
Mique (builder), 143, 159, 169
Mirabeau, Marquis de, 112, 232, 233,
256, 257, 259, 260, 280, 296, 325,
378

THE FOREIGN POLICY
OF PALMERSTON
1830–1841

William Lamb, Viscount Melbourne

from the portrait by *John Partridge*
in the National Portrait Gallery

THE FOREIGN POLICY
OF PALMERSTON

1830-1841

BRITAIN, THE LIBERAL MOVEMENT AND
THE EASTERN QUESTION

BY

SIR CHARLES WEBSTER
K.C.M.G., Litt.D., F.B.A.

VOLUME II

LONDON
G. BELL & SONS, LTD
1951

PRINTED IN GREAT BRITAIN BY ROBERT MACLEHOSE AND CO. LTD.
THE UNIVERSITY PRESS, GLASGOW

CHAPTER VII

TSAR AND SULTAN:
THE DEVELOPMENT OF THE
EASTERN QUESTION
1835–1839

1. RELATIONS WITH THE SULTAN AND HIS ADVISERS

2. THE ATTEMPT TO MODERNISE THE OTTOMAN EMPIRE
   - (i) PALMERSTON'S PROGRAMME
   - (ii) THE ARMY AND NAVY
   - (iii) THE COMMERCIAL CONVENTION, 1838

3. THE CONTEST WITH RUSSIA

4. THE SECOND FAILURE OF THE CONCERT

5. THE SULTAN AND HIS VASSAL

" I have a thousand times said that war is not necessary. I repeat it ; but it is necessary to shew that war is not dreaded through fear but avoided through principle."
PONSONBY, 17 October, 1838.

CONTENTS OF VOLUME II

v

150418

CHAPTER VII

TSAR AND SULTAN: THE DEVELOPMENT OF THE EASTERN QUESTION, 1835–1839

During these four years the situation in the East developed along lines similar to that in the West and was strongly influenced by it. The story is confused by the strange and emotional personalities of Ponsonby, Durham and the Sultan himself, each of them intent on a personal policy and each seeing only a small part of the European picture and imperfectly realising the interests at stake and the forces at work. Palmerston used each of his subordinates in turn, prevented them from doing harm by their extravagances, defended them from their enemies and ultimately brought his curious team into some sort of harmony.

He had also to cope with the extraordinary conduct of the half-mad David Urquhart who, through the patronage of the King and a lapse of judgment on Palmerston's part, was given a position at Constantinople for which he was altogether unfitted. Finally he had to keep along with him his too ardent Monarch, his diffident Prime Minister, and a Cabinet which sometimes seemed to forget the Eastern Question altogether.

His own conviction that British interests could only be maintained by a strong and determined policy, that the mistake of 1833 must never be repeated, that Russia would yield if she realised this, that time was on the Sultan's side if only the crisis could be prevented from arising too soon, that Britain could by the mutual fears and jealousies of her rivals and the strength of the British fleet and British commerce and finance obtain a mastery of the situation, was ultimately triumphantly justified.

Thus he tried with little success to reform the Ottoman Empire, with much more to increase British influence at Constantinople and reduce that of Russia; he more than anyone else kept Mehemet Ali quiet; he shewed a strong face to Russia, doubtful of her ultimate intentions, pretty sure she could not act at once, preparing to resist her when the time came, but ready to compromise on inessentials; finally he attempted to keep the centre of diplomatic

525

action in London and to devise a new European treaty to replace that of Unkiar Skelessi.

In none of these objects did he have complete success in these years. The time had not yet come. His attention had to be devoted mainly to the struggle in the Iberian Peninsula. Only when that had worked itself out with its effect on the Franco-British *entente* could the Eastern Question become once more the central problem of European diplomacy. Meanwhile he more than held his own. Both at Constantinople and at the capitals of the Great Powers the determination and strength of Britain were realised. In every government, Turkish, Russian, French and Austrian, he had strong opponents. But in each he had powerful assistance. In Russia the realism of Nesselrode and Orlov, in Turkey the influence of Vogorides, the Prince of Samos, and, after many experiments and disappointments, the capacity of Reschid Pasha, in France the help of Broglie at the beginning, then of the remnant of the Doctrinaires as well as of the French Ambassador in London. In final analysis also, Metternich aimed at the same ends, though he wanted different methods, and Vienna, not London, as the diplomatic centre.

The story is a complicated one. An attempt has been made, therefore, to describe its different aspects in separate sections, even though this involves occasionally some reconsideration of an incident already discussed.

1. RELATIONS WITH THE SULTAN
AND HIS ADVISERS

In 1834 Ponsonby had made a good beginning to reestablish at Constantinople British prestige and authority, so fatally weakened by the events of 1833. For four years the struggle continued there with every resource of oriental diplomacy. The Sultan's one aim was to recover from his hated rival, Mehemet Ali, the territory yielded in 1833. For this purpose he turned to Britain and Russia. Neither were ready to give him what he wanted, the power to attack, though both were ready to defend him and accepted his authority as Sultan over the whole Ottoman Empire. Each was afraid that the other might use its position as champion of the Sultan to establish its own ascendancy at Constantinople. Each was associated with an ally whose interests and methods were different. Both Austria and France, uneasily consorting with Russia and Britain respectively, wished to control events so as to accommodate their particular interests in the Eastern Question with their necessities in other parts of Europe. The representatives of all these states at Constantinople endeavoured by bribery and by the use of the favourites and indirect methods of approach to get past the official machinery to the source of power and decision, the Sultan himself. All were imperfectly served and Mehemet Ali himself, who used much gold, was better informed of the secrets of the Porte than any of the European Powers. The dragomans and other agents whom they used were constantly revealing these secret discussions to their rivals who, only partially informed, always tended to believe what most suited the policy which they were recommending to their chiefs. The difficulty of translating Turkish language and ideas into Western idioms added to the confusion in everybody's mind.[1]

---

[1] The methods of Ponsonby are now pretty well completely revealed and much light has been thrown by recent researches on those of the French and of Mehemet Ali himself. But we are still very imperfectly informed of those of Russia and Austria, the correspondence with Constantinople having been only very cursorily surveyed. Campbell told Mehemet Ali "that it was easy for him to foresee what would happen at Constantinople as he was better informed than the Sultan himself of what passed in the Divan there. Mehemet Ali laughed and said perhaps such is the case." From Campbell, 17 July, 1838, *F.O.*

Ponsonby had waited, he told Palmerston later, to see what happened to the Tory Government before he resigned, and in any case he preferred dismissal to resignation. It very nearly came. Wellington told Esterhazy that Ponsonby had been encouraged from London to send alarmist reports from Constantinople to mislead public opinion about Russia. He promised to recall Ponsonby but later said that he could not do so because of the Government's weakness.[1]

Meanwhile Ponsonby had continued on the course which he had mapped out for himself, to destroy the Russian control over the Sultan and to substitute that of Britain in its place. He used his own strange methods throughout these four years and, extravagant in language and action as he often was, he succeeded to a very large extent in intimidating his rivals, who never ceased to complain of him, and in imposing his personality on the Sultan and his advisers.

He was never, partly owing to the foolish parsimony of the Treasury, given an official residence during these years. The house at Pera was not large enough and not sufficiently isolated to save it from the fires of Constantinople. Ponsonby wished, therefore, to build a new one in the country. "Pera", he wrote, "is the most detestable place in Europe." He did in fact live mostly outside Constantinople at Therapia. Palmerston, on the other hand, insisted that he should live at or near Pera so as to be easily accessible to the Sultan's Ministers and to British merchants. Perhaps this is the reason no house was ever obtained. Ponsonby got very tired of his job at times. He asked in 1838 to be transferred to Vienna which he had heard Lamb was leaving. He was also worried because he had not served long enough to get a pension.[2]

In 1835 the three most powerful men at Constantinople were Husrev, the Seraskier or Commander-in-Chief, Pertev, the Kiahay Bey, or Grand Vizir, and Achmet Pasha, the Sultan's reigning favourite. Of these Pertev was the most patriotic and incorrup-

Turkey, 343, Pt. 1. Palmerston himself recognised that Pisani, whose brother was in the Russian service, probably told him most of what he did. To Melbourne, 30 Oct., 1835: *B.P.*

[1] From Ponsonby, 21 April, 1835: *B.P.* Esterhazy to Metternich, 11, 27 March, 1835: *V. St. A.*

[2] From Ponsonby, 7 Dec., 1836. To Ponsonby, 8 Feb., 1837, 22 May, 1838: *B.P.* From Ponsonby, 1 June, 1833: *F.O. Turkey*, 223. "I have fifty people to lodge and feed." He had to keep large stores because of the plague when he could buy nothing.

tible of all the Ministers, though he took money as a matter of course; old Husrev was Mehemet's mortal foe; Achmet was pro-Russian and in their pay. The Reis Effendi, Akif, a weak creature, was also soon bought by the Russians. In these circumstances Ponsonby's real diplomacy, as distinct from formal demands which could be openly avowed, had to be by subterranean methods. He seems early to have made a deep impression on the Sultan who conferred on him in December 1835 a decoration, "the highest in the Empire and were it an order which it *is not*, might be described as the Garter of Turkey." He could, however, only see the Sultan himself at rare intervals and nothing of great importance passed at these interviews. He was never sure of obtaining one and in 1838 thought of trying to establish the right of Ambassadors to see the Sultan on their demand. But close touch was kept through Vogorides and MacGuffog, whose devotion never failed, and was certainly not mainly due to the meagre sums which Ponsonby obtained for them out of Secret Service funds. Ponsonby himself also saw Pertev on occasions. His intercourse with the Reis Effendi was mainly through the Chief Dragoman, Frederick Pisani, whose interviews were recorded in formal notes and reports. Throughout 1835 and the first part of 1836 Ponsonby was able to report a satisfactory position in the Sultan's councils and the jealous despatches of his fellow Ambassadors confirm his claim.[1]

Palmerston had hoped that Urquhart, who became Secretary of Embassy in 1836, would be able by his knowledge of Turkish to assist Ponsonby to establish close confidential relations with the Sultan and his Ministers which might be revealed if left to the

---

[1] From Ponsonby, 8 April, 1836: *B.P.*; do., 6 Dec., 1835; 15 Feb., 1837 (with minutes by Backhouse and Palmerston), 7 May, 1837, *F.O. Turkey*, 256, 303. Presents were only given on a very limited scale for Palmerston pointed out that his small Secret Service funds could not compete with the unrestricted liberality of the Tsar which Ponsonby constantly reported. No money was available for bribes to the Ministers such as the Russians used. Gifts of horses and a carriage, weapons and scientific instruments, were sent to the Sultan and a few presents of special English products such as sporting rifles and pistols were given to the Turkish Ambassador. Ponsonby secured permission to accept for himself the special honour from the Sultan, but in spite of his entreaties Palmerston peremptorily refused the high order which the Sultan pressed upon him. Vogorides said he only wanted a present of small value just to shew the esteem of the British Government. Ponsonby asked for £1000 for Pertev. Backhouse said it was difficult to give open presents to Turkish Ministers and Palmerston told him to leave the matter alone. The Russians shortly afterwards gave Pertev a snuff box worth £1500, but Husrev, his enemy, admitted that "no bribe would move that old *Tartar*". (7 July, 1837: *B.P.*)

Dragomans. But the insane vanity of Urquhart prevented what in any case could hardly have been allowed by the Ambassador. So far from helping Ponsonby, Urquhart did his best to undermine his position both at Constantinople, in England, and in Palmerston's confidence. Urquhart's own extravagances made these treacherous attempts of little importance, but Ponsonby was more than ever alone, and the quarrel prevented him from taking that leave at the beginning of 1837 which would have renewed his contact with Palmerston and perhaps moderated his extravagance of language.[1]

He had all the more need of it because of the attacks upon him in 1836 when a special effort was made by his enemies to get him recalled over the Churchill affair. This is generally described as a great defeat and humiliation for Ponsonby and it certainly caused him great trouble and anxiety. But he got out of it eventually with considerable success, and in the long run his instinct was probably right and the attitude that he took increased his prestige with the Sultan's Ministers while the dislike of his colleagues could hardly be made greater than it was already.[2]

Churchill, a journalist, who represented the *Morning Herald*, accidentally injured a boy while shooting on 5 May and was put into gaol and beaten in a specially humiliating manner. He was of course entitled to the substantial compensation which he loudly demanded. Achmet, the favourite, a Russian partisan, and Akif, the Reis Effendi, a creature of his, were thought by Ponsonby to be thwarting justice as they probably were. It was necessary "for the Sultan's own good to break down the insolent pretensions of the Pashas" and Achmet was more to blame than Akif. Ponsonby regarded the affair as a contest between himself and Russia for the control of the Divan, refused any intercourse with Akif, and suggested to the Sultan the dismissal of both Ministers. He indicated to Palmerston in a private letter that he would resign rather than give way. "I hope", he wrote, "that you will take what I am about to say, in the sense I intend it to have, and not as an offensive expression of sentiments. I mean that if His Majesty's

---

[1] See my article "Ponsonby, Urquhart and Palmerston", *Eng. Hist. Rev.*, July 1947, 327–351.

[2] Professor Puryear gives an interesting account of the Churchill incident (*International Economics*, etc., 45–49) but he relies largely on Roussin's reports which were very biassed and does not seem to have followed the later developments of the controversy.

Government disapprove of what I have done in the matter they should send out somebody to perform such orders as they may give in contradiction of it. His M. Govt. ought not to depend on me for executing them." Butenev rallied to the side of his creatures and Stürmer naturally supported him. But there was less reason for Roussin to take such an uncompromising position. His colleagues apparently persuaded him that Ponsonby had threatened to join Russia in a partition of the Ottoman Empire if his demands were refused. What Ponsonby did say was that Britain could hardly be expected to support a state whose Ministers refused such just claims as had been made in the Churchill case.[1]

Both Roussin and Stürmer wrote a series of alarming reports to their Governments which in due course were sent to London in order that representations might be made to Palmerston. Pozzo di Borgo and Hummelauer were delighted with so congenial a task and they got Nourri Pasha, the Turkish envoy at London, to join with them. Sébastiani shewed himself more cooperative on this than on any other question and at the orders of Thiers supported them in a private letter. Metternich told Fox that Ponsonby was 'mad', and Thiers Granville that Ponsonby was endangering the peace of Europe.[2]

Palmerston was the last man to accept foreign complaints against an Ambassador in such a case. He gave short shrift to them. He realised at once the issues at stake, refused to believe the accounts sent home by Stürmer and Roussin of Ponsonby's conduct, and, though he was afraid Ponsonby had gone too far, sent strong letters to Granville and Lamb. "All the other Ministers and Ambassadors at Constantinople", he wrote at the outset to Granville, "think they have now got Ponsonby into a hobble and even Roussin, who is jealous of him, has, it seems, joined. Metternich has sent me quires about the matter. I tell everybody that as yet I have only half the story. . . . They would all, and their Courts too, exult at getting rid of Ponsonby; he has been too active and successful to be forgiven by any one of them. I hope that in this instance he has not gone too far, though I half fear he

[1] From Ponsonby, 15 May, 10, 28 June, 14, 22 July, 20 Aug., 7, 22 Sept., 18 Nov., 1836: *F.O. Turkey*, 273–278. do., 7, 16 May, 11, 17, 20 June, 21 July, 1836: *B.P.* The number shows how much the question occupied Ponsonby's attention and there are others on smaller points.
[2] From Granville, 27 June, 1836: *F.O. France*, 523. From Fox, 23 June, 1836: *B.P.* Sébastiani to Thiers, 28 June, 29 July, 1836: *A.A.E.*

has." To King Leopold, who had ventured to convey Louis Philippe's 'grief' to Palmerston and thought that Ponsonby was playing into the hands of Russia, Palmerston sent an impassioned defence of his Ambassador who "has like many other English Ambassadors and Ministers at home and abroad been grossly . calumniated by the Tory Party in Europe."

After he had received Ponsonby's reports he wrote even more strongly to Paris and Vienna, both officially and in private letters: "Ponsonby has acted, I think, with much skill and judgment. . . . All the others have been caballing against him from personal or political jealousy. We shall have a difficult job to determine what to do. The outrage was atrocious." And he added scathing comments on Roussin's conduct in cooperating with the three Eastern Powers before ascertaining what he had to protest against. To Lamb he admitted that the conduct of the representatives of the three Eastern Powers was not so bad as that of Roussin: "However we have triumphed and it is an important victory. It is now an English victory. They might have made it an European one." These letters produced an immediate effect at Paris. Thiers at first defended Roussin, but Desages admitted to Aston that the Ambassador was wrong, and under his influence Thiers lowered his tone. Metternich, of course, never admitted anything. The Russian Court kept outside the whole affair, and Durham attributed the comparative reticence of Butenev to his own influence at St. Petersburg.[1]

Palmerston himself was, indeed, perturbed when he first heard of the incident. "We should only be playing the game of Russia", he told Ponsonby in a hasty note, "if we were to break unnecessarily with the Sultan upon a separate quarrel of our own." He even consulted Backhouse as to the policy to be adopted, almost the only time such a course is recorded. The Under-Secretary, who

[1] To Granville, 5, 14 July, 1836; *F.O. France*, 517, do., 28 June, 5 July, 1836: *B.P.* To Aston, 19 July, 1836: *F.O. France*, 517, do., 18 July, 1836: *Aston P.* From Aston, 22, 25 July, 1836: *F.O. France*, 523; do., 25, 27 July, 1836: *Aston P.* Desages to Bourqueney, 27 June, 1836. "Le traitement infligé a Churchill est une abomination'" He had told Thiers he had gone too far in his strictures, though Ponsonby should not have demanded the resignation of the Reis Effendi but made 'un tapage infernal' until he got satisfaction. *Bour. P.* To Lamb, 18 July, 1836: *B.P.* From Lamb, 5 Aug., 1836: *F.O. Austria*, 257; do., 26 July, 5 Aug., 1836: *B.P.* From Durham, 14 July, 1836: *F.O. Russia*, 225. From Leopold, 30 June, 1836; To Leopold, 5 July, 1836: *B.P.* Metternich was impressed by the dismissal of Akif, and Tatischev thought Ponsonby had been far from 'mad'. Lamb wrote that this time Stürmer had over-reached himself in writing pro-Russian reports against Ponsonby.

had his own information, did not consider Ponsonby's demands justified. The Prime Minister, as always critical of Ponsonby, took the same view. But when Ponsonby's full account of all he had done reached him, Palmerston took up his cause with great vigour. "Ponsonby has really done us a valuable and important service and has acted with courage, firmness and ability," he told Melbourne. In spite of the opposition of all his colleagues the Ambassador had achieved a 'signal triumph', whose good effects would be felt beyond the incident itself. Palmerston wanted, therefore, the Government to approve the action taken and to mark that approval to the whole world by giving Ponsonby a step in the Peerage. He added that Lord John Russell agreed with him. The King was also violently on Ponsonby's side and the news of the dismissal of Akif announced in the *Morning Chronicle* was looked upon by public opinion as a triumph over Russia to such an extent that Palmerston had to damp the feeling down by the insertion of a leader next day. But the battle in the Cabinet was lost and it was decided that Ponsonby's demand for the dismissal of Achmet could not be supported. How long this took to settle is not known, but the final instructions were not sent till the beginning of November. Palmerston explained that he had de-layed them to give Ponsonby a chance to carry out his own policy first. "It is very possible you may be right", he wrote, "in wishing us to demand the dismissal of Achmet, but we are not up to so vigorous a measure, and we do not think the occasion requires it. We should not have insisted on the dismissal of the Reis Effendi; and the accomplishment of that was your merit." And he went on to explain the difficulties of enforcing such a demand and the resulting loss of prestige if it were made and not enforced.[1]

Meanwhile Ponsonby was waiting for instructions. The dis-missal of the Reis Effendi, which even Metternich admitted to be a 'great triumph', did not satisfy him. Moreover, owing to the pressure put on the Porte by the other Ambassadors, it was given

---

[1] To Ponsonby, 5, 11 Nov., 1836. *F.O. Turkey*, 272; do., 23 June, 11 Nov., 1836; Minutes, Palmerston and Backhouse, 5 July, 1836; To Melbourne, 19 July, 1836 *Appendix* p. 847; From do., 24 June, 1836: *B.P.* Hummelauer to Met-ternich, 17 July, 1836: *V. St. A.* From Will. IV, 22 June, 4, 7 July, 1836: *B.P.* It is hard to account for the long silence in spite of Ponsonby's urgent requests for a decision. The course adopted seems peculiarly cruel at such a time. Ponsonby who had asked for an Earldom some time before, did not of course know at this time that Palmerston had tried to make him a Viscount as he succeeded in doing in 1839.

out that the dismissal was due to other causes and other officials connected with the case were promoted. No compensation was paid to Churchill who had demanded a very large sum. Finally, Husrev, Achmet's rival, was dismissed from the position of Seraskier. Ponsonby, therefore, persisted in his demand for the dismissal of Achmet himself and was sure that with Palmerston's support he could obtain it. But this never came and the uncertainty was painful. Ponsonby had to report the triumph of his enemies and the substitution of Russian for British influence in the councils of the Sultan. Husrev's dismissal, he said, might cause him to promote a revolution at Constantinople to regain it and thus bring the Russians to the Bosphorus. He recognised that Butenev was entitled to do all he could to destroy his influence but that Stürmer, and above all Roussin, should join him was a betrayal of the interests of their Governments.[1]

When the instructions at last reached him, he had, as perhaps Palmerston anticipated, accepted the situation, and at once said that he would carry them out however much he disliked them. Then he made a surprising recovery. For though Achmet was promoted to be Capitan Pasha, he was thus removed from the Sultan's immediate entourage. Pertev, who had overthrown Husrev and succeeded him as the main instrument of power, was a devoted and incorruptible Moslem which meant that he was anti-Russian. Indeed he offered to Ponsonby to do whatever he demanded about Achmet. Faithful to his instructions, Ponsonby refused to embarrass the Sultan or his Minister by asking for more than they would do by themselves. His Government, he said, had delayed in order that the Sultan might act of his own free will. They would not press him to do what his natural inclinations should have suggested. Pertev was much relieved. For some time Ponsonby still failed to get compensation for the insistent Churchill, but eventually through the interposition of Vogorides that also was obtained from the Sultan's private purse. Before the year was out Roussin explained his role in the affair and Ponsonby agreed to bury the past. Reschid Pasha was appointed Reis Effendi in June, Sarim acting as his deputy until he could come back from London [2]

[1] From Ponsonby, 20 Aug., 7, 22 Sept., 18 Nov., 1836, 4 Jan., 1837: *F.O. Turkey*, 276–278, 301; do., 30 Oct., 7, 20 Dec., 1836: *B.P.*

[2] From Ponsonby, 18, 29 Nov., 1836: 4 Jan., 19 Feb., 14 June, 16 Sept., 1837: *F.O. Turkey*, 278, 301–6. Reschid was appointed Under-Secretary for

Palmerston described this handling of a difficult situation as 'perfect'. He took pains to tell Reschid Pasha, who was still at London, that the dismissal of Halil which had led to his own appointment as Reis Effendi, was due to Ponsonby's action and he praised Ponsonby warmly to him.[1]

The incorruptible Pertev only survived the malignant attacks of his enemies a few months before he too was dismissed by the Sultan, who was told he was only a 'puppet' in his Minister's hands. His fall had been partly due to an endeavour to follow British advice to create a militia which the Sultan suspected was aimed at reducing his own power. But by that time Reschid had become Reis Effendi and was gaining steadily in the Sultan's favour. The contest for the control of Mahmud continued and lasted until his death, a fact which was perhaps one of the reasons why the Great Powers at last agreed on a common solution. For, as Mehemet more than once bitterly complained, it was the rivalry between the Great Powers on which the Sultan relied and he was as much afraid of their agreement as of their quarrels.[2]

However that might be, Ponsonby had no option but to fight for the Sultan's confidence and he might claim that, in spite of the treachery of his subordinate, Urquhart, and the refusal of his Government to accept his advice, he had succeeded as well, perhaps better than, any of his rivals. "I do enjoy at least as much influence here as any other Minister," he claimed in July 1837.[3]

Pertev's overthrow made new combinations necessary. Akif Pasha, a more flexible *intrigant*, had the Sultan's ear, while it was Halil Pasha, his nominee, Husrev's ungrateful protégé, who succeeded to Pertev's position, though Husrev was always in the background and often saw the Sultan. Reschid Pasha, now Foreign Minister, was already by reason of his superior qualities of mind playing a considerable part in affairs and it was he who undertook the main burden of the commercial negotiation which was just

Foreign Affairs in November, 1836. This was a new post. From Ponsonby, 7, 20 Dec., 1836: *B.P.*

[1] To Ponsonby, 11 Nov., 1836, 17 Jan., 1837: *B.P.*

[2] From Ponsonby, 16 Sept., 13 Nov., 1837: 31 Jan., 6 June, 25 July, 1838: *F.O. Turkey*, 305, 329B, 331–332. It was the failure to save Pertev that made Ponsonby desire at this time to secure the right of Ambassadors to an audience with the Sultan. But Roussin would not support him and with Palmerston's approval he dropped the idea. (To Ponsonby, 6 June, 25 July, 1838: *F.O. Turkey*, 329A.)

[3] From Ponsonby, 7 July, 1837: *B.P.*

about to begin. Ponsonby found him rather timid and afraid of Russia, but with "somewhat more belief in the *will* and ability of England to resist Russia than some of his colleagues". It was, perhaps, only natural that Reschid felt he would be safer away from Constantinople and he made a deal with Akif Pasha to be appointed Ambassador at Paris. He would, however, be able to influence policy from there, he told Ponsonby, whose opinion of him gradually grew very favourable. "He has pleased the Sultan. There is no other man I know of capable of conducting at all to the taste of the Sultan a large part of the affairs of the Government." Meanwhile Reschid was to negotiate the commercial convention and since it was dangerous for him to see Ponsonby often, the latter established relations with the clique of Rayahs, some of whom had been with Reschid in Paris and London, who were now advising him. The Prince of Samos also acted as intermediary. Thus Ponsonby could report, at the beginning of 1838, "our influence here when considered in one point of view is very great—that is to say, the Sultan and his Ministers believe what I say to them and I doubt if they believe one word that is said by any other Minister." But he added the next month: "The Porte will not trust you until you shall have committed yourselves by some act that will prove you to be in earnest in your declaration of the *intention* to support the independence of Turkey."[1]

In March Halil and Akif were deposed by the joint efforts of the Sultan's favourite, Riza Bey, Husrev and Reschid, the latter delighted to avenge the murder of his friend Pertev. The Sultan, indeed, reorganised the whole system of Government and the Grand Vizir's office was reduced to a nullity. But Husrev now had a commanding influence in the three Camarillas that took its place. Achmet Pasha, the Capitan Pasha, had now lost all influence and Riza Bey, the favourite, was Husrev's man. Reschid was growing in influence and remained at the Foreign Office until the commercial convention was finally approved in August. Ponsonby had still some doubts about him but believed that he did not take money and was anti-Russian.[2]

[1] From Ponsonby, 5 Jan., 5 Feb., 1838: *B.P.* A more coherent description than usual of the position of the Sultan's Ministers and an interesting appreciation of Reschid. Among Reschid's advisers was M. Cor, a Frenchman, whom Palmerston described as a remarkably intelligent man (13 Sept., 1838: *B.P.*) He later acted as French Dragoman.
[2] From Ponsonby, 15, 26 March, 19 April, 1838: *F.O. Turkey*, 330; do., 21 April, 1838: *B.P.*

Bulwer came out in the spring of 1838 as Secretary of Embassy. He was by now an experienced official and Ponsonby liked him. Though Bulwer criticised his chief's policy to Palmerston, he recognised his good qualities, remained loyal to him and was of great assistance in getting the right contacts with the Sultan's officials. This was all the more necessary as the Seraglio were intriguing against Reschid and Husrev's loyalty to him was doubtful.[1]

The success of the commercial convention, and the joint cruise of the British and Turkish fleets produced an immense impression on the Tsar. Butenev, who had been on leave, was sent back post-haste and did a good deal to retrieve the position. He was helped by the increasing jealousy of Roussin who never quite forgave Ponsonby for his success in negotiating the commercial convention. Butenev began his usual policy of corrupting or influencing the favourite Riza Bey and old Husrev. The Turkish and British fleets were not allowed to go to the coast of Syria. Ponsonby found his position less favourable. Husrev became less dependable with the result that Reschid's position became a dangerous one, and he remembered the fate of Pertev. It was partly for this reason that Ponsonby eagerly supported his immediate despatch to Europe where he was to visit Vienna, Berlin and Paris on his way to London. Meanwhile the Sultan reinsured himself with Russia, and partly for that reason Ponsonby failed to obtain the military and naval cooperation which he had planned. Nevertheless it was to Britain that the Sultan was looking for a solution of his problem. The diamond necklace for the Queen was especially magnificent and the Misham Order was pressed on Palmerston. But Ponsonby was well aware that British influence depended on whether Palmerston could satisfy the demands which Reschid was soon to make on behalf of the Sultan, and, as will be seen, the refusal to overthrow Mehemet Ali almost destroyed Ponsonby's influence completely.[2]

[1] From Ponsonby, 21 May, 1838: *B.P.* Bulwer began a private and very free correspondence with Palmerston not shewn to Ponsonby of which only a very discreetly edited version is given in his book. He wrote on 4 Aug., 1838: "I have been uneasy at the thought that anything in the letters which I write . . . should seem from any accidental difference of opinion, if such there be, to impugn in the slightest degree Lord Ponsonby's judgment." *B.P.*

[2] From Ponsonby, 24, 27 Aug., 17 Oct., 7 Nov., 18 Dec., 1838: *B.P.* P. E. Mosely (*Russian Diplomacy*, etc., Chap. VI) gives an interesting account, based on the Russian Archives, of Russian action in the autumn of 1838 to overthrow Ponsonby's position.

The Sultan and his advisers were always dissatisfied with the representatives of the Great Powers at Constantinople but they had neither the wish nor the men to transact their business in foreign capitals. However, in this period the Sultan began to be more consistently represented abroad. At Vienna Mavrojeni continued his long mission and through his intercourse with Metternich and Frederick Lamb was able to present a point of view different to that of Ponsonby. A succession of envoys went to the Western Powers and particularly to Britain to obtain that support which Ponsonby, for all his ardour in the Turkish cause, was forbidden to promise. Namick Pasha got on so well that he was recalled at the behest of the Russians. His successor, Nourri Pasha, had no French and Palmerston found him an 'oaf' on whom he could make no impression.[1]

It was, perhaps, for this reason that the Sultan in 1836 determined in the greatest secrecy to send a Frenchman, M. Blaque, a lawyer and journalist, the head of the Sultan's Printing Establishment, personally well-known to the Sultan and a friend of the Sultan's reigning favourite. This mission was arranged by Ponsonby and Vogorides. The Reis Effendi himself was not informed. Unfortunately M. Blaque died at Malta on his way to England and the exact object of his mission which Ponsonby announced with the greatest portentousness was never fully stated.[2]

Reschid on his first mission in 1836 (which had included Paris) brought for a short time an entirely new atmosphere to Turkish diplomacy in London. When he was recalled to take the office of Reis Effendi, Sarim Effendi, sent on a special mission on the accession of Queen Victoria, was quite acceptable, but here again Palmerston confessed that "to us who are not used to interpreters it is heavy and desperate work, to do business by these intermedi-

---

[1] To Ponsonby, 16 July, 1835: *B.P.* "Nourri is a greasy stupid old Turk, without an idea in his head": do., 14 Aug., 1835: *B.P.* "A perfect nullity with whom it is impossible to get on at all. He is like a Turk in a melodrama on the stage: one of Bluebeard's attendants." His interpreter, "young Vogorides", was also quite inadequate. This unfortunate intercourse lent aid to Urquhart's advocacy of Turkish-speaking British officials at Constantinople.

[2] From Ponsonby, 6, 8 Feb., 8 April, 1836: *B.P.* "The object will be to afford to His Majesty's Government official and formal knowledge of the Sultan as it is understood by *himself*: and to explain his wishes and his expectations from his Majesty." (6 Feb.) Later Mme Blaque threatened to publish her husband's papers which might have been inconvenient and Ponsonby got Reschid to stop it by the threat of the loss of her pension. (11 May, 1838.) There is no evidence for Urquhart's assertion that M. Blaque was murdered by the Russians.

aries."[1] Ahmed Fethi Pasha, who came over from Paris for a short time, was better able to talk to British ministers but had no great weight. Not, therefore, until Reschid Pasha came back once more at the end of 1838 was a real negotiation attempted in London. Reschid, as had been seen, was only gradually trusted and recommended by Ponsonby and he had not the Sultan's full confidence, but he was of course a man of quite different measure to the others and was able at the end of 1838 to transfer for a short time the centre of negotiation to London, while Ponsonby was left neglected at Constantinople.

[1] To Ponsonby, 21 March, 1838: *B.P.*

2. THE ATTEMPT TO MODERNISE THE OTTOMAN EMPIRE

(i) PALMERSTON'S PROGRAMME

The principles of the Liberal Movement could not be applied in the East and Palmerston never thought of so doing. But his conscience would not have been comfortable if he had made use of the Ottoman Empire without attempting to improve it. He hoped also by reforming it to make it more capable of resisting its enemies and able to play its part in the balance of power in Eastern Europe.

He had laid down his programme in a letter to Ponsonby at the end of 1833:

"Our great aim should be to try to place the Porte in a state of internal organization compatible with independence, and to urge the Govt. to recruit their army and their finances, and to put their navy into some order. The latter is the least important of the three because England and France can supply the deficiencies of Turkey in that respect. The army ought to be their first object; and why is it necessary to put their provinces into a state of rebellion as they have done in Albania by forcing men into the ranks? Cannot they obtain recruits by voluntary enrolment? If pure Mussulmen will not enlist, will not their Christian subjects do so? especially if they were to admit officers of the same class into regimental commands." He then suggested employing half-pay British officers as instructors and went on to consider finance. "Is it hopeless to get them to put their finances into better condition? If, instead of granting out monopolies which ruin commerce, they would allow people to trade freely and levy moderate duties on commerce, they would find their revenue greatly improved. If instead of sending Pashas to eat up the provinces they govern, and then be squeezed in their turn by the Sultan, they would *pay* their Govt. officers and not allow them to plunder, the security which such a system would afford to the population would be a wonderful stimulus to industry and production."

He had no illusions, he said, as to the difficulty of all this: "You will ask whether I fancy myself writing to the Prophet or to

his earthly Vice-Regent, or how I imagine that a British Ambassador is to accomplish this regeneration of a rotten empire? I imagine no such impossibilities; but I see how active you are, and what influence you have obtained, and what channels of information you have opened for yourself, and I therefore point out to you the great landmarks by which your efforts should be directed."[1]

In answer Ponsonby stressed some of the difficulties. He could not even mention the army to the Sultan or his Ministers—yet. Ponsonby himself at that time believed that the best barrier to Russia was in the "strength vigour and interests" of the Rayah population. But it was at present impossible to arm them: "To enlist Rayahs in a Turkish army, is, I believe, against the law of the Empire, and I doubt if Turkish soldiers could be at present induced to associate in the necessary intimate manner with the Giaours." Nevertheless, possibly under the influence of the Prince of Samos, one of whose main objects was to raise the status of his coreligionists, Ponsonby considered with some hope the possibility of setting up Rayah municipal and provincial governments which might have a militia under their control: "The various Rayah provinces under the administration of coreligionists elected by themselves will I think cheerfully submit to the sovereignty of the Sultan and find their own best interests upon resisting the dominion of Russia." But he had to admit that arming the Rayahs would upset the whole balance of the Empire: "The fact, however, will be that the Rayahs armed will soon obtain entire equality with the Turks, but possibly, being themselves divided into so many nations, and having such diversity of interests, they may be content with equality and not seek for more. I think this even likely provided the Turk shall not attempt to persecute or insult and I also think the Turk will not attempt either [because of the] over ruling necessity derived from his own weakness." Needless to add, he claimed that the best way to obtain all these reforms was to send a fleet into the Dardanelles and relieve the Sultan from his fear of Russia.[2]

Ponsonby was to become even less optimistic as he learnt more about the Ottoman Empire. But Palmerston did not take these

---

[1] To Ponsonby, 6 Dec., 1833: *B.P.* On this subject see a good article by Professor F. S. Rodkey, "Lord Palmerston and the Rejuvenation of Turkey, *1830–1839*," *Journal of Modern History*, Dec., 1929, June, 1930, and F. E. Bailey, *British Policy and the Turkish Reform Movement, 1826–1853*.

[2] From Ponsonby, 17 Jan., 1834: *B.P.*

or later cautions to heart and went on advocating a Rayah army until the catastrophe of 1839. Neither he nor Ponsonby could of course do much to improve the central or provincial administration the iniquities of which the Consular reports described. How strongly Palmerston felt about it is seen by a minute he wrote on one of these from Trebizond which gave an account of the ill-treatment of the Kurds: "This is a curious paper and shews what has been one of the most active causes in converting into desert wastes those fertile districts which under the vigorous police of the Roman Empire were full of cities and of fixed inhabitants." All that Ponsonby could do was to support the Prince of Samos in his slow and cautious approach to the problem.[1]

Whatever the influence of the Prince of Samos there is little evidence that the Sultan was working to emancipate the Rayahs in this period. Akif and Halil caused the Sultan to sanction Pertev's death by tricking the Minister into advocacy of a militia instead of the Sultan's regular army. The Sultan, reported Ponsonby, was moved by motives of self-preservation: "With the fall of the Janissaries all control over his power fell also, and his authority was established by a new army recruited from distant Provinces, having nothing to connect the soldier with the mass of the people or with the chiefs of the nation and separated into small divisions placed in barracks at considerable distances one from the other." A militia would have deprived the Sultan of power because, like the Janissaries, they would have been armed instruments of the chiefs of the nation.[2]

Nothing could be done, therefore, to effect any real reform in the Ottoman army which was as badly led and supplied in 1839 as in 1832. As to the fleet, the Turks are not natural sailors. Before the Greek revolution the working crews were largely Greek. They supplied the seamanship while their loyalty was secured by the presence of Turkish soldiers and officers. But, according to Stratford Canning, in 1832 two-thirds of the crews were landsmen

[1] Minute Palmerston, 25 Dec., 1835, on a memoir of Brant, Consul at Trebizond: *F.O. Turkey*, 256.

[2] Professor Temperley stated (*Crimea*, 40) "That the improvement of the lot of the rayas was the supreme and last object of Mahmoud seems clear." But he produced but little evidence for this judgment. From Ponsonby, 31 Jan. 1838: *F.O. Turkey*, 329. There is no certainty of course about the causes of Pertev's death. The Seraglio never yielded up its secrets completely and Ponsonby later thought Mehemet Ali had a hand in the plot. But the judgment of Ponsonby, who by this time knew the Sultan better than any other Englishman had ever done, is a valuable one.

and the fleet was quite inefficient. The Turk, however, has always been a good soldier when he has been given a modicum of organisation, supply and leadership. The army had resisted Russia stubbornly in 1828. Its collapse in 1832–1833 was due to incapacity in high places and the same was true in 1839. Palmerston was right in thinking that it could play an important part in the balance of power of the Near East. What he did not realise was that the Sultan only maintained the Ottoman Empire because the Turk monopolised, or nearly so, the use of organised force. Palmerston failed to perceive that if the Rayahs were armed or a local militia created whose allegiance to the central authority was doubtful, the Empire was bound to disintegrate. Nor could the command of Ottoman troops be given to an infidel. Sève Pasha had to become a Mahommedan before he could become Ibrahim's trusted general. When Husrev was urged to employ the Polish general, Chrysanowski, in a similar position, the Seraskier made it a condition that he should make a formal change of religion. It took Palmerston a long time to realise these limitations to his planning.[1]

Still less was it possible to do much about administrative reorganisation. Partly under the influence of Reschid, but also because he distrusted all his servants, the Sultan reduced the status of the Grand Vizir, and the favourites became even more influential: "The Sultan fears the establishment of any Corps in the state, even one of Ministers of his own selection, as has been seen by the degradation of the powers of the Grand Vizier, who is almost a nullity and by the capricious elevation of sometimes one favourite and sometimes another to be the temporary instruments of his Govt, whereby all the Ministers become little more than chief clerks of their respective departments executing a will, itself moved by the intrigues and misrepresentations and falsehoods of the Seraglio."[2]

The Executive was, it is true, reorganised in March 1838 to suit this situation. Three Councils were established; (1) at the Seraskier's palace where military affairs were settled; (2) at the Porte, the old centre, where finance and commerce were discussed and (3) at the Sultan's palace where final decisions were to be taken. Old Husrev presided at the third, but every question was a matter of intrigue in the Seraglio with the Sultan's favourites, as

---

[1] From Stratford Canning, 17 May, 1832: *F.O. Turkey*, 210.
[2] From Ponsonby, 31 Jan., 1838: *F.O. Turkey*, 329.

Ponsonby reported to Palmerston in the autumn in a very intimate letter: "There is no such thing as a Minister here who has either will or influence or courage enough to discuss any point with the Sultan. Everything is done in the Serail by the favourite or in case of great difficulty the Sultan asks Husrev's opinion." No wonder Ponsonby asked for authority to give a handsome present to Riza Bey, the reigning favourite, which, he said, would please the Sultan also.[1]

Nothing could, indeed, be done except by the subterranean methods which Ponsonby had learnt to apply through Vogorides and MacGuffog. One cannot help but admire the persistent and methodical manner in which the Prince of Samos worked towards his ends. Nearly always it was by his intervention that Ponsonby obtained the Sultan's consent to some necessary step. Vogorides had long had a plan to get the system set up at Samos used in other Greek islands and in 1838 he succeeded in obtaining the Sultan's consent to apply it to Cyprus.[2] But for the larger schemes of Palmerston nothing could be done. Yet even late in 1838 after so many disappointments we find Palmerston again urging the same programme that he had put forward in 1834 of reorganising the army, navy and finance so that the Sultan could beat Mehemet by his own means, "that instead of harassing his subjects by a conscription carried on with every species of violence he should try to procure voluntary recruits and should take Christians as well as Turks if they chose to enter, just as we in India enlist Mahommedans and Hindus indiscriminately."[3]

In fact only two of the items on Palmerston's programme were attempted, the despatch of British officers and the negotiation of a new commercial convention. The first was a rather humiliating failure, with some redeeming indirect advantages, the second was a triumphant success.

(ii) THE ARMY AND NAVY

As regards officers the Sultan passionately desired to strengthen his army and naturally desired expert advice. His first instinct was to seek assistance from the French army which had done so

[1] From Ponsonby, 26 March, 1838: *F.O. Turkey*, 330; do., 17 Oct., 1838: *B.P.*
[2] From Ponsonby, 10 Feb., 1838: *F.O. Turkey*, 329.
[3] To Ponsonby, 13 Sept., 1838: *Bulwer*, II, 281, and *B.P.* The passage quoted is omitted by Bulwer.

much for Mehemet. Reschid Bey had supplied some French officers during his first visit to Paris. Russia protested and played on the religious objections of the Turks. Consequently Nourri was ordered to approach Palmerston for some assistance in equipment and training, though he does not seem to have been authorised to ask for British officers to be sent to Turkey. One of the results of the interest thus awakened was the despatch of the Polish General, Chrysanowski, whom Tsartoriski himself had recommended. He was described by Palmerston as "a remarkably intelligent well informed little fellow" who had served in the Russian army in the war against the Turks in 1828–1829 as a Captain of Artillery. Consequently his appointment was bound to be obnoxious to the Russians and Chrysanowski had no illusions on that head. He suggested that he should be attached unofficially to Reschid Pasha's headquarters and he got his payments arranged from British sources. Ponsonby got Husrev to view the appointment favourably at first and Chrysanowski gave some advice and learnt some of the conditions of the Turkish Army. But then the Russians moved and the little Pole hastened to fly. He was afraid of being handed over to Russia and shot as a deserter.[1]

Palmerston got the Pole to go back by giving him letters of 'denization'. These were only a partial protection against Russia, since Britain recognised the inalienable character of nationality, but Ponsonby gave him the protection of the Embassy. Reschid backed Ponsonby's request that Chrysanowski should be given a command but at the last moment Husrev shewed jealousy and the Pole had to act only in an advisory capacity. In 1838 he moved to Baghdad for a time. But his reports on the Turkish army were the best Palmerston received and throughout the critical years 1839–1840 the advice and information of Chrysanowski were of the greatest value to him.[2]

Nourri had also asked for young Turks to be trained as instructors in British ships of war. Palmerston was only too glad to

[1] From Ponsonby, 29 Dec., 1835: *F.O. Turkey*, 256.
[2] To Ponsonby, 4 Nov., 1835, 7 March, 1836; From Ponsonby, 30 July, 1838: *B.P.* The despatches and private letters abound in references to Chrysanowski who from the first made a most favourable impression on Palmerston. The General treated the Turkish officers with great tact and, unlike the British officers sent out, was content to serve in any capacity. His weakness was that his natural dread of being betrayed to the Russians made him avoid Constantinople. Tsartoriski said there were 100 Poles living quietly there. Professor Rodney (*Journal of Modern History*, Dec., 1929) has collected together many of the references in the despatches.

arrange this, but urged the superior advantages of employing British officers: "The military and naval art is the art of war; and that art can be fully learnt only in war itself. We have a vast number of officers who have so learnt it, and we could send the Sultan now British officers to instruct his army and navy who are much more competent as teachers than these Turkish young gentlemen will be five years hence." As a result, in addition to various stores, Colonel Considine and Captain du Plat with other officers were sent to Constantinople. No doubt they were fairly competent and Captain du Plat performed prodigies of valour in surveying the defences of the Balkan towns in the height of winter. But they wanted a command and Considine was soon dissatisfied with his position and returned to England. Command was, however, just what the Turkish Government could not give and it is surprising that Palmerston did not at once realise the fact. "Unless they have command I do not see that they can be of much use," he wrote at the outset, and he continued to press this view on the Porte. The failure of Considine's mission, he thought, "makes us ridiculous", and with his usual pertinacity he sent him out again. But the Turks, alleging Russian opposition, refused to employ him or pay him and Palmerston had to admit that he could not go on paying for British officers to advise the Turks. Considine was sent to Tunis where he seems to have done little better. He was, indeed, not the sort of man to win the Turks' confidence and all that Palmerston got out of this attempt was a certain amount of military information, and the Turks nothing at all.[1]

The Turks had less need for such inadaptable assistants because they had already secured expert advice from other quarters in Captain Helmuth von Moltke, who du Plat reported had come there disguised as a merchant in 1835. Palmerston thought this was a Russian trick and protested strongly against it. Ponsonby and others suspected that Moltke was to be used to fortify the Dardanelles. Lord William Russell's report of the mediocre quality of the greatest soldier since Napoleon has caused much derision but he obtained the information from the most competent authorities in Berlin. Shortly afterwards he insisted that Moltke was not to be trusted, and Palmerston hastened to inform Pon-

[1] To Ponsonby, 4 Nov., 1835, 7 March, 1836, 17 Jan., 1837, 12 Feb., 1838: B.P.

sonby that he was dangerous. But the Prussian Government sent out other officers whom Russell and even Ponsonby admitted were good Russian haters. Moreover they made no fuss about their status. They were also provided with plans made in the Prussian General Staff for the fortification of the Balkans as well as the Straits. Russell, who kept bombarding Palmerston with schemes to preserve the Ottoman Empire, attached great importance to these. It does not seem, however, that the Prussian officers did very much to improve the Turkish army though Moltke's eye detected all the mistakes of strategy in 1839. More important was the Hanoverian General, Jochmus, whom Palmerston sent out in 1838, who with the "little Pole" was to be of real service in 1840.[1]

Palmerston did not have much greater success with his renewed efforts to improve the Turkish fleet which he began after his failure with the Army—and for the same reason. "If the Sultan would let us send him some naval officers", he wrote in 1838, "it would be the making of his fleet and a good fleet would be the salvation of his Empire. But I do not think any naval officer would go or could be of any use unless he had command. The Sultan should man a couple of line-of-battle ships with Greek sailors and give them English officers and then put a number of young Turkish naval officers to learn their business on these ships and he would soon have an efficient navy without bringing religious and national prejudices into play." This last clause was added because of what he had gradually learned about the army, but it did not really meet Turkish prejudices. Ponsonby dutifully did his best to get the programme carried out. But Captain Walker who was sent out with other officers was refused command, ostensibly because of the fear of Russian protest. Not until 1840 was he given such a position, one of Ponsonby's greatest triumphs. The

[1] To Lord William Russell, 11 May, 1837: *F.O. Prussia*, 209. From Lord William Russell, 17, 24 May, 1837: *F.O. Prussia*, 210. In a private letter, after further enquiry, Russell repeated his view of Moltke: "His abilities are only considered to be of a very second rate nature and the value of his counsels, however well meant they may be, is much abated [sic]." (13 July, 1837: *B.P.*) do., 4, 11 Jan., 26 March, 21 Dec., 1837, 3 Jan., 1838; To Ponsonby, 12 Jan., 1838; To Lamb, 30 April, 1837: *B.P.* Palmerston took no notice of the plans sent by Russell, who said he acted so because Ponsonby was not a military man. Some lie in the Broadlands Archives apparently unread. Ponsonby reported most hostilely at first on the secret and suspicious conduct of Moltke, and the other officers, but by 1839 he was convinced of their anti-Russian attitude though, he wrote, they might be inciting the Sultan to war. From Ponsonby, 26 March, 1839: *F.O. Turkey*, 355.

cruise of the Ottoman fleet with the British in the autumn of 1838 no doubt helped to improve its efficiency and morale. But little had been done when the crisis came in 1839 and that little was of no avail since most of the fleet deserted to Mehemet.[1]

This was not much to have effected in four years on so important a question. But it must be remembered that Palmerston had little time to devote to Turkish affairs. His military talents were absorbed in Spain until the end of 1837. When the crisis came in 1840 he was able to apply the lessons of these years with remarkable ability and success.

(iii) THE COMMERCIAL CONVENTION, 1838

There is a very different story to tell about the commercial convention where in the end, after many doubts and hesitations, Palmerston and Ponsonby had a veritable triumph.[2] The origin of this instrument has been vehemently claimed by Urquhart and his claim has been supported by many historians. It is certainly true that after his travels in the East he saw more clearly than anyone else the necessity of change and what its effects might be. The report that he sent home at the beginning of 1834 won Ponsonby's warm approval because it was so hostile to Russia whose exports to Britain, Urquhart claimed, could be supplied by Turkey if the impediments to trade were removed. Thus would be provided a "two edged sword against Russia, Turkey would be strengthened and Russia weakened". But, Ponsonby insisted, Russia knew this fact well enough and would never allow the change to be made if she could prevent it. The Turks had received his first suggestions extremely well, "but all the favor engaged in that quarter is and must be totally unavailing so long as the Russian nightmare lies upon the bosom of Turkey." Nothing could be more true. It took four years before Ponsonby could create the necessary confidence in the Sultan to enable him to get a new treaty sanctioned.

---

[1] To Ponsonby, 14 April, 1838: *B.P.*

[2] The negotiation of the commercial convention and its later effects have been discussed at length by Professor Puryear in his *International Economics etc.*, chaps. 3 and 4. There are more concise descriptions by F. E. Bailey (*British Policy, etc.*, 122–127) and Professor Temperley (*Crimea*, 31–39) where the political implications are more clearly shown. All that is attempted here is to assign the responsibility for action and to shew the immediate political effects. The economic results belong to a later period.

Meanwhile the agitation for a new commercial treaty continued in many quarters. The traders in Constantinople had long been pressing for something to be done. Palmerston himself had begun to urge the abolition of monopolies before Urquhart paid any attention to the subject. The trading connections with nearly every country were being overhauled with a view to finding an outlet for the growing production of Britain. It would have been remarkable if the trade with the Ottoman Empire had been over-looked.[1]

But monopolies were only one aspect of a complicated problem. The relations between the Christian Powers and Turkey were based on the Capitulations made when their subjects first began to trade in a country where the infidel could not be put on an equal footing with the true believer. These had been in the course of time implemented in commercial treaties which laid down the maximum tariffs for exports, imports and goods in transit. The Porte had had to accept special regimes for its land frontiers with Austria and Russian by treaties made after it had been defeated in war. Britain and France had generally been on the Sultan's side and their treaties contained no such stipulations. Nevertheless the tariffs were low, three per cent, and had they really been put into practice they would have allowed a freer exchange of goods than existed between any two European states.

But to the duties at the Porte were added so many other charges that, as Bulwer pointed out, "our imports were taxed, forty, fifty, sixty per cent, and Turkish exports sixty, seventy, a hundred." This result was produced by inland charges (as later in China where the treaties were based on similar Capitulations) and also by monopolies. For the Sultan, needing money, created monopolies in order to sell them and his Pashas did likewise. But while Mehemet Ali managed his own monopolies a far less propor-tion of the profits of Turkish monopolies went into the Sultan's pocket. Much of them was taken by intermediaries. The regu-lations were such that only by bribery could trade be carried on at all. There were also financial difficulties, for the ex-penses of the war had inflated the currency. In addition there were (as in many European countries and especially Austria

---

[1] From Ponsonby, 31 Jan., 1834: *B.P.* To Ponsonby, 6 Dec., 1833, *F.O. Turkey*, 220. In an admirable economic lecture Palmerston shewed to his own satisfaction at any rate that the Sultan would gain financially by the abolition of monopolies.

and Russia) prohibitions against exporting or importing many articles.[1]

The Sultan, deprived of his Greek provinces and saddled with a war indemnity, needed, as everybody admitted, more money. The first move to change the system came indeed from Turkey, and Nourri Effendi was ordered to raise the question in London. As we have seen, Palmerston had no opinion of Nourri who could speak no European language and found the greatest difficulty in carrying out his mission. He sums up his negotiation on this subject as follows: "He is a great hog and not a diplomatist. We have made no advance about commercial matters; he wants me to agree to pay more than 3 per Cent Import Duty; I say, what equivalent advantage can you offer us in exchange? He says, the satisfaction of doing a good and generous action by a friend. I reply commerce knows nothing of philanthropy and romance, and we must have a quid pro quo; but he cannot think of any quid."[2]

Poor Nourri's position was made all the more uncomfortable by the fact that Urquhart, now working on the subject in London, was constantly giving him unnecessary advice, demanding to know what Palmerston had said to him, and warning him not to visit the Russian Ambassador. Nourri could not ascertain that Urquhart had any authority, but was afraid that he would write injurious reports to Constantinople. He was told not to take any notice and to let the Foreign Office know if Urquhart annoyed him again.

This is an excellent example of Urquhart's manners and methods. He was working at the tariff at the orders of the Foreign Office and furnishing the Board of Trade with valuable information, but he had of course no authority to decide a matter on which the Board of Trade and Foreign Secretary had not come to any conclusion. He apparently then left Nourri alone and at the beginning of 1836 was told by Backhouse, at Palmerston's orders, to

---

[1] The best account of the system is given by Professor Puryear who has seen many of the consular reports of these years. There was, indeed, naturally a constant stream of complaint. Professor Temperley well illustrated the difficulties by shewing that twelve different processes were necessary to secure permission to pass through the Bosphorus (*Crimea*, 33). No firman was, however, required for vessels to go up to Constantinople and return into the Mediterranean. (Minute, Backhouse, 1836: *B.P.*)

[2] To Ponsonby, 16 July, 1835: *B.P.* The demand for the revision of the tariff and the intimation of the '*quid pro quo*' had previously been exchanged in writing. To and from Nourri Effendi 11, 13 May, 1835: *F.O. Turkey*, 268.

come to an understanding with Poulett Thomson. The reports and memoranda which he was submitting were no doubt of considerable use in view of his local knowledge, but they were only part, though an important one, of a large documentation and insisted on lower duties than the Turks were likely to accept.[1]

What Urquhart was stressing was the total abolition of the internal duties, a sensible proposal but one which had necessarily to be compensated by a considerable increase in the tariff. He made every effort to get complete control of the negotiations. "I have no hesitation", he wrote, "in saying that I feel perfectly certain of the failure of the proposal with regard to the tariff if the negotiations are undertaken through the machinery of the Dragomans." Urquhart's dislike at being kept in a subordinate position which left the final decisions to those responsible to Parliament is shewn by his next suggestion that a parliamentary inquiry should be made into British trade in the Levant. On this Palmerston wrote a characteristic minute. "I see no practical object to be gained by such an inquiry but I do see a great loss of valuable time that would ensue from it to me and the President of the Board of Trade. It might be very amusing to a number of idle gentlemen about Town to come down and speak pamphlets in the Committee in answer to preconcerted questions and thus to have their works printed at the expense of the public, but I should oppose any such inquiry if moved by others and certainly shall not move it myself."[2]

The result of these discussions was that a draft convention was sent to Constantinople with instructions that the Consul-General,

[1] See my article, "Urquhart, Ponsonby and Palmerston," *English Historical Review*, July, 1947. Memorandum of a conversation which took place between Nourri Effendi, M. Vogorides [the younger] and M. V. Salamé [a Foreign Office representative] at the Levy [Undated] *F.O. Turkey*, 268. From Nourri Effendi, 23 Oct., 1835: *F.O. Turkey*, 268. Backhouse to Urquhart, 11 Feb., 1836: *F.O. Turkey*, 279. Minute by Palmerston, 11 Dec., 1835: *F.O. Turkey*, 266. Mrs. Robinson (*David Urquhart*, 59–60) quotes a correspondent's assertion that it was Urquhart that inspired the Turkish Government to ask for the revision. Urquhart no doubt made the suggestion, but all commercial circles in Constantinople were talking along similar lines. The document quoted in the text shews the Turkish Ambassador's real attitude towards Urquhart and Urquhart himself later alludes to "my rupture with Nourri Effendi". (Urquhart to Backhouse 27 Jan., 1837: *F.O. Turkey*, 309.)

[2] From Urquhart, 4 Feb., 1836: Urquhart to Backhouse, 18 April, 4 May, 1836; Minute, Palmerston: *F.O. Turkey*, 279. Urquhart later reported that the Commercial Bank of Liverpool would set up a bank in Constantinople —but only if the British banking laws were altered so that all property of the stockholders was not answerable for banking debts.

Cartwright, and two merchants were to enter into negotiation with the Porte concerning it. Urquhart had no doubt considerable influence on the terms proposed. He was, however, given no authority by Palmerston, though no doubt the idea that he would be useful in the negotiations was one of the motives which induced Palmerston to insist on his taking up his position as Secretary of Embassy at this time.[1]

But of course Ponsonby had the responsibility for the negotiation as for all else at Constantinople. Once there Urquhart began discussions in which he tried to insist on very low duties. As soon as Ponsonby's quarrel with Urquhart began he ordered the latter to cease negotiating about the commercial convention. It is, therefore, Ponsonby who is responsible for the delay which took place. Bulwer attributed it to his indolence, but this seems hardly fair. There were many other reasons. His plan to go on leave, and the row with Urquhart, rendering it quite impossible for the latter to be allowed to give any assistance, necessarily prevented immediate action. Ponsonby added later the illness of Houloussi, the acting Reis Effendi, and of Pertev, and the plague. But above all it was necessary to create the right political atmosphere in order to obtain so great a change as the abolition of the monopolies and inland duties in which so many powerful vested interests were concerned. Ponsonby could not be expected to concern himself with the details of the complicated negotiation any more than Lamb did at Vienna with the Austrian Treaty. It was the function of the Ambassador merely to exercise a very general supervision and to intervene at the highest level if a deadlock occurred.[2]

Ponsonby was not on very good terms with Cartwright, who in any case was hardly the man to tackle so big a problem. He had already found that the Sultan wished to obtain political advantage from the negotiation. In April 1836 when the Minister of Finance advised the abolition of the export duties on grain the Sultan told Ponsonby he dare not do it because of Russia. It is hardly surprising, therefore, to find Ponsonby refusing to put the plan into operation immediately. Other governments were moving at Constantinople in the question of monopolies, but in 1837 while

---

[1] To Ponsonby, 28 July, 1836: *F.O. Turkey*, 272.
[2] Urquhart to Backhouse, 27 Jan., 1837: *F.O. Turkey*, 309. As early as 24 Oct., 1836, Urquhart had insinuated in a letter to Ponsonby that the latter did not care about the convention. They then became reconciled again but the final rupture occurred in the early days of January.

Roussin was on leave Ponsonby got on very intimate terms with the French Chargé d'Affaires, D'Eyragues, and decided to act with France alone. This should be remembered in connection with the French protests in 1838. D'Eyragues took up the matter enthusiastically and made some progress with the Sultan and his advisers. But these latter were at this period still determined to raise the tariff without making the concessions concerning the other duties and monopolies. These obstacles were not overcome and the Ambassador even suggested at the end of 1837 that perhaps a new convention was not really necessary. It could only be secured, he said, if England and France threatened to insist that they would claim back the duties levied in defiance of the Capitulations. He clearly did not want to take a step which might play into the hand of his pro-Russian opponents in the Seraglio.[1]

It was the hope that the convention would have political effects that induced the Sultan to shew the necessary energy and decision to overcome the vested interests which were opposing change. However great Mahmud's reforming zeal in his earlier years, by 1838 he was in no mood to carry out so great a departure from established custom. His support of Reschid Pasha, for example, was more due to that Minister's connection with the Western Powers, with its possibility of obtaining help against Mehemet, than any real sympathy with Reschid's reforms. Reschid, indeed, had to leave Constantinople to save his life immediately after the convention was concluded, so powerful were his enemies. But the Sultan as his health declined was all the more eager to settle matters with his rebellious vassal. The convention would serve that purpose in two ways. By aiming a blow at Mehemet's monopolies it would weaken him and might even provoke him to such action as would bring on him the might of Britain. And it would predispose the British Government and British public opinion in the Sultan's favour and make more likely the success of Reschid's mission. This is, of course, a matter of speculation since the Sultan did not reveal his mind even to his nearest subordinates and favourites. But, despite Bulwer's later assertions, Ponsonby's claim that he carried the convention by an appeal to political

[1] From Ponsonby, 8, 16 April, 26 Dec., 1836, 15 March, May, 27 Aug., 1837: *F.O. Turkey*, 274, 278, 302–304. D'Eyragues was given a snuff-box by the Sultan for his work as Chargé d'Affaires, about which Ponsonby wrote enthusiastically.

motives is in accordance with all the contemporary evidence available.

Palmerston had not as yet taken any very special interest in this problem. The struggle in Spain was absorbing his attention. But at the beginning of 1838 here, as in Austria, he endeavoured to get action. He then did two important things. He wrote despatches, partly at Ponsonby's suggestion, threatening the Sultan with reprisals if he refused to negotiate but urging that the abolition of monopolies, while not really injuring the Sultan, would strike a blow at Mehemet Ali whose whole financial system depended on them. And he appointed Bulwer Secretary of Embassy, despite Ponsonby's intimation that he did not want one. Clearly someone was needed at Constantinople to do the work which MacGregor was doing at Vienna.[1]

Ponsonby, though he did not welcome the suggestion of a new Secretary, liked Bulwer and at this juncture took up the question of the treaty with far more energy since it might strike a blow at Mehemet. His claim that he obtained the treaty is obviously justified and Bulwer's romantic account written long afterwards is nothing but a fairy tale. The Ambassador immediately pressed Palmerston's argument on the Sultan and in April, before Bulwer arrived, had got the commercial convention brought to his personal notice. The vested interests were, however, working strongly against the abolition of monopolies and Ponsonby urged Palmerston to tell the Turkish Ambassador in London that, if British demands were not accepted, an account of the Turkish disregard of the Capitulations would be demanded. Reschid Pasha was now gaining influence and no doubt the convention could hardly have been secured without his help, which Ponsonby secured by backing him against his enemies, and threatening to leave him to the mercies of Husrev if he refused. Part of the price was the European mission which may have saved Reschid's life. But this, as Ponsonby pointed out, was only the *formal* part of the work: "It is in the Seraglio and with the Sultan himself I have been and still am endeavouring to bring it to a satisfactory conclusion."

In this situation Palmerston's plan for a political treaty described in Section 5 of this chapter, which made a deep impression on the Sultan and his advisers, must have counted for a great deal. It is quite probable that without it the negotiation would not have suc-

[1] To Ponsonby, 6 Feb., 14 April, 6 June, 1838: *F.O. Turkey*, 328, 329.

ceeded. For the convention added to the Sultan's difficulties with Russia and might perhaps finally determine Mehemet to declare his independence. It was the promise of guarantee against Russian threats, and the hope that the step would lead to a treaty countenancing an attack on Mehemet that caused the Sultan to take so momentous a decision against such powerful opposition.[1]

Bulwer, who came at the end of April to put the convention into shape with the Turkish Ministers, seems to have performed his minor, but all-essential, part of working out the detail with efficiency and tact and above all without worrying Ponsonby too much. But he never realised the political conditions of his work since he did not believe Mehemet could be overthrown and indeed did not desire it. Palmerston later pointed out his errors on this subject on which of course Bulwer had no influence. But meanwhile Bulwer with the help of Cartwright conducted well the negotiation as to the exact rates of duty. He eventually, no doubt under pressure from Ponsonby, accepted higher rates than had originally been intended in order to get the treaty through quickly. For Ponsonby saw that it was necessary to take advantage of the political position established by the prospect of armed cooperation against Mehemet. Roussin's suspicions, which Ponsonby turned aside by a denial that a treaty had been made, were justified. But the secret was also kept from Bulwer. The Secretary's assurances to the French and Austrian Ambassadors that no political issue was in question no doubt rang quite truly.

But Ponsonby's claim that he decided the main issue is surely justified: "It was carried", he wrote later, "by acting upon the passions of the Sultan and the fears of his Minister." Palmerston realised this and responded to the appeals to get the ratification through the Board of Trade as quickly as possible and without changes so that no opportunity could be given to Tahir Bey, the Chief of the Customs, and the rest of the opposition, "Armenian or Greek Bankers, of some of the Greek merchants, of many of the Pashas and other functionaries and a crowd of their dependants whose illegitimate gains will be cut off."[2]

---

[1] From Ponsonby, 12 March, 21 April, 10 May, 19 Aug., 1838: *F.O. Turkey*, 330–332; do., 7 Nov., 1837: *B.P.* He was delighted that Palmerston had arranged for Bulwer to live outside the Embassy.

[2] Bulwer's letters on the treaty were legitimately much cut down for print (*Bulwer*, II, 273, 283), but he also omitted significant sentences about Mehemet, e.g. "Egypt and Syria if regained could not be maintained" on which Palmerston

The treaty was hailed everywhere as a great triumph for Britain. "There has been nothing like it since Canning's speech on sending the troops to Portugal," wrote Lyons from Athens. "Joy and gladness, hope and confidence are revived all over the Levant, the eyes which shrank from the Russian flag with astonishment and dismay now look once more upon the British flag with pride, and all men say England is herself again." Butenev hastened back to his Embassy to repair the shattered Russian influence. Roussin also was furious at Ponsonby's success. He had perhaps some reasonable grounds for thinking that Ponsonby might have given to him the same confidence previously accorded to his Chargé d'Affaires, and he suspected not unjustly that political arrangements were secretly associated with the commercial. But the treaty was in fact to the advantage of all the Western Powers, and, though Molé was only too ready to see in it another excuse to break away from the English alliance, Desages soon admitted as much to Aston. Though Molé tried to get Egypt exempted from the convention he soon gave way. France was, indeed, one of the first states to follow the British example. Roussin himself took steps to deny at Constantinople that the attack by the *Journal des Débats* on the convention in any way represented the opinion of his Government, and asked Ponsonby for a copy of it in order to make one like it.[1]

The Russians on the other hand were much more cautious. They were not sure that the increase of duties would suit them better than their present position. It was on this fact that Urquhart, furious at his dismissal and the success of the negotiations which he had prophesied were bound to fail without his assistance, based his futile opposition to the treaty. But Russia made a new treaty in 1842 and by that time most other trading states had done the same. A great increase of trade resulted especially of that of Britain. Corn from the European provinces of Turkey came to British markets as Urquhart had prophesied. No doubt much of this expansion of trade was inevitable. But the indirect effects

wrote "why not?" His reply is in *Bulwer*, II, 286. From Ponsonby, 15 Dec., 1838: *F.O. Turkey*, 333. This interesting and important despatch describes some of the obstacles that had to be overcome.

[1] From Lyons, 7 Dec., 1838: *B.P.* For the Russian reaction see Mosely, *Russian Diplomacy, etc.*, 115–118. Butenev was more alarmed about Reschid's mission than the convention and was reassured by Bulwer's assertion that there were no political clauses. From Bulwer, 28 Aug., 1838: *B.P.* From Aston, 10 Sept., 1838: *Aston P.* From Ponsonby, 23, 29 Oct., 1838: *F.O. Turkey*, 332.

on the Ottoman Empire were considerable, part of that gradual westernisation which was ultimately bound to destroy it.[1]

One of Roussin's main objections to the treaty had been that Mehemet would refuse to accept it and the resulting clash with the Sultan would bring the Russians to Constantinople. Mehemet did demur at first but soon gave way. His admirers said that his control over all trade and commerce in Egypt and Syria was such that the treaty would really be a dead letter there. Ponsonby was immediately on the alert with plans to force the submission of the Pasha, whose legal position, he claimed, was most vulnerable. But the question was never really tested, for before the effect of the treaty on Egypt could be seen the attack on Mehemet had begun. The same cause hindered the immediate application of the treaty in Turkey itself but gradually its full operation was ensured, not without some struggle between British representatives and the reactionaries.[2]

[1] For the later Russian action see Puryear's detailed description and analysis in *International Diplomacy, etc.*

[2] From Bulwer, 16, 26 Sept., 12 Oct., 1838: *B.P.*; From Campbell, 28 Sept., 1839. *F.O. Turkey*, 343; From Ponsonby, 14 Oct., 1838: *B.P.* "I believe the Pasha possesses no property whatsoever and that he cannot possess any, being considered as the slave of the Sultan. . . . If therefore Mehemet Ali shall pretend to evade the commercial treaty made by his Sovereign under the plea of being himself the sole proprietor in Egypt, it is easy to destroy that plea."

3. THE CONTEST WITH RUSSIA

As we have seen, the Tsar had gradually lost interest in the attack on the Liberal Movement in the West. He carried out the promises which he had made to Metternich, sent funds to Don Carlos and hated Louis Philippe as much as ever, but he put no great zeal into the contest. But in the East he had his own struggle with Britain and at times it looked as if the war which so many expected was bound to come. The manoeuvres for influence extended to all the countries bordering on Russia, and the main lines of her relations with Britain during the next hundred years had been laid down by 1840. It says a good deal for the statesmen who directed these affairs that in 1841 they were on better terms than they had been at any other period since the Napoleonic wars. Palmerston's attitude to Russia has been the theme of many scolding pens. But his actions in these years resulted in a brilliant success and it seems clear that it could not have been obtained by a policy of appeasement, instead of a vigorous assertion of British interests.

The quarrel over Stratford Canning and the Lievens meant that Palmerston had two new Ambassadors to deal with. Orlov, who like all intelligent Russians would have liked to escape from the deadly routine of the Imperial Court, had hoped to succeed Lieven, and had perhaps worked against him for that reason, but the Tsar could not spare him from his side. All the world was surprised, however, when in February 1835 the Tsar transferred Pozzo di Borgo from Paris to London. This was considered partly as a hit at Louis Philippe. It was more likely due to the lack of trained Russian diplomatists and the Tsar's thought that Pozzo di Borgo's appointment would be pleasing to Wellington. Whatever the motive, the change had a disastrous effect on the ageing diplomat who had struck deep roots into Parisian life during his twenty years' residence. Granville wrote that he was 'mystified' and 'indignant' at the transfer, adding sarcastically: "He quite feels for the embarrassment of Apponyi and Werther and other minor members of the Corps Diplomatique bereaved as they now will be of their daily counsellor and guide."[1]

[1] Bligh to Wellington, 10 Jan., 1835. *F.O. Russia*, 217; Granville to Aston, 10 Feb., 1835: *Aston P.*; Esterhazy to Metternich, 31 July, 1835: *V. St. A.*

Pozzo di Borgo might perhaps have recovered from the shock to his pride and habits of life but for the publication of his secret despatches in the *Portfolio*, Urquhart's journal, for which the Poles provided the Russian documents. In a sense they did him credit. "Pozzo need not be ashamed of his," wrote Palmerston, "for they are most ably written." But this revelation of his hostility to both Wellington and Metternich in 1829, two men whom he had in the eighteen thirties assiduously flattered, put him in a most difficult position. Wellington forgave both Pozzo di Borgo and Matuszewic easily enough. He laid the main blame on Princess Lieven. But Metternich, as usual, was vindictive. He confessed his bitter feelings to Hummelauer but told him not to reveal them. Meanwhile he made an attempt to get Pozzo di Borgo removed from his post. It was rumoured, indeed, that Nesselrode would be appointed in his stead. Metternich's move failed. But the Ambassador had lost the confidence of the Tsar, who in 1836 actually spoke slightingly of him to Barante, words which Louis Philippe repeated to the Austrian Ambassador and must have penetrated everywhere in diplomatic circles. Pozzo di Borgo lost all his usual poise and nerve. He tried to court the Whigs and only succeeded in losing the confidence of the Tories. He was quite inadequate to the strain of the controversies of 1838, and the Russian Government consulted Clanricarde as to who should succeed him.

Palmerston failed to treat him with sufficient courtesy, but got on with him well enough. It was convenient to have an Ambassador who was hardly likely to be trusted by Austria or the Tories, and could, therefore, give no trouble. He wrote kind words about him to Durham. Even when he described Pozzo di Borgo as in his 'dotage', he said that suited his convenience. But the Ambassador became quite incapable of serious business and when the crisis of 1839 came a special envoy had to be sent to London.[1]

[1] To William Temple, 14 Jan., 1836: *B.P.* Hummelauer to Metternich, 16 Feb., 27 June, 1836; Metternich to Hummelauer, 13 March, 1836: *V. St. A.* From Lamb, 5 Aug., 1836; To Durham, 9 May, 1836; To Clanricarde, 1 March 1839: *B.P.* Barante, *Mémoires*, V, 243. Apponyi to Metternich, 27 Jan., 1836, *V. St. A.*, *Frankreich.* From Hummelauer, 15 April, 1836: *V. St. A.* He communicated to Wellington and Aberdeen Metternich's despatch to St. Petersburg about the *Portfolio*. Wellington in return communicated a letter to Fitzroy-Somerset to whom Matuszewic had written an exculpatory letter concerning the accusations made against the Duke's character. Matuszewic, the Duke wrote, had got his brief from "a certain lady, not fat, but fair and more than forty, who had a good deal of influence in the Russian Embassy". (Wel-

Meanwhile Palmerston, anxious to avoid another incident, incurred the displeasure of William IV by ascertaining informally that Durham would be acceptable to the Tsar before securing the King's assent. The King at first strongly objected to Durham's appointment and, as Nesselrode interpreted Palmerston's informal and confidential enquiry as a sort of recantation of the course taken over Stratford Canning, the King became very indignant and it took a very tactful and well-reasoned letter from Melbourne to secure his approval. The King naturally distrusted the accounts of Russia sent by his Ambassador who, he wrote, "really appears to forget that His Lordship is the servant of His Britannic Majesty and not of the Emperor of Russia." No doubt he repeated this view to others and Ellice with his usual malice reported it to Durham. The Ambassador's indignation was intense and he wrote bitter letters to Palmerston about it. Palmerston wrote him a friendly warning and got him to write a despatch pointing out the need of special vigilance over Russian activities even if they were not immediately dangerous. This produced some effect and though the King still spoke of Durham's 'delusions' and 'gullibility', he did not question his good faith. Durham was duly grateful, but the King's suspicions mounted again in 1837, because the increased prominence of Princess Victoria caused Durham to be talked about as her adviser. Palmerston, who throughout this Embassy treated Durham with exceptional tact and skill, arranged that the Ambassador should send him a 'private letter', in appearance not intended for royal eyes, which he could shew to the King to justify Durham. This was done, and just before the King's death Palmerston was thus able to get the G.C.B. for Durham and a friendly royal message. Durham was also allowed to accept Nicholas's gift of the Order of St. Andrew, an exception from the strict rule that Ambassadors should not accept foreign Orders which would not have been made under any other circumstances.[1]

lington to Fitzroy-Somerset, 12 Jan., 1836: *V. St. A.*) To Granville, 2 Feb., 1836: "Pozzo lives quiet and gives little trouble, and as it was said of George 4th that he was as good as no King at all, a similar remark may be made upon Pozzo"; do., 29 March, 1836: *B.P.* From Melbourne, 24 Dec., 1838: "No doubt you will agree with me that we should not interfere at all in the choice of an Ambassador." (*B.P.*)

[1] From Melbourne, 29 June, 1835: *B.P.* Lloyd Sanders, *Melbourne Papers,* 333. Palmerston was not supposed to see the King's letter to which this was a reply and there is no copy at Broadlands. To Durham, 2 May, 1837; From Durham, 3 June, 1837; From Will. IV, 28 Feb., 28 March, 23 July, 21 Oct., 1836: *B.P.* S. Reid, *Lord Durham,* II, 124. C. New, *Lord Durham,* 291–292.

Durham's character was already known at St. Petersburg and the Ambassador was again given an exceptional position which produced its full effect. The Tsar found genuine interest in a sort of intimacy with a brilliant and unconventional personality. Durham delightedly recounted the special honours paid to him at which both Court and diplomatic circles were astounded. He had, however, gone with the full intention of endeavouring to reconcile the two countries, a role which suited his vanity if not his political interests. He came, therefore, after no very profound enquiry to conclusions about both the strength and intentions of Russia different to those held by Palmerston. They were both agreed that the danger of war was not immediate. But Durham thought that better relations would be established by moderating public opinion in Britain and making every possible concession to the Tsar. Palmerston thought that Russia could only be checked if the Tsar and his Ministers were fully convinced that the British Government and people were determined to resist Russian aggression. In the circumstances, the two got on extraordinarily well. Durham was throughout most careful to avoid any possible charge of disloyalty to his chief, whose rival he had been thought to be, and Palmerston's differences of opinion were couched in friendly and restrained language.[1]

The Ambassador was convinced that he had the Tsar's confidence. When the Tsar was away on his long tours, of which there were many in 1837, he made little or no effort to get in touch with other diplomatists. Barante, the French Ambassador, was not intimate with him and, partly because of continual illness but also by choice, he saw little of the other members of the diplomatic circle. Their reports about him are pointed with irony—and perhaps with jealousy. Meanwhile by bribery, Cayley, an unpaid Vice-Consul who knew Russian well, obtained copies of secret information from the Finance Office about the military establishments and financial situation of Russia. Palmerston suspected

Palmerston thought Nicholas had given Durham the Order to embarrass him. To Granville, 27 June, 1837: B.P. Neither of Durham's biographers knew of Palmerston's last move to justify Durham who wrote (12 April, 1837): "I see in the papers a sharp war going on in which I am made a party respecting the Princess Victoria's establishment. The whole is a lie from beginning to end. . . . The object of all this is no doubt to confirm, if not encrease, the prejudices existing in a certain quarter—and I have little hopes of the measure not being successful." Palmerston cut out the last sentence and sent the rest to the King.

[1] Durham told Palmerston (5 April, 1836: B.P.) that he wrote to no one else about his mission. (To Melbourne, 31 Oct., 1835: B.P.)

that some of this information had been planted on Durham but admitted that it was a useful check and later authorised Clanricarde to spend money to continue it. Durham himself boasted so much of his exceptional information that it was clear that he had some special machinery of this kind, and Londonderry after a visit almost said as much in a book which he presented to Nesselrode! Durham, however, did thus supply factual information as well as hasty impressions, and his advocacy of the Russian case on many subjects may have had some effect on the Cabinet, if not on Palmerston.

Durham told Esterhazy on his return that he had improved relations with Russia in the face of the opposition of King, Cabinet, Parliament and the Press, and the Ambassador admitted the claim. Durham added that the Tsar wished him to become Foreign Minister, but he had refused because of the kind way Palmerston had treated him personally. Esterhazy believed, however, that he was still quite ready to accept the position if he got the chance to do so. But it seems pretty certain that Durham's mission was not really so important as he thought. Perhaps its main effect was to keep a little quieter some of his Radical followers in England. The depth of the Tsar's real feelings for him may be gauged by the fact that he told Clanricarde in 1839 that he would like to hang him with his own hands for his conduct in Canada.[1]

Clanricarde, who got the Embassy by a species of political blackmail, had been an old enemy of Palmerston, and his wife, Canning's daughter, though with some of her father's brilliance, was a tartar. Melbourne who was strongly against the appointment, described her as "a clever, lively woman thinking and talking of nothing but politics, a decided enemy of us and our Government, always having been so, even when Clanricarde was in office". But Palmerston, perhaps, thought he had a debt to pay to Canning and in the result the appointment turned out quite well. Clanricarde

[1] From Durham, 20 May, 1837; To Clanricarde, 20, 28 Nov., 1838, 28 Jan., 1839; From Clanricarde, 31 Oct., 1838, 7 Jan., 1839: *B.P.* Both Durham's biographers, Mr. Stuart Reid and Professor Chester New, while writing from Durham's point of view, do justice to Palmerston. But they exaggerate Durham's influence on his chief, and accept too easily Durham's own accounts of what he accomplished during his Embassy which is by no means borne out by other observers. Durham's estimate of his own importance may be gauged by his claim to have reestablished British influence at Constantinople by staying a few days there en route to Russia! (Reid, *Lord Durham*, II, 16.) Esterhazy to Metternich, 22 July, 1837: *V. St. A.*

had a point of view almost the same as that of his chief to whom he sent many amusing comments on his predecessor's activities. They got on well together and Clanricarde was a competent representative during his two years' stay. His Secretary of Embassy, Bloomfield, was no more than a functionary.[1]

Before Durham arrived public opinion in Britain was already moving strongly against Russia.[2] This was partly due to Urquhart's propaganda in the *Portfolio*. Palmerston was in no way responsible for that publication, but there can be no doubt but that he welcomed the attacks made on Russia and was glad that the British public had become thoroughly aroused. Edward Ellice, his greatest foe and critic, wrote to Grey from Constantinople whither he had accompanied Durham, urging what was in effect a policy of appeasement towards Russia, silence on her policy and the removal of the British fleet from the Mediterranean. As regards the last suggestion, Palmerston pointed out that it was just the absence of such a fleet that caused the Cabinet to refuse his proposal to assist the Sultan in 1833. He was even more emphatic on the necessity of speaking out about Russian policy. "It is not true", he told Melbourne, "that every tyro understands that policy; on the contrary not one man in a hundred thousand has until very lately been sufficiently aware of it; and Russia has advanced specially because nobody observed, watched and understood what she was doing. Expose her plans, and you half defeat them. Raise public opinion against her and you double her difficulties. I am all for making a clatter against her. Depend upon it, that is the best way to save you from the necessity of making war against her."[3]

The clatter grew to an uproar in the succeeding years. But the attack could not have succeeded had it not been based with all its extravagances on genuine reasons for alarm and suspicion. There was generous indignation at the Tsar's treatment of Poland which was increased by his brutal speech to the Poles at Warsaw in October 1835; there was intense irritation at the policy of commercial prohibition, which Durham, who could not mention

[1] From Melbourne, 13 Feb., 1838: *B.P.* The reappointment of Durham was considered at the end of 1839 but Melbourne wrote that there were many reasons against it and it would have been quite impossible.

[2] There is a good account of the growth of public opinion in Britain in Mr. C. W. Crawley's *Anglo-Russian Relations, 1815–1840.* (*Camb. Hist. Journal,* 1929, 47–73.)

[3] To Melbourne, 30, 31 Oct., 1835: *B.P.*

Poland to its tyrant, told the Tsar was the main cause of ill-feeling; there was the resentment at the treaty which the Tsar had made with the Sultan, not only at the treaty itself but at the manner in which it was made; there was a gradual realisation that Russian expansion menaced not only the Ottoman Empire and the overland route to the East, but Persia and thus indirectly Britain's Indian possessions. But above all, as Palmerston wrote, there was "the apparently threatening naval armaments which are so naturally calculated to give umbrage to the people of this country." The Russian fleets were kept in the summer on a war footing both in the Black Sea and the Baltic, a course no other country, and least of all Britain, could adopt because of the expense.[1]

In Palmerston's eyes the fleet was the most important aspect of the situation. Though it may be that Durham and others were right in thinking that it was in no condition to fight Britain, so many Sail of the Line within striking distance could not be ignored. An increase in the British fleet was made in 1833 as a result of Unkiar Skelessi, and another in 1838, after Palmerston had tried in vain to obtain a reduction in the Russian fleet. In 1836 steps were taken to make the striking force of the fleet more efficient, Minto, the new First Lord, having reported that Britain had practically no fleet at all. He explained the situation to Pozzo di Borgo, who was an old friend, and promised that the reorganisation should be done as quietly as possible so as not to seem to menace Russia. Palmerston himself later told Pozzo di Borgo that while Russia kept her fleet in summer on a war footing Britain must have more ships on the seas. The Cabinet readily agreed to these increases, Melbourne in 1838 suggesting that though Britain on many occasions had been under the special protection of Providence "no man ought to count upon such interposition of Divine favour". The necessary funds were also obtained without much difficulty from the House of Commons, but everyone grudged the expenditure the Tsar had forced on them.[2]

Palmerston naturally constantly demanded reports about the Russian fleet. Durham was able to supply a good deal of factual

[1] To Durham, 31 May, 1836: *F.O. Russia*, 221.
[2] To Durham, 14 Jan., 1836: *B.P.* do., 12 Feb., 1836: *F.O. Russia*, 221. To Clanricarde, 29 Dec., 1838: *F.O. Russia*, 243. Only informal enquiries were to be made. Palmerston suggested that Russia should equip only one division of the Baltic fleet and one-third of the Black Sea fleet instead of as usual putting the whole of the two fleets on a war footing. Hobhouse (Broughton, *Recollections*, V, 169) reports Melbourne's attitude with some surprise.

information from his secret sources. He inspected the Baltic fleet as the Tsar's guest and gave it as his opinion that, shut up as it was seven months in the year, it was not a formidable fighting machine. When, in the Spring of 1836, he thought that he had demonstrated the good will of the Tsar towards Britain he wished to shew it to the world in some striking form. "A public and marked alliance", he wrote, would be perfectly compatible with British relations with France. He even proposed that a British squadron should be sent to the Baltic to exercise with the Russian fleet. Such a demonstration would shew, he claimed, that Russia was under British influence. It would at any rate have served to advertise Durham's position, but of course Palmerston refused to agree, and in an unusually sarcastic answer gave in brief his whole attitude towards the problem: "We should not be disposed to send our summer exercise squadron into the Baltic to assist at the Water Kalisch. First of all we think the said 'Naumachia' not over complimentary to us. We have complained for some years of the Russian practice of parading a great fleet every summer in time of peace; our complaints have produced no effect; we have at last thought it necessary to arm on our side and the main reason understood by all parties for this increase of force in the discussions about it in Parliament was the necessity of not leaving our own shores and commerce entirely unprotected with a fleet of 20 Sail of the Line swaggering away within a week's sail of us. What does Russia thereupon? Why she resolves to add 9 Sail of the Line to her fleet to overtop the 8 which we are adding to ours. Her proceeding is very offensive, and it would not be fitting for us to send our ships to witness the bravado—besides our squadron would play second fiddle as the Prussians did by land [at Kalisch]. Then again, if we are better than them by sea, the less we are with them the fewer opportunities they will have of profiting by our example; and, lastly, if our fleet were to go this year into the Baltic, theirs would return the visit next year in the Channel."[1]

The Tsar, indeed, might have been pleased because he was anxious to learn as much as possible from British experience, and Russian officers were inspecting British dockyards and naval establishments for that purpose. Palmerston claimed the right to

[1] From Durham, 22 March, 1836; To Durham, 19 April, 1836: *B.P.* Melbourne had commented: "I concur with you that there would be nothing but evil in the appearance if a more intimate union than in fact exists." (5 April, 1836: *B.P.*)

similar facilities in Russia, and, not considering the response adequate, withdrew the privileges of which the Russians had made such abundant use. The Tsar scoffed at British fears of Russian attack, but when Durham first asked him the reasons for the increase of the fleet, he replied, so it was reported at St. Petersburg, "to prevent questions of that kind", and, after an inspection of Sevastopol and the Black Sea fleet, he said, "Now let the English come if they want their nose made bloody." It would have been a grave lapse of duty if Palmerston had failed to watch closely the construction of so large a navy, and he never ceased to ply Durham's successors with demands for accurate information about it.[1]

Less than six months after his arrival Durham embodied his views in a long and comprehensive report of 3 March, 1836, on which he spent great pains. It is well written and both his biographers compare it to the more famous report on Canada. But it was much inferior to that great document. It was necessarily superficial, as Durham himself confessed, and much of it was based on speculation. It concluded with an eloquent passage on the weakness of Russia in attack: "Abroad her soldiers fall by thousands sullen and dispirited, evincing the passive devotion of fatalism, but neither the brilliant chivalry of the French nor the determined unyielding courage of the English. At home they fight with desperate unconquerable fury, for national and domestic objects, consecrated by religious feeling and patriotic traditions. Such a nation, therefore, cannot be successfully led over her frontiers." This was hardly convincing to those who, like Palmerston, remembered 1813-1814, and it took no account of Russia's Eastern expansion which Durham himself agreed was a most difficult problem. Grey praised it warmly, but there is no evidence that either this or Durham's constant advocacy of the Russian point of view made any impression on Palmerston.[2]

Durham did his best to popularise his views among his own supporters, but was not very effective against the efforts of the refugee Poles and the *Portfolio*. The latter made a prodigious sensation over all Europe. Durham complained bitterly that it was circulated abroad by the Foreign Office and also of the personal

[1] To Durham, 8 Nov., 1836: *B.P.* "Fas est hostes doceri," Palmerston wrote, "but not 'docere'." T. Schiemann, *Geschichte Russlands*, III, 284, 328.

[2] There is an excellent summary of the report (*F.O. Russia*, 223) in Stuart Reid, *Lord Durham*, II, chap. XVIII. Melbourne wrote on it: "There is nothing in it that one has not heard fifty times." (27 March, 1836: *B.P.*)

attacks on himself. Tatischev was involved and was summoned
back to Russia. Metternich hoped at least that he had got rid of
this tiresome check on his conduct. Though he was studying the
Portfolio carefully and sent a vindication of some of the charges
against himself to the Tsar, he told the Archduke Louis and
Kolowrat that he had burnt his copy of the first number and they
tried to borrow one from Fox. Metternich was much afraid of the
effect at St. Petersburg, but in London, though he never ceased to
complain of the *Portfolio*, he hoped that the revelation of Austrian
opposition to Russia would do good and Hummelauer at the outset
wrote enthusiastically of the good effect on public opinion.[1]

The naval question and the commercial negotiations were the
only issues between the two countries in which Durham played
an important role. The Polish question he avoided as much as
possible and recommended Barante to do the same and concentrate on the East where the real danger of war was. "The continual junction of this dead body to living Russia", he wrote, ". . . .
is a source of continual and irremediable weakness." He did, of
course, by means of appeals to Nesselrode and other officials try
to mitigate the lot of the Poles. He claimed to have produced
some effect but there is little evidence that he in fact did so. In
the Cracow dispute, it is true, the Tsar, in order not to offend
Durham, allowed Austria and Prussia to bear nearly all the burden
of the British protests and carefully concealed the fact that
Russia had been the real author of the occupation and purging
that so moved Palmerston.[2]

But the Polish question could not be ignored. The Emperor's
speech at Warsaw in 1835 was made with such brutality that it had
to be edited for publication. The Emperor himself was conscious
that his anger had led him too far. "Be indulgent to me in your
reports," he said to Barnett, the British Consul at Warsaw.[3]

---

[1] From Durham, 18 July, 1836; From Fox, 14 March, 1836; From Lamb,
5 Aug., 1836: *B.P.* Hummelauer to Metternich, 27 Feb., 1836: *V. St. A.*
He, however, got less enthusiastic as the numbers came out, suspected that
Palmerston was behind it, as he was not attacked, and asserted that the Cabinet
could have stopped it if they had not been divided in opinion about it. (do.,
15 April, 1836: *V. St. A.*)

[2] From Durham, 27 Jan., 18 June, 1836: *B.P.* The appointment of the mild
Kozlowski, he thought, was due to his efforts. Durham believed Nesselrode
at once when he indignantly denied that any Polish children were removed from
Poland (C. New, *Durham*, 296). Yet we know that this was done. Probably
Nesselrode himself did not know the truth.

[3] From Barnett, Warsaw, 23 Oct., 1835: *B.P.* The circulated version omitted
the words "Je ne suis plus qu'Empereur de Russie et c'est à ce titre que vous

The debate in the House of Commons was milder than that in the French Chambers where the Tsar was violently attacked. But nevertheless indignation in Britain was immense and Hummelauer reported that the Tsar's speech had entirely reestablished Palmerston's popularity. Palmerston seriously considered whether it was necessary to make an official protest against the Tsar's claim that Poland no longer existed, but Melbourne deprecated taking notice of words of which there was no official report. Palmerston was indeed well aware that he could do no more for the Poles now than in 1832. He protected their refugees so far as he could, for the Tsar's hand reached out towards them wherever he could put pressure on a Government. Nicholas had naturally an intense jealousy of those in the free state of Cracow, though Barnett reported that they were comparatively harmless. But, indeed, that free state was an intolerable challenge to the Autocrat and at the Kalisch Conference in 1835 the Tsar forced Austria and Prussia to sign a secret agreement that it should be abolished. That fate was only deferred because of Prussia's opposition to the incorporation of Cracow in Austria to which the Tsar had agreed. But meanwhile Cracow must be cleaned up and above all no connection allowed with any other Government than those of the three Eastern States.[1]

Palmerston did not know of this document, but Cracow had been established by a treaty to which Britain was a party and its independence, therefore, was a matter with which Britain had a right to concern herself. Thus in 1836 when, after the murder of a Polish spy, the three Courts began their campaign against Cracow by a joint occupation and expulsion of undesirable elements, Palmerston at once decided to protest. He was careful about his facts, took legal advice and surrounded himself with textbooks on international law from which he had always a quotation ready at hand in his interviews with Bülow and Hummelauer. He admitted that action to prevent a hostile attack by refugees was perhaps justifiable. But the occupying Powers rested their claim on the quite insignificant unrest that had occurred. Palmerston then wrote a tremendous indictment. Melbourne at first was hardly

m'appartenez". Metternich strongly condemned the Warsaw speech. Poland's independence could be crushed, he said, but not her nationality (From Fox, 7 Nov., 1835: *B.P.*).

[1] From Melbourne, 14 Dec., 1835: *B.P.*, *Appendix, p.* 849. Hummelauer to Metternich, 17 Nov., 1 Dec., 1835: *V. St. A.* F. Martens, *Recueil*, IV, 472, first printed the correct version of the secret agreement, but the *Portfolio* had got hold of the truth. To Granville, 17 Nov., 1835: *B.P.*

prepared to go so far but eventually agreed that Britain could not keep silent: Geography, however, has left to Britain as to France whatever their rights, "only the faculty of remonstrance and the appeal to moral opinion which you say is so strong. I think that this power should under these circumstances be exercised, but with caution and dignity, because tho' a great deal of what you say is true yet, after all, admonitions which you cannot enforce and complaints of wrongs which you cannot redress do run risk of becoming ridiculous—at least they have a tendency that way." But Palmerston was thinking of Parliament and it does not seem that this advice had much effect. After a well-argued historical review the despatch suggested that this attack on the Treaty of Vienna tended to invalidate other parts of it which the three Powers were concerned to preserve. Lastly Palmerston said he would appoint a British Consul to Cracow to keep in touch with events.[1]

Both the Tsar and Metternich received the despatch with due recognition of its importance. The former, indeed, said so little that he earned Palmerston's thanks while Hummelauer reported with alarm and indignation that Pozzo di Borgo only gave the most perfunctory support to the efforts of Bülow and himself at London. Metternich entered into long explanations of the revolutionary centre at Cracow which he managed to link up with the latest attempt to assassinate Louis Philippe. But Metternich, wrote Palmerston, has behaved like the gentleman he is. It was Ancillon who got into the worst position by refusing to receive the despatch from Lord William Russell. Seeing that he had already told Bülow in London to communicate a Prussian despatch on the same subject, though that wary diplomat had ignored the instruction, his position was quite untenable. Palmerston simply threatened to break off diplomatic relations and though there was a long controversy, in the end Ancillon had to eat his words. He only complicated matters for Metternich whose main aim was to prevent Palmerston making public the refusal to allow a British Consul to be appointed to Cracow.[2]

[1] From Melbourne, 8, 12 April, 1836: *B.P.* To Lord William Russell, 15 April, 1836: *F.O. Prussia*, 204. Similar despatches were sent to Vienna and St. Petersburg. From Hummelauer, 27 June, 1836: *V. St. A.*
[2] To Lord William Russell, 3, 10 May, 1836; To Fox, 10 May, 1836: *B.P.* Hummelauer to Metternich, 3, 17, 24 June, 1836: *V. St. A.* Professor Bell (*Palmerston*, I, 267–271) devotes a surprisingly large space to this incident and gives the main references to the despatches in the *F.O. Archives*. There is a

The contest with Metternich about the appointment of the Consul continued hotly, much to the alarm of Louis Philippe, who Granville said was "terribly excited". Palmerston threatened him with violent attacks in the House of Commons unless he gave way. But Metternich called his bluff and said that he did not mind such abuse, if Ministers behaved in a restrained way. He insinuated also that Palmerston was trying to stir up discontent among Austrian subjects, an argument which, Granville wrote, "shews how deeply irritated Metternich is against you". He was profuse in historical explanation of how the situation had arisen through Tsartoriski's desire in 1815 to maintain "in however narrow a corner a shadow of Polish independence". This independence, in spite of the agreement he had signed at Toeplitz, he, with even more than his usual duplicity, promised to respect.

Lamb in reporting this urged that it was impossible to preserve real independence anyhow and that it was not a British interest to persist. "Deploring as much as any man the loss of the independence of Poland," he wrote, "I yet feel, that being lost, Europe would stand much better off if the very memory of it were effaced. We have questions yet to be solved which divide the three Powers, but this one unites them, and, if we alarm them in this, we sacrifice the present to the future—that which is full of hope to that which is irreparable." This attitude is a good example of Lamb's limitations and it was of course never accepted by Palmerston, who persisted for a long period in defending the position which he had taken up, though his words in the House were perhaps made more diplomatic by the pains and courtesy with which Metternich had argued his case.[1]

The serious incident of the *Vixen* in 1837 is one of the best examples of Palmerston's good sense and diplomatic skill in handling an awkard position. Public opinion was stirred because the seizure of a British trading ship naturally aroused much

good deal of explanatory material in the private letters. Professor Bell makes much of the fact reported by Barante from St. Petersburg (*Memoirs*, V, 344) that Metternich had informed Paris but not London of the intention. But there was no more than verbal communication and I cannot find evidence to shew that this distinction had any effect on Palmerston. Thiers took little action on this matter, partly because he was at the time applying pressure to Switzerland to get rid of refugees (see above p. 229) and partly to curry favour with Austria. Louis Philippe thought it might complicate matters just when the Duke of Orleans was to visit the Central Courts. From Granville, 27 May, 1836: *B.P.*

[1] To Lamb, 8 Dec., 1836: From Lamb, 23, 26 Dec., 1836: *B.P.* From Granville, 6 June, 1836: *B.P.*

feeling and the question of the Circassian revolt which Urquhart had advertised in the *Portfolio* and made popular was connected with it. Indeed Urquhart had planned or at least encouraged the whole affair. He and Hudson, who had visited the locality, had constantly urged support should be given to the tribesmen who had for so long resisted the attempt of Russia to control the whole of the Caucasus. Ponsonby suggested some munitions should be sent to them. The King was interested and Palmerston himself considered that Russia was establishing a position which would threaten the flank not only of Turkey but of Persia. But he had warned Ponsonby in 1834 at the time of Urquhart's visit that he could do nothing for them. He later tried to use his good offices to get the war between Russia and the Circassian rebels suspended on the basis of an assurance not to attack each other. But he was forced to agree with Melbourne that however sympathetic he might be to the rebels, he had no power to help them and that, if he did, whether they were considered to be Russian subjects or an independent state (as Urquhart claimed they were) Russia would have grounds for war against Britain. He has no shadow of responsibility for the *Vixen* and it seems certain, in spite of Urquhart's charges, that Ponsonby only gave Bell such advice as he could not as British Ambassador refuse.[1]

The arrest of the *Vixen* had been preceded by that of another ship, the *Lord Charles Spencer*, taken on the high seas. Nesselrode admitted the illegality of this action for which he was prepared to pay compensation, and that question would have been closed but for the fact that by implication he claimed a position for Russia in the Black Sea which Palmerston could not accept.

This matter was still under discussion when the *Vixen*, sent

---

[1] To Ponsonby, 31 Oct., 1836: *F.O. Turkey*, 272; do., 28 Oct., 1834: *B.P.* From Ponsonby, 1 Sept., 1834: *B.P.* To Durham, 21 Dec., 1836: *F.O. Russia*, 222. From Durham, 14 Aug., 1836: *F.O. Russia*, 225. I have treated this question at some length for though the *Vixen* case has received great attention, the respective roles of Palmerston and Metternich have been much misunderstood (e.g. V. J. Puryear, *International Economics etc.*, 52. H. C. F. Bell, *Palmerston*, I, 283). They are revealed in the public despatches of which a number were laid before Parliament and can be seen in *B.F.S.P.*, XXVI, 2–60, but the Broadlands Papers add a good deal of important detail. Professor Chester New (*Durham*, 295) corrects Mr. Stuart Reid's view (*Lord Durham*, II, 67) that it was Durham and not Palmerston to whom a peaceful settlement was due. From Ponsonby, 28 Oct., 1836: *F.O. Turkey*, 277; do., 30 Oct., 1836: *B.P.* Hudson to Sir H. Taylor, 8 Feb., 1836: *F.O. Turkey*, 273 (a long letter describing the heroic struggle of the Circassians). See also on the question of Ponsonby's responsibility my article, "Urquhart, Ponsonby and Palmerston," *Eng. Hist. Rev.*, July 1947.

2 O

from Constantinople by a British merchant, George Bell, in November 1836, was captured in the port of Soujouk Kalé, of which the Russians were in occupation. The vessel and its cargo were confiscated and its captain and crew were sent as prisoners to Odessa, but soon released. With the best of intentions a notice was published in the *St. Petersburg Gazette*, exonerating the British Government, but making incidentally claims of full sovereignty over the Caucasus. This was reproduced in the *Morning Chronicle* and caused an immense sensation which Urquhart's journalistic friends increased by all means in their power. Meanwhile Durham reported that Russian public opinion was just as strong on the subject and the Tsar could not give way even if he wanted to, which he did not.

Palmerston was angry at being forced into a position of this kind against his will. He was not going to be made to go to war by Urquhart and Bell. At the same time he was anxious not to recognise Russia's claims on the whole of Circassia, where he hoped some independence might remain, nor in any way to allow her to claim special rights over the navigation of the Black Sea. He approached the subject with great caution. The prestige of both Russia and Britain was at stake. "All Europe", wrote Minto, "has its eyes upon us." "The question is a serious one", Palmerston told Durham informally, "and goes to nothing less than peace and war between the two countries." He, therefore, referred the papers to the King's Advocate and told Pozzo he could make no comment until he had legal advice. Meanwhile he hoped to enlist the sympathies of both France and Austria in favour of the Circassians. From France there was no response. Indeed Granville would not even make the suggestion to Molé who he was sure would refuse all help. But Palmerston received a very different communication from Vienna. Metternich, Lamb reported, wanted Palmerston to stand on his rights. He consented to publish the British case as he had already done the Russian. He agreed that Austria's policy should be to get peace in the Caucasus and this Lamb noted "is more than neutrality, for peace in the Caucasus is independence". Though Metternich was a little vague on the legal aspect of the question and said that he must preserve his position as the advocate of Nicholas, Lamb was certain of his sympathy and cooperation and hoped much from his influence at Berlin as well as at St. Petersburg. Lamb himself

strongly urged Palmerston to stand firm. The smaller Courts would be on Britain's side and the Sultan himself, he said, whose mother, seven wives and two sons-in-law came from Circassia, would be deeply impressed. Meanwhile it would only be politic to be a little more cooperative on the question of a free Press in Malta.[1]

For once Palmerston put his trust in Metternich's promise. Melbourne on the other hand said that he was most afraid of Metternich when he was friendly. He was strongly against pressing British claims to trade with the whole of the Black Sea coast. "Recollect", he told Palmerston, "that powerful ministers have in general found themselves unable to incline this nation to vindicate her rights in distant countries." Lord Holland also was against a strong course. Though he promised to warn Pozzo di Borgo that Government, Parliament and people alike would refuse to acknowledge Russian claims on Circassia, he urged Palmerston to say as little as possible. He also distrusted Austria and was doubtful of the case put forward by the lawyers and the British representatives in the Levant. Such arguments in any case it was doubtful wisdom for Britain with her large Colonial possessions to put forward: "Peace in this is my dear delight and she often dwells with silence."[2]

Palmerston seems to have been in agreement with these views from the outset. He had also, as Esterhazy pointed out to Metternich, his hands full in Spain. He, therefore, devised a plan by which neither Britain nor Russia should give up their claims. He would not admit the blockade under which the Russian officer had acted. But he would recognise the sovereignty of Russia over the port of Soujouk Kalé which had been legitimately ceded by Turkey to Russia in the Treaty of Adrianople, and thus the legality of the seizure of a ship which was breaking Russian regulations for that port. If Nesselrode did not put forward his claim to the rest of

---

[1] From Minto, 18 March, 1837: *B.P.* To Granville, 3 Feb., 1837: *Bulwer*, II, 248; do., 7 Feb., 1837; From Granville, 20 Feb., 1837: *B.P.* Esterhazy to Metternich, 4, 27 Feb., 23 March, 1837: *V. St. A.* To Lamb, 11 Feb., 1837; From Lamb, 3, 7, 25 Feb., 5 March, 1837: *F.O. Austria*, 262, 264, do., 3 Feb., 1837: *B.P.* The British claimed that the cargo was salt and the Russians gunpowder. The matter was never made clear, since it made no difference to the argument.

[2] From Lord Holland, 17 March, 1837; From Melbourne, 4 and 17 March, 1837: *B.P.* Of Metternich he wrote: "He ruined Napoleon, when Napoleon trusted him most. I know not what object he may have in pushing us forward against Russia."

the Circassian coast the matter would be over. As for the future, in case some other *Vixen* appeared, the best solution would be for Russia to abandon her claims on the whole of Circassia which he insisted had been independent in 1829. Nesselrode did not, of course, accede to this last suggestion. But he was glad to accept Palmerston's way out of the immediate difficulty. A series of notes were exchanged on the lines Palmerston had stipulated. A flurry was caused by Pozzo di Borgo mixing up the case of the *Lord Charles Spencer*, where Palmerston had laid down the British doctrine of the open sea, with that of the *Vixen*, but Palmerston was able by June to regard the whole matter as settled. As to the future, he had no power to stop British ships, he told Durham, but would do so if he could. He was aware that such a settlement would not please the Radicals and the Tories. *The Times* and the *Morning Post* had already begun the attack. "I expect to be properly blown up in the House of Commons when I have to state that the *Vixen* affair is arranged and *how*," he confessed to Durham. But by confining the dispute to the occupation of a single port he had made it very difficult for his opponents to raise the whole issue before Parliament.[1]

It was fortunate that Palmerston had taken the safe course and not relied on Metternich's good offices. For on the news that the Tsar was displeased with his attitude and that Tatischev was coming back to Vienna immediately, the Chancellor got into a panic. He reinsured himself with a despatch to Esterhazy which reaffirmed all the objectionable doctrines of blockade. It was accompanied by a more informal one full of hostility to Palmerston whose bluff, he said, had been called. His Ambassador was too sensible to shew the official despatch to Palmerston as Metternich had directed, but Metternich used it to disillusion Lamb. That

[1] To Durham, 21 March, 23 April, 2, 22 May, 1837: *B.P.* do., 19 April, 1836 (2 despatches). The second gave the method he wished Nesselrode to pursue, of which Durham had already been apprised in a private letter. Durham did not communicate this, to Pozzo di Borgo's annoyance. He got the method accepted without putting it formally on record; do., 22 April, 1837 (the *Lord Charles Spencer* despatch which Pozzo di Borgo mixed up with the others), *F.O. Russia*, 231. Palmerston claimed that, "It will require as great sagacity [as his own] in those who may want to bring the real question to an issue to see where and how they may do so." (22 May, 1837: *B.P.*) The Foreign editor of the *Morning Post*, Honan, explained to Esterhazy that the attitude of his paper towards the question of the *Vixen* had been dictated to him by the 'Party' which saw in it an opportunity to attack Palmerston. *The Times* was actuated by the same motive. (Esterhazy to Metternich, 23 March, 1837: *V. St. A.*)

Ambassador was very crestfallen. This was the nastiest trick
Metternich had played on him since 1833. He could only report
in long despatches and letters Metternich's assurances that he
would never allow Europe to become Cossack. Metternich would
be with Britain on the great issue against Russia, he wrote, but he
could not be relied upon for smaller matters. Lamb's opinion of
Metternich sank rapidly. He regarded the *Vixen* settlement as a
defeat. It had revealed to the world that we were not prepared to
fight for our rights in the Black Sea. Meanwhile he could not
help admiring the cunning Esterhazy. "What tact Esterhazy has
shewn! not the dupe of Metternich's momentary velleité of
independence, and then not weak enough to go to you with his
silly arguments but treating him like a child and telling him they
had done wonders." This was as near a confession of bad judgment as Lamb ever got. But for some time he was very bellicose
and talked of war with Russia and the entrance of British ships
into the Black Sea quite in Ponsonby's style.[1]

Palmerston took the whole matter much more coolly. "I own
that for once Metternich has taken me in," he wrote, "and I
believed that, seeing that Austria and England have a common
interest as regards the encroachment of Russia, he meant to take
a straight line for the moment. I shall be more just to him in
future." He put on record for Metternich's edification his view
of the Austrian suggestion that a blockade of the Circassian coast
should be recognised, and urged Austria to advocate Circassian
claims at St. Petersburg. But he had not relied on Metternich
and the solution did not seem to him so great a defeat as it did to
Lamb. On the contrary, whatever Metternich might say, Russia
had accepted the method that Palmerston himself had suggested
and made no effort to make Britain admit Russian claims to
sovereignty and blockade. The situation remained exactly as it
was before the incidents. Palmerston had got out of an awkward
fix, at the price, it is true, of hot attacks by Tories and others,
which Urquhart, now dismissed for his part in the plot, was on the
way home to stimulate. Meanwhile Orlov was sent in July to

[1] From Lamb, 21 April, 14 May, 1837: *F.O. Austria*, 265; do., 21, 30 April,
10, 23 May, 1837: *B.P.* Lamb thought that Esterhazy had not even confessed
to Metternich that he had not used the despatch of 8 April. But the Ambassador told his Chief that he had suppressed it so as to avoid argument and
preserve Austrian influence for the future. Metternich to Esterhazy, 8 April,
1837; Esterhazy to Metternich, 12 May, 1837: *V. St. A.*

congratulate the young Queen on behalf of the Tsar, and Esterhazy
saw in this visit a desire to establish better relations with Britain
by direct contact. Orlov told him that he had not yet found
Palmerston very responsive. There were, indeed, to be other
very sharp passages of arms before the two countries could come to
an understanding. But Metternich, who had played a humiliating
role in the *Vixen* incident, might have taken the point that Russia
did not want his interference, but preferred to come to terms with
Palmerston by direct negotiation.[1]

Austria had failed lamentably to assist Britain in the Caucasus.
But that was far from Vienna. Lamb and Palmerston hoped for
better things in enlisting her aid in two threatened localities nearer
home, Serbia and the mouth of the Danube.

The first of these episodes shews Palmerston at his worst.
Urquhart after his visit home in 1834 had first drawn attention
to Serbia's importance, but now that the whole position of the
Ottoman Empire was under review it could hardly have escaped
notice. It seems to have been the Under-Secretary of State, Fox-
Strangeways, who first suggested consular representation at Belgrade on the model of that already established at Bucharest.
Ponsonby had long ago pointed out the necessity of attacking in
European Turkey Russian influence "which under the novel title
of Protector assumes indefinite powers". It was clear that Serbia
was coming more and more under such influence with obvious
dangers both strategic and economic. But Palmerston began to
tackle the problem before he had made any diplomatic preparations to ensure success. "The British Government has two objects
in view with respect to Servia," he informed Lamb, "first that
Servia should form a barrier against the further encroachments of
Russia, secondly that Servia should afford an opening for the
extension of the commerce of Great Britain."[2]

---

[1] From Melbourne, 29 April, 1837, *Appendix*, p. 854; To Durham, 2 May,
1837: *B.P.* Esterhazy to Metternich, 22 July, 1837: *V. St. A.* To Lamb,
10 June, 1837: *F.O. Austria*, 262.

[2] To Lamb, 7 Oct., 1837: *F.O. Austria*, 263. From Ponsonby, 15 July,
1836: *F.O. Turkey*, 276: "Servia, Bulgaria as well as Moldavia and Wallachia
are more or less under Russian protection (a protection indeed extended to all
the Rayah subjects of the Sultan)." Minute, Fox-Strangeways, 26 May,
[1836], "a Vice-Consul at Belgrade might be of use in watching the opening of
trade in that quarter and in finding sure and regular conveyance of correspondence to Bucharest and Jassy—as well as for superintending the exchange of
despatches between Mess[enge]rs and Tatars, fumigation, etc.": *F.O.* 96
(*Miscellanea*), 18.

These were reasonable ends but Palmerston refused to estimate with any sense of reality the methods by which he was to achieve them. Obviously the only state that could assist him much was Austria whose interests in checking Russia were clearly the same as those of Britain. Yet he told Lamb he distrusted Austria who would try to prevent Serbia from improving herself and might even make a deal with Russia for the partition of her territory.

But the only way that the problem could be solved, answered Lamb, was to enlist the interests of Austria, already irritated by Russia's control of the Danube mouths, though at present blind to the Russian danger in Serbia: "If we do not instigate and assist Austria to resist her, the chances are all in favor of Russia. Without direct interests with Servia, without a point of contact with her, what assistance can we render her? If she counts upon us in the hour of need, we shall assuredly disappoint her. I defy any Govt. that can exist in England to move the nation to raise a finger in her defence."

And, indeed, Palmerston, much as he disliked it, had to encourage Lamb to obtain Austrian assistance when the situation grew worse owing to the action of his own agent. He had sent out to Belgrade a vigorous representative as Consul, Colonel Hodges, a man who knew nothing of the Balkan peoples and languages but, claimed Palmerston, "firm, resolute, bold in character", and one whose "political principles are according to the most approved standard of the present day". Hodges, like Palmerston himself, could not try to advance British interests without associating them with an attempt to improve the lot of those who were to be used as instruments for that purpose. He obtained the confidence of the Obrenovitch Prince, Milosch, who was uneasily ruling, under the Sultan's suzerainty, a people who were determined not to accept too much government from anybody. Hodges thought, and no doubt rightly, that if the condition of Serbia was to be improved, that could only be done by a vigorous exercise of power from above. He encouraged Milosch, therefore, to assert himself for that purpose against the Serbian leaders. These latter relied on their native customs, which might be termed 'constitutional', and the Russian Consul, in order to undermine Hodges' influence, naturally supported them. The curious result, therefore, was that in Serbia Britain was supporting autocratic rule and Russia, with

the active countenance of the Austrian Consul, a sort of constitutionalism.[1]

Lamb saw at once the danger of this method of handling so complicated a problem. "Colonel Hodges", he wrote, "seems to me to be an active politician and I think you had better keep him quiet. It is hardly probable that even in Servia we can agree with Austria upon the mode in which the country ought to be governed. If she will secure us against its falling under Russian influence it is all we want and we must not thwart her in a natural dependency of hers, where our main object is that she should retain her influence and exclude other protectors. If the Colonel meddles even for Milosch's good unless by previous understanding with Austria, be assured he will do mischief and sacrifice great interests to a trifling one." Nevertheless Lamb made every possible effort to get Metternich to help, and remove the obnoxious Austrian Consul. When he found that Metternich would do nothing he worked through the Austrian military and financial authorities, as he began to do more and more at this time. He got fair words and many promises of action from the soldiers who were anxious to keep Russian influence out of Belgrade and the Danube. But without Metternich's active support the cumbrous Austrian machine could produce no results and Lamb had to confess that he was baffled. There was, indeed, much to be said for Metternich's argument that Hodges' activity had simply roused the Russians to greater exertions and the best policy for Britain was to leave Serbia alone.[2]

Melbourne early saw that Britain could do nothing effective. "If, as is certain," he warned Palmerston, "you have little hope of inducing Austria to assist Milosch against Russia, you should take care that he is not induced to go further than he otherwise [would do] relying upon assistance from us which I do not see how we can afford him." But Palmerston would not give in. He thought of inviting the French to nominate a Consul, much to Metternich's alarm, but his relations with France were now such as did not encourage him to rely on her. He told Ponsonby to

[1] To Lamb, 10 Jan., 18 May, 1838: F.O. Austria, 270; do., 11 Jan., 1838; To Ponsonby, 17 Jan., 1837; From Lamb, 16 July, 1837: B.P. T. Schiemann, Geschichte Russlands, III, 295. Metternich suggested that all the three states should withdraw their Consuls, a course which Palmerston indignantly rejected. (18 May.) Hodges was recommended to him by some of his old constituents in South Hampshire.
[2] From Lamb, 3, 26 Jan., 1 April, 23 May, 1838: F.O. Austria, 271: do., 22 Sept., 1837, 1 April, 1838, 4 May, 1839: B.P.

get the Sultan to support Milosch. Ponsonby had no very great opinion of Milosch, but he gradually warmed to the contest and thought that here was a means of striking a great blow at Russia. The Sultan was, however, by no means inclined to increase the power of a subordinate over whom he had only a shadowy control, and on his return to Constantinople, Butenev, who succeeded in ousting the Prince of Samos from the discussions, found it comparatively easy to get the Turkish Ministers to accept the Russian point of view. Ponsonby got the Porte to order Milosch to send a deputation to Constantinople to discuss the new constitution, but the decision was to decrease not increase the power of the Prince.[1]

The result was what might have been expected. The unrest in Serbia increased until it became a revolution. Hodges had to retire into Austria, and to his chagrin Milosch first followed him and then made a humiliating reconciliation with his opponents and the Russian Consul. "I fear that Servia, Wallachia and Moldavia may now be considered to belong wholly to H.I.M. the Emperor of Russia," wrote Ponsonby. Milosch did not in fact manage to appease his enemies sufficiently and was later removed in favour of his son. But by this time Palmerston had abandoned the struggle. Hodges, after remaining some time near the Serbian frontier, where he was naturally suspected of intrigue, went to Vienna and thence departed for the more suitable job of tackling Mehemet Ali at Alexandria. And Metternich was so far right, that the Russians were less happy in Belgrade when left to themselves, and the elevation of the Karageorgevitch family in place of the Obrenovitch brought them many problems. Nor, if the Serbs were for long deprived of the benefits of modern civilisation and the trade of Britain was still largely excluded, was the strategic situation much impaired by the result. The arm of Russia was not strong enough to control such hardy and freedom-loving people as the Serbs. She could only produce a negative result.[2]

In the question of the Danube mouths Palmerston had more success. Even Metternich responded to the suggestion that the control by Russia over the Sulina Channel, which she had acquired

[1] From Melbourne, 11 April, 1838; To Ponsonby, 12 Feb., 21 March, 22 May, 1838: B.P. From Ponsonby, 5 Oct., 1837, 7 March, 18 April, 30 July, 20 Oct., 18 Nov., 8, 16 Dec., 1838: F.O. Turkey, 306, 330–338; do., 11 March, 21 May, 18 Nov., 1838: B.P.

[2] From Ponsonby, 15, 27 Jan., 1839: F.O. Turkey, 354. To Lamb, 17 Aug., 28 Nov., 1839; From Lamb, 17 Feb., 4, 8 May, 9 June, 31 Aug., 8 Sept., 16 Nov., 1839: F.O. Austria, 279–282.

by doubtful means as a result of the Treaty of Adrianople, was a threat to Austrian commerce down the Danube to the Black Sea. Quarantine regulations were applied by the Russians in such a way as to hamper both Austrian trade and that of the Principalities, and other irritating restrictions were resented by the trading classes of both countries. Lamb was at first not optimistic that anything could be done, though he reported the growing realisation that Austrian commercial interests were at stake and the consequent increase of illwill towards Russia. But until Austria revised her commercial system of prohibitions he thought British interest was slight and suggested waiting until the commercial treaty was negotiated.[1]

This negotiation had been begun in 1836 by McGregor as part of the general campaign for the extension of British trade. 'Intolerable delay' was caused by the complications of the Austrian internal system. Kolowrat himself confessed that the question had fallen into 'inextricable confusion', but the Archdukes, who entirely failed to understand the problem, refused to allow the fundamental law of the Empire to be changed. "Against the treaty", wrote Lamb, "are the whole of the bankers of Vienna who make great profit by the present state of things, Eichoff, the Minister of Finance, who is reported to share in these profits, the Archduke Louis, moved by narrowness of understanding, obstinacy, timidity and conscientiousness as to introducing changes in an Empire where he is but a locum tenens, and the real difficulty of combining partial changes with the absurd and embarrassing relations in which they stand to Hungary. In favor of the treaty are Metternich and Kolowrath, weakly, without much knowledge or confidence in themselves upon this subject, and the latter in the hands of Eichoff and opposed by all the subalterns in the offices who are the real rulers of these affairs in this Empire. Notwithstanding this discouraging state of things, I have in the fire all the irons it will hold to stir it to my purposes, but without much hope of success." Fortunately Metternich had the good sense to enlist the aid of Neumann, who had negotiated the commercial treaty of 1829 with Britain, and with his expert assistance the treaty was at length completed. It contained provision for the free navigation of the Danube and everyone saw in it an intention of Austria to

---

[1] From Lamb, 2 Nov., 1836, 30 April, 5 May, 16 July, 1837: *B.P.*; do. 14 May, 1837: *F.O. Austria*, 265.

trade through the Black Sea to a greater extent than before. Lamb claimed great political results for the treaty as likely to throw Austria into the forefront of resistance to Russian encroachment there. It was, indeed, considered a great blow by the merchants of Odessa, who had done all they could to prevent the Danube mouth from being freely opened, and it enabled the grain of the lower Danube to compete with Russian grain in Western European markets, mainly British. There was much negotiation with Russia concerning the freedom of navigation of the Sulina Channel, but on the whole that Power acceded to all demands with a good grace and the problem caused at this time little friction between the two countries.[1]

[1] From Lamb, 20 Dec., 1837: *B.P.* On the connection between the commercial treaty and the Danube problem see Puryear, *International Economics*, 132–139, 141–145. He has collected together much interesting information from the Foreign Office Archives to supplement A. Beer, *Die Oesterreichische Handelspolitik im neunzehnten Jahrhundert.* Here, however, as in his study of the Turkish treaty he is apt to give too much political effect to economic motives. For the negotiation of the commercial treaty see A. F. Pribram, *Oesterreichischer Staatsvertrage*, and From Lamb, 3 July, 1838: *F.O. Austria*, 272, an interesting review of the treaty which Prof. Puryear does not seem to have used: and E. B. Chancellor, *Diary of Neumann*, II, 78–82. Aberdeen affected to think the new treaty no different from that of 1829 concluded under his auspices. So he told Princess Lieven. E. Jones-Parry, *Corres. of Princess Lieven and Aberdeen*, I, 121.

4. THE SECOND FAILURE OF THE CONCERT

Throughout these years in spite of the divisions between the Governments there was recognition in every capital that the only alternative to war over the Eastern Question was a new treaty concerning the Straits and the integrity of the Ottoman Empire. The Tsar himself was, it is true, adverse to any step which would enable the Western Powers to share the special position which Russia had acquired by the Treaty of Unkiar Skelessi. But Nesselrode and others were fully conscious of Russia's inability to accept their challenge successfully if it were made. Metternich always dreamed of establishing Vienna as the centre of mediation between Russia and the West so that he could himself find the means by which a new treaty could be negotiated.

In 1835, on the other hand, both Broglie and Palmerston thought that the best course was for Britain and France to make a treaty with the Sultan and thus nullify the Treaty of Unkiar Skelessi. Austria could be associated with it when she had overcome her fear of revolution sufficiently to detach herself from Russia. That Power would then either have to accept a 'European' solution or find herself isolated. If Austria refused, Britain and France together would be able to protect the Sultan from both Mehemet Ali and Russia. In 1835 they made a great effort to achieve this end but neither of them were able to get the consent of their Governments to such a course. The pro-Austrian party in the British Cabinet insisted on Austria being approached before a treaty with France and the Sultan was negotiated, while Louis Philippe insisted on putting forward Talleyrand's old device of a European conference to obtain a treaty not merely to guarantee the Ottoman Empire but the territorial limits of all European states. This suggestion, in spite of its impracticability, seems to have been sincere. But Louis Philippe also used it as part of his manoeuvre to disentangle himself from Britain and draw nearer to the Eastern Powers and especially Austria, as has been described in Chapter VI. The fall of Broglie in February 1836 removed any chance of obtaining a treaty in that year, but Palmerston took up the project once more in 1838 in a new manner adapted to the

changed circumstances of that time.   He again failed, but his effort prepared the way for his success in 1840.

Metternich was left in 1835 to a régime of Chargés d'Affaires as Palmerston had been in 1834.   He justified his conduct to them on the Eastern Question with much allusion to the consistency of his own conduct.   The fatality of Navarino had been due to the action of France and England.   What could Austria do when they joined Russia?   But neither Palmerston nor Broglie believed that Metternich would subscribe to any treaty or declaration which, however phrased, was bound to be considered as aimed at the Treaty of Unkiar Skelessi.   All they could expect, Broglie declared, was a *sous-entendu*, a sort of understanding, that cooperation would be possible between the three Powers, if Russia resumed her policy of conquest.[1]

When, therefore, Palmerston first put his plan before the Cabinet in November 1835, his own idea was that Britain and France alone should make a treaty with the Sultan; that the latter should promise not to make any cession of territory and that they should promise to support him.   This was clearly a treaty directed against Russia rather than against Mehemet.   The Cabinet were in favour of something being done, but Melbourne and others wished that Austria should be invited to be a party to the treaty from the outset.   This was far from being Palmerston's view.   He was at this time specially indignant with and suspicious of Metternich.

When the plan was communicated to Sébastiani at the beginning of December, that Ambassador agreed with Palmerston that Britain and France should make the offer to the Sultan first and at once wrote to his King and to Broglie.   The latter laid the matter before the French Cabinet who were favourable except for a slight hesitation at the moment chosen, because of the dispute then going on with the United States.

Broglie desired, however, a rather different treaty and a rather different procedure.   He agreed with Palmerston and Sébastiani that the negotiation should in the first instance be confined to France and Britain, and the resulting treaty then offered to the other Great Powers and the Sultan.   He had no hopes that Austria would be ready to sign it immediately and feared that Metternich

[1] From Fox-Strangways, 25 Aug., 1835: *B.P.* With memorandum approved by Metternich of his views. He had tried, he said, to remedy the bad position in which the false policy of Joseph II had placed Austria. From Granville, 16 Nov., 1835: *F.O. France*, 505.

might even try to prevent the Sultan from signing it. If that Sovereign, however, was given the treaty at the same time as the other Powers he might be induced to sign it before Russian influence could be brought to bear on him, though Broglie was clearly doubtful also about the Sultan and enquired if Palmerston had any grounds for believing that his signature could be obtained. He, therefore, wished to include an attack by Mehemet Ali in the *casus foederis*, in order to forestall Russian objections that the treaty was solely directed against her and to induce the Sultan to accept the treaty.[1]

It was naturally assumed in London that Louis Philippe approved of Broglie's point of view, but he subsequently denied that he had ever given his consent. It seems clear that Broglie had gone on with the discussions with Palmerston in the hope that an agreement between the two governments would force the King to give way.

Palmerston at once accepted the view that the treaty should only be offered to Austria after Britain and France had signed it. He was less favourable to Broglie's other suggestions. He thought that it was impossible to sign a treaty against the cession of Turkish territory without the Sultan being a party to it. Supposing the Sultan did sign away some territory to Russia, they would have grounds for war both against Russia and against Turkey. There was no need to mention Mehemet Ali, he said, because all the territory the Sultan would ever offer to him was "so many feet of earth as may equal the length of his body".

However he began to discuss these questions with Sébastiani and they seem to have moved far towards agreement on them. The object of the treaty was to be any 'menace' to the 'indepen-

[1] To Granville, 8, 15 Dec., 1835, 9 Feb., 1836: B.P. From Granville, 11, 28 Dec., 1835: *Granville P.* This discussion was not recorded in the despatches but dealt with by private letters. Some of these are missing but that of 9 February is a résumé of the whole transaction until February, 1836. I have not been able to find any official letters in the series *Angleterre* of the Archives of the French Foreign Office, but Thureau-Dangin (*Histoire de la Monarchie de Juillet*, II, 421) gives a French point of view from Broglie's private papers. He exaggerates Broglie's reluctance to agree to a treaty. William IV much approved the exclusion of Austria and as usual considered that the treaty should be backed up by the reinforcement of the Mediterranean Squadron. (16 Dec., 1835: B.P.) Leopold, whose opinion was asked by Louis Philippe, strongly supported the view that France and Britain should first make a treaty and then offer it to the Sultan. The latter would accept it if it was already made, he insisted, but not it if it were a mere project. The hostility of Russia to Belgium made Leopold desire that France and Britain should unite against her (From Leopold, 22, 29 Dec., 1835; Leopold to Louis Philippe, 12 Dec., 1835: B.P.).

dence and integrity' of the Ottoman Empire, whose existence was essential to the balance of power in Europe. The Sultan was to be mentioned as an acceding party in one of the articles. The final drafts do not appear to have been settled, but it seems probable that they could easily have been so had not an obstacle arisen on the question of the exclusion of Austria from being a party to the original treaty.[1]

Palmerston vehemently supported Broglie's view—and surprisingly enough Lamb, who was in London, took the same side. Palmerston's reason was his distrust and dislike of Metternich who he still suspected of casting a greedy eye on Bosnia and desiring a deal with Russia about the Ottoman Empire. But in a cogent memorandum he shewed that whether Austria refused, as he anticipated, or supported the treaty and tried to persuade the Tsar to accede also, the result was likely to be much more satisfactory if France and England had first signed the treaty and asked the Sultan for his adhesion.[2]

He tried for a whole month to get Melbourne to accept this view but failed entirely, though he had a majority in the Cabinet and the King was wholeheartedly on his side. Melbourne, who, it seems likely, did not want anything done at all, consulted Grey. The latter in a verbose reply expressed the opinion that no treaty was necessary, since the danger from Russia was not pressing. He was afraid of the complications which might arise and particularly urged that nothing should be done to assist the Sultan to recover Syria from Mehemet, who he thought might again "become an important element in the future policy of the East". He distrusted both Russia and France. The best thing, therefore, was to shew a readiness to cooperate in resisting any further encroachment on the Ottoman Empire but to avoid any formal engagement. He closed with a reference to Fox's famous quotation, "Iniquissimam pacem justissimo bello antefero." "I am always inclined", he added, "to take the chances of time, which may by their own working prevent that tremendous result."[3]

Palmerston wrote a furious reply to what he considered to be a pusillanimous judgment and the Cabinet seems not to have accepted Grey's policy of appeasement, in which he may have been

[1] So I judge from the drafts of the treaty in the Broadlands Papers, one in English and the other in French.
[2] Memorandum in Palmerston's handwriting dated 1836: *B.P.*
[3] Grey to Melbourne, 8 Jan., 1836: *B.P.*

influenced by Durham. But no doubt it added to the difficulty of getting them to agree to Palmerston's own plan which was far more likely to result in a treaty than one in which Austria was to be consulted first. Melbourne remained sceptical. "The Black Sea and the Caucasus and these great Asiatic Empires", he wrote, "inflame imaginations wonderfully." "I have", Palmerston told Granville, "during the last six weeks used every endeavour in my power and employed every argument I could think of, but in vain; Melbourne remains immoveable and the natural consequence of that is, that other members of the Cabinet who originally agreed with me begin to partake Melbourne's opinion. People who do not follow up questions in the way that the person at the head of the department is obliged to do are generally for the doubting line."[1]

By this time Broglie's Government had fallen and, though Palmerston directed Granville to approach his successor, Thiers, he can have had little hope of success. Granville, though he much regretted that the idea of a treaty with France had been given up, put with much force to Thiers the suggestion that Britain and France should approach Austria with a view to the negotiation of a treaty. When Thiers asked for details Granville could only say that if he agreed to go on with the plan the two governments could discuss the instructions to be sent to their Ambassadors at Vienna on the subject. When Thiers consulted the King he found that Louis Philippe had very different ideas and Granville was soon made aware of them by the King himself. When Granville began to discuss the treaty the King replied "that they must be settled by a conference of the Ministers of the five Powers and that Vienna seemed the natural place for that conference". "This language", suggested Granville, "very much chimes in with Talleyrand's views, who has made no secret of his wish to end his political life in such a conference. The King also seemed desirous to efface any impression that may have been created in England that Talleyrand's predilections for the English Alliance had at all

---

[1] To Melbourne, 12 Jan., 1836; From Melbourne, 23 Jan., 1836; To Granville, 9 Feb., 1836: *B.P.* Lansdowne was inclined to the bolder course if a more trustworthy French Minister than Thiers could be found, and the rumour that Thiers was to be Broglie's successor probably finally decided the Cabinet (Lansdowne to Melbourne (Tuesday), 1836). Commenting on Grey's letter Lansdowne thought Palmerston had hardly been quite fair, but he agreed with him rather than with Grey. Lord Holland had a plan of his own. William IV was very much on Palmerston's side and rather embarrassed Palmerston by his continual interest in the treaty after it had been dropped. (From Will. IV, 9, 11 Feb., 1 March, 10 April, 1836: *B.P.*)

changed; he said his [Talleyrand's] opinions were the same now as when at the Congress of Vienna in 1815 he exerted himself to unite France with England and Austria against Russia."[1]

The effect of this communication on Palmerston was, of course, to cause him to drop the project altogether.   The last thing he would have agreed to at this time was a conference at Vienna which might well have been used to draw Western affairs away from London in addition to giving Metternich the control of the diplomacy concerning the Eastern Question.   He told Granville that he would not accept such a conference and, shortly afterwards, to let the whole matter sleep.[2]

Louis Philippe seems to have been sincere in putting forward this fantastic plan of a Treaty of Guarantee for all Europe to be negotiated at a special conference at Vienna.   He may well have been persuaded by Talleyrand into a real belief in it.   But of his immediate object there can be no doubt.   He was already preparing that propitiation of Austria which has already been described in Chapter VI.   He had in January informed the Austrian Ambassador of the British scheme, said he would never agree to it and adumbrated his own idea of a territorial guarantee.   He kept recurring to the theme throughout this year in his conversations with Apponyi.[3]

Nevertheless the idea of sounding Austria was still in the minds of the Cabinet and especially of Melbourne, who doubted whether Constantinople could be saved from Russia without her cooperation.   Thus when Lamb at last began his tardy journey to Vienna in May 1836, he had orders to take the question up there and secure the cooperation of St. Aulaire.   As has been seen, he visited Paris on the way and in the course of his conversations discussed the question of the Ottoman Empire both with the King and with Thiers.   It was piquant for Lamb to report from the King himself that he had always refused to agree to the separate treaty with Britain, the question on which Palmerston had fought with Melbourne for six weeks on the supposition that it was the considered

---

[1] From Granville, 26, 29 Feb., 1836: *F.O. France*, 520; do., 29 Feb., 1836: *B.P.*

[2] To Granville, 1, 8, 12 March, 1836; To Lord John Russell, 7 March, 1836: *B.P.*   To Melbourne, 1 March, 1836: L. C. Sanders, *Lord Melbourne's Papers*, 337.

[3] Apponyi to Metternich, 24 Jan., 1836: *V. St. A. Frankreich.*   See on Louis Philippe's communication to Austria my Raleigh lecture in *Proceedings British Academy*, 1934, 143–145.

decision of the French Government! The King and Lamb, however, agreed on their objective, viz., to support the Ottoman Empire by peaceful means, and Lamb was surprised to find Louis Philippe desiring that Syria should be restored to the Sultan, "by the assistance of England, France and if possible Austria, without, however, landing a French soldier in Syria."

But on the question of method the King not only said that Austria needed to be conciliated by the abandonment of the patronage of all 'Propaganda', a hit at British policy in Spain, but began to develop his project for a general treaty of territorial guarantee for all European states. Lamb enjoyed himself in a devastating attack on this idea. Could the King for example, he said, guarantee Poland to Russia? Certainly Britain could not. And he pointed out that the frontiers of Belgium were still to seek. He then found that the King was specially anxious for such a treaty in order to protect Belgium. Leopold's army was unreliable, he said, and he could not go on indefinitely in the present situation. The King's next object was "to prevent the future cessions or sales of territory either in Germany or Italy from which he apprehends the absorption of the smaller states by the larger ones." "What childishness!", was Lamb's comment, and he told Palmerston that he need not, of course, take up these suggestions. At the same time the King had made it so clear that he would never consent to a separate treaty between France and England on the Eastern Question that Lamb advised Palmerston he must abandon that idea whatever Ministry might be in power in France, until he heard that Louis Philippe himself had changed his mind.[1]

Meanwhile Lamb turned to Thiers for a policy and found that they were in pretty close agreement. Austria, Thiers thought, would not sign a treaty and the only thing to do was what Grey had suggested, to see how far Britain and France could get her to come to some understanding with them. He promised that St. Aulaire would work with Lamb to that end. The French Ambassador was well prepared for the task. It had long been Broglie's policy, and St. Aulaire fully shared his views, to lead Metternich back to cooperation with the Western Powers by small concessions, association in mutual conveniences and an assurance that the con-

[1] From Melbourne, 29 Feb., 1836: *B.P. Appendix*, p. 851. From Lamb, 13 May, 6 June, 1836: *B.P.* He told Palmerston he had better not try to find out how the mistake occurred. Clearly he thought Broglie had been disingenuous.

stitutional governments were the only alternative to the revolution in its most extreme form. Louis Philippe himself wanted something more and, as has been seen, it broke up the Anglo-French entente. But for a time Britain and France could on the Eastern Question pursue the same policy towards Austria.[1]

As might have been expected Lamb's discussions at Vienna did not lead to any very tangible result. Metternich reiterated his confidence in the Tsar and asserted once again that any attack by Russia or any other Power on the Ottoman Empire would make Austria join forces with Britain to prevent it. But he refused any suggestion of a treaty which he said was not necessary for such a hypothetical case. The three Eastern Courts, he added, worked perfectly well together without one. In response to skilful questioning by Lamb he said that his guarantees of Russian good faith were given just as much for the Asiatic dominions of the Sultan as for the European, thus answering an old suspicion of Palmerston's. What Metternich wanted was quiet at Constantinople, not the restless activity of Ponsonby—and Lamb shewed how much he agreed with him in this respect. At the same time Metternich saw no reason why Britain should not declare to the Sultan that she would guarantee the integrity of his dominions, a course which Lamb thought might satisfy Ponsonby who was so much against joining with Russia in a Five Power treaty for that purpose. Metternich also was wholeheartedly in favour of supporting the strengthening of Turkey internally. All this, thought Lamb, was excellent. The interests of Austria and Britain were so identical on the Eastern Question that matters could be left to work themselves out. Meanwhile he, like Metternich, was more concerned about Western affairs.[2]

Lamb thought this approach had made a substantial impression on Metternich. But the latter was in fact just as hostile to Palmerston as before. The despatch which Palmerston wrote in the

[1] From Lamb, 26 May, 1836: *B.P.* Thureau-Dangin, *Histoire de la Monarchie de Juillet*, II, 421. Even Melbourne was ready to accept a 'general treaty', since it would tend to "break up the union of the three Powers". He added, however: "Treaties of this comprehensive character are very dangerous transactions; they have rarely answered the purpose for which they were formed, and have often involved consequences, which were in no respect foreseen." (5 April, 1836: *B.P.*)

[2] From Lamb, 5 Aug., 1836: *F.O. Austria*, 257; do., 2 Nov., 1836: *B.P.* The first of the two despatches of 5 August was shewn to Metternich and approved by him as a correct account of his attitude after one or two minor alterations.

autumn, of his gratification that the views of Austria on the Eastern Question were the same as those of Britain, only aroused Metternich's suspicions. He was, he told Esterhazy, not susceptible to flattery. As for the Eastern Question, "There is no Eastern Question," he said. Nor was Palmerston satisfied. He had in fact been offered nothing but Lamb's assurances of Metternich's assurances. But he was occupied with Spain and the Eastern Question must be left alone for a time. After all, he told Ponsonby, "Metternich is not immortal. . . . He will pass away in due time and then we shall have Austria with us on Turkish affairs." Molé was even less anxious to do anything and when Roussin, home on leave, proposed action at the end of the year both Molé and Palmerston agreed that nothing need be done.[1]

Thus nothing had been done when the Eastern Question again became acute in 1838, because Mehemet threatened to declare the independence of all the territories which he controlled. Mehemet, as will be described in Section 5, was stopped by the diplomatic action of the Great Powers. But the Treaty of Unkiar Skelessi still threatened to disturb European peace since Palmerston was determined that Russian forces should not again dominate Constantinople. His idea of making a special treaty with France as a counterbalance to that of Unkiar Skelessi had been shewn to be impossible. He abandoned it, therefore, in favour of an attempt to negotiate, by means of an Ambassadorial conference in London, a European treaty to replace that of Russia.[2]

He was undoubtedly encouraged in this view by the reports which came from Vienna. On two occasions Metternich had agreed that the immediate problem of tackling Mehemet should be settled by an arrangement in London. Lamb had interpreted these remarks as an agreement to the negotiation there of a new treaty or convention about the whole problem. This was far from

---

[1] Metternich to Esterhazy, 29 Nov., 1836: *V. St. A.* To Ponsonby, 7 Nov., 1836: *B.P.* To Lamb, 11 Nov., 1836: *F.O. Austria*, 256. From Granville, 28 Nov., 1836: *F.O. France*, 526. William IV was sorry that Roussin's suggestion was not followed up. He never ceased to regret the dropping of the treaty of guarantee. (11 Dec., 1836: 23 Jan., 1837: *B.P.*)

[2] This incident has been studied in some detail by Mr. Philip E. Mosely from the evidence of the Russian Archives in his *Russian Diplomacy and the Opening of the Eastern Question in 1838 and 1839* (1934). See also my Raleigh Lecture, "Palmerston, Metternich and the European System, 1830–1841," *Proceedings of the British Academy*, 1934, which is based on the British, French and Austrian Archives and Granville papers. The two accounts substantially agree though the emphasis is different. The Broadlands Papers add only a few details.

Metternich's intention. He was concerned with the immediate issue produced by Mehemet's action and not with the negotiation of a substitute for the Treaty of Unkiar Skelessi. He had no intention of allowing the management of the whole Eastern Question to fall into Palmerston's hands. At any rate, as soon as he encountered Nesselrode at Toeplitz he completely altered his tune. He ordered Esterhazy to consider the instructions to Pozzo di Borgo as addressed to himself. This despatch, which Esterhazy thought it most imprudent of Pozzo di Borgo to communicate to Palmerston, indicated that in certain circumstances Russia might find it necessary to base her action on the Treaty of Unkiar Skelessi. Metternich did not of course confess to Lamb how much he had changed. That Ambassador still thought that he would accept a conference if Palmerston insisted, though he would only give "indirect assistance". "He will not face Russia, but will try to lead her into his path; the pushing her into it must come from you." Palmerston did not receive this advice until 15 August, but the previous communications may well have contributed to the decision to take the dramatic step of summoning the Ambassadors to consultation.[1]

Molé, on the other hand, when Lamb's information was communicated to him, roused Granville's indignation by suggesting that the conference should take place in Paris, a more neutral place. Were not the interests of France and Britain identical, asked the Ambassador? But he explained this attitude to Palmerston as due to Molé's extreme jealousy of Sébastiani. Palmerston had seen such objections overcome in 1830 and might hope that he could do so now, especially as Sébastiani now, like Talleyrand then, was wholeheartedly on the British side.[2]

Palmerston persisted in separate negotiations with the Ambassadors until he received on 8 August Nesselrode's despatch to Pozzo di Borgo. He at once pointed out to the Russian Ambassador the alarm that would be caused by separate action on the part of Russia. His attempt to meet the immediate threat from Mehemet had already shewn how difficult it was to arrange

---

[1] From Lamb, 19 June, 1838: *F.O. Austria,* 271; do., 19 July, 10 Aug., 1838: *B.P.* See P. E. Mosely, *Russian Diplomacy, etc.,* 76, for the Russian pressure on Metternich. M. Sabry has pointed out (*L'Empire Egyptien,* 416) that Metternich was the first to suggest a conference but he does not realise the issues at stake nor pursue the development of the question.

[2] From Granville, 9 July, 1838: *F.O. France,* 562.

concerted action by an interchange of views between the capitals.
But over all lay the menace of separate action by Russia on the
basis of her treaty. Her intentions even now were obscure. The
only way, therefore, was to endeavour to obtain a negotiation in
London to work out a substitute for it and arrange the methods
by which common action could be obtained.[1]

It must be admitted that the means by which Palmerston sought
to obtain this result were very unorthodox. For Esterhazy, Pozzo
di Borgo and Bülow each received on 13 August a little note
inviting them all to meet him at the Foreign Office next day.
Only Sébastiani had been admitted to Palmerston's confidence.
To the others no reason had been given and the subject of discussion might well have been the Belgian Question then under
consideration in conference. Palmerston confessed to Sébastiani
that he took this course for fear Pozzo di Borgo would stay away
if he knew the object of the meeting. The three Ambassadors,
however, consulted together and were pretty sure that it was
Palmerston's intention to bring the Eastern Question before
them. They eventually decided to go, but only after Esterhazy
had agreed to see Palmerston first and warn him that he must not
ask his visitors to make any statement but simply inform them of
the views of his government. Palmerston admitted that his procedure was irregular, but promised that his object was no more than
Esterhazy had suggested. He in fact next day expressed to the four
Ambassadors the pleasure of the British Government at the unity
of ideas manifested in the instructions sent to Alexandria, pointing
out, however, that Britain had gone further than the others by
declaring that Mehemet's persistence in his determination would
mean that he must consider himself in a state of war with Britain.
It might be hoped that these declarations would be effective for
their purpose. But it would still be desirable to concert together
in London as to the measures to be taken by the five Powers in
case Mehemet Ali committed an act of aggression against his
Sovereign and so disturbed the peace. He asked them to obtain
the instructions of their Governments for that purpose. Sébastiani, primed by Palmerston, immediately said that he had such
instructions. Esterhazy and Bülow said they would ask for them.
Pozzo di Borgo said nothing at all. Perhaps that was what
Palmerston anticipated. For his object, according to Sébastiani,

---

[1] P. E. Mosely, *Russian Diplomacy, etc.*, 79.

who seems to have been much in his confidence at this time, was either to confine Russia more and more in the bonds of a 'concert préalable' or else to force her to reveal clearly by her refusal the true secret of her oriental policy.[1]

Metternich, as we have seen, had already agreed that this particular crisis should be settled at London. Esterhazy tried to make matters easier by insisting that there was no question of setting up a 'conference' in London but only of establishing a 'concert' between them. Both Melbourne and Palmerston, he said, appreciated that point fully. Metternich knew well enough that this distinction of form, which he had often used himself, meant very little. The real question was where the issue between Russia and Britain was to be decided. In any case he was already pledged to Russia, though he could not very well confess this to Lamb. The fact that he had gone to Italy for the coronation ceremonies caused some delay and when Lamb, who went to attend them, pressed him for instructions he always promised them but none were sent. Lamb put this dilatoriness down to old age and feebleness but Metternich knew very well what he was doing.[2]

Meanwhile Pozzo di Borgo had reported the incident in an agony of fear and indignation. Palmerston increased the Ambassador's dismay by following up the meeting with a note in answer to Nesselrode's despatch. It was only at Esterhazy's urgent desire that he omitted from it an explicit reference to the Treaty of Unkiar Skelessi. But he insisted that, though Mehemet had given way on this occasion, he might try again unless means were taken to see that the Five Powers were really united on the Eastern Question. These must not be unprepared in the future. "Unanimity can be arrived at", he stated, "only by previous concert." He pressed Pozzo di Borgo, therefore, to obtain instructions from his Court to enable him to take part in discussions on the subject at London. All this took place while the Persian dispute was beginning and Pozzo di Borgo was frightened to death. But he had little influence on the decisions of his Court who recognised his inadequacy to the occasion.

[1] Sébastiani to Molé, 14 Aug., 1838: *A.A.E.* Esterhazy to Metternich, 18 Aug., 1848: *V. St. A.* Molé revealed Sébastiani's despatch to the Russian Envoy, but the motive had been fairly obvious. (P. E. Mosely, *Russian Diplomacy, etc.*, 80.)
[2] Esterhazy to Metternich, 18 Aug., 1838. From Lamb, 25 Oct., 1838: *F.O. Austria*, 272.

The answer which Nesselrode despatched at his master's orders simply reaffirmed the previous note, declared that the British position was perfectly well appreciated by the Emperor and that no 'concert préalable' was necessary. On the contrary, it would be more likely to create differences than produce unanimity. Palmerston now determined to make the issue perfectly clear by explicit reference to the Treaty of Unkiar Skelessi. In a reply, sent to the British Ambassador at St. Petersburg, he reaffirmed with great emphasis his view that "Europe never would endure that the matter should be settled by the single independent and self-regulated interference of any one Power, acting according to its own will or without concert with any other Power." Russia had no doubt acted with the best intentions in 1829 and in 1833. But in each case she had obtained advantages for herself, in the one case increase of territory, in the other the Treaty of Unkiar Skelessi. Britain could not allow such a thing to happen again "to the detriment of other Powers", and he believed that the French government took the same view.

This was plain speaking, indeed. But Palmerston used the opportunity to point the moral. "That, therefore", he went on, "the only way in which the Turkey could be assisted without risking a disturbance of the peace would be by the establishment of that concert between the Five Powers which Her Majesty's Government have proposed." When this despatch was read to Nesselrode he appeared a good deal moved. He protested that Russia considered the Treaty of Unkiar Skelessi a burden and added that the sole condition to their advantage, the closing of the Dardanelles, applied only to a state of war. The acquisition on the Danube had been trifling. He denied that he had ever intimated that Russia would occupy Syria if Mehemet attacked, but only that she would defend the Sultan if Mehemet approached Constantinople. On the question of the concert he was silent. The incident was now closed and only formal despatches followed. But there can be no doubt that Palmerston's emphatic warning had great influence on Russian policy when the crisis came next year.[1]

The attempt to establish a concert to negotiate a new European

---

[1] Esterhazy to Metternich, 10 Sept., 1838: *V. St. A.* To Pozzo di Borgo, 3 Sept., 1838; To Clanricarde, 10 Oct., 1838, From Clanricarde, 20 Nov., 1838: *F.O. Russia*, 247, 243, 244.

treaty was, therefore, again a failure. But, like the attempt to organise joint forces described in Section 5, it was a great contribution towards a settlement. It made clear to the other Governments exactly what the British position was. Russia profited by the warning, France did not. Metternich saw that he could rely on British determination and with that support proposed to follow at Vienna the very course Palmerston had suggested should be taken at London. But there could be no question in anyone's mind, including his critics in the Cabinet and the diplomatic service, that Palmerston had shewn himself more 'European' than any other statesman. He had accepted action with Russia; he had urged France and Austria to join with him. He had abandoned, no doubt largely because France was unreliable, the policy of the two maritime Powers acting together against the three Eastern ones. He had placed British policy on the strongest possible basis. The Eastern Question was for all the Great Powers to decide in concert, not for any one of them to control by a special treaty.

5. THE SULTAN AND HIS VASSAL

The contest for the Sultan's favour revolved round the problem of driving Mehemet Ali out of Syria, the Sultan's passionate desire. Mahmud preferred British help to Russian for that purpose because he knew that Britain wished to preserve the Ottoman Empire and that Russia wished ultimately to destroy it. He relied in the last resource on the British fleet to keep him safe from Russian aggression. He also made effort after effort to induce the British Government to give him help to attack his vassal but always without success. He had, therefore, to keep a way of retreat to Russia who had protected him from the Pasha in 1833 and was bound by treaty to do so again if necessary. But Russia also denied him all help to attack; the Treaty of Unkiar Skelessi was purely defensive. Of the discussions between the Porte and the Russian Ambassador on that question we are not yet very accurately informed, but at any rate the Sultan met with the same refusal at St. Petersburg as in London.

The Sultan often threatened to attack by himself. He thought —and events after his death showed he was right—that the Great Powers would be bound to come to his aid whatever happened. The risk of a defeat was better than the prolongation of the armed hostility that existed between him and the Pasha and the consequent exhaustion of his financial resources. He had to be restrained. Palmerston continually sent peremptory orders to Ponsonby to stop him and inform him that his plan was impossible, that he would be beaten and that an appeal by him to Russia might cause the overthrow of his Empire. Ponsonby carried out these orders in his own way. He always gave hope that the Sultan's desire would one day be carried out. In this sense he encouraged him to keep an attack on Mehemet in mind. But he always advised against the attack at that particular moment. He also preferred, if possible, to allow the representatives of other Courts to take the lead in such action which always angered the Sultan and made him less amenable to advice. Butenev, the Russian Ambassador, acted in exactly the same way, though his quieter methods drew less attention to himself and the Russian Government some-

times managed an affair behind his back so as not to embarrass him.

Ponsonby's recipe for gaining the victory over Russia continued to be the same as he had advocated in 1834, the British fleet in the Sea of Marmora. Once it was there, the Sultan was safe from Russian naval attack and British influence would be established at Constantinople. He continually claimed that Russia would accept this situation without war, though sometimes he—and Palmerston had the same thought occasionally—did not see how the problem could ever be resolved until war came and Russia's supremacy in the Black Sea was destroyed. But Palmerston saw clearly the consequences of such a struggle, and desired to avoid or at any rate postpone it. If Russia insisted on isolated action he would not shrink from war. But he would not be the aggressor and he always had hopes, which ultimately proved to be well founded, that once the situation in the West had been cleared up, he would be able to get without war a solution satisfactory to British interests.

That solution necessarily involved the expulsion of Mehemet from Syria. Ponsonby now vehemently supported the Sultan on that question and Palmerston agreed wholeheartedly. Indeed all the European Powers accepted this view. Even Russia advocated it strongly and Broglie and other French Ministers. Metternich never wavered regarding it. Russia was the most suspect, and Ponsonby was convinced that not only did she wish the Pasha to remain in Syria in order to weaken the Sultan, but even had an agreement with him to that effect, and Palmerston was sometimes almost ready to share that opinion. There is no substance in this charge, but Russia's conduct often seemed suspicious and she always insisted that she had no obligation to defend more of the Ottoman Empire in Asia than the Straits.

Wellington, as we have seen, was shocked at Ponsonby's attitude, which the Ambassador made no effort to change when the Tories came in, and would have dismissed him if he had dared. This judgment was partly due to the summoning of the fleet from Malta to Vourla Bay by Ponsonby because of the situation at Constantinople and the Sultan's determination to break with Mehemet. Wellington told Esterhazy that the summoning of the fleet was a proof of Ponsonby's incapacity. Accordingly he cancelled the general instruction concerning the fleet, which, he said, enabled

an Ambassador to involve his country in war. The French
Government was immediately informed by him of what he had
done.[1]

When Palmerston came back he told Ponsonby that the sending
of the fleet to Constantinople would not solve the problem. In any
case Britain must tackle first the more pressing one of Spain.
Ponsonby for a time said little about it. No doubt he thought the
position of the Whig Government precarious. In August, however, he made a frank confession of his views. The new Government, he thought, had not the energy to solve the Eastern Question,
though Palmerston's own nerves were strong and his opinion
sound. He did not wish to remain at Constantinople if England in
fact abandoned the Sultan. "This, I think", he went on, "depends
upon accident. It depends upon the decision of the Sultan as to a
war with Mehemet Ali. If that takes place the British Government will have no choice; it will be bound to act with arms in its
hand or give up the ghost. I think the Sultan will make war on
Mehemet Ali. I am certain he ought to do so. He cannot long
support the present state of things in comparison with which defeat
by Mehemet in the field would be an advantage. . . . Remember
I tell you that I think it probable the Sultan will make war and
that if so, unless he shall be completely victorious you must interfere, and even if it be so, I doubt if you will be able to avoid taking
a strong part."

In the autumn Ponsonby ("that I may acquire a certain responsibility," he explained) began to put these views in rather more
guarded language in his despatches. In 1835 the Syrians showed
much opposition to Ibrahim's administration and the fanatical
Druses of the 'Mountain', Lebanon, had to be repressed. Ponsonby
announced that the Sultan was contemplating attack, giving details
of movements of Turkish troops and fleet, and implied that the
Sultan hoped to bring in the Russians and then the British and
French and so emancipate himself from his two enemies at the
same time. "It will be madness in you to oppose the Sultan's
resolution," he said in a private letter, . . . "I will assert that you
will never be able to do any good with Turkey until Mehemet
Ali is destroyed and he will be destroyed by any war he shall

[1] Esterhazy to Metternich, 11, 27 March, 1835: *V. St. A.* Wellington to
Ponsonby, 16 March, 1835: *F.O. Turkey,* 251. Wellington to Aston, 17 March,
1835: *F.O. France,* 497. Medem told Wellington that if the British fleet went
to Constantinople the Russians would attack by land.

make on the Sultan even though he should obtain another great victory."[1]

These prophecies were fulfilled to the letter in 1839, but everything depended on when the crisis would come and what the diplomatic situation would be when it did come. Palmerston, as has been seen, was engaged in endeavouring to produce a treaty which would make it possible for Britain and France to act together at Constantinople and perhaps use their fleets. But these negotiations had hardly begun and clearly it was necessary to wait. Palmerston instructed Ponsonby to use his utmost endeavours to stop the attack. Time, he repeated, was on the Sultan's side. And he ordered him to warn the Turkish Ministers that if the Sultan forced the issue, "the British Government will never allow itself to be thus forced into war by the caprice or wrongheadedness of another Government; and . . . would find means to protect her own interests without regard to those of a Government which would thus have deliberately sought to bring on a general war in Europe for its own selfish interests."[2]

Ponsonby consistently refused to speak in this way to the Sultan's advisers. Such a course, he said, would throw Turkey into the arms of Russia, undermine all his own influence and produce the very result Palmerston was anxious to avoid. But he was able to announce that he had taken steps to make it certain that Turkey would not attack. No doubt one of the means used was to support the mission of M. Blaque which came to such an untimely end. The Sultan promised not to attack until the result of that mission was known. Though the British agent, Richard Wood, reported that Emir Bechir and his subjects were ready to cooperate with the Turks in driving out the Egyptians, the crisis died down.[3]

Ponsonby could be sure of Palmerston's approval so long as the immediate attack was prevented. For he knew that his chief was in sympathy with his main thesis. "You have all along taken a just view of the position of affairs," Palmerston wrote privately,

[1] To Ponsonby, 16 July, 1835: *B.P.* From Ponsonby, 11, 30 Oct., 1835. *F.O. Turkey*, 255, 256; do., 19 Aug., 27 Sept., 1835: *B.P.*

[2] To Ponsonby, 4 Nov., 8 Dec., 1835: *F.O. Turkey*, 251. The strong wording of the first dispatch was partly due to a wish to satisfy Melbourne to whom Ellice had complained after his passage through Constantinople with Durham. To Melbourne, 31 Oct., 1835: *B.P.*

[3] From Ponsonby, 29 Dec., 1835, 4 Jan., 5 Feb., 1836: *F.O. Turkey*, 256, 276. Richard Wood's reports were consistently hostile to Ibrahim and Campbell insisted that he did not do him justice. But the events of 1840 showed that Wood had judged rightly.

"and perhaps you are right in the remedies you propose, that is to say the employment of force, but considerations connected with home affairs and the circumstances of other parts of Europe prevent us from adopting these means. For my part I believe that England alone and unaided by any other power would enable Turkey to defend herself against Russia, for that, if we and Turkey had, as we should have, the command of the Black Sea, Russia would not be able to get access to the Balkans."[1]

Thus encouraged, Ponsonby continued to expound his views in private letters. "In this question", he wrote on 8 April, "the possession of the Sultan is the main spring. If we have him our voluntary and real friend we can so arrange matters as to obtain *against* Russia whatever we may think necessary without giving Russia the least stateable or just cause of complaint." If Russia did oppose, she would expose her whole position. "It is wholly impossible", he went on, "for H.M.'s Govt. to prevent a war between the Sultan and Mehemet Ali, and I think it folly (excuse the word) to attempt it, for in the attempt the sacrifice will be made of the greatest strength we have for the preservation of a general peace, and this will be made clear, by events, to all the world, and the Government be answerable for bringing on that war which they may easily avoid by acting so as to keep the Sultan their fast friend. I have placed you in the situation to obtain this great good. If you do not chuse to avail yourself of it I am not to blame."[2]

Meanwhile there had been an incident which had added to the growing criticism of Ponsonby at the capitals of Europe and of which the Russian representatives, chagrined at the increase of British influence over the Sultan, took full advantage. At the end of January 1836 Roussin told Ponsonby that the Turkish Ministers had informed him that the Russian dragoman had warned them that, convinced that England meditated attack, the Tsar intended to put the Treaty of Unkiar Skelessi into operation and occupy the Dardanelles with Russian troops. Roussin had replied that England and France were united and now consulted Ponsonby as to the necessary action. The latter told his colleague that he was not authorised to act, but that if the crisis came and the Sultan "demanded *privately but officially*" the support of the British

---

[1] To Ponsonby, 15 Dec., 1835: *B.P.*
[2] From Ponsonby, 6 Feb., 8 April, 1836: *B.P.*

squadron, he would write to the Admiral saying that it was necessary to protect the Sultan and would personally take the responsibility. According to Ponsonby the French Ambassador said he would do likewise. Ponsonby reported his action home and said that if he had done wrong he hoped that he might be informed in order that he might tell the Sultan to make the best terms he could with the "victorious Muscovite". The declaration of Roussin, he added, had done much good in encouraging the Turk and alarming the Russians. Austria, he claimed, would side with England and France, if they showed that they were determined to resist Russia.

In a private letter, sent at the same time, Ponsonby wrote that he thought the Russians were convinced that they had lost their influence over the Sultan, and that they could not accept such a situation: "I think Nicolas *dares* not lose the game here for fear of the consequences of his defeat upon his subjects. I am confident he cannot win the game if he be opposed by the will of the Sultan and that if he risk any movement unsanctioned by the Sultan he will be ruined by that measure. . . . I suspect that a black cloud hangs over him and will destroy him. I think Poland will press him down and finish him, as human, if not poetical, justice requires should be the case." He asked for Palmerston's approbation: "I am certain that if war can be avoided it will be by the measures I have so long and patiently matured and that the overthrow of the Russian influence here was necessary to preserve peace."[1]

When, at Palmerston's desire, Granville asked the French Ministers about this incident, they at first denied all knowledge of it, but subsequently Desages produced a report of discussions of a very different colour. Roussin did not admit that he had agreed to act with Ponsonby, but stated that he had warned Ponsonby that it was his language that was provoking the Russians and that the Ambassador had replied "that it was true England did not wish for an immediate war with Russia and that Lord Palmerston had written to him in this sense in a private communication, but Lord P[onsonby] said, I will nevertheless bring it about because

[1] From Ponsonby, 7 Feb., 1836: *F.O. Turkey*, 273; do., 8 Feb., 1836: *B.P.* cf. Sabry, *L'Empire Egyptien*, 307. Professor Puryear (*International Economics*, etc., 45), gave Roussin's account of this incident in a note, but did not check it by the British archives. Dr. Bolsover had succinctly and correctly reported it from that source. (*Slavonic Review*, July, 1934, 12.)

I conceive it to be in the interest of my country." When Roussin said England and France were unprepared for war, Ponsonby insisted that Russia was also unprepared, that he could at any moment order the English Admiral to station his fleet in the Dardanelles and the Admiral would have to bear the responsibility if he refused.

There seems little doubt that this is a garbled account of the interview, possibly due to difficulties of language. It is near enough to Ponsonby's account to make a mistake quite possible. It must also be remembered that Roussin was jealous of Ponsonby's success and that the latter was on far better terms with the French Secretary of Embassy, D'Eyragues, than with Roussin himself. The French Government took little notice of the despatch until Granville made enquiries, though they had hinted on more than one occasion that Ponsonby was not carrying out his orders. They cannot have taken Roussin's report very seriously. Palmerston not only believed Ponsonby but in a sense accepted his point of view. "What we ought to do", he told Granville, "is to sign our treaty, offer it to Turkey, and send our two fleets to the entrance of the Dardanelles, with orders to go up to Constantinople the moment they were invited to do so by the Sultan. We *ought* then to tell Mehemet Ali to evacuate Syria and retire into his proper shell in Egypt. To this many members of our Cabinet would I fear object, and I suspect the French Government is not quite prepared for it. But it is clear that while Mehemet Ali has a great army in Syria, the Sultan must keep the greater part of his forces in Asia Minor, and leave his northern frontier undefended." Thus the Sultan was in the power of Russia and Mehemet, and, while Britain and France could control the latter, they must wait until the Sultan had reorganised his forces before trying to redress the balance against Russia.

But at the same time Palmerston, as he promised Granville, instructed Ponsonby that Britain's aim was peace and for that reason the Sultan must be kept quiet: "Our line is simply this. We wish to maintain peace and shall certainly not provoke war; we hope to keep at peace; but there are certain things we shall not stand; and we are resolved to uphold the integrity and indepen-dance of the Turkish Empire. Pray conform your language to this." And then he warned him that he had many detractors who tried "to make out that your language is too warlike," Edward

Ellice among them, and of a "cock and bull story" that Ponsonby had said that "we were determined to go to war with Russia". Though the Ambassador might adapt Palmerston's language if he thought it too severe, he must exhort the Sultan in the strongest measure to keep the peace. This advice he reiterated a month later when he heard of M. Blaque's mission. Until the secret agent arrived he would not give an official answer "upon the subject of the attack which the Sultan contemplates making upon Mehemet Ali." But Mehemet had turned seventy. "Is it not better", he asked Ponsonby, "for the Sultan to wait the cooperation of his sure ally than to risk his own existence by precipitate rashness?"[1]

The proof of Palmerston's confidence that Ponsonby would carry out these orders lies in his renewal of the Ambassador's power to summon the fleet to Constantinople, if the Sultan asked for it. This would be a defensive measure against Russia rather than an aggressive one against Mehemet. It was clear that if Russia did intend to occupy the Dardanelles, which not only the incident at Constantinople, but much information from Russia showed was possible, the situation could only be saved if the British fleet got there first. Palmerston must have had some difficulty in obtaining these instructions, but no record has come down about them and possibly the fear of Russian aggression, which was felt in all quarters at this time, helped the Cabinet to approve an action which was after all only precautionary.

Ponsonby himself had shown no great desire to be given back his instructions and in reporting the incident he had said that he had no need of them. "Have you ever known", he wrote, "the cause why the Duke of Wellington withdrew from me the powers entrusted to me by your instructions of 10th March 1834? I know his reasons and I think them very discreditable, to his understanding at least. I may however be glad to be free from the responsibility they would have laid upon me, were I not always willing to risk everything to serve the Govt. and the country. I think these instructions were like the last trump at Whist and sure to win the game under the circumstances that *they* anticipated. You have now before yourself the facts upon which to act and I have no need of the instructions as things are."

[1] To Granville, 1, 12 March, 1836. From Granville, 11 March, 1836; To Ponsonby [Blank] April, 10 May, 1836: *B.P.*; do., 7 May, 1836: *F.O. Turkey*, 271.

But Palmerston obviously thought it better to regularise the position. Suggestions had been made for the use of the fleets in 1833 and the French Admiral had contemplated going through the Dardanelles. Such a situation might well recur. What was Ponsonby to do if the Sultan appealed to him for aid? There would be no time for reference to London. Power was, therefore, given him with the same restrictions as before. Only if the Sultan himself invited the fleet and only if the Admiral agreed that there was no naval risk could the Ambassador order it to pass the Dardanelles. Ponsonby had already given assurances that his power to summon the fleet would only be used as a last resource to anticipate a Russian entry. Palmerston endorsed this attitude with a solemn warning that the power was only to be used in "case of urgent and demonstrable necessity", because if a precedent were so created the Russian fleet was in a position to take advantage of it more often than the British.[1]

By this time the return of Silistria to the Porte by the Tsar had convinced some of the Cabinet of the truth of Durham's reports and even made an impression on the public, though Ponsonby declared that it was simply done to humbug Britain and France. No doubt this was one of the means by which the Russian Government regained to some extent the confidence of the Sultan. Then occurred the Churchill incident narrated above, which was used by the Russian party for the same purpose, and, as we have seen, Ponsonby's reputation and spirits fell to a low ebb in the autumn of 1836 and winter of 1837.

Palmerston on the other hand was especially anxious to keep things quiet in the East because the struggle in Spain had reached its height. "We are defending Turkey in the Basque Provinces," he wrote, "and John Hay and his squadron are rescuing the Dardanelles from Russia at Passages and St. Sebastian." Ponsonby did keep things quiet, and it seems unlikely that he had any responsibility for the dispatch of the *Vixen* which was entirely due to Urquhart's influence on Bell. Palmerston naturally refused to consider a suggestion derived from Roussin, which Molé made Sébastiani put forward as his own invention, that France should take the initiative in a mediation between the Sultan and Mehemet. He wanted, he said, the *status quo* preserved. Roussin on the

---

[1] From Ponsonby, 8 Feb., 1836: *B.P.* To Ponsonby, 20 June, 1836: *F.O. Turkey*, 271.

other hand was a busybody. He got the Sultan himself to make some sort of approach to Mehemet Ali, and at the end of 1836 Sarim Effendi, an experienced official of the second rank, had been sent to Alexandria to sound the Pasha as to a reconciliation. Some suggestion that he should be guaranteed the succession of his children in Egypt and part of his Syrian dominions seems to have been made in return for the surrender of the rest of his territory, but the negotiation was conducted on the most oriental lines and neither Campbell nor anyone else seems to have discovered what exactly took place.[1]

At any rate no arrangement was arrived at and it is improbable that the Sultan expected any other result. After this failure he made another appeal for help to Ponsonby in vague language which the Ambassador did not press on Palmerston with his usual vigour. It was of course refused. "We can give the Sultan no encouragement in his warlike propensities against Mehemet; and you may extinguish all hope he may entertain of that," wrote Palmerston. Ponsonby as usual altered the terms of the refusal in order to avoid "serious discouragement" of the Sultan. The Sultan remained quiet, but Ponsonby continued to assert throughout the years that he could get the Sultan to allow British ships to enter the Black Sea if Palmerston would permit him to insist on doing so. Austria and Prussia would be only too glad, he claimed, and what could Russia do? Palmerston made no response.[2]

Thus the situation remained until the middle of 1838. The Sultan was enjoined to improve his army and wait. Ponsonby claimed credit for "the exertions I have made to keep the Sultan upon the strictest line of pacific policy consistent with measures of self defence", and for "the counsel I gave him not to permit his

[1] To Ponsonby, 17 Jan., 1837: *B.P.* For the *Vixen* incident see above, p. 571. From Campbell, 20 Dec., 1836, 9, 21, 24, 27 Jan., 7 April, 1837: *F.O. Turkey*, 284, 319. The negotiation broke down on the rank to be accorded to Ibrahim, but there was much communication between Pertev and Mehemet of which little is known. cf. Sabry, *L'Empire Egyptien*, 321-322. Note to Sébastiani, 7 Nov., 1836, Sébastiani to Molé, 11 Nov., 1836, *A.A.E.* Desages wrote long accounts of Roussin's action to Bourqueney, explained how he had ordered D'Eyragues to refute it after Roussin had gone on leave. Sarim Effendi, he wrote, was "un espèce de *moi* ou de Backhouse" (8 Nov., 1836, 14 April, 1837: *Bour. P.*) Metternich's advice to the Porte was to give way on Egypt but on nothing else and to take advantage of Mehemet's refusal to withdraw the offer of Acre. From Lamb, 31 March, 1837: *F.O. Austria*, 264.
[2] To Ponsonby, 11 May, 1837; From Ponsonby, 7 June, 7 July, 1837: *B.P.* Mavrojeni urged the same course on Lamb at Vienna.

army to fight a general action under any circumstances of provo-
cation". The Ambassador continued to insist that Russia was
pushing the Sultan on while at the same time secretly encouraging
Mehemet. This last charge is, of course, not true, but Russia
preferred to leave to Ponsonby the task of restraining the Sultan.
Moreover, we now know that the Russian Government was ready
to seize the Dardanelles and Bosphorus in force if the Sultan were
to call on Britain and France to assist him at Constantinople.
Palmerston's endeavours to obtain a European concert on the
Eastern Question already narrated aroused great suspicions, and
the Tsar put pressure on the Austrian Court during the Toeplitz
meeting of this year to wean Metternich from Lamb's dangerous
influence, while at the same time he behaved in a more conciliatory
manner towards France.[1]

Thus Ponsonby's expectations that he might wake up one morning and find a Russian squadron on the Sea of Marmora were not
quite so foolish as his critics thought. He reluctantly admitted
that Palmerston would not apply his own remedy, a British squadron at Constantinople, before the Russians could get there. But
he was pressing now for the right to apply to the Sultan for
permission for British frigates to pass through the Straits and
explore the Black Sea. He rightly thought that the Tsar intended
the Black Sea to be a *Mare Clausum* and wished that no other
warships sail on it. Since all the Powers were at peace, Russia, he
said, could not object. He wrote Lamb a bullying despatch to
urge Melbourne to accept his plan. That Ambassador was
indignant and suggested that Palmerston should make Ponsonby
realise that it was time enough for Ambassadors to be warlike when
their Governments were. Palmerston had contemplated sending surveying vessels through the straits but he was in no mood
for Ponsonby's plan. "To do what?", he wrote on Ponsonby's
letter. He entirely agreed with Lamb's strictures. He knew
that the diplomatic situation was not yet sufficiently favourable for
action.[2]

Then came the news that Mehemet was about to declare his
independence. Throughout these years Palmerston had grown
more and more hostile to the Pasha and come to regard him as the

---

[1] From Ponsonby, 11 March, 1838: *B.P.* The Russian policy of this year
has been revealed by P. E. Mosely (*Russian Diplomacy*, 40–42).
[2] From Ponsonby, 27 May, 1838; From Lamb, 4 May, 25 June, 1838: *B.P.*

great stumbling block to the solution of the Eastern Question. Nearly all his agents succumbed to the wiles of Mehemet. The British agents in Syria reported, it is true, the discontent of the population with Ibrahim's rule and especially his methods of conscription. Richard Wood and Farren were especially critical. But Campbell grew more and more favourable to Mehemet and refused to admit the validity of these reports. Though he carried out Palmerston's orders there can be little doubt that his sympathetic attitude had some effect on Mehemet. When Bowring went out in 1838 to investigate the commercial possibilities of Egypt, he too fell under Mehemet's spell and undoubtedly encouraged him to think that he would have some support in Britain for his plans.[1]

Since 1834 Palmerston had supported every move to break down Mehemet's power and to keep him subordinate to the Sultan even though it was not yet possible to turn him out of Syria. He welcomed for that reason the Sultan's abolition of monopolies in the commercial convention. He had already strongly insisted on Mehemet carrying out the abolition of the silk monopoly in Syria. He suspected Mehemet of wishing to annex the Pashalik of Baghdad (quite wrongly for it was not in the Pasha's view worth having) and protested against the occupation of Dair by Ibrahim which he thought was a preliminary to such a plan. He viewed with growing anxiety the Pasha's gradual conquest of the Arabian peninsula which was intensified in 1837. The Government of India in 1838 had already taken steps to exclude Mehemet from further penetration of the Red Sea by the negotiation for the lease of Aden to Britain.[3]

This was the situation when Mehemet suddenly announced to

---

[1] Palmerston told Campbell to "undo the mischief" Bowring had done (4 Aug., 1838: *B.P.*). Bowring later tried to repudiate the accounts of his language and said Mehemet Ali had misrepresented him, and Campbell reported that Bowring had always told Mehemet that he could not speak for his Government on official questions. The Pasha's move, he claimed, was due to Prokesch and French influence. It was at this time that Campbell sent home Prokesch's report of 1833 first published by M. Sabry (*L'Empire Egyptien*, 271). It was no doubt sent at this time to divert Palmerston's attention from Campbell himself and Bowring, whose attitude Campbell had welcomed.

[2] For the action as to Aden see the admirable account by Dodwell (*The Founder of Modern Egypt*, 145–151) who has used the India Office Papers, and a recent article by Halford L. Hoskins, "Background of the British Position in Arabia," *The Middle East Journal*, April, 1947. Researches are now being made in the Egyptian Archives into this significant but little known activity of Mehemet Ali. For the connection of this problem with the Persian attack on Herat see Chapter VIII, Section 5, p. 749.

the Consuls-General at Alexandria that he intended to declare his independence of the Sultan. The motives which prompted him to do so at this time are not exactly known, but in spite of the fact that his son Ibrahim was strongly against such a step, Mehemet's patience seems at last to have given way and he determined to make an attempt to get his family established, relying on the disunion of the Powers to prevent any action against him. The Sultan was greatly alarmed. If Mehemet became independent, Mahmud would no longer be sovereign of the Holy Cities on which to some extent his whole claim to rule the Ottoman Empire depended.

Palmerston took up the challenge at once. Such a threat might bring on immediate war and the Russian fleet to the Bosphorus. He thought that the crisis which he had so long tried to prevent had come at last and was resolved to use it if he could to clear up the whole Eastern Question. His first thought, in spite of Melbourne's opposition, was joint action by France and England on the lines suggested in 1836. He did not expect Austria to do anything, but a treaty of the two Powers with the Sultan would at any rate legalise the entry of the British and French fleets into the Dardanelles if necessary. Indeed, he wrote, a treaty with Britain alone might be sufficient. He proposed, therefore, a plan to Melbourne for an Anglo-French Turkish convention. But Granville poured cold water on this project which he did not think Molé would accept. And the Cabinet when consulted wished an offer to be made both to Russia and to Austria to join the Maritime Powers in defence of the Sultan. The former might send her fleet to act conjointly with those of Britain and France, while Austria might furnish land forces in Syria, an old idea of Palmerston's, which he had already without much hope of success suggested to Lamb when the first rumours of Mehemet's intentions reached him.[1]

[1] From Ponsonby, 25 June, 1838: *F.O. Turkey*, 331. To Granville, 5, 8 June, 1838: *Bulwer*, II, 266–7, and *B.P.* (Bulwer's version gives a very inadequate idea of these letters). To Granville, 16 June, 1838: *B.P.* This letter described a one-article convention by which Britain and France would provide naval aid at any time in the next eight years if Mehemet attacked or declared himself independent. The Sultan was to promise not to ask for aid from any other source except on urgent necessity and with the agreement of the French and British Ambassadors. Melbourne deprecated a treaty. France, he wrote, was an unreliable partner and would merely look after her own interests. "It may be necessary to defend Turkey but I should not like to be bound to defend her. . . . I agree with you that there is every appearance of the coming on of considerable difficulties, but our policy is to have our hands free." (3 June, 1838: *B.P.*)

The first thing, however, was to get all the Powers to protest energetically at Alexandria. This was the more necessary as the French Consul-General was showing every sign of sympathy with Mehemet's demands and Campbell was not much better. In this matter there was no great difficulty. Molé refused, it is true, to make joint representations. But no doubt Desages gave him some good advice. At any rate Molé and Palmerston consulted together and each was entirely satisfied with the despatches of the other. The despatch which Palmerston sent to Alexandria was written in his best manner and warned Mehemet that he was much mistaken if he relied on the jealousies of the European forces to protect him from Britain's wrath. Metternich readily agreed to do likewise, thought Palmerston's despatch admirable and engaged to get Russia to send a similar one at the Toeplitz meeting. Nesselrode did do so, but, in his despatch to Pozzo di Borgo concerning it, he hinted that Russia was in a different position to the other Powers because the Treaty of Unkiar Skelessi bound her to assist the Sultan if he demanded her aid. As has been noted in Section 4 it was this claim which produced such a great effect on Palmerston and led him to make a special effort to force Russia to substitute a general European treaty for that of Unkiar Skelessi.[1]

But meanwhile no common plan for action against Mehemet could be made. Palmerston discussed the problem with Sébastiani, Esterhazy and Pozzo di Borgo in a series of interviews. All were most helpful. Pozzo di Borgo, though he was alarmed about Constantinople, suggested that the British fleet should go to Egypt. Sébastiani not only wished the British and French fleets to cruise together, but agreed with Palmerston and recommended to his Government that a land force might be necessary and that Austrian forces would cause the least jealousy if used for this purpose. He was ready for the Russian fleet to act with the British and French fleets in the Mediterranean. Louis Philippe professed himself delighted at this idea of Austrian troops but unfortunately Molé, whose jealousy of his own Ambassador was almost equal to that which he had had of Talleyrand in 1830, was furious at Sébastiani taking so much on himself. He absolutely

[1] To Campbell, 9 June, 7 July, 1838: *F.O. Turkey*, 343. To Granville, 3 July, 1838: *F.O. France*, 557; do., 6 July, 1838, *Bulwer*, II, 370 and *B.P.* From Granville, 11, 15, 18, 22 June, 1838: *F.O. France*, 562. Esterhazy to Metternich, 26 June, 1838: *V. St. A.* Nesselrode to Pozzo di Borgo, 23 July, 1838: *F.O. Russia*, 247. See above, Section 4, p. 591.

refused to agree, stating that such a move would be unpopular in France, though he professed himself ready for the British and French fleets to act together if Mehemet persisted in his intention. He added that the two Governments might also consider how to reconcile the Sultan and the Pasha on the basis of the hereditary succession of Mehemet's family not only in Egypt but in Syria. These hesitations naturally confirmed all Palmerston's suspicions of French good faith, though Granville and Louis Philippe himself attributed them to Molé's jealousy of Sébastiani. It was in fact, as Louis Philippe well knew, something more than this. Molé was much more ready to get into touch with Russia than with Britain. The effect on Palmerston was apparent, as Esterhazy noted, though with Sébastiani his relations continued to be as intimate as before. Nor could Lamb get anything further out of Metternich who was off to see Nicholas at Toeplitz. The dispute with Russia concerning Persia also complicated matters. In the final result nothing was done but to get the British and Turkish fleets ready.[1]

Thus no international naval action was obtained, and for long Palmerston was very anxious lest Russia should send a force to Constantinople or to Asia Minor at the Sultan's request. This anxiety was increased by the Persian dispute which was now becoming acute. Palmerston was, it is true, prepared to invite a Russian squadron to cruise with the British and French fleets in the Mediterranean. But we know in fact that preparations were being made for isolated action by Russia, and that Pozzo di Borgo himself had already suggested that the right place for the Russian troops was Constantinople and that the task of stopping Mehemet in Asia Minor could be left to others.

Fortunately Mehemet was impressed by the series of warnings received from the Consuls-General and with many protestations and complaints gradually withdrew from his position. Further action was not necessary. But Palmerston's efforts had been worth while. They were to be repeated with better success in 1840 and had taught him much of the manner in which he could obtain

[1] To Granville, 3 July, 1838: *F.O. France*, 557; do., 8 June, 6 July: *Bulwer*, II, 268, 270 and *B.P.* From Granville, 11, 15, 18, 22 June, 2, 6, 9, 13, 16 July, 1838: *F.O. France*, 562; do., 2, 9, 16 July, 1838: *B.P.* Esterhazy to Metternich, 26 June, 3, 22 July, 1838: *V. St. A.* Sébastiani to Molé, 12, 29 June, 12, 19 July, 1838; Molé to Sébastiani, 7 July, 1838: *A.A.E.* Esterhazy early noted that Palmerston seemed almost as suspicious of France as of Russia.

his ends without a European war. And his energy, directness and readiness to accept the suggestions of others for a common object had impressed all those with whom he had come into contact.[1]

Meanwhile Ponsonby had made the Sultan keep quiet while his defence was being prepared. The Ambassador believed that Mehemet had been stirred up by Russia, and Palmerston at the outset was inclined to agree, but not because of the reports that the Turkish Ministers thought so. "It is natural", Palmerston wrote on 23 June, "that they who know we are jealous of Russia and also want to set us against Mehemet should tell us that their enemy and ours are secretly friends to each other. But it is in the nature of things that it should be so: and no assertions will make me disbelieve it." Moreover, though British and French fleets could intercept Egyptian vessels if the Sultan ordered them to do so, they could not touch neutrals. He wanted, therefore, the Turkish fleet to cruise with the British and French fleets, after a convention had been made between the two Governments and the Sultan. "Such a convention", he went on, "might lead naturally and without the appearance of any intention hostile to Russia to a part of our squadron coming up to Constantinople either to escort the Turkish ships down, or to help to fit them out, or to accompany them."

Ponsonby had already sent for the British fleet to move from Malta. He sent a letter through the Austrian post which claimed that the Sultan could defeat Mehemet and implied that Mehemet was following Russian advice: "*Disorder* and *difficulties* in Turkey", he wrote "are the means for bringing about Russian ends." But his conduct was otherwise unimpeachable, though, of course, he supported the Sultan's position by every means in his power. Reschid declared that the Sultan would never consent to his vassal's demand, and Ponsonby himself pointed out that Mehemet's assumption of independence would mean that, since the Sultan would no longer be the Sovereign of the Holy Cities, a new Caliph might be set up. He suggested that Chrysanowski should be put in command of the Turkish forces. But even though he was informed that the Russians had offered naval and military forces to the

---

[1] Sébastiani to Molé, 14, 24 Aug., 1838: *A.A.E.* Pozzo di Borgo to Nesselrode, 3 July, 1838: P. E. Mosely, *Russian Diplomacy, etc.*, 148. From Campbell, 16 Aug., 5 Sept., 1838: *F.O. Turkey*, 343.

Sultan, his conduct was most circumspect. He urged the Sultan to be quiet and when the French Ambassador objected to the Turkish squadron going to sea lest it should come into collision with Mehemet's fleet, he advised that it should go to Tripoli or Malta and avoid Syria.[1]

He was naturally immensely moved by Palmerston's proposal for a convention for the defence of the Sultan and immediately tackled Reschid on the subject. But even here he was, though verbose, very careful, and while suggesting the employment of a British fleet if the Sultan entered into the necessary contracts to obtain it, explained that only if Mehemet persisted was such a contingency possible and made no mention of the entry of British ships into the Dardanelles, lest by some leakage Russia should get to hear of it and use it as an excuse for action. There followed a series of conferences with Reschid Pasha and Mustapha Kamil Bey in which the relations with Russia were discussed. The Sultan authorised the Ministers to declare that he would not apply for Russian aid, but in return asked for an assurance that England would protect him from Russian attack. Ponsonby, who of course had no official authorisation to make any such declaration, handled the matter very skilfully by appealing to promises made in the King's speech in Parliament of maintaining the integrity of the Ottoman Empire and of Palmerston's recent assurances to Reschid in London which that Minister confirmed. In the end he obtained a letter from Reschid in which it was stated that the Sultan had not the slightest intention of asking Russia for help, that none such had yet been offered and that the Porte was ready to seek British naval aid along the lines Ponsonby had suggested.

These proceedings, which occurred during the negotiations for the commercial convention, excited the greatest suspicion of Roussin who was already very jealous of Ponsonby's success. He imagined that a loan had been offered as part of a treaty of alliance and demanded information from Ponsonby. Ponsonby did not disclose the subject of his meetings and thought that he had convinced the Ambassador that they were solely concerned with

---

[1] To Ponsonby, 23 June, 1838: *B.P.* From Ponsonby, 6, 11, 14, 24, 25 June, 1838. *F.O. Turkey*, 331; do., 6 June, 1838: *V. St. A.* Husrev objected to Chrysanowski's appointment (30 July, 1838: *B.P.*). Ponsonby on several occasions sent letters by the Austrian courier containing criticisms of Russia. Lamb protested; but it may be that Ponsonby's apparent carelessness was calculated.

the commercial convention. Roussin, however, naturally sent home an account of the incident to his Government and made the uncooperative and suspicious Molé still more unready to allow the French and British fleets to act together.

The French Government suspected that in order to obtain the convention Britain had offered an alliance. This is of course untrue, and there is nothing in the communication which Ponsonby made to the Porte different from the plans which Palmerston had for long discussed with the French Government. But the desire to obtain British help in an attack on Mehemet was one of the reasons why the Sultan agreed to the commercial convention, and it is probable that it would not have been obtained at this moment if these discussions had not made it seem more likely that such aid could be obtained.[1]

Since Mehemet withdrew his claims nothing tangible could immediately result. The French fleet did not cooperate with the British but the Turkish fleet did. Palmerston now suggested a joint cruise as a means of showing the friendly relations between the two Governments and exercising the Turkish navy rather than as a demonstration against Mehemet. It served that purpose, but the absence of the French fleet did not go unremarked in Europe.

There was of course no question in Palmerston's mind of the fleet now going up to Constantinople. The danger had passed. Ponsonby refused to believe it and insisted that the *status quo*, rejected by both the Sultan and Mehemet, was only supported by Russia and France for their own interests. The Pasha would act in order to get out of enforcing the commercial convention. Ponsonby still hoped, therefore, to be allowed to bring the fleet up to Constantinople, a course which he claimed was not a breach of the Treaty of Unkiar Skelessi. He was furious when Admiral Stopford refused to stay in the neighbourhood of the Straits in spite of all appeals. "It is one thing to face iron bullets," he wrote, "and that Admirals will always do, but some of them are devilishly afraid of paper bullets." And he urged Palmerston to clinch the

---

[1] From Ponsonby, 30 July, 1838; Reschid Pasha to Ponsonby, 28 July, 1838: *B.P.* and *Bulwer*, II, 272, who omits the concluding passage. Professor Puryear has given an account of Roussin's suspicions. He, like other historians, found it difficult to account for them, since there is no mention of Ponsonby's discussions with Reschid in the official correspondence. (*International Economics, etc.*, 82–83.)

success just obtained in Persia by sending the British fleet into the Dardanelles. But Palmerston thoroughly approved of Stopford's action and again warned Ponsonby that there was nothing to be gained in getting the fleet to Constantinople unless it had a definite object. Nor when he heard of Reschid's mission to London did he give the slightest encouragement that an offensive treaty could be made. On the contrary he suggested that perhaps the best arrangement was to offer Mehemet the hereditary succession of his family in Egypt in return for the evacuation of Syria.[1]

Thus the action at Constantinople amounted to little more than a joint fleet exercise. But this also contributed to the solution in 1840. It showed the hesitations of France, the possibility of the British fleet acting with the Turkish and thus obtaining a better legal and moral position than if it acted alone, and the fact that the Tsar was not prepared to give the final orders to occupy the Bosphorus even when the Turks were clearly acting under the guidance of Britain in their defence against the Pasha.

The ageing and ailing Sultan, though again disappointed, had noted the vigorous action of Palmerston, more prompt and effective than that of any other Government. He determined to make one more attempt to obtain the countenance and support of Britain before he forced the issue by attacking Mehemet on his sole responsibility. That was, in his mind, the object of Reschid's mission. The Ambassador was to explore the situation at Vienna, Berlin and Paris on his way to London. But it was to Palmerston that the Sultan's appeal was really directed. This step was apparently concerted between Reschid and the Sultan without much consultation with Ponsonby who believed it much more important to get the fleet to Constantinople than to make a treaty. He was afraid of Russia using the threat from Mehemet to reestablish her ascendancy once more. But for the Sultan it was Mehemet and not Russia that was the enemy. He wanted the British fleet on his side, to crush him.

---

[1] To Ponsonby, 15 Sept., 11 Dec., 1838: *F.O. Turkey*, 329A; do., 10 Aug., 13 Sept., 2 Oct., 1838: *B.P.* (*Bulwer*, II, 282, gives part of the letter of 13 Sept.) From Ponsonby, 19, 27 Sept., 3, 13, 20, 29 Oct., 1838: *F.O. Turkey*, 332; do., 27 Sept., 17, 20 Oct., 1838: *B.P.* Ponsonby had, however, told Stopford to keep away from the entrance to the Dardanelles when the Russians complained that his fleet was a threat. V. J. Puryear (*International Economics, etc.*, 94–96) describes Ponsonby's manoeuvres in some detail but does not mention Palmerston's despatch of 11 December approving the Admiral's action. On one private letter of Ponsonby (20 Oct.) Palmerston pencilled 'Stuff'.

Reschid's mission was ill-starred from the beginning. He got no encouragement at Vienna or Berlin on his way. At London he found Palmerston absorbed in other matters and in no mood to respond to the Sultan's entreaties. At the end of December Reschid tried to spur him into action by urging that the Russians had the ear of the Sultan and had persuaded him to refuse all conference on the Eastern Question at London. Britain and France must shew proofs that they were ready to act against Mehemet if they were to prevail. But the discussions still went on slowly while conflicting reports as to the Sultan's intentions came from Constantinople. Reschid of course had to recognise that Palmerston could only consider a defensive treaty. But the exact shape of this was not easy to devise and Palmerston had much other business. Not until the 13 March, 1839, was Palmerston able to tell Ponsonby that the Cabinet had agreed on the principle of the defensive treaty which Reschid had proposed. The fall of Molé, he added, would enable Britain to cooperate with a French Government at Constantinople.

Just at this time Reschid, who seems to have given up hope of action, informed Palmerston that a defensive treaty was now useless since Ibrahim's preparations had caused the Sultan to order an immediate attack. Palmerston sent immediately instructions to Ponsonby to urge the Sultan to remain quiet, while Reschid sent to Constantinople a draft treaty on which he and Palmerston had agreed through of course nothing had been signed. It amounted to no more than an agreement for the British and Turkish fleets to act together in case Mehemet or his sons were 'disobedient'. Nothing was said of depriving him of Syria and his other possessions outside Egypt.[1]

[1] From Reschid Pasha, 28 Dec., 1838, 12 March, 1839; To Ponsonby, 13 March, 1839: *B.P.*; do., 15 March, 1839: *L.P.*, I, No. 7. The best account of Reschid's Mission is in P. E. Mosely, *Russian Diplomacy, etc.*, 120–133. It is founded on what the Turks told the Russian Ambassador about it. There is little about it in the Foreign Office Archives or the Broadland Papers. In an interview with Tsartoriski in March 1839 Reschid dwelt pessimistically on the situation of the Sultan, a cruel tyrant whose camarilla was the worst he ever had and wholly under Russian influence. Though ostensibly advising peace the Russians were secretly urging the Sultan to attack. He himself would not return to Constantinople except with a British fleet. He had no wish for the same fate as Pertev. (*Tsartoriski Archives*, Cracow, XX, No. 5294.) Tsartoriski also had an interview with Palmerston who explained to him how impossible it was to attack Russia in the Black Sea or to send a British fleet to Constantinople. When Tsartoriski reminded him of British actions at Naples and Copenhagen, Palmerston replied that Britain would only use moral force which, with that of France and Austria would be sufficient to stop Russia. (do.)

Since the Sultan now determined to attack, this proposal was useless. The Turkish Reis Effendi, Nouri Pasha, informed Ponsonby that it would do more harm than good. The Ambassador who knew little of what had passed between Palmerston and Reschid pressed the Sultan's Ministers to accept it, but without avail. Henceforward, as later events were to shew, the Sultan was determined to force the hands of the Great Powers by attacking Ibrahim. Nouri, it is true, asked both Stürmer and Ponsonby for a treaty the object of which should be to deprive Mehemet of his possessions. But this cannot have been done with any expectations that it would be accepted. The intention of the Sultan was more clearly indicated by the anger with which Nouri received Ponsonby's transmission of Palmerston's entreaties not to attack. For once the Ambassador could not make up his mind as to how far Russia was behind these warlike moves. Officially she was reported as urging the Sultan to keep the peace, but Ponsonby suspected, quite erroneously, that her agents were secretly inciting the Sultan and Hafiz Pasha, the Commander-in-Chief, to attack Ibrahim. He had, indeed, lost the Sultan's confidence and was out of touch with what was planned. His faithfulness in carrying out Palmerston's instructions had, as he had so often prophesied would be the case, deprived him at this critical moment of the commanding position which he had enjoyed in the counsels of the Porte.[1]

Meanwhile, had not Peel behaved so stiffly to the Queen over her Ladies, Palmerston would have been no longer Secretary of State. Among the last things he did before the Melbourne Government resigned on 7 May was to get Melbourne to make Lamb Baron Beauvale and reward Ponsonby with a Viscountcy for his great services at Constantinople. Reschid had informed him at the end of April that better news had come from Constantinople and that peace was assured. He prepared, therefore, when the Whigs resumed office, to go on with the negotiations for a defensive treaty with the Sultan in spite of Reschid's insistence that it would not be well received. Reschid had in fact been warned by Pozzo di Borgo and Orlov of the Russian opposition

---

[1] From Ponsonby, 27 Jan., 12 Feb., 7, 19, 23 March, 7 April, 1839: *F.O. Turkey*, 354–356. All references to Russian policy were cut out in the *Levant Papers*. From Ponsonby, 22 April, 1839: *F.O. Turkey*, 356 (part in *L.P.*, I, No. 26) with minute of draft treaty; do., 1 May, 1839. Nouri Pasha to Ponsonby, 28 April, 1839: *L.P.*, I, No. 37; do., 21 May, 1839: *L.P.*, I, No. 47.

to the treaty and received fresh instructions from Constantinople. Palmerston did not know this, and, as, after much manoeuvring, a new Government had been formed at Paris under Soult, he hoped for French cooperation. Meanwhile the young Tsarevitch was making an excellent impression in London. But Palmerston had hardly begun to take stock of the situation when news came that the Sultan's armies had crossed the Euphrates and the conflict with Mehemet Ali, so long expected and feared, had at last really begun.[1]

[1] From Reschid Pasha, 27 April, 1839: *L.P.*, I, No. 21. P. Mosely, *Russian Diplomacy, etc.*, 132–133. To Ponsonby, 14 May, 1839: *B.P.* "Recid tells me the Sultan will not thank us for any treaty which shall not bind us to turn Ibrahim out of Syria. We shall see. We have got a French Government and France is an European power again, at least for the present." To Granville, 10 May, 1839: "The Grand Duke succeeds here amazingly. . . . I gave him a dinner of fifty people at this office." *Granville P.* T. Schiemann, *Geschichte Russlands*, III, 363. Pozzo di Borgo had tried to stop the visit on the ground that the Tsarevitch would be badly received.

CHAPTER VIII

MEHEMET ALI AND THE STRAITS: THE TRIUMPH IN THE EASTERN QUESTION
1839–1841

" Never, I will answer for it, was a great measure undertaken upon a basis of support so slender and so uncertain."
MELBOURNE, 14 September, 1840.

" Mehemet Ali is like a lie and will be destroyed as that is by truth." PONSONBY, 12 August, 1840.

CHAPTER VIII

MEHEMET ALI AND THE STRAITS: THE TRIUMPH IN THE EASTERN QUESTION
1839–1841

THE triumph of Palmerston in 1840 was perhaps the greatest which he ever won in his long connection with foreign affairs. At one time he stood almost alone, not only in Europe but in his own country, for a policy which he thought essential for British interests and the preservation of peace. His energy and resource, both diplomatic and administrative, obtained results which astonished nearly all his contemporaries. At the same time, in the long-drawn-out negotiation he shewed a patience and readiness to wait for the right moment such as he rarely achieved. No British Foreign Minister, save perhaps Canning, won such a diplomatic victory with a Cabinet so divided on the main issue. He wielded every weapon in the diplomatic armoury with unerring skill; intimidation, conciliation, flattery, personal appeal were all employed at the appropriate time. Meagre military resources were used with their maximum effect. Palmerston could not control the appointment of Admirals and Generals. But he got the inadequate military leaders who were supplied by the Admiralty and the Horse Guards provided with more skilful and bold subordinates. At the end even his enemies recognised the greatness of the achievement.

This result was obtained because Palmerston sought ends which in the long run even those who opposed him saw were necessary. The time was not ripe for a dissolution of the Ottoman Empire which would almost certainly have occurred if Palmerston had not had his way. The failure of Mahmud's final fling at his vassal, so disastrous in its results, would have deprived the Porte permanently of the rule of all the Arab-speaking lands, including the Holy Places, unless it had been rescued by European, mainly British, action. Had Mehemet obtained the hereditary rule of these large dominions, the prestige of the Sultan would have been so reduced that his control over the European provinces could

hardly have been preserved. Europe was not ready to face such a problem nor were the subject populations of the Porte ready for liberation. It is most probable that the result would have been a war between the Great Powers. All came in time to see the dangers of inaction and the necessary remedies, but it was Palmerston who ensured that they were applied. Amongst them was the closing of the Straits, which by the wise agreement of Palmerston, Metternich and the Tsar's advisers, was for the first time made part of the public law of Europe. No deviation from its principles has ever been successful.

Palmerston succeeded partly because London became the diplomatic centre where these problems were discussed. That advantage was obtained by a policy of self-abnegation which he must have found it hard to apply. He abandoned without protest both his desire to have the problem settled under his personal supervision and his scheme to guarantee the integrity of the Ottoman Empire. He thus won Austria and later Russia to his side. He allowed France to make the running at the start. It seemed at the outset, indeed, that France and Austria would play a far larger part than Britain in the settlement. Both took the initiative and in the early stages of the discussion were far more prominent in devising schemes to meet the danger. Metternich succeeded at last, so he thought, in making Vienna the diplomatic capital of Europe. Louis Philippe had confronted Russia, so he thought, with a combination not only of France and Britain but of Austria and Prussia as well. Palmerston, far from shewing jealousy of either of these two Powers, cooperated wholeheartedly with both of them. In April his Government had fallen and in May, when it was first realised that this time Mahmud meant business, it had scarcely recovered sufficiently for Palmerston to take the lead. He himself seems to have realised rather slowly the gravity of the danger. But though it came somewhat late neither France nor Austria could complain of the support which he gave them when he had obtained Cabinet approval. Vienna was accepted as the place of negotiation and France's desire to check isolated Russian action supported to the full. This close cooperation finally resulted in the five Great Powers undertaking the responsibility of settling the problem in such a manner that the integrity and independence of the Ottoman Empire should be maintained.

Then two things transformed the situation. The complete defeat and death of the Sultan and the skilful propaganda of Mehemet Ali led many Frenchmen to imagine that a great Arab state could be brought into existence under French auspices. The Tsar with some justice suspected that Metternich was as much opposed to Russia as the maritime Powers and preferred to deal directly with Britain. He accepted the view that it was in the best interests of Russia, as well as of Europe, that the Sultan's Empire in Asia Minor should be preserved and that the Straits should be put under European protection. Palmerston had already proclaimed these principles and remained faithful to them so that he was able to come to terms with Russia. France abandoned the first while seeking to enforce the second and thus lost all control over the negotiations. Metternich, made ill by the Tsar's contemptuous dismissal of his services which the Western Powers had accepted, never recovered his powers of decision and vacillated interminably. Palmerston assumed the leadership thus offered him and mastered the appalling difficulties of the situation, not only preserving the Ottoman Empire but winning the respect and cooperation of Russia. This he obtained also as regards Persia and Afghanistan as well as in the decisions concerning the Straits and Asia Minor. He lost, it is true, the *entente* with France, but, as has been seen, that was already worn out. The situation in Western and Central Europe had been stabilised and the greatest threat to British influence there was not that of the Eastern Powers but of France herself.

The story has been told many times, but there are still some parts of it which are difficult to unravel. In Russia the final decisions were taken by the Tsar and the arguments which decided him are not exactly known. Louis Philippe, who decided those of France, was the most prolific talker of all the actors in the drama, but the advice of the permanent civil servants, the gold of Mehemet Ali, the ambitions of French politicians and the pride of the French people had all to be taken into account by him and the rest of the world. Palmerston's hardest fights were in his own Cabinet and with sections of public opinion in Britain, partly inspired by attachment to France and hatred of Russia, partly by personal dislike and jealousy of Palmerston himself.

As courageous men always do he found some devoted and able supporters. Minto and Hobhouse were strong allies in the Cab-

1. COOPERATION WITH FRANCE AND AUSTRIA
1839

The Sultan's attempt to obtain British support for an attack on Mehemet had been due to his determination to make one in any event in the spring of 1839. However disappointed he might be at the result of the negotiations at London, the attack was still to take place. No doubt Mahmud felt his health failing and that he could not back his own life against the tough old vassal who had so long defied him. He could not continue, as he frequently explained to Ponsonby, to remain indefinitely in a state of armed suspense. Such a situation was worse than the defeat which his friends warned him was likely to come. He continued, therefore, to accumulate men and provisions and prepare his Seraskier, Hafiz Pasha, for an attack on Ibrahim's forces. His hopes of success were increased by the news of unrest in Syria, which might even be optimistically called an insurrection against Ibrahim. But there can also be no doubt that he relied in the last resort on the intervention of the Great Powers, and especially of Britain. He thought that she was bound to come to his aid in a new clash of arms however much Palmerston refused to pledge himself. His diagnosis was a correct one. Though he did not live to see the success of his plan, his final fling was one of the most astute of his long and chequered career.

From the beginning of the year there were indications of the Sultan's intentions in the movements of troops, and indeed he made no secret of them. But all this had been said and done before and for a considerable time they were not taken very seriously by anyone. In the spring both the British and French Governments were in a state of dissolution. In Britain the Whig Cabinet resigned in May on the weak support given by the House to its West Indian policy, but the tactless conduct of Peel and Wellington over the Queen's Ladies had brought it back to office for another two years. It was, however, much shaken and was preoccupied with domestic questions. The Prime Minister was more than ever absorbed in the special problems of his royal mistress and had little time for foreign affairs.

In France there was a long period of intricate negotiation before

Louis Philippe obtained a Cabinet which would satisfy the Chamber while remaining sufficiently obedient to himself. Neither the Doctrinaires nor Thiers were members of it and Soult was both Premier and Foreign Minister. He was a strong Anglophil, for he had been immensely touched by the attention paid to him in London by his old enemies during the coronation festivities. The relief to Palmerston and Granville after dealing with Molé was immense. But Soult was a vain and emotional man who never fully understood the intricate foreign questions with which he had to deal. Policy was as before decided by the King, but the despatches of the officials received even less control from Soult than from either his predecessors or successors. It was only natural that France failed to find a consistent line of action under his leadership. Neither Roussin at Constantinople nor Sébastiani at London were able to interpret to the satisfaction of the Quai d'Orsay the shifts and subtleties of French policy and both had to go. Barante at St. Petersburg shewed excessive zeal. But Soult himself was all for action and under his inspiration France pressed eagerly forward to take control of a problem in which she thought she had a very special position.

Metternich also saw in the crisis an opportunity. He perceived the seriousness of the situation sooner than anyone else and thought that out of the clash of interests he could at last realise his dream of making Vienna once more the diplomatic centre of Europe. Remembering Palmerston's attempt to draw the Eastern Question to London in 1838, he was determined this time to anticipate him and with unusual energy set all his machinery in motion to get the Great Powers to settle it at Vienna, not by a formal conference, for that was not the medium in which he best excelled, but in informal discussions. He expected to be the intermediary between the maritime Powers and Russia and instead of playing the inactive and humiliating role of 1833 to emerge as the dominating figure of European diplomacy. He seems to have been in no doubt that, if France and Britain accepted this position, the Tsar would welcome such assistance from the man who had been most closely associated with him since 1830.

For the Tsar himself the crisis came at a most inconvenient time. He had not yet settled his dispute with Britain over Persia though the tension had eased. But his main attention was concentrated on family affairs. For him the marriage of his daughter

Marie to the Leuchtenberg Prince was an event of great importance, all the more so in that it was ill-received by his German
relations. He was also engaged in considering the marriage of the
Crown Prince whose attachment to a Polish lady was causing him
grave anxiety. For reasons of which the Tsar was unaware the
Prince's choice of a wife had widened the breach with Prussia.[1]
Finally he was preparing to celebrate the unveiling of a memorial
on the field of Borodino with a reproduction of the battle on a
magnificent scale, a task all the more congenial because it was not
likely to please the French. London, Paris and Vienna were all
without a Russian Ambassador and the Chargés d'Affaires were
men of no great ability or influence. All the Tsar and his Ministers
wished was for the Sultan and Mehemet to keep quiet and nothing
could be less true than the suspicions which Ponsonby sent home
by every courier, and which Palmerston for a time shared, that the
crisis had been produced by the secret encouragement of the
Russians in order that they might reestablish their position at
Constantinople before the Treaty of Unkiar Skelessi came to an
end in 1841.

Though Ponsonby's reports grew increasingly alarmist Palmerston took little notice of them. As has been noted he repeated
officially his usual warning to the Sultan not to attack and he was
of course reiterating the same advice to Reschid Pasha in London
while he pressed on him a purely defensive treaty between Britain
and Turkey. He was occupied with the final stages of the Belgian
Question, the dispute with Persia, the question of Afghanistan and
the growing difficulties in Canton. He responded less promptly
than usual to the warnings from Constantinople and made no
diplomatic preparation to implement the policy which he had laid
down in 1838. It may be, though there is no indication of it, that
he thought that his position would be stronger if he allowed others
to take the initiative instead of taking the lead himself as he had
done the previous year. At the same time he was determined, as
we have repeatedly seen, that the situation of 1833 was not to recur.
If Russia attempted to use the Treaty of Unkiar Skelessi to send
her fleets and soldiers once more to Constantinople to protect the
Sultan, the British fleet would go there also. He could be certain

[1] From William Russell, 2 Oct., 1839: *B.P.* The Princess of Hesse Darmstadt was believed by the Prussian Court to be the daughter of a Frenchman, the
tutor of the elder children of her mother, a fact "which has almost brought about
a rupture between the Courts".

that Louis Philippe, after nearly nine years of contemptuous treatment from the Tsar, would be ready for the French fleet to accompany it.

But in addition Palmerston, as Mahmud foresaw, was determined that a solution must also be found for the conflict between
the Sultan and the Pasha and that that could only be the return
of Syria to the Sultan's control. He had made up his mind that
Mehemet possessed so large a portion of the Ottoman Empire
that its very existence was threatened. The relation of Sultan and
vassal was no protection while the Sultan had no control over the
Egyptian army and fleet. The desert must be placed as a frontier
between the Sultan's dominions and Egypt. The latter was in
effect lost to the Sultan as much as the rest of North Africa, and
Mehemet could be allowed to establish his family there. But
Asia Minor was different. There was no barrier to the expansion
of Mehemet's power there and the valley of the Euphrates might
well pass under his control with what Palmerston thought was the
best short route to the East. But even more important than this
was the weakening of the Sultan's power and prestige to such an
extent that he could not perform his function of guarding the
Straits and preserving Balkan Europe from Russian aggression.
To prevent this catastrophe was Palmerston's object from the very
beginning of the crisis and he never departed from it, though
forced to compromise on some points by the opposition of some
of his colleagues. He was almost alone in Europe in thinking it
possible to expel Mehemet from Syria, though Metternich agreed
also from the outset that it was by far the best solution if it could
be obtained.

Early in May news reached Constantinople which made war
appear certain. The Sultan's troops had crossed the Euphrates.
"The Sultan", wrote Ponsonby, "would rather die or be the vassal
of Russia than not endeavour to destroy the rebel subject." His
entourage hoped much from the Syrian revolt but, they added, "if
we should be beaten we are still sure of succour from Russia."
Ponsonby—and it was no bad judgment—thought that Russia
would merely attempt to mediate and settle with Mehemet by
giving him hereditary succession of Syria and such new conquests
that he made. Such a settlement, he said, would destroy the
Ottoman Empire. The only way to prevent it was "that England
should immediately resume the right of *equal interference* with

Russia in the settlement of the question." He made no secret of his opinion that Mehemet should be thrown out of Syria. Palmerston himself from the first thought that the opportunity had come to expel Mehemet from Syria while allowing him to have the hereditary government of Egypt. His colleagues, he told Granville, agreed with him, though the Cabinet had not considered the question formally.

"For my own part," he added, "I hate Mehemet Ali whom I consider as nothing by an ignorant barbarian who by cunning and boldness and mother wit has been successful in rebellion and has turned to his own advantage, by breach of trust, power which was confided to him for other purposes. I look upon his boasted civilization of Egypt as the arrantest humbug; and I believe that he is as great a tyrant and oppressor as ever made a people wretched; but there he is and one can not get rid of him altogether without war and all its concomitant evils." He hoped that Austria and Britain would be able together to bring Russia and France to adopt a common policy.[1]

Soult at any rate wanted action to restrain Russia and it was Paris that acted first. Soult on the 28 May sent his aide-de-camp, Captain Callier, to Mehemet to urge him to keep his armies back and to proceed to Ibrahim's headquarters with orders to that effect. Similar pressure was to be put upon the Sultan at Constantinople. Meanwhile Bourqueney's reports and Granville's private letters shewed that so far as the attitude to Russia was concerned the outlook of France and Britain was very similar. Both wished to use Austria to put pressure on the Tsar to accept joint action at Constantinople by all the Great Powers. Palmerston, it is true, shewed some distrust of Metternich's ability and influence which he thought had deteriorated and even suggested a conference in St. Petersburg, while Louis Philippe was more convinced of the value of Austria's assistance and was obviously more ready than Palmerston to see Metternich take control of the situation. There was also complete agreement on joint naval action by France and Britain to enforce their policy. A vote of credit of ten million francs for the increase of the French fleet was hastily passed through an enthusiastic Chamber. In these circum-

[1] From Ponsonby, 20 May, 1839: *F.O. Turkey*, 356. All this is left out in *L.P.* I, No. 44, and the whole character of the despatch is thus changed. To Granville, 10 June, 1839: *Granville P.*

stances the French Government took little notice of Palmerston's emphatic statement to Bourqueney that, whatever the rights and wrongs of the dispute, the Great Powers could not be neutral towards Mehemet Ali. They must settle the question this time by getting him out of Syria altogether. Granville's first opinion on the other hand was that Mehemet must get an increase of power. Soult "who was out of his element as a foreign minister" let the question go by, so eager was he to secure Great Power cooperation against Russia.[1]

At Vienna Lord Beauvale saw at once all the implications of the news from Constantinople. He suggested to Palmerston that a conference would be necessary and that Austria should be called upon to shew her flag in the Orient. This plan he did not communicate to Metternich who had told him that this affair would blow over as others before it. In reality, however, Metternich had already determined to act and by the medium of France. He told St. Aulaire, the French Ambassador, that he had already suggested to the Porte to appeal to the five Powers. That would necessitate a conference, or rather a centre of decision, which Metternich implied could only be Vienna. His Ambassador, Count Apponyi, was ordered on 18 May to make the same suggestion at Paris. For some little time Soult rather demurred and told Granville that he would prefer London or Constantinople. But Metternich knew that he could rely on Louis Philippe's passionate desire to break down the isolation from the Eastern Courts which Nicholas had imposed for so long. Thus France accepted Metternich's offer and it was through the medium of France that Palmerston's consent was first asked unofficially. He found it hard to make up his mind. He sent his apologies for the unavoidable delay adding: "If we could get Russia to join in a conference perhaps there would be no harm in having that conference at Vienna as Soult suggests. There would be some advantage in the nearness of Vienna to Constantinople; on the other hand Russian intrigue would be more powerful at Vienna than elsewhere to the Westward." He was unable to get a Cabinet to consider the question during the first part of June and it was a step to which he could

---

[1] Bourqueney to Soult, 25 May, 1839: Guizot, *Mémoires*, IV, 479; do. 27 May, 1839: *A.A.E.* From Granville, 27 May, 1839: *B.P.* Soult to Cochelet, 28 May, 1839: E. Driault, *L'Egypte et l'Europe*, I, 34. The Prussian Chargé d'Affaires reported from Paris that the vote of credit was inspired by hostility to Britain rather than Russia. A. Hasenclever, *Die Orientalische Frage*, 39.

hardly agree on his own responsibility. The Cabinet also were doubtful: "We do not know what to say about a conference at Vienna. Metternich is so feeble and timid and tricky and so much swayed by Russia, and by nature so prone to crooked paths, to playing off one party against the other; and so fond of staving off difficulties and putting off the evil day, that I greatly doubt whether a Vienna conference would lead to anything good. On the other hand Russia might perhaps consent to a conference there and not elsewhere, knowing Metternich and reckoning upon the influence which she exerts over him and which is not less real because he and Russia hate and distrust each other."[1]

Metternich had, however, also sent Esterhazy back to London and the Ambassador shewed as usual great understanding and tact. Palmerston told to him as well as to Bourqueney all the doubts and hesitations of the Cabinet and their reluctance to increase Metternich's control of the situation by accepting Vienna as the centre of discussion. He was doubtful, he confessed to Beauvale, whether Metternich would carry through such a plan as he himself thought necessary. The Chancellor was too timid to adopt wholeheartedly the Sultan against Mehemet. But if he could be worked up to 'concert pitch', "he would do more to consolidate the peace of Europe than any man has done since the 18th June 1815." Britain would of course give him enthusiastic support. How could Russia object? And, if so, France would be bound to overcome the resistance of the little cabal at Paris that supported Mehemet.

But Palmerston put great faith not only in Beauvale's ability and energy but in the Ambassador's influence over Metternich. If Austrian support was to be obtained, the Ambassador, who had so long been certain of securing it when the emergency came and whose words now seemed to be justified by Metternich's action, was a suitable instrument of British policy. Thus Esterhazy was at last able to report triumphantly to his chief that he had conquered Palmerston's secret desire to make London the centre of the negotiations on the Eastern Question and obtain over them the same influence that he had exercised over those on Belgium. The result had been obtained, he thought, largely because French

---

[1] From Beauvale, 21 May, 1839: *B.P.* St. Aulaire, *Souvenirs*, 246. From Granville, 31 May, 1839: *B.P.* To Granville, 10, 19, 21 June, 1839. To Beauvale, 20 June, 1839: *Granville P.*

support had first been secured. The gratified Chancellor noted on the despatch that it was for that very reason he had chosen this method of approach.[1]

Metternich was delighted with the new position in which France and Britain had placed him, and his Ambassador's despatches were covered with enthusiastic comments. There was not to be a 'conference' at Vienna, he explained to everybody concerned, but only a centre of discussion in which joint decisions could be arrived at. He gave as a reason for this insistence the right of Turkey to claim representation at any formal conference by appealing to the Protocol of Aix-la-Chapelle. The Belgian discussions had shewn how little this formal right was respected by the Great Powers. But Metternich had always preferred less formal methods and he seems also to have thought that the Tsar would be more ready for Russia to take part in discussions of that kind. Palmerston was ready to agree for the same reason though he noted that by this method Russia would be less bound than if she became a member of a formal conference. One motive of the British Government, he wrote in a despatch, was their confidence in their Ambassador at Vienna. However, as Soult pointed out, the use of the word conference made little real difference; the great thing was to get Russia to cooperate with the rest of Europe.[2]

At any rate, once the decision was taken it was necessary to make it effective. Palmerston at once suggested that the Ambassadors at Vienna should concert with Metternich joint instructions to the Ambassadors at Constantinople and the Admirals of the fleets. This was my plan, wrote the delighted Chancellor on the despatch, and he informed Esterhazy immediately that he accepted the responsibility of obtaining agreement at the 'point central' of Vienna on the instructions to be sent to Constantinople. Beauvale had been more doubtful. He praised Metternich's energy and pointed out to his critical chief how much had already been done to get things going. But he was very conscious of the difficulties of concentrating all decision in Vienna: "Metternich is really anxious that the term conference should not be applied to the discussions upon Eastern Affairs here. At the same time he

[1] Esterhazy to Metternich, 29 June, 3 July, 1839: *V. St. A.* Bourqueney to Soult, 20, 26, 27 June, 1839: Guizot, *Mémoires*, IV, 493; *A.A.E.* To Beauvale (as previous note).
[2] To Beauvale, 28 June, 1839: *F.O. Austria*, 278. From Granville, 22 June, 1839: *L.P.* I, No. 67.

wants something strong enough to give orders both at Constantinople and Alexandria and be obeyed, and above all if there are
affairs of importance to be treated of, he wants everything to
proceed from this centre, and the separate French action threatening at Constantinople, stopping the Turkish fleet, protecting and
counselling Mehemet Ali at Alexandria, to cease. How this is to
be unless you could come here I don't know and I told him so, to
which he said that a reunion of the Cabinets would be the best
thing. Think about it." This was generous of the Ambassador
who much appreciated the importance of his own position in the
affair. But it shews the inconsistency of Metternich and that he
had not yet grasped all the implications of the position which he
had so eagerly seized.[1]

Strangest of all was his delay in approaching Russia. Tatischev,
the Russian Ambassador, was at St. Petersburg and his Chargé
d'Affaires, Struve, was unable to give Metternich any advice on
the subject. Metternich's explanation was that he must first
secure the agreement of France and Britain. Once that was done
he prepared a monumental expedition for St. Petersburg full of
flattery for the Tsar but practically announcing a *fait accompli*
which he assumed would be accepted. He recommended that the
British and French fleets should join the Russian fleet in the Sea
of Marmora if Constantinople were threatened. How ill prepared
the Tsar was for this communication will be seen.

But in the intervening month of July there was a real 'Concert'
at Vienna which obtained results of the greatest importance. For
it was here that the steps were taken to deal with the terribly
critical position which arose at Constantinople. Metternich was
right in claiming that geography made Vienna the natural seat of
operations. Had action had to wait for Paris and London to
receive the bad news, it would have been too late. For Ibrahim
had routed Hafiz Pasha at Nezib on 24 June. Captain Callier had
reached him too late to prevent the clash but it was perhaps his
influence that caused Ibrahim to refrain from following up the
action immediately.[2] The Sultan himself had died of his many

[1] Esterhazy to Metternich, 9 July, 1839; Metternich to Esterhazy, 19 July,
1839: *V. St. A.* From Beauvale, 5 July, 1839: *B.P.*
[2] Thiers stated later that Callier promised Mehemet the hereditary possession
of Syria. N. Senior, *Conversations*, I, 4. A. Stern, *Geschichte Europas*, V, 390,
stated that no such report is in the French Archives. Callier's report in E.
Driault, *L'Egypte et l'Europe*, I, 142, shews that he at any rate encouraged him
to hope.

disorders on 1 July even before the news of the battle reached him. The new Sultan was not yet seventeen years of age. Old Husrev reestablished the office of Grand Vizir in his own person and attempted to deal with the situation. But his first thought was to make a deal at almost any price with the enemy at the gates. This disposition became something like panic when the Ottoman Fleet left Constantinople and deserted to the enemy. Instead of appealing to the Great Powers Husrev prepared to send emissaries to Mehemet with the offer of almost everything which he demanded. The British and French Ambassadors were kept in the dark as to this step as long as possible. When they found out what was going on they reported on it in the most pessimistic terms. Ponsonby had already attributed the weakness of the Ministers to Russian intrigue. Russia would prefer, he thought, that Mehemet Ali should be satisfied rather than send her fleet to Constantinople to oppose him. Now that Mahmud was dead there was no one to whom to appeal, and, though Husrev had promised to do nothing without the assent of the Great Powers, he could not be trusted. The only remedy was his usual one of the British fleet at Constantinople whether the Turkish Ministers asked for it or not. On the 26 July Ponsonby sent a despairing despatch. Appeasement had been decided and he believed not only Russia but Austria would countenance it. In this he was not far wrong. Russia was trying to get Mehemet to make peace on the basis of adding Orfa and Diarbekir to his Syrian territories and Metternich later told Beauvale that Stürmer had confessed that he had advocated concessions. "I consider", wrote Ponsonby, "the Ottoman Empire to be delivered over to Mehemet Ali and that Russia has been the chief director of what has been done."[1]

But at the last moment the situation was saved. For Metternich had already acted. The 'point central' had from the first shewn zeal and efficiency. St. Aulaire had cooperated eagerly and Beau-

[1] From Ponsonby, 8, 21, 22, 26 July, 1839: *L.P.* Nos. 149, 216, 225 and *F.O. Turkey*, 357. These despatches, written with more than usual emotion, were much mutilated before publication, e.g. "The Liberals of Europe will see what may be called the fortress of the world placed in the hands of the chief support and representative of despotism". From Beauvale, 11 July, 1839: *L.P.* I, No. 137. "It is clear that Vienna in its relation to that place [Constantinople] is nearly a month ahead of London and Petersburgh." From Beauvale, 1 Aug., 1839: *F.O. Austria*, 282 [as to Stürmer]. Goriainow, *Le Bosphore, etc.*, 58–59. Nesselrode reported to the Tsar that the Porte had intended to offer the hereditary possession of all his territories to Mehemet Ali—and was angry that this had been stopped.

vale had of course been zealous to get Palmerston's ideas adopted. He was less confident than his chief of the possibility of throwing Mehemet out of Syria and that negotiation had made little progress. But, in concerting fleet action for entry into the Dardanelles, France and Britain had Austrian support and Austrian ships with an Archduke were to be associated in the joint squadrons. That this demonstration seemed more aimed at Russia than at Mehemet Metternich was shortly to find out, but for the moment the union of the three Powers seemed most cordial and the Russian Chargé d'Affaires was not the man to challenge Metternich. When therefore the bad news came pouring in from Constantinople there was a centre ready to deal with it, as both Metternich and Palmerston had hoped. Afraid that the Sultan's Ministers would come to a separate arrangement with Mehemet, Metternich was determined to act at once. He sent an instruction to Stürmer to warn them that they should entrust the future fate of Turkey to the Great Powers who were agreed to maintain its integrity. The Russian Chargé d'Affaires, Struve, also carried out Metternich's request to write to Butenev. The French and British Ambassadors immediately did likewise, Beauvale, though he felt that he was to some extent exceeding his powers, St. Aulaire, influenced by the desire of retaining Austrian and British support against Russia, who might otherwise act alone. But as Beauvale later insisted, the measure was entirely Metternich's own. The others only followed his lead.[1]

These communications produced an immediate effect at Constantinople. Baron Stürmer, however suspect his previous conduct, took instant action and the Prussian representative, as always, of course followed his lead. The French and British Ambassadors felt authorised by their communications from Vienna to associate themselves with him, and in such circumstances the Russian Minister thought it wise to give his support also. Thus resulted the famous collective Note of 27 July, actually presented by the Dragomans of the Five Powers to the Sultan's Ministers on the

[1] From Beauvale, 24 July, 3, 10 Aug., 1839: *B.P.* St. Aulaire, *Souvenirs*, 253–254. There is no clear account in Beauvale's despatches and consequently none in the *Levant Papers*. Metternich himself, because of the shock from Russia which followed, advertised his action but little. This is one reason why historians have never given him due credit for his energy and foresight at so critical a moment. Ponsonby gave the main praise to Beauvale who disclaimed it. St. Aulaire admits that he yielded to the pressure of Metternich and Beauvale.

2 S

28th. This stated that instructions had been received by the five representatives so that they could inform the Porte that "agreement among the Five Great Powers on the Question of the East is secured" and "invite it to suspend any definitive resolution without their concurrence, waiting for the effect of the interest which those powers feel for it." Ponsonby, recovering from his despair, had himself taken the first action by sending Chrysanowski at 5 a.m. to warn the Grand Vizir of the news from Vienna. He reported that the note had been delivered just in time to prevent Husrev's resignation and enable him to resist both Mehemet and Russia. He gave warm praise to his old antagonist Stürmer. Butenev's signature, he said, did not surprise him: "I have long been convinced that Russia would yield whenever really opposed."[1]

The responsibility of settling the dispute between the Porte and Mehemet was thus thrown squarely on the Five European Powers. No solution had been agreed but the Porte had at least a moral claim for better terms than it could have got for itself. The Great Powers were bound to one another as well as to the Porte. The dispute had been recognised by all as one for the 'Concert of Europe'. France through her Ambassadors was bound by this declaration to this point of view, and Russia also. The obligations of this step affected all the future course of the negotiations. None of the Five Powers ventured to denounce the action of their Ambassadors.

But in actual fact before the news of this important step reached the capitals of the Powers open differences of opinion on fundamental points had occurred. France and Britain had realised that their policies towards Mehemet were in contradiction and Russia had repudiated the use of Vienna as a centre. It is now necessary to retrace the manner in which these two cleavages occurred. They were revealed at almost the same time and produced a diplomatic revolution almost as far-reaching in its effects as the famous one of the eighteenth century. The cleavage between France and Britain was to prove the deepest and most intractable, for in the long run the Tsar accepted Metternich's policy, though

[1] From Ponsonby, 29 July, 1839: *F.O. Turkey*, 357. The version in *L.P.* I, No. 226, leaves out all mention of Ponsonby's own action and of course of his remarks on Russia. St. Aulaire places the main responsibility for the promptness at Constantinople on Roussin, but he could hardly know. Metternich attributed Butenev's cooperation to long standing orders to follow the Austrian lead and Struve's letter from Vienna. (From Beauvale, 10 Aug., 1839: *B.P.*) cf. Hasenclever, *Die orientalische Frage*, 55–56, where Stürmer's report is quoted.

not his conduct of it. But the issue between France and Britain could not be resolved until France was forced to withdraw in humiliation and defeat.

During June and July Palmerston had been full of praise for Soult. The reason for the delay in appreciating the situation is a very simple one. During June and July Palmerston had been as eager as France to prevent Russian isolated action. He had followed the French lead in organising measures to prevent such a step. France had gone ahead both in securing Austrian support and in organising a joint naval squadron in the Eastern Mediterranean which should enter the Dardanelles if Russian ships passed the Bosphorus. Palmerston regarded these fleets as directed against Mehemet also. He had from the first put forward his view that Mehemet should be driven out of Syria, whatever the immediate issue of the struggle between him and the Sultan. Soult had not accepted this view and neither had any of the other Powers though Metternich had gone very far in that direction. But both Soult and Louis Philippe had shewn themselves sympathetic to a reduction of Mehemet's power.

When Russia put forward the view that the contest between the Sultan and Pasha should be left alone provided Ibrahim's armies did not advance across the Taurus, and even suggested that Orfa and Diarbekir should be added to the area under his control, both Soult and Louis Philippe—all the more emphatically since Russia had completely ignored France—shewed sympathy with Palmerston's indignant criticisms. Soult, it is true, said that he could not agree that the whole of Syria should be taken from Mehemet, but at any rate he disapproved the policy of inaction which Russia recommended. Louis Philippe went much further. "He agreed", wrote Granville, "not only on the desirableness of restoring the whole of Syria to the Sultan but with all the arguments you adduce in support of your opinion; he thought that the desert between Egypt and Syria was a better boundary between the possessions of the Sultan and of Mehemet Ali than any that could be found in Syria itself." Louis Philippe had, however, also a reservation as to the possibility of obtaining this desirable end. "He was not prepared to say at present", continued Granville, "that we must go to war with Mehemet Ali rather than not obtain it—much must depend upon the opinion of the other Great Powers; if they were all disposed to make that proposition to the Pasha, France would

join in it." This was not an absolute promise of the use of force
but it naturally left in Palmerston's mind the conviction that,
if he could get Austria to agree, France would not lag behind.

On the news of the death of the Sultan the French Government
again took the initiative and sent a circular despatch to the other
four Powers suggesting that they should all guarantee the independence and integrity of the Ottoman Empire. Palmerston was
quite ready to see his old device brought into the foreground
again and hastened to send a favourable reply. It was in response
to this overture that he used the often-quoted words "Soult is a
jewel". Metternich also gave a favourable reply, and Prussia
therefore did the same. The effect on the Tsar of this proposal
was very different and was one of the causes of his change of front
in the next month. But for the moment it seemed to make France
the champion of the Ottoman Empire and Palmerston, who of
course printed it in the *Levant Papers*, was often to refer to it in
later months.[1]

By "independence and integrity" the French officials, if not
Soult himself, meant something very different to Palmerston's
interpretation, but, though there was considerable difficulty
in establishing exact uniformity in the instructions to the Ambassadors and Admirals, the relations between the two Governments
remained on an excellent footing until the end of July when the
difference between them was first realised. For the defeat of the
Sultan's attack, which he ascribed to Russian scheming, seemed
to Palmerston to make the reestablishment of the Ottoman Empire
all the more urgent. It could not be divided. They must choose
between the Sultan and Mehemet as ruler—and the choice could
not be doubtful. At the same time, Soult expressed to Granville
an opinion "that neither the disastrous overthrow of the Turkish
Army, nor the traitorous conduct of the Capudan Pasha, nor the
prostrate attitude of the Divan, should affect the course which the
Great Powers of Europe intended to pursue." Granville also re-

---

[1] Nesselrode to Pozzo di Borgo, 3/15 June, 1839: *L.P.*, I, No. 74. To Granville, 29 June, 1839. *F.O. France*, 575; *L.P.*, I, No. 82. From Granville, 2 July,
1839: *F.O. France*, 584; *L.P.*, No. 101; do., 2 July, 1839. *B.P.* Palmerston's
suspicions of Russia and his proposals for a combination of the other Great
Powers against her are of course not given in the *Levant Papers*. They tended
to predispose Louis Philippe in his favour. The vagueness of Soult and Granville as to where the desert was much amused Louis Philippe, who was far better
informed, and Granville had to ask Palmerston to correct the despatch after it had
arrived in London. Soult to Bourqueney, 17 July, 1839 (circular) *L.P.*, I, No.
128. *Bulwer*, II, 295.

ported that Louis Philippe was ready to follow Austria and Britain as regards the conditions of peace between the Sultan and the Pasha, though he warned him that the French Press took a different view and if action were delayed he might not be able to count on French support. Palmerston was delighted and in an official despatch recorded his Government's rejoicing "at the complete identity of opinion on these most important matters between France and England."[1]

In reality the breach had already occurred, for Soult had already signed, but not read, a despatch written by Desages which took a very different line. Cooperation was, indeed, to be maintained but, it was suggested, Mehemet's victory made it necessary to offer better terms than before if he was to be restrained from further attack. This despatch was clearly in complete contradiction with what Soult had said. Bourqueney reported Palmerston's surprise and indignation. Soult found it difficult to explain his conduct when an outspoken despatch arrived at Paris, though Granville acquitted him of any intentional double dealing. He had intended, Soult said, to ascertain Palmerston's view as to what ought to be done. He himself was still inclined to exclude the Pasha from Syria but account must be taken of the views of Austria and Prussia. Thus, while Palmerston demanded that the French and British fleets should be sent to Alexandria to bring back the Turkish fleet by force if necessary, Soult would agree to nothing of the kind. It would be dangerous, he said, to remove the fleets from the Dardanelles. When Granville saw Louis Philippe he found him in full agreement with his Ministers. He would not be easily induced, thought Granville, to run counter to French public opinion which Mehemet's recent successes had caused to run strongly in his favour. Only if Austria would also agree and thus break up the Triple Alliance against France would Louis Philippe consider taking such a step.[2]

This deadlock continued and the difference of opinion grew deeper and deeper. It was in no way composed by the arrival of the news of the joint note of 27 July. Palmerston was of course

[1] To Granville, 23 July, 1839: *Granville P.*; do., 30 July, 1839: *L.P.*, I, No. 157. From Granville, 26 July, 1839: *L.P.*, I, No. 156; do., *B.P.*
[2] Soult to Bourqueney, 26 July, 1839: *L.P.*, I, No. 158. Guizot, *Mémoires*, IV, 519. Bourqueney to Soult, 31 July, 1839: Guizot, *Mémoires*, IV, 523. To Granville, 30 July, 1839: *L.P.*, I, No. 159; do., *B.P.* From Granville, 2, 8 Aug., 1839: *L.P.*, I, Nos., 181, 209; do., 2, 8 Aug., 1839: *B.P.*

delighted with it and claimed that it bound the other Powers to adopt his views. The situation, he told the House of Commons, had been entirely transformed by it and the previous instructions were now out of date. In spite of the reports about the defection of Russia, he still looked to Vienna as the centre of action whence new instructions would be issued.

The French Government on the other hand received the news of the note with some dismay. Soult suggested that Russia would repudiate the action of her Ambassador and obviously hoped she would. He got very excited at the suggestion that instructions should be issued from Vienna to the Admirals to act against Mehemet. And, in spite of Sébastiani's contrary advice, Louis Philippe strongly supported the view of his Cabinet, that the question of the Straits must first be settled, since any action against Alexandria might cause Ibrahim to march on Constantinople. The French Government did not venture to repudiate Roussin's action. But it had already suggested to Palmerston that the two Governments should send new Ambassadors to Constantinople. Palmerston had naturally refused to remove Ponsonby and merely ordered him to cooperate more closely with Roussin. Now the French Government decided to recall their own Ambassador and substitute for him someone less sympathetic to the Sultan and more favourable to Mehemet. Meanwhile they refused with growing impatience all Palmerston's suggestions to send, through the Vienna centre, instructions for action against the Pasha. The French Press began to attack British policy, revealing in the process that they had been given information of the confidential discussions between the two Governments. Soult said he was as pained as Palmerston at these criticisms and the simulacrum of friendship was maintained by the special mention of France in the Queen's Speech, the first time for two years that this had been done.[1]

In these circumstances Palmerston began to look more and more to Vienna for help. There for a short time there had been much

[1] To Granville, 16 Aug., 1839; To Bulwer, 20 Aug., 1839: *L.P.*, I, Nos., 223, 236. To Granville, 9, 16 Aug., 1839: *Granville P.* From Granville, 12, 16 Aug., 1839: *B.P.* The suggestion about Roussin and Ponsonby was made in July. Roussin was reprimanded at the beginning of September, for transmitting a letter (which he had not read) to the Commander of the Turkish fleet at Alexandria and recalled a few days later. His successor Pontois was appointed as Minister only, to save Roussin's face. From Granville, 5 July, 1839; From Bulwer, 6, 9 Sept., 1839: *B.P.* Bourqueney to Soult, 13, 15, 20, 27 Aug., 1839: *A.A.E.* To Beauvale, 25 Aug., 1839: *V. St. A. Varia.*

diplomatic activity.   Both St. Aulaire and Beauvale were pressing for
further measures.   St. Aulaire was urging Metternich to join with
France in insisting on the entry of the fleets into the Dardanelles
to support the Turkish Government.   Beauvale did not agree to
this step and Metternich also refused it.   The British Ambassador,
on the other hand, was ready to support Soult's proposal of a
declaration of the Great Powers that they would maintain the
independence and integrity of the Ottoman Empire, and notes
were exchanged on this subject.   Metternich was shewing, it is
true, much hesitation, but his views concerning Mehemet seemed
in harmony with those of Britain.   Accordingly Palmerston
directed to Beauvale his important despatch of 25 August in which
he laid before the Great Powers his opinion that Mehemet must
be driven out of Syria and the unity of the Ottoman Empire thus
be reestablished.   In this he suggested, for the first time officially,
that the refusal of one Power to agree to such a course of action
need not prevent the others from carrying it out.   This was meant,
of course, as a warning to France as much as to Russia.   The
'Concert' at Vienna was to issue the necessary instructions to the
Admirals to go to Alexandria and get back the Turkish fleet, or,
if that was not possible, to break off diplomatic relations by
recalling the Consuls-General.   In the private letter that accompanied the despatch he asserted his belief that Soult and Louis
Philippe still wished to act with the other Great Powers, but were
prevented by the powerful clique of a few hundred Frenchmen
who had vested interests in Mehemet's administration.   He hoped,
however, that France would be drawn in, if action was taken: "I
am still not without hopes that all five may be brought to insist on
the evacuation of Syria and I am sanguine in expectation that, if
that demand is resolutely made, it will be complied with, not,
perhaps, at first, but after some little time, if the five Powers shew
by their acts that they are in earnest.   If that is done, we can get a
treaty of restitution [sic] for the Porte by all five Powers or by
three for the next ten years."[1]
But before this despatch reached Vienna the whole situation
there had been transformed, the 'Concert' had virtually been

[1] From Beauvale, 30 July, 1 Aug., 1839: *F.O. Austria*, 281, 2.   *L.P.*, I, Nos.
202, 207.   From Beauvale, 24, 25 July, 1839;   To Beauvale, 25 Aug., 1839:
L.P., I, Nos. 248, 249 (circular); do., *V. St. A. Varia*.   The letter, which went on
to deny that Turkey was worn out, is quoted by F. S. Rodkey, *Journal of Mod.
Hist.*, June, 1930, 202.

dissolved and Metternich had retired a shattered man to recover his health at Johannisberg.   For he had received from St. Petersburg an even more humiliating blow than in 1833.   At the beginning of the negotiations at Vienna he had confidently expected Russian approval to all that he was doing and had constantly told Beauvale that he would answer for the Tsar.   Such news as he had from St. Petersburg seemed to shew that this was so.   When no official despatch came from his Ambassador, Ficquelmont, he grew somewhat uneasy.   Then immediately after his important instructions had been sent to Constantinople a courier arrived with despatches which he for a little time tried to conceal from Beauvale and St. Aulaire.   The contents, vague and mainly concerning the fêtes and celebrations at St. Petersburg, were disquieting.   The news of the death of the Sultan was considered there to have put an end to the crisis and ensured peace.   More extraordinary still, Ficquelmont was taking advantage of a leave of absence granted long before and coming home.   "I can understand this from Russia," wrote Beauvale, "it is her game; but Ficquelmont, the flower of the Austrian diplomacy, what can it mean from him?" It seemed clear that Russia did not accept Vienna as the main centre of discussion.   But Metternich refused to believe it.   He thought, Beauvale reported, that he could still drag her along: "Il faut l'envelopper avec nous et elle marchera."   Thus the discussions about guaranteeing the Ottoman Empire, the entry of the fleets into the Dardanelles, still went on, but with a good deal less zest than before.   It made it all the more necessary, Beauvale thought, that France and Britain should be closely united.   He might then be able to detach Austria from Russia and get action taken at Vienna, if Palmerston would give him the necessary powers. Metternich, he said, was enchanted with Palmerston's condemnation of Mehemet Ali, though he doubted the possibility of taking such strong measures against him and thought he should have some part of his Syrian territories for life.[1]

A few days later when Ficquelmont arrived it was realised that Russia refused all cooperation at Vienna.   Metternich was completely out of favour with the Tsar.   He had appeared to join France and Britain in a menace to Russia.   Barante's insistence on the right of entry into the Dardanelles and the exuberant

---

[1] From Beauvale, 25 July, 1 Aug., 1839:   *B.P.*; do., 31 July, 2 Aug., 1839: *F.O. Austria*, 282.

claims at Paris that Austria had been entirely won over, prevented the Tsar from sending Tatischev back to Vienna to negotiate there the solution of the Eastern Question. At least that was Metternich's explanation. For some time he tried to bear up under the blow, heartened a little by the news that came from Constantinople of the success of his last effort. He wrote to London and Paris to ask that instructions should be sent to Beauvale and St. Aulaire to work out a common policy at Vienna. He entirely approved Palmerston's attitude towards Mehemet Ali. "He adopts", wrote Beauvale, "all your principles and reasonings but thinks your means of attack upon the Pasha weak."

Discussions still continued for a time between Metternich, St. Aulaire and Beauvale on the different questions. But all the heart had gone out of them. The French and British points of view diverged. The French Ambassador refused to agree to any coercive action against Mehemet. Metternich, deprived of confidence and prestige by the Tsar's attitude, could do nothing to bring them together. How great was the blow to his pride was seen by his sudden collapse on 11 August which rendered him quite incapable of business. He retired to Johannisberg to recover his health. He had designed the Anglophil, Clam, to succeed him, but the Archdukes intervened. They had been much perturbed at the rupture with Russia, and preferred Count Ficquelmont, naturally the most favourable to Russia of all the Austrian diplomats. His first step was to urge that the fleets might be removed from the Dardanelles so that the Tsar might be placated. In these circumstances Beauvale could only assume that the great role he himself had hoped to play in the negotiations was over. He had come to realise as much as Palmerston that Louis Philippe was trying to force Austria into an acceptance of the French view of Mehemet. Both France and Austria were unreliable. Perhaps it was only from Russia herself, the Ambassador even ventured to suggest, that the necessary support for action against Mehemet could be obtained.[1]

[1] From Beauvale, 3, 7, 8, 10, 24, 27 Aug., 8, 9 Sept., 1839: *B.P.*; do., 3, 8 Sept., 1839: *F.O. Austria*, 282; *L.P.*, I, No. 301. St. Aulaire to Barante, 10 Aug., 1839: Barante, *Souvenirs*, VI, 298. St. Aulaire, *Souvenirs*, 256–262. There is little of the story in the British despatches, but Beauvale's private letters give all the details which he could find out. Princess Mélanie narrates the course of the illness which at first seemed very serious, and was thought by some to be a kind of stroke. Metternich, *Mémoires*, VI, 327–330. St. Aulaire's *Souvenirs*, written in retrospect, are perhaps not quite trustworthy as to details. He certainly gets his dates wrong.

2. THE RAPPROCHEMENT WITH RUSSIA
1839
(i) The First Failure

There had been less excitement at St. Petersburg over the crisis than at any other capital of the Great Powers. The desire most expressed was to leave matters alone. Neither the Tsar nor his Ministers had any wish to put the Treaty of Unkiar Skelessi into effect and send ships or troops through the Bosphorus. They hoped that the Sultan would again come to some arrangement with his vassal. The autocrat was preoccupied with his family affairs and was much annoyed at this distraction. It was even said that he would have dismissed Nesselrode for not stopping the Sultan had there been anyone to replace him. In addition, owing to his own extravagance and the rapacity of his Ministers and courtiers, his finances were in an exceptionally bad state and in no condition to bear the expenses of an expedition. Nesselrode's formal despatch, therefore, laid it down that there was no need to do anything unless Ibrahim crossed the Taurus. He might even add Orfa and Diarbekir to Mehemet's dominions if he wished. When in response to this Palmerston at last sent Clanricarde information of the British contrary view, Nesselrode admitted that Mehemet ought to give up Syria—and perhaps the Sultan would get it back when his vassal died. When the news came of the death of the Sultan, neither Minister nor Tsar concealed their pleasure and again their first reaction was to hope that a settlement would now be arranged between the Ministers of the Porte and Mehemet.[1]

It was while this was the mood of the Emperor that Nesselrode received from Barante and Ficquelmont the results of the activities of their Courts. Barante, pleased to revenge innumerable slights on his monarch, pressed hard the fact that France would not tolerate the Russian fleet at Constantinople without her own ships going there also. "Thereupon", reported the British Ambassador,

---

[1] From Clanricarde, 8 June, 1839: *F.O. Russia*, 252. Nesselrode to Pozzo di Borgo, 15 June, 1839: *L.P.*, I, No. 74. From Clanricarde, 15, 18, 27 July, 1839: *L.P.*, I, Nos. 132, 160, 184; *F.O. Russia*, 252; do., 26 June, 3 July, 1839: *B.P.*

"Count Nesselrode changed colour and became violently excited. He said these constant feelings of suspicion and distrust of the Emperor and of his intentions that were evinced by France were unjust and intolerable." The effect of this communication on Nesselrode was indeed so marked, wrote Clanricarde, as to "make him ridiculous to all the Court. . . . And I believe no school-boy ever approached a master with more dread than he will the Emp^r to discuss the subject." Neither the Emperor nor Nesselrode, he added, had asked him whether similar instructions had been sent to the British fleet and so he remained silent on the subject. The Tsar and Orlov seemed well pleased with him.

It was thus from Austria rather than Britain that support for the insistent Barante seemed to come. Metternich's communication of the agreement of France and Britain to coordinate their actions under his auspices at Vienna could not have been worse timed, especially as Austria seemed to have agreed that her flag should fly with those that threatened the Dardanelles. Metternich was probably right when he ascribed the action of the Tsar to the excessive zeal of the French Ambassador. But Nicholas had shewn more than once that he put no trust in Metternich's view of the Eastern Question and had no desire to make him the arbiter between Russia and the West. He was told—and it was true—that Metternich had claimed that he could answer for the Tsar. The paean of joy at Paris seemed to shew that Metternich thought a solution could be obtained on any terms. The Tsar neither intended nor desired to send ships to the Sea of Marmora and the actions of the Porte gave him plenty of excuse to refuse. But he did not wish to appear as intimidated from action by a European combination against him. Nesslerode's dislike of Metternich is clearly revealed in his private letters. Thus instead of sending Tatischev back to Vienna to control Metternich, as seems at first to have been the intention of Nesselrode at any rate, the Tsar sent Ficquelmont to inform the Chancellor that the negotiation at Vienna was refused. When Tatischev returned he was only to negotiate with Metternich not with the other Ambassadors at Vienna. Constantinople was suggested instead as the centre where the Ambassadors should act together, but this was before the news of the note of 27 July reached St. Petersburg, which shewed that action there was by

no means along the lines which the Russian Government had desired.[1]

On the other hand, in contrast to France, Britain had seemed to shew a desire to get on good terms with the Tsar. The latter was much moved by the reports which now reached him of the great success of his son's visit and had already decided to shew his appreciation by a present to Queen Victoria of a vase at the Hermitage, "the finest specimen of Malachite in the world." In these circumstances it is not surprising to find Nesselrode turning to Clanricarde with confidential assurances which he gave to no other Ambassador. Metternich, reported the British Envoy, is entirely wrong if he thinks he can guide the Tsar. On the contrary all the evidence at St. Petersburg shewed that the Russian Government was aggrieved and irritated at his conduct. "If Austria would separate from France and England," Clanricarde went on, "Russia might lean to her side in a difference of policy. But such would be the case, I believe, in a still greater degree if England were to separate herself from France and Austria or from France alone. Russia fears England more than Austria and therefore she respects her more and is more inclined to court her." This excessive simplification of the position was characteristic of the Ambassador, but it seems obvious that Palmerston's determined conduct in 1838, coupled with the friendly reception of the Tsarevitch, had a considerable effect on the Tsar. At the same time, there can be no doubt that the opportunity presented of driving a wedge between France and Britain by accepting Palmerston's view of the contest with Mehemet appealed strongly to both the Tsar and his Ministers after the affront they considered they had received. "The Emperor", wrote Clanricarde, "is extremely pleased at the sentiments of the British Cabinet with regard to Mehemet Ali which are, he says, in unison with his own. And it has been made very evident that the prospect of any separation between the French Govt. and that of the Queen gave him great satisfaction." Nesselrode assured the Ambassador: "You may be sure that we shall not desert you."[2]

[1] From Clanricarde, 3, 9, 10 Aug., 1839: *F.O. Russia*, 252; do., 3 Aug., 1839: *B.P.* Barante's own accounts, given in vol. VI of his *Souvenirs*, still shewed complacency, but he had become aware to some extent of the effect which he had produced. Nesselrode to Meyendorf, 24 July, 1839: Nesselrode, *Lettres et Papiers*, VII, 287. From Beauvale, 2 Sept., 1839: *F.O. Austria*, 282; do., 29 Aug., 1839: *B.P.*

[2] From Clanricarde, 15, 17, 22 Aug., 1839: *F.O. Russia*, 252 253. (Only small extracts are given in *L.P.*); do., 28 Aug., 1839 (with undated despatch from Medem): *L.P.*, I, No. 292; do., 24 Aug., 1839: *B.P.*

For these reasons the Tsar decided to enter into direct negotiations with Palmerston and for that purpose sent to London Baron Brunnow, of no higher rank than his Minister at Darmstadt and Stuttgart, but a man who until recently had been Nesselrode's principal assistant at St. Petersburg and consequently knew all the shades of Russian policy and had, as Nesselrode said, "the unreserved and entire confidence" of his Government. He was to arrange matters concerning Persia as well as the Ottoman Empire. Nesselrode had no doubt, he told Clanricarde, that Brunnow would be able to satisfy Palmerston on both questions.[1]

The British Ambassador insisted on going to Borodino, where the Tsar had now encamped, more in order to see the spectacle than the Tsar. The Tsar had been annoyed at Ponsonby's support of French action at Constantinople in refusing the Russian request that the fleets should be sent away from the Dardanelles, but he paid the most flattering attentions to Clanricarde, and an opportunity was thus given to make him aware of Palmerston's despatch of 25 August which first laid down uncompromisingly the necessity of throwing Mehemet out of Syria. The Tsar was delighted with it and the Ambassador was assured he could reckon on Russian support for his policy. Nicholas added that "he did not care a straw if we took and kept Egypt if we liked. He said it was no business of his, that he should not even interfere to prevent the French having it, altho' he said he never could look on the French in the same light as the English." This insidious suggestion made no appeal to Palmerston; but the Russian view of French policy was being confirmed by every despatch from Paris. "The whole gist of the observations of the Emperor and his Minister on this subject", wrote Clanricarde, "was that France would while away time in negotiations in order to protect and strengthen Mehemet Ali and would then laugh at England whose policy would thus be entirely frustrated." It was clear that the Russian Government hoped to use this position to get Palmerston to accept their own views as to the Straits.[2]

Ere Palmerston received these later despatches Brunnow had

---

[1] The appointment was attributed to the influence of Orlov, whose secretary Brunnow had been during Orlov's visit to London in 1833. He had since been one of the six higher officials of the Russian Foreign Office dealing with Western affairs—all Germans. (T. Schiemann, *Geschichte Russlands*, III, 368.)

[2] From Clanricarde, 27, 31 Aug., 16 Sept., 1839: *F.O. Russia*, 253; do., 10 Sept., 1839: *B.P.*

arrived in London with the Russian proposals. As to Mehemet Russia not only accepted all Palmerston's views but wished Britain to act at once, whether France—or Austria, though the latter was not mentioned—would join in the action or not. Brunnow even produced a memorandum shewing the necessary steps which the British fleet should take to raise Syria against Mehemet very much on the lines actually put into operation in 1840. He offered full support together with the assurance that if the Russian fleet had to go to Constantinople it would act as the mandatory of Europe, and not under the terms of the Treaty of Unkiar Skelessi. The Russian Government had now fully determined to accept the policy of closing the Straits to all vessels of war, thus securing that the Black Sea should be a *mare clausum* to all but its riparians, which meant Russian supremacy in it.

Palmerston had, as we have seen, already come to the conclusion that because of the nearness of Russia to the Bosphorus the closing of the Straits was also the best policy for Britain. Only if the Porte were the ally of Britain against Russia would a British fleet in the Black Sea be necessary. Thus the Straits would be closed while the Sultan was at peace but not while he was at war. The Russian Government had for a moment hoped that it could get agreement on the closing of the Straits even if the Porte were at war. But it was clear that the Porte could not be denied the right of summoning an ally to defend it if it were attacked. Palmerston always saw this point very clearly but he did not put it in the foreground. It shewed too clearly the advantage of the treaty to Britain. Lastly the Tsar and his advisers were strongly against any general guarantee of the Ottoman Empire by the Great Powers. This might threaten some of the special treaty rights which Russia had secured in the last sixty years, and perhaps prevent Russia from succeeding one day to territories to which she would always aspire even if Constantinople itself were given up. Palmerston had of course only just recently welcomed the French revival of this project, an old one of his. But he may have well thought that the interpretation put on it by the French Ministers made it of little practical value at this juncture. The question of a general guarantee of the Ottoman Empire though raised by him was not pressed, all attention being concentrated on the Straits. As Esterhazy reported, Brunnow tried

to keep away from theory and concentrate on the immediate issues.[1]

Palmerston himself was from the first strongly tempted to accept Brunnow's offer in order to obtain the necessary support for his plans against Mehemet Ali. The French attitude towards it drove him further in this direction. The Russian despatch suggesting action against Mehemet had already produced from Louis Philippe a declaration that the Powers would never agree to use force for that purpose. The news of the Brunnow mission produced in the excitable French Prime Minister a veritable phrensy. Bulwer, who was obviously delighted to be left in charge while Granville was on leave, described in detail the emphatic manner in which Soult cried that France would never, never agree to such terms. If England agreed with Russia instead of France, Bulwer added, all the old accusations of perfidy would be brought up once more and the feeling of the country would be little short of fury. The Government's attitude was due to confusion and wounded vanity rather than to any deep-laid scheme of aggrandisement such as Palmerston had suggested to account for the inconsistencies of French conduct. Whatever their vacillation as to Mehemet, they had maintained the same viewpoint on the Straits and they were not likely to abandon it.[2]

Bulwer, like Granville, would at this time have liked to make large concessions to Mehemet to get French agreement, but he was considerably shocked by an interview with Louis Philippe at the end of the month. The King got as excited as his Prime Minister at the idea of Britain breaking the Alliance of which he claimed to be the 'Papa'. In response to Bulwer's expostulations and flattery, he would only say that he could never get a Ministry to join in coercive measures against Mehemet. It was clear also that he already thought that Austria would take the same attitude now that Ficquelmont was in charge at Vienna. Bulwer, reporting the

[1] Goriainow, *Le Bosphore, etc.*, 63. T. Schiemann, *Geschichte Russlands*, III, 386. Esterhazy to Metternich, 4 Oct., 1839: *V. St. A.* Goriainow makes it clear that Brunnow was to refuse a guarantee and discusses the point raised by Metternich as to whether the Straits would be closed if the Sultan was at war with Russia. But, with his usual imprecision he mixes up the various questions and it is impossible to know exactly what were discussed with Palmerston. Schiemann also is vague and confused. A. Hasenclever (*Die orientalische Frage*, 92) states on Werther's authority that the question of guarantee was discussed. The account drawn up by Brunnow and accepted by Palmerston at the end of the negotiations (*L.P.*, I, No. 353) deals only with Mehemet Ali.
[2] From Bulwer, 14, 23 Sept., 1839: *B.P.*

situation in long and detailed letters and despatches, could only surmise that it was unlikely that this resolution could be overcome. Even Sébastiani urged the necessity of conceding Syria to Mehemet and the humiliation of allowing Russia to act alone at Constantinople.[1]

Palmerston on the other hand was receiving from Esterhazy assurances that he agreed with all Palmerston's views on the Levant and the opinion that the best way to keep France right was to shew her that the other Powers could get on without her. Esterhazy, whatever the disposition of his Court, abounded in hostility to Mehemet, though he evaded Palmerston's demand for Austrian troops to throw him out of Syria. His main object was to bridge the rift that had grown up between Russia and Austria, and for this purpose he agreed with all Brunnow's conditions and tried to get himself accepted as a co-worker in the negotiation with Palmerston. He had considerable success. He won Brunnow's confidence and the latter confessed to him that his first object had been to exclude Austria from the discussions with Britain, so strongly had Russia resented Austrian participation with the Anglo-French squadrons. But he was glad of the support on the question of the Straits which Esterhazy was able to give to him, for with his usual analytic ability Metternich had always been able to see further into this question than anyone else.

Esterhazy also tried to overcome Russian dislike of Prussian cooperation which had gone so far that Brunnow was not prepared even to discuss matters with young Werther, the Chargé d'Affaires in Bülow's temporary absence. Esterhazy thus turned the negotiation to some extent into a transaction between Britain and the three Eastern Courts, and Palmerston's disposition to agree to Brunnow's demands was increased by the thought that, even if France held aloof, the other Great Powers would be with him. He later told Beauvale that Esterhazy's conduct had been 'perfect' throughout the negotiation.[2]

---

[1] From Bulwer, 30 Sept., 1839: *B.P.* Sébastiani to Soult, 23 Sept., 1839: *A.A.E.*

[2] Esterhazy to Metternich, 25 Sept., 1, 4, 8 Oct., 1839: *V. St. A.* Metternich's observation on the despatch of 4 Oct. agreed that the Austrian attitude towards the Straits was the main reason for Russian distrust of him. He noted also: "L'employ de force de terre Autrichien en Syrie comme en Egypte est un rêve creux," while he told a French official at Johannisberg that the best thing would be for the Porte to make its own arrangements with Mehemet Ali though no one would dare to suggest such a course (Desages to Bourqueney, 21 Oct., 1839: *Bour. P.*). To Beauvale, 25 Oct., 1839: *B.P.*

In these circumstances Palmerston himself would have accepted the Russian offer, as regards the Straits and Mehemet. He pressed Sébastiani hard to receive them favourably and pointed out that it was not England alone but Europe that France would desert if she refused to agree to any coercion of Mehemet. He was, moreover, still coquetting with the idea of a convention guaranteeing the Ottoman Empire for a period of years. The French Government still held strongly to this plan and Soult desired the guarantee to be perpetual. Palmerston shewed a readiness to agree and produced a draft of his own.[1]

This was of course not something which Brunnow could have accepted, but it was not the main point nor the one on which the negotiation broke down. The Cabinet refused to break with France over the question of the Straits. Palmerston proposed that coercive measures should be taken against Mehemet along the lines which Brunnow had suggested, if necessary without the participation of France. Naval forces were to be used on the Syrian coast and as a last resource troops landed in Egypt itself. Mehemet was to be offered the hereditary governance of Egypt alone and, if he refused to agree, that concession was to be withdrawn and even the temporary possession of Egypt was to be taken from him if he ordered Ibrahim to attack. In this last case the use of Russian ships and troops in Asia Minor to protect Constantinople was envisaged. But the Cabinet unanimously rejected this plan. The strong pro-French section had the powerful argument that in such a case it would be Britain that would be inconsistent, for from the outset Palmerston had supported the French demand that Russian ships must not be allowed to enter the Sea of Marmora without those of the maritime Powers. Until this point was settled discussion of the future regime of the Straits was useless. Other influences working against agreement, reported Esterhazy, were the financial classes interested in Egypt, and the Liberals who could not bear to desert France for the Russian Tsar.[2]

Brunnow, therefore, had to be told that Britain could not agree

[1] Sébastiani to Soult, 14, 17, 27 Sept., 1839: *A.A.E.*; do., 23 Sept., 1839: Guizot, *Mémoires*, IV, 550.

[2] Memorandum, 19 Sept., 1839: *B.P.* It is noted on it in Palmerston's hand that the proposals in it were subsequently almost entirely carried out except the landing of troops in Egypt. Esterhazy to Metternich, 4, 8 Oct., 1839: *V. St. A.* I do not know whether the Memorandum itself was placed before the whole Cabinet or only discussed with Melbourne. The correspondence with him referred to in the Memorandum is missing.

that only Russian ships should enter the Straits even though the Treaty of Unkiar Skelessi was abandoned. In such circumstances, the attack on Mehemet could not be immediately begun, as Russia had suggested, for it might raise the question of the entry into the Straits on which it had not been possible to agree. Brunnow urged that inaction was dangerous. Palmerston did not conceal his sympathy with this point of view and the discussions were throughout marked with the greatest cordiality and frankness. Brunnow, for example, suggested that Palmerston should remove Ponsonby and send Durham to Constantinople. Naturally Palmerston refused this proposal as also Brunnow's suggestion that Britain should take Candia. But he was convinced of the genuine nature of the Russian offer. "I believe that Power to be acting honestly," he told Beauvale, "and I hope we may be able to come to an understanding with her." But neither Palmerston nor Brunnow had the power to accept the indispensable conditions laid down by the other, and all that could be done was for the latter to report to his Court and await the decisions of the Tsar.

On his way back, however, he paid an important visit. He passed through Dover and sought out Wellington. The Duke had long ago in 1835 advised Palmerston of his view that the closing of the Straits was to the interest of Britain. He found no difficulty, therefore, in agreeing with Brunnow on that topic which was not explored in detail. But in addition he was emphatically of the opinion that Mehemet should be confined to Egypt, and he judged the strategic situation much more favourably than the civilians. Ibrahim would never be able to march on Constantinople, he said, if his sea communications were cut and by the same means he could be turned out of Syria. This opinion undoubtedly had an immense effect on Brunnow who regarded it as confirming the wisdom of the plan he had proposed to Palmerston. If it were true, it was unlikely that the question of the entry into the Dardanelles would in fact occur and this seems to have exercised considerable influence on the decision of the Tsar. Brunnow also hastened to inform Esterhazy, as the most delicate way of communicating immediately to the British Government the views of a leader of the Opposition. He also emphasised its importance to the British Minister at Frankfurt and asked him to make sure Palmerston knew about it.[1]

---

[1] To Beauvale, 25 Oct., 1839: *B.P.* Brunnow to Esterhazy, 15 Oct., 1839, enclosed in Esterhazy to Metternich, 15 Nov., 1839: *V. St. A.*, and in Esterhazy to Palmerston, 15 Oct., 1839: *B.P.* From Abercrombie, 26 Oct., 1839: *B.P.*

The French Government was informed that the rejection of the Russian offer had been done in deference to the French view. If Palmerston hoped to obtain concessions concerning Mehemet by presenting matters in this way he was immediately disappointed. He made, as a result of the Cabinet discussions, an offer to Sébastiani of the Pashalik of Acre to Mehemet for life, without the renowned fortress, and asked if France would support him in imposing such a solution. This perhaps did not go very far. But it was the first time Palmerston had yielded on his desert frontier. The offer was treated at Paris with contempt. No attempt was made to negotiate about it or even to answer Palmerston's arguments. Both Soult and the King refused to consider the exercise of force against Mehemet in any event. Louis Philippe, when reminded by Bulwer that he had long ago agreed that Mehemet should give up the Holy Places, replied, "Mon Dieu, qui les prendra?" Soult, reported Bulwer, had become "irritable and very disagreeable if contradicted". He said that, in fifty years of active life, "it is extraordinary that I have never once been wrong." "Prince Metternich", added Bulwer, "is the only other Providence who would say the same thing."

The French Government denied also that Austria and Prussia accepted Palmerston's plans, and the despatches from Vienna had been so uncertain that they had much material to support their view. It was clear that they thought that now that the Russian negotiation had broken down Palmerston was helpless and must in the long run give way. Now that Brunnow had gone, the Foreign Minister had left London and, reported Sébastiani, diplomatic affairs were in a state of complete stagnation. Many members of the British Cabinet did indeed share the French view. They were sick of the question. At the end of October Melbourne confessed to Esterhazy that he was against the coercion of Mehemet because it was a source of division among the Great Powers, and that he almost wished that the note of 27 July had never been presented since it had prevented direct agreement between the Porte and the Pasha.[1]

Esterhazy delayed his own departure to see Wellington and Peel. The former confirmed these views. Peel on the other hand disagreed with him and shewed much jealousy of Russia. Palmerston had told Bourqueney in July of Wellington's opinion expressed in 1835. Guizot, *Mémoires*, IV, 510. He now passed Brunnow's letter on to several colleagues.

[1] From Bulwer, 14 Oct., 1839: *B.P.* Esterhazy to Metternich, 8 Oct., 1839: *V. St. A.* Sébastiani to Soult, 27 Sept., 1839: *A.A.E.*

Not so Palmerston. His determination to secure his objective was only increased by the intransigeance of France, and the refusal of the Cabinet to accept Brunnow's offer. His first step was to withdraw the offer to France which had been so contemptuously refused. Poor Sébastiani, who tried to keep the negotiation open, found the usually genial Foreign Minister absolutely 'glacial'. The offer was cancelled and Palmerston refused even to discuss it. He was, he told Esterhazy, convinced that there was more to hope from Russia than France.[1]

It was in this mood that he, using for this purpose, during a short stay at Broadlands, the 'stagnation' which Sébastiani had reported, composed the first of the trenchant indictments of French policy which wounded and embittered Louis Philippe and his Ministers all the more deeply because they were practically unanswerable, so vulnerable had the French position become. In response to the pleadings of Granville he twice softened its wording. But, as Melbourne pointed out, these changes made little difference. It was the exposure of the whole trend of French policy rather than any details which was bound to hurt and humiliate France. The survey shewed that France, after joining with the rest of Europe in the agreement to protect the Sultan against Mehemet, now refused to take part in any action necessary to make the promise good.[2]

As Palmerston had, perhaps, expected, this despatch produced no effect at Paris. Louis Philippe professed to be deeply wounded at it and said that it was not the will but the power to overthrow Mehemet that was lacking. Soult's reply was of the lamest and Palmerston had no difficulty in refuting it. But more serious was it that all the efforts of Esterhazy, who spent three weeks at Paris on the way back to Austria, produced absolutely no effect, though he pressed hard all the arguments for action. Public opinion, he said at the end, was less in favour of Mehemet than he had expected but Louis Philippe far more so. The King insisted that Palmerston had a personal grudge against him because of his Spanish

[1] Sébastiani to Soult, 10 Oct., 1839: *A.A.E.* do., 3, 10 Oct., 1839: Guizot, *Mémoires*, IV, 553, 555; do., 18 Oct., 1839: *A.A.E.* There is a note in the margin of Sébastiani's despatch of 10 Oct. about Palmerston's offer to the effect that it was absurd to suppose it possible.

[2] From Granville, 1, 8, 15 Nov., 1839; From Melbourne, 16 Nov., 1839: *B.P.* The despatch is dated 29 October (*L.P.*, No. 358) but it not despatched officially until later. Copies of it were sent to the other capitals of the Great Powers.

policy. It was impossible, he added, to coerce Mehemet. Conciliation was the only possible policy. Soult's only concession was to ask Esterhazy to see if he could get Palmerston to renew his offer of the Pashalik of Acre. Esterhazy did his best to find some means of compromise and in a letter to Palmerston himself acquitted the French Government of desiring Mehemet to be established in Syria, even though they refused to employ the slightest threat against him. Before he left he thought he had done some good, but that was not Granville's opinion. The French Government, now that the negotiation with Russia seemed to have ended was convinced that its point of view must prevail. And though Esterhazy had tried to remove the effects of Austrian vacillation they could still hope that Metternich would ultimately come over to their side. Beauvale attempted to defend Metternich's twists of policy but he had himself become defeatist as regards Mehemet. And no one could have been more so than Admiral Stopford who practically refused to take the responsibility for using the fleet to coerce him—a refusal which Lord Holland warmly commended. The Chancellor of the Duchy was only one such in a Cabinet which Palmerston knew was deeply divided and doubtful of his policy.[1]

Encouragement now came from the Porte itself. All through the late summer Ponsonby's despatches had dwelt on the precarious nature of the situation there. He could never be certain whether underground negotiations were not taking place with Mehemet—and in fact in one subterranean channel or another these never ceased. Pontois was reported to be urging the Porte

[1] From Granville, 18, 25, 29 Nov., 1839: *L.P.*, Nos. 385, 395, 399; do., 29 Nov., 2, 7 Dec., 1839: *B.P.* To Granville, 22 Nov., 1839: *L.P.*, 386. From Esterhazy, 4 Dec., 1839: *B.P.* Esterhazy to Metternich, 15, 29 Nov., 1839: *V. St. A.* From Beauvale, 19 Nov., 1839: *B.P.* It was at this juncture that the suggestion was made by Ponsonby that the British fleet should find shelter inside the Dardanelles at the White Cliffs. The idea was originally Stopford's to get shelter from the autumn weather. Ponsonby pronounced it inconvenient and Reschid forbade it, but some refuge had to be found for the fleet. Palmerston was for a moment tempted to advocate that course but Melbourne was against it. Wiser counsels prevailed and the fleet was ordered to Smyrna. It could leave the entrance to the Dardanelles, Palmerston explained, because of the new disposition of Russia. Though there had been precedents for using the entry as a haven, the Russians might certainly have suspected an attempt to enter the Sea of Marmora. From Beauvale, 14 Oct., 1839: *B.P.*; do., 8 Nov., 1839: *F.O. Austria*, 282. Ponsonby to Beauvale, 9 Oct., 1839: *B.P.* To Beauvale, 25, Oct., 1839: *B.P.* From Ponsonby, 9, 22 Sept., 8 Oct., 1839: *F.O. Turkey*, 358, 359. To Admiralty, 29 Oct., 1839: *L.P.*, I, No. 356; To Ponsonby, do: *B.P.*

to come to an understanding with the Pasha on the basis which had been put forward in Paris of the return of Adana and the Holy Places to the Sultan. Russian activities were thought to be in the same direction and her Ambassador was also trying to get the fleets away from the entrance of the Dardanelles. Husrev, reported Ponsonby, was too old to cope with all these difficulties and liable to be bought by Russia. Fortunately Stürmer was now working closely with Ponsonby and it was largely by his influence that the dangerous intrigues in the Seraglio connected with the Sultan's Mother were frustrated.[1]

The one hope was the new Foreign Minister, Reschid Pasha, who had been sent for from London by Husrev when the crisis came in July. He arrived on 21 September and at once told Ponsonby of his faith in Britain, his suspicions of Russia and his doubts of France. In less than a month he had got rid of the least reliable of the Turkish Ministers, Nourri, Sarim and Mustapha Kiamil. With Husrev as the figurehead, Reschid got two other pro-British Ministers, Halil and Ahmed, into power, to help him. They warned the Sultan against the intrigues of his Mother. Correspondence with Mehemet still went on and no one was sure of Husrev himself. But though rumours of plots persisted, Ponsonby believed that Stürmer and he could maintain Reschid and Halil in office and prevent the interference of the Seraglio. "The Seraglio", he wrote, "was everything in the time of Sultan Mahmoud. The young Sultan has agreed not to consult with or listen to the men who surround him as domestic officers."[2]

This increase of Reschid's power gave him the opportunity for the grand stroke which he seems to have contemplated ever since his last visit to London. For on 3 November the famous Edict of Gulhané was issued. Reforms of the most drastic character were promised and Ponsonby hailed them as a blow against Mehemet: "It is a victorious answer to those who say that the Empire cannot be saved by its ancient Government and that the spurious regeneration to be worked out by the Pasha of Egypt is its only preservation. The enemies of Turkey and the friends of Mehemet

---

[1] From Ponsonby, 18, 19, 21, 22 Aug., 1839: *F.O. Turkey*, 358.
[2] From Ponsonby, 10, 23, 30 Sept., 8, 16 Oct., 1839: *F.O. Turkey*, 358–359. Some of this, much emasculated, is printed in *Levant Papers* where is also given the official correspondence between Mehemet and the Porte, which is, however, less important than the hidden intercourse.

Ali are said to feel the weight of the blow that has fallen upon them."[1]

Palmerston also thought the Edict a master stroke. He gave Ponsonby credit for the achievement. "Your Hathi Sheriff", he wrote, "was a grand stroke of policy and it is producing great effect on public feeling both here and in France. I never have despaired of seeing Turkey rear her head again as a substantive element in the balance of power." He warmly commended Reschid, though Melbourne, with some wisdom, thought it safer not to single out a Minister by name. But even more important was the change in Russian policy which rendered the presence of the fleet no longer necessary at the mouth of the Dardanelles. Ponsonby was urged to work as cordially as possible with the Russian Ambassador: "It is not necessary to enquire what the reasons are which have led Russia to adopt her present course, nor to examine whether among them may be a hope that she may thus at least retain some portion of her influence at Constantinople. It is our business to take advantage of her present temper, and to encourage her to work with us for our own objects, as long as she is willing to do so."[2]

(ii) The Tsar accepts the British Conditions

While his sympathetic account of the failure of his first mission was on its way to his master Brunnow returned to his post at Stuttgart via Frankfurt. On his way he paid another important visit. He spent several days with Metternich at Johannisberg and Frankfurt (19–24 Oct.). His tact and authority, which Princess Mélanie reveals in her naïve diary, produced a great effect. It shewed the Chancellor that agreement could be obtained only on the basis laid down at London and made him anxious that these negotiations should be successful. He was ready to second them if the Tsar agreed to go on.[3]

At the same time Metternich was far from accepting all Brunnow's propositions. He emphasised the necessity of recognising the sovereignty of the Sultan over the Straits and won Brunnow's assent to seeking a solution of the problem in this manner. But

[1] From Ponsonby, 5 Nov., 1839: *F.O. Turkey*, 360. For the scene, which Ponsonby and others describe in detail, see H. W. V. Temperley, *Crimea*, 161
[2] To Ponsonby, 29 Oct., (undated) 1839; From Melbourne, 9 Dec., 1839: *B.P.* To Ponsonby, 2 Dec., 1839: *F.O. Turkey*, 353.
[3] Metternich, *Mémoires*, VI, 341–344.

how anxious Metternich was to keep in with all parties was seen in Leopold's report of a conversation which he had at Wiesbaden on the 22 October. The Chancellor was full of suggestions for reconciling the French support of Mehemet with the necessities of the Porte. Metternich, according to Leopold, was anxious to establish Five Power unanimity and saw the danger of using force against the Pasha. Leopold urged him to mediate between France and Britain and at Metternich's suggestion wrote an account of his views to Louis Philippe.

Palmerston no doubt thought that this epistle was not likely to exert much good influence at Paris, and he immediately sent Leopold a terrific indictment of French policy. If France, he wrote, were to be judged by her Press, which was primed with confidential information, she must be considered more dangerous to Europe than Russia. But he was ready to attribute her apparent bad faith more to timidity than worse motives. Mehemet had in his pay five or six leading newspapers, many of the talkers in the Salons and perhaps a friend or two in the Cabinet, and the Government was afraid to stand up to them. But what sort of a figure would France cut when the papers were published as they must be? In Spanish affairs, while secretly betraying Britain, she had preserved appearances. Now she had behaved like a weathercock and substituted a policy of dismembering the Ottoman Empire for that of preserving the integrity which she had promised to defend. Such a course was not even in her own selfish interests. For, even if she did not mind Russia possessing Constantinople, provided that she could establish an Arab Empire, "she would find that if such did come into existence England would have far more influence over it than France, and this for a great many reasons, moral, political, geographical."[1]

Meanwhile the Tsar was awaiting at St. Petersburg Palmerston's confirmation of Brunnow's reports and proposals for a new agreement. Clanricarde recounted the impatience to receive it and Brunnow complained bitterly to Sir George Shee at Stuttgart of Palmerston's neglect to instruct his Ambassador. Meanwhile, he said, the way was left open for French intrigue at St. Petersburg where Barante was insinuating that Britain was not to be relied upon, and had three times pressed Nesselrode to accept the French point of view about Mehemet. Nesselrode had replied

[1] From Leopold, 24 Oct., 1839; To Leopold, 4 Nov., 1839: *B.P.*

with a despatch to Paris which played for time, but which the French Government interpreted as a distinct advance in their direction. Eventually in order to satisfy Nesselrode's impatience Clanricarde used an extract from one of Palmerston's private letters. At last on the 14 November Palmerston's long-awaited despatch arrived.

The result was that the Tsar agreed to the British condition that, if the necessity arose, both fleets should enter the Sea of Marmora. He seems to have grasped quite eagerly at the opportunity of agreement. No doubt the probable effect on France was a strong inducement to him to come to terms with Britain. But there were also other reasons. The effect which might be produced on the struggle in the Caucasus and generally a desire to get things quiet again in the Middle East were also powerful motives. Nesselrode, indeed, insisted that it was no part of the Emperor's intentions to cause a breach between Britain and France. It will be seen, however, that Brunnow's instructions were so drawn as to make that breach almost inevitable unless France gave way completely.[1]

The notice of this change first reached Brunnow at Stuttgart at the beginning of December, in the shape of a private letter from Nesselrode. He at once got in touch with Shee who assured him that Palmerston would be delighted to receive him back in England. The Russian Minister was much pleased with the compliments paid to him by Palmerston in his despatch and was, stated Shee, *"thoroughly English*. His eyes seemed quite to *fill* when he talked of the probable renewal of friendly feelings between Russia and England." Shortly afterwards a formal despatch authorised him to resume his negotiations in England on a new basis.

Brunnow had hoped to persuade Esterhazy to go back from Paris to London to help him. But as usual that Ambassador was immersed in personal affairs. Metternich, however, as the result of Brunnow's diplomatic handling at Wiesbaden, was completely

---

[1] From Clanricarde, 5, 18 Nov., 1839: *F.O. Russia*, 253. *L.P.*, I, No. 377. To Clanricarde, 25 Oct., 1839: *L.P.*, I, No. 352. From Shee, 3 Dec., 1839: *B.P.* Palmerston had promised to send to St. Petersburg a report similar to that drawn up by Brunnow. He subsequently said that he accepted Brunnow's as his own. Pressure of work had delayed his sending instructions. Later he said he had expected the Russian Government to make new proposals on the basis of Brunnow's report. There seems to have been a genuine misunderstanding but Palmerston may well have desired to rest his case on Brunnow's report than on one of his own which the Cabinet would have to see.

won over to the necessity of Austrian participation in the discussions at London. He therefore sent Neumann on a special mission for that purpose. Neumann had left London six years before on the worst of terms with Palmerston, but all that was forgotten and, as will be seen, he was to play an important part in assisting Palmerston to get his way with the Cabinet. Palmerston's agents abroad had for the most part little confidence that Metternich would act without France. But from Vienna Beauvale once again expressed confidence in the Chancellor's resolution, and reported his advocacy of the conference system. If only Palmerston and the Tsar could meet—with Metternich himself perhaps to act as a catalyst—all would go well. But the centre of discussion must now, Beauvale solemnly pointed out, be at London, a fact which was apparent to all the world.[1]

The news of Russian agreement naturally caused the greatest excitement in French circles. Officially both Louis Philippe and his Minister had to profess to be delighted that the Russians had given way. The main object of their diplomacy had ostensibly thus been achieved. But they could not help being aware that Palmerston, instead of being isolated, was now the centre of a new negotiation which would be directed against Mehemet Ali. Sébastiani was given no inkling of what was in Palmerston's mind. But he was congratulated on France's return to the alliance, and the two agreed on the vacillation and unreliability of Metternich who had been saying different things to Britain and France. More significant was it that Sébastiani announced to Hummelauer, who was used to keep a line out to France, that he would be able to defeat Palmerston's plans by his influence on those members of the Cabinet whom he knew did not accept the Foreign Minister's policy as their own.

Neumann shewed wonderful zeal and caught up with Brunnow at Calais. The two journeyed to London together and won each other's confidence at the outset, a fact of great importance at the subsequent negotiations. It was not at London but at Broadlands that these negotiations began. For on 16 December, two days

---

[1] From Sir George Shee, 3, 7, 8, 9 Dec., 1839; From Beauvale, 8, 17, 31 Dec., 1839: *B.P.* Neumann was at first only given instructions as to the Straits because it was thought that Brunnow was limited to that topic, but when it was realised he was also to deal with the question of Mehemet he was given further instructions to enter also into that negotiation. He had at first only a letter to Palmerston, no Full Powers to negotiate.

before they landed at Dover, Palmerston had married Lady Cowper. He did not, however, allow his honeymoon to interrupt his diplomatic labours. He invited Brunnow and Neumann to visit Broadlands and discuss the situation. Sébastiani thought the action most precipitate and that the Cabinet would disapprove. It had in fact Melbourne's warm approval. Thus at Broadlands on Christmas Day the foundations were laid of all the subsequent negotiations. Palmerston saw Brunnow twice on the 23rd and 24th, discussed matters afterwards with Neumann and spent the first Christmas Day of his married life in going over the whole question with both of them together.[1]

Brunnow's instructions were complicated. The Sultan was not himself to be a party to the treaty which was to be made between the Great Powers, who offered the Sultan their assistance and, after he had accepted it, would proceed to make their help effective. There were many different possibilities according as Austria, France and Britain came to an agreement. A good deal of discretion was, therefore, allowed to Brunnow in the interpretation of his orders and of this permission he was to take full advantage.[2]

There was, however, one cardinal point which brought all the strands of the negotiations together and ensured that the result should be a comprehensive settlement if it were secured at all. It also made almost certain a breach between Britain and France which was always one of the objects of the Tsar even if Nesselrode did not desire it. For Brunnow was instructed to make Russian assent to the entry of the fleets into the Dardanelles depend upon an agreement on the dispute between Mehemet and the Sultan. It was most unlikely that Britain and France would agree on this question and the means might thus be found of completely destroying the Franco-British Alliance. Brunnow from the first insisted that he had no latitude on this point. Neumann made some attempt to get him to divide the two questions when they first

[1] From Hummelauer, 21, 31 Dec., 1839; From Neumann, 21 Dec., 1839: *V. St. A.* Soult to Sébastiani, 9 Dec., 1839: Guizot, *Mémoires*, IV, 556. Sébastiani to Soult, 12, 18 Dec., 1839: *A.A.E.* From Melbourne, 21 Dec., 1839: *B.P.*

[2] Brunnow's Instructions are given in a confused form in Goriainow, *Le Bosphore, etc.*, 73–75, and discussed with equal obscurity in T. Schiemann's *Geschichte Russlands*, III, 391–392 and F. Marten's *Recueil, etc.*, XII, 111. Neumann's despatches and private letters make them pretty clear. (See *Appendix D.*)

discussed it. But the Russian Minister was adamant and he said the same thing to Palmerston, who of course wished for the same procedure—if he could get his Cabinet to agree.

Subject to this consideration Brunnow was to suggest a definite method by which, if the need arose, the fleets of the different Powers should take up their stations. The British and French fleets, reduced to a few vessels, were to be stationed inside the Dardanelles, the Russian fleet of indefinite number was to take up the same position as in 1833, i.e. on the Asiatic side of the Bosphorus and away from the Dardanelles. Austria's station was not laid down but it was intimated that, true to her role of mediator, she might like to send a vessel or two to lie somewhere between the ships of Russia and those of the maritime Powers.

This was, however, to be a special exception to protect the Sultan from Mehemet Ali. It was not to derogate from a general rule to which Russia was prepared to agree, the closing of the Straits. Here Russian instructions had been much influenced by Metternich's insistence that what had to be done was to recognise the right inherent in the Sultan's sovereignty of closing the Straits rather than to impose any restrictions upon him. Thus the Powers were to agree with one another that they would respect this right and the Sultan was to declare that he meant to uphold it. The words "in peace and in war" still remained but Brunnow already told Neumann that he was prepared to withdraw them if pressed. Nothing was said about any guarantee of the Ottoman Empire as a whole. That had now been abandoned by every Power save France.

Lastly the Powers were to come to agreement about the steps to be taken against Mehemet along the lines laid down in Brunnow's previous memorandum. Here Brunnow was given much latitude. He could of course agree without the assent of France. But he could also in the last resource agree even if Austria did not consent to take part. If, however, the Porte and Mehemet had already come to an agreement—as the news from Constantinople at St. Petersburg when the instructions were written seemed to indicate was possible—he was to do nothing to overthrow this. In this case it was assumed that the crisis would cease to exist.

Palmerston, as might be expected, received all this with the greatest pleasure. He told Neumann that it left nothing to be desired, though, as was soon to be seen, there was much in it which

he wished to alter when he had had time to examine the document carefully. But for the moment all that he suggested to Brunnow was that the question of the Straits might be regulated separately in a convention recognising, in the same way as Britain had done in 1809, the Porte's ancient right to close the Straits. But he at once gave up this suggestion when Brunnow told him he was expressly ordered to include everything in one transaction. Neumann was received with equal cordiality and frankness.

Palmerston could not of course pledge the Cabinet. The best method of winning their assent was frankly discussed with the two Envoys, who were well aware of the difficulty and delicacy of the task. The only concession which could be made to Mehemet, said Palmerston, was that which he had made to France and withdrawn, the Pashalik of Acre without the fortress itself. There was much discussion as to the force to be used and Palmerston recurred to an old idea of bringing Indian troops to invade Egypt. The detailed application could not obviously be immediately worked out. Meanwhile it was decided that it would be better for Palmerston himself to lay a plan before the Cabinet rather than merely submit that of Brunnow, and this task he promised to undertake at once. Palmerston pointed out that though Brunnow had the necessary authority to sign the treaty, Neumann, and of course the Prussian representative also, had not received Full Powers for that purpose. He engaged to write to their Courts to obtain them. The two representatives meanwhile promised to do everything possible to assist Palmerston to obtain the assent of the Cabinet.[1]

How necessary such assistance might be was shewn by Sébastiani's conduct. Furious at being left out of the discussions, he forced an invitation to the country house where Palmerston went immediately after this negotiation. There, in response to his insistent enquiries, Palmerston told him little or nothing. He would, the Ambassador assured his Court, wrap himself up in 'calm' and 'indifference'. But he indicated to both Hummelauer and Neumann that he would fight Palmerston in the Cabinet, the majority of which he knew were against a breach with France. Faithful to his promise Neumann spent two days with the Hollands whom he knew were the most likely to be on Sébastiani's side, following Palmerston who had been engaged on the same

---

[1] Neumann to Metternich, 31 Dec., 1839: *V. St. A. Appendix*, p. 875.

MEHEMET ALI AND THE STRAITS

task. He reported that he had had great success in seconding Palmerston's views. Brunnow meanwhile had seen Wellington and received his congratulations on the success of his diplomacy. The French, the Duke said, would be fools if they did not agree also. But all the news from Paris shewed that the French took an entirely different view. And it was under these circumstances that Palmerston began to draft the convention he was to submit to the Cabinet.[1]

[1] Hummelauer to Metternich, 31 Dec., 1839; Neumann to Metternich, 30 Dec., 1839: *V. St. A.* Sébastiani to Soult, 27 Dec., 1839: *A.A.E.* It was noted on the despatch that to be 'calm' was all right but 'indifference' was the last thing Sébastiani ought to shew. On the contrary he ought to make every effort to know all the threads of the negotiation and insist on taking part in it as he had been ordered to do. This was perhaps the last straw which made Soult and Desages determined to overcome Louis Philippe's reluctance to recall Sébastiani and substitute a less Anglophil ambassador. Brunnow told Sébastiani that he had simply come to resume the discussions broken off in October but he admitted that plans were being made to coerce Mehemet as Holland and Portugal had been coerced. (28 Dec., 1839: *A.A.E.* partly in Guichen, *La Crise d'Orient*, 187–188.)

3. THE CONVENTION OF 15 JULY, 1840

The agreement of Russia to share the defence of the Straits with the Western Powers seemed to have removed a major obstacle to agreement. But it was not long before Palmerston found out how many other difficulties lay in the way of that combined action against Mehemet Ali which was necessary to reestablish the Sultan's authority over his Asiatic dominions. The negotiation of the next six months is, indeed, one of the most intricate and curious in the annals of diplomacy. Until the month of July was reached it seemed impossible that a satisfactory result could be obtained. Throughout these months Louis Philippe, the French Government and nearly all their advisers were confident that Palmerston would fail in his primary object, the use of force against Mehemet. More than once Brunnow and Neumann, as well as their chiefs, Nesselrode and Metternich, were ready to give up in despair. At Constantinople intrigue never ceased to obtain a separate arrangement between the Sultan and the Pasha, which would have made Palmerston the laughing-stock of Europe and was only prevented by the ceaseless vigilance and powerful authority of Ponsonby. The majority of the British Cabinet under the leadership of Lord Holland and the new recruit, Clarendon, were always opposed to Palmerston and ruthlessly rejected almost every plan that divided Britain from France. The French Ambassadors were fully informed of their proceedings and assisted many of them with advice. The Prime Minister, though his first desire was to avoid at all hazards a split in the Cabinet and the consequent downfall of his Government, was, so far as he took a determined line at all, on the side of compromise and peace.

But Palmerston himself, though he was forced to manoeuvre and delay, never lost either his courage or his patience. He forbore to force the issue until the situation was such that he could insist on his own way. Then with dramatic intensity he compelled the unwilling Cabinet to follow his advice by the threat of his resignation. He was throughout overwhelmed with work, for there were other important problems to be dealt with, and a Queen's marriage which necessarily threw many duties on him. This was no doubt one reason why events moved so slowly while Neumann

665

chafed impatiently and wrote stinging despatches to his Court. But Palmerston believed, and rightly, that time was on his side and that Mehemet would not dare to forestall him by a vigorous action. The Egyptian army indeed was losing strength all through this period of delay and Ponsonby had begun to overthrow Ibrahim even before the Powers had come to agreement.

Palmerston's first task was to produce a draft for the Cabinet as he had promised to Brunnow and Neumann at Broadlands. As soon as he set himself to examine closely the project which Brunnow had laid before him he found that he was far from agreement on several essential points. In the first place he now adopted the view which Metternich had so constantly put forward that everything must be done in the name of the Sultan. This made it necessary that the Sultan should be a party to the convention and, therefore, that a Turkish Plenipotentiary with Full Powers should come to London, a condition inevitably causing delay. Palmerston was very conscious of this and even before he obtained the assent of Brunnow and Neumann ordered Ponsonby to urge the Porte to send to London its representative at Paris, the 'oaf', Nourri Pasha, who, he assured him, would not have to sign anything which "a good Turk ought to hesitate to subscribe to". Secondly, Palmerston could not accept the Russian proposal that the fleet of the Western Powers should be limited in numbers while that of Russia was unrestricted. He accordingly suggested that the Russian fleet should be equal to the combined strength of France and Britain. Lastly he did not wish at the outset that the military and naval coercion of Mehemet should be too nakedly announced, and confined himself to the promise of aid to the Sultan to cut off supplies to the Syrian army and omitted all mention of an attack on Alexandria. These last two changes were probably more due to the advice of Cabinet colleagues than to Palmerston's own desires, for he consulted some of them informally about his draft. These consultations revealed the intense desire of many members of the Cabinet not to break with France and Palmerston was forced, therefore, to use language which would at least postpone the issue.[1]

For the same reason he entered into communication with

---

[1] To Beauvale, 26 Jan., 3 Feb., 1840: *B.P.* Neumann to Metternich, 14, 17 Jan., 1840: *V. St. A.* To Ponsonby, 25 Jan., 1840: *L.P.*, I, No. 455; do., *B.P.*

Sébastiani, revealing to him the substance of Brunnow's proposals and asking him to obtain the agreement of his Government to his own modifications of them which took into account French susceptibilities to a much greater degree. This was a bold step for Brunnow had given him no authority to do so, but, after all, Sébastiani was to a large extent himself on Palmerston's side and was likely to find out from other members of the Cabinet what was going on.

All these negotiations took time and it was not until 20 January that Palmerston communicated the result to the impatient Brunnow and Neumann. They were both dissatisfied, but Brunnow was so shocked and indignant at what Palmerston had done that he even refused to discuss the draft with him. There was no need at all to summon a Turkish representative, he said, and thus incur a long delay. But the other two alterations were inexcusable. His master would be insulted at the idea that his ships were to be limited in number, while the communication of the Russian plans to France before they had been officially placed before the British Cabinet, much less accepted by them, was against all the rules of diplomatic behaviour. The lack of precision regarding the coercion of Mehemet was also regrettable. In fact the draft seemed still to be aimed more at Russia than at the rebellious Pasha and his French backer. Neumann felt less strongly on these points, but he thought it necessary to support Brunnow and maintain the Austro-Russian front, and it was he who at Brunnow's request conveyed these criticisms to Palmerston. But Palmerston refused to yield on the first point, the participation of the Sultan. He insisted to Neumann and emphasised in his private letter to Beauvale that he was merely following Metternich's advice. Nor could he admit that Britain and France were to be placed in a different position to Russia as regards entering the Straits. On the question of the coercion of Mehemet he was more ready to listen to Neumann's arguments. He did himself in fact agree with them, but he pointed out that the experience of Spain shewed how difficult it was for an outside Power to exercise the right of blockade in a civil war, and intimated that he could only gradually get his colleagues to accept the full implications of coercion on which indeed he had as yet no very clear idea himself. Neumann had objected to the mention of an Austrian squadron in the draft. It was needed, Palmerston explained, for moral effect

2 U

not material aid.   And it was clear that it was on the British Cabinet that moral pressure was most needed.[1]

Neumann criticised severely Palmerston's handling of the Cabinet of which he seems to have been well informed.   Since they had approved of the despatches to Clanricarde and Granville of October they had, he insisted, committed themselves to Palmerston's view of French policy.   But Palmerston's communication to Sébastiani of Brunnow's proposals had enabled the latter to influence several members of the Cabinet.   The effect on Melbourne particularly was very noticeable.   The result was that Palmerston was enjoined by his colleagues not to make a separation from France inevitable.   Palmerston had shewn them the two drafts and they had preferred his to that of Brunnow.   But he was under an illusion, wrote Neumann, if he thought he could overcome their resistance.

Thus, though Palmerston said that he would go on without France, Brunnow, whose instructions were to return to Darmstadt by the middle of February, was already in despair and urging Neumann to leave London at the same time.   All that the Austrian envoy could suggest was that Metternich should get Beauvale to use his influence with the Prime Minister.   He asked for instructions as to how far he was to go in standing solidly with Brunnow.[2]

Meanwhile nothing had come from Palmerston's approach to Sébastiani and his strong appeal to France to join the other Powers.   He had rather to protest at the increase of the French fleet in the Mediterranean and intimated that unless it was stopped Britain would have to follow the French example.   Sébastiani's attempt to get his Government to agree met with no response. The debates in the Chambers had shewn them to be strongly in favour of Mehemet and the whole Cabinet was opposed to Sébastiani's advice.   Louis Philippe said no French Cabinet could consent to limit the French force for the Dardanelles to two or three ships.   Though a clause had been put in the King's Speech in response to the mention of the Alliance in that proroguing the

---

[1] Neumann to Metternich, 21, 23 Jan., 1840;   *V. St. A.*   To Beauvale, 26 Jan., 3 Feb., 1840: *B.P.*

[2] Neumann to Metternich, 23, 26 Jan., 1840: *V. St. A.*   He reported that Baring, the Chancellor of the Exchequer, had personal financial interests in France, Lord Holland thought the French alliance indispensable and Melbourne feared the expense of an expedition to Syria or Egypt.

last session of the British Parliament, many speakers had criticised British policy. A notable exception was Thiers who warmly defended the alliance. But he also had had to advocate Mehemet's cause and he hastened to tell Bulwer that no Ministry could join in sanctions against him, an opinion strongly endorsed by Bulwer himself.[1]

In these circumstances it was only natural that no mention was made of the French alliance in the Queen's Speech opening the new session of the British Parliament. Nevertheless Louis Philippe and his Ministers were very hurt and Granville, who recorded with a kind of melancholy satisfaction the outcome of Palmerston's *démarche* on which he had not been consulted, also reproached his chief. "But how", replied Palmerston, "could we with any truth have talked about our union and alliance with France, when France has left us on the most important question of the day and when no real unity of views continues to exist? Such phrases are worse than unmeaning when they are not in accordance with the truth."[2]

It was not very likely, therefore, that Sébastiani's advocacy would have any success. On the contrary, its principal result was to produce the recall of Sébastiani himself. Soult had long distrusted him and been jealous of his position at London. Now the French Cabinet by a threat of resignation forced Louis Philippe to withdraw his protection from an Ambassador who had been in very intimate relations with himself. All that he could obtain was that Sébastiani should remain to represent France at the Queen's wedding. His successor was to be no less a person than Guizot, and one of the causes of the King's acquiescence was that the appointment gave some prospect of Doctrinaire support in the Chamber for the approaching vote on the grant to the Duc de Nemours; for his son's marriage to a Saxe-Coburg princess ranked in Louis Philippe's mind as of almost equal importance to the Eastern Question. Soult meanwhile could avoid an official refusal by asserting that he had only received an unofficial communication of the new plan. When Granville, who complained that

[1] To Sébastiani, 5 Jan., 1840: *B.P.* This is written from Holland House, no doubt after discussion with Lord Holland. It refuses to communicate to Sébastiani the despatch to Brunnow which contained the details of the plan, but Palmerston had shewn it to him previously. To Granville, 3, 7 Jan, 1840: *B.P.* From Granville, 13 Jan., 1840: *L.P.*, I, Nos., 447, 448; do., 17 Jan., 1840, *F.O. France*, 601; do., 3, 6, 10, 13 Jan., 1840; From Bulwer, 13 Jan., 1840: *B.P.*
[2] From Granville, 20 Jan., 1840; To Granville, 23 Jan., 1840: *B.P.*

he himself had little knowledge of what was going on at London, spoke to the King about it, he made the same excuse.[1]

Soult was encouraged in this course by Apponyi, the Austrian Ambassador, who assured him that Metternich did not like the Russian plan. When Sébastiani reported that the British Cabinet had agreed to negotiate a treaty with the Sultan he said it would take two months for a Turkish representative to reach London. The official French answer eventually sent welcomed the new situation with regard to the Straits but insisted that no means existed for the coercion of Mehemet. There was thus no hurry and Guizot, in spite of Palmerston's urgent entreaties, remained at Paris to vote in the debate, and France, since Sébastiani had lost the confidence of his Government, was virtually unrepresented at London. It was clear also that Granville was now an inadequate representative of Palmerston's views, closely connected as he was with the policy of a French alliance. He said that the coercion of Mehemet by Britain might cost Louis Philippe his throne.[2]

Naturally this failure had its repercussions at Vienna and St. Petersburg, but the reaction was very different in the two places. At Vienna it sensibly reduced the boldness of Metternich, who, on the first news of Brunnow's plan, had promised that he would go on even if France refused, had hastened to send Neumann instructions to negotiate a comprehensive treaty and had even talked of sending Austrian troops to Crete. The effect was all the greater because he had heard from St. Aulaire of the refusal of the Cabinet to accept Brunnow's plan long before Neumann had realised all the implications of Palmerston's hesitations. The truth was, explained Beauvale, that members of the Cabinet were betraying its secrets to the French before Palmerston could adjust his official policy to their decisions. Metternich's confidence was shattered and he was now trying harder to repair his bridge with Russia than to press on with the coercion of Mehemet. Unless Palmerston stood firm against France he would find himself

---

[1] From Granville, 24 Jan., 1840: *L.P.*, I, No., 458; do., 27 Jan., 1840: *F.O. France*, 601; do., 24, 27 Jan., 3, 10, 14 Feb., 1840: *B.P.* Bulwer said that Sébastiani was recalled because he kept the Cabinet in ignorance of what he was doing, Granville that they felt his faculties were impaired, Palmerston, in 1843 (*Bulwer*, III, 429), because he was not sufficiently favourable to Mehemet Ali. Louis Philippe was greatly pleased at the handsome tribute paid to Sébastiani by the British Government and made him a Marshal, but that hardly helped him to exercise much influence when he got back to Paris.

[2] From Granville, 13, 27 Jan., 14 Feb., 1840: *B.P.*; do., 31 Jan., 1840: *L.P.*, I, No. 470. Soult to Sébastiani, 26 Jan., 1840: Guizot, *Mémoires*, IV, 568.

isolated.   Beauvale himself dared not entrust his thoughts to an official despatch lest it be seen by members of the Cabinet who would disclose them to the French.   Metternich, he added a little later, was sending new instructions to Neumann which he hoped would make Palmerston's task easier.   These in fact were of little assistance.   They exposed, indeed, the inconsistencies of French policy.   But they recommended that the question of the Straits should first be settled separately by the Great Powers and the coercion of Mehemet be postponed until a more favourable moment.   This was exactly what the French party in the Cabinet desired and Lord Holland wrote a note strongly urging that Metternich's scheme be accepted.[1]

At St. Petersburg, on the other hand, both the Tsar and his Minister had been made even more bitter against France by the communication by Bloomfield, who was in charge in Clanricarde's temporary absence, of a despatch of Soult strongly critical of Russian policy.   They had received Brunnow's reports of his first interviews with great satisfaction, and Orlov said that any attack on the British fleet at the Dardanelles would be looked upon as an attack on Russia itself.   Nor did they react so strongly as Brunnow had feared to the changes which Palmerston subsequently proposed.   Nesselrode suggested that all mention of the number of ships should be left out of the agreement.   But though the Tsar's hatred of France made him ready to accept almost anything that Britain offered, his Ministers, while moved by the same anti-French feelings, were not so complaisant.   Nesselrode was shocked at the delay in the negotiations and by a speech of Peel which strongly advocated the French alliance.   He also complained of the proposal to send for a Turkish Plenipotentiary. The truth was, confessed Clanricarde, that there were two opposite motives acting on Russian policy.   Nesselrode above all wanted peace and talked of making some concession to Mehemet. The Tsar's main object was to isolate France.   The communication of Soult's despatch, for which he took full responsibility on his return, alone enabled him to get the necessary action by Russia.   But at any rate when this came it was very satisfactory. The Treaty of Unkiar Skelessi was virtually abandoned altogether

[1] From Beauvale, 12 Jan., 1840: *L.P.*, I, No. 453; do., 12 Jan., 3 Feb., 1840: *B.P.* Metternich to Neumann, 7 Feb., 1840: *F.O. Austria*, 293, with Minute by Lord Holland, 29 Feb., 1840.

and Britain placed on complete equality with Russia in any action in the Straits. And, most important of all, Brunnow was not to leave London but to remain as Envoy and Minister Extraordinary to carry on the negotiations. Both Tsar and Minister were convinced that France would never agree to action against Mehemet. This fact made the Tsar all the more ready to join with Britain for that purpose.[1]

At London, meanwhile, little could be done because of the new situation in France. On 20 February the refusal of the Chambers to make the grant to the Duc de Nemours drove Louis Philippe to violent expostulation, his wife to tears and the Cabinet to resignation. It was some time before a new Government could be formed. Thiers, in spite of the King's dislike of him, was the obvious successor to Soult. He shewed no great desire to assume the responsibility and tried to get Broglie to become Premier and Foreign Minister. But Broglie would not listen to Thiers whose return to office he was anxious to prevent. Soult was ready to resume office and much hurt that no one else, except the King, thought such a course desirable. The latter devised many other combinations but none were possible and eventually Thiers became President of the Council and Foreign Secretary; for nearly three weeks, however, the precarious nature of his position was almost the sole topic of Parisian society as he and Louis Philippe manoeuvred for position. Thiers' strength lay in the fact that he had control of a considerable portion of the Press, including the *Siècle*, which had a larger circulation than any other French newspaper. At last they came to an understanding, the King stating that Thiers' pacific views and attachment to the British alliance had won him over, and a handsome majority on the very controversial question of the disposal of the secret funds firmly established the new Ministry in office, too firmly indeed for Louis Philippe's liking. He was soon jealous of his Prime Minister.[2]

[1] From Clanricarde, 2, 14, 29 Jan., 11, 24 Feb., 3 March, 1840: *L.P.*, I, Nos. 491, 511 and *F.O. Russia*, 260. The dislike of the Russian Government to the inclusion of Turkey in the negotiations is carefully excluded from the *Levant Papers*. Brunnow's rank was not sufficiently high for him to be given the title of Ambassador. T. Schiemann (*Geschichte Russlands*, III, 393) states that it was a speech by Soult in the Chamber concerning Poland that made the Tsar go on.

[2] From Granville, 23 March, 1840: *B.P.* The principal influence on the French Press, however, was at this time Mehemet Ali himself whose subsidies were larger than those of the French Government. "He annually expends", reported Hodges, "350,000 francs on his mission in France over which Mons.

Thiers was later to claim, as Louis Philippe assured Granville at the time, that "the cornerstone of my policy has always been the English alliance".[1] He interpreted his policy, however, in a manner peculiarly his own. He made no concessions himself and expected the rest of Europe to give up their demands entirely. The situation was such that he had no alternative but to refuse to join Britain in the coercion of Mehemet Ali. His policy was, therefore, one of delay and obstruction, a course which, so he later stated, Granville advised him to pursue. But his imagination and energy and the influence on him of his study of the revolutionary and Napoleonic age made it impossible for him merely to remain passive. There is still some doubt as to how far he went in actively promoting a settlement between the Sultan and the Pasha while he was ostensibly still bound to pursue a common policy with the other Great Powers in accordance with the note of 27 July. But it is clear that up to the last minute he hoped to force Palmerston to abandon his policy completely.[2]

Guizot had arrived in London on the 27 February before Thiers came to power and it was for some time uncertain whether he would remain to serve the new Ministry. The advice of his friends on that point was conflicting. But Guizot was anxious to keep out of the melée at Paris for the time being and undoubtedly attracted by the new and unexpected position which he now occupied. He had never before been out of France and had no knowledge of diplomacy—except perhaps what his intimate connection with Princess Lieven had taught him. She was, however, not a very suitable instructress for one of Guizot's habits and temperament. There was much amusement when she followed him across the Channel at the crisis of the negotiations in which, as will be seen, she played no very helpful part. Guizot was enthusiastically received by the Hollands who were delighted to have an Ambassador so cultured and interested in the kind of table talk

---

Ouvrard presides. I know for a fact that he has given 100,000 fr. to the Journal des Débats, 35,000 to the Semaphore of Marseilles and 20,000 each to those other French newspapers as a remuneration for the advocacy of his cause for 12 months, and I believe that he places more reliance on the sympathies of the French nation as generated and fomented by the above organs than on the virtual support of the Executive Government." (To Palmerston, 23 Jan., 1840: *B.P.*)

[1] N. W. Senior, *Conversations with M. Thiers, M. Guizot, etc.*, I, 4.

[2] In an interesting article ("La politique de Thiers pendant la crise orientale de 1840", *Revue Historique*, Jan., 1938, pp. 72–96) Professor C. H. Pouthas comes to conclusions about Thiers very much the same as those put forward here.

that filled the Holland House circle. In other quarters his rather undistinguished mien and stiff bourgeois manners did not make a very powerful impression. But he was always a good foil to the flamboyant Thiers and could be held up by those who attacked Palmerston's policy as a model of pacific and orthodox behaviour. Ostensibly he was on excellent terms with his chief but there was no real confidence between them. Louis Philippe, on the other hand, as the situation developed grew more and more to trust Guizot.

The uncertainty in France and the inevitable delay before the Russian attitude could be known prevented any progress being made in the negotiations in February and March. Brunnow kept himself in the background. The French Ambassador began quietly, explored London society and the London suburbs with a rather naïve curiosity but gradually learnt the cross-currents of the political situation. Neumann's new instructions reached him in the middle of the month and brought him, after a long delay of which he bitterly complained, once more into communication with Palmerston. Metternich's caution had moderated the rather excessive zeal with which Neumann had cooperated with Brunnow while at the same time his support of coercion was toned down. The ostensible instructions were communicated to Palmerston and the Cabinet, where, Neumann reported, they won strong approval. Metternich himself moved steadily in the direction of concession to Mehemet. He would, reported Beauvale in the middle of March, be prepared to give him Syria for his own life. He considered that the policy of coercion had practically been abandoned and that all that the Great Powers could do was to guarantee the Sultan against further attacks and await Mehemet's demise before further action was taken. The death of Clam at the beginning of March was a heavy blow to Metternich and to Beauvale's attempts to get active Austrian cooperation. He had now no means, the Ambassador confessed, of persuading Metternich to allow Austrian troops to join British naval forces.

Meanwhile Guizot had preliminary and non-committal discussions with Palmerston in which the difference between France and England was frankly reviewed. Guizot said that Mehemet could only be coerced with the help of Russia, a greater danger to the Ottoman Empire than the evil it was to remedy. Indeed the Sultan could not govern Syria if it were given back to him and his

power did not depend on the extent of his territory.   All this was
said in as conciliatory a manner as possible in accordance with the
advice of Desages who in a friendly note had warned the new
envoy not to reproach Palmerston but to help him to find his way
back to the alliance. •But Palmerston shewed no signs of yielding.
He replied that all history showed this last assertion to be false,
that Russia would be no danger if controlled by a Concert, but a
menace that might well cause war if she were forced to act by
herself.   But Russian troops would not be necessary.   And he
proceeded to sketch out a plan for "an expedition to Alexandria
to strike at the heart of the Pasha's power. . . .   I reminded him
that about 13000 English had made good their landing in Egypt in
face of a French army of 20 and 30000 men, and that a combined
Austrian and Turkish expedition would drive like dust before
them the artisans of the dockyard and the wretched Egyptians
whom Mehemet Ali has now in Egypt, and that if he brought
Mehemet's army from Syria to defend Egypt, the expedition
would only have to change its direction and go and take possession
of Syria then left defenceless."[1]

Thus it was necessary to look to Austria for help and the prospect there was not too good.   Nevertheless Palmerston still saw in
Austrian cooperation the main means of influencing the British
Cabinet in the right direction.   While he waited to see what
would happen in France he tried to prepare the way for action.
If Guizot refused to cooperate he would go on without France,
he told Neumann in February, and he believed that he could get
his Cabinet to agree to do so.   "Let the French say what they like,"
he replied to Granville's warnings, "they *cannot* go to war with the
Four Powers in support of Mehemet Ali."   Brunnow had of
course promised him all support.   But it was necessary, Palmerston said a little later, to have some Austrian troops, so that it
would not seem that the policy of coercion was only approved by
Russia.   Neumann could not help but admire the patience and
persistence with which Palmerston opposed the French party in
the Cabinet.   Clarendon, he said, was the head of it and indeed

[1] Desages to Bourqueney, 2 March, 1840: *Bour. P., Appendix p.* 897. To
Beauvale, 12 March, 1840: *B.P.* Guizot's account (5 March) in his *Mémoires* (V,
33–45) attributes to Palmerston the suggestion of a Russo-Turkish expedition, but
this was written long afterwards and dressed up the despatch to Soult on which
it is founded. (*A.A.E.* and Guichen, *Crise d'Orient*, 213–216, which gives an
imperfect summary of it.)

from now on people began to talk of Clarendon as a possible successor to Palmerston. Neumann was induced to assist Palmerston to overcome the reluctance of his colleagues and had conversations with Lansdowne, Minto, Clarendon and Lord Holland. The promise of Austrian help would, Neumann informed Metternich, make all the difference to the situation.[1]

The instructions of Thiers to Guizot were necessarily only a repetition of the usual formula, the impossibility of coercing Mehemet since France could not do so. They went indeed beyond previous instructions for they insisted that it was necessary to take into account not only "l'ambition raisonnable mais encore l'amour propre" of the Pasha. His son, Ibrahim must, therefore, succeed to all Syria. A solemn warning was added that the Alliance depended upon the agreement of Britain and France on a question so fundamental. When Palmerston in answer to this said that he could not give the hereditary possession to Mehemet and take it away from his children, Guizot made a lame reply and, as he reported, the conversation then languished. Palmerston's reticence had the effect which he no doubt desired. Guizot warned Thiers that while the British Government was anxious not to destroy the alliance, they saw in the present situation an opportunity to protect their own interests in the East against both Russia and France which they did not wish to let slip.[2]

Palmerston informed Neumann immediately of this unpromising beginning and told him frankly that everything depended on the attitude of Austria. If she would give some help, say troops to Candia, not only would she satisfy his colleagues and British public opinion which disliked acting with Russia, but France herself would be forced to go with them. He would make a new attempt, he told Neumann, when Nourri arrived. The Turk could appeal with great moral effect to the joint note of 27 July, 1839. Meanwhile he needed, he said, all the help Neumann could give him with the Cabinet. He had, indeed, the latter reported, only four members of it on his side, Lansdowne, Minto, Hob-

---

[1] From Clanricarde, 24 Feb., 1840: *B.P.* Metternich to Neumann, 7 Feb., 1840: *F.O. Austria*, 292. To Granville, 11 Feb., 1840: *B.P.* Neumann to Metternich, 9, 10, 11, 18 Feb., 9, 11 March, 1840: *V. St. A.*

[2] Thiers to Guizot, 12 March, 1840; Guizot to Thiers, 16 March, 1840: *A.A.E.* (small extracts in Guichen, *La Crise d'Orient*, 262–263). The original draft had referred to the 'vanité' of Mehemet which Thiers altered to 'amour propre'.

house and John Russell.   All the rest with Lord Holland at their
head refused to break with France.   He urged Metternich to give
Palmerston the necessary support.

The test of the Austrian attitude would come when the Turkish
representative appeared.   Ponsonby had been able to get Reschid
to send orders to Nourri Pasha to go at once to London while
Chekib, considered a more reliable envoy, would shortly follow
from Constantinople with the ostensible object of congratulating
Queen Victoria on her marriage, a happy thought of the young
Sultan himself.   Meanwhile it was encouraging to know that the
Russian representative had received orders from St. Petersburg to
cooperate with Ponsonby in inspiring the Porte with confidence
in the Great Powers, while, though Ponsonby himself wished to
have specific instructions in case of an attack by Ibrahim, Hodges
reported from Alexandria that there were no signs of Mehemet
being bold enough to order his son to advance.[1]

Meanwhile Neumann, who had been warned by Metternich not
to be too intimate with Brunnow, reported with a certain satisfaction the Russian envoy's growing irritation and sense of frustration at the delay.   Brunnow had expected to accomplish his
mission in a few weeks.   Now he had given up hope and was preparing to return to Darmstadt.   But towards the end of March he
received the new instructions from Nesselrode which informed
him of his permanent appointment to London and the acceptance
by his Court of practically all Palmerston's demands.   This new
concession which Neumann attributed to the fear of a new clash
with Britain in Central Asia at a time when Russia was especially
weak, was conveyed in a private letter.   It was, therefore, some
time before his new position could be made generally known in
London, and Brunnow's influence on the negotiations was to
Neumann's great pleasure sensibly diminished.   On the other
hand, Bülow had been sent back to replace the young and inexperi-
enced Werther.   In accordance with Metternich's instructions
Neumann did everything possible to bring him into the negotiations.   The two determined to work together for a solution of the
Eastern Question by making great concessions to France.   At the
same time the *amour propre* of Neumann, who had now such a

---

[1] Neumann to Metternich, 17, 23 March, 1840: *V. St. A.*   From Ponsonby,
26, 28 Jan., 18, 26 Feb., 1840: *L.P.*, I, Nos. 513, 516, and *F.O. Turkey*, 392.
From Hodges, 6 Feb., 1840: *L.P.*, I, No. 504.

central position in the negotiations, made him strive his hardest to produce a result.[1]

The diplomatic moves were now concentrated on Nourri Pasha, the rather stupid and somewhat suspect Turkish representative who came to London from Paris at Reschid's orders. Granville reported that he was against coercion and he had told Thiers, who tried to get him to promise to advocate a direct arrangement between the Sultan and Mehemet, that he had no Full Powers and would sign nothing. But, as Palmerston had foreseen, once Nourri got to London he subjected himself entirely to the advice of those on the spot. "Poor old Nourri", he told Beauvale, "is a perfect cipher but he can hold his pen and sign his name." This is exactly what Nourri did. He had indeed some difficult moments. Palmerston advised him to appeal to the note of 27 July and claim the support of the Powers because the Porte had been so weakened since Navarino by the Great Powers themselves. To draft such a note was far beyond Nourri's powers and he had no capable assistant. In this extremity he turned to Neumann who was delighted to supply the necessary document. Neumann left out, it would seem wisely, all reference to Navarino, but drafted a vigorous note. Palmerston, unaware of the real author, made one important alteration and so Nourri was able to send a compelling appeal to the representatives of the Great Powers. It emphasised the promises made by them to the Porte, narrated the nefarious conduct of Mehemet, and demanded their cooperation in order to put an end to evils of so serious a nature, for which purpose, Nourri informed them, he was empowered to conclude a Convention. It was expressly said that Mehemet ought to surrender all territory outside Egypt. This claim was due to Palmerston for Neumann had tried to leave the way open to the largest possible concessions.[2]

This was an important step forward but what difficulties still remained were seen when the Powers came to consider how it should be answered. Palmerston invited Guizot to join the other four Powers in a conference to draft a joint reply. Guizot of course could do no more than acknowledge the receipt of the note

---

[1] Neumann to Metternich, 24 March, 1840: *V. St. A.*

[2] Neumann to Metternich, 11 April, 1840: *V. St. A.* In order to leave nothing in his handwriting Neumann dictated the note to Nourri's interpreter. Guizot saw that Nourri could not have drafted it himself and thought that Palmerston had done it. (Guizot to Thiers, 13 April, 1840: *A.A.E.*) Bülow alone was told the truth. Nourri to Palmerston, 7 April, 1840: *L.P.*, I, No. 541.

and refer it to his Government. Thiers at first said that no answer would be given. He refused, he told Guizot, to take it seriously. It simply repeated the old arguments which had been so often refuted. Whatever France meant by her signature of the note of 27 July she did not mean what Nourri demanded. And if she were criticised for not going on with the others at London, had she not the same right to withdraw, if she were in a minority, as Russia had to refuse to negotiate at Vienna? This would indeed have let the other Powers know exactly where France stood and Guizot with great wisdom refused to act on it. It would simply leave open the way for a Four Power treaty without France. But though no formal answer was made by Guizot, Thiers stated frankly to Granville that France must refuse to enter into any conference to discuss the coercion of Mehemet Ali because her views on that subject differed so radically from those of the other four Powers.[1]

Even agreement between the Four was, however, found to be difficult. Brunnow had disliked bringing in a Turk, partly, so Neumann alleged, because it deprived him of the premier role in the negotiations. He joined with Palmerston in wishing to emphasise the threat of sanctions in the reply, but Neumann and Bülow, who met his violent and insistent tone with a concerted coolness of manner, insisted that the cooperation of the Powers to implement the note of 27 July should only be stated in the most general terms in order to enable France to subscribe to it. "The negotiation is thus well launched," wrote Palmerston, "and I hope it may be brought to a satisfactory end, *with* France, if possible, but *without* France, if she will not concur." But when France made her vague response nothing had really been agreed by the rest and it could hardly be claimed that much progress had been made.[2]

Events in other parts of the world now threw obstacles in the way of agreement. The violent quarrel which had arisen between

---

[1] From Granville, 13, 17 April, 1840: *F.O. France*, 602 (*L.P.*, I, Nos. 545, 547). Thiers to Guizot, 14 April, 1840: *A.A.E.* Guizot, *Mémoires*, V, 78. Granville's despatch of the 17 April was often used by Palmerston in later discussions of the French attitude at this time.

[2] Guizot to Thiers, 7 April, 1840: Guizot, *Mémoires*, V, 76. Neumann to Metternich, 11 April, 1840: *V. St. A.* Palmerston to Nourri Effendi, 11 April, 1840: *L.P.*, I, No. 543. Neumann wrote that Palmerston insisted on the word 'immediately' and redrafted the note so that it enabled the other Powers to act together without France.

Britain and Naples over the British sulphur mines alarmed Metternich and made him still more pacific on the Eastern Question,
while it gave Thiers an opportunity for shewing his friendship
for England by acting as mediator. The situation in Central Asia
was causing both Britain and Russia anxiety. Bülow indeed
informed Neumann that according to Russian information both
Nesselrode and Orlov were sick of the Eastern Question and only
the Tsar's hatred of Louis Philippe, on which Brunnow played in
his despatches, prevented them from giving way to France. The
Tsar himself showed some impatience at the long delay and
told Clanricarde that moderation so far from bringing France in
would have the contrary effect.[1]

Palmerston, while maintaining his position in all essentials
during this period and urging that the Four should find a way to
act without France, had necessarily to wait on events. His principal object was to keep Austria firm and here he had but indifferent success. Metternich told Beauvale that he had come to the
conclusion that coercion at this time was impossible, that Mehemet,
had better be given Syria for life, care being taken that it was on
his death split up amongst his descendants. Meanwhile the Great
Powers should guarantee the *status quo* and prevent any attack.
He promised to await Palmerston's reply before stating this view
definitely to the other Powers, but on 25 April in a long and
pessimistic review he shewed behind a mass of verbiage his conviction that the situation was hopeless if France did not join the
other Powers. Palmerston meanwhile used every effort to shew
Neumann that the coercion of Mehemet was perfectly feasible
without France. He was encouraged in this view by the optimistic
reports and letters which Ponsonby was sending from Constantinople.[2]

Ponsonby had, it is true, plenty of difficulties to cope with. His
confidence in the good effects of the new reforms ebbed rapidly
and it was soon seen that they increased rather than diminished
the rapacity and corruption of the provincial governors. The
combination of the modern Reschid with Husrev and the old gang
at the Porte was an uneasy one, and Ponsonby was soon once more

[1] Neumann to Metternich, 3 May, 1840: *V. St. A.* From Clanricarde,
4 May, 1840: *F.O. Russia*, 260.
[2] Neumann to Metternich, 3, 8 May, 1840: *V. St. A.* Metternich to Neumann, 25 April, 1840: Metternich, *Mémoires*, VI, 454. From Beauvale, 24,
25 April, 1840: *F.O. Austria*, 290.

in the thick of intricate manoeuvres concerned with changes in the Ministry. Reschid himself was surrounded by Frenchmen, and Ponsonby occasionally suspected his complete loyalty to the British view. But on the main point of holding the Porte firm on the question of Mehemet Ali he was always able to report satisfactorily. The negotiations and intrigues between Alexandria and Constantinople never ceased, and on occasion Mehemet seemed to have made some progress. But Ponsonby was always able to pull back the Sultan's Ministers on to the right line by an exertion of his vigorous personality. Thus, when Reschid wished to make a vague reply to Mehemet's official offers to restore the fleet if the rest of his demands were conceded, he insisted on the despatch of an uncompromising rejoinder. Though he reported more than once that Pontois was urging Reschid to come to a separate arrangement with the Pasha, that Minister always informed him at once of the approaches made to him. Husrev, however, though in the eyes of the world the symbol of opposition to Mehemet, could not be trusted. Mehemet was gradually penetrating the Harem of the new Sultan who proved to be no less susceptible to the influence of favourites than his predecessors, and the Sultan's Mother was very suspect. But no one was found courageous enough to defy the Ambassador, especially as he now had the support of the representatives of the Eastern Powers.

Ponsonby was also using all his energy not only to make the Porte safe from attack by Ibrahim but even to prepare the way for an offensive against him. By incessant pressure he got troops collected to oppose any advance of the Egyptian forces and Chrysanowski placed, though unofficially, in control of them. This necessitated the removal of both the Commander-in-Chief and the Minister of War, and it was not until the end of May that the process was completed and Ponsonby could advise Palmerston that Constantinople was safe from attack by Ibrahim.[1]

But in addition Ponsonby began to prepare for the attack on Mehemet, and his foresight and energy and the advice which he now gave to Palmerston contributed greatly to the rapid success of the autumn. He assured Palmerston at an early stage that the

[1] From Ponsonby, 15, 22, 27 April: *B.P.*; do., 26, 28 Jan., 7, 23 March, 10, 25, 26 April, 7, 14, 15, 17, 26 May, 1840: *F.O. Turkey*, 392–396. *L.P.*, I (Nos. 494–496, 504, 513, 526, 530, 570, 571, 582–588) leaves a great deal out.

Sultan would facilitate the establishment of a blockade and be able to send ships to join in it. Even at the beginning of January he claimed "I will raise the Druses against Ibrahim if you choose" Then reports began to come in of the growing discontent of the Syrians, in which the powerful chief Emir Bechir shared, at the enforcement of conscription and other arbitrary measures of Ibrahim. As early as March the Druses, the most warlike of the tribes, secretly appealed to British agents for help from Britain. Ponsonby suggested that he should get the Porte to promise them their ancient rights and perhaps the city of Acre. The reply given to them was that Britain was the upholder of the Sultan's authority, but Ponsonby had no doubt that he could raise the whole country if Britain shewed that she intended to act. "I could if you direct it bring this [unrest] to a head," he wrote in March . . . "I know how to act upon the Druses. I think it much to be desired that the inhabitants of Lebanon should have privileges secured to them by our aid and I think it could be done." He admitted that it was essential for either France or Russia to be on the British side so that the other would be held in check. In that case the task was an easy one. "Neither will stir and whatever we desire can be done. As to the power of Mehemet I think it is despicable. I have told you I can raise the Druses. All Syrians that can get a musket will act against the Pasha. The Sultan's flag united with the English will bring all Mussulmen to our side." This was an exact prophecy of what was to take place later on, but at this period Ponsonby almost alone of those in a position of responsibility believed such a course to be possible.[1]

Hodges, indeed, was sending in his private letters a somewhat similar view. According to him Mehemet was depending on the dissensions of the Great Powers which he thought would prevent effective action. The Russian Consul, Medem, spoke Turkish and had many private interviews with the Pasha, and to a late date Hodges continued to reiterate his suspicions that Russia was behind Mehemet's obstinacy. But at the same time he asserted that Mehemet would not stand up to Britain if she acted alone. He deprecated an attack on Alexandria which would need 15,000 troops, but naval action would he thought intimidate the Pasha.

[1] From Ponsonby, 8 Jan., 23 March, 8 April, 1840: *B.P.*; do., 3 March, 1840 (with Consul Moore to Ponsonby, 21 Feb., 1840), *L.P.*, I, 526; do., 3 March, 1840: *F.O. Turkey*, 392.

Hodges' judgments are emotional and rash but he also foresaw that Mehemet could be easily defeated.[1]

Palmerston had need of all the encouragement that Ponsonby could give during the next six weeks. He got little from other sources and those on whom he had counted most were most urgent that he should give way. Guizot was allowed by his chief to negotiate, though not to take part in a conference, but every communication from Paris shewed that Thiers would not accept less than Mehemet demanded. Palmerston had agreed immediately to Thiers' request to bring back the remains of Napoleon from St. Helena and hoped the French would be more malleable: "This will amuse the public mind for six months to come and make those full grown children think less of other things." Neumann told Metternich that he by no means shared Palmerston's illusion that effective sanctions could be taken without the assistance of France. He and Palmerston, however, were still working closely together and it was at his insistence that a new and important offer was made to Guizot.

The new offer was better than that made and withdrawn in October, 1839—not only the Pashalik of Acre, but the fortress and part of lower Syria to Beirut to Mehemet for life. The French official answer was that Mehemet Ali must be consulted before they could reply, but Thiers told Guizot that he would not accept it. No other reply was made until June when it was said that Syria could not be cut in two. Palmerston attributed this obstinacy to the influence of Edward Ellice, who, whatever his language to Granville, had been intriguing against Palmerston at Paris. The Embassy staff also, he said, was not without blame, a remark at which Granville was much hurt. Thiers, he wrote, had given his reason for the refusal, the impossibility of coercing Mehemet, and Granville clearly agreed with him.

Neumann was indignant at French intransigeance, but Palmerston said there was nothing to do but wait. He would go on without France if she refused, he told Neumann. But for the Cabinet, the latter thought, he would do so at once. In order to overcome the Cabinet's reluctance Austrian cooperation in sanctions must be obtained. The real difficulty lay not in Paris or Alexandria but in London itself. When Palmerston warmly defended Russia's good faith in the House, his opponents in the

---

[1] From Hodges, 23 Jan., 1, 21 April, 1840: *B.P.*

Cabinet said that he was being duped by her. Melbourne told him that, though the "large majority" of the Cabinet would support him, it would be with fear and reluctance. It was true that Brunnow was doing everything he could to prevent an arrangement with France. Thus Neumann had to report complete failure to his chief, though, as will be seen, the fact that this offer was made and rejected in such a manner had an important effect on the last stage of the discussions. But Metternich by no means approved the step. The offer should only have been made, he said, after it had been agreed to by the other three and the British Cabinet. He scolded Neumann for taking so much on himself. Nevertheless the incident seems to have produced considerable effect. Metternich noted on Neumann's despatches that Britain and Russia had the means of action if they chose to employ them and that while the cooperation of Russia was indispensable to success that of France was not.[1]

This situation came to a head in June when Chekib Pasha arrived from Constantinople to replace Nourri who was only too glad to get back to Paris. Chekib, who was from the first anxious for a settlement, received shortly after his arrival new instructions which seemed to make one urgent and was ready for almost any concession to obtain it. He claimed with some reason that Britain ought by now to have settled what action should be taken. Neumann agreed with him and determined to use Chekib to force a solution on Palmerston even if it meant conceding the whole of Syria. Thus after Palmerston and Brunnow had told Chekib that there was no necessity for haste, Neumann and Bülow gave him contrary advice and without Palmerston's knowledge Neumann drafted a note from him to the Great Powers, and another to Palmerston, pressing for a decision. The note made no stipulations but the language used implied that great concessions to the Pasha would be made. Since Palmerston knew that he could not get the reply to Chekib's communication which he desired, he played for delay and refused to do anything, in spite of a stiff note

---

[1] To Beauvale, 12, 19 May, 1840: *B.P.*; do., 20 May, 1840: *L.P.*, I, No. 575 and *F.O. Austria*, 288. Neumann to Metternich, 9, 12, (*Appendix*, p. 876–7), 19, 22 May, 10 June, 1840: *V. St. A.* with Metternich's notes. Guizot, *Mémoires*, V, 85–88, 189–190. To Granville, 29 May, 1840; From Granville, 1 June, 1840: *B.P.* "I have seen a great deal of Ellice," wrote Princess Lieven to Earl Grey, 19 May, 1840 (G. Le Strange, *Corres. Princess Lieven and Grey*, III, 317). From Melbourne, 7 June, 1840: *B.P.* Lord Holland was already talking of recording a minute of protest.

sent to him by Neumann which enclosed his official report to Metternich of the urgent necessity of immediate action. Chekib himself was rebuked by Palmerston for telling the other representatives that he would settle at any price, a thing he protested he had never done. Neumann's exasperation and frustration were so great that he prepared to appeal to Melbourne and the Cabinet. They should at least be made aware, he said, how far Austria was prepared to go to obtain French assent and thus a pacific solution of the whole matter. And in his desire for action he took an even graver step. For, in a private and unofficial conversation with Guizot, he offered him the whole of Syria including Aleppo and Scanderoon, though of course not with hereditary tenure. When Guizot transmitted this offer to Thiers he obviously thought that France had won the game. He told Neumann that if Palmerston delayed much longer he would send Chekib an answer himself.[1]

When the situation was at this critical stage, more critical perhaps than was realised by Palmerston, who never lost his confidence or sangfroid, it was transformed by further news from Constantinople and a change in Metternich's attitude. From Constantinople came reports of three important alterations in the situation. First the deposition of Husrev, which had been foreseen and indeed welcomed by Ponsonby, who thought that the old man's "persevering venality and corruption" entirely justified it. But by the world it was regarded as a symbol that the Porte was going at last to make terms with Mehemet, and the Vice-Roy himself received the news of the fall of his old enemy with loud demonstrations of joy. He sent at once an emissary, Sami Bey, to offer to return the Turkish fleet. He had high hopes that he would be able to retain all his conquests and obtain the hereditary possession of Syria. The situation at Constantinople was at any

---

[1] Neumann to Metternich, 10, 12, 15 June, 1840: *V. St. A.* Guizot, *Mémoires*, V, 197–201. (Neumann made the offer on the 12 June, Guizot reported it on the 15 June, Thiers on the 19 sent a reply which was not clear, Guizot asked for an explanation on the 24 June, Thiers replied on the 30 June that he could only accept hereditary Syria which he had meant in his previous reply.) Chekib to Palmerston, 31 May, 1840: *L.P.*, I, No. 580. This was addressed to the representatives of all the Great Powers. There is another addressed to Palmerston personally (do., No. 579) asking for quick action. From Neumann, 10 June, 1840, (with his ostensible despatch of 10 June): *B.P.* In a letter of 15 August Neumann confessed to Palmerston that he had offered the Pashalik of Aleppo to Guizot who had demanded it 'hereditarily' which he had refused. *F.O. Austria*, 292.

rate growing more serious and the Russian and Austrian Ambassadors reported on it to their courts with far more alarm than Ponsonby himself at first shewed.

The British Ambassador, however, added more definite information on a topic to which he had previously alluded, the endeavours of M. Coste, a French journalist, on intimate terms with Thiers, to persuade Reschid to make a deal with Mehemet Ali. Though the final proof is not extant it is almost certain that Thiers was cognisant of and had perhaps inspired this attempt to defeat the negotiation at London on which France was still ostensibly engaged. It was at any rate one of the main reasons why he refused Guizot's advice to accept the offer of Syria for life and told him that, now that Husrev was gone, the matter would soon be arranged at Constantinople.

Lastly, Ponsonby was able to report that the Syrian insurrection had begun, that the insurgents were appealing to England and France and that he had advised Reschid to encourage the revolt and promised to try to get the British Admiral to send ships to Beirut. Since the mission of Sami Bey was supported by the Sultan's mother and the Sultan was anxious to get back his fleet, the situation was not without danger, though he and Stürmer hoped to prevent any yielding to Mehemet.[1]

The news of these events had important effects both at St. Petersburg and Vienna. They likewise startled Brunnow, who also received peremptory orders from Nesselrode, and made him almost as anxious as Neumann to bring the negotiation to an end. He had, hitherto, like Palmerston, been playing for time. He now joined Neumann in urging Palmerston to force the issue. But above all they helped Metternich to a decision, which he seems to have been contemplating for some time, to contribute Austrian

---

[1] From Ponsonby, 20 May, 23 June, 1840: *B.P.*; do., 29 May, 8, 9, 23 June, 1840: *L.P.*, I, No. 613, and *F.O. Turkey*, 394. For M. Coste's intrigue see Major John Hall, *England and the Orleans Monarchy*, 270–272. These letters were obtained by the ubiquitous Vogorides. (From Ponsonby, 13 Sept., 1840: *B.P.*) Thiers always denied that he had tried to make a separate arrangement between the Porte and Mehemet and no doubt this was true so far as official action was concerned. For his confident belief that it would ensue see Guizot, *Mémoires*, V, 206, and his comment: "C'était précisément là le vœu du cabinet français, et le but vers lequel il tendait constamment en dépit des entraves que lui imposait l'engagement d'action commune contracté entre les cinq puissances par la note du 27 juillet 1839." Cochelet to Thiers, 26 May, 1840: E. Driault, *L'Egypte et l'Europe*, 1839–1841, II, 295. In June Thiers tried to send Bresson to Constantinople but that wily diplomat, one of Louis Philippe's personal appointments, refused to go. (From Will. Russell, 24 June, 1840: *B.P.*)

forces for joint coercive action even if France would not agree to associate herself with the other Powers.[1]

Palmerston himself, though imperfectly aware of the intentions of Neumann and Bülow, could not help but be moved by the insistence from so many quarters that the decision must be taken. For long he resisted all their attempts to make concessions to France. When asked for an alternative plan he confessed that he had not got one but was waiting on events. Finally he agreed that part of Syria should be offered to Mehemet and the fact stated in the reply to Chekib. Neumann meant that part to extend to Aleppo and hoped that, if the Cabinet agreed, France would then be forced to come in by the threat that the Four Powers were united and would go on without her. He then with great energy tried to influence all the various parties whose consent was indispensable. He urged on Melbourne the necessity of Cabinet backing for Palmerston if France was to be brought in. Melbourne, however, was most pessimistic and said that without France it would be impossible to get more than Adana from the Pasha, perhaps not even that. He talked of the dangers from Russia and was in no way comforted when Neumann tried to shew him that there was every prospect of obtaining agreement. With other members of the Cabinet Neumann had more success and got them to agree that they would consent to such a plan as he had proposed if Palmerston put it before them.

Guizot, as he had long threatened to do, now replied to Chekib himself in a note which promised nothing at all. He could not say more because Thiers refused to make any concessions. This was a mistake on Guizot's part as it emphasised the isolation of France. But when Neumann pointed out how much Palmerston's reputation was involved, Guizot promised to do his utmost to get a new offer accepted. It looked both to Guizot and to Neumann as if agreement was in sight on the basis of giving to Mehemet all

[1] Neumann to Metternich, 12 June, 1840: *V. St. A.* The fall of Husrev was not reported officially by Ponsonby until the 8 June, but he had indicated it must happen on the 24 May. The news seems to have reached London on 11 June. The reports of the Austrian and Russian Ambassadors had been pessimistic before the final denouément and it must have been before the news of Husrev's fall reached him that Nesselrode instructed Brunnow to press for a decision. Bloomfield knew nothing of this and reported on the 20 June that the Russian Government had become 'indifferent' to the subject. *F.O. Russia,* 261.

Syria for life, as Metternich had proposed in April, if France would agree to ensure Mehemet's acceptance.[1]

It is improbable that Palmerston would ever have consented to have gone so far, but Neumann had in fact pressed his scheme too fast. Chekib himself, indeed, professed satisfaction and Bülow was assisting Neumann with all his power. But Brunnow said that he refused to pass under the Caudine Forks of France. He urged Palmerston not to give way. Even more important was it that Guizot could not get his chief to move an inch from his position. Thiers naturally refused contemptuously, when Guizot at Palmerston's request pressed for an answer, the offer of the Pashalik of Acre, thus giving official proof of refusal to compromise which Palmerston could lay before the Cabinet. But he also would have nothing to do with the suggestion that Neumann and Bülow were putting forward with Chekib's consent of all Syria, though without hereditary possession. The news of Husrev's fall confirmed him in the belief that the question would be settled at Constantinople. There was no hurry, he told Guizot. Both his Ambassador and Neumann were helpless. In his *Mémoires* Guizot claims that he himself was aware of the danger of the situation. He does not mention what provoked the mingled amusement and irritation of the Diplomatic Corps, that Princess Lieven had arrived from Paris to join the pedantic but obviously lovesick Ambassador. What advice she gave is not exactly known but it seems certain that she led Guizot astray on one all important point. For the King of Prussia had died on 7 June, and she extracted from Bülow the information that he had not received Full Powers from his new monarch and deduced from that fact that a treaty could not be signed at once.

Thus the Austrian plan could not go forward with the prospect that France would accept it. Nevertheless Neumann insisted that the Cabinet should be informed of how far Austria was prepared to go, and Palmerston promised that if they would not accept his own line he would put the other before them, though he did not say he would support it himself. Since Brunnow declared that the Austrian plan was nothing less than the French plan in disguise he was backing Palmerston strongly. On the 30 June Neumann had

[1] Neumann to Metternich, 22, (*Appendix*, p. 878) 23, 26 June, 1840: *V. St. A.* Note of Guizot to Chekib, 21 June, 1840: Guizot, *Mémoires*, V, 443. A. Hasenclever, *Die orientalische Frage*, 155–156, gives Bülow's account of the intricate negotiations of these days.

little hopes of what to him would seem a satisfactory result. In either case Russia stood to gain. If the Cabinet accepted Palmerston's plan, France would be isolated, secretly the real desire of Russia. If not, then the affair would most probably fall into Russian hands to settle at some future date.[1]

But Palmerston was by no means in despair. The news of the Syrian revolt had at last revealed a method of expelling Ibrahim from Syria, if the chance were taken at once. "I will fairly own", he wrote later to Ponsonby, "that till this insurrection broke out I did not clearly see my way as to the means by which we could drive Mehemet out of Syria." Now that had appeared he was most eager of all to get an agreement and ready to force the issue with the Cabinet. And Neumann just in time was given hope by receiving from Metternich the new instructions which authorised him to offer Austrian assistance in coercion without the participation of France. He at once communicated the despatch to Palmerston for use with his colleagues at the meeting of the Cabinet, where it had a decisive influence on the course of events.[2]

The discussions had now reached an acute stage. When Palmerston pressed for a decision, Melbourne was now of the opinion that the majority of the Cabinet would not agree to his plan. A meeting on 5 July shewed that this forecast was correct. Clarendon, who with Holland was the most intractable, complained to Melbourne that it was too vague. Palmerston immediately sent his resignation to Melbourne who, however, entreated him to await another Cabinet before he finally made up his mind. The Cabinet, he added with characteristic insouciance, might very likely be forced to resign on another difficulty, and was that not better than revealing their differences over the Eastern Question? He suggested that Palmerston should wait for the result of next day's division.

[1] Neumann to Metternich, 29, 30 June, 1840: *V. St. A.* Guizot, *Mémoires*, V, 199–203. Neumann's acid comments on Princess Lieven were no doubt specially meant to please her old lover. He says that she in vain tried to pump Lady Palmerston and to extract information from Bülow.

[2] To Ponsonby, 15 July, 1840: *B.P.* Metternich to Neumann, 24 June, 1840: *F.O. Austria*, 292. Palmerston received on 28 June a despatch of 10 June from Ponsonby (*L.P.*, I, No. 596), giving Hodges' opinion that Mehemet could be overcome by naval action on the Syrian coast and confirming the news which had already been sent of the discontent in Syria. This seems to have been the information to which he alludes in his letter. Much previous information had already come in of a less definitive kind. Moore's report of 10 June, as sent by Ponsonby did not arrive till 12 July, but it may have reached Palmerston earlier by another route. (*L.P.*, I, No. 613.)

Palmerston's reply was crushing. His letter reviewed the whole course of the negotiation and came to the conclusion that if Britain now refused to go forward with the three Governments the Ottoman Empire would be divided into two parts, one of which would be under the control of Russia and the other of France. Twice before, in 1833 and in 1835, had Palmerston been overruled by the Cabinet when he tried to find means to preserve the Ottoman Empire. He was so certain now that he was right that, if he were wrong on this, he could, he wrote, be of no further use to the Cabinet.

Melbourne was at last fully aroused to the gravity of the situa-tion. He entreated Palmerston to await the result of another Cabinet before he took the fatal step. This Palmerston agreed to do stating that he had thought it fairer to give Melbourne a free hand and had not thought his resignation would necessarily break up the Cabinet. To this Melbourne replied in a note obviously written in great haste and agitation, that his resignation would dissolve the Government. A last attempt by Lord John Russell to find some compromise seems to have had no effect at all.

A further Cabinet was held on the 8th and this time, after a long discussion, Palmerston was triumphant. Melbourne's endeavours to prevent a rupture at the last minute may have influenced Lord Holland and Clarendon. Palmerston's threat to break up the Cabinet was no doubt the most important factor in forcing the decision. But the news of the Syrian insurrection gave him a powerful reason for acting immediately. The official refusal of France to agree to the scheme which Palmerston and Neumann had proposed shewed that he had made concessions which had been contemptuously put on one side. He was also able to shew, partly by means of a despatch of Apponyi, that Thiers was playing false and seeking to make a separate arrangement at Constantinople. And the news that Austria would join in coercive action without France made just that extra bit of difference that turned the scale. There were no resignations. Holland and Clarendon contented themselves with adding a formal record of their dissent to the Minute which, in view of the gravity of the decision, was submitted to the Queen.[1]

[1] To Melbourne, 5, 6 July, 1840: *Bulwer*, II, 356, 361. The draft at Broad-lands of the first of these shews how carefully Palmerston prepared one of the most trenchant of his letters. From Melbourne, 4, 6, 7, 8 July, 1840: *B.P. Appendix*, p. 857. The letters between Melbourne and Clarendon, 6, 7 July, is

The representatives of the other Powers were summoned to hear
the details on 9 July in an atmosphere of mutual congratulation.
Chekib, whose name signified 'patience', was overjoyed, thus, as
Palmerston told Ponsonby, refuting by his manner the allegations
that he was pro-Mehemet. Palmerston congratulated the others
on their patience also as he informed them that he had been given
authority to draw up a convention by the Cabinet.

Now that he had gained his object Palmerston moved at a pace
which astonished Neumann. He and Bülow agreed immediately
to all Palmerston's proposals which were worked out with the
greatest clarity. Brunnow was far more afraid of responsibility
and wanted to insert once more the exact number of ships to be
employed in the Sea of Marmora, and to refer the whole question
to St. Petersburg. But Bülow and Neumann got him to agree by
promising to force Palmerston to accept such an arrangement over
the Straits as would ensure him against censure from his Court.
This was done by means of a note from Palmerston assuring Brunnow that only a small number of British ships would be sent
through the Dardanelles in any event. Neumann wrote in pity and
contempt of Brunnow's senile fears and the miserable life of a
Russian agent who must always be afraid of the anger of the Tsar
if he made a false move. As for Princess Lieven, he added, after
recounting her attempt to extract information from Bülow, she
had indeed fallen from the high position that she once held in
Society.[1]

In Palmerston's view, however, the agreement to close the
Straits to warships satisfied the interests of both Britain and

in Sir H. Maxwell, *Clarendon*, I, 194–195. To Beauvale, 9 July, 1840: *B.P.*, in
which Palmerston lays special stress on the refusal by Thiers of the offer, which
he said had much influence in the Cabinet, but this may have been due to a
desire to shield Neumann who had acted in this way without Metternich's
instructions. The authority for the minute of Lord Holland and Clarendon is
given by Professor Bell (*Palmerston*, I, 485) as Windsor Archives, and Professor
Temperley (*Crimea*, 486) actually printed it as an appendix from that source,
but it had of course long been in print in Sir H. Maxwell, *Clarendon*, I, 196.
Nor is it as is stated (*Crimea*, 113) "almost unprecedented", though such minutes
and dissenting opinions were only used infrequently. Neumann to Metternich, 9 July, 1840, who had an account of the Cabinet discussion from Lord
Normanby, stresses the points made above and adds that even Lord Holland had
admitted that Austria had given the "casting vote". *V. St. A.*, *Appendix*,
p. 878. From Minto, 6 July, 1840: *B.P.* pressing Palmerston to get a decision.
Broughton, *Recollections*, V, 277.
[1] To Beauvale, 15 July, 1840; To Ponsonby, 15 July, 1840: *B.P.* To
Brunnow, 15 July, 1840: *L.P.*, I, No. 622. Neumann to Metternich, 16 July,
1840: *V. St. A.* Appendix, p. 883.

Russia. "What the Emperor really wanted in all this transaction", he told Beauvale, "is the article about ships of war not passing the Dardanelles and I do not think that Brunnow would have lightly run the chance of losing that by postponing signature till he could refer to the Emperor. On our part I consider this article as an advantage gained. We were bound to this by the Treaty of 1809 but Russia was free; now both are bound alike and the Porte is as secure as paper can make her against uninvited visitors from the Black Sea. Notwithstanding all the clamour raised for an opposite system, I much prefer that the Straights should be closed rather than that there should be a thoroughfare. It is an additional security for peace."

This general rule, of course, remained suspended during the immediate emergency which was the occasion of the convention. This was mainly directed to the coercion of Mehemet, should he refuse the conditions offered to him by the Sultan of which the Powers had approved. His communications were to be cut by British and Austrian naval forces. Should he advance on Constantinople all the Powers were entitled to come to the Sultan's defence. This act was, however, to be an exception to the ancient rule of the Ottoman Empire that, "as long as the Porte is at peace", no foreign warship should pass the Bosphorus or the Dardanelles.

In another convention the terms to be offered to Mehemet Ali were laid down in a very Palmerstonian manner, the hereditary rule of Egypt and the Pashalik of Acre for life if he at once accepted. If he did not do so in ten days the offer of the Pashalik was to be withdrawn. If he did not do so in another ten days the offer as regards Egypt itself was no longer valid. All other possessions of Mehemet were to be given up and the Turkish fleet with its crews and equipment was to be returned to the Sultan. It was also expressly provided that the laws of the Ottoman Empire were to apply to Mehemet's possessions and that his army and fleet were to be part of the Imperial forces. Egypt would thus be a province of the Empire, even if hereditarily ruled, and not independent as it had been, save for the payment of tribute, during Mehemet Ali's Pashalik.

In a separate Protocol, due entirely to Palmerston, it was laid down that action could be taken on the treaty before it was ratified. This was unprecedented and it was the most courageous action of the signatories. "Success alone could justify a resolution so bold

and energetic," wrote Neumann, and added that Palmerston might have to get a bill of indemnity from Parliament. The British Constitution did not make such a step necessary, and the wisdom of immediate action was obvious for it was necessary to take advantage of the rising in Syria before Ibrahim could put it down. One can imagine, however, how such a measure would have been criticised if Mehemet had been able to make a successful resistance.

Finally it was agreed that the convention should not be disclosed to France. Nothing was said to Guizot until the messengers were well on their way with the fateful despatches. Then Palmerston gave him a Memorandum which informed him in most general terms of what had been agreed upon.[1]

Whatever Guizot had suspected he was clearly quite unprepared for such an announcement. He had assumed that France would be informed before the treaty was signed and given a last chance to join the other Powers. No doubt he had been preparing himself for a final struggle against Palmerston. The latter said that the four Powers were only putting into force a plan which Guizot's predecessor had at one time proposed to him. Since France had refused to contemplate force in any event the others would have to act without her. Guizot denied both assertions. He said that Sébastiani had only acted in his own name and Palmerston had to admit that there was no official record, but implied that Louis Philippe himself had authorised the offer. When Guizot denied that France had refused all use of force and had always offered to defend Constantinople, Palmerston said this was not coercion and added that "many believed that France aims at dismembering the Turkish Empire and erecting a new and independent state to consist of Egypt, Arabia and Syria." Guizot was taken aback when Palmerston said the action would begin immediately and not await an answer from Alexandria. He indicated that France would need to be in great force in the Levant to protect her interests. Palmerston trusted that she would give no encouragement to Mehemet to resist. When Guizot regretted

[1] The Conventions of 15 July were of course printed in *L.P.*, I, No. 615, and have often since been published. There was also a Protocol regulating the admission of light vessels of war in the service of the Legations (*L.P.*, I, No. 617), a topic which was often to be a subject of discussion in later years. To Beauvale, 15 July, 1840: *B.P.* Neumann to Metternich, 16 July, 1840: *V. St. A. Appendix*, p. 881.

that such serious consequences had arisen out of "three or four wretched pashaliks in Syria", Palmerston said their value could be judged by the tenacity with which Mehemet Ali clung to them. The Ambassador retired in high dudgeon and maintained in Society his attitude of cold hostility, which his mistress also displayed. "Guizot and Madame de Lieven have looked as cross as the devil for the last few days," wrote Palmerston. The representatives of the three Powers, he added, accused the Princess of betraying her country and becoming the tool of France.[1]

It was only natural that Guizot should take such a line. Palmerston had expected it. He continued to assert in despatches to every capital that France would not resist by force the decision of the Powers, and awaited with complete calm the reaction of the French Government and people to the measures which had at last been taken.

[1] To Bulwer, 21, 22 July, 1840: *F.O. France*, 600A, and *L.P.*, II, Nos. 10, 11, do., 21, 22 July, 1840: *Bulwer*, II, 315, 318, and *B.P.* Guizot, *Mémoires*, V, 220 ff. In recounting the interview Neumann insisted that only after every effort to get France to come in had failed did Palmerston suggest they should act without her. (To Metternich, 25 July, 1840: *V. St. A.*) Both Brunnow and Neumann were following the Princess's actions closely. Brunnow after watching her at a reception warned Neumann in a hasty note that she was already intriguing with the Opposition against the convention and urged him to use his influence with the Tory chiefs to frustrate her plans—a task which he immediately carried out with great success. She told Neumann that her Russian heart rejoiced in the fact that the old Quadruple Alliance had been reconstructed, at the same time remarking that Palmerston had undone the work of Canning by recreating the Holy Alliance. She was much taken aback when Neumann said he for his part was sorry that France had left the Alliance and especially when he told her that the final step had been taken by Guizot himself in his reply to Chekib of the 21 June (25 July: *V. St. A.*). Bulwer cut out all references to the Princess in his *Palmerston*. He wrote at this time from Paris that she was accused there of misleading Guizot.

4. THE CONVENTION OF 15 JULY, 1840 IN OPERATION

That the convention obtained with so much effort was carried out in its entirety was due to the strong will, steadfast courage and sustained energy of Palmerston. It is perhaps the incident in the whole of his long career which best displays these qualities. He had to overcome obstacles that seemed certain to wreck the plan. He had to contend with the opposition of those who had joined with him to make it, both Cabinet colleagues and continental allies, while the instruments chosen for him to apply the necessary force in Asia Minor were hesitant and unimaginative and did not believe in the possibility of success. To cope with the former Palmerston had the consistent backing of the Tsar; the Admiral and General were supplemented by more capable younger men whom Palmerston himself selected for the purpose. They were spurred into action by the faithful Ponsonby and still more by Palmerston's own urging and that of Minto, who was his greatest support in Britain during the crisis. But the essential thing was that Palmerston himself saw the situation more clearly than anyone else, knew exactly what he wanted to do, and never doubted that he could do it.

The convention was not signed until five o'clock and was followed by a Cabinet dinner, but late that same night Palmerston had already written despatches and letters to Vienna and next day the instructions were sent off to Constantinople to set the naval and military forces in action, and a long series of despatches and letters to the other Courts followed in rapid succession. Speedy ratification was essential in order to deprive France of the last opportunity to delay and thus frustrate Palmerston's plans. It was secured from all the signatories with ease except in one case— Prussia. Palmerston had urged that she should give money, expert officers and artillery. Werther's answer was "that Prussia would contribute nothing, nothing whatever." The ratification was accompanied with the reservation that she was not bound to use force. This was the Minister's decision rather than the King's, who promised Metternich shortly afterwards at Dresden to withdraw it. But Austria was little more helpful, her main

addition to Bandiera's small squadron being the young Archduke
Frederick, the son of the Archduke Charles. She would promise
nothing more. The Tsar, who was delighted with the convention,
was far more eager; an expedition was got ready in the Black Sea.
But this was for use only if Mehemet threatened Constantinople;
neither the Tsar nor Palmerston wished it to be employed in
Asia Minor. All depended, therefore, on the Turks themselves,
the British fleet and the insurrection of the Lebanese, and it was
not long before news came that this last had miscarried and that
Ibrahim's authority had been reestablished.[1]

When Thiers received the news of the convention he did not
at first shew more surprise and indignation than Guizot had done.
He complained bitterly that a final offer had not been made to
France, though in the same breath he admitted that he would
have refused it, an attitude which Metternich thought was non-
sensical. He had told Bulwer only a day or two before that he had
not in any way endeavoured to get the Sultan to yield to Mehemet
Ali's demands, so he could hardly claim that the convention had
prevented an arrangement being made at Constantinople. But
Thiers, like Desages and indeed most people in Europe, believed
that Mehemet could not be deprived of Syria without French
assistance. The *entente* he bitterly insisted was at an end. He
poured out to Bulwer a flood of expostulations and explanations
of his own conduct, but, though he made vague statements as to
the actions that France might take to protect her interests, the
reception was better than might have been expected, as Palmerston
himself confessed. The first treatment of the news in the organs
of the French Press controlled by Thiers, while angry and hostile,
was not threatening, and the official memorandum that was
sent in reply on 24 July was moderate and pacific in tone. In
fact Leopold told Palmerston a little later that Thiers would
have accepted Palmerston's memorandum as a friendly gesture

[1] To Beauvale, 15 July, 1840: *B.P.* From William Russell, 29 July, 1840:
F.O. Prussia, 229. From Bloomfield, 30 July, 1840: *F.O. Russia*, 261; do.,
8 Aug., 1840: *B.P.* The Tsar shewed his personal enthusiasm for the convention by sending Brunnow the order of the White Eagle and a year's salary, and
decorating every member of his mission. Guichen, *La Crise d'Orient*, 336.
From Beauvale, 25 July, 1840; Metternich to Beauvale, 22, 28 July, 1840: *B.P.*
Metternich chuckled over Princess Lieven's failure to find out that the convention was to be made, boasted that Palmerston had used Austria to overcome the
opposition in the Cabinet and was full of praise for both Palmerston and Ponsonby, but explained he could not give arms, money or officers. He suggested
Prussia might send an officer to join the Austrian Flagship.

if he had not been stirred up by Palmerston's opponents in England.[1]

However that may be, it was not long before a storm of passionate protest arose in France in which the whole nation joined and which neither Thiers nor Louis Philippe could have ignored had they wished to do so. They joined, therefore, in an uneasy alliance to direct and control it, each suspecting the other of the intention of using it for his own personal ends. Thiers began, as Bulwer said, to breathe fire and flames, and threats began to be uttered about Malta or some coup in Spain. Louis Philippe would never countenance such action, Bulwer believed, but he dared not openly shew himself too peaceful. "The position of the King and Minister is indeed most curious," he wrote. "Playing the game together as partners, each is jealous of the cards and skill of the other and afraid that he will find some means of pocketing the whole of the stake which should be divided between them."[2]

But though the King openly backed the arming of France, the increase of the fleet and, most discussed project of all, the circling of Paris with fortifications, his tone to Bulwer was more of grief than anger and he added that he had already himself sent off to Alexandria a messenger to prevent Ibrahim from crossing the Taurus and precipating a crisis. He had to arm, he said, to satisfy the nation. Nor could he get rid of Thiers who would be more dangerous in opposition than in office. In a private letter Bulwer told Palmerston that while the King was pacific, he must be prepared for anything.[3]

Granville, who came back to his post at the end of July, reluc-

[1] From Bulwer, 20 July, 1840: *F.O. France*, 604. *L.P.*, II, No. 9; do., 20 July, 1840: *B.P.* To Granville, 12 Aug., 1840: *B.P.* Metternich's note on Neumann's despatch (25 July, 1840), giving the assertion of Thiers that France should have been asked though he would certainly have refused, was 'fort sot'. *V. St. A.* French Note of 24 July: *L.P.*, II, No. 17. Leopold told Bülow, however, that it was the sarcastic letters of Princess Lieven and Mme Flahaut's assertion that he had been tricked that caused Thiers to take the line he did. (Neumann to Metternich, 15 Aug., 1840: *V. St. A.*)

[2] From Bulwer, 27 July, 1840: *F.O. France*, 604. *L.P.*, II, Nos. 33, 34; do., 25, 26, 27, 31 July, 1840: *B.P.*

[3] From Bulwer, 27 July, 1840: *F.O. France*, 604. This despatch and all other references to Louis Philippe himself are left out of the *Levant Papers*. Statements by him are sometimes attributed to the "French Government", From Bulwer, 2 Aug., 1840: *B.P.* The project for fortifying Paris has generally been ascribed to the desire of the King to have protection against internal disorder. But the forts certainly were an important contribution to the defence of France as 1870 was to reveal, and in 1840 the Prussian soldiers emphasised the fact that Paris would no longer be liable to immediate capture by an invading army. (From Lord William Russell, 25 Nov., 1840: *F.O. Prussia*, 229.)

tantly and full of gout, was much more perturbed and pessimistic. If the King dismissed his Minister, he said, he might lose his throne so strong was the feeling of the country. The publication of the British memorandum had done good and so had Palmerston's moderate and friendly speech in Parliament, but the Prorogation Queen's Speech, by eulogising the convention and not mentioning France, had reawakened the storm. Ordinances had proclaimed an increase in the army and navy, though Granville was sure crews could not be found for the 16 sail of the line and 9 steamers contemplated in them. James Rothschild, in the first of many interviews of these days, was quite trembling with the idea that the warlike feeling of the public would force the Government into war, and pleaded for a conciliatory word. Then, as the King left for Eu, Granville also went off to the seaside to nurse his gout and apprehensions which grew daily more painful. Macaulay, who paid a short visit to France, shared these fears and, though agreeing with Palmerston on the necessity of carrying out the treaty, "thinks war very probable".[1]

Bulwer's reports continued the story in a more cautious strain. Though he warned Palmerston of the possibility of an 'Anconade' against Malta or Crete, he made more of the arguments for peace. The fury was not always sustained at the highest pitch, the papers had been ordered not to attack Palmerston personally and only one or two had repeated the accusations of Attwood and the absurd crew of Urquhart's friends who had come over to Paris. Moreover the persistent rumours that Thiers had made money on the crisis by stock-jobbing had done him much harm with the public, though Bulwer himself did not believe them.

Meanwhile the news had come that the Syrian insurrection had failed and the communications from Vienna were so vague and contradictory that Thiers described them as 'twaddle' and Apponyi had confessed to Granville that he did not know what they meant. In these circumstances it was natural that Thiers should hope for some new offer from Britain, especially as his British visitors all assured him that Palmerston represented only himself and not the feeling of his country. He told Bulwer unofficially

---

[1] From Granville, 3, 5, 7, 10 Aug., 1840: *F.O. France*, 604, partly in *L.P.*, II, Nos., 48, 56, 61; do., 6, 10, 14, 17 Aug., 1840: *B.P.* Palmerston's replies to attacks by Hume and Leader had described the failure of the negotiation with France in such friendly terms that Brunnow was quite alarmed. (Neumann to Metternich, 9 Aug., 1840: *V. St. A.*)

that he would accept the temporary occupation of Syria for the lives of Mehemet and his son. He would not promise coercion if Mehemet refused the offer, but he indicated that it would not be necessary. Louis Philippe also reiterated his desire for peace and said he would aim at preventing Ibrahim from crossing the Taurus, or the French fleet from going into a dangerous zone. He hoped for a compromise and promised to dismiss any Minister who refused what he considered to be a reasonable one. Since the continual Bourse rumours had weakened Thiers' position, it was Bulwer's opinion that the King would prevail if such a clash came.[1]

Palmerston received these reports with equanimity. Bulwer was told to leave Thiers alone if he was rude—and to let him know the reason. It was the influence of Ellice, furious at having failed to dictate British policy, which had caused Thiers to act thus, Palmerston thought. But he was not afraid of the combination: "There are other clever people in the world besides Thiers and Ellice. Of course both Thiers and his English jackal are much disappointed, and for a time will both of them try to make as much mischief as they can; but we must stand them both." If the French threatened to use their temporarily superior naval force in the Mediterranean, he would, he said, summon the Russian fleet—and they would be challenging Austria too. Thiers, he wrote a week later, had, he knew, been warned by Guizot of the probable consequences of his policy and if "he has pinned his faith on Ellice instead of Guizot or if he has deliberately preferred that France should be left by herself, he has no right to blame anybody but himself." Meanwhile he urged that the defences of Malta should be looked to and worked in close conjunction with Minto. The latter shewed great zeal and energy. By the end of the month the British had 15 sail of the line and six steamers in commission in the Mediterranean, and Palmerston told everybody they could now feel safe that France would not put her threats into action; with an army in Algiers and no superiority of naval force it would simply be madness, and, though Thiers might talk loudly, he was not mad enough to act thus—and still less so was Louis Philippe.[2]

[1] From Granville, 10 Aug., 1840: *B.P.* From Bulwer, 21, 28 Aug., 1840: *F.O. France*, 604, 605. *L.P.*, II, Nos. 72, 78; do., 17, 21, 22, 28 Aug., 1840: *B.P.*

[2] To Bulwer, 22, 29 July, 1840: *B.P. Bulwer*, II, 318, gives the first but leaves out the sentence quoted. Princess Lieven had written to Lady Palmerston on 7 May: "I have reason to believe that Ellice has been his [Thiers] sole informant about your political situation." (Sudley, *Corres. Princess Lieven—Lady Palmerston*, 188.) To John Russell, 5, 11 Aug., 1840. To Sir Hussey Vivian,

Unfortunately Thiers had made a far greater impression on others, both in Britain and abroad, and Palmerston's tone grew more dogmatic and bitter as he realised that so many people refused to accept what to him seemed so certain. He had to reiterate his convictions in letter after letter to his Cabinet colleagues and his representatives abroad. Hardly one except Ponsonby believed him, though the majority were as yet prepared to take the risk of war. Melbourne himself quite early began to shew his uneasiness and forwarded a letter from Lord Spencer condemning Palmerston for breaking up the whole system on which British foreign policy had been conducted during the last ten years.

This attitude was probably due to Ellice, Palmerston replied, but added that it was characteristic of Lord Spencer. Melbourne, however, continued to send hints and warnings. Louis Philippe, he wrote, had still a good deal of Jemappes in him. Towards the end of the month Lord John Russell had begun to press the same point of view in a series of notes and to demand a new approach to France through Austria.[1]

At Holland House these views were already openly stated and Bourqueney, left in charge while Guizot went back to France to consult the King, was able to report them to Thiers and, what was just as important, to Desages. When Guizot came back he found Leopold on the scene and began to concert action with him to get a new treaty by which Mehemet should be given possession of Syria for life. Leopold said he had prepared the way for the Ambassador in long interviews with Palmerston and Melbourne. When Guizot himself went into action he naturally got no concession on these lines. But Palmerston treated him with the greatest friendliness. He told him that the convention must be carried out, but that no commercial blockade of Syria would be instituted and that Russian troops would not be used.[2]

---

12 Aug., 1840: *B.P.* Minto in an able review of the naval situation stated that the real difficulty was not the ships but the crews. They were difficult to obtain in summer without a Press. Minto to Melbourne, 23 Aug., 1840: Lloyd Sanders, *Lord Melbourne's Papers,* 464.

[1] Spencer to Melbourne, 7 Aug., 1840. To Melbourne, 8 Aug., 1840; From Melbourne, 8, 12, 25 Aug., 1840; *Appendix,* p. 858. John Russell to Melbourne, 24 Aug., 1840: *B.P.*

[2] Bourqueney to Thiers, 8, 11 Aug., 1840; Guizot to Thiers, 22 Aug., 1840: Guizot, *Mémoires,* V, 286, and *A.A.E.* Neumann described how Palmerston gave a little dinner not only to Guizot and himself but also to Princess Lieven, taking Guizot aside to explain to him how impossible it was to negotiate a new convention (25 Aug., 1840: *V. St. A.*). Guizot does not mention the other guests.

These decisions had been made for other reasons and were only communicated to Guizot because Palmerston thought that the Ambassador would take a more reasonable view of the situation than Thiers. He now drafted a trenchant despatch designed to stop the protests in the Cabinet as much as the loud complaints of Thiers. It was another long review of the past conduct of France. The French Government, he pointed out, had refused all the offers made to them and secretly pressed the Porte to negotiate with Mehemet Ali. "I hope," he told Bulwer, it "will undeceive Thiers as to his notion that we are going to give up our Treaty of July 15. . . . Does Thiers imagine that such menaces and revilings that he has been pleased to deal out through his irresponsible organs have made the slightest change in our determination and intentions? If he does, he has yet much to learn as to the character and habits of the English nation." Melbourne at once admitted the cogency of this indictment: "It is a capital paper and completely proves that France has no right to complain of offence or surprise or of anything else in the game which has been done." But the French Cabinet were far from considering that they must accept defeat. Guizot had seen in Palmerston's moderation a desire to compromise and found many members of the Government more afraid of the use of Russian troops than of Mehemet himself. It was the challenge to the Euphrates route, he wrote, which had brought about the situation. Let the Pasha keep away from that part of Asia Minor. Desages was also writing with great confidence at this period. The Lebanon insurrection had been put down and he did not see how Palmerston could succeed with the means at his disposal. Meanwhile the French Consul-General, Cochelet, had persuaded Mehemet not to proclaim a holy war and to be content with assuring Ibrahim's supplies by means of a camel corps. Time was on France's side, Desages thought, and Leopold's intervention was not needed. He was the more inclined to think Palmerston's position was a weak one because of the half-hearted defence of the treaty that came from Austria. This illusion lasted for nearly a month until Desages realised that Palmerston not only intended to carry out the convention but had the means to do so.[1]

[1] From Melbourne, 29 Aug., 1840: B.P. To Bulwer, 31 Aug., 1840: F.O. France, 600A. L.P., II, No. 91; do., 1 Sept., 1840: B.P. Guizot to Thiers, 21, 22, 31 Aug., 1840: A.A.E. (Extracts in Guichen, La Crise Orientale, 351, 355.) Desages to Bourqueney, 7, 17, 20 Aug., 1840: Bour. P.

Desages' belief that Metternich was not too steadfast in attachment to the convention was unfortunately only too well-founded
and the same was true of Werther at Berlin. Throughout the
month of August Beauvale and William Russell managed to keep
both Foreign Ministers up to the mark, but it was significant that
they already had to seek help from outside. Metternich shewed
signs of yielding to the insistent pressure of St. Aulaire who had
hastened to Königswart where as usual Metternich was holding
his little court during the midsummer months. The Chancellor
pleaded that he could do nothing away from Vienna. This was a
strange excuse and Beauvale accordingly appealed to Esterhazy
for help to get the Archdukes to take action. The presence of
the young Archduke Frederic in the Austrian fleet was a great
argument in his favour. But neither money, arms nor officers
could be obtained. It was at any rate satisfactory that Metternich
had refused the suggestion already made by Leopold and Bülow
to transfer the conference to Vienna. He was far too comfortable
at Königswart. And, when the news reached him of the threats
Pontois, the French Minister, had made at Constantinople, he
sent a severe despatch to Paris which Palmerston of course
endorsed with a strong protest of his own. Metternich also
wrote a letter to Leopold which stated in firm language the necessity of France accepting the situation, though it did not meet
all Palmerston's wishes, since it implied some sort of concession to
French demands, and the resumption of negotiations concerning
the Eastern Question.[1]

Similarly Lord William Russell had appealed from Werther to
the King, whom he had insisted on seeing personally, and found
cool and collected. The Austrian and Prussian soldiers were
already at least talking of collaborating against France. But
Werther himself was clearly unreliable and Bülow, with his
countenance, was already in collaboration with Leopold who, with
a pretence of seeking Belgian interests, was exploring every means

---

[1] From Beauvale, 27, 29, Aug., 1840: *F.O. Austria*, 291A; do., 4, 9, 11, 12,
23, 25, 31 Aug., 1840: *B.P.* The Archduke Charles was delighted at the
opportunity his son had to go into action with the British fleet. Palmerston
naturally at once refused Bülow's suggestion which would have reflected on
himself and told him not to mention it again. (To Beauvale, 5 Sept., 1840:
B.P.) Metternich, *Mémoires*, VI, 412. St. Aulaire gives a vivid picture of the
scene at Königswart, where the Eastern Question was discussed interminably
day and night by the Ambassadors of the three Courts, Esterhazy and Ficquelmont. (*Souvenirs*, 301.)

to obtain concessions for France, while at Bresson's instigation he
was considering doubling his army. It was clear that the resolution of both Austria and Prussia had visibly weakened in the face
of the threats of France—and this was bound to encourage Thiers
to go on in the course he had chosen.[1]

Much, therefore, would obviously depend on how well and how
fast affairs went in Syria. Palmerston was fully conscious of the
value of the advice which Guizot himself had given to Melbourne
at the outset—to get the thing over as quickly as possible. But to
organise an attack on an army of 50,000 men with the resources at
Palmerston's disposal was no light task. Fortunately at Constantinople was a man as determined and energetic as Palmerston
himself and the situation was really much better than anyone in
Western Europe imagined. But the offer to Mehemet had first to
be made and a means of attack found if he refused. News took
two or three weeks to come, and during September there was not
much good that came, and the uncertainty entirely undermined the
faith both of the Cabinet and Metternich in Palmerston's promise
that all would ultimately be attained. The Syrian insurrection,
Ponsonby reported, had failed because the Turk had shewed no
sign of giving help and Emir Bechir, the King of the Mountain,
had therefore taken the side of Ibrahim who had wreaked savage
reprisals on the Christians and burnt monks alive. When the
convention arrived, therefore, the Admiral, Stopford, had considered his instructions to support the insurrection no longer
valid. This weak and hesitating approach to a problem which
could only be solved by prompt and confident action was the first
of a long series which drove Ponsonby nearly frantic and was
condemned by both Palmerston and Minto. "A superannuated
twaddler," Palmerston called Stopford on 30 August. It was held
to be impossible, however, to change the command in the middle
of the operation. All that could be done was to send orders to act
as energetically as possible, orders difficult to frame, since their
execution depended on local circumstances which could not be
accurately known at London. These ultimately produced their
effect on the mind of the Admiral, a man seventy years of age,
whose courage was stout enough but matched by an excessive

[1] From Lord William Russell, 5, 12, 22, 26 Aug., 1840: *B.P.* do., 5, Aug.,
1840: *F.O. Prussia*, 229. Lord William Russell had already written to his
brother John to leave the Eastern Question to Palmerston.

prudence. Already Ponsonby relied more on Napier, in command of a squadron of the fleet, than on the Admiral himself.[1]

But Ponsonby himself was sure that the convention could be carried out in its entirety. He only regretted that its terms were too lenient to Mehemet Ali, hoped he would reject them and consequently lose not only all Syria but also Egypt as the convention threatened would then ensue. He was confident that the Pasha's power could easily be destroyed because of the weakness of his moral position. He stated this opinion in a remarkable letter, a sentence of which is at the head of this chapter: "Mehemet Ali is like a lie and will be destroyed as that is by truth. He is believed to be strong and that belief has given him strength. He is weak and it will now be seen and felt that he is so and all those who seek to be on the strongest side will turn away from him. Despair is the origin of the insurrection in Syria. Despair cannot be cured by Mehemet who has created it, and when a chance of succour is offered to the Syrians they must wish to seize it. *That is doing. It will soon be done.* It almost appears as if people were not aware of the power of *opinion.* The greatest men and nations fall before it and now Mehemet Ali has it against him to the highest degree in his own country. . . . I have no doubt of success attending your plans if they [the instructions] are acted upon with spirit by our people and I hope that will be the case."[2]

This notable judgment was entirely accurate. No other diplomatist either at Constantinople or in Europe had made it and no one believed it but Palmerston himself. Ponsonby immediately used all his energy and resource to make it come true. Even before the negotiation at Alexandria took place arms and money were sent to the Lebanon mountaineers and Richard Wood sent back to complete the work he had already begun. The Grand

---

[1] From Ponsonby, 1, 5, 12 Aug., 1840; Stopford to Ponsonby, 3 Aug., 1840: *B.P.* The convention arrived at Constantinople on the 3 August. The details of the subsequent engagements are given in dramatic detail in Professor Temperley's *Crimea*, 123–135. The author studied the campaign on the ground. He was concerned to defend Stopford from the strictures of Palmerston and Napier. No doubt the responsibility was a great one but there can be little doubt that it was only the orders from Britain and the enterprise of Napier that enabled the campaign to be finished so quickly. Stopford would not have begun, would have removed the fleet at the end of October and refused to attack Acre unless others had forced him to do so. To Minto, 30 Aug., 1840: *B.P.* Stopford was "quite unfit for the mixed political and naval duties" he had to perform, Palmerston wrote (do., 2 Sept., *B.P.*).

[2] From Ponsonby, 12 Aug., 1840: *B.P.*

Vizir was persuaded to send a letter to the Emir Bechir promising the Sultan's forgiveness and countenance. A constant succession of notes was sent to Stopford urging action. There would be no need to employ Russian troops, Ponsonby asserted. The Turkish army, suitably advised, and the British fleet would be quite sufficient. Chrysanowski was used to give counsel to the Turks, though he soon found he could do little more now that action had superseded preparation. Even more remarkable was it that Captain Walker was put in command of the small Turkish fleet, all that was left to the Sultan outside Alexandria.[1]

Meanwhile Stopford himself had gone with a squadron to Alexandria where the Consuls-General of the Four Powers were pressing Mehemet to agree to the terms of the convention. They could get nothing out of him. His answers were given with characteristic reserve and mystery. The violence of Colonel Hodges did not fit in well with the suave manoeuvres of the others who carried out their orders with no great zeal. The real negotiation was taking place with the special envoy of Thiers, Walewski, and Cochelet, the French Consul-General. The latter, a sincere admirer of Mehemet, was urging his Government to support the Pasha wholeheartedly, but the supple Walewski succeeded in getting a request for French mediation without in any way committing his Government. Meanwhile the news came from Constantinople that, as Mehemet had not accepted the convention in the time limit laid down, the Sultan had deposed him from the Pashalik of Egypt, and named his successor. Ponsonby had certainly been the main influence in obtaining this decision but the Austrian and Prussian representatives, though not the Russian, Titov, had supported him. The Ambassador was well aware of what he was doing and defended his conduct in a vigorous despatch and private letter on the ground of the effect that it would produce on opinion in the East: "Half measures will be ruinous; one of our best arms is the prerogative of the Sultan. People will never believe in the sincerity and force of the Porte, if Mehemet be spared. Everybody knows the Sultan can exert his sovereign authority against him and will *suspect* that things are not right if it be not exerted. There is a vast deference paid by all the people

[1] From Ponsonby, 5, 8, 16 Aug., 1 Sept., 1840: *F.O. Turkey*, 395, 396; *L.P.*, II, Nos. 91, 94. Walker was also put in command of the transports for 5500 men and all the officers ordered to obey him. "No Giaour has ever commanded the Turks," added Ponsonby triumphantly.

to the Sultan's acts of a solemn nature, for religious feelings are by no means fallen in the way some superficial observers assert. I am told that the Ulemas are really offended at the pretentions of Mehemet Ali to be the Protector of Islam."

That there was much truth in this judgment events were to shew. Mehemet Ali, it is true, laughed off the move. It had happened before, he said. But the threat was there and it was against France as well as Mehemet. The news caused another storm of vituperation in France and Palmerston's colleagues and allies were indignant with Ponsonby. Nesselrode was displeased and Metternich and Werther were horrified. Palmerston himself would have liked to get rid of Mehemet Ali altogether as he more than once confessed. But he was aware that it was impossible to do so. The Cabinet, he later told Ponsonby, would never allow him to attack Egypt. But the move served him well; it was both a threat and something that could be used to make a concession to the importunities of colleagues without injuring the essential object, the removal of Mehemet Ali from all Syria. It was to be of use at a critical moment in the negotiations.[1]

Just as essential was it to reassure the Turkish Government. The French Minister, Pontois, had been ordered to do his best to intimidate them and if possible to prevent the ratification of the convention. With such ardour did he carry out his task that Reschid appealed in great alarm to the representatives of the Four Powers for protection. They hastened to reassure him, Ponsonby foremost but Titov and Stürmer shewing similar zeal. Pontois later denied that he had used the threats attributed to him by Reschid and was supported by the French Government, but Desages confessed to Bourqueney that he had been ordered to

---

[1] Professor Dodwell has described the negotiation at Alexandria from Medem's reports as well as Hodges' despatches. He is too hostile to the latter, who, however, was not the man to handle so delicate a negotiation. The French reports have subsequently been published in E. Driault, *La Crise Orientale*, 1839–1841, vol. III, but there must have been many private letters to Thiers and Desages which are not yet known. M. Sabry had already shewn from the French Archives the equivocal conduct of France. (*L'Empire Egyptien*, 499–509.) From Ponsonby, 3 Sept., 1840: *B.P.*; do: *F.O. Turkey*, 396. To Ponsonby, 5, 27 Oct., 1840: *B.P.* Palmerston's only criticism of Ponsonby was that in a matter of such importance he should have sent home the Protocol of the meeting between Reschid and the Ambassadors in which the deposition of Mehemet was determined so that the attacks on his conduct could be answered. To Beauvale, 5 Oct., 1840: *B.P.* Greville (*Memoirs*, IV, 312) recounts the row in the Cabinet when news came from Vienna that the Ambassadors had not been unanimous.

abuse (malmener) and intimidate Reschid, and there can be no
doubt that his dragoman, Cor, used violent language. At any rate
the opportunity was given to shew the solidarity of the Four, and
the incident did France no good and made even more unlikely
the success of M. Coste who was still engaged in his endeavours to get the Turks to use French assistance to settle the
dispute.[1]

All this was reassuring but there was still no proof that Ibrahim
was likely to be driven out of Syria, while during the next month
the clamour in France shewed no signs of ceasing, and produced
considerable effect on the minds of the European peoples and
statesmen. The impression was in any case a false one. Louis
Philippe and the majority of the French Government never
intended to go to war and by the end of the month Desages was
warning Bourqueney of the probable result. But they had got
into a difficult position and Thiers at any rate hoped that the high
tone he adopted would frighten the Four Powers into a compromise, and was ready for that purpose to risk allowing the situation
to get out of control. He would have succeeded in his object if
Palmerston had not resisted all attempts to shake the position of
the Four Powers.

It was Bulwer who reported the scene at Paris in a flood of
despatches and letters, while Granville remained on leave. The
French Press and the President of the Council grew more and more
bellicose. When Walewski reported that he had induced the
Pasha to give up both Candia and Adana and accept Syria for his
lifetime, Thiers indicated that France would feel bound to support a ruler who had made such concessions at French insistence.
But such threats were still conveyed in the vaguest manner and
Thiers always avoided making any definite statement as to what
would cause France to take up arms. Meanwhile reports had
come from Alexandria that Mehemet Ali might well have accepted
the offer of the Four Powers if he had not been deterred by the
joint efforts of Cochelet and Walewski, and the accusation was
openly made in Palmerston's organ, the *Morning Chronicle*.
Thiers hotly denied this and of course Granville supported him.
But Bulwer, who penetrated into the secrets of the Quai d'Orsay
far more deeply than his valetudinarian chief, was not far wrong

[1] From Ponsonby, 17, 19 Aug., 1840: *F.O. Turkey*, 396. *L.P.*, II, Nos. 96,
111. Desages to Bourqueney, 8 Sept., 1840: *Bour. P.*

when he explained the incident as arising from the reluctance of
Mehemet Ali to place himself in French hands and his preference
to use language which could be interpreted later according to
events.   As it was the French envoys only secured with great
difficulty the request for French mediation which they referred to
Thiers.

The French Government only intended to accept the position
of mediator if they knew that the Four Powers would offer better
terms than were contained in the convention.   It was towards
this end that all their efforts were now directed.   But the majority
of the French Cabinet never intended to oppose the Four Powers
if they failed to secure it.   They relied on a prolonged resistance
by the Egyptian forces.   This, they thought, would gradually
force the compromise on Palmerston which France could proclaim
to the world as a victory made in the teeth of all Europe.   In order
to achieve this end Thiers began to make vague threats that it was
not in the East but on the French frontiers that France would
attack.   Italy especially was ripe for invasion.   The German
people received these threats with a patriotic outburst of indignation that surprised both France and Europe.   But an impression
was certainly made on Metternich.[1]

The pacific resolution that underlay these threats was in the
nature of things as Palmerston realised.   France could not declare
war on all Europe to oppose an end which she had herself previously endorsed.   But the situation was made perfectly safe by
the attitude of the King.   He allowed just as much bombast and
solid preparation as would satisfy public opinion, reported Bulwer
in a private letter, but refused to sanction any steps which would
allow of war.   The French fleet which Cochelet naïvely thought
might be sent to shadow the British fleet was kept at Salamis away
from the theatre of war.   Thiers wanted to send it to Candia but
even there it would have done little harm.

The King played his part in frightening the timid Granville
by telling him that the concessions of Mehemet had been bought
at too high a price, thus insinuating that France had promised to
fight for them.   The Ambassador's entreaties to Palmerston grew
more and more insistent as the month drew to a close.   Bulwer,

[1] Many of the most important despatches of Granville and Bulwer appear in
Levant Papers.   But they give a misleading impression because all reference to
the attitude of Louis Philippe is omitted.   Granville, who returned on the 21
September, was much more positive of the danger of war than Bulwer.

on the other hand, who had pretty well sized up the situation, now told Palmerston that war would be more likely to result if he gave way to France's threats. The French nation would then be so exalted that it would demand impossible concessions. By this time the cooler heads in France had come to realise the folly of Thiers. Roussin prophesied that Ibrahim would not be able to hold out for long and Desages now warned Bourqueney that, however outrageous Palmerston's conduct was, he was likely to be successful. There was, he said, no real danger of war. "Lord P. n'y croit pas et moi non plus."[1]

Palmerston had not the slightest intention of giving way. In measured language to Granville and in the Palmerstonian extravagances to Bulwer, so often quoted, he told his envoys to make the French Government and the French King realise that Britain could not be intimidated by threats. That this judgment was true enough was eventually to be proved, but meanwhile the majority of Palmerston's colleagues adopted an attitude which inspired justifiable hopes in Guizot on his return from France. He could rely also on the help of Leopold whom he had visited on his journey, and he could soon report that Bülow and even Neumann were anxious that something should be done. Palmerston again peremptorily refused to give Mehemet Syria for life. But a much smaller concession would suffice to content France, Guizot told his British friends, and doubtless this was true, though Thiers continued to insist that Mehemet must at least have all Syria.[2]

The ramifications of the pro-French party extended in every direction. Greville's subterranean moves, surely disgraceful in a Clerk to the Privy Council, have been revealed by himself. His principal confidant was Clarendon, who, however, professed to Palmerston to have fully accepted the situation and sent him

<hr/>

[1] From Granville, 25 Sept., 1840. *F.O. France*, 606. *L.P.*, No. 168; do., 21, 23, 25, 28 Sept., 1840: *B.P.* From Bulwer, 11, 14, 18, 25 Sept., 1840: *B.P.* The last written apparently without Granville's knowledge gave his theory as to what had happened at Alexandria and his advice not to give way. The despatches of Cochelet and Walewski (E. Driault, *L'Egypte et l'Europe, La Crise orientale*, 1839–1841, III, Nos. 45, 48, 50, 70, 71) shew the manoeuvres of the two envoys to obtain the request of Mehemet for mediation. Walewski was careful to point out that their reply committed France to nothing. Desages to Bourqueney, 29 Sept., 1 Oct., 1840 (*Appendix*, p. 899): *A.A.E.* If a conflict came between Thiers and the King, Desages had no doubt who would prevail.

[2] To Granville, 22, 25 Sept., 1840: *B.P.* To Bulwer, 22 Sept., 1840: *Bulwer*, II, 327. (The celebrated letter which says that in a war Mehemet will "just be chucked into the Nile".) Guizot, *Mémoires*, V, 317–323.

objective reports received from Paris. Greville also was continually spurring on Lord John Russell and the Duke of Bedford to oppose Palmerston. He was in close touch with Barnes and through his protégé, Henry Reeves, who had just been brought into the service of *The Times*, hoped to wield that powerful weapon against Palmerston. Meanwhile Spencer, Morpeth, the Duke of Bedford and other Peers continually wrote pessimistic and disquieting epistles to one another and canvassed what could be done. They hoped to persuade Lansdowne to move and in the end even induced the phlegmatic and reserved Nestor of the Whigs to take alarm. The main centre of intrigue was Holland House where Guizot went nearly every day, to get his tears dried, Neumann said, and discussed how Palmerston could be forced to make some concession to France. Lord Holland no doubt did not realise all that he and Lady Holland revealed to their friendly and soft-spoken guest, but the Cabinet controversies thus became known to the French Government and were used by some of these to play with French bankers on the Stock Exchange. Beauvale wrote that Metternich had news of British policy in this way before Neumann could report on it from London. Palmerston protested to Melbourne against these leakages only to draw from the Prime Minister the admission that he could not stop them.[1]

But all this, with Minto and Hobhouse backing him wholeheartedly, Palmerston could overcome and his own control of the

---

[1] To Melbourne, 16 Sept., 1840: *B.P.* (and part in Lloyd Sanders, *Melbourne Papers*, 475). From Melbourne, 17 Sept., 1840; From Beauvale, 13 Oct., 1840: *B.P.* Neither in his diary nor in his letters to Henry Reeve did Greville shew any shame or consciousness that he was acting unworthily. His accounts of what the various actors said to him cannot be trusted, but he clearly knew a great deal. Ashley reported to Palmerston on him and Palmerston's bitter notes on the letters shew that he knew what Greville was doing. Clarendon wrote a number of letters to Palmerston giving news from French correspondents. Melbourne summed up Holland House as follows: "The talking at Holland House is irremediable. They do not know how much they talk themselves. The table and constant Salon there are great advantages. They form a great point of union for the party. But they have also their disadvantages and this perpetual talking is one and a great one. I begin to think that a Minister should never talk much promiscuously either about Politics or anything else. He loses something by this both as to what he may hear and what he may teach, but he gains more in point of safety. Nobody can talk much and be really prudent unless he be such a compound of skill and mystery as nature seldom produces, and then, if he is, he is liable to misconception and misrepresentation which will make him utter follies, even if he has not done so." He eventually warned Lord Holland that his indiscretions were being used for stockjobbing (Ilchester, *Chronicles*, 282). If so, they were obviously also known to the French Government.

Press ensured that all efforts in that direction would fail. But it was essential for him to have the support of the Prime Minister and Lord John Russell, the leader of the House, as well as Secretary of State for War, with whose assistance he had got the convention through the Cabinet. Unfortunately both of them began to lose their nerve and Lord John Russell started an active campaign to compel Palmerston to give way. Lady Palmerston was so alarmed that she urged Beauvale to come back from Königswart to get their brother into a better frame of mind, but the Ambassador was needed to keep Metternich straight.

Melbourne's conduct at this time displayed his characteristic qualities to the highest degree. He never took the initiative himself and answered the heated epistles of his colleagues with cool and detached little notes which pointed out their inconsistencies. He insisted that Palmerston's policy should be tried out but he obviously had no great belief that it would be successful and his natural disposition to compromise made him seek a way out. He was also preoccupied with the condition of the Queen, now far gone with her first child, and this anxiety must have been increased by the fact that an illness in October kept him for some time from his usual place at her side. Thus he was constantly expressing to Palmerston his scepticism and urging him to accept the suggestions of his colleagues though he always gave way when Palmerston, as was nearly always the case, refused to agree. But, as in July, at the last moment he took vigorous action which helped to save the situation.[1]

Lord John Russell's behaviour was far worse, especially as he had been amongst the strongest supporters of the convention. Some of it seems to have come from jealousy of Palmerston's commanding position, for in September he claimed the supervision of the operations on the Syrian coast. Palmerston settled this point by a courteous and moderate reply, which pointed out that Britain was not at war and that he had the same position now as in the Spanish question. At the same time Russell began an attack on Ponsonby and pressed that some more moderate man should

---

[1] Neumann to Metternich, 17 Sept., 1840: *V. St. A.* From Beauvale, 24 Sept., 1840: *B.P.* He had in June asked for leave of absence but he was now strongly of the opinion that he must stay near Metternich. Both Palmerston and his wife eventually agreed. The presence at Königswart of Maltzahn's daughter, whom Beauvale was to marry in 1841, may have contributed to his determination not to come home.

be sent out to Constantinople to conduct the negotiations. For some time Palmerston ignored this impertinence which was as much an attack on himself as on Ponsonby. Then in response to repeated reminders from Melbourne he sent a devastating reply. He refused of course to subject Ponsonby to such a mark of lack of confidence. But in addition he pointed out that his critics were all the while assuming the failure of operations which had not yet even been begun. Let them at least wait until the policy which they had supported in the Cabinet had been tried out.

This argument was indeed unanswerable, as even the Duke of Bedford told his brother, and for a little time it silenced Palmerston's opponents in the Cabinet, except Lord Holland whom, however, Palmerston treated with the greatest courtesy in spite of the harm which his indiscretions were producing. Though we know from other letters that Palmerston was indignant at being subjected to these attacks while he was directing a political and strategic campaign of such importance, his letters to his colleagues are couched in most temperate language when they are made. But he often evaded or ignored their suggestions, believing that time was on his side.

To win sufficient time to bring his forces into action was the main object to which he directed all his diplomatic resources—and it was clear that he could not wait too long, as Melbourne told him in one of his most pessimistic epistles. The dissolution of the Cabinet was threatened, he warned Palmerston on 14 September. The policy had been adopted against the will of two members of it and several others had only given it lukewarm support. "Never, I will answer for it was a great measure undertaken upon a basis of support so slender and so uncertain. The present state of things unless you can find a way out of it or something that will open a prospect of a speedy termination to it, will lead to a dissolution of the Government. This will be an evil for the country because it will appear, and it will be, that the English Government will have been changed by the outcry of the Press and populace of Paris and by the mere apprehension of a serious difference with France. What a prospect for the country and for those who are hereafter to administer its affairs!"[1]

[1] From Melbourne, 14, 16, 17, 19, 24, 30 Sept., 1840: *B.P.* To Melbourne, 22 Sept., 1840: *B.P.* From Lord Holland, 17 Sept., 1840. To Lord Holland, 19 Sept., 1840: *B.P.* Palmerston used the device of telling Lord Holland his answers to an unnamed correspondent who had expressed views which were

The attempts to prevent Palmerston directing operations in the East were easily overcome. But parallel to these was another line of attack which was more difficult to resist. Not only Lord Holland but all the Whig pundits, and foremost amongst them John Russell, began to urge that some new approach should be made to France to satisfy her wounded pride. What exactly was to be done was variously and vaguely hinted, but some concession was to be made and France thus brought back into the Concert of Europe. This is what Guizot had come back to obtain, and what was soon to be urged by both Prussia and Austria as their alarm grew. Leopold was already pressing it on the Queen in a series of avuncular letters in which high politics were mingled with family news, as well as on Palmerston himself. Palmerston was determined to resist it. The next move would be to suspend operations while discussion took place. The reaction in Syria and Turkey would be incalculable. Consequently, he used to the full his commanding position as the channel of communication to prevent any such move taking place. He had a strong technical position. He was able at once to get rid of John Russell's suggestion that the convention, now that it had been ratified, should be communicated officially by the Four Powers to France. Neumann objected that there was no collective body at London to take such a step and Melbourne at once agreed. This suggestion was meant to be the beginning of a negotiation with France as was another proposal to conclude a self-denying ordinance not to take territory which Palmerston also rejected as unnecessary and unwise. But Melbourne responded in characteristic fashion to his complaints of those who had pressed this course on him: "I agree with you as to the manner in which people, who have concurred in a measure which they do not approve, ought to act. But people do not act as they ought. You calculate a little too much upon nations and individuals following reason, right and a just view of their own interest. I do not say that these are not the great considerations which actuate individuals, but there are other motives which exercise at least equal power and influence."[1]

identical with those of Lord Holland himself. Lord Holland replied that he did not desire a 'boxing match' with Palmerston. Memorandum by Lord John Russell, 18 Sept., 1840; To Lord John Russell, 23 Sept., 1840: G.P. Gooch, *Later Correspondence*, I, 15, 19.

[1] For Lord John Russell's attitude see G. P. Gooch, *Later Correspondence*, I, 12–18, and Spencer Walpole, *Lord John Russell*, I, 348 ff. The correspondence with Leopold is given in *Queen Victoria Letters*, I, 288, 293. He pressed

This attack would have probably been no more dangerous than the first had not it received support from abroad. But early in September Metternich began to shew signs of weakness and it took all the efforts of Beauvale to keep him from giving way altogether. He began to despair of carrying out the convention without the aid of France and consequently wanted concessions to be made to her. He was prepared to leave the insurgents to their fate and accept Mehemet's rule over Syria for life. Kolowrat was as usual opposing his policy and Metternich was at first too comfortable at his country estate to go to Vienna and face him. The Chancellor gradually became really alarmed. He was much exercised about the condition of Italy which Thiers threatened to make the first objective of a continental campaign. He recommended a conciliatory gesture to France in order to prevent a general war. The Ottoman Empire, he said, would be destroyed in the course of it. He actually wrote a private letter to Neumann threatening to separate Austria from the other Powers in certain eventualities and only Beauvale's protests and scoldings prevented him from sending it. Gradually Kolowrat came out in open opposition to resistance to France. Eichof, who managed the finances, was altogether on the same side and said that war would mean that Austria must choose between Kolowrat and Metternich and there was no doubt what the decision would be. Beauvale, indeed, had to admit that Austrian public opinion, which cared little about Asia Minor, was on Kolowrat's side. Metternich refused Beauvale's advice to challenge his critic in the Council with the Archdukes, and the action of a Great Empire, lamented the Ambassador, was thus paralysed. "Metternich told me last night in as many words", he wrote on the 30 September, "that not only he should lose the confidence of Germany and Italy if he went to war, but, appealing to me, added 'you know enough of the position of this Empire to be aware that in such a case I should risk my situation in the interior'." A week later Metternich proposed that there should be a conference at Wiesbaden under his auspices. He could, explained the Ambassador in a bitter letter, manage it comfortably from Johannisberg. He was determined if possible to take shelter behind the neutrality of the Confederation

the same view on Palmerston in letters of 13, 19 Sept. from Wiesbaden (B.P.). From Melbourne, 17, 29, Sept., 1840: B.P. Neumann to Metternich, 6 Sept., 1840: V. St. A.

and Sardinia if war ensued as a result of the landing in Beirut of which news had just come.[1]

Nor during this month was the news from Prussia much more comforting. Bresson's activity and violence were increasing and Werther was visibly impressed. He was worried at the reported increase of Belgian armaments which was, he said, the clearest indication that war was intended. He was much alarmed also at the deposition of Mehemet, which Bresson told him would mean war, and discontented with the conduct of his own Minister at Constantinople. Lord William Russell placed all his hopes on the King but, though that monarch was braver than his Minister, he was clearly angry at Prussia being placed in a position of danger for a question in which she had no direct interest. Bülow on his return to Berlin wrote a pessimistic letter to Palmerston. Werther, he said, would not even discuss affairs with him, and the King while kind was visibly embarrassed. The country had not yet made up its mind to incur the expense of arming against France. If the matter was allowed to drag on he could not answer for Prussia's steadfastness. "It would suit us here", wrote William Russell in an accompanying letter, "if you could end the Oriental affair. We have a weak King and a pusillanimous Government."[2]

The Tsar of course remained as determined as ever and this attitude was reflected in his Minister at London. A Baltic fleet was got ready and it must have given Nicholas great satisfaction to offer it for the defence of the country which had protested against it for so long. But Nesselrode was by no means as firm as his master. He was perturbed at the deposition of Mehemet which he had not expected. His despatches to Vienna and elsewhere indicated more readiness to make some overture to France than might have been expected.[3]

[1] From Beauvale, 5, 11, 15, 20, 25, 30 Sept., 1, 8 Oct., 1840: *B.P.*; do., 25 Sept., 8 Oct., 1840: *F.O. Austria*, 291B. The long private letters give in detail the intricacies of the internal situation, and are full of interesting reflections on it. There is much less in the despatches on the subject. The two noted above recount Metternich's desire for a new offer to France, a meeting with France on the Rhine and to remain neutral. The Ambassador had necessarily to send a official account of these views since Metternich was putting them in despatches to Neumann. Palmerston wrote to him a little later: "the less you can put his [Metternich's] back-slidings into your despatches the better; for these things are caught hold of by those who are on the look out for difficulties, and are turned to bad account." (4 Nov., 1840: *B.P.*)

[2] From William Russell, 22, 30 Sept., 8 Oct., 1840; from Bülow, 7 Oct., 1840: *B.P.* From William Russell, 2, 23, 30 Sept., 7 Oct., 1840: *F.O. Prussia*, 229.

[3] From Bloomfield, 29 Aug., 12, 18, 26 Sept., 2 Oct., 1840: *F.O. Russia*, 261, 262.

Naturally the Austrian attitude became known in London even though Beauvale was careful to say as little as possible in his despatches. St. Aulaire was sending accounts of it to Paris and Guizot was informing his faithful friends in the Cabinet. Gradually the pro-French party began to look to Austria to force Palmerston to yield. In these circumstances it can be imagined how anxiously he was watching for news from the Near East which would convince his colleagues and allies that he could perform what he had set out to do. It came in time, thanks to the energy and foresight of Ponsonby and the boldness of Napier, but it might have been too late if Palmerston himself had not shewn great address and dexterity as well as determination and courage.

At Constantinople Ponsonby wore himself out in collecting money, arms and stores for the Turkish expeditionary force, as well as maintaining the courage of the timid Reschid and the other Ministers, and counteracting the intrigues in the Harem in which both Mehemet and the French still saw a means of obtaining their ends. Napier had appeared off the coast while Stopford was at Alexandria and begun to stir up the inhabitants of the Lebanon and blockade the ports before Mehemet's answer was known, thus producing a violent French protest of which Palmerston took no notice. When Stopford took over, the technical part of his job seems to have been done with great skill. The fleet was so distributed that Suliman Pasha did not know which part of the coast to defend, and Ibrahim shewed himself quite incapable of concentrating his forces. This was partly owing to the fact that a good part of them were unreliable and this was due to the work of Wood and others who got in touch with the men of the Mountain. Soliman Pasha placed a price on his head, and neither Stopford nor Hodges, who arrived later on, would take notice of him, but his work had been well done and deserved the warm praise which Ponsonby gave him. Nor would the Turkish troops have fought as they did if Ponsonby had not obtained the virtual command for Sir Charles Smith and Jochmus. Napier, as in Portugal, shewed that he was a soldier as well as a sailor. When the first Egyptian defeats came all hastened to get on the winning side, the Emir Bechir too late to save himself from having to give way to his nephew. Thus by 10 October Ibrahim had been driven from the coast, the inhabitants of the Lebanon were rising everywhere and the Egyptian army was doomed unless Acre main-

tained its usual reputation for prolonged resistance and winter weather drove the conquering fleet from the coast.[1]

The news of the first bombardment, though it caused an extra outburst of wrath in the French Press, gave little assurance of victory. But the fall of Beirut precipitated the final crisis. Palmerston had then to face the combination of all the forces arrayed against his policy. There was of course no real danger of a continental war though Beauvale wrote on 25 September that only a miracle could prevent it. But there was always a chance that Palmerston's enemies and allies would force him to compromise before the hollow nature of the French position had been revealed. Granville was completely taken in by the French Government and in his private letters constantly urged concessions to France on the ground that otherwise war was almost inevitable Thiers, he said, could not give way completely after all his boasting. According to Broglie, who was brokenhearted at the situation, if the King dismissed Thiers he would be brought back in triumph when the Chambers met. If the Egyptians were beaten then France would seize some place for herself as a protection of her interests, Candia perhaps, or the Balearic Isles. The news that the French fleet had been brought back to Toulon seemed ominous though the move was in fact only due to the King's desire to keep it out of harm's way. Thiers still believed that the expedition to Syria would fail. The King was using all his power to prevent war and had stopped an angry note on the deposition of Mehemet Ali. But he could not dictate to the French Cabinet which in its turn was responsive to the great surge of public opinion in France.[2]

---

[1] From Ponsonby, 8, 14, 15, 23, 26, 28 Sept., 1840; Wood to Ponsonby, 7 Sept., 1840; Ponsonby to Stopford, 8 Oct., 1840: *B.P.* (protesting against the intention of leaving the coast). Ponsonby's condemnation of Smith as a General and Stopford for dilatoriness was endorsed by Palmerston and Minto. The other side of the case is given by Professor Temperley (*Crimea*, 119-130). Smith, however, had a sort of apoplectic stroke (To Fitzroy Somerset, 17 Oct., 1840: *B.P.*), and this in itself was surely sufficient cause for his removal. See also p. 726, note. "A man who does not expect success rarely gets it," wrote Minto on 4 October, and on the 27th: "Old Stopford will be the death of me," though he was not quite so bad as Ponsonby made out. (From Minto, 6, 27 Oct., 1840: *B.P.*)

[2] From Granville, 5, 8, 9, 12 Oct., 1840: *F.O. France* 606, part in *L.P.*, II, Nos. 207, 214, 215; do., 5, 9, 11 Oct., 1840: *B.P.* Palmerston was much exercised about the French fleet and ordered Granville to use his Secret Service money to find out about it. Was it to be used to attack the Russian fleet if it came West or to seize the Balearic Isles? A member of the Thiers' Cabinet was later so foolhardy as to confess in the Chamber that the latter idea was in their

Bulwer's private letters to Palmerston were not nearly so alarmist. The heads of the army and navy, he reported, had backed up the King in opposing Thiers in the Cabinet. Bulwer recommended Palmerston to threaten to take away Egypt and then make a handsome concession about it. Palmerston had some such idea in mind. But he was in no mood to make any such concessions as Granville demanded. He told him to warn Louis Philippe that an 'Anconade' would mean war and a Russian fleet in Western Europe, a warning Granville refused to give, because, he said, Louis Philippe's conduct had already shewn that it was unnecessary, thus incurring Palmerston's official displeasure and almost completely losing his confidence.[1]

The pressure on Palmerston had much increased in intensity at the end of September and the Queen and Prince Albert, who had been continually urged to do something by Uncle Leopold, now at last began to use their influence with Melbourne to make Palmerston give way. The Queen wished some overture to be made to France, Melbourne told Palmerston on the 24 September, and he might as well do it as it would not affect the result. Prince Albert added his entreaties to hers and Lansdowne, inspired, Palmerston later said, by Broglie, also pleaded with Melbourne. Leopold himself joined in the attack on Melbourne with a portentous letter which, with many underlinings in the true Coburg style, argued the necessity of preserving the throne of Louis Philippe. He suggested that Granville should be told to propose to Thiers a general consultation on the Eastern Question, and the Queen and Prince Albert, at his prompting, repeatedly urged the same course on Melbourne, though always answering Leopold in language suggested by the Prime Minister.[2]

It was to Lord John Russell that all these critics looked for a lead. He had first threatened Melbourne with his resignation on

mind, but there does not seem to have been any real plan about it. Nevertheless at Palmerston's orders Granville sent post-haste to Madrid to warn the Spanish Government, and a messenger was sent off to Gen. Espartero who promised to take the necessary precautions. On the whole subject see C. N. Scott, *France and the Balearic Isles in 1840*, *Eng. Hist. Rev.*, April, 1912.

[1] From Bulwer, 5, 7, 8, 9 Oct., 1840; to Granville, 7, 8, 20 Oct., 1940: *B.P.* The letters of 7, 8 Oct. in *Bulwer*, II, 337, 339, are much emasculated. From Granville, 11 Oct., 1840: *B.P.*

[2] From Melbourne, 29, 30 Sept., 1840, enclosing Prince Albert to Melbourne, undated, and Lansdowne to Melbourne, "Tuesday night". "The inclination of my mind at present is very much to take John Russell's view"; do., 6, 10 Oct. 1840; *Appendix*, p. 860. Leopold to Melbourne, 1 Oct., 1840: *B.P.*

10 September.   Since then he had been bombarded by letters from the Whig pundits and particularly Lord Spencer, who, as Althorp, had always been the most pusillanimous of Cabinet Ministers.   He had seen Guizot who had also poured out his heart to other Whigs whom he met at Holland House or elsewhere. Russell now insisted on the whole question being brought before the Cabinet.   It was perhaps only Melbourne's appeal to him to respect the condition of the Queen that prevented him from resigning forthwith.   Lord Spencer had told him that if Britain went to war the Melbourne Government would at once be overthrown in the House of Commons.   But the Queen made a personal appeal and when the Cabinet met he was not yet prepared to press his resignation.

This decision may well have been influenced by the fact that in spite of the croakings of the Whig peers increasing support for resistance to France was coming from many sides.   The British people had taken longer than those on the Continent to resent the threats of Thiers and the expansion of French armaments on sea as well as on land.   They regretted the rupture of the 'Alliance' as it was still called.   But the conduct of France had at last begun to take effect.   The Tory party was by now almost unanimously on Palmerston's side.   Greville and Henry Reeve suddenly found that Barnes had swung *The Times* round to the same side, a change as much due to his deep-seated patriotism as to the advice given him by Aberdeen, now one of the strongest defenders of Palmerston amongst the Tories.   Peel was almost as decided and though the Duke made an imprudent remark to Bourqueney that France ought to be consulted, which was much quoted by Palmerston's enemies, he was really entirely of Palmerston's view.   The Whig Press was of course all on Palmerston's side and represented a good deal of the rank and file of the Party.   Considerable effect had been produced on the more religious of both parties by the proposal to find some means of helping the Jews to get back to Palestine, an element of public opinion to which Palmerston himself paid great attention.   Only the Radicals still clung to their opposition to the 'Holy Alliance', not very comfortable allies for Lord John Russell and his aristocratic supporters.[1]

The series of Cabinets began on the 28 September.   A comic

---

[1] Spencer Walpole, *Lord John Russell*, I, 348–354. Neumann to Metternich, 30 Sept., 1840: *V. St. A.* On the question of the Jews and Protestant interest in the settlement see below Sec. 6, p. 761.

turn was given to the proceedings by the fact that in each Minister's place was a copy of the letter written by Urquhart to Melbourne accusing Palmerston of High Treason. Palmerston used the incident to warn Russell that the Cabinet discussions would soon be known, if in distorted form, at Paris and Alexandria. The Cabinet arrived only slowly and reluctantly in London and some were absent from the first meetings. Palmerston tried to shew his colleagues that matters were going well enough and they had better leave them alone. But when the opposition refused to agree and insisted on a friendly reply to the conciliatory note which Guizot had communicated on 10 October, he made what seemed at first a great concession. He offered to concert with the signatories of the July Convention a soothing communication to France on the lines long ago laid down by Metternich in his letter to Leopold. This would have committed him to very little, but it might have led to dangerous discussions. It was, however, much less than was now insistently demanded by Lord John Russell, who had if not a majority at least a strong minority of the Cabinet with him. It was done, according to Neumann, after pressure from Melbourne who was now seriously alarmed at the effect of the crisis on the health of the Queen.

Whether Palmerston anticipated the result is not known. He certainly never intended to make any real concession about Syria. At any rate, when he summoned the Allied representatives to the Foreign Office and submitted his draft to them, Brunnow strongly objected. He could not, he said, take such a step without direct authorisation from the Tsar. Neumann, who had reflected the pessimistic attitude current at this moment in Vienna, wished something to be done. But he and others, including later Metternich himself, had to admit that there was no conference in existence at London from which a joint communication could be made to the French Government. Palmerston was thus able to report that it was impossible to do what the Cabinet wanted without a fresh negotiation with the other Great Powers. More time was thus gained and this was of vital importance. In a few days news had come which, if it for the moment increased the French fury, shewed the Cabinet that a serious impression had already been made on Ibrahim's defences.[1]

[1] See my article, "Urquhart, Ponsonby and Palmerston," *Eng. Hist. Rev.*, July 1947. Greville's (*Memoirs*, IV, 299–319) long reports of these cabinets

This situation was, as has been noted, influenced by the two French despatches which arrived in London at this time, the result of a long struggle in the French Cabinet. One dated 3 October was a belated official reply to Palmerston's despatch of the 31 August. It gave a French view of the course of the negotiations in a manner far too moderate for many of Thiers' supporters. It stressed the value to Europe of the Franco-British *entente* during the last ten years. It also tried to embarrass Palmerston by recalling the previous agreements made between France and Britain for action in the Straits against Russia. At the last minute, on the news of the Sultan's deposition of Mehemet Ali, there was added a declaration made in a second despatch dated 8 October. This stated more vigorously that France would regard such an act as a menace to the balance of power, but even here no explicit threat was made. These despatches were indeed a curious commentary on the violence of Thiers and the French Press during the preceding two months. Palmerston might have rated the first more highly than he did if it had not been published in *The Times* within a few hours of his receiving it, and before he could make it known to the Queen and the Prime Minister.

For Guizot communicated to Palmerston on 10 October the second despatch about the deposition before using the first one, of which he was thoroughly ashamed. This he only gave to Palmerston on 12 October. The publication of the latter, indeed, rather dismayed the 'French party' as they were beginning to be called. It seemed to justify Palmerston's estimate of French intentions. The Cabinet, however, still under the influence of the French threats, insisted so strongly that something should be done that Palmerston felt it necessary to make some concession to their alarm.[1]

shew that Palmerston's warning was only too justified. It is impossible to trust completely Greville's account which includes the famous statement that Melbourne fell asleep during the discussions, almost certainly untrue, unless it was a calculated action to lower the temperature. He can be checked by Melbourne's reports to the Queen given in *Queen Victoria Letters*, I, 293–304. From Melbourne, 10, 12 Oct., 1840: *B.P.*, Appendix, pp. 860. Neumann to Metternich, 5 Oct., 7 Nov., 1840: *V. St. A.* Guizot to Thiers, 29 Sept., 1840: *A.A.E.*

[1] Thiers to Guizot, 3, 8 Oct., 1840: *L.P.*, II, Nos. 217, 213. Guizot, *Mémoires*, V, 336–337. The first draft of the French despatch of 3 October had been made by Viel Castel (Desages to Bourqueney, 8 Sept., 1840: *Bour. P.*). There had been prolonged disputes about it in the French Cabinet and Louis Philippe himself had insisted on toning it down. Guizot does not comment on the fact, but there is no doubt that he presented the second despatch first. It was the despatch of 3 October that Thiers gave to Reeve and which he published in

The French note of 8 October had indicated, though not explicitly, that France would fight if Mehemet were turned out of Egypt. The other three Courts had shewn their dislike of the deposition of the Pasha when it was first announced, though as will be seen, Metternich was later to take a new line about it. Palmerston accordingly now saw Guizot and told him that the deposition of Mehemet was not a final decision and wrote a despatch to that effect to Granville. Palmerston had already told Ponsonby in private letters that he could not see his way to expel the Pasha from Egypt so he would have to be left there, though the nature of the hereditary tenure could still be determined in a manner most calculated to establish the Sultan's authority. The Ambassador now received a definite instruction to get the deposition reversed, while the French Government were immediately informed that this had been done. Since Palmerston had hardly dared to hope that he would secure Egypt for the Sultan no great concession had been made; the move served its purpose at this critical moment in quietening the Cabinet and shewing Louis Philippe that there was one extremity at least that he would not have to face at present.[1]

That harassed monarch had probably already determined to get rid of his bellicose minister but his resolution was certainly aided by a sudden move by Melbourne who, with one of the spasmodic acts of energy which he sometimes shewed, determined to make the situation quite clear. This action seems to have been as much due to his desire to protect the Queen from the constant pressure of her relatives, as to fear of war. Unknown to all his colleagues he wrote a letter in reply to Leopold's long epistles of October in which he roundly told him that Britain could no longer tolerate

---

The Times but in his note in Greville's *Memoirs* (IV, 314) Reeve mixed up the two despatches. He does not state whether Thiers gave him permission to do so, but though Granville later reported that the publication was not intended (19 Oct., 1840: *B.P.*) it seems likely that Thiers wished it. He probably thought, however, that it would be in Palmerston's hands two or three days before publication. It was the speed of Reeve and Barnes and the delay of Guizot that caused the incident. Guizot told Greville that he had never expected to receive anything so weak and inconsistent as the despatch of 3 October. Lady Palmerston told Princess Lieven that the revelation of the proposed measures against Russia had helped Palmerston with public opinion at home (Sudley, *Corres. Lieven-Palmerston*, 192).

[1] Guizot to Thiers, 4, 10, 16 Oct., 1840: Guizot, *Mémoires*, V, 329, 338, and *A.A.E.* Guichen, *La Crise Orientale*, 399. To Ponsonby, 17 Oct., 1840: *B.P.*; do., 15 Oct., 1840: *F.O. Turkey*, 391 and *L.P.*, II, No. 230. To Granville, 17 Oct., 1840: *F.O. France*, 600b and *L.P.*, II, No. 231.

the threats of France and still less her increase of armaments. If they persisted he would summon Parliament and demand the means to resist them. This letter was, as he knew it would be, immediately forwarded to Louis Philippe and contributed a good deal to the decision which the latter made a few days later. Louis Philippe's first step was to send for Guizot to assist him with the debates in the Chambers now about to meet, and on the 21 October he refused to accept the warlike speech with which Thiers proposed to open them and forced the resignation of his Ministry. Bülow, who saw Melbourne's letter when he passed through Brussels, told Palmerston later that he believed Louis Philippe's action was due to it, and Beauvale, informed from Prussian sources, wrote that it acted like a charm. "He never did a better thing than in writing it," he added, and Palmerston, far from taking umbrage at the concealment of such an important action from himself, seems to have been of the same opinion.[1]

The resignation of Thiers, the appointment of a new Ministry of which Soult was the nominal but Guizot the real head, and the news that soon came from the East ended the crisis. Henceforward Palmerston's attackers could do little. For another month, however, he still had an anxious time. For though the energy of Napier and Jochmus and the defection of the Maronites had defeated Ibrahim's armies and obtained possession of the sea coast, Acre was still there with its ominous reputation for long

[1] From Melbourne, 25th Oct., 1840; Leopold to Melbourne, 23 Oct., 1840: *B.P.* described the use made of the letter but implied that he would still keep Thiers in office. The fact of the letter has long been known. (Sir T. Martin, *Life of the Prince Consort*, I, 231.) To Beauvale, 4 Nov., 1840; from Beauvale, 14 Nov., 1840: *B.P.* "Melbourne did not mention to me that he had written to this effect," Palmerston wrote. But Melbourne had in fact communicated its general tenour on 25 October: "My letter to him [Leopold] was principally to urge upon him the bad effect of the French military and naval preparations and of the necessity of which they would lay us under of arming upon our part. I also shewed to him the poverty of the ground which Thiers had taken in asserting that the power of Mehemet was a necessary constituent part of the balance of power and these are the two points of the difference which has taken place between the King and Thiers." The exact contents of the letter are variously described, but all agree that it was very strongly worded. Bülow, who saw it at Brussels, told Neumann that part of it ran as follows: "I will lay before it [Parliament] the conduct of France, ask for supplies in order to increase our fleets. I will take care that they shall be placed upon the largest footing,—this is in a word, War, Sir. If I do take such a responsibility upon myself in the state in which is now Her Majesty, I know that the interests and honour of my country require it and that I will be approved by the whole nation." Neumann to Metternich, 7 Nov., 1840: *V. St. A.*; (in English in the original). cf. A. Hasenclever, *Die Orientalische Frage*, 228–229. Raikes (*Journal, New Edn.*, II, 262) noted the references in the French Press but completely misconceived the purpose of the letter.

resistance and winter was coming on. Stopford had for some time threatened to take the fleet away in spite of frantic appeals from Ponsonby. Bandiera, the Austrian Admiral, was strongly in favour of such a course. Many thought it inevitable, including Guizot's advisers in Paris, who still hoped to obtain something for the Pasha to satisfy French opinion and establish the new Ministry firmly in its place. Louis Philippe and Guizot, indeed, seemed to think it obvious that concessions should now be made for this purpose which had been refused to the threats of Thiers. Granville pressed this point of view with all his strength. If the Left came into power, he insisted, there would be war.[1]

That was not Palmerston's view. British policy, he always insisted, was founded on the necessities of the situation in Asia Minor and had nothing to do with the question of who was to be in power in France. He warmly praised Ponsonby for getting 10,000 more Turks despatched to Syria and continued to send all the aid he could. He authorised him to get the Porte to remove Sir Charles Smith and sent a capable engineering officer in his place, together with expert ordnance officers. He depleted the British arsenals to supply muskets for the Turkish troops. He stressed especially the necessity of adequate commissariat and medical arrangements and sent out officers to assist the Turks with these problems. He hoped that their advice would not only help to overcome Mehemet but establish new and better services in Turkey. He continued to urge Metternich to send help also. He did his best to get the bankers to back the Sultan though he had to refuse the British guarantee of a loan, which, like all their kind, they immediately demanded.[2]

Palmerston had already strongly supported Ponsonby's appeal

[1] From Ponsonby, 3, 7 Oct., 1840; from Beauvale, 13 Oct., 1840; from Granville, 2, 6 Nov., 1840: *B.P.* Ponsonby, in order to increase the ardour of the Sultan and the public morale, presented a standard captured by Napier's forces as one taken by the Turkish Army. The object of the Ambassador, in which he had great success, was hardly appreciated by Napier—or by some historians who have considered the incident.

[2] To Ponsonby, 17, 23, 27 Oct., 4 Nov., 1840: *B.P.* "I hope at Vienna they will feel ashamed to leave a young Prince of the Imperial Family fighting in the Levant with not two hundred men at his back. Put this strongly to Stürmer and get him to write to this effect to Vienna." When the Turks were asked to pay for the arms sent the total value was estimated at £41,928. (*F.O. Turkey*, 391.) "I hope our medical men will be able to make arrangements which will be useful to Turkey beyond the present crisis" (4 Nov.). By the time the missions arrived the fighting was over, the Turks received them coldly and they were able to effect nothing. cf. F. E. Bailey, *British Policy and the Turkish Reform Movement*, 203, n. 87.

to keep the fleet on the coast, even if it had sometimes to withdraw a little. The steamers at any rate could remain without danger, and Palmerston pointed out that Mehemet had kept his fleet there during the winter. It was difficult to frame explicit instructions on such a question at so great a distance. The Admiralty were naturally cautious, but Minto was altogether of Palmerston's view and wrote to Stopford that the attack was to continue. "I hope", Palmerston wrote on the 5 October, "that by this time our squadron has taken Acre. But I send an instruction to Stopford to attack it if he can do so with a prospect of success, in order to satisfy him that he was right, if he has done so already, and to spur him on, if he has hesitated. He is a brave and honourable man and a good officer; but rather old and worn out in mind, and I should think weak in judgment and liable to take a wrong turn, but I am sure that when he learnt, as he will have done from Minto, the wishes and intentions of his Govt. he will have set himself to work in good earnest to carry them into effect."

The official instructions signed by Palmerston reached Stopford on the 29th. They were no doubt the result of much consultation in London and their careful wording, which placed on Stopford himself the final responsibility for the attack, reflected the caution of the Admiralty and other members of the Cabinet more than Palmerston's own optimism. Melbourne, indeed, strongly advised against action and seems to have given way only at the last moment. A whole series of communications could have already left no doubt in the Admiral's mind of the intense desire to obtain Acre as soon as possible. Stopford was, however, still hesitating when the instructions reached him and it was not only Palmerston's firm conviction but also the opinion of many who had followed the events closely that they decided him to make the attack on 4 November. It was amazingly successful. Aided by the blowing up of the powder magazine by a chance shot, the fortress fell in a single day, the young Archduke of Austria being amongst the first to enter by the breach. Ibrahim had no alternative now but to get his army back to Egypt across the desert route. Had the attack been pressed as Ponsonby desired he might have lost the whole of it. Sir Charles Smith was eventually removed from his position as Turkish Chief of Staff. But though Jochmus did his best he got little support from Stopford, while Napier had been sent to Alexandria to summon Mehemet to surrender, a mission

with surprising results.   For two months longer Ibrahim kept his
army in Syria while Mehemet negotiated for its safety.   It was
finally allowed to go without pressure.   The bulk of the routed
army thus at last reached Egypt in safety with their commander,
a broken and despairing man, who sought refuge in the bottle
from the consequences of his defeat.[1]

The news of the fall of Acre did not reach the Western capitals

[1] To Ponsonby, 5 Oct., 1840; from Melbourne, 4 Oct., 1840: *B.P.* Broughton, *Recollections*, V, 298.   The whole question is discussed in great detail in
Appendix III of H. W. V. Temperley's *Crimea*, where the instructions of
5 October are printed, and all that can be said in defence of Stopford and Sir
Charles Smith will be found skilfully marshalled.   Professor Temperley rightly
pointed out the responsibility thrown on the Admiral and attacked Napier's
conduct during the bombardment where he took up a position contrary to the
Admiral's orders.   Though Napier demanded a court martial, which was refused,
it was he who was sent to Alexandria to summon Mehemet to surrender.
Much of the information on which Palmerston relied was sent in private letters.
Much of this was *ex parte* evidence from Napier and Jochmus who were strongly
supported by Ponsonby.   Ponsonby's letters were as usual written very freely
and by Palmerston's direction only short extracts were put on official record,
but he placed in the F.O. Archives part of the letter of Jochmus of 23 October in which he summed up Smith: "I never saw a person less qualified for his
present station, from nervous affection irascibility indolence and, as it appears,
to me a *decidedly narrow scope of mind*, than the man now unfortunately charged
with directing the movements of this war.   He seems entirely incapable of
comprehending the description of people he has to deal with and the nature
and genius of this mountain warfare, and, what is more, from fear of showing
that he does not, he wont consult others who do or who are capable to act.   He
has shown the most unwarrantable jealousy of Commodore Napier for no other
earthly reason than that the latter has been fortunate enough to succeed on shore.
. . . If your Excy wants to establish some probability of victory the Admiral
must go off Alexandria or into some winter Post where he can waver without
injury to the cause: Sir Charles Smith must be recalled to Constantinople to
be consulted on the general campaign and remain there or go to England, and
Commodore Napier and myself left to fight *in Syria*." (*F.O. Turkey*, 398 and
B.P.)

Jochmus, while personally interested in the result, was an experienced and
loyal officer and this letter is convincing.

Palmerston gave Ponsonby only conditional instructions to get the Porte to
remove Smith and substitute Jochmus on 17 October but Ponsonby promptly
put them into effect, though Jochmus did not receive his Firman giving him the
command until 15 December. (Wood to Ponsonby, 16 Dec., 1840: *F.O. Turkey*, 399.) The letter to Smith himself seems to have been more equivocal and
the latter protested bitterly to Ponsonby for the speed at which he had acted.
Melbourne certainly thought no decision had been taken (18 Nov.: *B.P.
Appendix*, p. 861). Jochmus later complained that his own despatches were not
published and in a secret report threw on Smith the blame for allowing Ibrahim's
troops to escape to Egypt. Napier, it is true, considered the position at that time
critical, but he was defending his own conduct at Alexandria.   The whole
question of these operations demands more extended treatment than can be
given here, but it would seem that the conclusion of Professor Temperley cannot
be accepted without further consideration of all the evidence available.   To
Ponsonby, 17 Oct., 1840; from Ponsonby, 9 Dec., 1840 (enclosing Smith to
Ponsonby, 25 Nov.).   *F.O. Turkey*, 391, 399. Jochmus to Ponsonby, 12 May,
1841 (with secret report): *B.P.* and *F.O. Turkey*, 434.

until 24 November. In the meanwhile Palmerston had to resist
another attempt to make him give Mehemet something more than
Egypt—Candia or some portion of the Acre Pashalik. Some
concession, Guizot reiterated in his appeals to his Whig friends,
was surely due to him for taking up his burden and was necessary
to ensure the stability of the new Government about to face the
Chambers where Thiers was expected to make a furious attack.
Louis Philippe and Leopold began a new campaign to obtain this
end and were supported by most of those in England who had
previously worked for France including Clarendon and Greville.
Lord Holland's sudden death on 22 October deprived them of the
great centre of cabal and intrigue, but the Whig peers and Greville
and his friends were as persistent as before.

It was no doubt partly to counter these moves that Palmerston
now sent to Guizot the despatch which he had prepared in answer
to Thiers' note of 8 October. This was another incisive exposure
of French inconsistencies and took no account of the fact that
Thiers had been thrown out of office. Since Thiers' had published
a despatch in *The Times*, Palmerston had his published in the
Morning Chronicle, thus adding to the chagrin of Guizot and his
British allies. This step was perhaps a little vindictive. But Guizot was already intriguing with members of the Cabinet, and
Palmerston wished to provide ammunition against Thiers for the
debates in the Chambers, a purpose the despatch served very well.
It caused, however, a 'great sensation' at Paris where in some
quarters it was regarded as a threat that Mehemet Ali might lose
Egypt as well as Syria. Guizot told the sympathetic Granville
that he was sure that Palmerston, who had been so nice to him on
his departure from London, could not have conceived the damage
it would do to the new Government.[1]

The attack in London had this time been led by Bülow, who,
after being indoctrinated by Werther at Berlin, had come back via
Brussels where he and Leopold had planned the new campaign
together. He was to tackle Melbourne and other Cabinet members before Palmerston, and the suggestion was that an armistice
should be immediately proclaimed in Syria and that the Pasha

---

[1] To Granville, 2 Nov., 1840: *L.P.*, II, No. 262. From Granville, 13 Nov.,
1840: *F.O. France*, 607; do., 16 Nov., 1840. Palmerston blandly replied to
Granville's protests that pressure of work had prevented him from completing
the despatch in time to send it to Thiers. To Melbourne, 26 Oct., 1840: *B.P.
Appendix*, p. 848.

might be allowed to possess for life such territory as he still held. Guizot meanwhile had been demanding much more from Granville. This offer, he said, was not good enough. Ibrahim's armies were still intact and their hold on the interior could not be shaken. The British fleet would have to leave the coast. Bourqueney was loth to take part in operations behind Palmerston's back which he knew would be regarded as underhand. He preferred to tackle him directly and of course got nothing but friendly conversation. He held back Guizot's despatches, however, until Bülow could make his approach to Melbourne and the Cabinet so that Palmerston could not conceal them. There was in fact an intrigue to undermine Palmerston's position.[1]

Clarendon and Greville had lent themselves to this intrigue with the same ardour as on previous occasions, though a severe attack of gout prevented the latter from doing very much. Clarendon discussed the possibilities with Bourqueney in a frank conversation in which he told him that Lord John Russell and Lansdowne shared his own desire to make concessions. Austria and Prussia would move with Britain, he said, if she left Russia to draw nearer to France. The Tsar had wished to provoke a European war and a revolution in France and he and his friends would leave the Cabinet before they allowed such a thing to occur. He promised that they would do everything possible in the Cabinet to assist Guizot. Bourqueney had even to remind him that it was with Palmerston that he must transact his business rather than with Clarendon and his colleagues.[2]

In order to obtain a result it was above all necessary that some concrete proposal should be at once made by Guizot that his friends in the Cabinet could support. That Minister was prolific in suggestions in unofficial conversations with Granville and in private letters to Bourqueney. But, either by design or through sheer ineptitude, he gave to neither any explicit or official proposal. When Bourqueney went to Palmerston in the expectation that he had already received from Granville Guizot's definite plan, the Secretary of State was able to show him that the despatch contained nothing of the kind. The Chargé d'Affaires dared not take

[1] From Granville, 6 Nov., 1840: *F.O. France*, 606. Bourqueney to Guizot, 2 Nov., 1840; Guizot to Bourqueney, 4, 7 Nov., 1840: *A.A.E.* Part of the last letter was shewn to Greville (*Memoirs*, IV, 328). Neumann to Metternich, 7 Nov., 1840: *V. St. A.*

[2] Bourqueney to Guizot, 28 Oct., 1840: *A.A.E.*

the responsibility on himself. Thus, though the Cabinet had decided that any such offer must be seriously considered, Palmerston was able to inform them that none had been received. When Granville inquired of Guizot what the situation was, the answer was that Bourqueney's informal approach had shewn that nothing worth while could be obtained and that consequently no official proposal would be made.[1]

In any case the news from Syria destroyed Bülow's effort almost as soon as it had begun. The population there had clearly declared itself on the Turkish side. The Ambassador's discomfiture was completed by the attitude of Metternich. For at Vienna the Court had become very warlike. The Archduke Charles was radiant at the conduct of his son. Kolowrat found he could get no support and abandoned his opposition. Once the danger from France had died down Metternich plucked up courage to be defiant. The uproar in Germany forced both the Prussian and Austrian Government to take the question of the defence of the Confederation seriously. There was much consultation amongst the soldiers and Prussia proposed that the defence of the Confederation should be extended to Piedmont, thus covering Italy about which Metternich had been so nervous.

Metternich now began to consider the extent of Austrian interests in the Levant and proposals began to be made for Austria to become the Protector of the Catholics in Syria. A promise was made to send arms for the Turks and even reinforcements of marines for the Austrian squadron. The result of all this was, wrote Beauvale, exulting in the successes in the East, that "We are now as bold as lions and have forgot we were ever afraid."[2]

This new strength was already reflected in Metternich's despatches. He was not only against any concession in Syria but would not even do what Palmerston had agreed to do, press the Sultan to withdraw the deposition of Mehemet. That, he said, could be left until the Pasha made his submission. Bülow, reported Bourqueney, was 'atterré' by this news. The Ambassa-

[1] From Bourqueney, 2, 6, 8, 9, 10 Nov., 1840: *A.A.E.* His embarrassment and chagrin are clearly revealed in the despatches. From Granville, 6, 9, 13 Nov., 1840: *F.O. France*, 606, 607. To Granville, 12, 13 Nov., 1840: *F.O. France*, 600, B. Greville (*Memoirs*, IV, 323–334) though ill with the gout, got most of the story from Clarendon and Bourqueney, and his advice helped Guizot to decide to do nothing.
[2] From Beauvale, 19, 27, 31 Oct., 14 Nov., 1840: *B.P.*

dor hastened to beat a retreat and, by an abject apology that he had mistaken the situation, to make his peace with Palmerston. Palmerston was easily appeased but he complained to Berlin that, as Prussia had done nothing, he had at least the right to her full moral support. The King was much pained at this complaint for he considered that the stout attitude of the German people had done a great deal to keep France from pressing her demands. Bourqueney and Desages began to fear that the grant of heredity for Egypt would be lost. The only comfort that the former could give Guizot was to stress the fact that Stopford had insisted that most of the fleet should go to Malta for the winter, and that Sir Charles Smith had reported that the whole Turkish army must be reorganised before it could attack again. There would thus be a long delay and meanwhile Metternich might change his mind again as he had so often done before and Prussia would assuredly follow his lead.[1]

It was at this juncture that the debates began in the French Chambers. They were a complete vindication of Palmerston's policy. Guizot used all the arguments that Palmerston himself had employed to shew that France had not been treated in such a manner as necessitated Thier's policy. Thiers in an effort to defend himself explained that he meant to attack Europe when French armaments were completed. The discomfiture of the Whig coterie was completed by Thiers' eulogy of Lord Holland who, he openly insinuated, had worked for France in the British Cabinet. Guizot also described how he had found allies among Palmerston's colleagues. "What a painful picture does the French Ambassador give of the British Cabinet", Palmerston commented, "when he quietly relates his cooperation with different members of it for the purpose of thwarting the Secretary of State for Foreign Affairs and to prevent him from promoting and securing the interests of England; and how much must Privy Counsellors have kept the secrets of the Cabinet when Guizot says that he knew almost everything from day to day that passed in our deliberations!"

But the effect of the whole debate was to justify Palmerston even in the eyes of his most determined critics. "I really think

[1] Bourqueney to Guizot, 13, 17 Nov., 1840: *A.A.E.* To Bülow, 9 Nov.' 1840; From Bülow, 11 Nov., 1840: *B.P.* To Lord William Russell, 17 Nov., 1840: *B.P.*; do., 16 Nov., 1840; from Lord William Russell, 25 Nov., 1840: *F.O. Prussia,* 227, 229.

you must have had Thiers in your pay during the last 3 weeks,"
wrote Clarendon, "for even in every lie he has told he seemed to
have no other object but to make out a good case for you," Lord
Lansdowne made the same jest. "He says", reported Macaulay,
"that he now sees where all your Secret Service money has gone.
It has been distributed amongst the opposition orators in the
Chamber of Deputies." Though the Left applauded Thiers and
Odillon Barrot, who also used warlike language, French public
opinion was not impressed and realised the futility of Thiers'
policy. It turned its attention to other matters. The reception
of Napoleon's remains was a great and moving spectacle but the
ordinary citizen was even more diverted by the sensational trial
of Madame Lefarge who, according to some cynical observers,
had done more to reduce the temperature of the political discussions than any of the statesmen.[1]

The result was a complete and unexpected triumph of Guizot
in the Chamber, Thiers' final discomfiture being increased by the
news of the total defeat of Ibrahim. The debate and the taking of
Acre finally also routed all Palmerston's opponents in Britain.
One and all had to confess that the facts had shewn him to be
right. Some grudgingly attributed his success to luck, but for the
most part it was admitted that the triumph was well deserved and
due as much to Palmerston's own energy and judgment as to the
unexpected weakness of his opponents. Thiers himself told Lord
Beauvale that he regarded Palmerston "as the first Statesman of
this age and perhaps of any other". Even Greville had to reverse
all his ideas and in his diary compare Palmerston to Chatham, a
standard which Disraeli was later to accept in *Tancred*. The most
portentous congratulation came from Wellesley who had nothing

[1] From Granville, 13, 20, 27 Nov., 4 Dec., 1840: *F.O. France*, 607. From
Clarendon, 6 Dec., 1840; From Macaulay (undated); To Granville, 30 Nov.,
1840: *B.P. Bulwer*, II, 365, leaves out this passage and a trenchant criticism
of French honesty and ability in foreign affairs. Lady Holland was much distressed at the implication that Lord Holland had betrayed Cabinet secrets, a
charge that was repeated in *The Times*. She wrote a number of letters about it,
including one to Palmerston asking for refutation. Lord Holland's friends took
a similar line. Unfortunately, as has been seen, there was too much truth in the
statement for any very convincing denial to be made. Lady Holland was
reduced to appealing to Bourqueney to get a letter from Guizot stating that
Lord Holland had never betrayed his country. (Bourqueney to Guizot, 29 Dec.,
1840: *A.A.E.*) But Palmerston's letters about Lord Holland to his colleagues
and Ambassadors were couched in the friendliest terms. Thureau-Dangon
(*Histoire de la Monarchie de Juillet*, iv, 384–403) gives the details of the debates.
Granville was not allowed to appear officially at the reception of Napoleon's
remains and watched the ceremony from afar.

to retract and nothing to gain from Palmerston's favours and came
to his conclusion before the final dénouement was known. After
recounting his long experience of political life, which included the
careers of both Pitt and Fox, he wrote: "It is a complete and most
splendid justification of your policy; and is the most important,
and I trust will prove the most salutary event which has happened
in the civilised world for the last half century or more. But I must
go further . . . and I sincerely declare that this is the ablest act
both of diplomatic and military policy that within my memory has
proceeded from the British Cabinet."[1]

Many Frenchmen thought likewise and Palmerston had incurred
their deep hostility because of the vigour and insight with which
he had resisted France. Those most deeply chagrined were those
who like Broglie and de Tocqueville had been most attached to the
entente with Britain. Previous opponents like Molé were much
less critical. And the more realistic members of the official class
saw that the sooner France got back to her normal position in
Europe the better for her interests. The question of Mehemet Ali,
Desages advised Bourqueney, should be regarded as only an
incident, like the Quadruple Alliance or the Treaty of 1827 concerning Greece. In due course the common interests of France
and Britain in some other question would bring them together
again. Unfortunately this was not Guizot's attitude, and he no
doubt reflected the view of the majority of Frenchmen. He still
pressed for some special recognition of France and as Bourqueney
did not seem zealous enough in the cause sent a special envoy,
Mounier, to expound his views, much to Bourqueney's distress.
Mounier had no more success than the Chargé d'Affaires and the
problem of bringing France back to her proper place in the
European polity was, therefore, yet to be solved and it was to
prove much more difficult than anyone yet realised.[2]

---

[1] Beauvale to Lady Palmerston, 5 Jan., 1846: Airlie, *Lady Palmerston*, II, 105.
From Wellesley, 4 Nov., 1840. "This", wrote Palmerston to Melbourne, "is
to be taken with the allowance which is always to be made for Lord Wellesley's
high flown style; but . . . I have good reason to believe that an immense majority of the British nation will likewise approve the conduct of the Government in
this affair." *B.P.* Lord Spencer wrote a private letter to Palmerston admitting
that he had been wrong and paid a tribute to him in the House of Lords. Lord
Morpeth, who had been an insistent critic, now wrote a handsome letter of
congratulation.
[2] Guizot to Bourqueney, 20, 29 Nov., 11 Dec., 1840; Bourqueney to Guizot,
24, 26 Nov., 2 Dec., 1840: *A.A.E.* He was deeply hurt at what would be considered as a 'supercession' of his functions and asked for a mark of confidence to
be inserted in the *Journal Officiel*. Desages to Bourqueney, 4 Nov., 1840: *A.A.E.*

Meanwhile Palmerston himself had been much exercised about the grant of hereditary tenure to Mehemet. He had begun to regret the concession already made and wished it to be limited as far as was possible. These views he communicated to Ponsonby in private letters, for the whole question was still hypothetical and he had no definite plan to put before the Cabinet. Already on 27 October he suggested that the grant of heredity might perhaps be limited to Ibrahim alone. But he had to admit that the Cabinet would not allow the British fleet to attack Egypt and it hardly seemed possible to force on Mehemet such a treaty in any other way. Metternich's unexpected attitude, however, encouraged his hopes of getting more than he had anticipated. The Sultan, he pointed out, could make his own laws about the kind of heredity to be granted, and in the act attached to the convention it had been agreed that Mehemet must accept and apply the laws of the Ottoman Empire. Yet he was anxious to get Mehemet's submission before the autumn gales. That would be difficult unless Acre was taken and in view of Stopford's hesitations he hardly dared hope that could be done. But the attempt was worth making. Accordingly on 14 November Stopford was instructed to send an emissary to Mehemet to tell him that if he surrendered all his conquests outside Egypt and handed back the Turkish fleet, the Powers would recommend the Sultan to re-appoint him to the Governorship of Egypt. Nothing was said of hereditary tenure, but in a separate instruction the officer was authorised to convey Mehemet's reply to Constantinople if he insisted on it. As Palmerston explained to Ponsonby: "If he makes his submission as we invite him to do he must have the hereditary Pashalik of Egypt; subject of course to all the restrictions mentioned in the separate act and annexed to the Treaty [of 15 July]. If he refuses and goes on fighting then the Sultan will be doubly free to do what he pleases." Palmerston did not communicate these reservations and interpretations to the Cabinet or his Allies and this is perhaps the most equivocal step which he took in all these years. The attitude which he took towards Mehemet was naturally welcomed by Ponsonby and accounts for all his subsequent conduct in the question of the grant of hereditary tenure. Palmerston did not in fact press his policy to its logical conclusion and, though he never admits it, it is probable that he regretted it during the long period

which ensued before the final settlement with Mehemet was made.[1]

The envoy sent to Mehemet, however, was imbued with very different ideas. Stopford had chosen Napier for this mission because he found him so hard to control in the Syrian operations. But Napier fell like other Englishmen under the Pasha's spell and tried to settle matters with his usual recklessness and flamboyance. Mehemet had for long seen that the game was up, and for some time it had taken all the efforts of Walewski and Cochelet to prevent him from throwing over the French and appealing to the Allied Powers. He received Napier with open arms and the two were soon on excellent terms. Napier went far beyond his instructions by negotiating a convention which gave Mehemet all that he could now hope to get. In return for a promise to recall his armies an immediate armistice was to be granted, thus ensuring the safety of Ibrahim's remaining troops, of which the bulk were to come by sea. Further Mehemet promised to make his submission to the Sultan and return the Ottoman fleet on condition that the Four Powers guaranteed to him the hereditary possession of Egypt. With his usual bombast Napier expounded what he had done in extravagant language and alluded to the Ptolemies looking down on the new state. "I have done", he wrote, "what I think you wish." Ponsonby was of course horrified and Stopford without consulting Constantinople promptly disavowed his subordinate. He had just received Palmerston's instruction and private letter of 14 November. He offered Mehemet Egypt, with no mention of hereditary tenure, if he would surrender the fleet.

Palmerston and Melbourne were also taken aback at Napier's action and laughed at the language used. But though Palmerston at once pointed out that the four Powers could not guarantee the hereditary possession but only advise the Sultan to grant it, he was ready to accept in substance what had been done. The Sultan, however, had already refused the submission under these conditions and the whole question had to be reconsidered. Austria and Prussia, reported Beauvale, saw in Napier's convention a sign that Britain was merely looking to her own interests now that the struggle was over.[2]

[1] To Ponsonby, 27 Oct., 14, 15 Nov., 1840: *B.P.* To Admiralty, 14 Nov., 1840: *L.P.*, II, Nos. 22, 23. Beauvale told Palmerston that Metternich would never agree to hereditary succession. (14 Nov., 1840: *B.P.*).

[2] From Napier, 26 Nov., 1840: *L.P.*, III, Nos. 85–87: 28 Nov., 1840: *B.P.* From Ponsonby, 8, 9 Dec., 1840: *B.P.* To Ponsonby, 12 Dec., 1840: *B.P.*

The news that followed from the East was, however, more cheering. Though the reply to Stopford contained some equivocal phrases it was so far satisfactory that Stopford's emissary, Captain Fanshawe, declared himself ready to convey it to the Porte. Shortly afterwards Captain Walker hoisted the Sultan's flag in the Ottoman fleet in Alexandria and prepared to take it to Constantinople. There was still some doubt as to Ibrahim's movements but he seemed to be making preparations to retire to Egypt. Provided the Porte did not impose impossible terms on Mehemet in granting the hereditary tenure of Egypt to him and his family, peace would be assured and the negotiation with France could be begun at once, the settlement of the Eastern Question be put into a treaty of the Five Powers with the Sultan and, even more important, the situation in Western Europe brought back to normal.[1]

For France still refused to reduce her armaments. Guizot had really shown in his speeches that they were not necessary but he would not abandon them at the behest of the other European Powers. After a great fight in the Chambers the fortifications bills were finally passed, though Soult shewed very clearly that he did not approve of them. Some Frenchmen were even talking of the possibility of a Franco-Russian alliance, a fact which Granville reported in great alarm only to get from Palmerston the reply that it was a quite natural development but would not come yet awhile. When Metternich proposed to begin discussions for a mutual return to a peace footing, Guizot warned him that such a negotiation would have the worst effect on French public opinion. All that must wait, he said, until France could be sure that the Eastern Question had been finally settled and Mehemet Ali's

From Beauvale, 26 Dec., 1840: *B.P.* To Beauvale, 4, 19 Dec., 1840: *B.P.* Esterhazy to Metternich, 4, 12 Dec., 1840: *V. St. A.* From Melbourne, 15 Dec., 1840: *B.P.* Melbourne was the only person able to discuss the appositeness of the allusion to the Ptolemies: "I do not recollect much of the nature of the power of the Ptolemies but I dare say it was in the first instance a delegated and dependant authority under the Roman General in Macedonia." Palmerston criticised the form and said it was 'diamond cut diamond' for Napier would not have attacked and Mehemet had already ordered his troops to return. Napier vigorously defended himself. The title given to Mehemet was a bad translation due to the haste necessary to prevent French intrigues; he would have attacked, the order had not been given; Ibrahim had concentrated his army and the Turkish troops were dispersed so that the issue was still doubtful. To Napier, 12 Jan., 1841; From Napier, 26 March, 1841: *B.P.*

[1] Much detail on all this is given in *L.P.*, III, Nos. 115, 117 and in E. Driault, *La Crise Orientale*, III, Nos. 1-42.

position in Egypt assured. He also desired the other Powers to state that this position was due to their regard for France, "or rather from fear of her", as Melbourne commented, "which is what she desires to be understood. Never heard of such a thing before."[1]

In Europe the alarm caused by Thiers' threats and armaments took some time to die down. The Prussian soldiers had been afraid that France would postpone her attack until the Eastern Question was finished and Britain had not the same interest in defending Central Europe. They had even in great secrecy asked the Duke of Wellington to command the European armies if the breach came, an offer which Wellington had seemed disposed to accept. This was done without the British Cabinet being consulted. But the Prussian Government also put forward the idea of creating a permanent alliance against France amongst the Four Powers. This was naturally welcomed by the Tsar but Palmerston would have nothing to do with it. He had no desire to make permanent the present situation. He was not afraid of France and had no desire to encourage the Central Powers to think that he would be on their side in all circumstances. The project, therefore, was soon abandoned though, as will be seen, it was to come up again when the Eastern Question was finally settled.[2]

Nor would either Palmerston or Melbourne give the slightest encouragement to a "very secret" scheme of Metternich to win back France to the Concert by recognising her position in Algiers. Such a concession, Palmerston wrote, would turn the "salutary moral humiliation" of France into a veritable triumph and undo all the good that had been done. Palmerston was determined that France should be compelled to accept such terms as he thought reasonable and right. He refused to see the advantage of conciliating her now that he had obtained all that was essential. And, as he a little later told Esterhazy, Algiers would be a hostage in the hands of her enemies if France again made war on Europe, a threat that would be less strong if her sovereignty had been recog-

---

[1] From Granville, 4, 7, 11, 25 Dec., 1840: *B.P.* A flock of Russian ladies including Mme Nesselrode had descended on Paris—but they were not allowed to go to Court. To Granville, 8, 29 Dec., 1840; to Beauvale, 19, 26 Dec., 1840; from Beauvale, 4, 15 Dec., 1840; from Melbourne, 15 Dec., 1840: *B.P.*
[2] From Lord William Russell, 21 Oct., 25 Nov., 16 Dec., 1840, 20 Jan., 1841: *B.P.* I have nowhere else found any allusion to the offer to Wellington but Russell reports it in the private letters of 16 Dec. and 20 Jan. in such a manner as seems to leave no doubt but that it took place, though of course informally.

nised by the Great Powers. Melbourne agreed entirely. To give France Algiers "would be treating her like a child", and make it more difficult to guard against the real danger in North Africa— further extension of French power.[1]

Thus, though the year closed for Palmerston in great triumph, he had still tangled and difficult negotiations in front of him which were to try the patience of the Cabinet and the European Allies for many months to come. Nor perhaps was he unconscious of the fact that he had incurred the bitter hostility not only of Guizot and Louis Philippe but of Leopold whose mediatory efforts he had treated so roughly. That he had expected, but it had consequences in Britain itself. For Queen Victoria and Prince Albert and especially the latter, now in full control of the royal prerogative, could not help but be influenced by the insinuations which Leopold conveyed to them in his avuncular letters. "Rex and autocrat" was the phrase applied by him to Palmerston in a specially damaging letter to Prince Albert. Meanwhile not only was Lord John Russell complaining to Melbourne that Palmerston did not keep him reasonably informed of what he was doing, but Queen Victoria, now entirely in the hands of her husband so far as public business was concerned, began to demand that the important despatches should be sent in good time so that they could be considered properly before they were sent off. This was Albert's first move to establish the Crown in that position of authority which it held in the minds of his tutors, Stockmar and Leopold.[2]

---

[1] From Beauvale, 15 Dec., 1840; to Beauvale, 26 Dec., 1840; from Melbourne, 28 Dec., 1840: *B.P.* Esterhazy to Metternich, 7 Jan., 1841: *V. St. A.* Palmerston said the British Government would declare to France that they would not allow her to do in Morocco what she had done in Algiers. For his watchful eye on that country see R. Flournoy, *British Policy towards Morocco in the age of Palmerston (1830–1865)*, chap. III.

[2] Leopold to Prince Albert, 26 Nov., 1840. *Queen Victoria Letters*, I, 315. The significance of the letter is brought out by Professor Bell (*Palmerston*, I, 320). A similar phrase, "King and Minister", had long been in Leopold's mind and its connection with the reestablishment of the royal power is more clearly shewn in an account by Lord Burghersh of an interview with Leopold at Laeken on 12 October. R. Weigall, *Corres. of Lord Burghersh*, 286. At this same period, reviewing her visit to England, Princess Lieven wrote to her brother, "Lord Palmerston *gouverne*." (15 Nov., 1840: *Lie MSS.*) From Melbourne, 28 Nov., 14 Dec., 1840: *B.P.*

5. THE CONTEST IN CENTRAL ASIA[1]
1837–1841

Palmerston recognised that he had obtained all his objectives in the Eastern Question with the cooperation of the Tsar who had supported him more consistently than any other person in Europe. His conduct, Palmerston avowed, had been 'perfect'. But all this time Britain was engaged in another struggle with Russia for power and influence which might ultimately have as important results as that concerning the Ottoman Empire. The whole future of Central Asia was at stake and to some minds that meant the future of India as well. At any rate great areas including Persia, Khiva, Bokhara, Afghanistan and even Sind and the Punjaub, were concerned. The two great empires in Asia were advancing towards one another. No one knew how fast they would go or where the contact would be made. In the employ of both countries were active and imaginative men, who were beginning to realise the possibilities of the situation. The old oriental despotisms clearly could not resist the pressure of the disciplined armies of the European Empires when these could be brought to bear on them. The distances were great, the conditions imperfectly known, the movements of armies or even of traders difficult and hazardous. The contest was largely one of logistics. The risks were great, but the prizes were dazzling and attracted many adventurous as well as patriotic men. The Governments as always lagged cautiously behind, but in these also were some who thought that the time had come for bold and prompt action.

Amongst these was certainly Palmerston, who was one of the foremost advocates of a forward policy. He summed up his position in a letter to Hobhouse in 1840:

"It seems pretty clear that sooner or later the Cossak [sic] and the Sepoy, the man from the Baltic and he from the British islands

---

[1] There were several Blue books on Persia and Afghanistan reprinted in *B.F.S.P.*, vols. XXV–XXVIII. There is also a large literature on this theme which H. W. C. Davis surveyed in his remarkable Raleigh lecture, "The Great Game in Central Asia", *Proceedings, British Academy*, 1927. There is a wealth of material from British actors in India. Here only an outline can be given of policies for which Palmerston was only partly responsible and the execution of which he did not control. The private correspondence at Broadlands on this subject is not extensive but has some significant letters.

will meet in the centre of Asia. It should be our business to take
care that the meeting should be as far off from our Indian possessions as may be convenient and advantageous to us. But the
meeting will not be avoided by our staying at home to receive the
visit."[1]

This was written when he had in his mind the Russian expedition
to Khiva which he thought would soon extend to Bokhara. His
policy had originally been determined by the Russian action in
Persia. It was only gradually that the wider possibilities of the
situation became clear to him.

In Persia Palmerston inherited a position of great weakness due
to the neglect and parsimony of the British Governments in London and India. During the Napoleonic Wars Britain had established her influence in Persia to thwart the French attempt to use
it as a base for an attack on India. For that purpose Britain could
either use force in the Persian Gulf or offer money to the corrupt
and avaricious rulers of Persia. The latter method was by far the
cheapest in the long run, and by the Treaty of 1814 Britain had
agreed to give a subsidy to the Shah if Persia was subjected to
attack, while in return Persia agreed to prevent hostile armies from
advancing towards India. The Persians readily accepted the
treaty, not only for the sake of the money, but also because they
considered that the two Powers had a common interest in opposing
Russia. The consequences of Russian control over Persia, however, had not been imagined and guarded against by British governments as the French schemes had been. When the Russo-Persian
war took place in 1826 Canning had insisted that Persia was the
aggressor. He was engaged at the time in establishing close
relations with Russia in his attempt to solve the problem of Greece.
Persia was given no support. Russia in the Treaty of Turko-
manchai of 1828 obtained the boundary of the Araxes which has
ever since been that between the two countries on that side of the
Caspian Sea. Persia had also to pay a heavy indemnity and
Britain took advantage of this fact to obtain the cancellation of her
promise of subsidy by one immediate payment which could be
used to propitiate Russia. Abbaz Mirza, who had borne all the
burden of defence, had to accept this convenient relief, though his

---

[1] To Hobhouse, 14 Feb., 1840: *B.P.* With his practised eye for a telling
phrase Philip Guedalla quoted this sentence from the letter which he found in
the Broughton Papers (*Palmerston*, 225).

father, Fath Ali, who would provide no other funds to meet the Russian indemnity, for long refused to agree to the suggestion. The result was that Russia became supreme at Teheran, the Persians feeling completely abandoned by Britain. Metternich told Lamb that this weakness was even worse than the policy which had permitted the Russo-Turkish war of 1828.

There had always been a conflict between the Indian and London administrations as to which should control relations with Persia. Serious harm had been done to British interests by this rivalry. The British Government had of course always the final decision if it cared to exercise its power. But when Palmerston came into office the British representative, Sir John Campbell, was under the orders of India and but little interest was taken there as to what was happening in Persia by those with most influence on affairs. Its Government was absorbed in the problems brought about by its contact with the Sikh power in the Punjaub and the congeries of weak states that comprised Sind and Baluchistan, many of them under the nominal suzerainty of Afghanistan which itself was convulsed by civil war. Sir John Campbell's recipe was a renewal of the subsidy. "If we want Persia, My Lord," he wrote, "we must pay the price of her alliance."[1]

One consequence of Persia's defeat by Russia was to drive her to seek compensation in the North-east for what she had lost in the North-west. She had plenty of excuse, for the Khans on her frontiers lived by raiding her territory. Abbas Mirza, the Shah's son, who had had to yield to the Russians, had considerable success and the Russian Minister at Teheran encouraged the Shah to exploit it. Persia was thus pressing on the frontier of Afghanistan just as the British were extending their power from the south and seeking trading outlets with central Asia through the Indus River. The Indian government had an uneasy alliance with Ranjit Singh, the great Sikh ruler of the Punjaub, now aged and in decline. On his flank the Indus ran through Sind to Afghanistan. Ranjit Singh was in conflict with his Afghan neighbours and had taken Peshawar from Dost Mohammed, the Afghan Khan, who ruled in Kabul. In 1833 he had made a treaty with Shuja Khan, the deposed ruler of Afghanistan, and a weak and unsuccessful attempt was made to put him back into power.

[1] From Sir John Campbell, 23 Sept., 1834: *B.P.*

Palmerston had little time for this problem in his first period of office. His gaze hardly went beyond the Ottoman Empire. Nor did he realise the danger to India from Russian penetration and control. Indeed in 1834 on the death of Fath Ali, the Russian and British Ministers at Teheran combined together to put on the throne his grandson, Mohammed Shah, the son of Abbas Mirza who had himself died a year previously. They did a great service to Persia in preventing a civil war, but the new ruler was young, ambitious and altogether under Russian influence. The Government of India had so far recognised the situation as to send a military mission, but its able officers, Stoddart, Sheil, Todd and others, were not well received and could do little. Sir H. L. Bethune sent out from London was somewhat more successful, and played a role in the decisions of 1834. But it was to Russia that Mohammed Shah looked for support in his plans.

When Palmerston came back in 1835 a change was made in the control of the British Mission in Persia which now depended on the Foreign Office. Sir Henry Ellis, who had succeeded Sir John Campbell on a special mission, had adopted a defeatist attitude. Persia, he wrote, was no use as a defence to India. She was more likely to side with Britain's enemies. An attack on Herat, a key town on the Afghan-Persian frontier, was already planned and the Russian Minister was urging the Shah to undertake it. In the face of Russian opposition it was not likely that the Shah would grant the commercial treaty which Palmerston had made one of the principal objects of the mission.[1]

In addition, as soon as he came back in 1835, Palmerston saw danger in a Russian advance across the Caspian to Khiva. "Once in possession of Khiva", he told Durham, "they command the Oxus which is navigable till you come very near the spot where the Indus is navigable, and this would be the route they would take to attack or threaten our Indian possessions." This would also threaten the independence of Persia, "and the independence of Persia is a great object to us not merely with reference to India, but as connected with the independence of Turkey. Russia pursues the same system of strategy against Persia and Turkey; she creeps down the Black Sea and wants to do the same down the

---

[1] *B.F.S.P.*, XXIII, 860–865. From Ellis, 6 Oct., 1835, 15 Jan., 17, 20 Feb., 1836: *B.P.* Ellis also objected to Sir Henry Bethune controlling the military mission because he did not belong to the Indian army.

Caspian and to take both Persia and Turkey on each of their flanks."

This was certainly thinking very far ahead, but at any rate a more vigorous policy and a more vigorous envoy were needed in Persia. Ellis was not anxious to return and Palmerston put in his place John McNeill, who had already had a subordinate position in the British mission to Persia. He was a man in touch with Urquhart and a good Russian hater. In 1836 he published anonymously a pamphlet directed against her. But it was not this, as is often said, that made Palmerston appoint him. McNeill was chosen as the most energetic and strong personality amongst those who had knowledge of Persia. He set out in June 1836 and was soon in the thick of a great controversy with the Tsar and the Russian Minister, Simonich.[1]

Meanwhile the Whig Government had refused to accept the nomination of Lord Heytesbury whom the Tories had appointed to succeed Lord William Bentinck as Governor-General. Lord Auckland was sent in his stead because he was reckoned to be a 'safe' and reliable man. He had worked well with Palmerston while First Lord of the Admiralty and the two were on excellent terms.

The threatened attack on Herat awakened all Palmerston's fears. He at once protested vigorously to St. Petersburg and secured a promise from Nesselrode that Simonich would be recalled. It was more than a year, however, before the promise was made good, and suspicions of Russian designs continued to grow. Durham himself at first deprecated such suspicions, but soon came to share them. It was the only part of Russian policy against which he warned his chief. The danger of Russian expansion towards India was, he thought, real and inevitable. Palmerston must prepare to meet it. Both the British and Indian Governments were indeed now fully alive to what the capture of Herat might mean. If Persia remained under Russian influence

[1] To Durham, 27 Oct., 1835; to McNeill, 21 Feb., 1836: *B.P.* Palmerston deprecated the publication of a pamphlet written in such a tone as likely to detract from McNeill's authority in Persia; "to give your acts the greatest weight," he wrote, "they should appear to be the fulfilment of a duty and an obedience to the orders of your Govt, and not the supererogatory works of individual animosity." *The Memoir of Sir John McNeill*, written by his granddaughter, contains a few of the not very numerous letters in the Broadlands Papers. McNeill attributed his appointment partly to Baillie Frazer who worked under Hammond in the Turkish department of the Foreign Office (*Memoir*, 180).

a forward base for the attack on India could be established there. All the contending rulers of Northern India were watching what would happen and there was talk in the bazaars that the end of the Company's rule in India was at hand.[1]

McNeill did his best to stop the Shah by every kind of persuasion and intimidation. His position was all the more difficult since by Article IX of the Treaty of 1814 Britain had promised not to interfere in quarrels between Persia and Afghanistan unless invited to do so by both sides. He nearly succeeded however and went himself to the Shah's camp before Herat and thence into the town itself to arrange a truce with its defenders. But the Russian Ambassador had the last word and the attack went on. Herat was saved by the bravery of its Afghan defenders under Yar Mohammed Khan, the energetic Minister of its weak ruler Kamran, and the encouragement given to them by the young lieutenant, Eldred Pottinger, whose more famous uncle had sent him to the town as the siege began. A grand attack on 24 June 1838 was beaten back with great slaughter and at last the Shah sullenly withdrew his starving armies. Ghorian, of almost equal strategic importance, still remained in Persian hands. Meanwhile, however, relations with the British Government had been broken off. A messenger to McNeill from Herat had been molested, and all reparation refused. Conscious that his prestige and that of his country was at stake, McNeill withdrew to Tabriz and threatened the grave displeasure of his Government. After waiting there for a long period he eventually returned home via Constantinople and St. Petersburg. The Shah, alarmed at what he had done, despatched an envoy, Hussein Khan, to get into direct touch with the British Government.[2]

Meanwhile in the spring of 1838 the Indian Government had at the demand of McNeill decided to put pressure on the Shah by

[1] From Durham, 21 Feb., 19 Dec., 1836: 24 Feb., 25 May, 1837: *F.O. Russia*, 223, 226, 233–234. The last considered in detail the Russian routes for an attack on India.

[2] *B.F.S.P.*, XXV, 1218–1299. The story of this famous siege in which Pottinger played so admirable a part has often been told. Mr. Archbold calls Yar Mohammed Khan "one of the vilest wretches in Asia". (*Cambridge History of India*, IV, 493) Hussein Khan's journey was reported by the British envoys as he made his way to Britain. Milbanke discovered that his interpreter had been bribed by the Russians to send them accounts of all his interviews. Hussein had, however, enough English to make himself understood alone. He said his main object was to obtain the recall of McNeill (18 Jan., 1839: *F.O. Austria*, 280). He was badly treated by the Shah after his failure, suffering corporal punishment.

the usual method of sending a naval force to the Gulf to occupy a strategic position. The island of Karrak was seized. But the Gulf was far off Teheran and, though the Princes of the South could no doubt be raised in revolt, the result might only be to play into Russia's hands. The decision was, therefore, come to almost simultaneously at Calcutta and London that the Persian menace must be warded off by some new arrangement with Afghanistan itself, the threatened point from which an attack on India might be based. This decision was indeed obvious enough. The Sikh Kingdom by itself was not a sufficient barrier and could be outflanked. The Afghan feuds provided great opportunities to their enemies. Their Khans were treacherous and unreliable.

Alexander Burnes, who had already made an adventurous journey through Afghanistan, had been sent back in 1836 to Kabul on a 'commercial' mission, whence he reported on the attitude of its ruler Dost Mohammed towards the attack on Herat. Dost Mohammed had promised assistance to its ruler, Kamran, if he were given back Peshawar. But this was just what the Indian Government could not do unless it was prepared to quarrel with Ranjit Singh, the ruler of the Sikhs. Accordingly Dost Mohammed reinsured himself by offers to Persia. Moreover, to Kabul had come a Russian envoy, Vikovich, to whom he seemed to be paying great attention. This 'commercial' agent had been despatched by Simonich to get Dost Mohammed's help in the attack on Herat. In these circumstances Lord Auckland, inspired by his Secretary of Council, Macnaghten, determined to recreate the alliance between the deposed ruler Shah Shuja and the Sikhs, and eventually to assist them with a British force. By this means it was hoped Afghanistan would become a friendly state under British influence, and thus be a barrier to Persian penetration behind which was the more dangerous Russian advance.[1]

---

[1] The despatches on these negotiations including Burnes' reports were laid before Parliament in 1839. They are the famous garbled despatches, for the reports of Burnes favourable to Dost Mohammed were omitted, and the unfavourable evidence left in. When this became known through Burnes' papers Palmerston was challenged in the House, but said the omissions were unimportant. Eventually in Palmerston's old age in 1859 the publication was obtained and Bright made in 1861 the tremendous indictment which has impressed itself on history. But omissions of inconvenient evidence were common in such publications. There is almost as significant evidence concerning Russia left out of the *Levant Papers*. It was the unfortunate end of the occupation that created the necessary emotional background for the attack on Palmerston, not the essential facts of the case.

This is the famous decision which has been the theme of so many pens, most of them roundly condemning the action of the Indian Government. The policy was certainly determined by Lord Auckland at Simla without the advice of many of those best qualified to pronounce on it, and some at the time and many more after the Afghan disaster were critical of it. It was clear, however, that something had to be done and an alternative policy was hard to find. It may be that it would have been better to risk Sikh displeasure and accept the first offers of Dost Mohammed. The abandonment of the siege of Herat might have been considered a sufficient reason at least to postpone the expedition. But that was hardly clear at that time. Indeed political and strategic points that later became obvious were then necessarily obscure. Even the geography was imperfectly known. The right line to which British government should advance and what its relations should be with its turbulent and treacherous neighbours could only be found out by experiment. The real criticism of the policy followed in 1838–1839 is not the decision itself, but of the manner in which it was carried out and especially after it had attained such signal success.

But even before the Indian Government had come to its decision a similar one had been taken by the Melbourne Government. In the autumn Ministers began to be much exercised at the threat to India. Grey was consulted about it by Lord John Russell, who received from Lord Howick the answer that his father, while unable to judge the immediate situation, had "for many years been convinced that sooner or later it would be necessary to resist the encroachments of Russia by force". If action was intended, now was the time while the Russian fleet in the Baltic was frozen in. Howick himself was far from agreeing with these bellicose opinions. On the contrary he avowed that if the decision to take Karrak had not already been made by Auckland on his own responsibility he would have resigned rather than agree to it. The Cabinet were neither so warlike as Grey nor so pacifist as his son. Its members were of course as usual scattered in the autumn, but the position was considered so serious that a meeting of seven Ministers was held at Windsor early in October at which it was decided to instruct Auckland to act in Afghanistan rather than in the South. The expedition to Herat was considered to be only one part of a Russian scheme to advance in Central Asia.

"It is evident", Palmerston told Clanricarde, "that the Schah's expedition against Herat was part of a scheme planned some time ago for extending Persian and therefore Russian influence all over Afghanistan; for the first steps had been taken previous to the Schah's expedition by endeavouring to establish a political connection between Cambul and Candahar and Persia. . . . But Auckland has been told to take Afghanistan in hand and make it a British dependency and there is no doubt of his being able to accomplish that object. We have long declined to meddle with the Afghans and have purposely left them independent, but if the Russians try to make them Russian we must take care that they become British."[1]

Meanwhile Palmerston had already sent a stern protest to Russia through Pozzo di Borgo who was so alarmed at his menacing tone that he became quite ill. This warning was now reinforced with a note which Clanricarde was ordered to deliver, recounting all the misdeeds in Persia. This was no doubt meant to be laid before Parliament eventually as, indeed, it was next year. "Russia", wrote Palmerston in his private letter, "does not I believe wish to go to war with us, but is always trying to push on just to the extreme point of encroachment and aggression to which she may be allowed to go without war. She then halts to take breath and waits till people are looking another way to make another step or two forward." However that may be the British attitude had immediate effect. Even before this despatch reached him Nesselrode had sent to Pozzo di Borgo a despatch which, if inaccurate as to past events, contained satisfactory assurances for the future, so that Palmerston was able to make a friendly reply. Pozzo di Borgo "has been an altered man," he wrote, "has cast his physic to the winds and hung his face with smiles." "This", Palmerston went on, "is a proof of two things. First that poor old Pozzo is in his dotage, which is the Emperor's affair not ours: secondly that as you say Russia fears above all things a war with England." Nesselrode had admitted, he said, that Simonich had "projected an entirely new organization of Afghanistan close to our frontier." However, he was quite prepared to bury the past and resume friendly relations with both Russia and Persia provided

[1] Howick to Lord John Russell, 8 Oct., 1838. To Clanricarde, 26 Oct., 1838: B.P. Lloyd Sanders, *Melbourne*, 452-454. W. M. Torrens, *Melbourne*, 463, 464. The seven Ministers were Melbourne, Palmerston, Hobhouse, the Lord Chancellor, Lord John Russell, Lord Lansdowne and Lord Glenelg.

these declarations were carried out. The recall of Simonich which now took place was a proof that they were sincerely meant, and Clanricarde was "convinced that no intention is entertained by this Govt. of taking any direct part in the hostile movements which agitate Asia."[1]

But neither the abandonment of the siege of Herat by Persia, nor the assurances of the Russian Government, were sufficient to cause the expedition to Afghanistan to be given up. That decision was taken in India but it was fully approved in London. Hobhouse was primarily responsible but Palmerston was strongly on his side, and no doubt helped him to a decision. There were indeed after what had happened strong arguments that British influence in the North needed to be reestablished by some special action. Palmerston considered the Russian withdrawal only a truce and wished to take advantage of it before her advance began again. The Persian Government also needed a lesson. The occupation of Karrak was maintained and Palmerston pressed the necessity for reparation so hard that Nesselrode protested on the ground that he might overturn the Shah altogether and throw Persia into a state of anarchy.

There was of course no intention of occupying Afghanistan permanently. "The measure", Palmerston told Lamb, "has been forced on us by the aggression and intrigues of others; it is purely defensive on our part, but we shall probably not carry our operations beyond the limits which effective defence may prescribe. We do not want to make Afghanistan a British province, but we must have it an ally upon whom we can depend." Afghanistan must be 'English' not Persian, he told Hussein Khan, but went on to promise that British troops would retire "as soon as Shah Shoojah [sic] was firm on the throne".[2]

[1] Nesselrode to Pozzo di Borgo, 1 Nov., 1838: *B.F.S.P.*, XXVII, 174. To Clanricarde, 20 Nov., 1838, *B.P.* W. M. Torrens, *Melbourne*, 466. From Clanricarde, 20 Nov., 1838: *F.O. Russia*, 244. At the beginning of 1839 Wellington informed the Cabinet of a plan for Russia to send her Baltic fleet with a large force to attack India. This information was communicated to him by a Hampshire gentleman who had a son in the service of the Emperor. The Cabinet did not take the story very seriously. Palmerston pointed out that it was too good to be true, though there might possibly be some idea of sending the Baltic fleet to the Mediterranean. (To Clanricarde, 12 March, 1839. Wellington to Melbourne, 2 March, 1839: *B.P.*) This in fact had been the Tsar's intention in 1838, cf. P. E. Mosely, *Russian Diplomacy, etc., Appendix* A.
[2] To Lamb, 13 July, 1839: *B.P.* Memorandum of a Conference between Palmerston and Hoosein [sic] Khan, 13 July, 1839: *B.F.S.P.*, XXVIII, 85. The Secret Committee of the Indian Board of Control insisted that instructions should be sent to Auckland whom they suspected of wishing to make the occupation permanent. (From Hobhouse, 10 July, 1839: *B.P.*)

Whatever its merits the enterprise against Afghanistan had an immediate success. By August Shah Shuja had been replaced on his throne and Dost Mohammed was a fugitive. A year afterwards the latter surrendered to the Indian Government, a fact which Palmerston thought was "more honorable to the British name than a great victory". Herat, it is true, was still well outside the orbit of British control and Yar Mohammed was suspected of a wish to intrigue with the Persian Government against Britain. But the effect of the entry of a British force into Afghanistan naturally made itself felt throughout all Central Asia. One consequence was to move Russia in the autumn of 1839 to attempt a similar expedition against Khiva, whose Khan by raiding caravans and enslaving Russian subjects had given her plenty of excuse for such action.

Palmerston got news of this just as he had begun the discussions with Brunnow at the beginning of 1840. He at once strongly protested against this new threat to approach the frontiers of India. Russia, he said, had been defeated when she tried to use Persia as a base; now she was making a second attempt along another route. The Indian Government, he warned Brunnow, would be forced to reply by a more active policy in Central Asia. The Ambassador insisted that the expedition had no political object but was merely meant to free the slaves and prevent the attacks on the Russian caravans. He even offered to see the Duke of Wellington about it and ask him to keep the Tories quiet—a course to which Palmerston took strong exception. Brunnow was told that the Emperor and Nesselrode should make the official assurances of their intentions in a formal manner to Clanricarde and then the British Government would see what they would do about it.[1]

It was this situation which led Palmerston to make to Hobhouse the epigram about the meeting of the Cossack and the Sepoy already quoted. He did not believe, he said, that Russia would try to conquer Khiva but she would set up a puppet Khan there. After Khiva would come Bokhara and the way to Afghanistan and India would then be open. The Government of India had also been alarmed. A British officer, Captain Abbott, was sent to Khiva to try to get the Russian slaves released and prevent the

---

[1] To Auckland, 22 Jan., 1841; to Melbourne, 2 Jan., 1840: *B.P.* To Clanricarde, 24 Jan., 1840: *F.O. Russia*, 258.

necessity for Russian armies going there. When Brunnow demanded explanations of this conduct both Hobhouse and Palmerston spoke with the greatest frankness, and even truculence, all the more surprising since Russia was their main support in the negotiation concerning Mehemet Ali. Hobhouse said that if the two Empires should meet in Central Asia he should regret it, but had no doubt as to the result. Palmerston warned Brunnow that if Russia went to Khiva he did not know how far north of the Hindoo Koosh Auckland might be compelled to go. The only way to avoid such embarrassments was for Russia to leave Khiva alone. "All we want of Khiva", he added, "is that it should be a non-conducting body interposed between Russia and British India, and separated from both by a considerable interval of space."[1]

The Russian Government were of course never for one moment prepared to accept the position that, while British influence should be supreme in Afghanistan, Russia should have no more interest in Khiva and Bokhara than Britain. But their expedition was a failure and had to stop 250 miles from Khiva. The British emissaries, sent from Herat to obtain from its ruler the release of the Russian captives, insisted on going on to St. Petersburg with Khivan envoys which the Russian soldiers had hitherto always turned back. By these means a sort of truce was patched up. It was indeed thirty years before Russian power was able to penetrate so far.[2]

Auckland meanwhile had been much less disturbed by the Khiva expedition. He was far more preoccupied at this time with the expansion of Mehemet Ali's influence in the Persian Gulf. He considered that Karrak should not be given up until Russian and Persian policy had been further defined. The surrender of Ghorian would be more convincing evidence of their goodwill

---

[1] To Melbourne, 2 Jan., 1840; to Hobhouse, 25 May, 1840; to Bloomfield, 23 June, 1840: *B.P.* To Clanricarde, 24 Jan., 24 March, 1840: *F.O. Russia*, 258. The Russians, reported Clanricarde, intended to control Khiva but not to attack India. (24 Feb., 1840: *F.O. Russia*, 260.)

[2] The appearance on the Russian frontier of Captain Abbott and later of Captain Shakespeare with news of the release of the prisoners and accompanied by Khivan envoys is amusingly recorded in the despatches. The Russians were clearly disconcerted at so much having been accomplished. The unfortunate envoy of Khiva was practically chased out of the British Embassy by the Russians when he tried to pay a visit there. With the ferocious ruler of Bokhara the British envoys were not so fortunate. Colonel Stoddart after a long captivity and the young Captain Connolly were both put to death by him as Palmerston noted in his own hand on the last letter he received from Stoddart.

than any number of fair words. The Russian expedition to Khiva, he thought—and thought rightly—would find the task a difficult one, but even if it succeeded with dangerous repercussions in Bokhara, the advance would be contained by the growing strength and prestige of Shah Shuja in Afghanistan, if that developed as he hoped and intended it should. He was above all anxious to avoid the necessity of sending a British force to Herat. There he reiterated they must depend on Yar Mohammed Khan who he hoped would be intimidated by the British position in Afghanistan from betraying them. Ghorian he considered so important that he even told Major Todd, who had succeeded Pottinger in Herat, that his Government would support him if he managed to get hold of it by a *coup de main*. The maintenance of the position in central Afghanistan was thus the pivot on which all his policy depended. If Russia would limit her own advance he thought Britain should not look beyond the Hindu Koosh, which ran across Afghanistan. Relying on the strength of prestige obtained in Afghanistan he hoped to maintain British interests in Khiva and Herat through negotiation.[1]

These views reiterated in private letters in the course of the year 1840 did not satisfy Palmerston. Elated with the success of his campaign in Asia Minor he pressed for vigorous measures in Central Asia. After a survey of the European situation, where he pointed out France had been humbled and Russia and Austria become the allies of Britain, he urged on Auckland that now was the time to make good the British position in Central Asia. "Make fast what you have gained in Afghanistan," he wrote; "secure the Kingdom of Cabul and make yourself sure of Herat." Everything should also be done to find new markets for British commerce by sending missions to Arabia and even Abyssinia. In a striking passage he stressed the duty of the Government to work for this end:

"The rivalship of European manufactures is fast excluding our productions from the markets of Europe, and we must unremittingly endeavour to find in other parts of the world new vents for the produce of our industry. The world is large enough and the wants of the human race ample enough to afford a demand for all we can manufacture; but it is the business of the Govern-

---

[1] From Auckland, 16 Feb., 20 April, 11 July, 14 Sept., 20 Nov., 1840; Auckland to Hobhouse, 20 Nov., 1840: *B.P.*

ment to open and to secure the roads for the merchant. Will the navigation of the Indus turn out to be as great a help as was expected for our commerce? If it does, and if we succeed in our China expedition, Abyssinia, Arabia, the countries on the Indus and the new markets in China, will at no distant period give a most important extension to the range of our foreign commerce, and, though in regard to the quickness of the returns, markets nearer home might be better, yet on a political point of view it must be remembered that these distant transactions not only employ our manufacturers but form our sailors."

The opportunity was all the more apparent because the weakness of Russia would compel her to keep on good terms with Britain for some years and was the explanation of her excellent conduct during the past year in Europe. "The fact is," he claimed, "she is fitter for shew than for action; she is apparently of gigantic strength, but really weak. Her finances are in a state of great embarrassment and she could not well undertake an expensive war; the whole system of her internal administration is a mass of abuse, mismanagement, roguery and peculation, her nobles are dissatisfied and her army discontented, being hard worked, ill paid and looked after, and governed with revolting severity." The Russian failure in Circassia and the new strength given to the Sultan by the overthrow of Mehemet Ali's power should render Constantinople safe. Only a Russian-French Alliance could again bring a threatening situation in Europe, and this was not likely so long as Louis Philippe and Nicholas lived and even if it eventually occurred could be met by the union of Britain with the German Powers.[1]

This optimistic survey had much truth in it. And it had seemed to be fulfilled, so far as Central Asia was concerned, by the failure of the Russian expedition to Khiva. But Palmerston was writing about countries of which he really knew very little, and shewed here, as in his dealings with Mehemet Ali in 1841, signs that he was perhaps somewhat too elated by his triumph and losing the sense of proportion and the realistic approach which he had hitherto shewn. Auckland was by no means ready to send out further expeditions. He refused to the end to send a British force to Herat as Palmerston desired, and when Yar Mohammed quarrelled with Major Todd, who wished to put down

---

[1] To Auckland, 22 Jan., 1841: *B.P.*

the Slave Trade and other iniquities, was disposed to blame his envoy rather than the Khan. Even here, however, the British object was soon afterwards achieved. For ultimately the Persian pressure died down, Russian again cooperated with Britain, and, though it came too late for Palmerston to claim the credit, he was able at the beginning of 1842 to write to McNeill, who had returned to his post, to congratulate him on at last obtaining the commercial treaty which Palmerston had put in the forefront of his instructions in 1836.[1]

Then came the news of the shattering blow of the collapse of the British position in Afghanistan, the murder of Burnes and, finally, that of Sir William Macnaghten himself and the destruction of a brigade of British troops. For the blunders and bad leadership that caused this disaster Palmerston was in no sense responsible. But it was of course the result of the forward policy which he had supported, and he can be fairly charged with having adopted it without counting all the risks. On the other hand, events also soon made it clear that the whole position in Northern India had to be transformed. The position in Afghanistan was soon retrieved and its ruler, the restored Dost Mohammed, looked for a time to India for protection and advice. In a few more years both Sind and the Punjaub were annexed. All that Palmerston had desired was in fact obtained. Though Russia was still unable to penetrate the natural obstacles that lay between her dominion and the strategic frontier thus given to India, her expansion was, as Durham and many others pointed out, only a question of time. In due course Russia did annex both Khiva and Bokhara and then Afghanistan became of vital importance, as Palmerston and indeed all sensible men always knew. Whether the same objectives could have been obtained with less bloodshed and intrigue is a question of Indian strategy and politics and not of British foreign policy.

---

[1] From Auckland, 24 March, 21 April, 20 August, 1841: *B.P.* In the last he wrote: "I know that you and others think that I have over-rated the difficulties of an advance on Herat and still more that I have over-rated the store of embarrassment which would await us if we were in possession of that city before the tranquillity of Afghanistan had been perfectly settled and secured." To McNeill, 31 Jan., 1842: *Memoir of Sir J. McNeill*, 257.

6. THE SETTLEMENT WITH MEHEMET ALI AND THE STRAITS CONVENTION OF 13 JULY, 1841

The struggle with Mehemet had threatened the total overthrow of the Ottoman Empire and it was only natural that it should take considerable time to settle the problems raised by it. 'Hereditary tenure' for a Pasha was in a sense a contradiction in terms for a Pasha was no more than the slave of the Sultan. Moreover, in an Oriental country where polygamy was the law, succession as often as not went to others than the eldest son, of whom the father was usually jealous, and whose life was often in danger. The relations between the Sultan and his vassal had also necessarily to be more exactly defined than had been done hitherto. Mehemet's enemies, including both Palmerston and Ponsonby, hoped to take advantage of this necessity to reduce his power to the lowest possible point, even if they could not get rid of him altogether. Reschid had already sent a despatch to London protesting against any grant of hereditary tenure. Meanwhile all kinds of plans were being hastily composed in Paris and Vienna about Syria, now brought once more under the control of the Sultan. Until all this was settled France would not resume her normal attitude. Guizot had peremptorily refused to discuss with Austria and Prussia the question of armaments before the Eastern Question was concluded. He made the same answer to a very mild remonstrance from Granville. And he also refused to sign a treaty on any aspect of the Eastern Question until the Sultan and the Four Powers solemnly declared that the object of the Convention of 15 July, 1840, had been attained, and that consequently there no longer existed any tie between them from which France was excluded.[1]

Neither Palmerston nor the Tsar was particularly eager for a speedy settlement. But Austria and Prussia felt the challenge of

---

[1] From Granville, 4 Jan., 1841: *F.O. France*, 622. Until the end of March Granville worked zealously to overcome the difficulties that prevented the convention from being signed. Then he had a serious illness which was thought to be a stroke and henceforward Bulwer took complete charge. It had been decided to replace Granville with a new Ambassador, but he recovered somewhat, and nothing had been done when the Whig Ministry fell and Granville consequently retired from his post.

France's armaments and were anxious therefore to conclude some
arrangement as soon as possible. It was Metternich's opposition,
it is true, which had prevented the grant of hereditary tenure from
being peremptorily urged on the Turkish Ministers before the
final defeat of Ibrahim. Metternich, however, had only wanted
delay as a means to force Mehemet to give in. As soon as Ibrahim
had been driven out of Syria he was urgent that the Sultan should
grant Mehemet favourable terms so that France might resume her
normal position in Europe and reduce the armaments which had
so alarmed the German States. Austrian opinion, reported Lamb,
was completely unable to understand how one British agent could
sign a convention with Mehemet Ali and another promptly disavow
it. Metternich, while agreeing that the convention was a mistake,
insisted that the Porte must be made to act at once. Both he and
Beauvale regretted that the centre of action was so far removed
from Constantinople that Palmerston's instructions could not
catch up with events.[1]

Palmerston meanwhile had been subjected to pressure from
Esterhazy and Neumann to send instructions to Constantinople to
force the Sultan to give in, and Brunnow had joined them.
Palmerston had conceded the principle of hereditary tenure
because, as he told Beauvale, his Cabinet would not take any other
line. But, though he had approved the substance of Napier's
convention, he now argued that that instrument only dealt with the
immediate problem of the armistice and that the main question
was still open. France, he insisted, would not fight for the
hereditary tenure and the idea of compelling the Sultan by force
to grant it was nonsense. "Hereditary tenure of delegated authority", he wrote, "is objectionable and inconsistent," and for a short
time he had some hopes that Metternich would take that view.
But letters from Vienna soon shewed that Metternich had now an
entirely different opinion. Esterhazy and Neumann plied
Palmerston with despatches from Stürmer which accused Ponsonby of encouraging the Porte to resist, and threatened that
Austria would withdraw all moral and material support from the
Sultan.

Palmerston's indignant reply to the charge that Britain was
responsible for the delay was made in a despatch to Beauvale of so
incisive a character that the Ambassador refused to communicate

[1] From Beauvale, 26 Dec., 1840: *B.P.*

it to Metternich as he was instructed to do. Metternich's insinuations against Britain were, Palmerston wrote, "entirely opposed
to facts and to truth." Ponsonby alone of the representatives of
the Four Powers at Constantinople had had instructions to advise
the Porte to grant hereditary tenure to Mehemet. Metternich,
who had been mainly responsible for the delay by refusing to
support Palmerston's note of 15 October, had suddenly changed
his tactics, a course which, Palmerston indicated in no very veiled
language, was simply due to fear of France and not to a consideration of all the circumstances of the problem.[1]

Ponsonby had in fact only carried out the instructions, which
Palmerston had given him in the autumn, to define the hereditary
tenure in such a manner as to reduce Mehemet's power. But
Palmerston, while he defended Ponsonby to his critics, saw that
he must not press his advantage too far. Before the end of
January he had written to Constantinople that, as the representatives of the Four Powers had already told Chekib in London, the
Sultan must give way on the main issue. "Pray get this matter
settled as soon as you can," he wrote, "and then let us set to work
to organise the Turkish system, military, naval and financial."[2]

But the decision at Constantinople had been taken before these
instructions arrived. Ponsonby had in fact loyally advised the
Porte to grant the hereditary tenure as soon as he had received
instructions to do so. But he had worked out with the Porte's
Ministers an elaborate set of conditions "that will be", as he told
Palmerston, "the performance of your engagements to the French
to give Mehemet the hereditary right and at the same time will
preserve intact the sovereignty of the Sultan." "It will be the
Sultan's fault", he concluded, "if he does not take proper care to
secure himself against the future rebellion of Mehemet Ali and to
protect his Egyptian subjects from an aggression worse than
slavery or death." The result was a Hatti Sheriff of the 13 February which not only gave the Sultan the choice of a successor

[1] From Beauvale, 17 Jan., 1841: *L.P.*, III, No. 136; do., 1, 6, 13 Jan., 1841:
B.P. To Beauvale, 26 Jan., 1841: *F.O. Austria*, 296; do., *L.P.*, III, No. 138;
do., 7, 26 Jan., 1841: *B.P.* From Neumann and Esterhazy, 25 Jan., 1841:
F.O. Austria, 301, with Stürmer to Metternich, 10 Dec., 1840: "Ld Ponsonby
ne cesse de nourrir l'espoir que le Sultan se refusera à accorder l'hérédité de
l'Egypte à Mehemet Ali. Il a fait jouer tous les ressorts pour déterminer
Reschid Pasha à entrer dans ses vues." Neumann to Metternich, 1 Feb., 1841:
V. St. A.
[2] To Ponsonby, 29 Jan., 1841: *L.P.*, III, No. 144; do., 26 Jan., 1841: *B.P.*

among the children of Mehemet Ali but also laid down that Mehemet was not to have more power than other Pashas, that his army was to be restricted to 18,000 men and the nomination of all officers above the grade of captain to be in the hands of the Sultan, that he was to build no ships, and, of course, that he be bound by the laws of the Ottoman Empire including the Edict of Gulhané. Moreover, a point to which Ponsonby himself attached the highest importance, the collection of the revenue was to be under the special supervision of the Porte. A quarter of it was to be paid to the Sultan as tribute. It was only natural that Mehemet immediately refused to submit on these terms, a course he was strongly advised to take by Napier who was now one of his greatest admirers and believed that the Pasha was now disillusioned about France and could be made into a strong supporter of Britain.[1]

Meanwhile, as is narrated below, the Four Powers and France had been working out the terms of the treaty which should mark the return of France to the Concert. By reducing it to the sole question of the Straits they had come to agreement when the news of the Sultan's action reached them. Since it prevented the signature of the treaty with France there were loud complaints from all those concerned and Ponsonby was again bitterly attacked as the man mainly responsible for the Hatti Sheriff. Metternich was especially indignant and Beauvale, reflecting this attitude, went further in his attack on Ponsonby than he had ever previously ventured. The Russian and Prussian representatives at Constantinople, he claimed, blamed Ponsonby as much as Stürmer did. He supported Stürmer's accusations that Ponsonby had deliberately deceived both his colleagues and his Government, thus playing Russia's game by keeping France outside the Concert. At the end of March he wrote to the Prime Minister urging that Ponsonby be removed forthwith. Melbourne accepted his brother's view and told Palmerston that when Ponsonby did not like his instructions he simply ignored them and that the Eastern Question would never be settled while it was in the hands of such an Ambassador.[2]

[1] From Ponsonby, 10 Jan., 1, 4, 14 Feb., 1840: *L.P.*, III, Nos. 154, 162, 163, 171; do., 4, 11, 27 Jan., 1841: *B.P.* From Napier, 26 March, 1841: *B.P.* Beauvale took the same view as Napier about the possibility of drawing Mehemet closer to Britain but Palmerston rejected the idea as impossible.

[2] From Beauvale, 5 March, 1841; Beauvale to Melbourne, 30 March, 1841; From Melbourne, 9, 13 April, 1841: *B.P.*

Palmerston of course refused to give up Ponsonby who after all had only been carrying out his own wishes by encouraging the Porte to establish the Sultan's authority in Egypt to the greatest possible extent. He continued to insist that the Ottoman law and treaties must prevail throughout the whole of the Sultan's dominions, especially the Edict of Gulhané. But he realised that Mehemet would never agree that the Sultan should choose his successor, and, while genuinely puzzled for a considerable time as to what was the best method of dealing with this delicate question in an oriental country, eventually accepted Esterhazy's advice that the succession should go to the eldest direct heir as in European countries. Some of the other points, he thought, were not worth pressing too far. The Egyptian army was organised on the French model, which was better than that of the Turks who might well imitate it, and the Pasha must be able to appoint the field officers. The tribute was a matter for negotiation and would no doubt be eventually settled by prolonged bargaining in the oriental manner. He had, reported Esterhazy, been tempted by the wholehearted support of Russia to go too far, but he was now coming back to a sane position. At any rate Palmerston pressed these points on Ponsonby during March and April in both private letters and public despatches. Austria was not reliable, he explained, and might back out altogether at any moment. He even threatened that Britain might have to do likewise if the Sultan proved too obstinate. The Sultan must fulfil, therefore, his promise to grant heredity. It was to his advantage to settle the question as soon as possible. It could be reopened at a later date, Palmerston added, if the situation became more favourable.[1]

Metternich was mollified by this attitude and scolded Stürmer for not carrying out his instructions properly. He urged that a settlement should be made as soon as possible. There was nothing more for the conference at London to do, he said, and it should be dissolved. Palmerston considered that the threat of

---

[1] To Beauvale, 2 April, 1841: *L.P.*, III, No. 210; do., 9, 16 March, 1841: *B.P.* Esterhazy to Metternich, 29 March, 10, 20 April, 1841: *V. St. A.* Palmerston was especially exercised about the difficulty caused if a minor should succeed. "A regency for a minor Pasha would be nonsense, you might as well appoint an infant to be Lord Lieut. of Ireland, and then have a Regent over him." (9 March.) Esterhazy drew up a table of Mehemet's descendants to shew that there was no likelihood of a minor succeeding. He had also a shrewd idea that Palmerston's private letters might have been couched in different language to his public despatches. To Ponsonby, 16 March, 1841: *L.P.* III, No. 186; do., 21 April: *F.O. Turkey*, 428; do., 11, 16 March, 2, 19 April, 1841: *B.P.*

action against Mehemet must be maintained, especially after he had learnt of his rather arrogant reply to the Hatti Sheriff. Metternich was forced to agree and meanwhile the four representatives at Constantinople were able to advise the Sultan, when the news of Mehemet's refusal to accept the Firman reached them, to consult his allies before making a reply. This caused further delay and the news that came at this time of the fall of Reschid caused much perturbation in Vienna. The answer of the Allies was of course not in doubt and was drawn up on the lines already agreed upon. It eventually produced its due effect on the Porte where it was seen that no support could be obtained to enforce the last Firman. Another Firman was issued which granted Mehemet's main demands and though there was to be a long wrangle about the tribute, agreement on all essential points had been obtained by the middle of June. Mehemet sent an emissary with rich gifts to Constantinople. He intended to settle the question of the tribute in the usual manner—by bribery He was glad, he said, that the European Powers had ceased to meddle, he could now handle affairs in the true oriental manner. In August the Consuls-General at last returned to Constantinople and relations with Egypt became normal again.[1]

Meanwhile the Four Powers and France had long concluded their negotiations as to the new instrument which they should sign with the Sultan. These resulted in the middle of March in a convention which dealt with the question of the Straits. But for a considerable period all kinds of schemes were canvassed, some of them bordering on the fantastic. Guizot at first thought that France should celebrate her reentry into the European Concert by a comprehensive treaty. Foremost among his demands was one for a Five Power guarantee of the integrity and independence of the Ottoman Empire. The Russians would of course have never consented to sign such a treaty. They had always refused to commit themselves not to obtain some part of the Ottoman Empire. Apart from this, Palmerston, remembering Thiers' interpretation of such a promise, saw no advantage in it. Metter-

---

[1] From Beauvale, 22 April, 3 May, 1841: *L.P.*, No. 242, *F.O. Austria*, 299. To Beauvale, 4, 8 May, 1841: *F.O. Austria*, 297. Four Powers to Chekib, 10 May, 1841: *L.P.*, III, No. 249. From Ponsonby, 22 May, 1841: *L.P.*, III, No. 278; do., 19 May, 1841: *B.P.* Ponsonby, true to his principles, refused to approve the new Firman, but he did not oppose its despatch. Mehemet Ali's final moves are given in E. Driault, *La Crise Orientale*, V, 126–224.

nich was even more hostile. Guizot suggested that the Powers might at least recognise it in the Preamble as had been done in the Convention of 15 July, 1840, in order to link it up with the Note of 27 July, 1839, but even in this mild form the proposal found no favour anywhere. Bourqueney had soon to explain to Guizot that it was impossible. The Porte in spite of this shewed some inclination to revive the idea at a later stage when Metternich wrote a specially incisive despatch. "A state placed under a guarantee", he wrote, "becomes a mediatised state . . . and if one protector, to say the least of it, is inconvenient, many protectors become an insupportable burden." Palmerston rather demurred at this, pointing to the success of the guarantee of Belgian neutrality. But such a guarantee of the Ottoman Empire was no longer necessary, he thought, now that the Sultan had reestablished his power in Asia Minor.

A more curious guarantee was suggested by Guizot, that of the routes across the Ottoman Empire to the East. He seems to have thought that in this way he would satisfy a main British interest while preventing her from obtaining political control of Turkish or Egyptian territory in order to obtain it. Metternich supported the idea as regards the isthmus of Suez and Palmerston was tempted to do something about it. Eventually however Guizot himself abandoned it, partly because its negotiation would have delayed the agreement which all were seeking to obtain.[1]

Far more eagerly canvassed by all the Powers were the proposals for some kind of European protection of the non-Moslem inhabitants of Syria—Catholics, Jews and the pilgrims to the Holy City —Protestant as well as the others. The idea seems first to have occurred to the French Government and to have been deliberately adopted as a means of countering the Russian influence exercised through the Orthodox Church. It looks forward, therefore, to the famous controversy which was a prelude to the Crimean War.

[1] Guizot, *Mémoires*, VI, 73, 84. Guizot to Bourqueney, 15, 23 Feb., 1841; Bourqueney to Guizot, 19, 25 Feb., 1841: *A.A.E.* From Beauvale, 22 April, 1841; to Beauvale, 10 May, 1841: *L.P.*, III, Nos. 244, 248. Esterhazy to Metternich, 14 March, 1841: *V. St. A.* This of course was a guarantee of the Suez overland route, though the idea of a canal was already being freely canvassed. Palmerston said he could not support Guizot's proposal because it would look as if Britain were seeking special advantage in the treaty. Palmerston was not at this time opposed to a canal for political reasons. He thought that it would be so costly to construct that the money could not be raised for it. (To Ponsonby, 25 April, 1841: *B.P.*) He long held this idea, cf. H. L. Hoskins, *British Routes to India*, 295–299.

But in Guizot's Protestant mind it became connected with the Holy City. "Guizot", wrote Granville, "has been expatiating with quite religious fervour in his conversations with Pahlen upon a project of making Jerusalem a Christian city separated from the Pachalik and guaranteed by all the European Powers." Granville poured scorn on the idea but he warned Palmerston that it might appeal to some religious enthusiasts in England. In reply to his chief's cynical comments on French motives he admitted that the suggestion of a Christian free city at Jerusalem "after the manner of Cracow or Frankfort" had been made as one means of reestablishing French influence in the Levant: "France always assumed a sort of protectorate of the Roman Catholic Christians but ... the idea of huddling them together within the precincts of Jerusalem seems to be the most wild and impracticable of schemes." Louis Philippe held the same view while Nesselrode and Orlov ridiculed this suggestion of a "Cracovie religieuse". Nevertheless the idea was canvassed quite widely and Palmerston was startled to receive from Castelcicala, the Neapolitan Minister, the suggestion from the King of Naples that his brother, the Prince of Capua, should be made the ruler of the new Christian State of Palestine which the Four Powers intended to set up.

Meanwhile Austria evinced a similar desire to assume the protection of the Catholic Church in the Levant. The idea had long been in Metternich's mind and discussions took place between the two Governments which did not get very far, but might conceivably have resulted in some form of general guarantee by the Powers of the rights of the inhabitants of Syria and the pilgrims to the Holy Land. Metternich suggested the appointment of a special Turkish emissary at Jerusalem to safeguard Christian interests there[1]

But the subject became complicated by the interest of Palmerston in the Jews and the desire of the new King of Prussia to

---

[1] Guizot to Bourqueney, 15, 16 Feb., 1841: *A.A.E.* Guizot, *Mémoires*, VI, 77, 79. To Granville, 7 Jan., 1841; from Granville, 4, 11, 24 Jan., 19 Feb., 1841: *B.P.* Guichen, *La Crise d'Orient*, 469, 471. "I assured Castelcicala that we mean to preserve the integrity of the Turkish Empire and not to dismember it; but he said the French had made very serious proposals and communications on this subject at Naples; and I could hardly persuade him that his master had been bamboozled by Louis Philippe." (To Beauvale, 26 Feb., 1841: *B.P.*) Esterhazy to Metternich, 13 Feb., 1841: *V. St. A.* Beauvale later reported that France had sent 100,000 francs for distribution amongst the Maronites while Austria had sent money to rebuild houses and churches, 100,000 francs having been collected for that purpose in the Churches of Vienna (5 May, 1841: *B.P.*).

establish a Protestant bishopric at Jerusalem. Palmerston was from the first afraid that any guarantee of the rights of the inhabitants of Syria would lead to undue interference by the Great Powers in their own advantage. But as has been seen, the interest of evangelical Britain in the Holy Land was a factor in public opinion during the crisis in the autumn of which Palmerston tried to take full advantage. In this he was assisted by Lord Ashley, naturally, as Lady Palmerston's son-in-law, admitted to close friendship though a member of the Tory party. This fervent evangelical was as much under the influence of Biblical prophesy as the King of Prussia himself, and had since 1838 been crusading for the return of the Jews to Palestine under some Great Power protection. Moreover, Palmerston seems to have had a genuine desire to protect the Jews in Palestine for humanitarian reasons as well as for the advantage which he thought might thus be obtained both for the Sultan and for Britain.

The ill-treatment of the Jews in Rhodes and Damascus in April, 1840, seems first to have increased interest in their position in the Holy Land. The Jews in the West were much moved by it and used their influence at the capitals of Europe to help their co-religionists. Thiers, who refused to admit that the French Consul at Damascus had shewn callousness, had a serious quarrel with James Rothschild about it, though it did not prevent the French Bourse from financing the French armaments. Ponsonby, on the other hand, shewed much indignation at the pogrom at Damascus which had occurred under Mehemet's administration, and Palmerston of course strongly supported his protests. In England, however, the subject took a wider aspect in evangelical circles and became connected with a mystical idea, never altogether lost in the nineteenth century, that Britain was to be the chosen instrument of God to bring back the Jews to the Holy Land. "We have on our side", Lady Palmerston told Princess Lieven on 13 November, 1840, "the fanatical and religious elements, and you know what a following they have in this country. They are absolutely determined that Jerusalem and the whole of Palestine shall be reserved for the Jews to return to; this is their only longing (to restore the Jews)."[1]

[1] From Granville, 22 June, 9, 12 Oct., 1840: *B.P.* Corti, *The Reign of the House of Rothschild*, 223. James was moved to protest by the Austrian Rothschild, for Laurin had sent to Vienna long reports on the incident and Metternich at once took action. Sudley, *Corres. Lieven-Palmerston*, 196. Thiers claimed

Lady Palmerston must have written with the knowledge that her husband, in response to this feeling, had already in August instructed Ponsonby to get the Sultan to respond to the Jewish idea that the time was approaching for their nation to return to Palestine by the promulgation of special laws in their favour. This would not only be a blow against Mehemet Ali but even if it did not attract many immigrants would spread a friendly disposition towards the Sultan among the Jews of Europe. The importance he attached to the subject is shewn by the manner in which he kept coming back to it in his private letters. "Pray don't lose sight of my recommendation to the Porte", he wrote in September, "to invite the Jews to return to Palestine. You can have no idea how much such a measure would tend to interest in the Sultan's cause all the religious party in this country, and their influence is great and their connexion extensive. The measure moreover in itself would be highly advantageous to the Sultan, by bringing into his dominions a great number of wealthy capitalists who would employ the people and enrich the Empire." And a little later he developed the idea in a wider manner: "The establishment of a good school of Medicine at Constantinople would have a great effect upon public opinion in Europe; and so would an edict giving security and encouragement to all Jews who might chuse to return to Palestine or to any other part of the Turkish Empire. The late barbarities at Rhodes and Damascus would afford the Sultan a good occasion for issuing such an edict, as he might say that being desirous of preventing the recurrence of such scenes, and being determined to give to the Jews full security for person and property within his dominions, he had thought fit to publish an edict declaring that the Jews should henceforth enjoy within his dominions all the securities which have been granted by law to his other subjects. I think it would be best that the Sultan should not place the Jews formally under the protection of foreign Consuls, because the principle of foreign interference between a sovereign and his subjects is bad; and Jews coming to settle in Turkey ought to be considered as subjects of the Sultan. But if any arrangement could be devised by means of which they could be sure of having their complaints brought to the knowledge of the

that the Jews had murdered a French priest and were responsible for the outbreak (22 June). This episode is rather sketchily discussed in N. Sokolow's *History of Zionism*, I, 115–132. Lord Ashley's well-known views are given in E. Hodder, *Life and Work of the Seventh Lord Shaftesbury*, I, 307–319.

Turkish Govt. it would be good; such arrangement, however, should be local. For if there was a Jewish High Priest or other representative established at Constantinople he would, like the Greek Patriarch, be liable to be bought by some foreign Power and through him the Jewish population might be influenced; but if some Turkish Minister of the Porte were bound to receive Jewish complaints, that evil would not be created; and our English Consuls might be instructed to make known to our Ambassador at Constantinople any causes of just complaint for which no speedy redress was obtained.

"The Jews and the Medical men of Europe are each a sort of Free Mason fraternity whose good word would be useful to the Sultan."[1]

The Porte did not then respond to this overture and Ponsonby gave it little support. But when the question of the future of Syria was discussed in the spring of 1841 Palmerston continued for some time to press that the British Vice-Consul recently established in Jerusalem should be used as the agent to transmit to the Porte the representations of the Jewish body, though without any success. The right thing, replied Ponsonby, was for the Porte to secure justice for all its subjects, not for any special section of them, and there is no doubt but that Palmerston felt as strongly as his Ambassador the danger to the Porte of allowing other Powers to have rights of interference in the internal affairs of Turkey. It was the eternal dilemma which he was to face all his life, the impossibility of reforming the Ottoman Empire without such interference as would destroy it.[2]

Palmerston had gone so far in this matter partly for reasons of humanity but mainly to satisfy an important section of public opinion. He was not a man to be moved by any mystical ideas about the future of Palestine. His action to obtain the establishment of a Protestant Bishopric in Jerusalem was determined by similar motives. The protagonist in this movement was the King of Prussia, the pupil of Ancillon, whose biblical instruction now bore rather strange fruit. For the King desired that the Protestant

[1] For Palmerston's despatches on this subject see F. S. Rodkey, "Lord Palmerston and the Rejuvenation of Turkey, 1839–1841." *Journal of Modern History*, June 1930, where they are all conveniently brought together. To Ponsonby, 4 Sept., 4 Nov., 1840: *B.P.*
[2] For the details see the article by F. S. Rodkey given in the last note. "Let me recommend the Jews to your special care," Palmerston wrote to Ponsonby on 26 Feb., 1841 (*B.P.*).

Church should share in the special rights of the other Christian
sects in the Holy Places, for which armed guards should be provided by the Great Powers. Metternich was much annoyed at
this suggestion which, he told Beauvale, threw the whole question
into confusion, substituting for his own practical scheme of the
appointment of a Turkish official proposals which would not be
accepted by the Pope and would cause great controversy between
the Christian Powers. He harped on the necessity of checking
Russia, who desired to get a monopoly of such rights in the
Turkish Empire for the Orthodox Church, and France, who was
planning to use the Catholic Christians for her own purposes.[1]

Palmerston sympathised with Metternich's desire to check the
pretensions of both Russia and France. But he had to go warily
on the question of Protestant representation. The subject was in
any case too complicated, he said, to be dealt with in the new
convention and must be treated separately. Melbourne on the
other hand had incautiously admitted the special position of Russia
and France in a speech in the House of Lords, much to the indignation of Wellington. But Melbourne like Palmerston soon saw
that the claims of the Protestant Churches must be taken seriously.
The subject became a burning one later in the spring when Bunsen
was summoned by the King of Prussia from Rome and sent to
London to urge the cooperation of the two Protestant Powers.
He had an enthusiastic reception from the English Church, both
High and Low. The diplomats, it is true, looked a little askance
and Melbourne at first thought that more trouble was in store for
him. But both he and Palmerston eventually won high praise
from Bunsen for their sympathy and cooperation. Palmerston
did his best to put the scheme on a practical basis before he
handed it over to his successor. He had joined Austria in urging
the Sultan to ensure adequate protection for all Christian creeds
in Syria and had got Bunsen to agree that Prussia should do no
more than this. The special Protestant claim, meanwhile, had
been reduced to an agreement to establish a Bishopric at Jerusalem
under the joint auspices of the Prussian and English Churches,
a Protestant combination that helped to drive Newman into the
Catholic Church. Palmerston set Ponsonby to work to get the

---

[1] From Esterhazy, 31 March, 1841, with Memorandum shewing difference
between Metternich's proposals of 3 February and those in the Prussian Memoir,
F.O. Austria, 301. Esterhazy to Metternich, 30 March, 1841: *V. St. A.*

necessary Firman from the Porte to build a Protestant Church in Jerusalem. It was not an easy task and the delay aroused the anger of the zealous Lord Ashley. He suspected the hidden hands of Rome and the Tsar. Pisani, the interpreter, was a fervent Catholic and as has been noted, his brother worked for the Russian Embassy. "We have thus", he lamented, "a double interest against us. I must say this is a sad issue to all our achievements in Syria. Can you not leave on record an opinion that the thing is just and ought to be completed." Palmerston complied with the request and one of his last communications to his faithful Ambassador was to pass on this warning: "I hope you will be able to manage the matter to which Bunsen's proposition relates," he wrote. "It is a matter which will excite great interest in this country and all through Protestant Germany." Great credit could be gained by ensuring its success. However sacred the object, Palmerston was fully aware that it was mundane considerations that would count most at Constantinople. "And if a thousand pounds of Secret Service money would carry the point," he added, "do not scruple to draw."[1]

All this effort in favour of the sects distracted attention from the central question of how to ensure for all the inhabitants of the Ottoman Empire the benefits of the new reforms. For it was already clear that the Edict of Gulhané, which Palmerston was so insistent must be applied in Egypt, was not producing the expected results in the rest of the Empire. The old Turk party had re-established its position as soon as the danger from Mehemet was past and the assistance of the Western Powers no longer necessary. The Sultan's first representative in Syria, Izzet Pasha, turned out to be even worse than had been expected and he had done much harm by his rapacity and cruelty before Ponsonby could effect his recall. Since then the British Consuls and soldiers had in vain tried

[1] Bunsen's mission is described in Baroness Bunsen, *Memoirs of Baron Bunsen*, I, 593–637. From Lord William Russell, 21 May, 1841: *B.P.* "He is very English. . . . If his Syrian propositions dont please you treat them with great indulgence for the King has set his heart on them"; do., 22 May, 1841: *F.O. Prussia*, 283. Neumann to Metternich, 18 Aug., 1841: *V. St. A.* Wellington thought there ought to be a centre for oriental affairs at Vienna, another working under it at Constantinople and a third under this at Jerusalem where consular agents would watch over the security of the Christians, so Neumann at any rate reported. From Ponsonby, 11, 27 July, 1841: *F.O. Turkey*, 432. Later reports were more hopeful (2, 8 Sept.). From Lord Ashley, 14 Aug., 1841: *B.P.* E. Hodder, *Lord Shaftesbury*, I, 364–380. To Ponsonby, 16 Aug., 1841: *B.P.* The whole subject has been illuminated by an article by R. W. Greaves, "The Jerusalem Bishopric, 1841" (*Eng. Hist. Rev.*, July, 1949).

to overcome the disposition of the Ottoman troops to treat the Syrians as a hostile and conquered population. The Albanian levies had been especially brutal and they had only gradually been removed. Wood had played a big role in all these efforts, but he had not the authority necessary for his task in spite of the energetic support he got from Ponsonby.[1]

Even more ominous was it that the author of the great reform fell from office in spite of the zealous defence of no less a person than Metternich himself. It was one of the charges brought against Ponsonby by Beauvale and Metternich that he had failed to give Reschid the support that so good a friend might be expected to have from the British Ambassador. This was true enough, though they were never able to substantiate their accusation. Ponsonby had come to the conclusion that Reschid's usefulness was over, that he had not the energy and courage necessary to get the reform working. Moreover, Reschid was surrounded by Frenchmen and seemed disposed to listen to Stürmer more than to Ponsonby himself. "It is not to be denied", Ponsonby told Palmerston, "that Reschid looks more towards others than towards us, notwithstanding, or it may be on account of, the fact that *I made him* what he is. I am therefore not inclined to lose the Sultan by attempts (that would be ineffectual also) to support a man who is not our man, however much I might be inclined to do Reschid good by the sort of personal partiality I have for him, and I hope after all that I shall do him essential good, if he must fall."[2]

Palmerston, while puzzled at Metternich's zeal for a reformer, thought it expedient to support Reschid officially and he did so in an instruction which was communicated to Vienna and received warm thanks. But in a private letter, though he summed up in Reschid's favour, he agreed with Ponsonby that it was not worth risking the loss of all influence with the Sultan in order to save him. His weakness and the fact that he had fallen under influences unfriendly to England were obvious enough. But Reschid was westernised and if he could carry out his ideas Turkey would be regenerated. Palmerston surveyed the problem in its widest aspect in words which shew perhaps more clearly than any others his general attitude towards the reform of the Ottoman Empire:

[1] There is much in the *Levant Papers*, III, on the situation in Syria in 1840–1841.

[2] From Ponsonby, 14, 26 Feb., 1841: *B.P.* From Beauvale, 5 March, 1841: *F.O. Austria*, 298; do., 31 March, 1841: *B.P.*

"It is difficult enough for a large political party in an enlightened country like England with abundance of instruments to work with, to carry into execution any great measures of reform; but how much more difficult must it be for a single man to accomplish such things in a benighted country like Turkey! . . . Though paper reforms are of course incomplete until they are carried out in practice yet it would be a mistake to suppose them to be *nothing*. It is a great step gained when the sanction of the sovereign in a despotic country has been obtained for the promulgation of any great measure of reform or for the practical enforcement of any great principle of justice; and though such laws may be a dead letter at first, it is far more easy afterwards to invoke them and to call them into activity than it would be at that later period to get them issued for the first time . . . and, if after we have done so much, our protégés the Turks were to sink back into their former lethargy we should lose much of the credit we have gained and we should not obtain that European security which was the great object and the main justification of all our proceedings."[1]

Before the instruction and this letter reached Constantinople Reschid had fallen as a result of the attacks of the old Turks. His reforming colleague, Ahmed Fethi Pasha, fell with him and Rifaat Pasha had his place and power. "Baron Stürmer weeps over his removal", wrote Ponsonby, "as if it was to occasion the advent of the day of judgment. You know that I have had my doubts of Reschid's honesty a long time past. I am now convinced that he is wholly unworthy to be trusted and I rejoice at his fall and I consider it as a *respite* for this Empire from the full establishment of French influence over its counsels." The reason for Ponsonby's attitude is evident enough, but Reschid's later career shewed that the Ambassador had not mistaken the character of the man whom he had done more than anyone else to elevate. Nor was Ponsonby ungrateful for what Reschid had done. It was largely due to his action that Reschid was protected from further molestation and his safety secured by his appointment once more to the Paris Embassy.[2]

[1] To Ponsonby, 1 April, 1841: *F.O. Turkey*, 427; do., 2 April, 1841; To Beauvale, 1 April, 1841: *B.P.* Many people were puzzled at the fall of Reschid. The French attributed it to Metternich and Palmerston himself was later, in view of Austrian support of Rifaat, inclined to think so. But Beauvale insisted that Metternich had always desired Reschid to remain in office. To Beauvale, 2 June, 1841; from Beauvale, 7 Aug., 1841: *F.O. Austria*, 297, 299.

[2] From Ponsonby, 7 April, 1841: *F.O. Turkey*, 433; do., 29 March, 27 April, 1841: *B.P.* Palmerston on the news of Reschid's fall instructed Ponsonby to

Chekib, Reschid's protégé and friend, tactfully told Palmerston that the change was "just as if in this country the Whigs were to go out and the Tories were to come in." For Palmerston that meant reaction and he expressed his alarm in public and private communications. "This would be very unfortunate," he told Ponsonby, "and would do the Sultan's cause great injury all over Europe; and it would also give great advantage to Mehemet Ali's partisans who hold him up as a pattern of an enlightened and regenerating Mussulman."[1] Chekib was, however, only too accurate a prophet. A period of reaction followed in which the reforms laid down in the Gulhané decree were completely forgotten.

In the short interval left to him Palmerston did what he could to stem the tide. But it was of little use and it was left to Stratford Canning, Ponsonby's successor in 1842, to resume the ungrateful and, indeed, impossible task of reforming the Ottoman Empire. Beauvale, who studied with care Stürmer's reports as well as those of Ponsonby, perhaps stated the real truth with more accuracy than anyone else dared use:

"Reschid Pasha's fall was intended to lead to the fall of his system, and will do so. Rifaat told Stürmer that the Edict of Gulhané would be kept in force in as far as it secures life and property, but that in as far as it limits the power of the Sultan it will be suffered to fall into disuse. Rifaat you will observe is a mere Secretary having no power of any sort. Now as nothing limits the power of the Sultan more than securing life and property, I conclude that no part of the Hatti Sheriff will last. It has been executed nowhere because it cannot be. Its execution demands a police, a graduated system of uncorrupted tribunals, an honest magistracy and all of them backed by a paid, obedient and disciplined force; which of all these things exists in Turkey? The existing discontent in Syria has its rise chiefly in the open shameless extorting corruption of all Turkish authorities from high to low. Go and reform this by an Edict! Where no principle of honour no feeling of shame exist, by what are you to govern if not by force? The question is how to substitute for this weak and faulty principle of Government a better and a stronger one, and the solution of this question is the work of centurys. By

protect his life. Stürmer had told Metternich it was in danger. But Ponsonby had already done far more than this. He had got the Sultan to give Reschid a large grant of money and promise him employment abroad.

[1] To Ponsonby, 22 April, 1841: *B.P.*

rapid sweeping reforms, imitated from countrys quite otherwise constituted, there is nothing but mischief to be done and no good, and the less we call upon them to execute the hasty and crude conceptions, into which they have run without knowing what they were about, the better. My belief is that the Empire is falling to pieces by a gradual dissolving process which nothing can arrest. The problem will be to retard it as long as may be, and where inevitable to direct it in the least mischievous course."

Palmerston did not accept this pessimistic judgment. His whole moral position in the Near Eastern Question depended on the supposition that the Ottoman Empire could be reformed. But in these last months of office he had to admit that his immediate hopes had been disappointed.[1]

But if Palmerston had failed to obtain the necessary basis of reform in Turkey, he had at last complete success in the question of the Straits. As has been seen, all the proposals to introduce other questions into the final document had failed. They were all too controversial or too complicated to secure agreement. And the convention as to the Straits was drawn up almost exactly as Palmerston himself desired, though Brunnow did a good deal of the drafting. Palmerston indeed claimed that there was nothing new in it. It simply repeated, with the all-important addition of French support, what had already been laid down in the Convention of 15 July, 1840. Guizot continued to insist that France would only sign the new convention after the Great Powers had solemnly asserted that the aims of the Convention of 15 July, 1840, had been attained, and that consequently its operation was over. The only representative of the Four Powers who seemed disposed to refuse these terms was Brunnow who, both Neumann and Bourqueney reported, wished to prevent a reconciliation with France. But he was isolated; Austria and Prussia were pressing strongly for an agreement, while the British people were anxious, to get on good terms with France once more. The debate in the House of Commons at the beginning of the Session surprised and pleased the French Government and people by its cordial tone, coming as it did after all the revelations in the French Chambers.

[1] From Beauvale, 5 May, 1841: *B.P.* Guizot also spoke most pessimistically about the future of the Ottoman Empire, and said that he meant to do something about it, but he did no more than order his agents to report all incidents. (From Bulwer, 4 June, 1841: *F.O. France*, 625.)

Brunnow who had so often spoken of the funeral of the Franco-British Alliance, did not, reported Bourqueney, know what to do about it.[1]

Brunnow continued to make difficulties throughout February and March and was reluctant to sign the agreement when it was at last made. He thought it made too great a concession to France. Palmerston, on the other hand, was anxious to get the signature of France to a document while Guizot was still in power. He did not consider that there had been any undue yielding. On the contrary, he told Clanricarde, "the convention contains nothing but the stipulation about the Straights taken almost verbatim from our Convention of July [1840] and therefore it is virtually and indirectly an acknowledgement of that convention by France." And he put great pressure on Brunnow to sign without specific authority from St. Petersburg, "because on the one hand the treaty is just what the Emperor wished it to be, that is to say a 'transaction' confined within the narrowest limits, and because . . . if we were to let slip this opportunity of binding France, Guizot might go out and then we should have fresh difficulties. For England and Russia this would not much signify, for it is to us a matter of comparative indifference whether France signs or not, but to our German allies it is a matter of importance."[2]

Brunnow gave way and thus by the middle of March Bourqueney had agreed with the others not only on the new convention about the Straits but on the Protocol which the Four were to sign concerning the end of the Convention of 15 July, 1840. But the news that came from Constantinople and Alexandria of the Sultan's Hatti Sheriff and the refusal of Mehemet to accept it prevented the signature of the Protocol. The German Powers would have signed it, but Palmerston refused to do so before the submission of Mehemet was complete. He suspected the French of planning to get rid of the Convention of 15 July, 1840, and then to encourage Mehemet Ali to demand impossible terms after the means of coercion had thus been destroyed. Since the Protocol could not be signed, the new convention could not be signed

---

[1] Bourqueney to Guizot, 29 Jan., 1841: *A.A.E.* From Granville, 1 Feb., 1841: *F.O. France,* 622.

[2] To Clanricarde, 12 March, 1841: *B.P.* From Granville, 19 March, 1841: *F.O. France,* 623. Bourqueney, reported Granville, "renders full justice to the zealous exertions of Yr. Ldship. to overcome the reluctance felt by Baron Brunnow to put his initials to the draft of the convention."

either. All that could be done was to initial the document as an agreed one, and there was no further change in it.

The uneasy situation in Europe, therefore, persisted. Palmerston was not much disturbed. Brunnow also was naturally not much disappointed. But Austria and Prussia and the friends of France in Britain were exasperated and heaped abuse on Ponsonby as the main cause of the delay. There was, however, nothing to be done until the new Hatti Sheriff was issued and it was seen whether Mehemet would accept it. When it came, it did, as has been seen, grant all Mehemet's main demands and in June it seemed as if the Protocol and the convention could be signed at once. But again Palmerston hesitated. He was still suspicious, Neumann reported, that France and Mehemet would play some trick if he formally stated that the obligations of the Convention of 15 July, 1840, were at an end. He could not, he told Bourqueney, do so until Mehemet himself had shewn that the convention was no longer necessary, and Guizot had to admit that his position was logical and consistent. It was not, therefore, until the news came from Alexandria in July that Mehemet had accepted the new offer (or at least almost all of it—for the tribute was not really settled) that the Protocol and convention could be signed. On 13 July the representatives of the Five and Turkey met for that purpose, Palmerston being especially cordial to Bourqueney and even Brunnow shewing no signs of repugnance.[1]

Thus came into existence the agreement of all the Great Powers concerning the Straits which determined that problem for the rest of the nineteenth century, and indeed in all its essentials the twentieth century as well. There was some alteration from the phraseology of the previuos year. The substance was however the same. The Sultan declared his intention of maintaining the ancient rule by which warships of foreign Powers were forbidden to enter the Straits and that he would admit no such ships "while the Porte was at peace". Brunnow did not renew the attempt, defeated in 1840, to substitute for this last condition "whether the Sultan is at peace or war", which would have left the Sultan to the Tsar's mercy in case of rupture. It was clear that if Russia were to go to war with the Sultan nothing could prevent him from

[1] Bourqueney to Guizot, 2, 5, 16 March, 14, 25 June, 1841; Guizot to Bourqueney, 8, 14 March, 1841: *A.A.E.* Guizot, *Mémoires*, VI, 72–117. Esterhazy to Metternich, 3, 14, 16 March, 8, 29 June, 13 July, 1841; Neumann to Metternich, 6 June, 1841: *V. St. A.*

inviting the assistance of other Powers and, if these were ready to give it, it shewed that they were ready to defend him by force of arms. The only sanction for such a clause was the threat of war by Russia and that was useless after war had already been determined upon by the other Powers.

But so long as the Sultan remained at peace Russia was protected from naval attack from the Mediterranean and this to the Tsar and his advisers seemed a considerable advantage. They gave up of course the right to attack in the Mediterranean. But this they had not possessed even under the Treaty of Unkiar Skelessi. Under that treaty, however, the Sultan had promised to consult the Tsar when a state of emergency arose, and it was this stipulation that to Palmerston was the most obnoxious part of the treaty. That privileged position was now lost and the Sultan was free to deal with all the Great Powers according to his own interests. Russia still possessed her special rights concerning the Orthodox subjects of the Porte and she had succeeded in preventing any reference to the territorial independence and integrity of the Ottoman Empire in the convention, even in the Preamble. The way was thus still open to that absorption of Turkish territory at the proper moment which it cannot be doubted was never absent from the mind of the Tsar and his advisers.[1]

But Palmerston also was satisfied with what had been done. He had secured complete equality with Russia as regards the Straits, and since Russia was so much nearer to Turkey than Britain the closing of the Straits was to the advantage of the latter. Moreover, Britain had no intention of attacking the Ottoman Empire and desired none of its territories. She was not likely therefore to go to war with the Sultan, and his control over the Straits was thus likely to be exercised in her favour so long as the Sultan was free to act according to his own desires. On the other hand the Sultan had the right to summon the British fleet to protect him if Russia went to war with him. How important this was was to be seen in 1854 and 1878.

Two variations from the Convention of 15 July, 1840, were both due to Russia. Brunnow not only insisted on adding the clause which enabled the Sultan to permit light vessels of war to

---

[1] Goriainow's long analysis of the treaty in *Le Bosphore et les Dardanelles*, 82–91, is designed to prove the Russian case concerning the outbreak of the Crimean war and the situation in 1877–1878.

pass through the Straits but made a special declaration on the subject for the record. It was, he said, necessary for Russian communications with Greece. It was due to Brunnow also that a clause was added allowing the Sultan to invite all the other Powers with whom the Porte was in friendly relations to accede to the treaty. This was an unusual step and the reason for it is not quite clear. None of the smaller Powers was likely to cause trouble at Constantinople. But Russia seems to have thought that the protection given by the treaty would be increased if all the smaller maritime Powers bound themselves to recognise it as the Great Powers had done. For the obligation which the signatories undertook was of course to one another as well as to the Sultan. They could not be released from it by any action on his part contrary to the treaty.[1]

At any rate both the Tsar and Palmerston were satisfied at the result of the long contest between them. Indeed the success of Palmerston's handling of the Tsar had already been shewn in dramatic fashion at the end of 1840. The armaments and threats of France had necessarily produced a great effect on Europe and, as has already been mentioned, the possibility of renewing the Quadruple Alliance against her had occurred to some of the Prussian soldiers and statesmen. But the Tsar's relations with Prussia had grown much cooler, even hostile, though this was largely due to the attitude of the Prussian Court towards the marriage of his son. He was also more suspicious of Metternich than he had ever been. He spoke of him to Clanricarde with the greatest contempt and distrust. It was to Britain, therefore, that he made the suggestion of a special Four Power Alliance against France, indicating in no uncertain fashion to Clanricarde that he had more confidence in her than in any other of the Great Powers. In a later discussion he explained the reason for this trust. "The fundamental principle", reported Clanricarde, "of His Imperial Majesty's Government—felt to be such by himself and his people —was their religion and their religious duty. . . . We [the British] maintained our respect for the principles of religion and of good order and of good faith throughout all our changes of opinion upon matters of policy." The danger from France was

---

[1] That these additions were mainly due to Brunnow is made clear by Gorisainow (see previous note). Palmerston wrote, "Brunnow has been of great use to us all with his pen." (To Clanricarde, 12 March, 1841: *B.P.*)

apparent and Britain ought, therefore, to make common cause with the other nations of Europe against her. "Such an engagement," the Tsar said, "no matter how contracted, verbally or otherwise, would make peace certain." Nesselrode subsequently made the offer more formally to Clanricarde in a much less enthusiastic manner, dwelling on the importance of the Treaty of Vienna with a hint that Poland was included in it, an approach that the Ambassador thought somewhat impertinent.

But of course Palmerston could not in any case accept such an offer. He took advantage of it, indeed, to explain the attitude of Britain towards such an alliance in a despatch which is reminiscent of the State Papers of Castlereagh and Canning. The doctrine of non-intervention was restated in unequivocal terms and the impossibility of a Parliamentary Government undertaking indefinite obligations was again laid down. At the same time it was once more affirmed that Britain would play her part in maintaining the balance of power in Europe. Perhaps the Tsar had not expected much more. At any rate he took no umbrage and continued to assure Clanricarde of the absurdity of the reports of a Franco-Russian rapprochement which were then rife in Western Europe. Palmerston warned the Russian Government not to encroach on Norway and the Tsar and his Ministers shewed some anxiety lest Britain should absorb too much of the Chinese trade. But these suspicions were overcome by frank explanations on both sides. As recounted in Section 5, the tension concerning Persia and Afghanistan was also by now sensibly reduced. The Ambassador had no doubt as to the Tsar's good faith which indeed all his actions seemed to prove. And as a final mark of his friendship Nicholas paid an informal visit to a party at the Ambassador's residence, an unprecedented condescension, such as Durham had never received.[1]

If the Tsar saw in Britain the key to European peace Metternich also looked to Palmerston to help him to reestablish a new system

---

[1] F. S. Rodkey, "Anglo-Russian negotiations about a 'Permanent' Quadruple Alliance", *American Historical Review*, Jan., 1931, gives the details of the Russian offer and Palmerston's reply, but omits the passage above quoted. From Clanricarde, 18 Jan., 1841: *F.O. Russia*, 271; do., 13 Jan., 24 Feb., 9, 23 March, 20 April, 1841: *B.P.* The private letters add nothing to the despatches except the remark: "You see they have formally made the Holy Alliance proposition. I think Nesselrode's allusion to the Treaties of Vienna impudent. But I don't like to say much about it because the Emperor is more violent than ever about the Poles." To Clanricarde, 2 March, 1841: *F.O. Russia*, 269.

of European diplomacy. He took advantage of the Porte's desire to obtain a guarantee to propose his own remedies. And, so Beauvale explained, since he had at last been cured of his strange illusion that he could answer for the Tsar, it was to Palmerston that he turned for help. He proposed once more the old device, once brought forward by Talleyrand in 1833, of a self-denying ordinance of the Five Powers such as they had given concerning Greece, a promise that they would not themselves acquire any Turkish territory. Palmerston knew that the Tsar would refuse such a proposition which he must consider as aimed at Russia, and would have nothing to do with it. Nor would he listen to the hints given by Metternich to Beauvale which the Ambassador said were feelers after his real object, the establishment at Vienna of a centre to deal with Oriental affairs. So little had Metternich learnt from his experience in 1840! Palmerston gave the proposal short shrift. Austrian policy, he wrote, had not been marked with such steadiness and consistency as to give her a claim to be trusted by the British Government. Moreover, such a centre was only useful and necessary when common action had to be taken to carry out treaty engagements. Metternich was much disappointed at the failure of this final attempt to make Vienna the centre of European diplomacy and roundly abused Palmerston to the Russian Chargé d'Affaires. He hoped to disrupt the cordial relations established between Russia and Britain, but his abuse did nothing to lower Palmerston in the opinion of the Tsar.[1]

Prussia made no such definite advances but it was clear that the Prussian King and the Prussian soldiers looked to Britain more than to any other state. With only one Power was Palmerston the stumbling block to better relations—France, whom he had defeated and humiliated. And it must be admitted that Palmerston himself did little to heal the breach. On the contrary he widened it in the last weeks of his tenure of office by a speech to his constituents at Tiverton which contrasted the success of Britain in India with the failure of France in Algiers, a failure which he attributed to the barbarous methods employed by the French soldiers. This was all the more wounding in that there was some truth in the accusation. The attack was no doubt drawn from Palmerston in the heat of the contest and not meant to

[1] The details are given in my "Palmerston, Metternich and the European System," in *Proceedings of the British Academy*, 1934.

attract the attention which it obtained. But it is a sign that his success had caused him to lose some of the restraint and tact necessary for the conduct of foreign affairs. Such an outburst might be defended if it was calculated and had some object in view. But Palmerston had nothing to gain by it. On the contrary, he was anxious to obtain Guizot's signature to a Five Power Slave Trade treaty on which he had spent a great deal of time and thought, and which would have been a fitting recognition of the unceasing effort he had made on that subject throughout his period of office. It is not surprising that, in spite of Palmerston's elaborate explanation to Bulwer, which however fell short of a real apology, Guizot refused to allow Palmerston to have this satisfaction.[1]

This was an unnecessary and humiliating setback. But, though the French Government naturally disliked Palmerston himself, they recognised that his policy had been justified by events and were anxious to renew the *entente cordiale*. Aberdeen, who had been one of the most zealous supporters of Palmerston's policy in 1840, had no difficulty in establishing the old relation of the early eighteen thirties with Louis Philippe and Guizot as soon as he had come into office.

[1] The details of this well-known incident are in *Bulwer*, II, 376–383. Palmerston's explanation was made at Bulwer's suggestion. After his failure Bulwer wrote: "I can only say I had good reason to think what I did and our first conversation on the subject entitled me to think even more than I did . . . and tho' I am much hurt and dissatisfied at the present little spiteful proceeding, I must say that Guizot himself always speaks of you, your public service and ability with respect and liking." (27 Aug., 1841: *B.P.*) He also altered for publication his own letter. For example, he had expressed his *conviction* not his *belief* that Guizot would change his decision on receipt of a letter of explanation to Bulwer and he omitted the sentence "Guizot is a Frenchman and like all Frenchmen vain and susceptible".

CHAPTER IX

THE CONTRIBUTION OF PALMERSTON TO BRITISH FOREIGN POLICY
1830–1841

" The system of England ought to be to maintain the liberties
and independence of all other nations ; out of the conflicting
interests of all other countries to secure her own independence ;
to throw her moral weight into the scale of any people who are
spontaneously striving for freedom, by which I mean rational
government, and to extend as far and as fast as possible civilisation all over the world.   I am sure this is our interest, I am certain
it must redound to our honour ; I am convinced we have within
ourselves the strength to pursue this course, if we have only the
will to do so ; and in your humble servant that will is strong and
persevering."   PALMERSTON, 21 March, 1838.

CHAPTER IX

THE CONTRIBUTION OF PALMERSTON TO BRITISH FOREIGN POLICY, 1830–1841

ALL estimates of these eleven years have necessarily been influenced by Palmerston's later career. He was nearly fifty seven at the close of this period and when he came back to the Foreign Office five years later he was still in full vigour. He shewed no signs of loss of energy when he became Prime Minister at the age of seventy. He had, however, the misfortune to spend nearly all the next ten years in that office. Palmerston wore out more slowly than anyone except Gladstone, but few men are fit for such responsibility after the age of seventy-five and Palmerston's reputation suffered from the mistakes which he made at the end of his life.

Moreover, he had himself to deal with the consequences of the actions of these years. Castlereagh died while the great experiment of the European Alliance was in the balance, and that fact is given as one of the explanations of its failure. Canning joined Russia in an attack on Turkish power and assisted to bring France and Russia together, a combination dangerous to his country. But he died just as this was accomplished and historians have generally thought that if he had lived he would have mastered the difficult situation which he had helped to create. But Palmerston had himself to face in 1848 the revolutions in Europe, which his work in the eighteen thirties had been designed to prevent, and in 1854 he was a member of a Cabinet which began the war against Russia which he had then so successfully guarded against—and there were many other subordinate parts of his policy which he had to reconsider and adapt to new circumstances. Instead of a Liberal France he had to work with an Emperor. It was inevitable that some of his later policy should seem inconsistent with that of his former period of office.

Palmerston also made enemies of some of the most active and influential individuals of this time. The fact is to his credit. He defeated manoeuvres that would have injured not only himself but his country. But Talleyrand and Princess Lieven were

attractive personalities and have left voluminous records behind them designed to deceive. Their insinuations and falsehoods have been believed to a far greater degree than they deserved. Both have repeatedly been shewn to be deliberate liars, yet their assertions have often been accepted in the most uncritical fashion by historians of repute and become part of the stock of text-book makers. The legends of the nineteenth century have done more to obscure the truth than those of the Middle Ages, because they have not been examined with the same scepticism and historical technique. Greville's diary also has had an immense influence on British historiography of the nineteenth century. It is written with such an air of candour that it has often been accepted without question. Yet it is full of misleading statements, and, though Greville was compelled at the end of this period to pay a great tribute to Palmerston's abilities, he sometimes had all the rancour of a man whose shafts have missed their mark. Urquhart's accusations were so absurd that they did little injury to Palmerston, even though some of them were repeated by no less a figure than Karl Marx. All this denigration was, however, only very partially answered in the official biography of Bulwer who never took the trouble to examine more than a fraction of the voluminous evidence left in Palmerston's private papers.

Palmerston himself certainly did much to injure his own reputation by the manner of his writings. His private letters often contain extravagant assertions. They were written in the heat of the moment to convey an immediate reaction. Unless they are set beside the official despatches which went with them they give a misleading impression of his attitude towards the problems with which he had to deal. But the despatches also are more direct and uncompromising than most of their kind. Palmerston was in these years always in conflict not only with foreign but with domestic opponents and all his writings bear the mark of the struggle. That is true of nearly all Foreign Ministers in some degree, but it is more apparent in Palmerston's case than in that of any other.

But, whatever judgment be formed on it, it is clear that Palmerston's work during this period was of immense importance. He set the course of British foreign policy for a generation. He signed the two treaties which throughout the century were most important to the position of Britain in Europe—the one securing

the neutrality of Belgium and the other the closing of the Straits. But he took an interest in every part of the Continent. His attitude towards Europe in these years was indeed more that of Castlereagh than of Canning. But to Castlereagh's conception of a Concert of the Great Powers he added that protection of Liberalism which Canning had threatened but never carried out. The combination was a difficult if not an impossible one. Yet Palmerston had an extraordinary degree of success.

In method he was of course as different to Castlereagh as it was possible to be and much nearer to Canning. In this respect indeed he can be regarded as that disciple of Canning as he is so often rather mistakenly described. Only in energy and perseverance throughout a long period of office is there any similarity between Castlereagh and Palmerston. Castlereagh who, it is true, in addition led the House of Commons, a task Palmerston escaped until he was seventy, died of the effects of his toil. Palmerston's freshness, resilience and eagerness to continue in office at the end of this period shew what his powers of resistance were. He could hardly perhaps have remained so had he not, so far as possible, confined himself to foreign affairs or questions closely connected with them. He was of course much interested in those of Ireland, but he seems to have succeeded in staying outside the controversies which arose about them in these years. When he did concern himself with them it was always to urge compromise and moderation.

This concentration, necessary for efficiency, had its disadvantages. He sometimes forgot that his colleagues could not be so conscious of the importance of what he was doing as he was himself. But generally Palmerston recognised as fully as anyone who ever held his office the limitations placed on his work by the processes of Cabinet Government. "There are very few public men in England", he wrote in 1838, "who follow up foreign affairs sufficiently to foresee the consequences of events which have not happened."[1]

The art of diplomacy depends upon timing as much as on anything else. But the right moment may come by preparation as well as by opportunity. Sometimes it is possible to take advantage of a fortunate combination of circumstances, but it is also possible to create them. Palmerston was perhaps better at the first than the

[1] To Granville, 5 June, 1838: *Bulwer*, II, 266.

second. He rarely missed an opportunity. But he also shewed great patience and skill in the gradual process of preparation which ultimately leads to success. His conduct of the Belgian negotiation as well as that of the Eastern Question in 1839–1840 shew his exceptional skill in this respect.

· Palmerston's directness of approach and clarity of exposition in speech and writing have not often been surpassed in his office. His State Papers are indeed not the equal of those of Canning. They do not lead the reader irresistibly to the conclusion of the writer. They are not so profound nor so subtle. But they are for the most part models of clear and incisive language. They come straight to the point, and the facts on which Palmerston relies are marshalled with great force. They perhaps do not take sufficiently into account the arguments on the other side. Palmerston could use effectively at times the method of stating the opposing case fairly and powerfully, but in such a manner that it could be demolished at a later stage of the argument, one of the best methods of convincing those to whom argument appeals at all. But, as he was always working against time, it was generally as much as he could do to state his own case. His despatches and letters are also often directed against prejudice and jealousy which he knew that he could not overcome. He certainly, however, devoted too much time to abuse and complaint of his opponents. He also tended to labour too much a point which was already won. Both Grey and Melbourne often pointed this fault out to him.

Palmerston's realisation of the strength and importance of public opinion in foreign affairs he undoubtedly learnt from watching Canning at work. He was not naturally an orator either in Parliament or on a public platform. This had been one of the reasons which kept him out of high office and he long refused to make the effort to attain to distinction in this field. But when he devoted sufficient preparation to a speech it could be very effective indeed. He much increased his reputation by this means during the Wellington Administration. When he came into office, however, he was less successful in impressing the House of Commons than might have been expected. This was partly due to its absorption in domestic affairs. But Palmerston seems to have learnt slowly the art of combining the responsibility of office with the ability to make a popular appeal. On the other hand, in informing public opinion by the publication of documents and

communication with the Press he set entirely new standards. He was ahead of any other Minister in Europe in this respect. In this way he helped to create an informed public opinion not only in Britain but on the continent of Europe which was of immense advantage to his work.

He could not have done this so well had he not possessed complete mastery over all the complicated problems with which he had to deal. Of some he had a greater knowledge than anyone else in Europe. He was so superior to all his colleagues in the Cabinets that they could never really engage in argument with him. Even Lord Grey, who more than anyone else entered into the problems of the foreign office, relied on Palmerston entirely for the facts on which he based his conclusions. The Lievens or colleagues like Holland or friends abroad were in constant correspondence with the Prime Minister, but it is clear that he trusted Palmerston's reports on and analysis of situations far more than anything he could get elsewhere. When other colleagues made complaints Palmerston could nearly always tear their case to pieces. No other Foreign Minister had a greater command of the information of his office.

The same was true when he met foreign diplomats either in conference or *tête à tête*. He had always all the business at his finger ends. They were overwhelmed by the completeness and certainty of his knowledge. This is clear in their reports which naturally try to make the best of their own share of the discussion. Palmerston's accounts of his conversations similarly give his own point of view, but they shew how terrific he could be in attack and how ruthlessly he could expose the weak side of his opponent's case. This ascendancy had its disadvantages. It cut Palmerston off from one source of information and influence. It was his own policy that he defended and generally obtained. But he had not the gift of stating his own aims in such a manner that others thought they had originated them. In this he was inferior to Castlereagh and Salisbury whose most important achievements sometimes passed without notice and became part of the common stock.

In all that part of his work which depended on technical skill rather than character Palmerston was above almost all holders of his office. His gift of language enabled him to talk to diplomats as easily in French as in English. When it was a question of drafting he could with speed and certainty do all that was necessary in either

language. He could master a complicated question with unusual rapidity when he gave his mind to it. He was not a lawyer but he knew much international law and kept the books on that subject constantly in use. "Some people not unqualified to judge", wrote Bagehot, "have said that his opinion on such matters was as good as any law officer's."[1] This was written about his later career but it applies to this period where more than one witness noticed his exceptional knowledge of this aspect of his work. The essays on political economy which appear at regular intervals, if a little naïve, are much more advanced than most statesmen of his time could have written.

The final impression is one of immense energy, power of concentration, courage and resilience. Palmerston faced combinations of internal and external foes that would have killed most men. A similar combination helped to kill Canning. No one could help but admire the resource and tenacity of his resistance. It is best seen in the final triumph in the Eastern Question, but is hardly less apparent in the problems of Belgium and the Peninsula. His optimism was unfailing. He always believed he could win—and he nearly always did. Clarendon, whose technique was pessimism, was irritated by this trait. "He always reckons that that *is* which he wishes," he told his brother.[2] But for Palmerston that was a method of obtaining what he wanted. He was more aware of the difficulties than he would confess to others—or even to himself.

But Palmerston must be judged by the ends to which these exceptional qualities were directed, by what he achieved for Britain and Europe. No one has ever questioned his devotion to his country's interests. He had indeed often been criticised for an excessive nationalism. This implies that he sought objects to the injury of the legitimate interests of other countries and did not take sufficient regard to the general interests of Europe. This is certainly untrue of this period. The objects which Palmerston tried to obtain were naturally those which he considered to be calculated to promote British interests. No Foreign Minister could hold office on any other terms. But he also pursued policies which were in the general interests of Europe. This may perhaps be disputed as regards the Eastern Question. It can be

[1] W. Bagehot, *Biographical Sketches*, 341. This is a hasty and inadequate sketch written two days after Palmerston's death but it contains some pregnant sentences.
[2] Sir H. Maxwell, *Clarendon*, I, 145.

claimed, though the balance of evidence is in the other direction, that the general interests of the world would have been better served if the Ottoman Empire had been allowed to disintegrate at this time. But in its defence Palmerston claimed no territory or special privilege for Britain. His policy in the Eastern Question was more European than that of any other Minister. And in Belgium, the Peninsula, Greece, Switzerland and Italy, he advocated policies which were meant to establish free, independent, prosperous states. There is no other period in British history of the nineteenth century where so much was done in peace time for objects in Europe, of which the benefits to Britain were only the indirect ones that come from the advantages of others. In China and India there was, it is true, the use of force for an immediate interest, in the one case commercial expansion, in the other the protection of the Indian Empire. But both these actions were the result of policies long pursued by Britain as by all other maritime states, and any criticism of Palmerston is one of the whole method by which Western civilisation spread over the world. British relations with the United States were during the greater part of this period exceptionally good, Palmerston was eager to help France and the United States to resume normal relations in 1834–1836 and certainly assisted to obtain the settlement of their unfortunate dispute. The Slave Trade, the United States' attitude to Canada and the Maine frontier problem disturbed their harmony in the last two years of this period, but the record is a remarkable one.

It is, however, his work in Europe which is surveyed in this book. Palmerston is more open to the charge that he interfered too much in European questions in which Britain had no real interest, or that he subordinated immediate British interests to general causes. This was the criticism constantly levelled at him by Frederick Lamb and his even more cynical brother, Lord Melbourne. Melbourne had no policy but doing nothing, but Lamb constantly suggested that Palmerston ought to make a deal with Austria whose interests were identical with those of Britain, instead of pursuing a quixotic policy of supporting the constitutional cause in Europe and driving the three Eastern Powers more closely together. France, the country with which Palmerston was associated, was the rival of Britain overseas and the greatest danger to British security. Central Europe was the natural ally of Britain against both France and Russia.

As has been seen, Palmerston had to take a view somewhat similar to this on his entry into office. He was uncertain of France and used the Eastern Powers to control her policy in Belgium. He was like others afraid that the aggressive policy of the first French Revolution might be repeated. But once that danger was shewn to be, if not entirely absent, more easily checked by cooperation with France, is it to be maintained that he should have subordinated his policy in the West to the necessities of Metternich? It is clear that he could have had a close alliance with Austria and Prussia at the cost of giving up all support to Liberalism. But even if such a course had been to the interests of Britain Palmerston could not have pursued it. No British Government could have supported a policy of repression in Europe.

But Palmerston had no doubt that British interests were entirely on the other side. In his opinion revolution could only be prevented by the progress of Liberalism and revolution was bound to threaten the peace of the Continent—the greatest interest of Britain. He tried hard to avoid the dilemma either of sacrificing British interests in the East or abandoning his position in the West, and it is possible that with a little more effort and financial expenditure the Eastern Question could have been tackled before the position in Western Europe was stabilised. Palmerston sometimes thought so, though perhaps his recognition of the dangers in the East came somewhat late. But if a choice had to be made he preferred to maintain the position in the West, and he was proved right in the end by securing most of his objects in both areas.

For in spite of the dramatic reversal of alliances Palmerston never gave up his defence of constitutional Government in Western Europe and Greece. He continued to the end to insist that its existence was necessary for both European and British interests. Melbourne often challenged this view. "All these Chambers and free Presses in other countries", he told Palmerston, "are very fine things, but depend upon it, they are full as hostile to England as the old Governments."[1] But Palmerston's belief in constitutional government was just as strong at the end of this period as at the beginning. He made some notable expressions of this belief, two of which deserve some quotation here for they sum up the faith that inspired his actions in these years.

[1] From Melbourne, 11 Feb., 1838: *B.P.*

As late as 1841, he replied to the never-ceasing criticism of his Ambassador at Vienna: "you say that a constitution is but a means to an end and the end is good government; but the experience of mankind shews that this is the only road by which the goal can be reached and that it is impossible without a constitution fully to develop the natural resources of a country and to ensure for the nation security for life, liberty and property. I hold that there is no instance in past or present times under a despotic government where these objects have been attained."[1]

This judgment was made in the intimacy of a private letter, but Palmerston wrote just as strongly a little later in an official despatch on the struggle in Greece which committed Melbourne and the Cabinet as well as himself: "It is always easy to say with regard to any country in which men do not wish to see constitutional government established that such a country is not fit for it and that it would not work there; but Her Majesty's Government do not happen to recollect any country in which a constitutional system of government has been established that has not on the whole been better off in consequence of that system than it had been before."[2]

It is of course true that Palmerston did not really succeed in establishing constitutionalism in Western Europe. Of all the countries with which Palmerston was concerned only in Belgium has the Liberal State maintained a continuing existence. Elsewhere it has often failed to cope with its difficulties, and been undermined by the corruption of its followers. But, though there have been intervals of autocracy or dictatorship, the conception of the Liberal state has remained for all Western Europe as the norm to which the body politic should return, as well as for those parts of the world to which the influence of Western Europe has extended. The failure of Liberalism to emerge in the new unified Germany has been a major cause of the two world wars of the twentieth century. Even in this period Palmerston was weakest in dealing with Germany and later on he was to shew that he did not realise how much depended on the manner by which its unity was brought about. But elsewhere he did a great deal to make possible the existence of constitutional Government. Its preservation is still the greatest issue in the world today. In the

---

[1] To Beauvale, 31 Jan., 1841: *B.P.*
[2] To Granville, 19 March, 1841: *F.O. France*, 619.

eighteen twenties Britain had put forward the doctrine of non-intervention but stood aside when it was disregarded. In the eighteen thirties Britain interpreted the doctrine of non-intervention in another manner. She claimed the right to protect the Liberal Movement if the Eastern Powers attacked it. She never did so much again in the nineteenth century. That so much was done even with imperfect success was mainly due to Palmerston.

The success of Liberalism in this period was in the first place due to France, a fact to which Palmerston gave full recognition. Indeed to the end of the period he believed that the French people were genuinely attached to the idea of the Liberal state, however Louis Philippe and some of his Ministers behaved. But he had the right to complain that the French King, who in the long run determined French policy, had deserted the cause which had given him his crown. Louis Philippe's policy in Spain was indeed treacherous and his relations with Austria, revealed in the Austrian archives, were in a sense a betrayal of the *entente*. Louis Philippe himself constantly attributed Palmerston's attitude towards France in 1840 to the latter's indignation at French policy in Spain. This is not true. Palmerston eagerly welcomed the apparently cooperative attitude of Soult's Government in 1839. But it is true that Palmerston considered that it was only the support of Britain that enabled the constitutional cause to triumph in the Peninsula, and the record of events given in Chapter VI would appear to prove him right. The rivalry of maritime and overseas power, and the fear of France of British commercial domination of the continent of Europe certainly contributed to this failure of the two countries to work together for a common end in which the mass of the peoples of both states believed. Palmerston's unfounded suspicions and immoderate language undoubtedly helped to divide them. But it has been seen that he genuinely desired to continue the cooperation with France. It was Louis Philippe and not Palmerston who destroyed the *entente*.

Palmerston's great contribution to the Liberal Movement has not received the attention which it deserved whatever opinion be held about it. But Palmerston's handling of the Eastern Question has been the theme of many pens. They have, however, concentrated on the attempt to modernise the Turkish Empire, and the vigorous opposition to Russian expansion. They have all been influenced by the fact that the Crimean War occurred and that

Palmerston shared the responsibility for it. How far the weakness and pacifism of Aberdeen was not more responsible for Britain's part in what is sometimes crudely called an unnecessary war is beyond the scope of this book. But it is in any case irrelevant to the issue of these years when Palmerston's success has to be admitted by all. That involved the protection of the Ottoman Empire and the limitation of Russian expansion and power of interference. But it should be noted that Palmerston's object was to do this by means of the European Concert. The problem of the Straits was in a sense solved by this means during these years. The solemn recognition by the Great Powers that the ruler of Constantinople was to keep the Straits closed except when he was himself at war was one of the great acts of the nineteenth century.

As in the case of Belgium this achievement was the result of statesmanship in a number of different countries. Russia shewed a wise restraint and Metternich, in spite of his vacillation, made a real contribution to the solution. But Palmerston can claim a great share of the credit. He felt his way rather slowly, but without the energy and courage that he shewed in the years 1838–1840 it could not have been obtained. The overthrow of Mehemet Ali was a necessary preliminary, for the Sultan could not have been accepted as the guardian of the gate if he were under a perpetual threat from the South. Palmerston accomplished that task almost singlehanded. But he never lost sight of the greater objective, the safeguarding of the Straits, and was the first to insist that the solution should be a European one. For long it is true he almost despaired of Russia accepting such a solution, but he always thought that if the rest of Europe shewed the necessary resolution she would be compelled to take part. When the Tsar evinced his readiness to do so, nothing could have been better than Palmerston's immediate resolve to take advantage of the opportunity. The conflict that arose with France is now recognised by French historians to be largely due to the faults of Thiers, though they condemn Palmerston's methods, hardly realising that they were necessary under the circumstances to obtain the desired ends. But on the whole the course of history and the analysis of historians have shewn that Palmerston deserved the admiration and praise that he then received in such large measure from all Europe.

He did not then obtain the larger objective, which Castlereagh

had been the first to attempt, of a guarantee of the independence and integrity of the Ottoman Empire. His readiness to abandon it was due to the opposition of Russia and it clearly could not have been obtained without her defeat in war. But it is also true that he had by 1840 come to regard it as something of much less importance than what it symbolised, the recognition that the fate of the Ottoman Empire was of supreme importance to all the European community of nations and that any changes in it should be worked out round the Council table and not produced by the unilateral action of one Power as had happened in 1829 and 1833. This is the real issue with Russia both in 1854 and 1877 and Palmerston's policy was the same as that which Salisbury laid down in the great despatch of 1 April, 1878.

Palmerston considered that he had obtained the cooperation of Russia by shewing her the determination not only of the Government but of the people of Britain to resist her encroachments on the Turkish Empire or her control of the Straits. All the evidence goes to shew that this judgment was correct. No doubt the Tsar was glad to take advantage of the opportunity to humiliate Louis Philippe and separate Britain from France. But it can hardly be doubted that the impression made on him and his advisers by the attitude of the British people as well as by Palmerston's action in 1838 was a major factor in causing him to take the course he did.

It must be remembered also that the British resistance extended to Central Asia. No other European power could have anything to say in that quarter. But as regards the Ottoman Empire Palmerston had always offered a European solution, while making it absolutely clear that Britain would fight rather than allow any unilateral action. Never was a policy more successful. Palmerston won from Russia such cooperation and respect as was never attained again in the nineteenth century. The course of history might have been changed had he been able to represent Britain to the Tsar in 1844 instead of the weak and incompetent Aberdeen.

With this policy of resistance to Russia Palmerston combined that of reforming the Ottoman Empire. It is obvious that he did not understand this problem and critics have fastened on this weakness. Palmerston himself shewed some dismay as the evidence accumulated that once the Turk was out of immediate danger he was just as corrupt and tyrannical as he had ever been. He admitted that Britain shared in the discredit because she had

been the principal instrument in preserving the Empire intact. But there was in fact nothing else to do but to persist in the policy of reform and Stratford Canning made his great attempt to accomplish the impossible in the immediately succeeding years. Had Palmerston then been his chief more success might have been obtained but the final result could not have been very different. It was, however, at that period impossible to apply to the Ottoman Empire the policy of later years. Time was needed before the subject races of the Balkans could create viable states and even in 1919 those in Asia Minor were not ready for self-government. This dilemma, the defence of a state which denied the elementary human rights to its subjects, persisted throughout the century. Lord Salisbury's conscience was to suffer from it. But it has still to be seen how far the division of the Ottoman Empire into separate states will secure the independence and welfare of the inhabitants of the Balkans and Asia Minor.

It is surely obvious that Palmerston was a good European as well as a patriotic Minister of Britain. He came near at this time to devising for Europe some permanent form of Council to express its common interests. The success of the Belgian negotiation and the obvious need for a European policy on the Eastern Question drove him in this direction. Modern apologists for Metternich sometimes paint him as the only really European minister in the first half of the nineteenth century. But Palmerston like Castlereagh was well aware of the complexity of European problems, the interest of Britain in them all and the need of some machinery to deal with them. If, like Canning, he inveighed against the "Holy Alliance" he meant merely the use of the Alliance as a means to repress Liberal institutions. He did not adopt Canning's dictum of no more congresses. On the contrary, as has been seen he wished to develop the conference system. Metternich indeed accused him of a design to make the Belgian Conference a sort of permanent Council of Europe. Palmerston himself hardly thought on those lines. But he obviously wished to repeat in another field the success that he had had in the Belgian question. Like Metternich he attached too much importance to his own position in the scheme. Partly for this reason, but apparently still more because of the opposition of the Cabinet, he abandoned the attempt. He tried once more in 1838 to make London the centre of negotiation. But in 1839 he surrendered the control of the machine because he

was so convinced of its necessity. The acceptance of Vienna as the centre in 1839 was one of his wisest acts in these years. The subsequent events are perhaps sufficient excuse for his refusal to consider at the end of this period any suggestion for the creation of a permanent centre. Europe was not yet ready for such a scheme and he would have had no support in Britain. But Palmerston at this time went further in accepting the idea of a permanent European Concert than any of his successors until the First Great War. It was one of his greatest failures in the eighteen sixties that he reacted so violently to the proposals of Napoleon III to use the method of conference as an alternative to war.

Like Castlereagh Palmerston regarded a balance of power in Europe as indispensable to British interests. But Castlereagh's conception of Europe was far more static than Palmerston's. Palmerston realised that change must come. But he relied on the balance of power to prevent aggression and in that he was in full agreement with his predecessor. His skill in creating the combinations to defeat the schemes of France, Austria, Russia and France again is a remarkable piece of diplomacy. He was aware that the ideological basis of the earlier years could not always persist. He foresaw the combination of France and Russia which was so dreaded, but believed that Central Europe would be able to resist it with British help. His famous phrase in the debate of 1849 that no country was either the eternal ally or the perpetual enemy of England but "that with every British Minister the interests of England ought to be the shibboleth of his policy" came to him partly as a result of the experience of this period. But it is often forgotten that that expression of national egotism was preceded by a recognition of ethical values which Gladstone himself could not have bettered: "As long as she [England] sympathises with right and justice she will never find herself altogether alone. She is sure to find some other state of sufficient power, influence and weight to support and aid her."[1] It would be a mistake to think such a statement to be mere hypocrisy, any more than the sentences which are placed at the head of this chapter. In all he did at this time Palmerston was fully convinced that right and justice were on his side. And by the end of this period, if many Courts and Cabinets disliked him, his name was already known all over

[1] E. Ashley, *Palmerston*, I, 62–63.

Europe as that of a Minister who had often been the foe of tyrants
and the champion of the oppressed.

Two views of Palmerston have often been put forward which are
contradictory of one another. There is clearly some truth in both
of them. Mr. Philip Guedalla ended his brilliant summary of
Palmerston's long career with a phrase that has often been
quoted, "the last candle of the Eighteenth Century was out."[1]
But this was surely mainly true as regards externals and acciden-
tals. In manners and social habits Palmerston retained the outlook of a previous age. But, in his attitude to Liberalism, to
nationality and to economics, Palmerston was a true Victorian
though he may have tempered his beliefs with some of the prag-
matism of the earlier century.

But Palmerston has also been described as a typical John Bull
who expressed the outlook of the British middle classes. He
certainly became their idol. The Russian exile, Alexander
Herzen, wrote of "the finest meteorological instrument in England,
Palmerston, who indicated with the greatest fidelity the temperature of the middle classes."[2] Palmerston did indeed share many
of their prejudices as well as their belief in themselves and their
determination to get their own way. But no one could have been
further removed from their insularity and ignorance of Europe.
Palmerston was passionately interested in the Continent and at
times commented bitterly on the inability of Parliament and
public opinion to realise the great issues at stake both in the West
and East of Europe. Nevertheless the Victorian age that was just
beginning was a great age of enterprise and adventure, and
Palmerston's enthusiasm and self-confidence were shared by many
of his countrymen.

It was this intensity of feeling that caused Palmerston to use the
language which did his reputation so much harm. The charge
that it led him into unnecessary interference, by advice and criticism, of the actions of other countries is not justified, at any rate
in this period. He was entitled to make his views known by the
treaties which Britain had not only signed but largely devised.
He had a right—some might say a duty—to express his opinion
about the affairs of Italy, the German Confederation or Cracow.
The states concerned had been brought into existence largely by

[1] P. Guedalla, *Palmerston*, 459.
[2] A. Herzen, *Memoirs* (translation by Constance Garnett), IV, 281.

the effort of Britain. But the manner and method of his interference was often unfortunate. It gave him an appearance of
arrogance which was not really a true expression of his feelings.
He was genuinely indignant at acts of cruelty and repression.
But the language which he used about Metternich or Otto of
Greece or Mehemet Ali, though not meant for other than intimate
friends or colleagues, cannot be defended. And that which he
used in despatches and letters which he meant foreign statesmen
to see was often unnecessarily offensive and far too insistent.
And at the end this verbal extravagance became something more
dangerous. He shewed some sign of losing the balance and sense
of reality which he displays in these years. His pressure on
France and Mehemet Ali was unnecessary, his eagerness to obtain
all the advantages of the forward move in Asia was excessive. He
shewed the same excess of zeal in later dealings with Greece and
after the victory of the Crimean War. This was a great defect in
his character but in this period it is not apparent until the end.

Final judgment on Palmerston must wait until the whole of his
career is further explored. But surely enough is known of the
period considered in this book to place him very high on the list of
British Foreign Ministers. During the years between the Great
Wars when pacifism and appeasement were rated highly as methods
of obtaining peace Palmerston's work and character were often
unduly deprecated. The Liberalism which he helped to establish
in Europe also had few defenders in an age in which the bourgeois
state was fiercely attacked and its undoubted weaknesses revealed.
The danger of Russian aggression was imperfectly appreciated.
The realisation of national self-government to which, though
mainly in a later period of his career, Palmerston also made a great
contribution, was thought to have brought as much evil as good.
Palmerston's work was not as unknown as that of Castlereagh for
it had been done much more in the open. But a good deal of it
in this period was overshadowed by the more dramatic revolutions
of 1848. Palmerston himself worked for immediate ends and the
last thing that he expected was any recognition of what he had
done. "The gratitude of individuals may be reckoned upon
sometimes," he wrote at the end of this period, "that of masses of
men or even of any number of men in a corporate capacity never."[1]
This is one of the harsh utterances that he sometimes made in a

[1] To Beauvale, 1 April, 1841: *B.P.*

bitter moment, and it is fortunately not entirely true. But whether gratitude is due to him or not, there are some important things in the world which owe much to Palmerston's influence. If the substantive is to have any meaning in social democracy, if Belgium and the Straits are to remain as independent areas, if the colossal mass of Russia can be contained and fitted into a world system, if effective international cooperation is to be obtained by the use of the Council table, these results will be due in part to Palmerston's work in these years.

APPENDICES

A. LETTERS FROM PALMERSTON TO WILLIAM IV, 1832–1837

B. CORRESPONDENCE BETWEEN PALMERSTON AND GREY, 1831–1833
   - (a) LETTERS FROM PALMERSTON TO GREY
   - (b) LETTERS FROM GREY TO PALMERSTON

C. CORRESPONDENCE BETWEEN PALMERSTON AND MELBOURNE, 1835–1840
   - (a) THE RETURN TO OFFICE IN 1835
   - (b) LETTERS FROM PALMERSTON TO MELBOURNE
   - (c) LETTERS FROM MELBOURNE TO PALMERSTON

D. DESPATCHES AND LETTERS FROM NEUMANN TO METTERNICH, 1839–1840

E. LETTERS FROM DESAGES TO BOURQUENEY, 1836–1840

APPENDIX A

LETTERS FROM PALMERSTON TO WILLIAM IV[1]
1832–1837
(i)

Foreign Office, 5 *August*, 1832.[2]

... Viscount Palmerston would humbly submit that the measures which Your Majesty has been advised to adopt in your Majesty's character of King of Hanover, are no bar to the course which, as King of Great Britain, Your Majesty is now advised to pursue.

It is well known throughout Europe that the Kingdoms of Great Britain and Hanover have little in common, except the Sovereign whom both have the happiness to obey. That, placed geographically in situations essentially different, they must frequently have interests and engagements differing no less; and that to expect that Hanover should submit her policy to the decision of Great Britain or that Great Britain should make hers follow the guidance of the Hanoverian Cabinet would be to require that, which would be equally repugnant to the feelings of both nations. But the object of your Majesty's Servants, being to preserve things as they are in the German States, Viscount Palmerston humbly conceives that the spirit in which they are desirous of acting, is the same which has guided the Hanoverian councils; and that the only difference between the two Cabinets lies, in the different anticipations which they form of the probable effect of certain measures.

Viscount Palmerston would rejoice to find that he has taken an exaggerated view of the aim of those who have planned these measures, or that he has over-estimated the effects which those measures may possibly produce; but in either case Viscount Palmerston would humbly submit, that no inconvenience can arise from the communications which he proposes to Your Majesty to authorize him to make. It is better that the British Cabinet should be taxed with entertaining groundless or premature apprehensions, than that it should be accused of blind indifference to events which might place the peace of Europe in jeopardy.

Viscount Palmerston begs further most humbly to submit that the course proposed to be pursued is by no means inconsistent with the doctrine, properly understood, of not interfering in the internal affairs of other countries. The interference in the internal affairs of other States, which your Majesty's Servants object to, upon principle, is an interference by force of arms; such an interference as France exercised in

---

[1] From the Broadlands Papers. The correspondence is, of course, always in the third person.

[2] The first part of this letter is in *Bulwer*, II, 415–418, with no indication that anything is omitted.

Spain and Austria in Naples ;[1] and such as the latter of these two
Powers seems at present disposed to exert, in Italy, in Swisserland, and
in Germany. Such an interference has for its object to subject the will
of an independent nation to the military dictation of a powerful neighbour; it is founded on injustice, and leads to the destruction of the
balance of power. But an interference which consists merely of
friendly advice, tendered by one ally to another, upon questions of
general interest, which may at will be accepted or declined, which has
for its object to prevent the collision of arms, and to dissuade from
measures of force by which peace is disturbed, such an interference,
Viscount Palmerston humbly submits, is sanctioned by the most
approved principles of international law, and is consistent with the
strictest regard for the rights of independent states.

Viscount Palmerston wishes to abstain from any minute examination
of the Resolutions of the Frankfort Diet, because the object of the
communication which he has humbly submitted to Your Majesty, is
rather the possible consequences of those Resolutions if pushed to their
full application, than their accordance with the spirit of the Acts, by
which the Confederation was constituted. But upon that latter point
the recent despatches from your Majestys Ministers at several of the
German Courts shew that the general opinion is not favourable to those
Resolutions. . . .

It appears, therefore, to be the opinion of Mr. Cartwright[2] judging
from personal observation on the spot, that the immediate effect of
these Resolutions will be, to create a serious breach between the constitutional Sovereigns and the great mass of their subjects, upon
questions of the deepest national importance, and which call into action
the strongest passions of mankind, a state of things which cannot exist
in any country without serious inconvenience and great danger, even
if that country were entirely cut off from all external contact. But
Mr. Cartwright goes on to point out a probable result, which it must be
far from the wish of Your Majesty to see realized, and he says that
"the *mass of the inhabitants* of the constitutional states finding their own
Governments lending themselves to measures having for their object
the restriction of the Liberal institutions, to which they are attached, will
turn to France for protection; and a strong French party may be created
in the heart of Germany which may ultimately produce a material
change in the political relations of the country."

Such then are the grounds of the alarm with which Viscount Palmerston views the present state of affairs in Germany. The intention of
Your Majesty's Servts is to endeavour to prevent and not to promote
revolution. . . .

Viscount Palmerston has only further most humbly to state to Your
Majesty that he has again revised the draft of the Despatch and has
made some alterations in it, which he hopes Your Majesty may approve.

[1] France in 1823 and Austria in 1821.
[2] From Cartwright, 16 July, 1832: *F.O. Germany*, 38.

(ii)

Foreign Office, 8 *October*, 1832.

Viscount Palmerston presents his humble duty to Your Majesty, and has had the honor of receiving Your Majesty's memorandum of yesterday, containing a succinct review of the prominent points of the latter stages of the negotiation on the affairs of Belgium, together with Your Majesty's just reflections thereupon, and Viscount Palmerston will not fail to lay that paper immediately before his colleagues.

Your Majesty will no doubt read with satisfaction Mr. Jerningham's last dispatch[1] from the Hague of the 5th July giving an Account of the instructions which the Prussian Minister at that Court had *at last* received from his Government, and Viscount Palmerston is not altogether without hopes, that this step, however tardily taken by Prussia, may have some effect upon the Cabinet of The Hague. The resolution of Prussia to take this step may, as Viscount Palmerston most humbly submits be in some measure ascribed to the circumstance, that the three Courts have found themselves baffled in all their endeavours to sow dissension between England and France, and to separate those two Governments; that they are conscious that the united determination of the two, to execute the treaty could only be impeded by the armed resistance of the three, and that they shrink from an unjust and groundless war with England and France, the avowed object of which must be deliberately to violate their plighted faith; that, therefore, when they found that they had pushed forbearance to its utmost limit, and that their schemes for further delay had proved abortive, they have set themselves in earnest to procure from Holland an acquiescence which at an earlier time they might have commanded.

Viscount Palmerston hopes the attempt may not be made too late.

The course of the Belgian negotiation seems to afford an illustration of the policy, which Viscount Palmerston very humbly conceives to be most for the advantage of Great Britain in the present state of Europe—

Your Majesty will remember in the earlier period of the transaction, France was unreasonable and encroaching. She wanted Philippeville and Marienbourg as a beginning of the dismemberment of Belgium; she wanted to put the Duke de Nemours on the Throne; she wanted to continue indefinitely to occupy Belgium after the Dutch had been expelled; and she wanted to demolish almost all the fortresses. Upon the occasion of all these pretensions the British Government brought the three Powers to bear upon France, and France was upon all compelled to yield; latterly the three Powers have in their turn been unreasonable and deficient in good faith, and have endeavoured, under false pretences, to defeat the treaty they had ratified and to mar the arrangement they had guaranteed. The British Government then brought France to bear upon the three Powers, and it is to be hoped with ultimate success. Rivals in military strength, as France and the three Powers are, Your Majesty may be said practically to hold the

---

[1] *F.O. Holland*, 182.

scales of the balance of Europe. France will not venture to attack the three Powers, if she is also to be opposed by England; and the three Powers will pause long before they attack France, if they think that France could in that case reckon upon the support of England. Thus, then, it appears to Viscount Palmerston, that Your Majesty has peculiarly the power of preserving the general peace and that by throwing the moral influence of Great Britain into one scale or the other, according as the opposite side may manifest a spirit of encroachment or injustice, Your Majesty may from the peculiar circumstances of the times, more than perhaps many of Your Majesty's Royal Precedessors, but certainly with far less exertion of physical strength, become on many occasions the arbiter of events in Europe. For in acting upon this system of practical mediation, it is hardly possible that it should ever become necessary for Your Majesty to send an army to the Continent to take part in operations by land; on most occasions the moral influence of Great Britain would probably be effectual; but if that should at any time fail, a prompt and vigorous employment of the powerful naval resources which Your Majesty can at any time command, would be sure to give adequate effect to just and moderate counsels. It is then by supporting and strengthening, on one hand, that party in France who are for peace abroad and order at home, and by tempering, on the other, the zeal of those in other countries, who think that the whole art of government consists in the application of military force, that the propagandists and the republicans may be kept out of power in France, and pretences for disturbance may be avoided in other parts of the Continent. And, if it should be possible to prevent, for a few years longer, any war between the great nations, and any serious civil commotions in Europe, Viscount Palmerston humbly hopes, that the widespread agitation which has been produced by the unfortunate measures of the illfated Charles 10, may at length subside into a comparative calm.

(iii)

Foreign Office, 29 *September*, 1833.

Viscount Palmerston presents his humble duty to Your Majesty, and has had the honor of receiving Your Majesty's memorandum of yesterday's date, upon Earl Granville's private letter of the 23d instant.[1]

Viscount Palmerston begs to assure Your Majesty, that it never was his intention to submit to Your Majesty, a remonstrance to be made to the Russian Government by Your Majesty's representative, and that of the King of the French *jointly*. Viscount Palmerston would humbly submit, that it would be expedient to follow at Saint Petersburgh the same course which was pursued at Constantinople, where the British and French Ambassadors presented *separately*, though at the same time, the protests which each had been instructed by his own Government to deliver. Each acted with perfect independence of the other, although

---

[1] *B.P.* This contained Broglie's draft of the protest to Russia.

the similarity of wording in the two protests, and the circumstance of their both being given in, in the course of the same day, added essentially to the effect of each, by proving that Great Britain and France, though acting each for itself, as independent Powers, yet concurred in taking the same view of the matters to which the protest related.

Viscount Palmerston begs most humbly to assure Your Majesty, that neither he, nor any others of Your Majesty's confidential Servants wish to shackle this country by any unnecessary engagements with the Government of France, and Viscount Palmerston is fully alive to the propriety of keeping a watchful eye upon the proceedings of that Power. National character can not at once be changed, and the spirit of enterprise and military activity, which was so sedulously excited among the French by Bonaparte, can only die away gradually and slowly.

While Monsieur Lafitte was at the head of the French Government, many things happened which were calculated to require the vigilance and the resistance of the British Government; and Viscount Palmerston humbly trusts, that upon those occasions Your Majesty's Servants were not found wanting in a proper sense of what was due to the interests of the country and the honor of Your Majesty's crown.

When Monsieur Casimir Perrier [sic] succeeded to power, the policy of the French Government underwent a change; it became more friendly to England, more straightforward, and more pacific. With the conduct of the French Government, the course, but not the principles of action, of Your Majesty's confidential Servants changed also; and it appeared to them to be wise to meet the proffered friendship of France with corresponding demonstrations; to encourage confidence by confidence; and, by drawing closer to the French Government, to confirm their inclination for peace, and render it more difficult for them to fall back to a system of war.

Since the Duc de Broglie has directed the councils of France, the good understanding between the two Governments has every day become more intimate. The Duc de Broglie possesses all the good qualities of Monsieur Casimir Perrier, with some which the latter had not. In integrity and a desire to do right, there is perhaps no difference between them; but the Duc de Broglie is a man of more attainment, is more of a statesman, and, therefore, better able to accomplish his purposes.

Monsieur Casimir Perier cultivated the friendship of England, because he saw that the union of England and France was the only means of preserving that peace which he was so anxious to maintain. The Duc de Broglie, besides this political motive, feels that personal goodwill towards this country, which arises from a perfect knowledge of its language, a complete acquaintance with it's institutions, and an intimate friendship with many of the most distinguished of Your Majesty's subjects. As long therefore as the influence of the Duc de Broglie predominates, Your Majesty will probably find the policy of the French Government friendly to this country, and pacific; and, while the policy of France bears that twofold character, Your Majesty will no

doubt be desirous of encouraging that Power, and of confirming it in this system, by a corresponding manifestation of confidence and friendship.

Your Majesty has most wisely determined, to make the preservation of peace, as long as it is possible to preserve it, the chief object of Your Majesty's solicitude in the direction of the foreign relations of this country; and, indeed, every year of peace is most valuable for the future, as well as for the present. For not only does Europe, in the mean while, remain free from the calamities of war, but also on the one hand, the French nation are insensibly led to turn their thoughts and energies to the pursuits of commerce and the other occupations of peace, and will gradually lose that military taste which has heretofore rendered them so restless and encroaching; while on the other hand, the German Powers are saved from all the dangers to which they might be exposed, if a war of political principle were now to break out; and thus the great bulwark of Europe against future aggression either from France or from Russia, is preserved unimpaired. Nor are these advantages purchased by any subserviency to France, derogatory to the dignity of Great Britain. On the contrary, it may safely be affirmed, that there never was a period when England exercised so great an influence over the councils of France, as she does at present, nor when the French Sovereign paid so great a deference to the King of Great Britain.

Viscount Palmerston, therefore, humbly trusts that, if he and his colleagues are anxious under present circumstances to cultivate the best understanding with France, Your Majesty will not suppose that it arises from any blind and unreflecting confidence on their part. But they believe, that at the present moment the French Government are conscious that the friendship of England is of the utmost value to them, and its forbearance and neutrality in the event of war absolutely necessary for their existence. Your Majesty's Servants are therefore desirous of taking advantage of this peculiar posture of affairs, and, without abating any of that circumspection which prudence may dictate, they would wish not to repulse the friendly demonstrations of the French Government by any outward shew of coldness or distrust and they are not without hopes, that by continuing to keep even the balance of power, by a due application of the moral influence of Great Britain, Your Majesty may still be enabled to enjoy the satisfaction of preserving the peace of Europe.

(iv)

Foreign Office, 12 *April*, 1834.

Viscount Palmerston presents his humble duty to your Majesty and has the honor to submit, that he has felt it his duty to bring under the serious consideration of his colleagues in the Cabinet, the note[1] from the Marquis de Miraflores, which he has recently had the honor of

[1] Dated 10 April, 1834.

laying before Your Majesty and the verbal communications which he has received upon the same subject, from the Marquis himself and from M. de Sarmento.

It appears as the result of these verbal and written communications, and this result is further confirmed by various despatches recently received from Mr. Villiers and Lord Howard de Walden, that the Governments of Portugal and Spain are agreed upon the necessity of a joint military operation in Portugal; that the Spanish Government would wish to confine that operation to the expulsion of Don Carlos, and wants to send its troops into Portugal without any formal engagement previously contracted with Portugal; that the Portuguese Government requires a previous convention, as a security for the future retirement of the Spanish troops, and insists that the action of these troops shall be directed to Portuguese as well as to Spanish objects, the expulsion of Don Miguel as well as of Don Carlos. But both the Spanish and the Portuguese Governments concur in one thing; they are both equally anxious that Your Majesty should be a party to the arrangement by which their joint operation is to take effect.

Spain solicits this upon the ground that Your Majesty, by concurring, might impose upon Don Pedro conditions as to amnesty, which Spain alone could not exact, but which are necessary for that future tranquillity of Portugal, which it is so important for Spain to see established. She also fears, that if she were, singly and uncountenanced by any other Power, to undertake operations against Don Miguel, she should draw down upon herself the resentment of Austria, which resentment might be injuriously felt through the agency of the Court of Rome acting upon the priesthood of Spain; while on the other hand, if she were supported by the sanction of Great Britain, she would be indifferent as to the displeasure of other Powers.

Portugal on the other hand, is most anxious for the concurrence of Your Majesty, because she feels jealous of the entrance of Spanish troops into her territory, unless under the controul of engagements to which Your Majesty should be a party; for she looks to Great Britain as her trusty friend and as the Power bound by ancient treaties to watch over and to defend her independence.

It appears, moreover, that if Spanish troops are to enter the territory of Portugal, it is most consistent with the dignity and most fitting the engagements and obligations of Your Majesty's Crown, that their entrance should be preceded by a convention, recording that they enter with the free consent of the Sovereign of Portugal, stipulating what shall be the purpose for which they go in, and declaring beforehand when they shall withdraw, and that this convention should be one to which Your Majesty should be a party.

Your Majesty's Servants having given their most serious attention to all these considerations, convinced that a speedy termination of the civil war in Portugal is the only foundation upon which the tranquillity of the Peninsula can be established, sensible that Great Britain has no right to object to the entrance of Spanish troops into Portugal upon the

invitation of the legitimate Sovereign of that country, and has no power
to prevent it except by sending thither British troops instead, conscious
that the treaties between the British and Portuguese Crowns oblige
this country to defend the independence of Portugal, and that therefore
Your Majesty might hereafter be called upon inconveniently to interfere, if, after the Spanish troops were in Portugal, any dispute were to
arise between the Spanish and Portuguese Governments as to their
conduct or their continued stay, upon all these grounds, Your Majesty's
Servants have come to the opinion, that it is expedient that a convention
should be concluded between Spain and Portugal, and that Your
Majesty should be a party thereto.

But it would scarcely be consistent with the power and position of
Great Britain, or with the influence which she ought to retain in Portu-
gal, that the operations in that country, which it would be the object of
such a convention to regulate, should be exclusively carried on by a
Spanish cooperation, and it is therefore the opinion of Your Majesty's
Servants, that the convention should stipulate a naval cooperation on
Your Majesty's part.

But when Your Majesty affords your countenance and cooperation
to measures which can scarcely fail to be effectual for ridding the
Portuguese territory of Don Miguel and the civil war which his presence keeps alive, Your Majesty is justly entitled to require from the
Portuguese Government a sufficient provision for Don Miguel as a
Prince of the House of Braganza, and pardon for those Portuguese
subjects who have hitherto followed his banner; and the proposed
convention ought to contain on the part of the Portuguese Government
stipulations to this effect.

The position of France with respect to Portugal is essentially different
from that of Great Britain. France is to Portugal at present a friendly
Power, but is bound to her by no special engagements; Great Britain
is to Portugal as it were a trustee for her estate. The same reasons,
therefore, which render it almost necessary that Great Britain should be
a party to this convention, do not apply to France.

Nevertheless it is the opinion which Your Majesty's Servants are
most humbly led to entertain, and to submit for Your Majesty's consideration, that it would, for more reasons than one be desireable to
connect France in some way or other with this transaction.

In the first place the moral effect of the convention would be greater,
if it is signed by the four Powers than if it signed only by the three, and
Your Majesty's servants are not without some hope that the moral
effect, which will be produced by the promulgation of such a convention
as that which is suggested, may in a great degree render unnecessary
the employment of the physical force for which it would provide.

In the next place, so much pains have been taken of late by the agents
of Russia, Austria and Prussia, to spread reports of disunion between
Great Britain and France, and those reports, if credited, are likely to be
so prejudicial to the policy of Your Majesty's Government in many
matters, but more especially with reference to the affairs of the Levant,

that it would be desireable to give those reports some public and practical contradiction. But the association of France with Great Britain,
Spain, and Portugal in such a convention as that in question, would be
such a contradiction, whereas her exclusion from such a convention
would not fail to give much credit to the reports of growing disunion.

But, lastly, it is always advantageous, considering the rapid changes of
men in the councils of France, to obtain by the binding engagement of
treaty, some controul over the conduct of her Government more permanent and secure than what arises from the personal character of the
individual who may at any given time be in office.

For all these reasons it appears to Your Majesty's Servants that it
would be desireable to invite the accession of France to any such
convention, and to propose to her to stipulate, that she will, *if called
upon by the other three contracting parties*, give such aid towards the
accomplishment of the objects of the convention, *as may then be agreed
upon between her and her three allies*.

Such an accession would strengthen the alliance, while it tied up the
hands of France.

Viscount Palmerston has accordingly prepared the draft of a convention for the above mentioned purposes, which, with the concurrence of
his colleagues, he now most humbly submits for Your Majesty's gracious
approval. . . . [Details of procedure and request for immediate signature.]

(v)

Foreign Office, 15 *April*, 1834.

Viscount Palmerston presents his humble duty to Your Majesty and
has the honor of submitting to Your Majesty the draft of the proposed
treaty such as it has been finally agreed to between himself, the French
Ambassador, the Spanish and the Portuguese Ministers, subject to
Your Majesty's gracious approval.

The substance of the treaty remains precisely the same as when
Viscount Palmerston previously submitted it to Your Majesty, with the
exception of a stipulation in favor of the Infant Don Carlos, which has
been introduced, with the consent of the Marquis de Miraflores, in
compliance with Your Majesty's desire.

Some slight changes of form have been made in parts of the treaty
which Viscount Palmerston would humbly submit, have in some degree
improved it. The accession of France has been introduced into the
body of the treaty instead of being made by a subsequent act; this was
done at the request of the Prince de Talleyrand and it had the advantage
of giving more unity to the transaction.

The Prince de Talleyrand also expressed a strong wish that the treaty
should mark distinctly that it was in consequence of the union between
England and France rather than in consequence of any particular union
between France, Spain and Portugal that France became a party to the
treaty; and the wording has been altered so as to express this idea.

Viscount Palmerston would humbly submit that as a Frenchman he

might perhaps have felt some hesitation as to a change, which instead of stating France to be spontaneously invited by the three other Powers jointly, represents Spain and Portugal as applying to her to join in the treaty, chiefly on the ground of the good understanding between her and England; but as an Englishman, Viscount Palmerston would submit to Your Majesty, that the proposed wording is, of the two, the most complimentary to this country. If Your Majesty should be pleased to approve of this draft, the treaty will immediately be prepared in conformity with it, and may be ready for signature on Thursday. The Spanish and Portuguese Ministers are delighted with the measure; and the Marquis de Miraflores in particular says he has only one regret upon the subject, and that is that he cannot himself have the pleasure of presenting the treaty with his own hands to his Government.

(vi)

Foreign Office, 20 *April*, 1834.

Viscount Palmerston presents his humble duty to Your Majesty and has the honor of reporting to Your Majesty that some difficulties have still arisen with respect to the Quadruple Treaty.

In consequence of the delay necessarily incident to a careful and as far as possible a literal translation of the original into the Spanish, Portuguese and French languages, the copies for signature had not been prepared yesterday, when at an early hour yesterday morning Viscount Palmerston received from Earl Granville the accompanying Note No. 1, and the altered Draft No. 2.[1]

Viscount Palmerston immediately wrote to the Prince de Talleyrand expressing his extreme regret at the difficulties which had thus unexpectedly sprung up, in a quarter where they were not looked for, pointed out the objections which he felt to the new proposal and requested the Prince to call on him in Stanhope Street.

The Prince came soon after twelve. Viscount Palmerston stated to him that it is the interest as well as the wish of Your Majesty's Government to avoid any thing which should unnecessarily tend to lower the French Government in the eyes of the French nation, and consequently, if as appeared from the Princes explanations, the French Government feared that to be mentioned in the latter part of the treaty would be considered by the public in France as derogatory, and that the national feeling would be gratified by a change of form in introducing the King of the French into the treaty, to such change of form Your Majesty's Government certainly could not object. But Viscount Palmerston said that the alteration proposed, was a change of substance as well as form. That the proposed addition to the Preamble as written in red ink, founded the accession of France upon recent applications made to her by Spain; that your Majesty's Government well knew that the only applications made to France by Spain, were for the assistance of French

[1] Not printed.

troops *in Spain*; that the British Government thought it very unwise in Monsieur de Zea to have made that application, and very prudent and proper in the French Government to have declined complying with it; that instead of recording and proclaiming that application in a treaty, it would be better to consign it to oblivion; but that Great Britain who disapproved of the application, and who would still advise Spain not to renew it, and France not to yield to it, never could sanction its principle by recording it in a treaty as the ground of French accession to such treaty. Prince Talleyrand in reply pointed out, that even if such a construction could fairly be put on the proposed Preamble, which he denied, the subsequent article 4 corrected the evil, since by that article France was to do nothing except in concert with her Allies.

Viscount Palmerston, however, said that right or wrong he saw in the proposed Preamble a meaning coupled with French interference in Spain and, if this impression struck his mind, it might very possibly occur also to other persons; that the whole object of the present treaty was a military operation by the Spaniards in Portugal, and no operation by any body in Spain; and that, for the reasons which he had assigned, he should positively refuse to sign the treaty with that passage in it.

After much discussion and some communications between Prince Talleyrand, Viscount Palmerston, and Your Majesty's other confidential Servants, with which it is not necessary to trouble Your Majesty, Prince Talleyrand agreed to such a change in the manner of introducing France into the treaty as appears in the altered copy No. 3.[1] . . .

[Discussion of drafting details].

(vii)

Stanhope St., 12 *June*, 1835.

Viscount Palmerston presents his humble duty to Your Majesty, and has had the honor on his return home tonight from the House of Commons, to receive Your Majesty's communication of today,[2] upon the subject of the selection of Colonel Evans to command the Corps about to be raised in this country for the service of the Queen of Spain, and he begs most humbly to submit to Your Majesty the following considerations on this matter; and in the first place with respect to the political opinions which Colonel Evans may entertain, Viscount Palmerston has no other knowledge of them than that which he has gathered from speeches made at elections, and in Parliament, but he would humbly submit for Your Majesty's consideration, that he is not aware that these opinions, though they may go to considerable lengths on some points, such as a ballot, suffrage and duration of Parliaments, have ever been otherwise than entirely consistent with an attachment and with loyalty to monarchy.

Experience moreover has frequently shewn that the real and settled opinions of men may often fall short of the speeches which they are

---

[1] Substantially as in the Treaty as signed.   [2] *B.P.*

led to make on the hustings, in the excitement of a contested election; or even of the language which they may hold in debates in the House of Commons, when striving to make themselves prominent, as leaders of the popular party.

Viscount Palmerston, therefore, would humbly submit, that (although he is far from agreeing with Colonel Evans on a variety of points) there is nothing, as far as he is aware, in the political tenets of that officer which should justly disqualify him from being employed in any military capacity for which his professional qualities might render him fit.

Viscount Palmerston would beg also to submit that it has been remarked by all foreign Governments, and even by those who are most jealous of strangers, that British subjects, whatever may be their opinions, are scarcely ever found engaged in intrigues or cabals against the Governments of the countries in which they are residing, and there seems to be no reason to suppose that Colonel Evans would be an exception to this rule.

Viscount Palmerston would further most humbly submit that the Spanish people are of all others the most jealous of strangers; that this jealousy has been shewn lately in a striking manner by the prejudice which has been created in Spain against the mission of Lord Eliot and Colonel Gurwood, that it is, therefore, essential that the officers who may be employed on the present occasion, should be men of Liberal opinions; because if they should be persons at all favourable to the cause of Don Carlos, or even lukewarm in that of the Queen, they would immediately be exposed to every kind of suspicion on the part of the officers of the Queen's army; and distrust and dissension would inevitably lead to failure.

It is also to be borne in mind that if it is desirable, as it undoubtedly is, that the Catholics of the South of Ireland should be induced to volunteer, it is necessary that the expedition should be commanded by persons in whom those Catholics may be disposed to place confidence, and whom they may be inclined to follow.

Viscount Palmerston would also beg humbly to submit that the contest in Portugal affords an instance very much in point. The political opinions of Admiral Napier are probably not very different from those of Colonel Evans (and in each case it may well be doubted whether those opinions are not as much a means as an end) but during the whole time that Admiral Napier was employed in Portugal, though he had political power, which Colonel Evans never can have in Spain, he never was found to exert his influence with a view to bringing his political opinions to bear upon the internal affairs of Portugal, but invariably confined himself, to his professional duties; or if he ever stepped beyond that line, did so, to assist your Majesty's Minister at Lisbon, and to support the Government of the Queen.

Viscount Palmerston therefore would humbly trust that considering the vast importance to England and to Europe of success in this war on the part of the Queen, considering how the national honor would be affected either by a failure in raising men, or by a miscarriage on the

part of the Corps when raised, Your Majesty may be disposed not to
disapprove of the choice which General Alava has made of Colonel
Evans, and may be induced to sanction such facilities as may be useful
towards giving the measure the best chances of success.

(viii)

Stanhope St., 10 *September*, 1836.

... Viscount Palmerston would also beg most humbly to submit
that the expression "revolutionary proceedings"[1] is one which has of
late been so much used by some of the Governments of Europe to
describe indefinitely anything whether real or imaginary which is at
variance with their own views and policy, that Viscount Palmerston
would be reluctant to insert it in a despatch for which he was to become
the responsible adviser of Your Majesty, unless it were accompanied by
some explanation stating the precise nature of the proceedings to which
that phrase was by anticipation applied, and shewing why those proceedings ought to call for a protest on the part of Your Majesty. For
Viscount Palmerston would further most humbly submit to your
Majesty, that the mere circumstance that proceedings in another
country are revolutionary, has not been of itself considered a conclusive
reason why your Majesty should protest against them, or even refuse
to countenance them.

There could not be a proceeding more purely and strictly revolutionary than that which took place in Paris in July 1830, when by a popular
insurrection the Royal troops were defeated, and the King together
with his own family expelled from France, and another person was
raised to the Throne by the tumultuous decree of the inhabitants of the
capital; and yet Your Majesty by the advice of the then Ministers of the
Crown, wisely given as Viscount Palmerston humbly ventures to think,
was the first Sovereign in Europe to acknowledge the new King of the
French; and the British Government by that immediate acknowledgement, and by the uninterrupted continuance of diplomatic relations
with France, undoubtedly gave a direct countenance to the results of
that revolutionary proceeding.

But, in truth, independently of the great political interests which at
that time rendered such a decision urgently and immediately expedient,
it would perhaps have been difficult for Your Majestys Servants to have
assigned the revolutionary character of the events which had led to a
change of dynasty in France, as a reason why that change should not be
acknowledged by Your Majesty, seeing that in this country a similar

---

[1] In reply to the King's amendment of a despatch to Villiers, on the situation
after the acceptance by the Queen Regent of the Constitution of 1812 at La
Granja, as follows: "He never will consent to give his countenance, direct or
indirect, to the revolutionary proceedings of any Government which the Queen
Regent acting on behalf of her infant daughter may accept or which may be
forced upon her, nor become a party to measures against the character of which
it is his bounden duty to protest."

change brought about in a similar manner was the foundation of the title of the present Royal Dynasty, and is considered by all political parties as the epoch, from whence they date the real and practical liberties of the nation.

With regard to the dispatch itself Viscount Palmerston had humbly hoped that the passage to which he has already adverted would sufficiently announce to the Spanish Government that Your Majesty will not be a party to any proceedings inconsistent with Your Majesty's engagements, and incompatible with the honor and dignity of Your Majesty's Crown; and to go into further detail would rather weaken and limit than strengthen and amplify that declaration. On other points the draft contains observations which Viscount Palmerston thinks ought to be stated to the Spanish Government through the British Minister at Madrid, and which with a view to his own responsibility he is anxious to place upon record as having been so communicated to the Spanish Cabinet at the present crisis.

(ix)

Foreign Office, 21 *February*, 1837.

Viscount Palmerston presents his humble duty to Your Majesty and has had the honor of receiving Your Majesty's memorandum of the 19th instant,[1] in which Your Majesty observes that the matter to which the accompanying draft to Lord Howard[2] relates, is entirely a Portuguese concern, and therefore not one in which Your Majestys Government ought to interfere.

Viscount Palmerston in explanation begs humbly to submit that it has never been the practice of the Government of England, and more especially in its intercourse with the Government of Portugal, to consider it improper or unbecoming to offer advice and to express opinions upon matters even connected with internal affairs, with regard to which such advice or opinion might be thought to be useful to a friendly Government.

But in the present case Viscount Palmerston would humbly beg to submit that he proposes to do no more than he did some little time ago, with Your Majestys sanction, with regard to Spain.

General Sevane stated to Mr Villiers that in a certain contingency, a system of terror and of legal murder would be established in Spain, and Viscount Palmerston felt that it was due to the character and honor of Your Majestys Government that it should not be in the power of any man to say that so revolting a plan had been communicated to them, and that they had by their silence approved it. In the same manner Viscount Palmerston begs on the present occasion to submit to Your Majesty, that it would not be consistent with the character and honor of

[1] *B.P.*
[2] To Lord Howard de Walden, 18 Feb., 1837: *F.O. Portugal*, 460. The despatch protests against any attempt to suppress the insurgent bands in the Algarves by laying waste the countryside.

your Majesty's Government, that such a scheme as that to which the accompanying draft relates, should have been communicated to Your Majesty's Minister at Lisbon by the Portuguese Government and that Lord Howard should not have been instructed to express thereupon those sentiments of disapprobation which so barbarous and impolitic a plan must inspire in every impartial mind.   To be silent would be to approve; and to approve would be in the highest degree reprehensible. Viscount Palmerston begs further to submit, that the tendering of the proposed opinion is not the sort of interference in the internal affairs of Portugal which Austria and Prussia and Russia are in the habit of exercising in the detailed administration, or in the constitutional arrangements of other countries, but that it stands on entirely different grounds.   The measure in question is a military operation which the Portugueze Government propose to have recourse to, in furtherance of the objects of a treaty to which Great Britain is a party, and if that measure were executed, it is impossible that some part of the disgrace attending it should not be shared by the allies of Portugal.

(x)

Stanhope St., 2 *June*, 1837.

Viscount Palmerston presents his humble duty to Your Majesty and has had the honor of receiving this evening Your Majesty's communication upon Sir Frederic Lamb's Despatch No. 44 of the 23rd May,[1] and he is much gratified to find that the opinion which Viscount Melbourne and himself had come to in a conversation on this subject and which Viscount Palmerston intended to submit for Your Majesty's consideration in the shape of a draft of a dispatch, has already received the sanction of your Majesty's immediate judgement.

Viscount Palmerston entirely subscribes to Your Majesty's opinion that it would be extremely inexpedient to act upon the suggestion of Prince Metternich, who proposes that the British Government should, through him, recommend to the Court of St. Petersburgh to establish a blockade of the coast of Circassia.

Such a course would, as Your Majesty most truly observes, be an abandonment at once of the whole of the Circassian question, which it is at least expedient to keep open, for this country to act upon as may be deemed advisable.   Russia would, as Your Majesty observes, interpret such a recommendation, as a virtual acknowledgement of her claim of sovereignty; and she would take care to let the Circassians know that in attempting their subjugation she was advised and encouraged by England.

Viscount Palmerston in his reserved despatch[2] to the Earl of Durham which he shewed to Count Pozzo di Borgo, in alluding to a blockade as a measure which was more applicable than municipal regulations, to the existing relations between Russia and Circassia, took care to throw in

[1] *F.O. Austria*, 265.
[2] To Durham, 19 April, 1837: *F.O. Russia*, 231.

precautionary words, stating that "with such a blockade foreign Powers would deal as they might think proper"; intending thereby to intimate to Russia that it did not follow as a mere matter of course, that such a blockade *would* at once be acknowledged by England. But if the English Government were to advise the blockade, no doubt as to acknowledgement could possibly exist.

Again supposing the right of Russia to establish such a blockade to be clear, still the blockade must be effectual, in order to be legal; but if the English Government had counselled the blockade, it would be difficult to insist too strictly upon degrees of effectiveness.

Viscount Palmerston begs humbly to say, that he entirely concurs in the opinion that Your Majesty has expressed with respect to Prince Metternich. That statesman may or may not be, a wise and prudent Minister for Austria, according to Austrian interests; that is a question between him, and his Sovereign and his country; but it cannot be denied that Prince Metternich is a most frail support and a most dangerous ally for any foreign Power to trust to. His timid and temporizing character, his love of indirect ways of attaining his purpose, his habit of sacrificing future interests for the convenience of the moment, his proneness to side with the party he thinks the strongest, all these combine to render him an object of distrust rather than of confidence; and make it vain to speculate what his conduct would be in any given future contingency. No reasonable man can doubt that a partition of Turkey between Austria and Russia would be highly injurious to the interests of Austria; but he would be a bold prophet who would foresay that Prince Metternich would not consent to, and join in such a partition, rather than make war with Russia, in order to maintain the integrity of the Ottoman Empire.

With regard to the suggestion, which has often been made by others and which has recently been adverted to by Sir Frederic Lamb of sending a British fleet into the Black Sea, Viscount Palmerston would beg most humbly to suggest that there are many important considerations connected with such a proceeding, which would require to be well weighed before it was adopted. In the first place the fleet to be so sent, ought to be clearly stronger than the Russian fleet of 12 or 14 Sail of the Line stationed in the Black Sea; and it would require some land force on board, to be used in case of need, to occupy commanding batteries.

But in the next place such a step would of course be considered by Russia as a threat; she would therefore immediately call upon Turkey to close the Dardanelles under the Treaty of Unkiar Skelessi; and to allow a Russian land force to occupy the batteries on one side at least; and this might lead to a military occupation of Turkey by Russia, before Turkey has sufficiently recovered from her late wars to be able to resist by her own means, and while Austria under the councils of Prince Metternich would not dare to do more than protest against such a proceeding.

But further the entrance of a British Squadron by force into the

Black Sea, as a menace against Russia, would justify the Emperor in sending his 29 or 30 Sail of the Line from the Baltic, upon a similar errand to the coast of England; and the position of this country during the interval that would elapse before an equal force could be got together would not be one in which it would be desirable to place Great Britain.

Viscount Palmerston would, therefore, humbly submit, that the forcible entrance of a strong British fleet into the Black Sea, would be a proper and advisable step, as a first and a preliminary measure of war against Russia, and might in such a case obtain advantages of position for this country; but that such a step would not be expedient unless it were simultaneously accompanied by a very large naval armament at home. And Viscount Palmerston would beg further to submit, that in order to obtain from Parliament the considerable funds which would be necessary for a naval armament on so large a scale, it would be requisite to shew that some very great and important national interest was directly at stake.

APPENDIX B

CORRESPONDENCE BETWEEN
PALMERSTON AND GREY, 1831–1833[1]

(a) LETTERS FROM PALMERSTON TO GREY

(i)

Stanhope St., 1 *February*, 1831.

[Talleyrand suggested, "in terms sufficiently plain not to be mistaken that we should agree to Nemours becoming King of Belgium."] To this I at once replied that it was impossible we could agree to any such thing; that we looked upon Nemours on the throne of Belgium as tantamount to the union of Belgium with France and, as we could not agree to the one, so neither could we to the other; that I was quite sure the other Powers of Europe would see the matter in the same point of view and that my personal opinion was that the acceptance of the crown for Nemours would produce a general war in Europe and it was for the Government and King of France to consider whether any possible advantage they could gain by the former would be an equivalent for the almost certain dangers which, to them at least, (let the nation face as it might) the latter would bring with it; that Sebastiani himself had said in his speech the other day, that even in war it is well to have right on ones side, but that in this case France would be violating the spirit, if not the letter, of those treaties, the promise to observe which was the condition upon which Louis Philippe obtained the recognition of Europe, and would be manifestly departing from all the recent pledges upon the very matter itself; that I could hardly think that he, Talleyrand, could press a point so entirely inconsistent with the engagements which he had recently entered into, nor that the King would expose himself to such an imputation as this would cast upon his good-faith; that by a recent Protocol the five Powers had renounced all exclusive influence and separate advantage to be derived from the arrangements to be made for Belgium and that, if the placing a son of the King of the French on the throne of Belgium was not precluded by this renunciation, I was at a loss to see the meaning of those words. I said that if there could be any doubt as to the fair meaning of those words or as to the intentions of the King, which I would not believe, I should propose in the conference about to take place a Protocol, to the same effect as a passage in that of the 22nd March, 1829 about Greece, by which the three Courts, who were engaged in the settlement of

---

[1] From the Broadlands Papers. Palmerston's letters begin "My dear Lord Grey" and end "Yours sincerely"; those of Grey begin "My dear Palmerston" and end "Ever Yours".

Greece, agreed that the Sovereign should not be taken from any of their respective royal families. Talleyrand let drop his proposition, alleging, however, that there would be a wide difference between positive union and the election of Nemours, as it was not to be supposed that the King, who is so attached to his family, would think of dethroning his own son.

He said my proposition was new and he would write this night for instructions about it; he had no doubt he should be authorized to agree to it, but could not do so without specific instructions, but he thought that if he agreed to this, we ought to agree entirely to give up the Prince of Orange whose election would bring civil war to their doors. I said I thought this was the moment for such an engagement while the election was not yet made rather than the time when it should actually have taken place and that, if the King and the Government wanted strength to resist the party which might urge them to accept the offer, I was tendering to them the best argument they could wish for a fresh and incompatible engagement; that as to the P. of Orange we had done nothing but express our wishes for him in concurrence with Talleyrand, founded upon the notion that his was the most numerous party, and that I much doubted whether civil war would not be the certain consequence of any other choice but him.

Talleyrand again wanted to return to the subject of Philippeville and Marienburg, but I declined opening a question already disposed of. He begged me not to make any proposition to the conference as it might produce *dissentiment*; I told him that I could not help doing so, but that it would be for the conference to dispose of it. . . .

(ii)

Stanhope St., 12 *August*, 1831.

Bulow has just told me in confidence that having arrived for our conference early, and found only Talleyrand come, the latter immediately began upon Belgium, told him that Belgium could not go on upon the present footing; that Leopold had proved himself a poor creature unfit for a throne, and that the Belgians have shewn themselves unworthy of independence; that if the French troops were to retire Perrier's [sic] administration would fall, and, if they do not, your Government could not stand. That some new arrangement therefore must be tried, and the only good one is a *partition of the country*. That Holland would be for it, and if Prussia united with France and Holland there could be no effectual resistance, especially if public opinion in England was reconciled by making Antwerp a free port.

Bulow said he supposed France meant to have the lion's share and wished to know what was to fall to the lot of Prussia. Talleyrand said all that could be easily settled—and their conversation was interrupted by the arrival of the other Ministers.

Bulow's notion is, that this move of the Dutch has been planned between Talleyrand and Falck, who have been much together since the

latter has removed to Portland Place, and that Russia has not discouraged it, partly wishing to help Holland to a share of Belgium, and partly thinking that war in the West would leave her elbow room in the East.

I send you a note from Melbourne[1] confirming Bulow's statement as to the views of France, and the papers say that the French Government is collecting another corps as a reserve for Gerard.

(iii)

Foreign Office, 27 *December*, 1831.

I saw Goblet yesterday evening and found from him that by the last of a succession of different instructions, he was desired not to exchange ratifications till further orders. I told him what we had settled in Cabinet and said I would write to Granville and to Leopold and see Talleyrand. I send you a draft of a dispatch to Granville, and I have written privately to him and to Leopold. To-day I have seen Talleyrand and told him that the Cabinet felt that they could not agree to any change in the stipulations of the convention. Our conversation was very calm on both sides, excepting a little warmth on his part when, in reply to a regret that his communications appeared to have added to the excitement at Paris, he assured me fervently that he had invariably tried to quiet his friends there upon this question and would continue to omit no efforts to do so. We went over the well known arguments on both sides and he ended by asking me what he should write to his Government. I said I concluded he would report that which I had told him as to the opinion of the Cabinet and that I wished him to add such of my arguments as he might think likely to have any weight with his Government; that I begged him to entreat his Government to consider that this question was important or trifling just as they chose to consider and to make it; that, if they chose to create an excitement about it, they as a Government leading the way on such a matter might undoubtedly succeed in doing so; but that if they chose to treat it as a trifle, which in fact it is, we should probably hear very little about it.

He said that what they dwelt upon most was the notion that this convention is a revival of the Holy Alliance. I pointed out all the absurdity of such an idea and he begged me to write to Granville to tell Sebastiani that he had urged that point, and that I had laughed at him for pressing it.

I then requested him to point out to the attention of his Government how foolish it would be to quarrel with us on such a matter as this, when there are so many important affairs pending in question, upon which cordiality and good understanding between France and England are so important for the attainment of objects which interest both. We parted very good friends after discussing several other subjects and my impression is that this little storm will subside. He did not even mention that he has any communication to make on this subject to the con-

[1] Missing.

ference and if he has received any I have no doubt he will do on this occasion, as he has on similar ones, and abstain from acting up to instructions, which a change of circumstances, or his nearer view of things here, may lead him to think it is better to postpone.

(iv)

Stanhope St., 3 *August*, 1832.

I have just received this[1] from the King. With respect to his first objection, that can very easily be removed by acting upon the suggestion contained in your note[2] of yesterday and making our communication to Austria and Prussia as well as to all the other German Courts with which we have relations.

With regard to his difficulty in doing anything as King of England which is not consistent with what he has done as King of Hanover, the answer is, that if the politics of the two countries are to be thus bound together, England being the most powerful and important is entitled to lead Hanover, and not Hanover to lead England; that if the English Government is to be tied by that which the Hanoverian has done, they ought to be previously consulted, and to have a voice in the deliberation. But neither you nor I could venture to tell Parliament that the European policy of England must be shackled and governed by decisions taken by the Hanoverian Cabinet without our knowledge or concurrence.

Such a doctrine would go further than anything else to shake the root of the Hanoverian family in this country.

With regard to the matter itself the real truth is, that the Resolutions of the Diet to which the constitutional Sovereigns have assented, are nearly as inconsistent with the German constitutions as the proceedings of Charles 10th or James 2nd were with those of France and England, and if carried into full execution may produce in Germany consequences similar to those which followed the errors of those monarchs.

I do not see how the English Government can avoid communicating to its allies its opinions and its fears as to the present menacing state of affairs in Europe.

(v)

Stanhope St., 8 *October*, 1833.

Your demur about presenting our protest at Petersburg disturbs and embarrasses me greatly, for I had so entirely considered that this was part of our original decision as to the presentation of the protest, that I have never imagined that any doubt could arise upon the subject; and the last passage in the despatch to Ponsonby of the 7th Aug.[3] distinctly announces our intention of presenting the protest at Petersburgh.

I can quite understand that Madame de Lieven should wish to persuade us not to do so, because not only as a general principle is it,

---

[1] From William IV, 3 Aug., 1832: B.P.   [2] B.P.
[3] *F.O. Turkey*, 220.

under present circumstances, her great object as Russian Ambassadress to paralize us, and to keep the English Government in a state of inaction and nullity, but as we know from Berlin, the presentation of this protest at Constantinople has much annoyed the Imperial Government and staggered them, and it would be a great coup, if the Lievens could persuade us *not* to present the protest at Petersburgh, and thereby could render entirely vain, or still worse than vain, the step we have taken at Constantinople.

I say worse than vain, because I must say, that if, knowing as we do, that the treaty against which we have protested, was forced by Russia upon Turkey, and it being manifest from the nature of the engagement, that the acts which we wish to prevent (and to prevent which in certain cases we are sending ships to the Mediterranean) are to be committed by Russia, and not by Turkey, I must say that, if under these circumstances we should hold a high tone to Turkey, the weaker Power and the tool, and not dare even to whisper our dissatisfaction to Russia, the stronger Power and the plotter, it would have been far better for our national honor, and not less useful towards the accomplishment of our objects, to have held our tongue to Turkey as well as to Russia. If we were to quail before Russia on the question of protest, and fear to risk with her a contest of words and notes, who would ever believe that we should venture to face her in a contest of a more serious kind? We should lose caste in Europe, and Russia would henceforth treat England as a Power from whom no serious resistance need ever be apprehended. She would be mistaken, but the error into which we should lead her might inspire her with a dangerous presumption; and she might be tempted by her reliance on our acquiescence, to do things, which, when done, we could not submit to; and thus our desire not to give offence to Nicholas, might draw us into a situation in which public opinion would force us to go to war with him.

I confess I cannot see any advantage in waiting for the despatch which Mme de Lieven expects from Nesselrode before he leaves Berlin. That despatch may probably contain nothing about Turkish affairs, but if it does, it *can* contain nothing which ought to make us abstain from presenting our protest; and if our protest *is* to be presented, there would be great advantage and convenience in presenting it *before* Russia has offered us her explanations, rather than delaying it till afterwards. In the one case the explanations are the answer to the protest, in the other the protest is the answer to the explanations; and in the second case, it might become necessary to go into a controversial correspondence, and not to give the same simple protest which we gave at Constantinople; whereas, if we have given in our protest before the explanations arrive, we might answer them more shortly, referring to the protest already given in.

I do not know what I shall say to the King on this subject tomorrow if he asks me about it, nor how I can account to the French Government for our apparent hesitation.

(vi)

Stanhope St., 23 *November*, 1833.

It is a saying of old that trouble is inseparable from power, and certainly the King's correspondence with us verifies the maxim.

The main object of this letter[1] seems to be to show that Governments, not being members of the Confederation, have no right to meddle with the deliberation of the Diet; and to shew that the German Confederation is exactly similar to the Swiss.

As to the first point, we do not contemplate any interference, but reserve ourselves to watch the progress of events. As to the second, the difference between the two Confederations is manifest and great. Swisserland is like the United States of N. America, an aggregation of independent elements, politically known to other Powers only in its united mass, and, however divided in its internal jurisdiction, acting externally upon all occasions but as one body. Its aggregate character was, indeed, by the Treaty of Vienna made the condition of its acknowledged political existence.

The German Confederation on the contrary is a treaty of union for certain purposes, entered into voluntarily by a number of previously existing states, who have all a separate existence among the Powers of Europe, who have each a separate policy of their own, who may take different courses in peace and war, and whose sovereigns hold their crowns independently of the general compact.

I explained indeed all this with some care to Ompteda before he went and pointed out to him, that the Act of Confederation was nothing more than a treaty voluntarily entered into by a number of independent states; that if any one state was unable, by the refusal of its legislature to vote supplies, to fulfil the obligation it has entered into towards the rest, of furnishing a contingent of men and money to the common stock, the other Confederates would undoubtedly have a right of war against the defaulting state, in order to compel it to make good its treaty engagement. But that in such a case the forcible action of the Confederates against the contumacious member would be *war*; war namely between independent states, and not civil war between a sovereign Power and its subjects; and that it is quite untenable to say that such a war having begun, other Governments, not members of the League, have not a perfect right to espouse the quarrel of the single state, if they should think it their interest to do so. This is nearly the case contemplated by the triple declaration launched at France,[2] and it would not be difficult to prove, that if the quarrels between the members of the Confederation should lead to an appeal to arms, France would have as good a right to take part in that war, as in any other.

[1] From Sir H. Taylor, 22 Nov., 1833: *B.P.* A long defence of the King's view of the approaching conference of German states at Vienna.
[2] See page 363.

(b) LETTERS FROM GREY TO PALMERSTON

(i)

Downing St., 22 *January*, 1831.

These dispatches strengthen the impression under which I woke this morning; and I come more and more to the opinion that we ought now to take no further part in the election of the sovereign, than that of representing amicably the circumstances which, in any particular case, might render the choice of a sovereign, to whom they might apply, objectionable.

When the representation came from Lord Ponsonby, of the increasing strength of the party of the P. of Orange, and of the means which he thought might be effectual in making it prevail, I consented to the measure of the proclamation, and concurred in passing it; but I did this, meaning to confine myself distinctly to such measures only as might afford the Prince a chance of success by an appeal to the people without any other interference on our part.

Now Lord Ponsonby's dispatches lead to measures of a very different description; to concert with the Orange party, for the overthrow of the present Government, at the risk of a civil war, in which we should be implicated as being parties to the measures which had produced it.

Than this nothing, in my opinion, could be more indefensible or more fatal. I think it therefore very necessary to explain to Lord Ponsonby, without delay, to what extent and on what principle we, in concurrence with the conference, had sanctioned the proclamation of the Prince, with a positive instruction to abstain from any measures, either direct or indirect, which might have the effect of instigating his party, under an assurance of our support, to attack the Government.

I have written hastily and perhaps indistinctly but I think you will be able to understand the sort of alarm which these dispatches have created in me.

A further inducement not to take any further or more active measures in this business of the P. of Orange, is the obstinate determination of his Father to resist to all extremity any proposal for settling the crown of the Netherlands on any head but his own.

(ii)

Downing Street, 21 *May*, 1831.

I have just read the Protocol[1] which has been agreed upon today, and I must say that I am a good deal disturbed by it.

The alternative you had before you was, either to adhere strictly to what you had determined upon by the last Protocol or to afford possibilities for an arrangement with the Belgians, according to the representations of Lord Ponsonby.

[1] Protocol No. 24, 21 May, 1831, *B.F.S.P.*, XVII, 798.

You seem to me to have done neither the one or the other.

You show in your preamble a disposition to give up something of what you had insisted upon; but, when you proceeded to state distinctly the propositions that are to be made by Lord Ponsonby, you put forward, in the first place, the necessity of adhering to the bases of the separation between Holland and Belgium in a manner that will provoke immediate opposition, and then state the inducements which are held out to engage them to acquiesce with so little certainty and decision as must necessarily expose them to criticism.

I fear, therefore, that you will not have advanced a step by the present proceeding, more especially if, as I greatly fear, King Leopold cannot be persuaded to authorise Ponsonby to say that he will accept the sovereignty on the terms you now propose.

I had hoped that the terms, as they were shaped in the paper, which Lord Ponsonby brought back from Claremont[1] would have been adopted clearly and explicitly in the Protocol, and I do not understand why they were not.

This is a matter of vital importance, the question of peace or war depends upon it; and I could not take upon myself the responsibility of a measure inviting this dreadful alternative, without the sanction of the Cabinet.

(iii)

East Sheen, 3 *September*, 1831.

That we have a right to insist on the immediate evacuation of Belgium by the French is undeniable. The question is whether it is advisable to rest immediately upon the right, or to wait, without showing timidity, or altering our tone, or doing one thing that would bear the character of fear and hesitation, to see what France will do upon the very clear and distinct intimation which has been given to her, that we cannot consent to any portion of her army remaining in Belgium, before we press its retreat in a peremptory tone, which might offend her national pride, and produce a resistance, which patience and management might prevent. It would give us time too to get Leopold, if it be possible, to assist us by desiring that the French troops should retire; whilst on the contrary, if he persists in requiring their presence as security to his safety, it will give a plausible pretext to the French, which will have the greatest effect here, as be assured the prevalent feeling of an infinite majority of the publick is strongly in favour of peace. If we suffer ourselves to be urged by a partial clamour into measures that may produce a war, we shall soon be convinced to our cost, that we have greatly miscalculated the support we are likely to meet with. I must add that I have a great distrust of the Ministers of the three Powers. I have seen, on more than one occasion, great reason to suspect their good faith. Some of them would not be sorry to see a war break out, from which they may expect advantage; and more than one of them I suspect

[1] The residence of Leopold.

is in communication with the Duke of Wellington and Aberdeen. I hope you will take care to let them know that, if a war takes place, they must be prepared to carry it on with their own resources, that we can act only by sea and that they must expect neither subsidies nor pecuniary assistance of any kind from this Country.

I retain, therefore, the opinion I expressed before, that, having stated in the most unequivocal terms our sense of the engagements into which France has entered with the Allied Powers, and our claim to the faithful performance of them, we should wait a short time, and see the effect of these representations before we take a step, which neither policy nor reason seems to me to require, and which might at once put an end to all amicable negociations.

I think we have the right to take a lead in these discussions, and to require of the other Powers an acquiescence in this course, which I again say is no departure from what either the general interest or our national character requires, which shows no want of firmness and determination, but is merely determined by the prudence, which would not precipitate matters into a hostile disaster, while there is yet room for amicable negociation.

I am to be with the King at three tomorrow, and will be in town by one; at which hour you had better summon the Cabinet.

I have only had time to read your letter being unwilling to detain your messenger, but I shall be prepared, after having carefully read the contents of all the boxes you have sent, to discuss these matters fully with you tomorrow.

(iv)

East Sheen, 29 *September*, 1831.

I see there is a Cabinet announced for to-day, but with a view to what subject, I am not informed.

Upon Belgium I think your opinion and mine certainly agree. An equitable arrangement between the parties, a good frontier of Holland, including Maestricht, and as much security as can be obtained for the new State of Belgium, founded on fair territorial arrangements and the establishment of a state of neutrality, are the principles upon which the settlement of this long depending [sic] question must be effected. With this view I entirely approve of your project. Can you mean when you say that Austria, Prussia, and Russia are becoming the partisans of Holland, that they think such an arrangement would not be sufficiently favourable to that Power? If they do, I think they should be told at once and without circumlocution that we cannot agree with them, and that, if they involve themselves in a dispute with France on such grounds, we cannot support them.

I am very glad that you have proposed an extension of the Armistice to the 10th of November. I hope the conference will support you in this demand, and urge it in a tone that will command obedience. If not, I think they should be told that we will resist any new attack, as an

act of hostility committed against us. Have you seen the Dutch Ministers separately? They ought to be made to feel that we are disposed and determined to do everything that can be fairly required of us for the advantage of Holland and for the security of the general peace, both of which may be endangered by their taking measures, which we feel ourselves compelled to resist.

[Lord] Holland has of course shown you Palmella's letter. It is ably written and contains much powerful argument. But I find it difficult to make up my mind to take a decided measure to overthrow a Government established de facto, and which is submitted to by the people. It is a most embarrassing question, and at all events one on which I think it would not be prudent to take any decided step, till we see whether we are to retain the power of conducting to a conclusion the measures, which we may think it right to adopt.

(v)

East Sheen, 8 *November*, 1831.

I now return the draft of your dispatch to Lord Heytesbury.[1] I have not had so much time as I could have wished for the consideration of so important a matter, but we shall probably have to revert to it, after you have had Lieven's instructions communicated to you. In the meantime I have marked such alterations as I think might be advisable in the draft. They are dictated chiefly by a desire to avoid as much as possible anything that might be felt to be offensive by Russia, and that might commit us too much on a question, which, if Russia should resist, approved as no doubt she would be by Austria and Prussia, we should not have the power of enforcing.

It seems to me too, that, after having suffered the Poles to be subdued without any interference, we should not carry publick opinion with us, if we were to get into a quarrel about the intended modification of the constitution. Experience has shown that the constitution has not been much respected, nor is it probable that it would be more so, even if we could get it formally re-acknowledged and established; nor do I know that the changes, as described by Lord Heytesbury are much to the disadvantage of Poland. Perhaps the Provincial Assemblies, which are working very well in the Russian Provinces, would at present be better suited than the Diet to the state of the people, and might lead hereafter to a better system of representation.

What Lord Heytesbury says of the vague provisions of the Treaty of Vienna is admirable. It would be difficult to make out a clear case upon them, and, upon the whole, I am persuaded that it would be our best course to satisfy ourselves with friendly representations made in such a manner as to prevent an offensive answer.

[P.S.] The dispatch will want a new conclusion.

[1] To Heytesbury, 23 Nov., 1831: *F.O. Russia*, 190.

(vi)

East Sheen, 25 *December*, 1831.

The Hollands lingered here so long after breakfast, that I was prevented sending back your messenger as soon as I wished. The delay, however, can be of no consequence.

The difficulty about the two fortresses,[1] if, confined to that point alone, it had led to a serious dispute, would have been almost ridiculous; and if it had occurred, whilst an alteration was yet practicable, one would have been inclined to do much to prevent it.

The more general objection now taken by Sebastiani is of a very different character, and entirely supersedes this minor question. It is in direct contradiction to the previous proceedings of the conference in the course of these negociations, and I am quite aware, even if we could have temporised upon it, that the other Powers would not have consented to give up a point, on which all right is clearly against France. I quite agree with you, therefore, that to retract is now impossible.

Seeing however, the very embarrassing and even dangerous consequences, which may ensue, I was and am anxious, that this matter, which has never been distinctly brought before the Cabinet, should now be submitted to their consideration; and I do not foresee any additional difficulty from the delaying the exchange of the ratifications, if the Belgian Ministers are still ready to exchange them, till five o'clock to-morrow.

I may, perhaps, regret that the treaty respecting the fortresses had not been postponed, till that of the separation was ratified; but I know the difficulties that were offered to this course.

Be this as it may, we have now only to look forward. I sincerely hope with you that this may prove to have been no more than a bluster on the part of the French Government and that it will blow over, when all hope of success has failed. But the events may disappoint our expectations, and the wolf which has been so often the cause of a false alarm, may at last come in earnest. All the accounts from Paris, and none more than the secret bulletin which I have read this morning, shew the insecurity of the present Government, and it is not at all impossible that Perrier and Sebastiani may, if they remain Ministers, take the desperate course of risking a war on grounds, which they might expect to be popular, or that they may avail themselves of what they might think a favourable opportunity of quitting office, to escape from the difficulties or dangers which surround them.

We should be, in either case, "dans notre droit". But I cannot conceal from myself that, if the negociations should break off and war ensue, we should be exposed to very severe attacks, in which plausible grounds would not be wanting; and that a war for the sake of maintaining the Belgian fortresses, for so it would be represented, would not be likely to have the support of publick opinion.

[1] Philippeville and Marienbourg.

This does not alter my view of the necessity of the case, but it renders it indispensable that we should have the full concurrence of the Cabinet in all the measures we are taking.

(vii)

Downing St., 21 *February*, 1832.

... I do not think we have much to fear on the subject of Algiers. To be sure if the French could establish a secure dominion to the extent mentioned, it would not be pleasant. But what chance is there of this? It can only be done, if it can be done, after a period of many years and at an immense expense of blood and money. There seems at present to be no chance of their being able to reconcile the native tribes, and if a war with this country should take place, before their dominion is established, all supplies from France being cut off, their army would probably have to capitulate. We have this hold over them on the one hand, if on the other this enterprise gives them the means of diverting the restless spirits, with which France abounds, to the purpose of acquiring a territory which may eventually be of advantage to them.

If you have no engagement that you can shew, it would be in vain to plead it; and at all events it is not probable that this Government would feel itself bound by what had been done by Polignac, unless it was of the most clear and specifick character. . . .

(viii)

Downing Street, 26 *May*, 1832.

The accounts we had before, confirmed by Lamb's assertion that he knew that such a project had been in contemplation some time ago, certainly gives a great air of probability to the scheme of establishing a single Republick in Switzerland.

Upon an attempt to carry such a scheme into effect, our natural and obvious policy would be to leave it to the people themselves, and not to interfere. This, from the influence it may have on the general system of European policy, cannot be done absolutely. But still we must bear in mind the necessity of keeping ourselves in such a situation as not to become parties in any questions that may arise.

My opinion, therefore, is that we should agree to make the representation to the Swiss States of the danger to which such a change in the present system of Confederation may expose them, as has been desired by the Ministers whom you saw yesterday, but separately, and not in conjunction with them, tho' you would of course communicate to them what you do. I think this the best course. It would be equally effectual for the purpose; and would save us from the danger of getting into a new conference, of which, I confess, I feel something like horror, and which you have reason to dread likewise.

3 G

But in whatever way we may determine to act, in the critical state into which things are getting in Switzerland, it is necessary that we should have an active and intelligent Minister there. I need not tell you that Mr Percy is far from being of this character, and it appears to me to be indispensable that he shall be recalled.

Whatever we may think right to say to France on this subject, should also I think be done in the same way, i.e. separately, but communicating to the others what we do. From Apponyi's dispatch moreover, it would appear that the French Government is disposed to do, what the other Courts wish, and has, indeed, given instructions to that effect to its Minister in Switzerland.

Ponsonby may go now at any time, and it seems better that there should be no further delay.

(ix)

Downing Street, 21 *July*, 1832.

Further consideration has confirmed me in the opinion which I expressed to you yesterday on the subject of this dispatch.[1] Whatever representations we may think fit to make respecting the late proceedings in the Diet, I think they should be made separately, as in the case of Switzerland, but with a confidential communication of them to the French Government.

I doubt the expediency however, and perhaps the right of interfering in a matter relating to the internal affairs of Germany in which the representatives of all the Governments at the Diet appear to agree, and the more particularly under the difficulty which would arise from the part taken by the King of Hanover.

But it does not appear to me that this objection would apply to a friendly and confidential exposition of our fears, that the measures may lead to consequences of a very dangerous nature to the peace of Europe, and of our conviction that the removal of the chances of war would be the most efficacious mode of putting a stop to the agitation which prevails in so many countries, and which must continue to prevail whilst hopes are entertained by those, whose object it is to excite discontent, that the renewal of hostilities may open a way to the accomplishment of their views. The most desirable thing of all, therefore, is to put an end to the Belgian dispute.

(x)

East Sheen, 31 *July*, 1832.

I have not been able to give so much time and attention to this dispatch[2] as the peculiar nature of the subject to which it relates, its extreme delicacy, and the dangers to which it may lead, would require: and I should like to see it again, if you are not too much pressed in

[1] The draft of the despatch of 7 September, 1832 to Prussia and Austria.
[2] See last note.

point of time, after you have remodelled it, if you think it right to do so, according to my suggestions.

I have used a good deal of freedom in the alterations which I have proposed; principally for the purpose of avoiding details, and confining the dispatch more to general views, which appears to me best in matters of this nature. It seems to me enough to point out generally the evil consequences which may result from the measures in contemplation, without entering into argumentation into the manner in which these consequences may take place, or the course that may be pursued both in producing and conducting the contest, if there should be one, between the Diet and the resisting members of the Confederation, or between individual Sovereigns, separate from the Diet, and their States; considering also the situation of the King, as King of Hanover, and the difficulties he may feel in consequence, it is also desireable to avoid entering into any speculations or discussions which are not absolutely required.

I have, however, some doubts, whether I may altogether have accurately conceived the view which you have taken of this matter; and I think the dispatch wants something to wind it up better at the conclusion.

It has also occurred to me that it may appear to encourage Bavaria, in some degree to resist, and that perhaps a friendly representation of this nature would be more properly made to the Courts of Berlin and Vienna; at all events instructions to this effect, in preparing which great care will be required, should, I think, be sent to our Ministers at these courts.

By the account in Durham's despatch, the interview between him and the Emperor appears to have been upon the whole, very satisfactory.

P.S. The more I think of the affair at Oporto, the less sanguine my hopes are in favour of D. Pedro.

(xi)

East Sheen, 3 *August*, 1832.

This is a very serious matter[1] and leads to very serious consequences; and it is necessary that we should come to a clear understanding with the King on the principles on which we are to act.

In one thing only he appears to be right. I think the instructions to Lord Erskine ought rather to have been addressed to our Minister at the Diet, or to our Ministers at Berlin and Vienna; and you may remember that I, at first, expressed some doubt upon this subject, and urged in my last note[2] the necessity of similar representations to Austria and Prussia.

But this is not much more than a matter of form; the question is as to the policy on which we are to act in regard to the proceedings of the Diet.

[1] See Palmerston's letter of the same date, p. 819.   [2] See No. (x) above.

In this view what you say as to the separate capacities of the King of England and the King of Hanover is quite unanswerable. Our conduct must be regulated by English principles and English interests, and we cannot be diverted from the line prescribed by these, because Hanover has taken a different course.

We expressly disclaim interference in matters which do not immediately concern us. But we are deeply interested in what may eventually affect the peace of Europe: and if we see the chief Powers of Germany engaging in measures which may lead to the most dangerous of all wars, a war of opinions, it surely is our duty as well as our right to offer, in the way of friendly counsel, the reasons which induce us to apprehend that such consequences may result from them.

It is in this view, and in this view only, as I understand them, that your instructions to Lord Erskine are framed, and the propriety of them, whether they are to be addressed to Munich or Vienna, must be maintained.

It is the more necessary that this should be clearly explained and understood, because there appears to reign throughout the King's letter, when he speaks of the [basis] of constitutional as opposed to monarchical Governments (a distinction by the way which it is rather odd that an English King should take), of Liberal principles as always revolutionary, and more especially of his disposition or rather his resolution to adhere to the *conservative* party, a spirit which indicates something more than the application of these feelings to German questions only.

It will be necessary therefore to send a well considered and full answer to this *manifesto*, for, to use the King's word, such it is. Nobody can do this better than you, and I shall be very glad to give you any assistance in my power in its construction, previous to its being laid before the Cabinet, which I think ought to be summoned for this purpose on Tuesday morning, that the answer may go the King with the full concurrence and sanction of the whole Administration.

This letter is evidently not the King's. Indeed he could not have written it: and though Taylor's opinions may be of this sort, I cannot help thinking that some more important person must have been consulted. Be this as it may, the question is brought to a point, that obliges us to come to a clear understanding as to the principles on which we are to act. I write in great haste that you may get this to-night. Pray consult Althorp on this subject.

(xii)

Howick, 26 *August*, 1832.

The packet with your letters, and the draft of your intended dispatch to Sir F. Lamb[1] reached me just as I was leaving Lowther Castle, but not in time for me to send an answer by the return of post.

As any instructions to Sir F. Lamb have been so long delayed it has lately more than once occurred to me that it might be as well perhaps

[1] 7 Sept., 1832: *F.O. Austria* ,233

to suspend them till the proceedings of the Diet had assumed a more decisive form, and appeared to be tending to immediate measures of execution. This idea just arose from the thought that the Resolutions of the 28th of June might after all turn out to be a mere brutum fulmen and that they might not proceed further. Perhaps my wish was father to that thought, but, if, now or hereafter, the Diet should proceed in the course which they have begun under the dictate of Austria and Prussia, my opinion, in which we had agreed, remains unchanged, that we should not stand acquitted to the publick here, if we abstained from making a firm but friendly representation of our opinions; nor to Austria and Prussia themselves, if we did not warn them against the consequence of measures to which, if they should produce war, they are not to expect any support from us.

I have, therefore, devoted the first moment of my arrival here, to as careful a consideration of your draft to Lamb, as frequent interruption would allow. It contains a fair expression of our views, and I do not think you will find in any of the alterations which I have suggested, any differences as to the line you have taken. The chief object has been not to commit ourselves by too confident a prediction of consequences, and in the latter paragraph to add a hint, which perhaps is not sufficiently intelligible, that they must be prepared to act without our assistance, if they get into a war. Not having the Treaty of Vienna here to refer to, I depend on your accuracy which I have never found at fault, as to the statement of its provisions.

(xiii)

Downing St., 17 *February*, 1833.

Stratford Canning's letter,[1] both as shewing the critical state of Spanish affairs, and his own ability, adds to my conviction that his continuing at Madrid would be of the greatest advantage; and raising the character of the mission there, if the Spaniards would agree to send an Ambassador here, would give weight to our Minister. The additional expence which would perhaps be balanced somewhere else, is not of that sort which, I think, would create much difficulty in Parliament.

I certainly feel no disposition to truckle to Russia, tho', I confess, I should be sorry to see the Lievens removed, to be replaced perhaps by Matusewitz [sic], as Russian Minister in an inferior rank. But the state of Spain and Portugal would of itself account for the change of Canning's destination, and leave no ground for its being subject to such an imputation.

I am sorry to hear of Granville's relapse and dread the consequences of his taking so much colchicum. . . .

---

[1] From Stratford Canning, 8 Feb., 1833: *B.P.* This is a long analysis of the situation which he found on his arrival.

(xiv)

Downing Street, 23 *April*, 1833.

... The state of affairs in the East certainly becomes very embarrassing. But I doubt very much whether it would have been less so, if we had taken a decided part in favour of the Turks when we were first pressed to do so. At all events it was not in our power, already engaged in the affairs of Belgium and Portugal, to enter into a third business of the same nature. We had no available force for such a [passage] and I am quite sure that Parliament would not have granted us one. The truth is that the fate of the Turkish Empire has long been sealed. It was sinking from internal decay, and the Greek affair, which led to the war with Russia, has produced the present crisis in the dangers of which we might have involved ourselves more deeply but could not have prevented them by an earlier interference. My great doubt is whether we may not now have committed ourselves too far. I believe Metternich's opinion in this matter to be well founded. It is evidently impossible to support the resurgence of the Turkish Empire without foreign force; and if this is to be afforded by Russia, it establishes at once a sort of Protectorate, the result of which cannot be doubtful. I agree with you and Metternich in thinking this question extremely difficult to solve, and it leads to another of no less nicety: how are we to proceed without producing on the one hand or the other dangers which it would be our desire and our interest to prevent? I will not go further into the discussion, but I shall be glad to enter upon it with you whenever you may find a convenient opportunity, and it is one which it is absolutely indispensable should be entered into by the Cabinet before any further measures are taken. The only good side of the business is that it may very possibly induce Prussia and Austria to assist us in settling the Belgian affair, and of this we should make the most, more especially as I quite agree on the probability, to which you allude, that similar motives may diminish the anxiety of France to bring that question to an end. I have written this amidst constant interruptions which I am afraid will be sufficiently apparent.

(xv)

Howick, 18 *September*, 1833.

Tho' I am awaiting with great impatience and anxiety the result of the operations before Lisbon, I cannot delay answering the letter[1] which I received yesterday, together with the very interesting communications from Ponsonby, and Sir Fredk. Lamb.[2]

I must however begin with a few words on the affairs of the Peninsula. The telegraphic account is good as far as it goes, and, coming from Spain, cannot be suspected of being too favourable to the cause of the Queen. But if Miguel's army, tho' repulsed, remained in its former

[1] Not found.
[2] From Ponsonby, 25 July, 1833; From Lamb, 9 Sept., 1833; *B.P.*

position, and was in a condition to renew the attack, there remains much cause for anxiety. But, it is only a waste of time and paper to speculate upon the probability of events, which probably must be known before this can reach you.

In the meantime, however, I cannot help saying that I do not like Granville's account of what has passed upon this subject between him and De Broglie. His expectation, derived probably from measures taken by himself, that Spain would make ouvertures to the French Government rather than to us, the repetition of the interest which France takes in the establishment of the Salick Law, tho' accompanied with an acknowledgement that the immediate interest of Louis Philippe is more connected with the succession of the Infanta, and his desire that French officers should be employed, and more especially that Marshall Clausel should have the command, which affords a striking comment on what passed respecting the Duke de Leuchtenberg, altogether seem to indicate, not only a desire, but a design to establish French influence both in Spain and Portugal. It would not be advisable to show any jealousy with respect to these matters in our conduct, but the indications seem to me sufficiently strong to put us on our guard, and to require an attentive observation of the proceedings of the French Government, and a firm language, which we are entitled to hold by the former admissions of that Government itself, in asserting our right to take the lead in any measures which may become necessary in the course of the present contest.

With a view to the same interests, it is also requisite that we should hold an equally plain language to the three other Powers, reminding them, that they concurred with us in reprobating the usurpation of D. Miguel, and that we certainly will not allow any interference on the part of those, whose interests are comparatively so remote, with the policy which, in accordance with the principles which have governed our connection with Portugal, we may find it expedient to pursue. I have been led to this by what Lamb says of his communications on this subject, which mark the spirit of distrust, if not of hostility, which, at this moment, seems to prevail on their part to us in the counsels of Austria upon all questions.

I am therefore much inclined to address the question suggested by Lamb to the three Courts, after the conference is over.[1] The manner in which this should be done, will however, require some consideration. It should of course be civil in terms, but at the same time such as to show that we are not to be made their dupes, and that we are determined to act upon our own views, without any fear of the consequences with which this union may threaten us.

The state of affairs in Turkey seems to afford an additional argument in favour of a proceeding of this nature and perhaps a separate question might be put to Russia, with respect to the existence of any separate Article, if it can be done without danger to the quarter from which we

---

[1] Lamb (9 Sept., 1833: *B.P.*) suggested that they should be asked if they had entered into any new engagements.

have derived our knowledge. If this consideration can be got over, it will be highly useful with respect to what may follow. If it is denied, it will place us on the most advantageous ground, if it should be acted upon hereafter. If the question is evasively answered, it will afford a complete justification of the precautionary measures which it may become necessary to adopt. How Metternich must have lied upon this subject! If he had been really kept in ignorance, is it likely that he would have so readily expressed his complete approbation of the treaty?

But Ponsonby distinctly says that the draft of the treaty was sent to Sturmer by Orloff; so much for the King's expectation of a separation between Austria and Russia.

It is, therefore, more than ever necessary, that we should be prepared to support our interests in the East, and that our Squadron should be increased, as soon as it can be done with convenience; and I should hope that the state of affairs in Portugal will soon set at liberty some of the ships, engaged in that service. From Ponsonby's account, it appears most probable that a revolution at Constantinople is at no great distance. There can be no question, that our true interests would engage us to support the new Government, if established, in the name of the Sultan's son, tho' really in the hands of Mahomet Ali, and rather more on that account, as this would afford a prospect of a really efficient Government, capable of resisting the designs of Russia.

But our conduct will require delicate management, and, above all things, that we should take ground to meet the charge, to which we may find ourselves exposed, of having acted upon a secret design of favouring the views of Mahomet Ali. Indeed the whole question is one involving so many important interests, and of so delicate a nature, that we ought to have the concurrence of the Cabinet before we can send to Ponsonby the instructions which he desires. It seems almost necessary that he should have power to call for the assistance of our naval force, if the necessity which he foresees should arise; but this is, in fact, to give him the power of doing what would be tantamount to a declaration of war, against Russia. I should not feel at ease either in sanctioning such a measure, unless we were assured that our naval force was quite adequate to insure its success. The whole matter therefore is, I must repeat, of such vital importance that the decision of the Cabinet seems to be previously indispensible.

I return Ponsonby's and Lamb's letters in the box, in which they came, with the dispatches. Ponsonby's to me, I enclose in this.

I need not say, after what I have written, that I think his views just. Pray send it back when you have read it, unless you should wish previously to send it with your own to the King. He ought I think certainly to be empowered to reward the person, from whom he has got his intelligence.[1]

I see Lamb alludes to a paper which you sent him on the state of Germany. I heard, before I left town, that such a paper had been

[1] The intelligence concerning the Treaty of Unkiar Skelessi was obtained by Vogorides.

drawn up, by Mr. Mellish, of your office and had intended to have asked you to let me see it. Perhaps you can send it to me. . . .

(xvi)

Howick, 23 *September*, 1833.

. . . I was very glad that the King asked Talleyrand to Windsor. The way in which it was brought about is rather curious, and I think was the work of Madame de Dino, who pays great court to the Queen, the Dukes of Gloucester and Wellington, and, I believe, also to Bulow. The result is good, let the motive be what it may, but it is rather extraordinary that in a matter of this nature, which must be considered essential, the King should receive the communications of the Dukes of Wellington and Gloucester through the Queen.

I have read the long paper transmitted by the King to you, on the subject of Turkey.[1] His views appear to me very just, except, perhaps, as to our not interfering to prevent the occupation of the Bosphorus by Russia. You will remember what Ponsonby said on this subject. How difficult it will be if Russia is once in possession to dislodge her, and the advantage it would give her in the contest which may succeed, by the controul she would thus acquire over the Turkish population!

To me who dread war like the plague, the turn that affairs are taking in this quarter, as well as in Portugal, is most disturbing; for I almost despair of our being able to preserve peace much longer. The Duke of Wellington's observation with respect to the necessity of our supporting Donna Maria is generally just. But I see at the same time great difficulties, from the evident indisposition of the people generally to her cause, from the character of Don Pedro's Government, and from the amount of force that might be required. 5000 men would I fear be insufficient to command certain success, and, in the present state of Ireland, I do not see how more could be spared: and time would be required for sending out even the inferior number. It is altogether, to use the French word, a complication which makes me very uneasy.

In the mean time any assistance that the Queen's party can get from other quarters, they should neglect no means or time in procuring: but I think you should be very cautious as to any communications you may have with them on this subject. We must not expose ourselves to a charge, better grounded than such charges have hitherto been, that in a case in which, if we interfered at all, it ought to be openly and effectually, we had confined ourselves to measures of an indirect, doubtful, and under-hand character. . . .

(xvii)

Howick, 29 *September*, 1833.

A fit of unconquerable idleness, during the last two days, has prevented my returning a more immediate answer to your letter of the 25th.[2]

[1] From William IV, 17 Sept., 1833: *B.P.*   [2] Not found.

I think I have nothing material to add to what I have already said in my former letters, as to Turkish affairs. When Mandeville comes we shall know more, and be able to judge better of the course to be taken. In the mean time there appears to be an entire agreement in our opinions. However desirable it may be to prevent a second occupation of the Bosphorus by the Russians, an instruction to oppose it by force cannot be given without the concurrence of the Cabinet; and there can be no question that the attempt should not be made without a force of *our own*, adequate to the object. For this therefore we ought to be prepared, and I hope no time will be lost in sending some of the ships now at Cork and at Lisbon to reinforce Malcolm, as soon as the state of Portuguese affairs will admit of it.

The plan of Lisbon will be very useful to me. I do not think there will be another attack there. I am more afraid of its being masked, and a force, that would be effectual, being marched to Oporto. There can, I think, be no doubt that with no very uncommon exertion of courage and discretion, the game may be won for Donna Maria; and that it should be won by the Portuguese themselves, without any assistance from hence but such as they may get without our departing from the assurances we have given, is on all accounts most to be desired. But we must look to the probability, according to the present course of events, of our being compelled to take a part, after due warning to Spain and her having refused her cooperation, to put an end to the contest. I hope therefore that troops to the largest amount that the present state of Ireland will permit (I agree with the D[uke] of W[ellington] that they should if possible be carried to the amount of 10,000) should be in readiness and placed in quarters convenient for embarkation. I think it would also be well if you and Stanley could consider with some safe and confidential military man what, if they should go, ought to be their plan of operations. My notion is that they should if possible act by themselves. This would avoid all jealousies about command, and all the embarrassments which the union of a force, probably not very well officered or disciplined, might occasion. It would also shew the Portuguese Government that they must do something for themselves, and that they must not hope to throw on us, from the moment of our landing, the whole burthen of the war. . . .

(xviii)

Howick, 14 *October*, 1833.

I return enclosed all the letters you sent me two days ago, respecting Turkey and Spain, together with those which I have received from you this morning.

With respect to the last, tho' there appears too much probability of a severe civil contest, I think there is enough in the accounts received from Madrid of the establishment of the Queen's Government, to justify, or rather render necessary, the immediate transmission of new credentials to Villiers, with a discretion to withhold them, if, in the interim,

circumstances should have arisen to make him think it expedient to do so. But the circumstances ought to be very strong to prevent, or delay a recognition, which is of the utmost importance in the effect it may have, in assisting to prevent the success of Don Carlos, which must necessarily prove extremely injurious to English interests, and which would render the preservation of peace almost hopeless.

But I have already written so fully on this, that it is unnecessary for me to do more. But I will only repeat that by an immediate recognition it appears to me that we risk little, for, if, after it, Don Carlos' party should prevail, it does not pledge us to any interference, which a consideration of our own interests, combined with the general state of Europe, might not require.

I hope William Russell is right in his estimate of the disposition of the army and the general feeling of the country. Much, as he says, will depend upon the Governor of Estremadura and if Don Carlos should be detained, a great advantage would be gained for the Queen, one, indeed, which would be, I think, nearly decisive. Another not less material, would be the success of Saldanha's concerted attack, which from the stated composition of the contending forces ought, if well conducted, to be hardly doubtful. Indeed with a Corps behind him at Torresvedras, I think Miguel could hardly risk a battle in his present position.

But I am much afraid of a Coup de Tête on the part of Pedro and his Ministers, which might increase all the difficulties already existing in Spain.

In Turkey our prospects are not attended with less anxiety. Ponsonby in a private letter to me, which only repeats what is contained in the letters you sent me, strongly urges the necessity of being beforehand with Russia in getting possession of the Bosphorus. But in the first place, have we any information, on which we can depend, that would justify our attempting the passage of the Dardanelles? That of [Landon] with respect to the rumoured state of the defences appears to be more than doubtful. It appears hardly credible, with the knowledge we possess of Russian officers having been sent to inspect and repair them, and he admits that an additional force of 3,000 men had arrived there.

But if these considerations render such an enterprise too hazardous to be undertaken, are there no objections to it, even with the probable or with an almost certain prospect of success? What pretext could we set forth for such a movement, without some more hostile demonstration, at least on the part of Russia? The effect of it, if successful, would assuredly be a revolution at Constantinople and the deposition of the Sultan; one consequence of this would certainly be the establishment of the power of Mahomet Ali, and how should we be able to defend ourselves against the imputation of bad faith, in view of all our professions of a wish to maintain the independence of the Sultan. I say nothing of the certainty of a war in consequence with Russia, and with the pretext it would furnish to Metternich for the course, which we know he is determined to pursue.

Upon the whole therefore, I concur in the opinion of De Broglie, that we should endeavour to keep Mahomet Ali quiet, and that he should make representations to him in accordance with these proposals by the French Government. The same thing should be done at Constantinople and for the present things should, in this manner, if possible be kept quiet.

In the meantime, I have strongly recommended to Graham, that our ships should winter in the harbour of Malta. They would then save the wear and tear, of cruising in the bad season; they would then be in a better state of readiness for action, and would be in a station where little, or any delay, would take place in their receiving, and proceeding to the execution of any orders, which it may be necessary to send; but, at the same time, that we should shape our course in this matter with respect to our affairs in the Mediterranean.

I give it without hesitation as my opinion, that we should hold a firm and decisive language both with Austria and Russia, in any discussions, which may arise on this subject, and that we should tell them frankly and explicitly, should it become necessary, that we are prepared to resist, by all the means in our power the accomplishment of a system which is evidently intended, and by the same process, to place Turkey in the same situation as Poland and to effect its ultimate subjugation and division.

It is all very well for Metternich to fly into a passion when matters are discussed. It proves at once how much he feels himself in the wrong, and how unable he is to defend the duplicity and treachery of his conduct. I confess I think Lamb was rather too forbearing in his conversation with him, and that he still leans too much to the opinion that we should become partners in the course which Metternich recommends.

Nothing can more easily be answered than Metternich's complaint that we did not do this sooner; if we had, we should have been the dupes of the scheme, which I have no doubt, has been long prepared between the Courts of Vienna and Petersburgh, and placed ourselves in a situation in which we should have been disabled from making any effectual opposition to it.

But, even it if had been right then, it would not be so after the Russian treaty, considering the nature of its stipulations and the way in which it was negotiated.

But in recommending a firm and decisive tone I should still have preferred waiting for an occasion, which something on the part of the Russia might have produced, and the expectation, announced by Ponsonby, of an answer to our protest has confirmed the opinion which I before expressed, but which I no longer wish to insist upon, that it would have been better not to send the protest to St Petersburg.

Pray write constantly, as I am getting more and more anxious, and should have been much inclined to return immediately to town, if I did not feel a little longer rest here to be absolutely necessary for my health.

APPENDIX C

CORRESPONDENCE BETWEEN PALMERSTON AND MELBOURNE, 1835–1840[1]

(a) THE RETURN TO OFFICE IN 1835

(i)

Melbourne to Palmerston

South Street, 14 *April*, 1835.

I wrote to Grey the result of your interview and I send you the reply which I have received.[2] It is in some places rather more strongly expressed than I should have expressed it, but upon the whole I agree with it.

(ii)

Palmerston to Melbourne

Stanhope St., 14 *April*, 1835.

I return you the inclosed letter from Lord Grey.

Nothing can be further from my wish than to embarrass you in the execution of the task you have undertaken; and the last thing I should desire to do, would be to render myself liable to the charge of appearing to force you to make in my person an appointment which you thought disadvantageous to the public service.

I have a right, on the other hand, to object to your making in my person an appointment which I think disadvantageous to my own personal honour, and to my public character.

But there is an obvious and simple way of reconciling our conflicting sentiments on this matter, and that is, that you should dispose of the Foreign Office in the manner which you may think most advantageous to the interests of your Government, and that I should be allowed to continue in the state of freedom from official labour in which I at present am; and I wish you to understand that I consider such an arrangement as being the result of our communication of this morning, and of this correspondence.

---

[1] From the Broadlands Papers. Palmerston's letters begin "My dear Melbourne" and end "Yours sincerely"; those of Melbourne begin "My dear Palmerston" and end sometimes "Yours faithfully", sometimes "Yours", and sometimes with only a signature, but the manner seems to bear no relation to the contents of the letter.

[2] See above, p. 420.

I should conclude here, but that I cannot refrain from some remarks suggested by Lord Grey's letter.

I am much gratified by the kind expressions towards myself personally which are contained in that letter; but it is not without some surprize that I find Lord Grey to entertain an opinion that "an objection is generally felt to me" as Foreign Secretary.

That the Tories when out of office objected to my manner of conducting our foreign relations, I know full well; though I also know, that since they have been in office, they have upon almost all the great questions followed the track which I had marked out.

That the Courts of Vienna, Berlin, Petersburgh and the Hague, objected to me as Foreign Secretary, has also been long and perfectly well known. But the course of policy with regard to Belgium, France, Portugal and Spain, which excited against me the ill will of the four Courts first mentioned, was approved of, and concurred in, during four years, by my late colleagues in the Government, and was in all respects consistent with the true interests of Great Britain. I do not think, however, that my conduct as Foreign Secretary is objected to by those parties in Parliament and in the country, by which your Administration was, and will be, supported; and I do not believe that it was objected to by any foreign Government with whom we have any established relations, except the four to which I have alluded. Indeed I have the very best reasons for being convinced of the reverse, not only by the nature of my intercourse while I was in office, but by communications which I have received from some of those Governments since I have been out of office.

It is always disagreeable to speak of oneself, but upon this occasion I must be permitted to say, that I consider myself to have conducted our foreign relations with great success, during four years of excessive labour, and through extreme difficulties arising not only from the complicated nature of the questions to be dealt with, but also from the resistance opposed to me by a combination of domestic with foreign opponents.

All the important questions connected with Greece, Belgium, Portugal, and Spain which essentially affected the interests of England, I left either virtually settled or in a satisfactory train of adjustment.

There was but one important matter which when we went out in November last, remained in an unsatisfactory state; and that was the condition of Turkey, with relation to Russia on the one hand, and to England on the other.

But with respect to that matter, the blame does not lie at my door; for if my advice had been taken by the Cabinet in the Autumn of 1832, and if we had then given to the Sultan our moral support against Mehemet Ali, the subsequent Treaty of Constantinople would never have been signed.

Excuse me for these details and believe me.

(iii)

Melbourne to Palmerston

South St., 15 *April*, 1835.

I only sent to you Grey's letter in order to prove to you that it was not my own notion and entirely from my own impressions that I had made to you the communication, which I did yesterday; but that others also were under similar impressions.

You will readily believe that it was very painful to me to have to intimate the least doubt of the propriety of your resuming the Foreign Office, but I was compelled by circumstances and a sense of duty to do so. All I said was that it appeared to me and to others that it would be of service to the Government, if you could reconcile it to your feelings to accept another office of equal rank and almost of equal importance.

I trust, that I am not to consider your communication of last night as going to this extent, that you would now decline the Foreign Seals if they were offered to you.

(iv)

Palmerston to Melbourne

Stanhope St., 15 *April*, 1835.

I have received your note of this morning. The intention of my letter of last night was to set you perfectly free with respect to myself; but undoubtedly the same feelings which I expressed in that letter, and the natural disinclination which every man must have to separate from his political and personal friends, would determine me to accept the Seals of the Foreign Office, if they were offered to me.

(b) LETTERS FROM PALMERSTON TO MELBOURNE

(i)

Stanhope St., 8 *June*, 1835.

I dare say this[1] is a pretty correct summary of Metternichs conversations with Strangeways; but after all what does it amount to? and what foundation does it afford for any system of European policy to be built upon the basis of Austrian alliance?

There are indeed abundant declarations of a desire to be the most intimate ally of England: and of a conviction that an alliance with England is the best and most useful for Austria. But when Metternich comes to explain the nature of the alliance which he contemplates, it turns out to be one, which is impracticable for us; and when we inquire what advantages we should derive from it, we are at a loss to discover any whatever.

[1] From Fox-Strangeways, 25 May, 1835: *F.O. Austria*, 253

He begins by describing France as the natural enemy both of Austria and England; and it is manifest that his notion of an alliance with England presupposes an estrangement of both Austria and England from France. Now it is needless to point out that to come to such a new system we must abandon all the objects we have been striving for during the last five years, undo all we have been doing, and, as we should at once become Tories abroad, we ought to begin by becoming Tories at home; for such a change of system would infallibly lose us the support of that party, by whom we are at present upheld. Metternich, in short, sighs for a return of the state of things which existed during the war against Buonaparte, when all Europe was united against France; and when, by the by, if the fate of Europe had depended upon the vigour of Austrian councils, and the enterprize of Austrian armies, we never should have had a Treaty of *Paris*. But he would wish all Europe to be leagued now against France in diplomatic and moral hostility, as it was at that period in active warfare. But here again he takes for granted, that, which to say no more of it, is in the highest degree doubtful, namely that if England was to abandon France in order to take to Austria, France would find no other ally to take the place of England; and what I should like to know, should we gain, if while we exchanged active, powerful, and neighbouring France for sluggish and temporising and distant Austria, Russia were to make the converse of our exchange and instead of being united with Austria, who, though subservient, acts as a clog, she were to strike up an intimacy with France, and gain a more active ambitious and a *naval* ally? It does not appear to me that such a change of partners would increase our chance of winning the rubber.

For what are the advantages he holds out to us as likely to result from this entire change in our system of policy? First of all, that we are to shape our course by his, and to make temporising not even a means but an end, and with respect to whom? Why, with respect to Russia, whom he admits to be a constantly increasing Power. Now nothing can be clearer than that if you pursue a system of temporising, which in other words means perpetually giving way, while your adversary pursues a system of perpetual encroachment, the only problem to be solved is, *how soon* you will be received. Metternich's principle is to submit to everything that is done, thinking that he has got out of all embarrassment by saying "c'est un fait accompli". This is an excellent doctrine for ones adversary to hold, but a very inconvenient maxim to serve as a rule of conduct for a friend and ally in difficult times.

Then again what flimsy and fallacious assumptions he puts forward, as grounds on which to build a system of measures upon great national interests! The personal character of Nicholas, for instance, is represented by him, as a sufficient guarantee for the *conservative* policy of Russia. Now we happen also to know something of the personal character of Nicholas; and I confess that I am disposed to draw from that personal character conclusions exactly the reverse of those which Metternich seems to have formed. I take Nicholas to be ambitious, bent upon great schemes, determined to make extensive additions to

his dominions; and labouring to push his political ascendancy far beyond the range of his Ukases, animated by the same hatred to England which was felt by Napoleon, and for the same reasons, namely that we are the friends of national independence, and the enemies of all conquerors. We are an obstacle in his path; he would cajole us if he could; he would crush us if he were able; not being equal to either, he only hates us.

The conclusion which seems to follow from all this is, that we should not quit or loosen our connection with France, but should encourage the friendly disposition of Austria towards us, as far as we can, without departing from our own course in order to please her; and to express on every favourable occasion a strong wish to see her friendly dispositions evinced by acts as well as expressed in conversations and despatches.

(ii)

Stanhope St., 30 *October*, 1835.

Ellice seems to me to take a very limited and erroneous view of these matters, unless he means that we should abandon the affairs of the East altogether to Russia, sit with our hands before us, and say "it's a great pity but we cannot help it".

If we are to stop Russia and encourage and uphold Turkey we must do so by following the maxim principiis obsta.

We must object betimes to things we dislike and encourage betimes the things we wish for. But what can be so ridiculous and unworthy as for a Government to be holding language of either kind in a remote quarter without any visible means of enforcing its objections or giving aid to those whom it may encourage? But the only force we *can* have and the only one that it can be *necessary* for us to have in the Mediterranean is a fleet; and as long as we have a respectable squadron there, we may express our opinions and wishes with some authority to all parties.

The Russians no doubt would be right glad that we should withdraw our ships, and the Austrians to *please Russia* would wish the same.

The French very likely are not particular glad to see us strong in the Mediterranean; but I am not aware that any of these circumstances are reasons *against*, though they seem to me to be good reasons *for* keeping our fleet there. If Portsmouth was where Toulon is, we might be content to keep our fleet at Portsmouth, as the French do at Toulon. But we well know that the keeping the French fleet at Toulon, and the not sending it to sea was an act of toadyism of Louis Philippe to Nicholas; but, if it was agreeable to Nicholas, it could only be so, because he felt that the absence of the French and a portion of the English fleet would be favourable to his influence in Turkey, and therefore conducive to his views in the East.

As to our having *a* Ship of the Line in the Mediterranean and steamers to go and fetch more when wanted, that is absurd. We want to act by moral effect produced by the presence of our fleet, and the

H   W.P. II.

uncertainty in the minds of others, what that fleet may do; and thus to prevent the necessity of its having to act by force of arms.

But if we keep a fleet in the Mediterranean it cannot be lying all the summer in the harbour of Malta; it must even for health and exercise go cruizing about; and it may as well visit places where matters of interest are going on as go and buy figs at Smyrna.

I am convinced that you will find that all the complaints of the bad effect produced by the *movements* of our fleet resolve themselves into a Russian wish to get that fleet out of the Mediterranean; once establish that, whenever it leaves Malta, explanations are to be given why it goes to one place more than another, and we may as well withdraw it.

Only remember that I wanted the Cabinet to let me write to stop Mehemet Ali, which if I had done, all these ills would have been avoided. The objection was, we must not hold strong language without the means of enforcing it *"and we have no fleet in the Mediterranean"*.

But people like Ellice will always find a peg on which to hang and find fault. If the fleet was at home, it would be said, why incur the expence of keeping ships to rot in harbour or to dawdle about the Channel, why not send them to the East where they might be of some use? Turkey is sinking under the grasp of Russia; you have six Sail of the Line doing nothing at home; why do you not send them to practise their duty in the Mediterranean, and thus obtain at once a naval and a political object?

Ellice says that all which passes between our Dragoman and the Reis Effendi is known to Russia. No doubt it is, each party is convinced that the other will tell, and, therefore, each hastens to have the merit of being first, and our "honest and valuable agent Pisani" and our friend and ally the Reis Effendi no doubt both make their report to the Russian, of every conversation they have together. Pisani's near relation is a Russian Dragoman, so he need not go from home to make his report.

Urquhart's appointment may, and I hope will, alter this state of things.

(iii)

Stanhope St., 7 *January*, 1836.

Those who like Mr Edward Ellice[1] labour under the ποιχιλομανια [sic] which shews itself by being busy in all sorts of matters with which the patient has no concern, and of which he knows nothing whatever, are

---

[1] This is a reply to a short note from Melbourne who passed on a message from Ellice adding, "as we have another Minister beside Granville at Paris to conduct our affairs, we may as well take advantage of his information." Ellice wrote: "Ld. Granville will write to you that the American squabble is settled, or is to be settled. The intriguers thought they saw a means in it of shaking de Broglie; but it will not do, he is safe for the present. If you wish, and it is a great object, to keep him so, advise Palmerston to communicate more with Sebastiani and to be less exclusive in his communications through Ld. G. with de B. here. I see that is a subject of jealousy even in the highest quarters, and others foment and wish to take advantage of it." *B.P.*

frequently led, as Mr. Edward Ellice has been in the present case, not merely to talk nonsense, but to say the thing which is not. To propose as a means of keeping a Foreign Minister in office, that we should make cyphers of him and of our own Ambassador, is stuff; the means have no adaption to the end, and, if employed, must render the end valueless. But Mr Edward Ellice's information as to my mode of doing business in the Foreign Office, is about as correct as his cock and a bull story about revolts and revolutions in Greece and probably comes from some authority as friendly and veracious as Admiral Count Dandalo. It is in fact merely a revival of one of the unfounded grievances which old Talleyrand racked his brains to invent during the last few months of his stay here by way of contributing his mite to the Unholy Alliance, which attempted to crush me, because they found me not a convenient tool for their purposes.

I have been much misinformed if Sebastiani complains of want of communication on my part; I have heard exactly the reverse and that he has expressed himself gratified with the confidence with which I have treated him. I am sure he could not with truth complain, because *"the exclusive dealing"*, of which Mr Edward Ellice accuses me, is a mere phantasy of his own distempered brain, an image which has remained upon his intellectual retina after reading an account of the practices of the Cambridge under graduate Pitt Club.

As to doing all ones business twice over, once to our own Ministers abroad, and then again to the Ministers at this Court, unless the sapient Ellice could *prove* that there are 48 Hours in every day (he very likely would *assert* it)—such a course of proceeding would be utterly impossible. Besides our Ministers abroad are our own agents; the Ministers here are the agents of other Governments. This is what Mrs Malaprop would call, one of the many *Ellice*cinations which bewilder the mind of our Right Honorable Friend.

(iv)

Stanhope St., 24 *May*, 1836.

I return you Hummelauer's letter and Metternich's dispatches, which afford a curious but by no means unprecedented specimen of Vienna diplomacy. The system of the Austrian and indeed of the other two courts also, is to endeavour to establish personal distinctions, and to create differences of opinions between members of the same Government, and to appeal to other authorities against the head of the foreign department. They were always trying this system here with Grey, and they pursued it at Paris against de Broglie. Grey gave in to it once in the case of a communication with Zuylen,[1] and his civility was made a bad use of, as you may remember, and he was very angry with Zuylen afterwards for the unfair turn which he gave to Lord Grey's communication. But it is quite true, as you say, that there is great inconvenience in departing from the established modes of communica-

[1] See p. 173.

tion, and those who seek to lead a Minister into such a course always
have their own views in doing so. Perhaps the best way of dealing with
this attempt on the part of Metternich would be to say to Hummelauer,
that you cannot as Prime Minister receive a *personal* communication
from a foreign Government upon a public question; that you can only
consider such communication as being made to you in your capacity
of head of the Government; and that in that capacity you would necessarily think it right to make the communication known to the King and
to your colleagues; but that the forms and arrangements of the English
Government have marked out the Secretary of State for Foreign
Affairs as the channel through which all communications between the
British Government and foreign Powers are to pass; and that there
always is great practical inconvenience in departing from long established forms of proceeding without any adequate necessity; that in the
present case you have a further difficulty in accepting the personal
communication which is offered to you, because while on the one hand
you could not withold it from the Government as a public and official
communication, there are on the other hand expressions in Metternich's
dispatch which seem to imply that he did not intend it to be so dealt
with; and that consequently you thought the best thing you could do
was to replace the despatches in Hummelauer's hands with these
observations, leaving it to him to take such further steps with regard to
them as he might think most comfortable with the intentions of his
Government. . . .

You ask what all this means; I should say it was only this, that
Metternich has gone on for so many years carrying his points in
Europe, by talking twaddle about "foyers d'intrigues" "et brandons de
revolution", that at last the language has become natural to him, and
he has persuaded himself of the reality of that, which he has so assiduously laboured to make all the rest of the world believe.

There is as you know a free Press in Greece. Metternich has for the
last twelve months being labouring hard to bully Armansperg to
suppress it. But Armansperg has stoutly resisted; but if we allow
Metternich to talk to us about a free Press at Malta, how could we say
anything in support of Greece, if we should be called upon to back up
our ally there, against the pressure of Austria and Russia?

Metternich's dispatch in fact goes straight to the great point of principle on which the continental Governments and the Liberal party in
England have long been at variance. The despotic Powers contend that
they have a right to prescribe to other nations what shall and what
shall not be their form of Government. In England on the contrary
it has been maintained by all with some exceptions, that every nation
has a right to chuse its own form of Government and institutions,
provided always that it abstained from attacking its neighbours.

(v)

Stanhope St., 19 *July*, 1836.

Ponsonby has really done us a valuable and important service, and has acted with courage, firmness and ability; he was openly opposed by the united influence of Austria, Prussia and Russia and betrayed by the representative of France. He had nothing to work with but his own energy, and the belief on the part of the Sultan that he enjoyed the confidence of his own Government and would be supported by it. The result has been a signal triumph of British influence, and the good effects will not end with the particular occasion out of which the matter arose. It seems to me that with reference to our own character as a Government, and with a view to the future interests of England, we ought not to accept coldly and timidly the success which has been achieved; by so doing, and by appearing to acquiesce in what Ponsonby has done, rather than to approve it, we should weaken the influence of all our foreign agents; and we should, with regard to Ponsonby, give a sort of tacit sanction to all the calumnies and abuse which the agents and Ministers of unfriendly Courts have so unsparingly heaped upon him.

I would therefore wish you to consider whether it would not be both a just and a wise measure to give Ponsonby a step in the Peerage. Such an act would be a better and more dignified rebuke to Metternich and the rest than any controversial and admonitory despatches to be read to them; and, by shewing the Sultan that we entirely approve Ponsonbys proceedings, would inspire the Sultan with additional confidence in the support of England.

With Ponsonby's fortune it would be better for him to be a Viscount than to have the Earldom he asked for.

P.S. You will find John Russell quite of this way of thinking.

(vi)

Broadlands, 29 *October*, 1837.

Glenelg spoke to me some time ago about the question whether a free Press should be established at Malta, and he has now requested me to write to you that which I said to him upon this subject.[1]

Upon the question itself I have as yet no formed opinion, because I have only hastily read the report of the Commissioners. But I have a very strong opinion upon the inexpediency of our admitting the objections of a foreign Government to be even an element of consideration in making our determination on the matter.

It seems to me that we cannot hold too high both in theory and practise the doctrine that no foreign Government can ever be allowed to talk to us upon matters belonging to the internal legislation and administration of any part of the Dominions of the British Crown.

To permit such interference even in the most mitigated shape would be extremely inconvenient to the Government and excessively dero-

---

[1] From Glenelg, 27 Oct., 1837: *B.P.*

gatory to the dignity and independence of the country. No Minister of the Crown could venture to acknowledge in his place in Parliament that such interference had been submitted to; and if it was known that a foreign Government had been allowed to remonstrate against a measure which upon other grounds had been abandoned, the Government would be taxed with having given up the measure, in deference to the foreign remonstrance, and would be much discredited thereby both at home and abroad.

But, if the precedent were once established in one case, it would be quoted in others, and there would be numerous repetitions of friendly advice and neighbourly warnings as to the dangerous consequences to other states of the measures which from time to time we might propose to adopt for ourselves.

Glenelg suggests that the Commissioners might prepare a report shewing how unfounded are the apprehensions of Austria and Naples of any danger to them that could result from a free Press at Malta. Nothing would be more easy than to draw up such a report, and to prove such alarms to be groundless; and if we determine to have a free Press, we might, after we have adopted the measure, make some such confidential communications to those Governments: but as to convincing them that a free Press anywhere is not an abomination, that I apprehend would be a task exceeding the powers even of Austin and Cornewall Lewis.

(vii)

Carlton Terrace, 26 *October*, 1840.

I return you these two letters.[1] Lansdowne's is evidently written upon the receipt of one from Broglie, who we know has been entirely won over by Thiers on the Turkish question. I cannot say that I share these great apprehensions as to L. Philippe's being able to hold his ground; I suspect on the contrary that he knows pretty well what he is about; he certainly understands his French subjects and their character, and has shewn that he knows how to manage them.

Guizot assured me the other day that there is far more stability in France than people seem to suppose; that the middle classes who are numerous and well to do in the world, are all for peace and internal order; that the agricultural population is well disposed and easily governed; but that there are in all the towns a certain number of turbulent men, without profession, occupation or principles, idle and thoroughly demoralized, passing their time in reading newspapers and talking politics, and that these people give a fictitious character to public opinion, and furnish in times of excitement individuals capable of the most atrocious crimes; but it would be a mistake to suppose the opinions of these men to be the opinions of the nation.

---

[1] Lansdowne to Melbourne, 25 Oct., 1840: *B.P.* John Russell to Melbourne, 25 Oct., 1840: G. P. Gooch, *Later Corres.*, I, 29 and *B.P.*

Of course we should all be desirous of supporting L. Philippe but, if the clamour of the Press and the Coffee Houses is to be taken as the true expression of public opinion in France, what the French want just now is not alliance with England, but the submission of England to the will of France, and it does not seem very politic to support L. Philippe in that way, nor can it be necessary to do so.

The French have on every occasion since 1830, when they wanted to drive us to make some concession to them, used this same argument; but we have on many occasions disregarded it, and without any realization of the predicted dangers. When they wanted Nemours to be King of the Belgians, when they wanted to alter the territorial arrangement between Belgium and Holland, and on several other occasions they used the same arguments; but we were hard hearted, and yet L. Philippe continued to reign.

It seems quite clear that we shall at no distant time recover for the Sultan the whole of Syria, and it would be exceedingly unwise to throw away so great an advantage. If we can accomplish this, doing it as we shall by our own means in conjunction with the Turks, and without any active assistance from either Austria or Russia, it will give us great additional weight in all the transactions and discussions in which for some years to come we may be engaged with any of the Powers of Europe, while, on the contrary, if we allow ourselves to be persuaded out of a success which we have almost in hand, we shall inevitably be made to suffer for our softness by the future difficulties which we shall in consequence thereof experience in our dealing with other Powers.

(c) LETTERS FROM MELBOURNE TO PALMERSTON

(i)

South St., 14 *December*, 1835.

With reference to the questions which may be asked in Parliament upon the subject of the Emperor of Russia's speech at Warsaw,[1] it appears to me that, whether any notice of that speech is taken or not, it will be easy in answering such questions to express, and that without giving great offence to Russia, such an opinion of that speech as will be satisfactory to the House and the country. I would consider the question therefore upon its own merits solely. Are we justified in taking any diplomatic notice of the speech, and if we are justified, is it prudent to do so? As you state in your letter[2] to Durham, the speech never has been published by authority and the reports of it differ the one from the other. It remains in fact uncertain what was delivered; and your despatch[2] adverts to expressions, which you can only state "to have been said to have been used by the Emperor etc, and which are not contained

[1] 16 October, 1835.
[2] Drafts are enclosed but it would seem that they were not sent.

in the published reports". These supposed expressions are the only ones which give you the least right to make any observations. Whatever may be your opinion of the prudence feeling or propriety of the Emperor's reproaches for the past, and menaces for the future, he has a right to employ them towards his subjects, if he pleases, and you have none to remark upon or remonstrate against his conduct in this respect. Is it nice or gracious to try to fix the Emperor with expressions from which he is himself anxious to withdraw and escape? Is it discreet to say to him upon the authority of newspapers, we believe you to have said so and so, and, therefore, we tell you what are our opinions upon that language; he can hardly reply "to assure you I never said so"; that would be beneath his dignity, and you almost, therefore, force, at least you provoke, him to avow and maintain words of which he is clearly desirous to disembarrass himself.

The question is large and difficult, but I own I am not prepared to lay down that "the events which have happened in Poland since the conclusion of the Treaty of Vienna, do not affect the stipulations of that treaty". I cannot think that this is practical sense or reason. One of these provisions, if I mistake not, was that the Polish army should be separate and independent; but can it be said that such a stipulation is to continue to be binding upon a Government against which that army has made a desperate rebellion and the existence of which it has endangered?

Besides it appears to me that if the opinions laid down in this letter are correct, we are doing too little. If the Articles of the Treaty of Vienna are still binding and we are guarantors of them, they have been so decidedly done away with, that we ought to be now at war with Russia, or at least we ought to have called upon those Powers, who are also parties to the treaty, to unite with us in enforcing the observation of it.

(ii)

South St., 8 *January*, 1836.

Adairs letter[1] is not only a proof of the intimate communication between the three Powers, but also of the great jealousy with which an overture made to one of them is viewed by the others. If Austria makes a proposition to us, it is considered as an attempt to detach us from France; if we say a word to Austria, it is interpreted into a design to divide her from Russia and Prussia, and in both cases perhaps truly; for I have never thought that we should effect a cooperation with Austria, but that an honest attempt to do so would put us in a better condition; but I am open to conviction upon the subject.

I feel the thing to be one of great importance.

[1] From Adair, 16 Dec., 1835: *B.P.* He reported Ancillon's suspicions that Britain was trying to detach Austria from Russia and statement that the three Eastern Powers would stick together.

(iii)

South St., 10 *February*, 1836.

. . . From all I hear of the real temper of the House of Commons, we must be very careful what we do in foreign affairs. They will vote our increased navy estimate with some alarm and reluctance, but they are determined against war, and if any step were proposed in that direction, they would leave us in the lurch. The evil consequences of such an event in encouraging Russia are sufficiently evident. It must upon no account be hazarded.

(iv)

South St., 17 *February*, 1836.

This event is, as you say, worthy of attention. I was pretty well aware of the acquisitions of Russia, of their extent, their direction and the time at which they had been made; a map of England with her acquisitions during the same period would make a very respectable figure and colour no inconsiderable portion of the globe. I quite agree also in the way she has made them and in her disposition to make them still. But the question is what is the best way to deal with her. Her proximity and her great military power give her great advantages. You would not make war to try to restrict her power and her dominion and to drive her back; any inconsiderate, ill-conceived hostilities will certainly have the effect of hastening and assisting her views. This big map shews most clearly the situation of Austria, the advantages of her position and the direct interest she has in the question. It appears to me to be very unwise not to try to carry her along with us and it appears to me that Metternich's own interest would prevent him from communicating any overture made to him to Russia.

Her advanced posts in Asia may be as distant from St. Petersburg as from our Indian Frontier. But how far are they from both? I take it nearly two thousand miles and their remoteness from St. Petersburg, the present seat of her Empire, is amongst others a source of weakness.

(v)

South St., 29 *February*, 1836.

I have not time to read all these papers about Circassia etc this morning, but will soon return them.

I fairly say I would leave the Circassians to themselves. If their own force enables them to make head against Russia they are sufficiently inclined to do so, and, if they have not of themselves sufficient strength for that purpose, you cannot give it them. I am against exciting people to commit themselves in a warfare in which you cannot give them effectual support.

Besides Russia will have great cause of complaint against you. They

are either her subjects in rebellion or an independent nation at war with her. In either case it is an act of hostility on your part to assist them.

Of course it is well known at St. Petersburgh who Hudson is and what he has been doing, and of course this knowledge must make a most unfavorable impression.

I see all the danger of Russia obtaining Constantinople etc.

I doubt whether you can keep her out of it, unless you obtain the [support] and cordial cooperation of Austria for that purpose.

There are great difficulties in the way of obtaining this cordial cooperation and none greater than the civil war in Spain, which I have no doubt Austria assists and supports.

It is quite evident that the position of Mehemet Ali forwards the views of Russia in every way whether he intends to come in as an ally or a conqueror.

Upon the whole these countries seem [at present] to be placed in a position and attitude in which they cannot long remain. I own myself to be much afraid of moving, least it should hasten the catastrophe we dread and wish to avert.

(vi)

South St., 2 *March*, 1836.

There is much, very much, in what you have written; but it takes for granted and certain that it is prudent and desirable to conclude this treaty with France. If it were so certainly desirable there is no question but that a great opportunity has been lost. The change in the French Government changes the case much and I suspect that you will find it so practically. Talleyrand will now be looking to his favourite scheme of a General Congress.

(vii)

Downing St., 4 *March*, 1836.

You know I always leaned to the opinion that the only mode of finishing this war in the North of Spain was by the intervention of the French; but Louis Philippe was always so decided against it, that I could not but suppose that he understood his own policy and situation better than I did, especially as I do not believe either that he wishes well to Don Carlos or that he can be indifferent to the result of the present contest in Spain, which must so deeply affect his permanent interests.

The King is deeply impressed with the notion that Louis Philippe has acted falsely, and he is also persuaded that the entry of French troops into Spain would be the immediate signal for war being made upon her by Austria and Prussia. You will, therefore, find it difficult to induce him to concur in making the proposition, you mention, to France, and I should think it would be better to sound the French Government upon the subject before it is formally made.

The state of these Spanish affairs is most serious and alarming. I fear

that pecuniary assistance might now come too late; otherwise I think it would not be difficult to collect what would be the opinion of our leading supporters upon giving it; at the same time the House of Lords, [as you observed] the other morning, is a formidable obstacle.

(viii)

Brocket Hall, 1 *April*, 1836.

This despatch of the 28th ult.[1] from Granville upon Spanish affairs is very bad. If the Queen changes her course in the manner there mentioned, it is all over with her and her Daughter too. Her success is identified with the success of the representative form of Government. It is possible that a constitution cannot be established and had [sic] in Spain. It is possible that absolute monarchy may be restored there, but she cannot change her course from constitutional to absolute. It will not be under her that it will take place. I am afraid from Rayneval's eagerness to announce the fall of Mendizabal that he has been contributing to it and also perhaps to the projected change of policy. It has been to be [sic] regretted from the beginning that he has not acted more in concert with Villiers. Whether this be his fault or the fault of his Government it is difficult to conjecture, as well as whether it is to be in any degree to be attributed to Villiers. I am afraid we are approaching a crisis in Spain. Many who know Cordova, have little confidence in him. If the Queen either throws herself upon the army for personal protection or attempts by means of the army to govern the country without a Cortes, it appears to me that it will soon be all over with her.

(ix)

Panshanger, 6 *April*, 1836.

It may be as you suppose and it is well to keep this probability in view; but do not permit pictures in your own mind and set them down for realities nor think that you see into a mill-stone further than the density of its material will permit you. Busybodies and tattlers like Ellice generally get credit for more steady views and deeper designs than they really act upon or entertain. I will however admit that there is a sort of general connection between Durham and Ellice, which is rather strange, but that it is the great object of the life of the latter to promote the views of the former, I cannot quite set down for a certainty.

(x)

Downing St., 6 *February*, 1837.

I had much rather send ships etc. than have anything whatever to do with these proposed money transactions. You know what I think

[1] *F.O. France*, 520.

of all that Villiers says about establishing influence in Spain, or in any other country. It is impracticable, and, if it were practicable, doubtful whether worth while. But with respect to the increased naval assistance I have no objection but of a prudential character—the King and Parliament. We shall certainly excite opposition by it, and if we push the thing too far, we shall hazard our power to give as much assistance as we have already done.

(xi)

South St., 29 *April*, 1837.

You may recollect that I have always felt and expressed the greatest surprise at Metternich's first language about the Vixen, and an entire distrust of it. I cannot now understand it; it was either the habit of deceit, or some scheme, which we do not yet fathom; but I entirely agree that neither in small nor in great affairs is any reliance to be placed upon Austria. She fears all revolutionary Governments and she considers ours as the most revolutionary Government in Europe. She may perhaps not fear us so much as she does France, because danger from us is neither so possible nor so immediate, but depend upon it she hates us more than she does France.

(xii)

Brighton, 18 *October*, 1837.

There is room for you in the Pavilion, and the Queen would wish you to come here. I did not mention it, as if you wished it, but I was aware from what she had said of there being room for two Ministers that she would wish you should come.

I return you Granville's letters.[1] Molé is right enough in his conjecture or rather his certainty that Talleyrand, when here, did everything in his [power] to make him (Molé) disliked and distrusted. I fancy that the French King and Government have had no difficulty in ascertaining the implacable animosity of the Emperor of Russia, which is very foolish in the Emperor, but not a bad thing for us.

I have received your box this morning. Your proposed application to the Continental Powers is a very serious matter. I will write to you in the course of the day what I think about it.

(xiii)

Brighton, 19 *October*, 1837.

... I rather doubt the prudence of stirring the question of Spain with the Northern Powers, unless you have previous reason to think that such a communication will be well received and tend to a good end.

---

[1] From Granville, 13 Oct., 1837: *B.P.* Molé had described Talleyrand's underhand conduct towards himself in 1830.

I think, unless this be the case, the consequences of your mentioning the subject will be; first they will deny that they have given any assistance or encouragement, and you will not be able to prove that they have; secondly, they will say, if you talk to us about Spain, we also have a right to talk to you and we shall have a long paper of Metternichs condemning the whole of our policy. This will lead to useless altercation. But the great danger of our moving in it appears to me to be this, least they should agree with you that something ought to be done and propose a Congress or some concerted measure for a suspension of arms etc. We should be unwilling to embark with them in such a matter, and yet, if we opened the business, it would be difficult to avoid it.

(xiv)

South St., 30 *March*, 1838.

I have always been against any negotiation or attempt at negotiation with the Northern Powers about Spain for the reason you mention.

The only objection to making an overture to the Basques is that you cannot promise for the Spanish Government, and that, even if you have the consent of that Government to the overture which you made, you cannot be sure of their afterwards observing the terms and thus you will be involved in the odium of their perfidy.

(xv)

South St., 3 *June*, 1838.

Send me back Leopold's letter with your notion of what should be written.

I cannot see the advantages of a treaty in as strong a light as you do. I do not see my way and, therefore, should not like to enter on it. It may be necessary to defend Turkey, but I should not like to be bound to defend her. France whether bound by treaty or not will be attending to her own interests and her own policy; what those interests and that policy may be in her opinion, it is impossible to say.

As to Servia, if Austria will not interfere, depend upon it we never can with any effect. I agree with you that there is every appearance of the coming on of considerable difficulties, but our policy is to have our hands free.

(xvi)

South St., 14 *June*, 1838.

If all this has been passing at Alexandria and the crisis is so imminent, is it not odd that you have heard nothing from Colonel Campbell?

The question itself is very important. I am unable of course at once to form an opinion of it.

Can you support and prop up the Porte? Suppose you deter Mehe-

met Ali from declaring his independence or force him to retract his declaration, would the Porte derive much strength from such nominal subjection?

The Porte has lost Egypt and Syria. Can the application of external force now restore them to her? What are we trying to preserve for the Porte? The tribute which it receives and the reversion of the dominions upon the deaths of Mehemet and Ibrahim? The tribute is the only thing of any importance. The reversion the Porte always has a good chance of.

For the balance of power I doubt whether this country will go to war, notwithstanding her hatred of Russia. I am sure that we will not long persevere in war, if its object be not attained at once.

(xvii)

South St., 16 *August*, 1838.

I do not like the despatches from Egypt and Constantinople, which I read last. By his own account in his despatch[1] of the 9th of July Campbell does not appear to have spoken half strongly or decisively enough to the Pasha respecting his intention of declaring his independence. I hope he has now instructions which will cause him to assume a firmer tone.

From the tone of Ponsonby's despatch and from his known opinions I very much think he will urge the Sultan to undertake [maritime] hostility on his side. In this point of view, I a little doubt the policy of allowing our fleet to cruise with the Turkish fleet. Its presence may encourage the Turks to act, and we may be engaged in an attempt to reduce Mehemet Ali and embroiled before we are aware and in a manner, which we do not intend.

[P.S.] Considine is at Tunis, I presume against the French. Do you mean him to act against the Turks, if hostilities should take place between them and the Bey?

(xviii)

Windsor Castle, 23 *September*, 1838.

I would give him a passport,[2] but not in a false name. He is a strange young man, and nobody knows what he intends to do, or what he may do. The only use of a Passport is to enable him to leave Switzerland. It is not necessary to empower him to come into England. Now if he should go to France and kick up a row anywhere there, as he did at Strasburgh, it would be an awkward thing, that he should do so under an English Passport, knowingly given by our Minister in a fictitious name.

[1] *F.O. Turkey*, 343.
[2] The note is endorsed: "Application of P. Louis Buonaparte to Morier our Minr at Berne for Passport under an assumed name to come to England."

(xix)

South St., 19 *June*, 1839.

I cannot think that in any case it would be wise or prudent to attempt to force the passage of the Dardanelles, if it is absolutely refused by the Porte.

Such a refusal can only arise in the case of determined hostility on the part both of Russia and Turkey, and in that case the enterprise would be most difficult and the situation of the fleet, even if it succeeded, most hazardous.

I think the Admiral should not be advised to go to Constantinople and the Black Sea, as the enemy of the Porte. He can only do it as her ally and with her good will.

In other respects I think the draft quite right.

I do not know whether the Admiral should not be simply instructed to take the measures necessary to prevent collision, without saying any thing about interfering between the fleets etc. He must take care not to act so as to give the advantage to the Egyptians. We must not have another Navarino.

(xx)

South St., 4 *July*, 1840.

Metternich seems to me to vex himself about very small points in diplomacy and to be very anxious about the exact manner in which his propositions are urged.

The more I think of the matter the more I am convinced that you will not be able to persuade a majority of the Cabinet to concur in measures which may lead to long and difficult operations. Some are, as you know, entirely for Mehemet Ali, others will be apprehensive of the House of Commons and the country, upon neither of which can any reliance be placed for support, and depend upon it that the intelligence from Alexandria and the disposition shewn by Mehemet with respect to the English fleet will, whether it ought or not, have a great effect upon their minds.

(xxi)

South St., 6 *July*, 1840.

I have received your letter. You have of course so entirely considered the general grounds upon which you are acting, that I do not pretend to argue them with you or to shake you in your conviction.

You are also no doubt fully aware of the necessary and immediate consequences of the step which you are taking. It must lead at once to the dissolution of the Government, the consequences of which both at home and abroad and particularly upon this eastern question must be most grave.

But what I wish earnestly to press upon you, is the consideration

whether this decided course upon your part is not premature, and whether the opinion of the majority of the Cabinet is sufficiently pronounced to justify you in taking it. Would it not be more fair to have another Cabinet upon the subject, a more deliberate discussion and a formal decision? It will now be said and with some truth that it was deferred to another time for consideration, and that the minds of many were by no means made up and certainly not declared upon it.

Consider also the peculiar position in which our affairs stand at present. Lord Hardwick's motion on Tuesday night may bring on a crisis. If the Calendar Bill were lost I do not think that John Russell would consent to continue in office, and if we are to resign would it not [be] better that we should do so upon that question, than upon an acknowledged difference upon these oriental affairs, which must be themselves so seriously affected by the knowledge and avowal of such a difference?

If we are beat tomorrow night, let us act upon that. If not, have a Cabinet on Wednesday on this question and act upon their decision.

[P.S.] I shall of course not mention the matter at present.

(xxii)

South St., 7 *July*, 1840.

Many thanks for you letter. For Gods sake do not think one thing. I have no notion that your resignation must not dissolve the present Government and how another is to be formed in the present state of parties and opinions I see not. I will call in the course of the morning.

(xxiii)

South St., 8 *July*, 1840.

I have received this from John Russell.[1] Would it not be possible to adopt it? What you propose is a convention between the four Powers upon the subject without specifying actual measures. Might it not be understood that this should be the point; we have proposed to the Sultan to undertake the management of the question for him, might we not now make the same proposition to the other party?

(xxiv)

Windsor Castle, 25 *August*, 1840.

I send you a letter[2] which I have received from John Russell this morning. It is most highly desirable that something should be done to withdraw us from our present state of uncertainty. We are now depen-

---

[1] Missing.
[2] Lord John Russell to Melbourne, 24 Aug., 1840: *B.P.* It suggested an approach to France through Austria.

dent entirely upon accident upon what may happen in the Levant, upon
the caprice of Mehemet Ali, upon the irritation of the French people,
upon the tone of the French and of our own Press.

Depend upon it also, you mistake Louis Philippe's character if you
suppose that he will act solely according to his interest, and not from
passion. He has a great deal of Jemappes left about him still.

I have a letter from Minto upon our naval state. There are two things
I do not at all like.

1st To trust to the French not being able to man their ships. It is
often found that people *can* do what they attempt with resolution.

2. To trust to Russia for naval assistance and defence.

The last great conflict in Europe brought Russia down into the middle
of Europe and gave her a power on the land which she never had before.
Take care that the next does not give her the same power upon the sea.
This is for France as well as for us to consider.

(xxv)

South St., 29 *September*, 1840.

I am going down to Windsor and shall be back perhaps tomorrow;
certainly on Thursday morning. I received a letter yesterday from the
Queen in which is the following passage: "The right way would be to
forget all irritation and to try to do what is fair by France without
appearing to bow to her. We should try, while we have still the chance
of success to make overtures to France to give in the principle [sic].
If we fail and then have recourse to France, she will exult exceedingly
and we shall be lowered. This is the Queens opinion and she wishes Lord
Melbourne would mention this both to Ld. Palmerston and Ld. John."

Now consider whether it is not possible to take a step in this direction.
If our measures fail, you must do something of this kind. If they succeed, you have said that you would then be ready to concert with
France the further steps to be taken. Things must be by this time in
such a state as to shew whether your measures will ultimately succeed
or fail. They must, in fact, have virtually done the one or the other;
any step you now take will, therefore, have no effect upon the result,
and it will have from the time at which it is taken the advantage which
the Queen points out. If you fail, it is better to have taken this course,
before you know of the failure. If you succeed, there will be no humiliation, but on the contrary all the credit which naturally belongs to
moderation in prosperity.

(xxvi)

Windsor Castle, 30 *September*, 1840.

I send you a note which I have this morning received from Lansdowne.[1] He is to be in town to-day and therefore you may probably
see him and hear his opinion from himself.

[1] Lansdowne to Melbourne, "Tuesday night": *B.P.*

31

I send you also a note which I have received this morning from Prince Albert,[1] who is of course very anxious about the matter. He thinks that a proposal to France might be based upon Metternich's proposition, that France should reaccede to and reassert the principle of supporting the Sultan. This is not a bad notion, but it requires France to take the first manifest step, which I fear that it would not suit her present purpose and position to do. It would not settle the affair because, I am afraid, that, France being readmitted into the negotiations, we should still differ about the further steps to be taken, but it might get France out of the present difficulty which is always worth while. I shall be in London by 12 o'clock to-morrow and will see you before the Cabinet.

(xxvii)

South St., 10 *October*, 1840.

I send you a letter which I received yesterday evening from Prince Albert. I have received one still stronger from the Queen.[2] I wish you would think seriously of some mode of reconciling matters. Provided the operations were not arrested, which now they cannot be, it has never appeared to me that it would be either a humiliation or a disadvantage to make an overture to France to the extent of asking her what ultimate arrangement she would agree to. [Health]. . . .

(xxviii)

South St., 12 *October*, 1840.[3]

Guizot wrote to me this morning desiring to see me and he has just been here. He came to state that he was desirous that I should know the actual posture of affairs in France and the importance of the moment, in which we were acting; that the Note [October 8th] which he had presented to you on Saturday, whether good or bad, well-argued or the contrary, he thought it unnecessary to discuss, was the result of a great effort of the party who were for peace in France; that this question, if now neglected, could not be resumed, and that affairs would infallibly fall into the hands of the violent and those who were disposed to war, and that the worst consequences would probably come. I said of course

---

[1] Prince Albert to Melbourne, [undated]: *B.P.*

[2] On 6 October he had written: "The Queen has also repeatedly asked me whether I had news that you had written to Granville, directing him to consult Thiers as to how he would receive a proposition founded upon Metternich's views."

[3] This letter was later endorsed by Palmerston:

"Giving me an account of Guizots (humbugging) conversation to him about the last French Note."

"Anxiety of Cabinet that negotiation should be *entered into with* France."

"That is, that we should yield to French threats and intrigues, which I was fully resolved never should be done by *me*."

little or nothing to him, and he added that he did not expect that I should; that all that he wished was to make me fully acquainted with the real state of things.

You must have observed how strong was the opinion of the Cabinet on Saturday, that this opening should be taken advantage of, and I urge you not to lose any time in proceeding with the negotiation. If you find any difficulty with the Ministers of the other Powers, it will be important instantly to inform the Cabinet of it. [Health] . . . .

(xxix)

South St., 18 *November*, 1840.

I have been very unwell this last two days or I should have written to you before upon the subject of this. I cannot help doubting the policy of this superceding of Sir C. Smith in the circumstances. In the first place it is doubtful into whose hands the command will fall, as it appears that Colonel Mitchell was only about to depart for Madrid on the 29th of October last.

Next from the news lately received from France it is probable that this dismissal will reach the force whilst engaged in active operations. If those operations are in a train of success, it is evident that the removal of the Commander will be prejudicial and may interrupt that success. If they are unsuccessful, it will probably add to the confusion and aggravate disaster.

These reasons make me think the step hazardous, yet, if it is to be taken, it appears to me that it would be best to take it simply and without giving the reasons contained in the draft [marked] circulated.

The opinion that Ibrahim has acted judiciously by withdrawing the [garrisons] of Tripoli and Latikea may be an erroneous opinion, but surely it is no more, and hardly affords a ground for so strong a measure.

It also appears to me to be impossible to pronounce so decided an opinion with respect to Napier without further information. All that you say is true, but what Sir C. Smith says, may be true also. The successes have been very brilliant, but they may have been accompanied by bold expressions of authority, which you cannot expect an officer of the army to approve.

Think again about superceding him and if you supercede him, it seems to me unnecessary to give reasons for it, which must bring on a vindication upon his part and a contest.

APPENDIX D

(i)

Private letter

Londres, 21 *Décembre*, 1839.

Je suis arrivé le 18 du courant après avoir été retenu tout un jour à Calais, où je ne trouvai pas de paquebot allant à Douvres dans la journée du 17.

Mr. le Baron de Brunow[2] étant arrivé quelques heures après moi à Calais dans la nuit du 16 au 17 et obligé de s'arrêter comme moi, je profitai de ce délai pour lui communiquer les instructions dont je suis muni et que Votre Altesse m'a chargé de porter à sa connaissance. Mr. de Brunow les lut avec un grand intérêt ainsique leurs volumineuses annexes dont il n'avait pas connaissance; j'ajoutai verbalement qu'il avait suffi du vœux exprimé par l'Empereur son Maitre de voir sa mission appuyée par nous pour que notre Gouvernement s'empressât à y déférer en envoyant une personne ad hoc, afin de mieux marquer cet appui et l'union de nos deux Cours aux yeux du monde. Mr. de Brunow observa que cette heureuse union avait produit de si grands bienfaits, qu'elle était de nouveau si essentielle pour la réussite de la grande affaire du moment, que sans un accord parfait entre nos deux Cours, il ne croyait pas pouvoir la mener à un résultat satisfaisant; je l'assurai qu'il ne dépendrait pas de nous que ce résultat ne fut atteint, que notre pensée à cet égard était suffisament connue de sa Cour et exprimée dans les expéditions du 19 et 25 Novembre adressées par notre Cabinet à ceux des quatre Puissances, qu'il sortait en outre de ces expéditions, traitant principalement de la pacification entre la Porte et l'Egypte, que nous étions d'accord sur le principe énoncé par l'Empereur Nicolas relativement à la clôture des détroits conduisant à la mer de Marmora, mais que nous devions y ajouter le desir, qui avait été apprécié à St. Petersbourg comme le constatait une dépêche du Comte de Nesselrode à Mr. de Tatischeff en date du 8/20 Novembre que ce fut le Sultan qui se prononçât à ce sujet et en fit la déclaration aux Puissances, en vertu du droit de souveraineté qu'il exerçait sur ces mêmes détroits. Mr. de Brunnow avec une franchise et un abandon de confiance dont je ne saurais assez relever le mérite, voulut bien me développer le plan qu'il comptait suivre et les propositions qu'il ferait

---

[1] Vienna, *Haus Hof und Staatsarchiv, England*, 290 and 295. I have noted the private letters. The others are despatches.
[2] Both the forms, Brunow and Brunnow, are used by Hummelauer and by others writing in French.

au Cabinet Anglais sur ces deux questions distinctes, celles de la pacification et de la clôture des détroits, mais qu'il compte réunir dans un même corps de transaction à formuler.

Cette transaction, dit Mr. de Brunnow, doit être tout au profit du Sultan, tendant à relever sa puissance et à le dégager de l'état de gêne où il se trouve placé vis-à-vis de son vassal ambitieux. Pour atteindre ce but salutaire il serait desirable de rédiger un acte qui ferait partie du droit public Européen; la pacification de l'Empire Ottoman formerait la base de cet acte; pour que cette pacification fut effective et durable, il faudrait rendre au Sultan une grande partie de la force et de l'indépendance qu'il possédait avant le traité de Kutahia, et obliger Mehemed Aly à rentrer dans des limites territoriales raisonables, le replaçant en même tems dans une position de vasselage dont lui ni ses successeurs ne pourraient plus jamais sortir sans s'exposer au ressentiment des Puissances signatoires de cet acte; elles conviendraient de plus entre elles des mesures à prendre pour faire exécuter cet acte dans toute son étendue et dans toute sa rigueur: il serait dit ensuite dans ce document que ces mêmes Puissances en vertu du droit qu'elles reconnaissent au Sultan de tenir clos les détroits, qui conduisent à la Mer de Marmora, aux vaisseaux de guerre étrangers—(principe d'ailleurs formellement établi et reconnu par la législation Ottomane)—prendraient entre elles l'engagement formel, tant pour rendre un hommage éclatant que pour mieux marquer encore le respect qu'elles portent à ce droit souverain du Sultan, de ne jamais l'enfreindre sous aucun prétexte quelconque, de considérer par conséquent la Mer noire et la Mer de Marmara comme des mers closes en tems de paix comme en tems de guerre; que cependant, si malgré tous les soins des cinq Puissances pour mettre le Sultan à l'abri d'une attaque de la part de Mehemed Aly ou de celle de l'un ou de l'autre de ses successeurs, le premier, ou l'un de ceux-ci, se portait à une agression spontanée contre leur Souverain légitime, qui mit celui-ci en danger dans sa capitale, et, qu'en suite de cette agression le Sultan crut dans ce cas devoir réclamer des secours matériels et simultanés des Puissances susdites, les détroits seraient alors ouverts, mais pour ce seul cas exceptionel, aux navires des dites Puissances Alliées, observant toute fois que ces navires prendraient selon leur nationalité, des positions fixes dans l'intérieur de la Mer de Marmara, de manière à empêcher tout contact entre les escadres étrangères.

Ces points convenus, on devrait alors se rendre compte de la nature de l'appui que nous avons promis à la Porte, des limites jusqu'où on croirait pouvoir l'étendre et des moyens à employer pour le rendre efficace, présenter ensuite à la Porte cet arrangement comme résultat de l'appui promis, lui demander s'il est conforme à ses vœux et si elle en accepte l'exécution par les Puissances. Après nous être assurés de son consentement et le consentement obtenu, on présenterait alors cet arrangement à Mehemed Aly pour l'obliger de l'accepter.

Voici, mon Prince, la substance du projet de transaction que Mr. le Baron de Brunnow compte présenter au Cabinet Anglais; s'il l'accepte,

avec ou sans modification, et si Mr. de Brunnow parvient à s'entendre
avec lui, il l'engagera alors à le présenter à la France; les observations
ou les objections qu'elle pourrait y faire, feront foi du degré de sincérité
qu'elle professe pour la conservation de l'Empire Ottoman dont elle a
ouvertement proclamé le principe; cependant, des objections, telles
qu'un refus d'adhérer à la proposition de stations fixes et convenues
dans l'intérieur de la Mer de Marmora, ne seraient pas acceptées et
prouveraient un obstacle insurmontable pour une entente avec elle, la
Russie étant fermement décidée à ne pas transiger sur ce point; dans
ce cas les quatre autres Puissances devraient aviser aux moyens d'aller
en avant sans la France et de faire exécuter l'acte dont elles seraient
convenues entre elles, dès qu'il aurait été accepté par le Sultan.

Mr. de Brunnow me demanda, si une transaction de cette nature
rencontrerait les vœux de notre Cabinet?—Je repondis à Mr. de
Brunnow que bien que les deux objets dont elle, se composait, celui de
la pacification de l'Empire Ottoman, et celui de la clôture des détroits,
étaient distincts en eux mêmes et qu'il eut été préférable de ne pas les
incorporer dans une même transaction; cependant tout ce qui pouvait
contribuer à relever et à rafermir l'autorité du Sultan, relativement au
premier point, celui de la pacification, et à constater le respect du à son
droit de souveraineté sur les détroits, me semblait d'après mon opinion
individuelle devoir rencontrer l'approbation de ma Cour; que pour
mieux m'en assurer, je desirerais qu'il me permit de porter à la connaissance de Votre Altesse les confidences qu'il avait eu la bonté de
me faire; afin qu'en les jugeant dans leur grand ensemble, Vous
puissiez, mon Prince, Vous en former une idée juste, malgré que Mr. de
Brunnow n'a pu encore rien faire dans l'objet de sa mission, vue l'absence
de Lord Palmerston, il a consenti sans hésitation et avec une complais-
ance toute particulière à ce que je transmette à Votre Altesse son
programme; en général je ne trouve point de termes suffisans pour
exprimer à Votre Altesse combien je dois de reconnaissance à Mr. de
Brunnow pour l'empressement avec lequel il est venu au devant de
tout ce que j'ai pu desirer d'éclaircissement de sa part ainsique pour la
confiance sans bornes qu'il me montre.

(ii)

Secret.

Londres, 21 *Décembre*, 1839.

Ma lettre précédente[1] a été écrite non seulement avec le consentement
de Mr. le Baron de Brunnow, mais pour être sûr de m'être bien
pénétré de ce qu'il m'avait confié sur son plan d'action, je lui ai fait la
lecture de ma lettre, à laquelle il a donné sa complette approbation. Il
met une grande importance à ce que Votre Altesse soit informée de
l'attitude qu'il va prendre ici—"je vois" me dit-il, "que le Prince de
Metternich n'a pas reçu de Petersbourg tous les renseignemens qu'il

[1] No. (i)

eut été desirable qu'il obtint sur l'ensemble de ma mission; c'est à moi
à remplir cette lacune, qu'il comprendra lorsqu'il saura que je n'ai
d'autres instructions que celles qu'il a vues et qui ne suffisent pas pour
lui avoir donné une idée claire et exacte de la tâche qui m'est imposée.
Je comprends donc qu'il soit dans le vague sur l'objet de ma mission,
et qu'il ait dans Vos instructions exprimé le désir de connaitre le terrain
sur lequel je me placerai en reprenant la négociation avec le Cabinet
Anglais. Le Chancelier de Cour et d'Etat a l'air aussi de croire que
l'objet le plus important de ma mission et celui qui nous occupe
uniquement est la clôture des détroits et que mes instructions ne
portent que sur cette partie de la question; je conçois qu'il ait pu en
juger ainsi, mais celle de la pacification nous interesse avant tout et
comme je possède à cet égard par mes premières instructions tout ce
dont j'ai besoin pour la discuter et la régler avec le Cabinet Anglais,
on me renvoie à ces instructions; je n'en possède pas d'autres que celles
que Vous connaissez hormi une lettre du Comte de Nesselrode qui
me dit au sujet de ma seconde mission;" "l'Empereur s'en rapporte
entièrement à ce que Vous ferez, Vous connaissez sa pensée et il Vous
laisse la liberté de faire ce que Vous croirez de plus utile pour amener
à une bonne fin l'affaire qui Vous est confiée." "Or" continua Mr. de
Brunnow "j'ai carte blanche et le premier emploi que j'en fais c'est
vis-à-vis de Votre Cabinet, en cherchant les moyens de venir au devant
de ses désirs et de me placer autant qu'il est dans mes facultés sur une
même ligne avec lui; nous le sommes déjà quant à la question de
principe; reste donc celle de forme; le Prince de Metternich met une
grande importance à ce que les droits de souveraineté du Sultan
relativement à la clôture des détroits se trouvent mentionés dans une
déclaration par laquelle le Sultan rappelle aux Puissances qu'il entend
que les deux détroits soyent et restent clos aux vaisseaux de guerre de
toutes les nations et dans une contredéclaration des Puissances qui
porterait qu'Elles sauront respecter ce principe."

Mr. de Brunnow croit la manière, dont il compte placer dans le projet
de transaction la reconnaissance de ce droit, plus forte encore, en ce
que les Puissances reconnaissent spontanément le droit *permanent* du
Sultan, sans qu'il ait été obligé de le leur rappeler; cependant il s'est
occupé à chercher un moyen de satisfaire le desir de Votre Altesse à
cet égard et Mr. de Brunnow croit qu'à l'époque ou l'on présenterait
à la Porte la transaction que l'on aurait faite dans son intérêt et comme
preuve et résultat de l'appui qu'on lui a promis, on devrait l'accom-
pagner d'une note, à laquelle la Porte répondrait en forme de déclaration
—(partant de la supposition qu'elle accepte la transaction)—elle s'y
exprimerait satisfaite et reconnaissante du genre d'appui qu'on lui
offrirait contre son vassal, ainsi que de l'hommage rendu par les Puissances à son droit de souveraineté sur la clôture des détroits ainsique
de l'engagement pris entr'elles de le respecter; elle mentionerait en
même tems le cas spécial et exceptionel où ils leur seraient ouverts,
celui d'une demande à ces mêmes Puissances de secours matériels
simultanés contre une attaque spontanée de Mehemed Aly ou de l'un

de ses successeurs. A cette occasion Mr. de Brunnow me répéta ce que j'ai mentioné dans mon rapport N. 1 Litt. B[1] et me dit avec plus de force et de solennité encore, de conjurer Votre Altesse de ne pas reculer devant des objets de forme qui pourraient nuire au fond, et le renverser peut-être. La bienveillance avec laquelle le Prince de Metternich m'a quelquefois écouté, dit-il, la confiance qu'il m'a montrée dans tant d'occasions me donnent le courage de faire ici un appel à sa haute intelligence pour que l'Autriche ne s'efface pas ou ne se tienne trop en arrière dans cette affaire et pour que le cas du traité du 6 Juillet [1827] ne se présente plus, ce qui porterait un coup fatal et irréparable à l'alliance. De son côté, pour l'éviter, Mr. de Brunnow m'a assuré qu'il apporterait dans le projet de transaction, qu'il m'a autorisé à soumettre à Votre Altesse, toutes les modifications qu'Elle lui suggérerait. Pour cela il faudrait qu'elles puissent arriver encore à tems et avant qu'il ne soit tombé d'accord avec le Cabinet Anglais sur l'arrangement qu'il discutera avec lui.

Egalement Mr. de Brunnow n'insistera pas sur l'insertion dans l'acte à conclure de la phrase relative à la clôture des détroits *en tems de paix et de guerre*, il ne la placera qu'en parenthèse pour remplir les ordres de sa Cour, mais il n'ajoute aucune valeur à cette phrase et prendra sur lui de l'écarter, si Lord Palmerston le desire. Quant à la séparation des deux objets distincts, celui de la pacification et celui du droit de souveraineté du Sultan sur les détroits, Mr. de Brunnow ne peut le faire, et le motif principal est à ce qu'il paroit, qu'on ne veut pas laisser à la France la faculté de choisir dans l'un ou l'autre des actes, s'ils étaient séparés, celui qui serait à sa convenance, il faut que la France, me dit Mr. de Brunnow, soit liée par l'ensemble de la transaction et qu'il ne lui soit pas permis de se prévaloir seulement des avantages sans les charges, ce qui lui deviendrait plus facile encore par deux actes séparés.

Relativement à la question de la demande d'un secours matériel par le Sultan en cas d'une attaque de la part de Mehemed Aly ou de l'un de ses successeurs, la refléxion que fait Votre Altesse dans mes instructions sur la nécessité d'une retractation de la déclaration faite par la Russie à cet égard à la Porte, tombe d'elle-même dèsque l'arrangement projetté sera conclu et accepté par elle.

Vous verrez, mon Prince, par ce récit long mais fidèle, tout ce qui occupe l'esprit de Mr. de Brunnow, il espere que Vous viendrez à son secours en lui accordant le bénéfice de vos lumières et de votre appui dans la tâche importante mais difficile qui lui est imposée. La franchise et l'abandon avec lesquels il est entré dans tous ces détails ne sauraient être assez appréciés; il est personellement dévoué à Votre Altesse et dans toutes les occasions s'occupe des moyens de remonter Vos desirs. La confiance qu'il me témoigne est due au dévouement et au respect qu'il Vous porte, mon Prince.

[1] Of the same date. An ostensible despatch shewn to Brunnow.

(iii)

Londres, 30 *Décembre*, 1839.

Je profite de l'occasion d'un courrier que Lord Palmerston expédie aujourd'hui à Lord Beauvale pour avoir l'honneur de rendre compte à Votre Altesse des entretiens que Mr. le Baron de Brunnow et moi avons eus avec le Principal Secrétaire d'Etat pour le département des affaires étrangères pendant les trois jours que nous avons passés chez lui à Broadlands. Nous nous y rendîmes le 23 dec.; Mr. de Brunnow m'y ayant précédé de quelques heures, entra d'abord en matière avec sa Seigneurie sur l'objet de son second envoi, après lui avoir annoncée que cette nouvelle mission n'était qu'un corollaire de la première, suspendue par un incident qu'il n'avait pas été en son pouvoir de résoudre, mais qui venait de l'être par une détermination généreuse de l'Empereur, Son Auguste Maître, détermination qu'il n'avait pas hésité de prendre dès qu'il avait appris qu'elle pouvait servir à faciliter une entente entre les Puissances pour la solution de cette importante affaire.

Mr. de Brunnow présenta alors le travail qu'il avait fait sur l'ensemble de cette grave complication et qui se trouve consigné dans la lettre qu'il a adressée le 21. de ce mois à Mr. de Tatistscheff;[1] c'est la minute de cette même lettre que Mr. de Brunnow lut au Principal Secrétaire d'Etat qui l'accueillit de la manière la plus favorable. Sa Seigneurie dans l'entretien que j'eus après avec elle me témoigna sa satisfaction sur ce travail et me dit qu'il ne laissait rien à désirer. En le lui présentant, Mr. de Brunnow dit à Lord Palmerston qu'il avait cherché à venir au devant des désirs de tout le monde, que, s'étant aperçu qu'à Vienne on avait été dans le doute sur le véritable objet de sa mission et qu'on y semblait croire qu'elle porterait plus sur l'arrangement de l'affaire des détroits que sur celui de la pacification, il avait cru devoir lever ce doute en présentant et y fesant parvenir sans délai le tableau fidèle de la marche qu'il allait suivre; dans un second entretien qu'eût cet Envoyé avec le Principal Secrétaire d'Etat, il lui déclara, qu'il était un point sur lequel il avait des ordres positifs, celui, de ne point séparer la question des détroits de celle de la pacification, de les renfermer dans une même transaction; Mr. de Brunnow fit cette déclaration à la suite d'une observation faite par le Principal Secrétaire d'Etat, qui avait proposé à côté de la transaction générale un article séparé relativement à la souveraineté du Grand Seigneur sur les détroits, dans le genre de celui convenu entre l'Angleterre et la Porte dans le traité de 1809 (Art. 11) entre ces deux Puissances. Sur cette déclaration de Mr. de Brunnow, sa Seigneurie n'insista plus et demanda le projet de cet Envoyé pour pouvoir le communiquer à Lord Melbourne. Voici, mon Prince, ce qui s'est passé dans le premier entretien qu'ont eu ensemble ces deux Ministres.

Arrivé le 23 une couple d'heures avant le dîner, Lord Palmerston me fit un accueil des plus flatteurs et bienveillans; je lui remis la lettre dont

[1] Russian Ambassador at Vienna.

Votre Altesse m'avait muni pour lui, et sa Seigneurie me dit que nous causerions le lendemain.

Le 24. après le déjeuner le Principal Secrétaire d'Etat me prit dans son Cabinet; je débutai par lui dire que l'Empereur Nicolas ayant manifesté le désir que nous donnions notre appui à la seconde mission de Mr. le Baron de Brunnow auprès du Gouvernement de Sa Majesté Britannique, nous nous étions prêtés avec d'autant plus d'empressement, à ce vœu, que nous avions cru voir dans la résolution que venait de prendre Sa Majesté Impériale un moyen efficace de lever l'obstacle qui avait arrêté jusqu'à présent une entente entre les Puissances tandisque nous pensions que cette résolution devait rencontrer l'entière satisfaction du Cabinet anglais; qu'alors nous avions voulu par en envoi spécial, qui n'aurait pas eu lieu si le Prince Esterhazy avait été à son poste, marquer encore davantage l'union intime de nos trois Cours dans la présente circonstance; que nous étions parfaitement d'accord avec son Cabinet et celui de St. Pétersbourg sur les principes fondamentaux des questions de la pacification et de la fermeture des détroits; que relativement à celle-ci, nous avions énoncé l'opinion qu'il appartenait au Sultan de s'expliquer sur le droit inhérent à sa souveraineté, qu'il possède sur la clôture de ces détroits; en même tems j'exprimai à sa Seigneurie notre désir anxieux de voir une solution prochaine de l'affaire turco-égyptienne; que le moyen d'arriver plus sûrement à un résultat satisfaisant, était de nous montrer unis d'intention et d'action; qu'il était de la plus haute importance que Mr. de Brunnow ne partit pas d'ici sans que ce résultat ne fut obtenu, qu'il fallait ne pas indisposer l'Empereur Nicolas qui venait de fournir une preuve si manifeste de Ses intentions bienveillantes et de Son désir pour le maintien de l'intégrité de l'Empire Ottoman; qu'il avait en Russie bien des personnes qui n'étaient pas de cet avis là; qu'il ne fallait pas renforcer ce parti et refouler peut-être ce Souverain, malgré lui, vers ce parti, si on exigeait de lui, ce que dans son intérêt particulier, il ne lui serait peutêtre pas possible de faire et ce qui alors pourrait compromettre la paix générale; que d'un autre côté, et malgré les difficultés qu'avait suscité la France dans toute cette affaire, il serait cependant plus facile de s'entendre avec un Prince de l'expérience de Louis Philippe, plutôt qu'avec son successeur qui pourrait être entraîné par le parti révolutionnaire et par un mouvement de fausse gloire dont il ne parait que, trop avide; que l'affaire manquée, il serait difficile de la reprendre tandisque nous avions dans ce moment tous les matériaux pour la conduire à une bonne fin.

Le Principal Secrétaire d'Etat voulut bien m'écouter sans m'interrompre et me dit que la résolution que Votre Altesse avait prise d'envoyer une spécialité dans la circonstance du moment répondait à tout ce qu'il pouvait désirer puisqu'elle manifestait l'union de nos deux Cabinets; qu'il y avait entre nos Gouvernemens tant d'intérêts communs qui formaient des points de rapprochement sans qu'il y en ait qui se croissassent; qu'en conséquence toute entente entre nous devenait facile; que le Cabinet anglais apprécie dans toute leur étendue

les services éminens rendus par Votre Altesse et l'intelligente activité
déployée par Elle dans tout le cours de cette importante affaire; qu'en
même tems il rendait une entière justice à la franchise que l'Empereur
Nicolas avait montrée dans cette grave complication et aux facilités
qu'il avait apportées pour aider à la résoudre, en un mot à la position
européenne qu'il avait prise.   Sa Seigneurie ajouta, qu'unis comme
nous l'étions, c.à.d. l'Autriche, l'Angleterre, la Russie et la Prusse, il
éspéroit que la France après s'être convaincue de cette union, jugerait
de son intérêt de se joindre à nous, surtout lorsqu'elle aurait acquis la
certitude qu'en dernière analyse on serait décidé à marcher sans elle.
Une coopération de la Prusse nous est surtout nécessaire à cause de sa
position géographique vis-à-vis de la France, ajouta-t-Elle.

Le Principal Secrétaire d'Etat voulut bien entrer en quelques détails
sur les moyens de la pacification: je m'étais, dit-il, d'abord déclaré pour
l'avis de votre Cour qui s'était prononcée pour le Minimum des
concessions à faire à Méhémed Aly; c'était la base la plus correcte,
puisque c'était celle adoptée par la Porte elle même, dans les offres de
réconciliation qu'Elle avait fait faire au Pacha d'Egypte, en le confir-
mant dans ce Pachalik et en lui promettant l'hérédité pour son successeur.   La France s'étant opposée à ce plan, je tâchai de la satisfaire en
fesant une part plus large à Méhémed Ali, mais celle-ci ayant également
repoussé cette seconde proposition, j'en suis revenu à ma première
idée, qui est la vôtre et celle du Sultan, le Minimum.   A la suite du
refus de Méhémed Aly et dans la crainte de quelqu'entreprise hardie
de sa part contre son Souverain légitime, nous avons promis notre
appui au Sultan, par une Note collective, dûe à la sagacité de votre
Cabinet et présentée par nos représentans à Constantinople; une
promesse faite aussi solennellement ne peut rester infructueuse; la
position usurpée par Méhémed Aly, continua le Principal Secrétaire
d'Etat, est incompatible avec l'existence du Sultan, un Vassal plus
puissant que son Souverain finit par le détruire et l'intégrité de l'Empire
Ottoman sous l'autorité du Sultan est indispensable au maintien de cet
Empire, de la paix générale et de l'équilibre politique des grands
intérêts européens.   Pour que cet ambitieux Vassal ne compromette
plus le repos de l'Orient, il faut qu'il rentre dans des limites territoriales d'où lui ni ses successeurs n'ayant plus les moyens de sortir, il
seroit donc à désirer qu'on le restreignit au Pachalick d'Egypte avec la
promesse de la réversion pour son fils Ibrahim; cependant si nous
trouvons de trop grandes difficultés de la part de la France à cet égard,
on pourroit alors étendre un peu la position territoriale de Méhémed
Aly, toutefois de manière à ce qu'il ne puisse jamais plus inquiéter son
souverain légitime; il faudrait placer entre lui et son Vassal, le désert
qui les séparait autrefois, lui enlever le district d'Adana, la Syrie, St.
Jean d'Acre, faire rentrer le Sultan dans la possession des villes saintes,
et de l'île de Candie; par la nouvelle délimitation Jérusalem resterait
probablement au Pacha: en un mot nous devons ôter à celui-ci tous les
moyens de jamais plus chercher à s'affranchir de l'autorité de son
souverain légitime; une plus grande étendue de territoire que celle

qu'il est de mon avis qu'on pourrait lui donner lui ferait toujours nourrir des idées d'indépendance qu'il chercherait à réaliser tôt ou tard si on ne lui en ôtait pas les moyens. Quant à ceux coercitifs pour l'obliger à se soumettre à cet arrangement, il faudrait en établir de différentes gradations selon le plus ou moins de résistance qu'il ferait. Les Puissances après avoir présenté au Sultan le résultat de leurs délibérations sur les moyens de pacification et ce résultat accepté par lui, il serait porté à Mehemed Aly; on lui promettrait une addition de territoire au Pachalick d'Egypte, s'il se soumet immédiatement à la première sommation; sur un refus de sa part, cette offre d'agrandissement de territoire serait retirée et on commencerait par intercepter les communications par mer avec l'armée d'Ibrahim; si cela ne suffisait pas, il faudrait s'emparer de l'île de Candie et la remettre au Sultan; on ne pourrait à la vérité mettre le blocus devant Alexandrie, parceque celui-ci ne se pratique qu'envers un état régulier sous un pouvoir légitime, ce qui n'est pas le cas de Méhémed Aly que nous considérons comme un rebelle, mais cela n'empêche pas que l'on pourrait saisir des vaisseaux de commerce ce qui tarirait bientôt les ressources de son trésor; ceux-ci seraient envoyés à Smyrne pour être placés sous l'autorité du souverain légitime; finalement il faudrait employer la force si toutes ces mesures échouaient. D'après des données que le Principal Secrétaire d'Etat a recueillies d'un officier expérimenté de la compagnie des Indes Orientales, qui connoit l'état intérieur de l'Egypte et de ses points vulnérables, données sur lesquelles il attend encore des renseignemens plus exacts, il semble qu'une expédition de 5000 hommes envoyée de Bombay à Suez, suffirait pour balayer toute l'Egypte dégarnie de troupes.

La Russie pourrait également envoyer un corps de troupes, mais le grand trajet qu'elles auraient à faire au travers de pays stériles et incivilisés, lui ferait mettre un long tems à arriver; ici sa Seigneurie a émis le désir que notre Cour voulût accorder de son côté un secours matériel en soldats qui pourraient à l'aide de bâtimens anglais être débarqués sur un point convenu de l'Egypte ou sur l'île de Candie pour agir simultanément avec des troupes Ottomanes; ce secours qui devrait être tout au plus de quelques mille hommes serait défrayé par la Porte. Si le Pacha laissait venir les choses à une pareille extrémité sa destitution et celle de toute sa famille, en serait la conséquence inévitable. Il est trop rusé pour s'y exposer et risquer le tout pour le tout, en supposant même qu'il tentât de se défendre et qu'il appelât l'armée d'Ibrahim à son secours, à mesure qu'elle avancerait vers Alexandrie, l'armée turque avancerait de son côté et s'emparerait de la Syrie, ce qui lui serait facile vû le mécontentement qui y règne.

Il est à présumer, dit Lord Palmerston, que nous ne serons pas obligés à aller jusque là, si nous fesons comprendre à Méhémed Aly que nous sommes fermement décidés à faire exécuter ce que nous aurons résolu, mais il sera bien d'être préparé à tous les contingens possibles.

Quant à l'affaire des détroits, le Principal Secrétaire d'Etat est

également d'avis, que le droit de souveraineté du Sultan à leur égard ne saurait assez être relevé; il m'a aussi parlé de la rédaction d'un Article séparé, semblable à celui de leur traîté de 1809 avec la Porte, mais il n'y a plus insisté après la déclaration que Mr. de Brunnow lui fit et que j'ai citée plus haut.

Dans une seconde entrevue que Mr. de Brunnow a eue le 25 avec Lord Palmerston où j'ai été invité d'assister, celui-ci après avoir passé avec lui en revue tous les points insérés dans la lettre de cet Envoyé à Mr. de Tatistscheff formant son projet de transaction, se montra satisfait de ce projet dans toutes ses parties, et dit qu'il allait faire la dessus un travail pour ensuite le présenter au Conseil, qu'il ne sera à même de pouvoir réunir avant 8 à 10 jours. Tous les moyens graduels de coercition à employer contre Méhémed Aly furent discutés et convenus en ma présence, je n'y pris aucune part et ne fis qu'écouter; mais le Principal Secrétaire d'Etat appuya fortement sur la nécessité d'en venir à un résultat, si non entre les cinq Puissances, du moins entre les quatre.

L'opinion du Conseil entendue et si elle répond aux vœux des Puissances, il désirerait que leurs Représentans à la Cour de Londres fussent munis de pouvoirs nécessaires pour conclure et signer l'acte qui renfermera simultanément la question de la pacification de l'Empire Ottoman et de la clôture des détroits, ainsique les mesures d'exécution qui auront été jugées utiles et mentionnées dans le présent rapport, pour obtenir les grands résultats qui feront l'objet de cette transaction. Lord Palmerston nous a dit, à Mr. de Brunnow et à moi, qu'il écrirait à cet effet à Lord Beauvale et à Sir George Hamilton pour demander de pareilles autorisations de la part des Cours de Vienne et de Berlin; Mr. de Brunnow s'est chargé d'écrire à la sienne pour réclamer d'Elle des pouvoirs spéciaux; il me montra la minute de la forme sous laquelle il les demanderait et voulut bien m'en laisser prendre la copie que j'ai l'honneur de joindre sous ce pli, observant toutefois qu'il avait formulé ainsi ce projet de pouvoirs, uniquement pour ce qui le concernait, mais qu'il n'avait pas la prétention de vouloir rien suggérer à cet égard aux autres Cabinets qui avaient leurs formes à eux.

Lord Palmerston observa même que Mr. de Brunnow n'aurait pas eu besoin d'en demander de plus spéciaux, qu'il considérait ceux qu'il possédait suffisans pour signer avec lui, mais qu'ayant annoncé ne pas être autorisé pour mon compte à prendre une part plus directe à la négociation, sa conclusion risquerait d'être retardée si nos Cours (celle de Vienne et de Berlin) ne levaient pas cet obstacle. Enfin le Principal Secrétaire d'Etat espère que cette transaction, si elle reçoit l'assentiment des cinq, ou à défaut de la France, des quatre Puissances, pourra être terminée et signée d'ici dans un mois, et toute l'affaire, c'est à dire l'exécution de la transaction dans trois mois. Dès qu'elle aura obtenu la sanction du Conseil de Sa Majesté Britannique, Lord Palmerston se chargera des démarches à faire auprès de la France, pour l'engager à se joindre à cette transaction et à marcher de front avec les quatre autres Puissances; il est trop pénétré de l'importance de gagner

cette Puissance dans nos rangs pour ne pas tout employer afin de l'y amener; lorsque le moment d'agir sera arrivé il ne croit pas qu'elle veuille et qu'elle puisse même s'isoler; il en résulterait pour elle une position de honte à laquelle elle ne peut s'exposer, puisque son impuissance d'empêcher l'action des quatre autres Cours serait démontrée et la placerait dans une attitude humiliante et de faiblesse qu'elle voudra éviter; une forte considération vient à l'appui de la nécessité de ne pas tarder à conclure l'affaire entre nous quatre, celle des embarras que le Gouvernement Français éprouve dans ce moment en Algérie; ils absorbent une grande partie de ses ressources militaires et pécuniaires.

Nous sommes convenus avec lui que lorsque le Conseil aurait prononcé son avis sur l'affaire que nous écririons aux représentans de nos Cours à Paris pour les inviter à seconder les efforts de l'Ambassadeur d'Angleterre auprès du Cabinet Français pour l'engager à se joindre à nous; en attendant nous sommes tombés d'accord de ne leur faire part que du langage qu'avec le Principal Secrétaire d'Etat nous sommes convenus de tenir ici au Général Sébastiani, savoir, que l'Empereur Nicolas ayant levé l'obstacle qui s'était opposé jusqu'à présent à une entente entre les Puissances pour la solution de l'affaire Turco-egyptienne et, cet obstacle ayant été levé non seulement pour une, mais pour toutes les Puissances, nous espérions que son Gouvernement voudra bien concourir avec les autres à l'acte de pacification qui forme l'objet de leurs vœux les plus ardens; le conseil de Sa Majesté Britannique allant délibérer sur les détails de l'arrangement à fixer pour la conclusion de cet acte, nous attendrions comme lui le résultat de ses déliberations, qu'en attendant nous nourissons l'espoir qu'il y aura unanimité entre toutes les Puissances qui doivent toutes désirer une fin prompte de cette crise.

Pour mon compte je me réserve d'ajouter, que l'Empereur Nicolas ayant manifesté le désir que de notre part on appuyât la nouvelle mission de Mr. de Brunnow, et ayant reconnu qu'elle était toute conçue dans un esprit de conciliation, offrant les moyens d'écarter les difficultés qui entravaient la solution de l'affaire et les gages les plus manifestes de la sincérité de l'Empereur Nicolas à cet égard, nous n'avions pas hésité à accorder notre appui pour l'atteinte d'un but qui intéressait également tout le monde; que c'était là une partie de mon envoi, indépendamment de l'injonction que j'avais reçue de fournir au besoin tous les eclaircissemens sur la pensée de notre Cabinet que l'on pourrait désirer obtenir.

(iv)

Private letter

Londres, 30 *Décembre*, 1839.

... L'affaire turco-égyptienne est plus près de sa solution qu'elle ne l'a encore été, tous les obstacles qui l'entravaient sont pour le moment écartés; mais je ne réponds pas pour cela que nous n'échouyons au port; les dispositions du principal Secrétaire d'Etat ne furent jamais

meilleures, il est placé sur le terrain le plus correct, il a le premier
Ministre et plusieurs membres du conseil pour lui dans cette affaire,
mais néanmoins il n'est pas possible de préjuger ce qui pourra arriver.
La majorité du conseil, composé d'élémens hétérogènes comme il est à
présent, peut suggérer quelque nouvelle difficulté, qu'il ne serait pas
possible d'écarter, Mr. de Brunow ayant déclaré qu'il avait dans ses
dernières propositions épuisé la latitude de ses instructions; Mr. de
Sébastiani travaille cette majorité, et non sans succès, comme il ressort
du langage de Lord Holland, qui est identique avec celui de l'Ambassadeur de France.   On peut prévoir de quelle nature sera l'opposition
dans le conseil, elle portera sur l'étendue des moyens coercitifs, que l'on
voudra peut-être restreindre et rendre par là ineffectifs, et sur l'objection que l'on pourra faire aussi, de marcher sans la France, ce qui
prouverait au monde que l'alliance entre les deux Puissances maritimes
a cessé; si même la réalité de cette union n'existe, le parti ultra libéral
du conseil voudra en conserver l'apparence et surtout empêcher que
l'Angleterre s'associe seule à des Gouvernements absolus, tandis qu'avec
la France, ce parti dirait que nous nous sommes joints à lui, et non pas
lui à nous; enfin Mon Prince je suis loin de voir le procès gagné, malgré
que Lord Palmerston était plein d'espoir et de courage; avant de se
fixer en ville il passera deux jours à Holland House, c'est ce qui a
particulièrement décidé ma visite.   Là il y trouvera les couleurs
autrichiennes fortement dessinées, et par les bonnes dispositions de
Lord Holland envers nous et par le langage que j'ai tenu à ce chef de
parti, s'il ne tient que la moitié de ce qu'il a promis de faire dans nos
intérêts, ce sera déjà beaucoup: tous les Ministres plus ou moins absens
ne seront réunis ici qu'entre le 3 et le 5; ce ne sera qu'après leur réunion
que l'affaire turco-égyptienne leur sera présentée, tout ce qu'il a été
possible de faire pour préparer les voies pour une heureuse solution de
cette immense affaire a été fait; le moment est grave, attendons en la
fin avec courage, et, sans vouloir être trop noir dans notre attente, il faut
être préparé à tout.

Il m'en coute de ne pas tenir Mr. le Comte Appony au courant de ce
qui s'est passé à Broadlands, mais comme il a été convenu que ce
serait Lord Palmerston qui prendrait l'initiative à Paris et que nous ne
ferions que appuyer les démarches qu'il fera faire à Lord Granville,
nous avons cru lui devoir par procédé ne pas anticiper sur lui; cependant dans l'intérêt de l'affaire, j'informerai notre Ambassadeur de
l'attitude et du langage de celui de France ici pour qu'il puisse y opposer
un contrepoids. Lord Palmerston compte beaucoup sur le M[aréchal]
Soult et se flattait que le Comte Sébastiani serait de son bord; nous
avons été tout étonné à notre retour de Broadlands de le trouver dans
des dispositions tout à fait contraires. Mais nous avons fini par nous
l'expliquer; plus l'homme du Roi que de son Cabinet, il appuie son
Maître, qui a dirigé toute la politique de la France dans cette affaire, et
il voudrait pouvoir le tirer d'embarras; Mr. de Sébastiani espère que la
majorité du Cabinet ne voudra jamais marcher sans la France; c'est ce
qui lui a fait dire "j'attends Lord Palmerston au Conseil", et celle-ci en

persévérant dans une attitude passive, en se refusant à l'emploi des mesures coercitives, espère de faire avorter toute l'affaire. Il était de l'intérêt du Principal Secrétaire d'Etat, de connaître le langage de celui sur lequel il avait l'air de compter; Mr. de Brunow et moi avons pensé qu'il serait utile qu'il en fut informé et j'ai requis Mr. de Hummelauer de lui faire parvenir confidentielement des extraits des deux rapports qu'il a l'honneur d'adresser aujourd'hui à Votre Altesse sur ses entretiens avec Mr. de Sebastiani; si je puis voir Lord Palmerston je l'informerai également de ma conversation avec Lord Holland; il est de notre devoir de soutenir les efforts du Principal Secrétaire d'Etat dans la lutte qu'il aura à soutenir dans le Conseil. Outre les objections qu'on pourra y faire et que j'ai signalées plus haut, il n'est pas impossible, que l'on ne trouve pas le rôle et les stations assignés aux deux Puissances maritimes assés brillantes; cependant Mr. de Brunow en les traçant a cherché à concilier tous les amours propres, il laisse Constantinople hors d'action, il croit cette Capitale suffisamment protégée par la place assignée à un chacun, elle ne serait donc pas occupée et je l'ai fortement encouragé à suivre ce plan; dans son projet relatif aux positions des escadres, il n'a pas fait mention de celle qu'il désirerait voir prendre par la nôtre; il croit que notre Gouvernement aimera à la tenir éloignée du pavilion tricolore et voici comment il pense que les escadres pourraient se placer:

Les escadres anglaise et française prendraient leur station depuis Gallipoli jusqu'au Golfe de Mudania, d'après une ligne qui serait tirée à partir de Ganos entre Gallipoli et Rodosto, atteindrait l'île de Marmora, de la l'île de Calokinnus et aboutirait au Golfe de Mudania.

L'escadre autrichienne prendrait une position intermédiaire qui au Sud aurait pour démarcation la ligne ci-dessus tracée et au Nord une ligne tirée à partir de Rodosto et Erekli au Sud des îles des Princes, jusqu'au Golfe de Nicomédie.

La station russe serait celle qu'elle a été en 1833. Il ne serait pas fait mention de Constantinople.

Pour ce qui regarde notre escadre, ce n'est qu'un projet, car la Russie fera à cet égard tout ce qui pourra être de notre convenance, mais Mr. de Brunow croit que cette position intermédiaire est conforme à notre attitude de modération et de médiation entre les parties directement intéressées.

Pour ce qui regarde le secours matériel en troupes nommé par Lord Palmerston, je ne lui ai pas caché que je doutais qu'on s'y prétât chés nous, une coopération avec des troupes ottomanes n'étant pas facile, sous le rapport militaire ni sous le rapport sanitaire; qu'il n'en était pas de même avec une escadre, où l'on tenait son monde reserré et hors de contact avec les turcs.

Le Sous Secrétaire d'Etat Backhouse, que j'ai vu hier, m'a dit que les dépositions d'Avedik coincidaient en grande partie avec celles qu'avait faites le Capitaine Walker à Lord Ponsonby, et qu'il était avéré que l'Amiral Lalande avait mis tout en œuvre pour que le Capudan Pacha ne communiquât pas avec l'escadre anglaise.

Le Baron de Brunow vient de recevoir l'ordre de son gouvernement de faire une communication à celui de S. M. B. sur la résolution qu'a prise l'Empereur Nicolas et la nécessité où il est de faire une expédition contre Khiva, dont les incursions du Khan sur le territoire russe, les déprédations que depuis trois ans il y a commises, outre plusieurs milliers de russes qu'il a enlevés et jetté dans l'esclavage, ne lui permettaient plus de laisser ces actes impunis; l'on a envoyé à Mr. de Brunow la proclamation du Général Peromoski, Gouverneur d'Orenburg, annonçant qu'il allait marcher pour punir ce Khan, délivrer les russes esclaves; la proclamation termine en disant que, l'objet atteint, l'expédition rentrera dans ses foyers. Malgré le bon droit de l'Empereur Nicolas, Mr. de Brunow n'en regrette pas moins le moment inoportun où cet événement se présente; il se flatte que Lord Palmerston comprendra la nécessité où Sa Majesté Impériale a été de ne pouvoir agir autrement, mais il craint que la partie moins raisonnable du Cabinet ne se prévale de cet incident contre la Russie.

Le parlement s'assemblera le 16. Janvier; on y annoncera le mariage de la Reine, dès que la dot du futur époux aura été fixée; on nommera le jour où la Cérémonie aura lieu; on croit que ce pourra être dans la première semaine de Février; elle sera toute religieuse et en famille, le corps diplomatique n'y sera pas invité; la Reine, dit-on, est très anxieuse que cela ait lieu dans le plus court délai possible.

Le Duc de Wellington m'a écrit pour me prier de remercier Votre Altesse de la lettre qu'Elle lui a écrite, il m'a invité d'aller le voir à Strathfieldsaye, mais je n'ai pu encore m'y rendre; peut-être irai-je après demain.

(v)

Private letter

Londres, 31 *Décembre*, 1839.

Le Baron de Brunow sort de chés moi; il a vu Lord Palmerston à qui il a fait la communication relativement à l'expédition de Khiva; le Principal Secrétaire d'Etat l'a fort bien prise et a compris la nécessité où a été l'Empereur Nicolas de la faire; Mr. de Brunow a dit que si Lord Clanricarde avait été à St. Pétersbourg, la communication eut été par lui, mais qu'à son retour on lui donnerait un gage écrit des intentions sincères de l'Empereur, de sa ferme résolution de rappeler ce corps d'expédition dès que l'objet serait atteint: la manière dont Lord Palmerston a pris la chose a mis Mr. de Brunow fort à l'aise. Il est convenu devant moi qu'il se sent soulagé d'un grand poids. Ce dernier lui a parlé de ma visite à Holland House. Le Principal Secrétaire a dit qu'il était enchanté que je l'avais faite et que j'avais parlé comme je l'avais fait à Lord Holland; il est convenu vis-à-vis de Mr. de Brunow que Lord Holland ne pensait rien moins qu'à voir Mehemet Ali à la place du Sultan; c'est une monomanie, dit-il.

Il est fort curieux que dans le courant de ma conversation avec lui, lorsqu'il fut question de l'ambition démesurée de ce Pacha, je lui dis si

3 K

on lui laisse la démarcation qu'il possède à présent, il ne reposera pas jusqu'à ce qu'il soit à Constantinople, et je ne lui cachai pas que nous ne le souffririons pas plus que la Russie, mais que ce serait la mort de l'Empire ottoman par la lutte qui s'engagerait.

Lord Palmerston est dans ce moment à 18 milles d'ici à Watton chés Lord Tankerville dont la femme est sœur de Madame de Sebastiani, toutes deux Mlles. Grammont; le Général Sebastiani a mis à profit cette circonstance pour aller chés sa belle-sœur sans y être invité; il a attaqué Lord Palmerston sur la mission de Mr. de Brunow et lui a dit: eh bien, Mr. de Brunow a libellé des propositions, dit-on. Lord Palmerston lui a fort sagement répondu que c'était lui qui était occupé à les libeller sur la base du plan qui avait été discuté lors du Ier envoi de Mr. de Brunow, qu'il les présenterait au Conseil d'où nous apprendrions tous l'accueil qu'elles y auraient reçu; dans le fait j'ai oublié de mander dans mon rapport principal A. qu'il a été convenu entre nous à Broadlands que les propositions viendraient de Lord Palmerston qui s'est approprié celles de Mr. de Brunow; cette forme aura plus d'effet sur le Cabinet et sur la France, toute apparence de propositions russes disparaîtra ainsi.

Lord Palmerston m'a fait dire par Mr. de Brunow de ne pas arrêter mon courrier, qu'il ferait ses expéditions à Vienne et à Berlin demain ou après bien surement, dans l'objet de demander pour Mr. de Werther et pour moi des pleins pouvoirs pour conclure, dès que l'affaire aurait obtenu le degré de maturité nécessaire à cet effet.

(vi)

Private letter

Londres, 9 *Mai*, 1840.

J'ai communiqué à Lord Palmerston mon rapport Litt. A. en date d'hier afin de m'assurer que j'avais bien saisi les paroles et les observations de la Seigneurie lorsque je lui communiquai l'expedition de Votre Altesse en date du 25 Avril.[1] Le Principal Secrétaire trouva ma rélation parfaitement exacte et observa au passage où je parle du secours maritime à demander à la Russie pour une action commune contre Alexandrie et la Syrie "Nous n'en aurions probablement pas besoin, dit-il, nous avons dix vaisseaux de ligne dans la Mediterranée, deux que l'on prépare ici et deux à Lisbonne feront quatorze, ajoutant à cela les fregates et autres batimens de guerre, c'est plus qu'il ne faut pour effectuer le blocus; cependant nous ne pourrions pas nous passer de votre pavillon, c'est un effet moral dont nous avons besoin, deux petits batimens de guerre autrichiens suffiraient *pour constater notre union dans l'affaire que nous donnerions au Sultan.*"[2]

[1] Metternich, *Mémoires*, vi, 454.
[2] Pencil note by Metternich: "Oui, l'union entre l'Autriche et l'Angleterre ; cette démonstration ne constaterait elle pas, par contre, la désunion entre ces deux cours et les 3 autres? Comment pourait-on obvier à ce mal? telle est la question."

Cet appui de notre part parait essentiel, autant vis-à-vis de l'Angleterre que de la France, non seulement pour justifier l'entreprise, mais
pour lui donner un effet plus puissant si elle se trouve placée sans
l'égide d'une alliance qui en Angleterre rencontre toutes les sympathies,
tandis qu'elle impose du respect et de la crainte sur le reste du monde.
C'est pour ce motif que Lord Palmerston a desiré que je parle à Mr.
Guizot vaguement de la possibilité que nous prétions un secours naval
dans le cours de l'affaire; la manière dont je l'ai fait, n'a pas permis à
cet Ambassadeur d'approfondir le *quid* et *le quomodo faciendum*, de
sorte qu'il ignore si notre action navale sera offensive contre la Syrie ou
protectrice pour le Sultan dans le cas où il dut se resigner à se refuser à
toute concession d'hérédité, à défaut d'en venir à la conclusion d'un
arrangement satisfesant pour l'honneur et les interéts de sa Hautesse.

(vii)

Cipher

Londres, 12 Mai, 1840.

Malgré la confiance avec laquelle Lord Palmerston envisage sa
position dans l'affaire turco-égyptienne, je suis loin de partager les
illusions qu'il se fait.   Ses collègues regardent toujours la coopération
de la France comme indispensable; si donc celle-ci ne souscrit pas aux
moyens de résoudre l'affaire en cinq, la solution en quatre en sera
beaucoup plus difficile; cependant le Principal Secrétaire d'Etat
l'essayera, et comme cette solution ne pourra avoir lieu sans l'emploi
d'une mesure coercitive telle que le blocus d'Alexandrie et des côtes
de la Syrie, envisagé par lui comme facile et suffisant pour atteindre
le but, il nous invite à y prendre part; s'il ne peut se tirer autrement
d'affaire, il se contenterait d'obtenir deux de nos vaisseaux de guerre,
uniquement pour constater par notre union que nous approuvons la
mesure.   Il est donc essentiel que Votre Altesse soit préparée à cette
demande.   Lord Palmerston paraît décidé à ne pas remettre l'affaire
à un avenir incertain en conseillant au Sultan de refuser l'hérédité sur
la Syrie et l'Egypte, dans le cas où l'on ne parvint pas à conclure un
arrangement favorable ou au moins honorable pour la Porte.   Lorsque
ce moment arrivera, les mêmes hommes qui sont au pouvoir à présent,
le seront-ils encore alors, observa-t-il, et nos successeurs partageront-ils
nos vues à cet égard?   Ceci est tellement vrai que si Lord Palmerston
devait faire place à un de ses collègues qui lui sont opposés maintenant
dans le Cabinet, tel que p.e. Lord Clarendon ou tout autre de ce bord,
l'affaire prendrait sur-le-champ un aspect tout franco-égyptien, et les
intérêts du Sultan seraient complètement sacrifiés.

(viii)

Cipher

Londres, 22 *Juin*, 1840.

Des nouvelles récemment arrivées de Constantinople à Mr. de Bülow et de Brunow, représentent les choses dans cette Capitale, et surtout dans plusieurs des provinces, sous un jour fort alarmant. Reschid Pacha a dit à Mr. de Buteneff que les délais des délibérations de Londres contribuent à alimenter l'inquiétude qui règne; que Chekib Efendi était autorisé à adhérer sans réserve à tout ce que les Représentans des Cours alliées du Sultan lui proposeraient. Nous convinmes, Mrs. de Bulow et de Brunow et moi, de demander une entrevue à Lord Palmerston pour lui communiquer ces nouvelles, et nous nous concertâmes sur ce que nous lui dirions. Nous tombâmes d'accord de lui représenter que les délais avaient atteint leur terme et qu'il fallait qu'il nous dise quel plan il comptait suivre. Le Principal Secrétaire d'Etat nous reçut hier; nous lui rappelâmes la teneur de nos instructions; je le ramenai à celle que Votre Altesse m'a transmise le 25 Avril[1] et à la dépêche N. 2 faisant mention de l'extrémité des sacrifices auxquels la Porte pourrait souscrire. Mr. le Baron de Brunow observa que l'on devrait tâcher d'obtenir en sus le Pachalik d'Haleb avec Scanderum; le tout dépend d'y faire adhérer la France. Je me suis déclaré pour le Maximum de la part à faire au Sultan, en autant qu'à défaut de ce Maximum, le Minimum ne soit pas perdu; mais je dis, que d'après mes instructions, j'étais autorisé à souscrire à ce Minimum si on ne pouvait gagner autrement la France dans l'arrangement; qu'il fallait lui présenter le plan en cinq, en y joignant le Pachalik d'Alep, se réservant toutefois de revenir au Minimum, si elle ne voulait absolument se rendre à notre proposition; qu'il fallait en même temps lui déclarer que, si nous étions obligés à faire l'affaire à quatre, la position de Méhémed Aly pourrait devenir moins bonne, puisquelle serait subordonnée aux événemens qui ressortiraient des moyens coercitifs que l'on serait dans le cas d'employer contre lui. Cette déclaration à la France servira de moyen comminatoire contre elle, pour l'engager à se joindre à nous et à faire l'affaire en cinq. Lord Palmerston a accueilli mon idée, à laquelle se sont joints mes collègues de Prusse et de Russie. Il est convenu, qu'on ne pouvait plus tarder à se mettre à l'œuvre; il nous a promis de s'en occuper dans le courant de cette semaine, de préparer un plan, qu'il présenterait à ses collègues, et il nous a invités à nous réunir dimanche prochain (28) chez lui pour examiner ce plan.

(ix)

Londres, 9 *Juillet*, 1840.

Mes rapports chiffrés du 22, 23, 26, 29 et 30 Juin auront fourni à Votre Altesse la preuve que nous étions allés Messieurs de Bülow, de

[1] Metternich, *Mémoires*, vi, 454.

Brunnow et moi au devant des instructions qu'Elle a daigné m'adresser le 24 et 27 Juin dernier.

Lord Palmerston, pressé par nos instances réitérées et par les nouvelles alarmantes qui venoient de Constantinople, dut enfin céder; il resista pendant quinze jours à l'urgence de nos démarches et ne nous épargna pas quelquefois les effets de sa mauvaise humeur; mais, cet intervalle fut utilement employé par Monsieur de Bülow et par moi pour travailler la partie du Conseil des Ministres la plus opposée aux vues du Principal Secrétaire d'Etat, sans en excepter Lord Melbourne, avec qui j'eus deux entretiens qui eurent le plus heureux succès, en ce que ce Ministre finit par comprendre qu'au milieu de la grande question orientale il y avait des intérêts anglais et autrichiens tellement identiques et d'une si haute portée, qu'ils ne pouvoient être négligés sans se créer pour l'avenir des complications de la nature la plus dangereuse pour le maintien de la paix générale.

Dans le conseil qui fut tenu hier sur cette importante affaire, Lord Palmerston doit avoir développé son plan et ses vues avec une prodigieuse habileté et une grande lucidité. Il prit pour base les démarches réitérées et infructueuses faites auprès de la France pour l'attirer dans nos rangs, cita les conversations que nous avions eues, lui et moi, avec Monsieur Guizot au mois de Mai dernier, sur un plan d'arrangement entre le Sultan et son vassal, plan qui n'étoit pas composé de propositions anglaises ou autrichiennes mais bien celui mis en avant par le Gouvernement français même, l'année dernière; que Monsieur Thiers, sans le nier ou l'avouer, disoit qu'il n'y objecteroit pas si Méhémet Ali y consentoit, ce qui rendoit l'affaire impossible, puisque le Pacha n'accepteroit que ce que la France lui conseilleroit; que même après avoir touché vis-à-vis d'elle le minimum des concessions à faire à Méhémed Ali, elle fesoit déjà entrevoir des doutes sur la restitution d'Adana; qu'en un mot elle cherchoit à s'assurer de la clef de toute la position comme le prouvoit la réponse faite tout dernièrement par Monsieur Guizot de la part de Monsieur Thiers, réponse dont j'ai eu l'honneur de faire mention à Votre Altesse par mon rapport chiffré en date du 29 Juin; que les desseins de la France étoient de fonder une grande Puissance arabe pour en faire une Alliée contre l'Angleterre; que d'un autre côté des événemens pouvoient surgir en Turquie qui obligeroient l'Empereur de Russie d'y intervenir; que l'Autriche y seroit attirée matériellement ou politiquement, et peutêtre de manière à déranger son équilibre; qu'il étoit important à l'Angleterre de conserver égale la balance de notre pouvoir; qu'il y avoit donc un intérêt anglo-autrichien qui tout en se présentant sur des points différens se réunissoit dans un même foyer politique; qu'il étoit de la plus haute importance pour les intérêts anglais de concilier ceux de notre Empire, de ménager une alliance qui avoit toujours été si utile à la Grande Bretagne et rencontroit toutes les sympathies de ce pays-ci, sans vouloir pour cela rompre avec le Gouvernement français; qu'il falloit au contraire, observer envers lui tous les ménagemens et les procédés qu'exigeoit sa position et lui faire comprendre qu'il pouvoit y avoir

des circonstances où des intérêts spéciaux imposeroient à l'une des obligations auxquelles l'autre ne pourroit pas s'associer, sans pour cela devoir se séparer; qu'on se retrouveroit plus tard sur un autre terrain d'intérêts communs; que le moment du reste étoit favorable pour marcher sans la France, puisqu'elle étoit trop occupée dans l'Algérie pour intervenir dans l'affaire en instance autrement que par des intrigues; que son action dans la Quadruple Alliance avec la péninsule Ibérienne avoit été plus gênante qu'utile et que l'on seroit plus à l'aise sans elle dans l'objet que les quatre Puissances vouloient atteindre.

Lord Melbourne a franchement soutenu le Principal Secrétaire d'Etat, et ceux qui voyoient avec peine et même avec répugnance le moment arrivé de devoir prendre une décision sur la nécessité de marcher *à cinq* ou *à quatre,* se sont divisés entre eux sur la question de savoir ce qui seroit plus utile, ou de ne pas se séparer de la France ou d'appuyer l'attitude de l'Autriche dans cette grave complication.　La dernière considération a été heureusement prépondérante, et Lord Holland même a dit que le "Casting Vote" (le veto) dans cette question appartenoit à l'Autriche, qu'à la suite de plusieurs conversations qu'il avoit eues avec moi, il avoit acquis la certitude que nous ne voulions pas les brouiller avec la France, et qu'au contraire le désir de notre Cabinet avoit été de marcher avec elle, mais qu'il entrevoyoit la difficulté.

Je tiens tous ces détails de Lord Normanby que j'ai rencontré hier soir et qui a assisté au Conseil.

Lord Palmerston a trouvé un grand auxiliaire dans les dernières nouvelles arrivées de Syrie; il s'en est servi pour prouver que tout ce que le Gouvernement français disoit sur l'état intérieur de cette province et sur la position du Pacha étoit des fables et qu'il ne falloit pas donner dans le piège.

La dépêche de Votre Altesse No. 1 du 24 Juin avoit parmi ses annexes la copie d'un rapport de Monsieur le Comte Appony en date du 16 Juin rendant compte d'une conversation avec Monsieur Thiers relative à l'effet qu'avoit produit sur Méhémed Ali, la nouvelle du renvoi de Chosrew Pacha.　Monsieur Guizot avoit reçu vendredi passé une soidisant dépêche télégraphique de Marseille annonçant la nouvelle (en date d'Alexandrie le 16 Juin) qui se trouve mot à mot dans le rapport de Monsieur le Comte Appony.　Je plaçai celui-ci sous les yeux du Principal Secrétaire d'Etat pour lui montrer que le tout étoit une mystification inventée pour jeter de l'indécision dans le Cabinet; que Monsieur Thiers prévoyoit devoir s'occuper de l'affaire turco-égyptienne après la réponse qu'il avoit chargé Monsieur Guizot de faire.　Celle-ci même fut faite deux jours après l'annonce de la dépêche télégraphique que Monsieur Guizot se hâta de communiquer au Gouvernement Britannique avec empressement et en y mettant un grand degré d'importance, comme devant mener à un accommodement à l'amiable entre le Sultan et le Pacha.

Cette démarche de Monsieur Thiers ne servit qu'à décider Lord Palmerston à marcher encore plus vigoureusement en avant surtout lorsqu'il vit qu'elle n'étoit qu'une ruse.

Je dois féliciter Votre Altesse de ce premier résultat; quoique tardif, il n'en sera peut-être que plus effectif. Le Cabinet Britannique, ramené à une saine politique, a fini par entrevoir que la marche sage, indiquée par notre Cabinet, étoit la seule vraie. La résolution, qu'il vient de prendre si Méhémed Ali ne cède pas de bonne grâce, sera exécutée avec force et promptitude pour en rendre le succès plus sûr et éclatant. Le Chef de l'Amirauté, Lord Minto, tout dans l'intérêt de Lord Palmerston, brûle d'impatience de faire agir la marine anglaise pour lui faire reprendre dans la Méditerranée la supériorité que les forces navales de la France cherchent à y usurper. Le Principal Secrétaire d'Etat m'a dit hier qu'il espéroit que dans le cas où Méhémed Ali ne se rendit pas à la sommation du Sultan, nous remplirions la promesse que nous avions faite de joindre notre pavillon au leur, moins pour son utilité matérielle, quoiqu'elle n'étoit pas à mépriser, que pour la force morale qu'il exerceroit en Angleterre et sur les populations de la Syrie. Il est question d'y faire figurer le pavillon ottoman comme partie soidisant principale dans l'action.

(x)

Londres, 16 *Juillet*, 1840.

L'affaire que nous venons de terminer est d'une importance majeure sous le double point de vue de son objet spécial et du bienfait qui en résulte de voir enfin l'Angleterre s'associer à nous dans l'intérêt du soutien de la légitimité et des principes conservatifs; la France révolutionnaire verra enfin que la solidarité avec le Gouvernement de la réforme avait des bornes; celles-ci ont été atteintes lorsqu'elles se sont rapprochées des intérêts matériels et politiques de la Grande Bretagne. Lord Palmerston est le seul qui les ait compris dès leur origine, mais il ne serait jamais parvenu à faire partager ses vues par la majorité de ses collègues, sans l'assistance de l'Autriche et sans le concours de plusieurs circonstances qui sont venues à son aide.

L'attitude sage, droite et honorable qu'a maintenue notre Cabinet dans tout le cours de cette négociation pénible et ardue a été un auxiliaire puissant pour le Principal Secrétaire d'Etat; on a reconnu que nous étions les seuls qui n'avions pas des vues d'intérêts personnels dans l'affaire; que nous nous occupions de celle-ci dans un but vraiment européen; que même vis-à-vis de la France nous avions été justes et franchement désireux de gagner sa coopération, tandisque Lord Palmerston, irrité par la résistance qu'il en avait éprouvée, n'était plus un agent impartial aux yeux de ses collègues qui recevaient ses opinions avec méfiance. Il lui fallait notre appui pour rétablir son équilibre; il l'a trouvé dans ma coopération auprès de Mr. Guizot et cette démarche qui n'a eu que la forme d'une conversation suivie à Paris par Mr. d'Appony avec Mr. Thiers, a été le Wedge (coin) (expression dont s'est servi Lord Palmerston vis-à-vis de moi) qui a rompu la résistance que jusque là on avait opposée au Principal Secrétaire d'Etat, accusé de prévention contre le Gouvernement français.

Une autre considération lui rendait notre soutien indispensable, celle de ne pouvoir se présenter au Conseil de la Reine avec le secours matériel de la Russie seul; il eut été rejetté à l'unanimité; l'alliage de notre pavillon lui était nécessaire pour la combinaison de l'entreprise dont l'Angleterre ne pouvait se charger à elle seule, puisque l'éventualité de l'ouverture des détroits en cas d'un mouvement hostile d'Ibrahim Pacha vers Constantinople devait y figurer en même tems que la conséquence qui devait en résulter de l'apparition de forces navales et militaires russes dans le Bosphore et sur la rive gauche de ce Canal.

La Russie sentait qu'on ne lui permettrait plus, comme en 1833, de se charger à elle seule du protectorat de la Porte et qu'il y aurait pour elle du danger à reparaître dans le Bosphore, si elle ne s'assurait en même tems de la clef des Dardanelles, ce qui devenait une affaire compliquée et grave; elle eut aimé à s'entendre avec le Gouvernement anglais à ce sujet et à marcher seule avec lui, mais celui-ci ne l'eut pu sans être accusée d'avoir renoncé à l'alliance française, et le parti dans le Cabinet Britannique attaché à cette alliance était trop fort pour réaliser un projet que le Cabinet Russe a certainement nourri et qu'il espérait faire réussir à l'aide de notre soutien, qu'il a recherché moins dans un intérêt européen que dans le sien propre. J'ai néanmoins donné à Mr. de Brunnow l'appui auquel j'étais autorisé, aussi longtems qu'il était pratique et raisonnable; il eut cessé d'être l'un et l'autre, si j'avais voulu me mêler de la question de détail dans laquelle cet Envoyé a désiré me faire entrer, savoir celle du plus ou moins de vaisseaux anglais à admettre dans la Mer de Marmora, et des stations qu'ils auraient à y prendre; j'ai fait sentir avec tout le ménagement possible à Mr. de Brunnow, que ceci ne me regardait pas, et que je devais lui rappeler ce que m'avait dit dans le tems le Duc de Wellington, lors de ma première visite chez Sa Grâce à Strathfieldsaye, savoir: qu'il fallait être facile sur les questions de détails, que de vouloir préscrire des conditions sur le nombre et les stations des vaisseaux anglais, était exiger ce qu'aucun Gouvernement, aucun parti dans ce pays ne pouvait accorder, que le Parlement et la Nation s'y refuseraient, qu'il devait se contenter de ce que Lord Palmerston avait exprimé à cet égard dans sa dépêche du 25 Octobre à Lord Clanricarde[1] et rendre confiance pour confiance; que, la France n'étant pas de la partie, les inquiétudes, qui auraient pu naître de la voir figurer dans la mer de Marmora, n'existaient plus; que par conséquent il y avait tous les motifs pour lui de se montrer conciliant, facile et confiant; que la question était de savoir s'il voulait faire l'affaire ou non; qu'en insistant sur une prétention que le Gouvernement anglais ne pouvait admettre, il ferait douter de la sincérité et de la générosité de l'Empereur Nicolas qu'il avait toujours mises en avant; qu'il prenait donc sur lui la double responsabilité de mettre celles-ci en question et de faire manquer l'affaire; que Mr. de Bülow et moi nous ne pourrions le soutenir jusqu'à là auprès de Lord Palmerston, et que s'il reculait après avoir aidé à pousser le Principal Secrétaire d'Etat tandisque celui-ci ne s'en souciait pas, et après lui

[1] *L.P.*, I, No. 352.

avoir dit devant nous que l'Empereur Nicolas ne l'abandonnerait pas
s'il allait en avant, ce serait manquer à sa parole et compromettre Lord
Palmerston devant ses propres collègues, ce qu'il ne lui pardonnerait
jamais. Mr. de Brunnow essaya ensuite de nous ébranler en disant
qu'il ne pourrait pas se décider à signer aucune transaction sans savoir
si elle aurait l'approbation de son Maître et qu'il préferait la Lui
soumettre pour mettre sa responsabilité à couvert. Nous lui prouv-
âmes que c'était également ne pas vouloir l'affaire, puisque les six
semaines, qui s'écouleraient avant d'avoir une réponse, la rendrait
impossible, tout dépendant de la célérité et du secret dans l'exécution;
que la France, une fois informé de ce que nous aurions fait, ce qui
serait impossible de lui tenir caché pendant si longtems, le contrarierait
par toutes sortes d'intrigues, qu'il ne nous serait peut-être pas possible
de déjouer. Enfin Mr. de Brunnow céda non sans peine et sans crainte
et nous dit qu'il préviendrait Lord Palmerston de la nécessité où il
était, pour mettre sa responsabilité à couvert, de lui écrire une lettre
dans laquelle il lui rappelerait la phrase de sa dépêche à Lord Clanricarde, relative à l'ouverture exceptionnelle des détroits. Nous lui
promîmes, Mr. de Bülow et moi, de l'appuyer en ceci auprès du
Principal Secrétaire d'Etat, qui trouva en effet la proposition de Mr. de
Brunnow naturelle et lui promit d'y répondre dans un sens propre à
tranquilliser sa responsabilité auprès de son Souverain. En résumé,
mon Prince, l'affaire était impossible sans le concours moral et matériel
de l'Autriche; ce dernier était nécessaire à Lord Palmerston pour
obtenir de ses collègues l'autorisation de formuler un projet de convention renfermant une éventualité telle que celle d'une répétition de l'action
militaire de la Russie dans le Bosphore. La convention est l'acte de
cinq Puissances, agissant chacune selon la nature de sa position et de ses
moyens vers un même but, c'est à dire dans l'intérêt de la légitimité et
des principes conservatifs. Ce qu'il importait était d'y voir figurer
l'Angleterre en première ligne par son action matérielle; une fois
engagée dans celle-ci, elle ne peut plus reculer, son honneur l'oblige à
mener l'enterprise vers une bonne fin; l'esprit d'insurrection qui vient
de se manifester sur plusieurs points de la Syrie présente des facilités
qui n'existaient pas avant; toutes les nouvelles que le Gouvernement
Anglais vient de recevoir annoncent que cette insurrection est devenue
presque générale en Syrie et qu'elle a pris un caractère formidable.
Les peuples qui cherchent à secouer le joug de Méhémet Aly, appelent
à grands cris la protection des Puissances étrangères; il est urgent qu'on
les aide le plutôt possible, afin qu'ils ne périssent pas par le glaive du
Pacha rébelle.

(xi)

Private letter

Londres, 16 *Juillet*, 1840.

Le quart d'heure de Rablais que Mr. de Bülow et moi avons eu à
passer avec Mr. de Brunow, n'a pas été le plus agréable de l'affaire

devant laquelle il voulait reculer après qu'elle avait été arrêtée entre nous.

Jamais un homme ne s'est montré plus pussillanime et servile que lui; l'Empereur Nicolas lui apparaissait comme un phantôme qui le poursuivait jour et nuit; lorsque je fais une affaire, nous dit-il, je vois toujours devant moi la grande image de mon Empereur ayant l'air de me dire: Brunow prends garde à ce que tu fais. A chaque pas en arrière que nous fesions faire à Mr. de Brunow, il fesait un signe de croix à la russe. La position d'un agent russe s'est montrée dans toute sa misère; celle de Mr. de Brunow est devenue fort sulbalterne dans le moment où il fallait du calme et de la dignité: nous avons vu celui où il allait faillir devant la crainte que lui inspirait l'image de son Empereur auquel il voulait, avant de la signer, soumettre une œuvre qui n'admettai pas un instant de délai dans son exécution.

Lord Palmerston, Mr. de Bülow et moi, avons plus d'une raison de croire que l'objet principal de Mr. de Brunow n'était pas de faire l'affaire, mais celui de la ramener dans les mains de l'Empereur son Maître, engagé maintenant dans une partie à cinq, tandis qu'il eut préféré jouer le jeu seul; plus Mr. de Brunow voyait ce jeu échapper des mains de son Maître et plus il tremblait. Ce n'est qu'après l'éloignement de Chosrew Pacha, entièrement dans les intérêts de la Russie, que Mr. de Brunow reçut les ordres les plus pressans de mener l'affaire à un résultat; il ne nous cacha pas qu'il voulait dégager l'Empereur de l'affaire pour qu'il ait la faculté d'agir selon les circonstances; on craignait à Pétersbourg qu'une autre influence à Constantinople prit la place de celle de la Russie.

Mr. de Bülow s'est loyalement serré à moi, je ne saurais assés louer le zêle et l'appui éclairés qu'il a prêtés dans les derniers momens de la crise.

Le billet ci-joint[1] qu'il m'a adressé en réponse à un rendés-vous que je lui demandais pour conférer avec lui sur la situation dangereuse où se trouvait l'affaire à la suite des tergiversations de Mr. de Brunow, prouve son courage et ses bonnes dispositions; ils sont d'autant plus méritoires que la position de la Prusse limitrophe de la France exige de grands ménagemens et que les instructions de Mr. de Bülow parlaient d'un arrangement à cinq et non à quatre; néanmoins il n'a pas hésité à se joindre aux miennes; il a donc pris beaucoup sur lui, mais il espère que Votre Altesse voudra bien faire exprimer son contentement à Berlin sur la conduite qu'il a tenue.

Madame de Lieven a dans les derniers jours redoublé ses importunités pour tâcher de pénétrer ce que nous ferions, elle a poussé la témérité jusqu'à dire à Mr. de Brunow que Lady Palmerston lui avait avoué que le conseil avait adopté les propositions de son mari—espérant par ce mensonge (car c'en était un) faire tomber Mr. de Brunow dans

[1] Dated 11 July: "Je passerai chez Vous après les 11 heures. Certes, le moment est grave,—mais j'ai bon espoir. Nous nous montrerons au niveau des circonstances et dignes de la confiance que nos Cours respectives ont placée en nous. C'est aprésent ou jamais! Calmes, réfléchis et résolus nous atteindrons le but. Tout à Vous"

un piège; il n'y donna pas, mais rendit le propos de Madame de Lieven
à Lady Palmerston; celle-ci, piquée au dernier degré, fit à son amie un
sermon très sec, lui conseilla de s'en aller pour ne pas accréditer
l'opinion, qu'on avait, qu'elle avait, été envoyée par Mr. Thiers pour
aider Mr. Guizot à entraver l'affaire orientale.

Telle est la fin de Madame de Lieven, qui après avoir occupé ici la
première position sociale est déchue au point de n'être plus que la
complaisante et l'entremetteuse d'un folliculaire et d'un professeur
d'histoire, tellement épris des charmes surannés et déséchés de la
Sybille ambulante, qu'il est devenu un objet d'amusement pour les
salons, où l'on épie les regards doux et peu lettrés qu'il lui lance; il ne
se doute pas que nous venons d'accomplir ce que son prédécesseur
avait su empêcher et que celui-ci saura faire valoir.

APPENDIX E

(i)

Paris, 14 *Juin*, 1836.

Mon cher Ami, J'ai reçu votre petit mot du 10 [Juin]. La lettre de congé est prête ainsi qu'une dépêche d'informations générales; elles partiront toutes deux aujourd'hui si le Ministre, qui doit avoir préparé, de son côté, une longue *Private*[2] pour le Général,[3] nous revient de la Chambre assez à temps pour l'heure de l'expédition du Portefeuille.

Je sais que le Ministre se proposait d'écrire au Général sur le caractère de ses rapports avec Lord Granville. Il y a dans celui-ci quelque maladresse et du soupçonneux; c'est chose incontestable, mais je ne crois pas aux mauvaises dispositions pour la personne. De son côté, M. Thiers n'a rien des habitudes anglaises et les comprend peu. Que le Général s'interpose avec ce tact qu'il possède à un si haut degré. On est ombrageux et trop insistant sur toute chose au Faubourg St Honoré.[4] On est susceptible et impressionable à l'hôtel des Capucines;[5] voilà les élémens à combiner et à amalgamer.

Vos observations sur le nez à nez des deux marines sont très justes. Nous veillerons de notre mieux à ce qu'il n'en résulte rien de fâcheux. Je regrette, pour mon compte, que le Commandant Roy, au Passage, n'ait pas obtempéré à l'invitation de son collègue anglais. Mais, en vérité, c'était trop que de nous demander de le blâmer et de le blâmer officiellement. Il ne pouvait quitter sa position qu'en commentant, en mettant de côté ses instructions qui, n'ayant pas prévu la circonstance qui a eu lieu, lui prescrivaient de rester au Passage. Il eut bien fait de commenter; mais nous ne pouvons le blâmer de s'en être tenu à la lettre, surtout lorsque le blâme est demandé du dehors. Ajoutons que, l'opération ayant réussi, la démarche évitée était une véritable querelle d'allemand. Enfin, et sous un point de vue plus général, je crois qu'il faut tenir compte de cette facheuse influence des on-dits, des propos de corps de garde et des relations de la Presse sur les Officiers respectifs. Il n'est pas de sottises qui ne soient dites au quartier général d'Evans et dans la Marine anglaise à propos de la chute de Mendizabal et de la prétendue part que nous y avons eue. Faut-il s'étonner ensuite que nos propres marins en concluent qu'il y aurait duperie à faire constam-

---

[1] From the *Bourqueney Papers, Fonds France*, 1899, in the Archives du Ministère des Affaires étrangères, Paris.

[2] Desages occasionally introduces English words such as this one, sometimes underlined, sometimes not.

[3] Sébastiani, the French Ambassador.

[4] The British Embassy.   [5] The residence of Thiers.

ment acte de condescendance pour ceux qui s'élèvent si fort contre l'ombre même d'une influence française; que Lord Minto avec son bon esprit, corrige ses compatriotes; nous obtiendrons alors sans peine que les nôtres mettent de côté toute susceptibilité d'amour-propre. Adieu, mon cher Ami, tout à vous de cœur.

(ii)

Paris, 16 *Septembre*, 1836.

. . . Revenant à l'Espagne, les nouvelles en sont fort peu rassurantes. Les paroles du Ministère espagnol sont tout ce qu'elles peuvent être; mais sunt verba et voces preterea qui nihil, ou à peu près. Avec une révolution purement politique on peut prévoir où l'on va et s'arranger en conséquence. Avec une dissolution sociale le plus savant calculateur s'y perd. Quoiqu'il en soit, si nous sommes bien renseignés, la chance tourne plus que jamais, en ce moment à don Carlos—sinon pour faire du définitif, du moins pour culbuter ce qui est. Dans cet état de choses, le thême ici est de se renfermer dans la lettre du traité—rien de plus, rien de moins. Il faut que je vous dise que tous les rapports qui nous sont venus d'Espagne, depuis quelque temps, rapports diplomatiques, rapports militaires et autres, sont unanimes à présenter la Légation anglaise comme ayant plus ou moins connivé aux derniers mouvements. Je ne croirai jamais que ce fut dans l'intention de les faire aboutir à ce que nous avons vu. Mais je crois volontiers que Villiers, par faiblesse pour une femme, par sympathie pour Mendizabal, par manie d'influence, a fait plus qu'il ne devait faire; et je crois aussi que les relations constantes de son attaché, Southern, avec les gens des Clubs et des Sociétés Secrétes ont eu, sinon pour but, du moins pour effet, d'encourager ces gens à se persuader et à persuader aux leurs que l'appui de l'Angleterre leur était assuré. En définitive, la différence qui n'est pas nouvelle mais qui se déssinera de plus en plus peut-être entre l'Angleterre et nous, consiste en ceci: Peu doit importer aux Anglais ce qui se passe en Espagne, pourvu que ce ne soit pas au profit de Don Carlos et de la Sainte Alliance; nous, limitrophes de la monarchie espagnole, en contact avec elle de mille manières et sous mille rapports, nous ne jugeons pas qu'il nous soit donné de pouvoir être indifférents à son état intérieur. . . .

[P.S.] Je m'apperçois que je n'ai pas répondu à ce que vous me demandiez de ma situation personelle. Merci d'abord, mon cher Ami, de ce que vous me dites d'aimable et de bon à ce sujet. Mes premiers rapports avec M. Molé sont très satisfaisants pour moi—du reste vous pouvez savoir que, dans mes habitudes, j'attends toujours la confiance et ne la provoque jamais.

(iii)

Paris, 28 *Mai*, 1839.

Mon cher Ami, J'ai retenu hier le Portefeuille, dans la pensée que le Maréchal[1] nous donnerait à temps la substance d'une réponse à votre dernière dépêche; mais il est revenu les mains vides et il en sera de même encore aujourd'hui, la discussion des fonds secrets l'obligeant à passer sa journée à la Chambre.

Je ne puis donc vous parler que de mes impressions et de celles qu'a fait éprouver parmi les initiés la lecture de ladite dépêche. La première chose qui nous a frappé ainsi que le bon Général, c'est la manière dont Lord Palmerston semble accepter la chance du retour des Russes à Constantinople, sous la seule condition que la Russie ne fasse point un nouveau traité d'Unkiar Skelessi ou quelque chose d'équivalent. *Quantum mutatus ab illo!* Cela, rapproché du singulier speech de Lord Melbourne sur le Czar, donne beaucoup à penser ici—(et par parenthèse, j'aurais bien voulu que vous *nous* ou *me* parlassiez de ce speech, de son but, de son effet et de sa portée); pour en revenir au plan de Lord Palmerston, il me semble que la Russie serait fort ingrate de ne pas souscrire à la condition posée. Car, à quoi bon un nouvel acte, quand, après avoir protesté contre en 1833, l'Angleterre accepte à si bon marché, le protectorat Impérial exclusif sur Constantinople? N'est il pas évident que c'est là le plus gros de ses gains possibles dans les circonstances actuelles? Pour moi, mon cher Ami, je suis disposé à croire qu'il vaut mieux subir en se taisant ce qu'on ne peut ou ne veut empêcher que de prévoir officiellement le fait et de négocier à l'avance pour une conclusion qui doit le sanctionner et le faire passer dans le droit commun.

Ce que je remarque ensuite, dans l'opinion émise par Lord Palmerston, c'est cette disposition marquée à frapper exclusivement sur Mehemet Ali. Dans l'état actuel des choses, ce n'est pas seulement une injustice, c'est une faute, à moins d'une arrière-pensée étrangère à la question du moment. Je suis d'avis qu'il faut frapper sur Mehemet Ali *vainqueur* pour l'arrêter, pour le contraindre à rester ou à rentrer en Syrie. Mais lorsque c'est le Sultan qui fausse promesse et qui attaque, s'il a des avantages, il faut aussi prendre immédiatement les moyens dont on dispose pour chercher à l'arrêter. Il faut tenir sa flotte à distance, ne pas lui permettre de paraître sur les côtes de Syrie ou de l'Egypte etc. Lord Palmerston part de la *doctrine de la légitimité*: Cela peut être beau à Vienne, mais cela me parait singulier venant de Londres. N'est-il pas naturel et plus sûr de partir de l'intérêt politique qui veut l'intégrité de l'Empire Ottoman, quellesque puissent être d'ailleurs les modifications de son régime intérieur, qui veut le maintien du trône du Sultan comme expression de cette intégrité, qui, pour ce faire, demande que l'Asie Mineure ne redevienne plus le théâtre d'une lutte entre les armées turques et égyptiennes qui, dans ce même but, conseille de se jeter entre les combattants et de peser sur l'un comme sur l'autre pour les séparer et les arrêter? Une médiation armée pour

---

[1] Soult.

faire cesser le combat, de quelque côté que penche la balance, voilà
notre rôle: il ne faut pas le compliquer inutilement de questions de
légitimité, de souveraineté de vassalité; ces questions ne doivent se
présenter qu'après la cessation des hostilités et lorsqu'il s'agira d'arbitrer
entre les prétentions respectives; jusque là, tout doit être égal autant
que possible dans le caractère des moyens à employer pour arrêter la
lutte matérielle. Et puis l'opinion publique de France, et j'imagine
aussi d'Angleterre, est-ce à nous de la compter pour zéro?

Couvrir Constantinople est le principal, sans doute, mais laisser
anéantir Mehemet Ali qui n'a point attaqué, c'est un *incident* qui, pour
le public, est presqu'aussi gros que le principal. Il faut se gouverner
d'après ces deux grosses considérations. Lord Palmerston, dans sa
théorie ou explication sur l'accord de Kutayeh est à la fois dans le vrai
et dans le faux. Il n'y a point une garantie positive dans le sens diplomatique du mot, mais il y a une garantie morale au profit de Pacha
comme de la Porte, dans les démarches et efforts incessants que toutes
les Cours ont faits à Alexandrie aussi bien qu'à Constantinople depuis
cinq ans pour exiger le respect du statu quo établi par ledit arrangement.
Je vous écris à bâtons rompus, mon cher Ami, et je ne sais trop où je
vais. C'est aujourd'hui notre jour d'expédition pour l'Orient. Nous
écrivons comminatoirement en Egypte, pour le cas où la guerre serait
déjà commencée—et où Ibrahim aura frotté les Turcs, ce qui est le
plus vraisemblable. En cas de lutte, nous écrivons à l'Amiral[1] de faire
les représentations les plus énergiques, en attendant le chapitre des
résolutions définitives. Nos lettres sont portées par deux officers
d'ordonnance du Maréchal. Mais, en fin de compte, mon cher Ami,
faisons des vœux pour que ce gros nuage se soit dissipé, car ni *vous* ni
nous ne me paraissons en état de parer convenablement à toutes les
éventualités extrêmes d'une pareille crise.

Si demain, nous sommes en mesure de vous dire quelque chose
d'officiel, nous vous enverrons un exprès.

Adieu, tout à vous de cœur; la suite de mon bavardage au prochain
Portefeuille.

(iv)

Paris, 30 *Mai*, 1839.

Mon cher Ami, Nous vous écrivons aujourd'hui à cette fin seulement
de vous dire ce que provisoirement nous avons fait pour la question
d'Orient. Le Maréchal, au lieu de débattre chacun des points de
l'opinion personelle et de premier jet que Lord Palmerston vous a
exprimée, a préféré attendre que vous nous fissiez connaître la pensée
arrêtée, sauf concert, du Cabinet de Londres. Nous n'avons rien reçu
d'Orient depuis les premières nouvelles. Dieu veuille, je le repète,
qu'il n'y ait eu qu'une *démonstration* turque sans plus, ni sans durée.
Vous verrez, parce que nous vous écrivons, que nous n'abandonnons
pas de prime abord le terrain de notre protestation contre le traité

---

[1] Admiral Roussin, the French Ambassador at Constantinople.

d'Unkiar-Skelessi. C'est bien le moins d'ailleurs que la Russie s'explique sur ce *casus foederis* de son œuvre. Je pense de plus que, même son dit traité à la main, on est parfaitement posé pour soutenir que la clôture des Dardanelles n'étant imposée à la Porte que pour le cas où la Russie se trouve attaquée ou menacée de l'être, rien ne doit s'opposer à ce que, pour la protection du Sultan, les grandes Puissances, les deux maritimes surtout, ne combinent les moyens qui leur sont propres avec ceux qui sont plus particulièrement du ressort de la Russie, vû sa situation topographique, afin de couvrir *ensemble* Constantinople. En Morée l'Angleterre et la Russie ont fourni des vaisseaux, nous des vaisseaux et des troupes. Qui empêcherait qu'on ne convint que, dans le but d'arrêter Ibrahim et de sauver la Capitale, la France et l'Angleterre s'y présenteraient avec tel nombre de vaisseaux, tandis que le contingent de la Russie, en vaisseaux et en troupes de débarquement, serait de telle ou telle force? Je sais bien que la Russie faisait une rude grimace à pareille proposition; mais, en vérité, je ne comprendrais pas qu'elle put y opposer les stipulations d'Unkiar-Skelessi; sa seule ressource plausible serait de suggérer et de se placer behind un refus de la Porte. Mais c'est là où l'intervention de l'Autriche pourrait être de mise et fort salutaire. Tout cela d'ailleurs est opinion mienne et je ne vous la donne que pour telle. Au surplus, pour ce plan comme pour tout autre, il faut avoir le temps de négocier: sans quoi, il n'y a qu'à subir l'impulsion du vent qui souffle dans le moment.

Comme vous le croirez aisément, mon cher Ami, je suis fort tiraillé et occupé, depuis l'installation du nouveau cabinet. Je fais un rude métier et mes services sont d'une terrible longueur. Enfin tant que les forces miennes le permettront, je me résignerai. Adieu, tout à vous de cœur.

(v)

Paris, 20 *Juin*, 1839.

A quo novis, mon cher Ami, car je suis très fatigué, très influxionné, et ma tête est faible—nous ne répondrons pas aujourd'hui à votre dernière dépêche; d'abord parce qu'il faut le temps de se reconnaître et, en second lieu, parce que votre dépêche s'étant croisée avec elle où nous vous donnions nos idées en gros, il est bon que nous sachions ce qu'en aura pensé Lord Palmerston.

Comme vous le savez déjà, nous différons, *vous* et *nous*, d'abord en ceci qu'à l'égard du Sultan vous prenez votre règle de conduite dans le droit rigoureux, dans sa *légitimité*, au lieu de la prendre dans les faits, dans la situation, dans l'intérêt qui consiste avant tout à prévenir ou à arrêter une colision entre Egyptiens et Turcs. J'applique surtout cette observation au plan proposé pour l'attitude et la conduite de nos Escadres. Si la mer est libre pour les Turcs sans l'être pour les Egyptiens vous jouez un jeu d'enfants. Les Grecs c'était aussi des rebelles et pourtant vous avez interdit aux vaisseaux ottomans l'accès des ports et côtes de la Grèce et vice versa. Vous avez bien fait alors; vous feriez mal d'agir autrement. Ce n'est pas connaître le terrain de Constan-

tinople que d'y porter ces distinctions et ces délicatesses qui partout ailleurs sont de rigueur. Voulez-vous avoir chance de sauver le Sultan, de l'empêcher de donner de la tête dans le précipice, *intimidez-le*, ne lui parlez pas de ses droits mais de vos intérêts, ou du moins dites-lui très nettement que les uns et les autres peuvent se concilier dans une juste mesure; vous n'aurez égard aux uns qu'au temps qu'il vous donnera, par sa déférence pour vos avis et représentations, sa garantie dont vous avez besoin pour les autres.

En résumé, si vous ne faites pas que le Sultan soit bien convaincu que nous empêcherons sa flotte d'aborder les côtes de Syrie, et de sortir même de l'Archipel, vous faites une sottise des plus compromettantes. Le second point sur lequel nous différons est celui de la part rigoureuse, *absolue* à faire à Mehémet-Ali. Ce que j'ai dit n'est point par sentiment de partialité pour le Pacha. Il nous importait fort peu en 1833 qu'il mit ou ne mit pas le pied en Syrie. Nous voulions qu'il ne s'étendit pas au delà du Pachalik *d'Acre*, s'il était victorieux, et, enfin, qu'en aucun cas il ne franchit le Taurus. Il a gagné cette dernière limite. Il nous importerait fort peu aujourd'hui qu'il y renonçât. Nous concevons même qu'il n'y a de négociation possible qu'à la condition de l'abandon à perte par lui d'une partie de ses possessions actuelles, en échange de la transmissibilité de son pouvoir sur le reste dans sa famille. Mais déclarer *a priori* qu'on ne lui laissera que l'Egypte (pas même *l'Arabie* et il y a peut-être de *l'Anglais* dans cette dernière restriction) c'est prendre l'engagement, coûte que coûte, d'exécuter cette sentence. Or cela nous serait d'autant plus impossible que, si les défilés du Taurus sont, de ce côté, la clef de Constantinople, St Jean d'Acre et Damas peuvent bien être les clefs de l'Egypte: et, dans ce cas, Mehémet-Ali aurait évidemment raison de vouloir d'autre garantie qu'un chiffon de papier signé Mahmoud, pour la sécurité des pays auxquels il se restreindrait. J'admets donc que l'on prenne pour base la seule possession d'Egypte mais non pour base inflexible, invariable. Il faut se réserver de faire pour le mieux suivant les circonstances et ne pas oublier que le *but* est, non pas de faire telle ou telle distribution de territoire, mais de raffermir ou de rétablir la paix, dans les conditions les moins onéreuses possibles, et le plus promptement que faire se pourra, le tout de telle sorte que le nouvel arrangement satisfasse aux diverses exigences nées de la situation.

Je finis, sauf à continuer un autre jour, mon cher Ami, tout à vous de cœur.

[P.S.] Encore un mot pourtant; je ne sais trop ce qu'on décidera ici pour l'éventualité du retour des Russes à Constantinople. Je tiens déjà pour certain toutefois qu'on reculera devant l'idée de troupes de débarquement. Quoiqu'il en soit, j'insiste pour qu'on se gouverne de manière à ce que tant à Pétersbourg qu'à Constantinople et même à Vienne on donne fermement à croire qu'à Paris et à Londres on ne reculerait devant aucune mesure extrême. Le tout pour avoir meilleure chance d'arriver à un concert.

(vi)

Paris, 11 *Juillet*, 1839.

Mon cher Ami, Nous avons reçu ce matin votre no 61 et ce soir, nous expédions notre courrier pour Vienne et Constantinople. Je n'ai pas trop compris les objections de Lord Palmerston contre le préambule de notre projet de note. Il me semble que le développement, en pareille circonstance, est moins blessant que le laconisme; quoiqu'il en soit, nous transmettons copie de votre dépêche à l'Amiral Roussin et nous l'autorisons à faire à notre projet de note les retranchements qu'il croirait convenables dans la situation. Si j'avais eu sous les yeux la rédaction même de Lord Palmerston j'aurais pu modifier moi-même mon premier travail. Mais, ne pouvant deviner comment *vous* serez entré en matière, je n'ai pu que proposer au Maréchal d'accorder à notre Ambassadeur l'autorisation en question.

Les explications de Lord Palmerston sur Lord Ponsonby m'ont paru fort embarassées et vos réponses ont été excellentes, jugez où nous pouvions aller, si l'on avait donné carte blanche au second pour disposer à sa guise des mouvements et opérations de l'escadre. Quant à Bassora et aux Iles Bahrim, il est bien que les Anglais n'aient point songé à des troupes de débarquement: mais si je conçois *qu'à la demande et pour compte du Sultan* ils fassent une démonstration, je ne comprends pas encore, je l'avoue, qu'ils puissent arguer *d'un droit-propre* pour s'opposer à ce que les Egyptiens s'établissent sur la côte est de l'Arabie, là surtout, où la suzeraineté ou souveraineté de l'Empire Ottoman n'est pas contestée même par eux. Ici l'opinion se réveille et se prend vivement à ces questions d'Orient: vous en avez pu juger par la dernière discussion. Déjà la prise de possession *d'Aden* par les Anglais a ébranlé beaucoup de gens. La disposition de nos voisins à s'établir en dominateurs dans le golfe Persique n'a pas non plus passée inaperçue. On en conclut volontiers que *la politique anglaise par un bout* n'est pas plus honnête et ne nous est pas plus favorable que la politique russe par *l'autre*; que toutes les deux se ressemblent fort et nous pourrions bien faire un métier de dupes en mettant tout notre enjeu sur la question de Constantinople de concert avec l'Angleterre etc. Je sais à merveille mon cher Ami, que nos imaginations vont vite et qu'elles tendent à nous entraîner bien au delà du but; mais il n'en est pas moins vrai que tout cela incite attention et que plus ira et plus nous serons obligés d'être regardants de très près aux faits et gestes de nos alliés, tout comme à ceux de nos adversaires. Déjà les Russes éclairés sont au désespoir de l'obstination aveugle de leur autocrate dans son aversion pour nous. Ils proclament, même assez haut, qu'il en faudra venir à tout faire, pour se lier de nouveau avec nous; que c'est là la politique naturelle de leur pays et du nôtre, la seule où les intérêts respectifs envers et contre tous puissent trouver une satisfaction légitime et assurée. Ici, à la vérité, tout cela n'a encore qu'un bien faible écho. L'aversion du Czar pour nous et son peu d'égard pour nos sympathies populaires envers la Pologne éloignent encore les russes de toute idée de rapprochement

avec lui: mais cela peut n'être qu'une affaire de temps et, dans quelques années, la réaction peut arriver. Je ne sais si à Londres on porte des prévisions dans cette voie.

Voilà bien du bavardage, mon cher Ami, mais ma plume demandait à courir et je l'ai laissée aller. Revenons au plus près. Je persiste à croire que Lord Palmerston a tort de vouloir sur des questions de paix ou de guerre, lutter de *douceur* à Constantinople avec les Russes. C'est ne pas connaître les Turcs, et je les ai vus assez longtemps à l'œuvre, pour savoir à quoi nous en tenir. Ce n'est pas que je veuille les brutaliser; ce serait donner dans l'excès contraire: mais avec eux, même pour les servir, il faut être froid et quelque peu austère dans son attitude et son langage, sans quoi ils n'en font qu'à leur tête. Nous attendons now votre réponse à la proposition Metternich sur la légitimité de la dynastie d'Othman. Nous écrivons à Vienne que pour nous, cela va sans dire; mais que quant à la forme d'une déclaration, nous voulons d'abord nous concerter avec *vous*. Si cette déclaration peut avoir une valeur, c'est comme acte plus ou moins explicite mais réel de garantie pour l'intégrité territoriale de l'Empire Ottoman et surtout contre tout démembrement au profit d'une quelconque des 5 Puissances ou plutôt des trois, Russie, Autriche et Angleterre. Nous sommes donc très portés à y donner les mains.

Adieu, mon cher Ami, je suis tellement interrompu que je ne sais plus trop ce que je vous écris. Tout à vous de cœur.

(vii)

Paris, 8 *Août*, 1839.

Mon cher Ami, Nous n'avons à vous envoyer aujourd'hui que ce que nous avons écrit hier à Constantinople et à Alexandrie. En communiquant nos écritures à Lord Palmerston, retranchez en ce qui est reproché à notre animal d'Amiral et ce que vous jugeriez pouvoir, d'autre part, disposer votre interlocuteur à chercher, comme on dit, *Midi à 14 heures*.

Notre dépêche en réponse à la proposition anglaise a été étrangement défigurée dans quelques parties de sa rédaction par nos MM. du Conseil; vous vous en seriez aperçu du reste; mais cela vous aura-t-il conduit à ne donner lecture que de ce qui était réellement lisible. Je le souhaite fort. Si j'avais pu renvoyer au lendemain l'expédition, nous aurions cherché à corriger les corrections pour mettre le tout d'accord; mais on s'était montré si pressé à vous, de recevoir notre réponse, que sans trop savoir ce qu'elle était devenue dans les mains de nos collègues du Ministère nous avons dû en précipiter l'envoi.

La Russie recule de plus en plus sur le chapitre des délibérations communes; bien que nous préférerions, comme vous le voyez, à chercher à entraver le système d'un arrangement *direct* entre la Porte et le Pacha, il est plus que probable que nous échouerons. J'ai prévu cela dès la nouvelle reçue de la mort de Mahmoud; jusque là le mal ne me parait pas très grand, je l'avoue. L'avantage d'un réglement de la

question *intérieure* par les Puissances était de rendre plus facile peut-être, comme conclusion de ce réglement et résultat de la médiation européennes, la garantie solennelle de l'Empire Ottoman *au point de vue extérieur*. L'inconvénient était, ou pourrait être, de donner, plus que de raison, *caractère* Européen, à l'établissement de Mehemet Ali tandis qu'il faut le maintenir établissement turc et partie intégrante de l'Empire, à durer ce qu'il plaira au Ciel. Donc, mon cher Ami, pour conclure, je crois que ce à quoi nous devons désormais nous attacher le plus, c'est à fortifier notre entente à trois, France, Angleterre et Autriche, c'est à lui imprimer un caractère de puissance qui nous donne toujours le droit de traiter d'égal à égal avec la Russie sur ce terrain du Levant et particulièrement de Constantinople. Si nous pouvions parvenir à transformer en traité nos trois déclarations récentes, je regarderais ce résultat comme le gage le plus fort de la paix générale et le frein le plus solide à l'ambition russe. Adieu, tout à vous de cœur.

[P.S.] ... Le Général parle de partir vers le 25 de ce mois pour retourner à son poste; ce n'est pas moi qui l'y pousse. Je trouve au contraire qu'il nous serait plus utile de l'avoir ici comme Conseiller.

(viii)

Paris, 19 *Août*, 1839.

Mon cher Ami, Nous recevons aujourd'hui votre no 77; avant-hier le 76 nous était parvenu. Lord Palmerston passe bien subitement d'un découragement extrême à une confiance sans limites. Cela me prouve qu'il connait imparfaitement le terrain d'Orient et qu'il se laisse aller, comme nos gens d'ici d'ailleurs, à toutes les impressions du moment. Il apprend que les Ambassadeurs à Constantinople, y compris l'Envoyé Russe, ont unaniment conseillé à la Porte de s'appuyer sur les Puissances et de suspendre toute négociation directe entre elle et Méhémet-Ali. Dès lors grande satisfaction, comme d'un succès non seulement inespéré, mais décisif; c'était pourtant chose toute simple: l'offre était convenue depuis assez longtemps déjà entre Londres, Paris et Vienne, et remarquez bien que si la Russie s'est adjointe à nous, c'est, *non pas à Vienne*, mais seulement à Constantinople où, dès l'origine, elle a déclaré vouloir concentrer et borner l'accord, parce que là elle échappe au contrôle, aux obligations d'un caractère Européen, et qu'il lui est plus facile d'y jouer un jeu double comme en 1827, à l'occasion du Traité du 6 Juillet. L'acceptation de l'offre par la Porte n'est pas moins simple et il était surtout aisé de la prévoir depuis que le Grand Vizir Kosrew s'est vu personnellement traqué par Méhémet-Ali: car, chez ces bienheureux orientaux les positions et les intérêts personnels sont la clef de tout. Je crois du reste que Méhémet-Ali a fait une faute en exigeant avant tout le renvoi de Kosrew. S'il s'était borné à lui demander des gages, à l'inquiéter sans menace directe, il en eut obtenu de suite tout ce qu'il eut voulu. Quoiqu'il en soit, il faut bien le dire que ce que nous pensons tenir par les dernières nouvelles de Constantinople

et de Vienne peut nous échapper d'un instant à l'autre; que si Méhémet-Ali reste militairement inactif, il ne l'est pas politiquement; que son appel à 16 Pachas pour les liguer avec lui contre Kosrew; que son or et le travail de ses partisans à Constantinople; que l'action souterraine des Russes pressés d'en finir et de pouvoir nous opposer un accommodement quelconque entre la Porte et l'Egypte; que tout cela enfin et mille autres circonstances encore, doivent modérer notre confiance. Au surplus, mon cher Ami, nous sommes parfaitement disposés à suivre cette voie des négociations de bon et entier accord avec nos Alliés. Que l'on propose à Vienne ce que l'on voudra, notre Ambassadeur à Constantinople et notre Consul à Alexandrie l'appuyeront, franchement et sans arrière-pensée; mais de mesures coercitives, d'intervention armée, tant que Méhémet-Ali ne bougera point et qu'Ibrahim restera là où il est, nous n'y pouvons recourir, et cela, croyez-le bien, ce n'est pas par faveur pour le Vice-Roi, ni parce qu'il entre dans notre pensée de l'aggrandir au détriment de l'autorité de la Porte; nullement, c'est uniquement parce que ce serait folie que de s'exposer aujourd'hui à pousser à bout des hommes qui sont plus que jamais en position de provoquer la réapparition des Russes dans le Bosphore et de soulever contre la Porte la plupart des Provinces mêmes qui ne relèvent pas directement d'eux.

Je vois que l'incident de la flotte turque donne toujours le cauchemar à Lord Palmerston. Je reconnais du reste qu'il est déjà bien loin de ses premières dispositions à cet égard; mais je ne goute pas non plus, je vous l'avoue, le rapport des Consuls. Doit-on ou ne doit-on pas exiger le renvoi de la flotte, *avant* d'abord la négociation du fonds, c'est-à-dire, celle qui est relative à la distribution des territoires etc. . . ? Si l'incident ne doit point, comme nous le jugeons, passer avant le principal, le rappel des Consuls n'a pas de sens; c'est se faire d'ailleurs, selon moi, une grosse illusion que de supposer que ce rapport puisse avoir une influence efficace sur les résolutions de Méhémet-Ali. Souvenez vous de 1833. Le Consul de Russie rappelé d'Egypte, les Russes dans le Bosphore, les autres Puissances agissant de leur mieux pour modérer les prétentions du Pacha et celui-ci néanmoins emportant tout ce qu'il voulait alors et les Cours elles-mêmes obligées d'engager la Porte à céder ainsi Adana, pour faire cesser au plus vite une situation aussi tendue; pensez-vous qu'aujourd'hui la situation (Mahmoud de moins et le reste de l'Empire plus ébranlé, plus *anarchisé* qu'alors) soit moins de nature à encourager Méhémet-Ali dans sa résistance? Laissons donc nos Consuls à Alexandrie où ils peuvent, d'un moment à l'autre, être utiles à nos vues, où ils peuvent contenir en surveillant et d'où leur départ serait sans influence sérieuse sur les déterminations du Vice-Roi. Attendons du moins que nous soyions mieux renseignés et sur la dernière démarche des Ambassadeurs auprès de lui et sur l'attitude que, par suite, il aura prise ou laissé pénétrer. Je ne parle point ici de l'idée d'entraver les communications entre la Syrie et l'Egypte; votre dépêche 77 n'y revient pas; cette idée du reste, je l'ai plutôt appuyée que combattue; mais, avant tout, il

nous faut voir comment on l'aura formulée à Londres dans les instructions pour Stopford, si on y a persisté. Quant au projet de la conversion des déclarations en un seul et même acte, vous savez qu'il est depuis longtemps nôtre, mais est, à Vienne, une question d'opportunité. Il faut, je crois, n'y pousser que quand M. de Metternich n'aura plus à nous dire: "J'ai encore confiance dans les Russes; ils viendront à nous, attendons les." Ce serait alors un coup dans l'eau; au surplus Saint-Aulaire est en mesure.

Notre dépêche de ce jour vous parle de la communication de Medem; elle est, *par le raisonnement*, de la dernière impertinence et repose sur le proverbe qui dit: "Il n'est pire sourd que qui ne veut pas entendre." Adieu; assez pour aujourd'hui. Tout à vous de cœur.

(ix)

Paris, 22 *Août*, 1839.

Mon cher Ami, Quelques mots seulement. Il se fait tard et le temps me manquerait pour étendre mon bavardage. Il me semble que nos rapports avec Londres se rembrunissent un peu; guerre de presse, des deux côtés; ici mille sottises impressées; là bas Morning Chronicle de plus en plus agressif; indiscrétions sorties, je le crains bien, de l'un ou de l'autre de nos Départements Ministériels; boutade étrange de Lord Melbourne. A Vienne, à Berlin, à Pétersbourg, Lord Palmerston écrivant à tort et à travers contre l'Egypte et notre manière d'envisager ce côté de la question, comme s'il voulait exciter contre nous les autres Cabinets etc... etc... etc., tout cela est déplorable et ne peut mener à rien de bien. On criera bravo dans les trois Cours et puis on rira *sous cape* à Pétersbourg surtout, de ce dissentiment ainsi affiché par un des deux alliés qui s'appelent *intimes*. En vérité, je ne comprends rien à tous ces soubresauts, à toutes ces illusions de Lord Palmerston, à cette façon de ne tenir aucun compte des éléments si variés de la situation. Pour nous, mon cher Ami, nous préférerons, je l'espère, du moins dans les voies que nous vous avons indiquées *par écrit*, des négociations à Vienne, pour que le résultat en soit porté de là à Constantinople et à Alexandrie; mais là rien que les moyens diplomatiques, les propositions, les avis, les représentations. Nous n'abandonnerons pas plus à St Aulaire qu'à Roussin le droit de discuter pour nous et de régler sans nous, l'emploi de mesures coercitives et l'action de nos forces navales. Si Mehémet Ali redevient agresseur, notre escadre qui a, dès l'origine, des instructions *ad hoc*, agira pour protéger la Porte; mais ce cas excepté, point de coup de canon, ni rien qui y conduise. Ce n'est pas par égard pour Mehémet Ali. Nous voudrions, je le repète, qu'il fit des concessions et de larges concessions à la Porte; mais jusqu'au jour où nous seront convaincus et bien convaincus qu'on peut recourir à la contrainte sans s'exposer à pis que ce qui est, jusque là nous persisterons à nous abstenir. Le mal est qu'à Londres on n'ait pas compris que pour avoir meilleure chance de peser avec fruit sur les déterminations du Pacha, il fallait avant tout, puisqu'on

nous suppose plus d'influence en Egypte qu'à d'autres, ne pas nous donner malgré nous, couleur d'être plus favorables à Mehémet Ali que nous ne le sommes, en nous traitant, sous ce rapport de pestiférés et en affichant partout qu'on avait une toute autre manière de voir. Je suis convaincu qu'une diplomatie très serrée à cet égard entre nous et Londres, appelant l'Autriche à son aide, aurait eu de meilleures chances à Alexandrie que ce dissentiment rendu public des deux Cabinets qui disposent de la mer.

Notre dépêche de ce jour est une querelle d'amants. Je désire qu'elle éclaire aussi Lord Palmerston; nous ne disons pas encore tout ce que nous savons de ses équipées en écriture; elles font un détestable effet au dehors—à Vienne surtout en ce sens que l'attitude de Lord Beauvale envers St Aulaire va flottant du haut en bas et du bas en haut suivant la couleur de ce que lui apporte chaque courrier expédié de Londres. Avec cela, dites moi un peu comment on parviendra à enlacer M. de Mett[ernich] pour la signature de l'acte qui nous ferait à tous une si bonne position parlementaire et autre. Ajoutez que Tatischeff arrive et que très certainement il arrive, moins pour prendre part à un accord que pour le faire manquer et imposer à M. de Mett[ernich] plus que ne saurait le faire le pauvre diable de Chargé d'Affaires russe qui a jusqu'ici l'*intérim*. Enfin, comme disent les vieux Turcs, Dieu est grand et nous verrons. Adieu, mon cher Ami, tout à vous de cœur.

P.S. Le Général part le 28 passant par Eu où il s'arretera un jour. Le Maréchal craint beaucoup sa disposition à abonder, en toutes choses, dans le sens anglais. J'aurais désiré, entre nous, qu'il ne retournât à Londres que lorsque le terrain aurait été déblayé; mais enfin, tâchez de l'empêcher de s'engager au-delà de ce que nous écrivons; car infailliblement, avec les dispositions d'ici, qui ont aussi leur excès que je combats, il serait désavoué et la brèche alors s'élargirait au lieu de se combler. Le bruit a couru que vous désiriez revenir, dès qu'il serait de retour; ajournez, si cela est, ajournez; car nous vous recevrions très mal, dans un tel moment.

(x)

Paris, 2 *Mars*, 1840.

Mon cher Ami, La crise est passée; souhaitons qu'il ne s'en présente plus de semblable d'ici à longtemps. Voici Thiers procédant à son installation; mais il lui faudra nécessairement quelques jours avant de se reconnaître et de pouvoir s'engager sur le terrain de nos affaires. J'ai lu le billet qu'il écrit à M. Guizot; c'est du private qui ne touche en rien à la grande question qui nous occupe. Donc un peu de patience. En attendant chercher à pénétrer au fond des instructions Brunow. Vous savez que les Russes ont des dépêches *officielles*, des dépêches réservées qu'on montre pour avoir l'air de faire de la confiance et des dépêches *secrètes*. Il me semble bizarre que la Russie, si elle est sincère, ne réponde pas nettement sur la proposition d'appeler un plénipoten-

tiaire turc; elle veut que le refus d'accord vienne de nous; et nous devons faire en sorte qu'il vienne d'elle. Le Général dont j'ai trouvé hier l'esprit remarquablement net et lucide, est d'avis que nous nous bornions, pour le présent, à appeler et à attendre l'envoyé ottoman. C'est deux mois de gagner, dit-il, et c'est déjà beaucoup; de part et d'autre, c'est à dire France et Angleterre, on s'est trop avancé, Lord Palmerston surtout. Il faut aider la disposition de rétrograder qui est dans les nécessités du Cabinet britannique et qui s'accorde avec les nôtres; pour cela point de reproche qui brise tout, et oblige ceux qu'on veut ramener, à prendre un parti tranchant et définitif. Cela me parait juste; vous jugerez jusqu'à quel point cela est pratique. Adieu, mon cher Ami, tout à vous de cœur. . . .

(xi)

Paris, 21 *Septembre*, 1840

Mon cher Ami, En arrivant ici ce matin, j'ai trouvé votre lettre de samedi. Je ne crois pas vous avoir écrit que, dans mon opinion, nous avions *certainement* le dernier mot de Méhémet-Ali. Je n'en sais rien et la correspondance de nos agents, dont j'ai d'ailleurs pour habitude de rabattre toujours beaucoup, n'est pas de nature à prévenir les doutes. Si M. Thiers a été plus affirmatif dans sa lettre à M. Guizot, c'est, 1^0) qu'il croit volontiers ce qu'il désire, et 2^0) qu'en se montrant sceptique, il craindrait que son scepticisme, passant en vous, ne nuise à votre action. Quant au résultat de celle-ci, je n'ai pas attendu votre lettre, mon cher Ami, pour le présumer négatif. Ce n'est pas qu'il n'y ait d'excellentes choses à dire pour appuyer le thème actuel et qu'en réalité il ne serait de saine politique à Londres d'en demeurer là. Je suis également porté à croire que, dans cette occasion, les membres modérés du Cabinet pourraient, avec moins de risque *intérieur* qu'en Juillet dernier, peser beaucoup plus sur Lord Palmerston: car, dans l'état, il serait plus difficile aujourd'hui, ce me semble, à Lord Palmerston de mettre honnêtement son portefeuille sur la table. Mais je ne compte passer cette chance. Lord Palmerston demandera qu'en tout cas on ne se presse point. Il demandera qu'on se donne le temps de voir si les dernières concessions du Pacha sont, ou ne sont pas, de la faiblesse etc. . . .; et ses collègues résisteront difficilement à ses arguments. Il y a réponse à cela sans doute: à des hypothèses, on peut aisément opposer des hypothèses; et puis la saison des opérations s'avance; et puis le Pacha est un barbare qui, s'il ne dit pas son dernier mot, peut-être à ses amis, soit dans un sens soit dans un autre, ne le dit certainement pas plus, dans l'un ni l'autre sens, à ses ennemis. Mais toujours est-il que je tiens pour assez naturel que Lord Palmerston fait comme il l'est, persiste dans sa voie propre et pour assez probable que ses collègues ne le pressent pas autrement de se déclarer pour la Syrie viagère.

Je ne puis pas dire que M. Thiers soit beaucoup plus confiant que moi dans le succès de vos efforts. Non! L'ensemble de ses démarches

à Londres, Vienne, Berlin, Alexandrie et Constantinople, au sujet du nouvel incident tend plutôt à se mettre à couvert pour le cas où le Pacha céderait davantage. La question est redevenue beaucoup pour lui une question *intérieure*. Cela a bien aussi son côté dangereux.

En résumé, mon cher Ami, pour un pays comme le nôtre, avec des têtes comme les nôtres, la situation est très grave. Comme ici l'on exagère tout, le succès et la défaite, personne ne peut prévoir ce qui arriverait, la défaite ou ce que l'on regarderait comme telle ayant lieu. Faites ce que vous pourrez: le reste à la garde de Dieu. . . .[1]

(xii)

Paris, 1 *Octobre*, 1840.

Mon cher Ami, Je réponds à votre lettre d'avant hier. Elle ne me surprend pas dans ce qu'elle a de peu rassurant sur ce qui peut sortir du Conseil d'aujourd'hui. Lord Palmerston est conséquent avec son passé et de plus il a pour lui ce qui parait s'être fait à Constantinople. Son dire est correct: comment dire *oui* à Londres, quand le Sultan a déjà dit *non?* et quand ce *non* repose sur un traité signé, en cours d'exécution depuis deux mois, quand on n'a point encore rencontré, dans cette execution, de ces obstacles qui expliquent une retraite et que, tout au contraire, l'adversaire a déjà fléchi considérablement devant sa simple menace? Il faut être juste en ce moment, Lord Palmerston a de forts arguments pour lui et, engagé comme il l'est et avec lui le Cabinet, je conçois très bien que des considérations générales et d'un ordre plus élévées soient d'autant plus mises de côté à Londres qu'on les avait déjà écartées à une époque où l'on n'était pas justifié d'amour propre à les méconnaître. Mais, direz-vous, la guerre ne menaçait pas alors, la guerre? Lord P[almerston] n'y croit pas et moi non plus je n'y crois pas. Il a donc raison dans le *présent* et pour le but qu'il se propose, il a raison de ne pas encore lâcher prise. Vous voyez, mon cher Ami, que j'accepte froidement le jeu et les nécessités de position d'un adversaire; mais nous, que ferons nous et quel jeu sera le nôtre? à cela, je ne sais trop que vous répondre. Si je ne consultais que mon sentiment propre et n'examinerait la question que pour elle-même, je dirais que rester isolés, regarder faire, refuser son concours pour tout ce qui ne serait pas le dernier thème, refuser sa signature à tout acte partiel ou général sur l'Orient, et accepter froidement au besoin le succès du traité du 15 Juillet dans ses limites et avec son caractère, *faire raide*, en un mot, et le marquer; je dirais qu'à mes yeux ce système serait le plus raisonnable, le seul digne, le seul propre à préparer, avant qu'il soit longtemps, notre rentrée sur la scène d'une manière un peu marquante: car le monde ne s'arrête pas plus que le soleil, mais, je le reconnais, je juge, j'apprécie là, en dehors des situations ministérielles, en dehors des situations des partis, en dehors de la question intérieure. Voilà pourquoi, mon cher Ami, je ne sais ce que nous ferons ni même ce

---

[1] The omissions concern some dresses for a lady to be sent to his own address, and the possibilities of Bourqueney being made a Minister.

que, placés comme nous le sommes, nous avons à faire. La guerre,
je vous l'ai dit, je n'y crois pas et surtout je ne la veux pas; ce serait
chose insensée et monstrueuse; mais, c'est aussi parce que je n'y crois
pas et que, d'autre part, on a trop tendu la corde dans ce sens, que ses
difficultés deviennent énormes pour nous. J'aperçois déjà, parmi nous
et dans nos propres rangs, des symptômes d'une vive réaction. Si elle
gagne du terrain, si, nos chambres assemblées, elle s'étend et, je ne dis
pas détruit, mais seulement balance notre influence et notre action, oh!
alors, il y aura déroute et déroute complète dans notre attitude et dans
notre politique au dehors—voilà ce que je redoute le plus à cette heure.
Tout cela, entre nous, comme de raison. Rien de nouveau d'Egypte
et de Constantinople, rien de Vienne, non plus. Adieu, mon cher Ami,
tout à vous de cœur.

(xiii)

Paris, 4 Novembre, 1840.

. . . Je vous ai dit ma répugnance pour un acte général de clotûre.
Je ne sais ce qu'on en pense autour de moi: mais je crois fermement que,
pour avoir chance d'être accepté just now dans l'opinion (je parle de
l'opinion des gens sensés de toute couleur), je crois dis-je que pour
être acceptable et accepté, il faudrait que cet acte mit tellement en relief
le sens que nous avons toujours attaché ici à l'indépendance et à
l'intégrité de l'Empire Ottoman, que cela en ferait un Etat Neutre
depuis l'embouchure du Danube jusqu'au golfe Persique et à l'extrémité méridionale de la Mer Rouge. Il faudrait que cet acte répondit à
la fois d'une manière explicite et aux préoccupations anti-russes et aux
préoccupations anti-anglaises. Cela vous parait-il possible? On dira,
mais en vous assoçiant à un Traité qui consacrera ce qui s'est fait au
point de vue de la pacification intérieure de l'Empire Ottoman vous avez
meilleure chance de couvrir éventuellement l'Egypte, si de nouveaux
incidents, de nouveaux tiraillements venaient à se reproduire entre le
Pacha et la Porte. L'argument peut être spécieux mais il n'est que cela,
à mon sens du moins. En réalité cette chance vous ne l'avez pas plus
au dedans qu'au dehors du traité. Dans un cas comme dans l'autre,
nous serons toujours un contre quatre, dès qu'il s'agira de parler pour
le Pacha contre la Porte: et cela doit être et, c'est parceque cela doit
être, que le Traité ne peut rien valoir pour nous à ce point de vue. Ce
qui a faussé toute notre Politique et fait des événements de Syrie, de la
dechéance, etc., une défaite pour nous, c'est ce sot engouement pour
Méhémet Ali, c'est cette absurde opinion qu'il y avait là pour nous un
point d'appui solide, durable, quelque chose, enfin, qui valait que nous
la protégassions envers et contre tous, fusse même par la guerre générale.
Cette opinion, dieu merci, commence à perdre de son empire. Je ne
souhaite absolument pas que Méhémet-Ali perde aujourd'hui l'Egypte.
Nous ne sommes pas encore assez guéris pour qu'une pareille secousse
ne nous exposât pas à voir tout remettre en question ici; mais d'autre
part je craindrais que le traité sur lequel je raisonne en ce moment,

n'eût aussi pour effet de ranimer cette même opinion qui veut identifier les intérêts présents et à venir de la France, avec ceux de Méhémet-Ali et des siens; et que tôt ou tard on se trouva ramené au point où nous étions il y a six semaines.

Tout bien considéré donc, mon cher Ami, je suis contre tout projet de convention générale de *clôture*, que le Traité du 15 Juillet soit, comme l'ont été celui de 1827 pour la Grèce et celui de 1834 pour le Portugal et l'Espagne, que ce Traité demeure un épisode, un incident dans l'histoire politique de notre temps; nous n'y pouvons plus rien retrancher puisqu'il est accompli, par la même raison n'y ajoutons rien. Maintenant mon sentiment prévaudra-t-il, je l'ignore. Nous avons des gens pressés qu'un peu d'isolement effraie, et qui se figurent qu'on se fait une situation par cela seul, qu'on donne *après*, ce qu'on a refusé *avant* et qu'on se met soi cinquième autour d'un tapis vert pour signer avec quatre autres. Vous savez que l'art des transitions est connu, parmi nous, de bien peu de monde, à coup sûr. Je souhaite plus que personne que le jour vienne où la France et l'Angleterre redeviennent l'une pour l'autre ce qu'elles étaient il y a trois et quatre ans. Mais pour qu'au vrai cela puisse avoir lieu, il faudra qu'une question bien et duement *anglo-française* par dessus tout, surgisse, et fasse oublier, en même temps, que les folies d'ici, le faux pas trop britannique (je parle poliment) de votre Secrétaire d'Etat.

Adieu, mon cher Ami, vous voyez par la longueur de cette lettre, que je redeviens bavard; prenez-vous à vous même, si je rentre dans cette habitude; vous m'avez reproché d'en être sorti. Tout à vous de cœur.

INDEX

*Volume I comprises pages 1–522,
Volume II pages 523–901*